Third Edition

GREAT CHRISTIAN CLASSICS

Volume 1

Five Remarkable Narratives of the Faith

GREAT CHRISTIAN CLASSICS

Volume 1

Five Remarkable Narratives of the Faith

EDITED BY

Kevin Swanson & Joshua Schwisow

First Master Books Printing: May 2017

ISBN: 978-1-68344-070-3
ISBN: 978-0-99617-191-5 (digital)
Library of Congress Number: 2017000000

Published in partnership with Generations
19039 Plaza Dr. Ste. 210
Parker, Colorado 80134
www.generations.org

Grace Abounding to the Chief of Sinners, Edited Version, used by permission of Moody Press.

History of the Reformation in Scotland, Edited Version, by Joshua Schwisow.

All other texts drawn from public domain sources.

Annotations written by Kevin Swanson.
All rights reserved.

Please consider requesting that a copy of this volume be purchased by your local library system.

Printed in the United States of America

Please visit our website for other great titles:
www.masterbooks.com

For information regarding author interviews,
please contact the publicity department at (870) 438-5288

Contents

GRACE ABOUNDING TO THE CHIEF OF SINNERS

THE AUTOBIOGRAPHY OF JOHN G. PATON

LIST OF IMAGES

❧ Introduction

You hold in your hands a singular compilation of the most remarkable life narratives ever recorded in the history of the Christian Church. For the first time, these outstanding autobiographical records are combined to form one powerful manual. It is the eye-witness account, or better, the heart-witness account of the work of the Spirit of God in the life of men in the New Testament era. It is the story of the siege of the city of Mansoul (to use Bunyan's analogy). Far more important than the historical narratives found in the city of man as it builds its proud empires, these narratives detail the powerful workings of the Spirit of God in the hearts of men.

The stories herein chronicle the building of another kingdom—a somewhat ignominious city in the eyes of the world around us. For what the world perceives as great accomplishments, based on its metrics of power and wealth, has little to do with the kingdom of God. This explains why such literature is largely ignored by the public and private schools in our day which have been commissioned to provide our children's education. We will refer to this material as *Christian classics*, as it is intended especially for those *Christians* who are profoundly impressed with the building of the kingdom of God and the Church of Jesus Christ through the centuries.

These narratives are true, real-life stories that recount the real battles against sin and evil, waged and won. Far more important than those battles fought by the world's great military leaders and statesmen, here are the men who overcame the world, by faith. For the greatest battles are those fought against the greatest enemies of the human soul—the world, the flesh, and the Devil. They are waged with the deadly weapons of the Word of God and steadfast faith in that Word.

Some stories are still read 1,000 years after they were written. But these stories will stand for eternity. They have already stood the test of time. Christian people everywhere have read these stories in every generation since they were first penned. But even more importantly, the men who tell their stories are great men and they will stand in God's hall of faith for eternity. They are men who worked hard to raise up a kingdom out of the dust of heathendom, paganism, statism, humanism, and ecclesiastical compromise and decay. All of them worked in the face of unbelievable dangers, including persecution, imprisonment, enslavement, and the devastation of war. Truly, these are the patriarchs and the pioneers in the faith. They built the Church from the bottom-up in places as far-flung as Africa, Ireland, Scotland, England, and the South Pacific.

Speaking as a father who has spent a lifetime seeking out the best literature for his children's education, aside from the Bible, I have never found a book or series of books as spiritually or intellectually edifying as the collection of narratives you are about to read in this compendium. These writings constitute rare, intimate, and transparent personal narratives concerning the work of the living God in the lives of some of the greatest Christian men in history. To witness in vivid, living colors the work of God in a man's life is to understand it better in our own lives!

If you want to raise up Christians in your home, there is nothing better than to put them at the feet of Christians. Disciples take on the thought and life patterns of those who disciple them (Luke 6:40), and when children read, they sit at the feet of the teachers who write the books. What better thing to do than to set them at the feet of the greatest Christians who have ever written anything? Too many Christian children sit at the feet of humanists in their high school and college literature classes while they have little or no knowledge of the deep truths of Scripture and the great Christian writings produced throughout history.

I pray God's blessings on all those that take up these powerful, impacting books; that God would first prepare their hearts to receive them, to comprehend them, and then to live them out for His glory! Amen.

A Father and Pastor,

Kevin Swanson
November, 2016 A.D.

THE CONFESSIONS OF AUGUSTINE

Augustine of Hippo
AD 401

translated by Albert C. Outler (Abridged)

An Introduction to the Testimony of Augustine

N o one influenced Christianity during the first one thousand years of the Church as profoundly as Augustine, Bishop of Hippo, in North Africa. Should one survey all of the sources favorably quoted by the Protestant reformers, he would find Augustine preeminent in the list. Indeed, to properly understand the development of the Christian faith and its impact on North Africa, Europe, and America, one must carefully consider the writings of this man.

Augustine was the son of a pagan father and a Christian mother, a scholar of the first order, and a teacher of rhetoric in the Roman schools. He experimented with various forms of unbelief, including the Manichean religion (a Gnostic cult that was active throughout the 4th and 5th centuries). He later converted to Christianity, thanks in part to his mother's relentless prayers and the faithful discipleship of Ambrose, the bishop (or pastor) of Milan, Italy.

His powerful intellect and penetrating discernment concerning human thought and action, combined with a self-abasing humility and deep piety, produced an outstanding orthodox Christian system of thought which has served to build the Church of Christ through the ages.

Hardly any other Christian author has so effectively captured the Pauline themes of man's depravity and God's grace.

This is beautifully communicated in the words of his own testimony, recorded in these Confessions as a prayer to God.

Unfortunately, too many Christians today think of Church history as the past ten years of the gathering of their local church, or the last one hundred years since their present denomination was organized. This narrow view of history denies the work of the Spirit of God over 1,900 years of Church history, and it betrays both a pride and an ignorance that, given enough time, is sure to land many in deviant cults and heresies. To read the work of Christians from the past is to consider the battles that they fought, the enemies they confronted, and the mistakes they made. We stand on their shoulders. From that viewpoint, we may not exactly replicate everything that they did but we respect their legacy, learn from their mistakes, and improve on what they have given us. Rejecting the Church fathers, imperfect as they may have been, is tantamount to cutting ourselves off at the knees and re-inventing the faith with each new generation.

One will not find a great deal of theology in this portion of Augustine's writings. *Confessions* serve more as a testimony, a godly example in humility, a self-analysis, and an apologetic for the Christian faith. In this study the autobiographical components of Augustine's great testimony are covered, which are particularly suited for this study of great Christian narratives.

❊ BOOK I

"Great art thou, O Lord, and greatly to be praised; great is thy power, and infinite is thy wisdom." And man desires to praise thee, for he is a part of thy creation; he bears his mortality about with him and carries the evidence of his sin and the proof that thou dost resist the proud. Still he desires to praise thee, this man who is only a small part of thy creation. Thou hast prompted him, that he should delight to praise thee, for thou hast made us for thyself and restless is our heart until it comes to rest in thee. Grant me, O Lord, to know and understand whether first to invoke thee or to praise thee; whether first to know thee or call upon thee. But who can invoke thee, knowing thee not? For he who knows thee not may invoke thee as another than thou art. It may be that we should invoke thee in order that we may come to know thee. But "how shall they call on him in whom they have not believed? Or how shall they believe without a preacher?" Now, "they shall praise the Lord who seek him," for "those who seek shall find him," and, finding him, shall praise him. I will seek thee, O Lord, and call upon thee. I call upon thee, O Lord, in my faith which thou hast given me, which thou hast inspired in me through the humanity of thy Son, and through the ministry of thy preacher.[1]

And how shall I call upon my God—my God and my Lord? For when I call on him I ask him to come into me. And

1. The preacher that helped to bring Augustine to faith is his pastor in Milan, a man named Ambrose.

what place is there in me into which my God can come? How could God, the God who made both heaven and earth, come into me? Is there anything in me, O Lord my God, that can contain thee? Do even the heaven and the earth, which thou hast made, and in which thou didst make me, contain thee? Is it possible that, since without thee nothing would be which does exist, thou didst make it so that whatever exists has some capacity to receive thee? Why, then, do I ask thee to come into me, since I also am and could not be if thou wert not in me? For I am not, after all, in hell—and yet thou art there too, for "if I go down into hell, thou art there." Therefore I would not exist—I would simply not be at all—unless I exist in thee, from whom and by whom and in whom all things are. Even so, Lord; even so. Where do I call thee to, when I am already in thee? Or from whence wouldst thou come into me? Where, beyond heaven and earth, could I go that there my God might come to me—he who hath said, "I fill heaven and earth?"

Since, then, thou dost fill the heaven and earth, do they contain thee? Or, dost thou fill and overflow them, because they cannot contain thee? And where dost thou pour out what remains of thee after heaven and earth are full? Or, indeed, is there no need that thou, who dost contain all things, shouldst be contained by any, since those things which thou dost fill thou fillest by containing them? For the vessels which thou dost fill do not confine thee, since even if they were broken, thou wouldst not be poured out. And, when thou art poured out on us, thou art not thereby brought down; rather, we are uplifted. Thou art not scattered; rather, thou dost gather us together. But when thou dost fill all things, dost thou fill them with thy whole being? Or, since not even all things together could contain thee altogether, does any one thing contain a single part, and do all things contain that same part at the same time? Do singulars contain thee singly? Do greater things contain more of thee, and smaller things less? Or, is it not rather that thou art wholly present everywhere, yet in such a way that nothing contains thee wholly?

What, therefore, is my God? What, I ask, but the Lord God? "For who is Lord but the Lord himself, or who is God besides our God?" Most high, most excellent, most potent, most omnipotent; most merciful and most just; most secret and most truly present; most beautiful and most strong; stable, yet not supported; unchangeable, yet changing all things; never new, never old; making all things new, yet bringing old age upon the proud, and they know it not; always working, ever at rest; gathering, yet needing nothing; sustaining, pervading, and protecting; creating, nourishing, and developing; seeking, and yet possessing all things. Thou dost love, but without passion; art jealous, yet free from care; dost repent without remorse; art angry, yet remainest serene. Thou changest thy ways, leaving thy plans unchanged; thou recoverest what thou hast never really lost. Thou art never in need but still thou dost rejoice at thy gains; art never greedy, yet demandest dividends. Men pay more than is required so that thou dost become a debtor; yet who can possess anything at all which is not already thine? Thou owest men nothing, yet payest out to them as if in debt to thy creature, and when thou dost cancel debts thou losest nothing thereby. Yet, O my God, my life, my holy Joy, what is this that I have said? What can any man say when he speaks of thee? But woe to them that keep silence—since even those who say most are dumb.

Who shall bring me to rest in thee? Who will send thee into my heart so to overwhelm it that my sins shall be blotted out and I may embrace thee, my only good? What art thou to me? Have mercy that I may speak. What am I to thee that thou shouldst command me to love thee, and if I do it not, art angry and threatenest vast misery? Is it, then, a trifling sorrow not to love thee? It is not so to me. Tell me, by thy mercy, O Lord, my God, what thou art to me. "Say to my soul, I am your salvation." So speak that I may hear. Behold, the ears of my heart are before thee, O Lord; open them and "say to my soul, I am your salvation." I will hasten after that voice, and I will

2. Augustine is sensitive to his sinful condition, yet still confident that God has forgiven him and "put away his iniquity."

lay hold upon thee. Hide not thy face from me. Even if I die, let me see thy face lest I die.[2]

The house of my soul is too narrow for thee to come in to me; let it be enlarged by thee. It is in ruins; do thou restore it. There is much about it which must offend thy eyes; I confess and know it. But who will cleanse it? Or, to whom shall I cry but to thee? "Cleanse thou me from my secret faults," O Lord, "and keep back thy servant from strange sins." "I believe, and therefore do I speak." But thou, O Lord, thou knowest. Have I not confessed my transgressions unto thee, O my God; and hast thou not put away the iniquity of my heart? I do not contend in judgment with thee, who art truth itself; and I would not deceive myself, lest my iniquity lie even to itself. I do not, therefore, contend in judgment with thee, for "if thou, Lord, shouldst mark iniquities, O Lord, who shall stand?"

Still, dust and ashes as I am, allow me to speak before thy mercy. Allow me to speak, for, behold, it is to thy mercy that I speak and not to a man who scorns me. Yet perhaps even thou mightest scorn me; but when thou dost turn and attend to me, thou wilt have mercy upon me. For what do I wish to say, O Lord my God, but that I know not whence I came hither into this life-in-death. Or should I call it death-in-life? I do not know. And yet the consolations of thy mercy have sustained me from the very beginning, as I have heard from my fleshly parents, from whom and in whom thou didst form me in time—for I cannot myself remember. Thus even though they sustained me by the consolation of woman's milk, neither my mother nor my nurses filled their own breasts but thou, through them, didst give me the food of infancy according to thy ordinance and thy bounty which underlie all things. For it was thou who didst cause me not to want more than thou gavest and it was thou who gavest to those who nourished me the will to give me what thou didst give them. And they, by an instinctive affection, were willing to give me what thou hadst supplied abundantly. It was, indeed, good for them that my good should come through them, though, in truth, it was not from them but by them. For it is from thee, O God, that all good things come—and from my God is all my health. This is what I have since learned, as thou hast made it abundantly clear by all that I have seen thee give, both to me and to those around me. For even at the very first I knew how to suck, to lie quiet when I was full, and to cry when in pain—nothing more.

Afterward I began to laugh—at first in my sleep, then when waking. For this I have been told about myself and I believe it—though I cannot remember it—for I see the same things in other infants. Then, little by little, I realized where I was and wished to tell my wishes to those who might satisfy them, but I could not! For my wants were inside me, and they were outside, and they could not by any power of theirs come into my soul. And so I would fling my arms and legs about and cry, making the few and feeble gestures that I could, though indeed the signs were not much like what I inwardly desired and when I was not satisfied—either from not being understood or because what I got was not good for me—I grew indignant that my elders were not subject to me and that those on whom I actually had no claim did not wait on me as slaves—and I avenged myself on them by crying. That infants are like this, I have myself been able to learn by watching them; and they, though they knew me not, have shown me better what I was like than my own nurses who knew me.

And, behold, my infancy died long ago, but I am still living. But thou, O Lord, whose life is forever and in whom nothing dies—since before the world was, indeed, before all that can be called "before," thou wast, and thou art the God and Lord of all thy creatures; and with thee abide all the stable causes of all unstable things, the unchanging sources of all changeable things, and the eternal reasons of all non- rational and temporal things—tell me, thy suppliant, O God, tell me, O merciful One, in pity tell a pitiful creature whether my infancy followed yet an earlier age of my life that had already passed away before it. Was it such another age which I spent in my mother's womb? For something of that sort has been suggested to me, and I have myself seen pregnant women. But what, O God, my Joy, preceded that period of life? Was I, indeed, anywhere, or anybody? No one can explain these things to me, neither father nor mother, nor the experience of others, nor my own memory. Dost thou laugh at me for asking such things? Or dost thou command me to praise and confess unto thee only what I know?

I give thanks to thee, O Lord of heaven and earth, giving praise to thee for that first being and my infancy of which I have no memory. For thou hast granted to man that he should come to self-knowledge through the knowledge of others, and that he should believe many things about himself on the authority of the womenfolk. Now, clearly, I had life and being; and, as my infancy closed, I was already learning signs by which my feelings could be communicated to others.[3]

Whence could such a creature come but from thee, O Lord? Is any man skillful enough to have fashioned himself? Or is there any other source from which being and life could flow into us, save this, that thou, O Lord, hast made us—thou with whom being and life are one, since thou thyself art supreme being and supreme life both together.

For thou art infinite and in thee there is no change, nor an end to this present day—although there is a sense in which it ends in thee since all things are in thee and there would be no such thing as days passing away unless thou didst sustain them. And since "thy years shall have no end, "thy years are an ever-present day." And how many of ours and our fathers' days have passed through this thy day and have received from it what measure and fashion of being they had? And all the days to come shall so receive and so pass away. "But thou art the same" And all the things of tomorrow and the days yet to come, and all of yesterday and the days that are past, thou wilt gather into this thy day. What is it to me if someone does not understand this? Let him still rejoice and continue to ask, "What is this?" Let him also rejoice and prefer to seek thee,

3. Augustine speaks of the ever-present day for God, in which there is no before or after with God. He also speaks of the doctrine of original sin, in that every infant is born in bondage to sin.

even if he fails to find an answer, rather than to seek an answer and not find thee!

"Hear me, O God! Woe to the sins of men!" When a man cries thus, thou showest him mercy, for thou didst create the man but not the sin in him. Who brings to remembrance the sins of my infancy? For in thy sight there is none free from sin, not even the infant who has lived but a day upon this earth. Who brings this to my remembrance? Does not each little one, in whom I now observe what I no longer remember of myself? In what ways, in that time, did I sin? Was it that I cried for the breast? If I should now so cry—not indeed for the breast, but for food suitable to my condition—I should be most justly laughed at and rebuked. What I did then deserved rebuke but, since I could not understand those who rebuked me, neither custom nor common sense permitted me to be rebuked. As we grow we root out and cast away from us such childish habits. Yet I have not seen anyone who is wise who cast away the good when trying to purge the bad. Nor was it good, even in that time, to strive to get by crying what, if it had been given me, would have been hurtful; or to be bitterly indignant at those who, because they were older—not slaves, either, but free—and wiser than I, would not indulge my capricious desires. Was it a good thing for me to try, by struggling as hard as I could, to harm them for not obeying me, even when it would have done me harm to have been obeyed? Thus, the infant's innocence lies in the weakness of his body and not in the infant mind.[4] I have myself observed a baby to be jealous, though it could not speak; it was livid as it watched another infant at the breast.

Who is ignorant of this? Mothers and nurses tell us that they cure these things by I know not what remedies. But is this innocence, when the fountain of milk is flowing fresh and abundant, that another who needs it should not be allowed to share it, even though he requires such nourishment to sustain his life? Yet we look leniently on such things, not because they are not faults, or even small faults, but because they will vanish

4. The sins of infants include jealousy and anger, sins which Augustine believes originate in the mind.

as the years pass. For, although we allow for such things in an infant, the same things could not be tolerated patiently in an adult.

Therefore, O Lord my God, thou who gavest life to the infant, and a body which, as we see, thou hast furnished with senses, shaped with limbs, beautified with form, and endowed with all vital energies for its well-being and health—thou dost command me to praise thee for these things, to give thanks unto the Lord, and to sing praise unto his name, O Most High. For thou art God, omnipotent and good, even if thou hadst done no more than these things, which no other but thou canst do—thou alone who madest all things fair and didst order everything according to thy law.

I am loath to dwell on this part of my life of which, O Lord, I have no remembrance, about which I must trust the word of others and what I can surmise from observing other infants, even if such guesses are trustworthy. For it lies in the deep murk of my forgetfulness and thus is like the period which I passed in my mother's womb. But if "I was conceived in iniquity, and in sin my mother nourished me in her womb," where, I pray thee, O my God, where, O Lord, or when was I, thy servant, ever innocent? But see now, I pass over that period, for what have I to do with a time from which I can recall no memories?

Did I not, then, as I grew out of infancy, come next to boyhood, or rather did it not come to me and succeed my infancy? My infancy did not go away (for where would it go?). It was simply no longer present; and I was no longer an infant who could not speak, but now a chattering boy. I remember this, and I have since observed how I learned to speak. My elders did not teach me words by rote, as they taught me my letters afterward. But I myself, when I was unable to communicate all I wished to say to whomever I wished by means of whimperings and grunts and various gestures of my limbs (which I used to reinforce my demands), I myself repeated the sounds already stored in my memory by the mind which thou,

O my God, hadst given me. When they called some thing by name and pointed it out while they spoke, I saw it and realized that the thing they wished to indicate was called by the name they then uttered. And what they meant was made plain by the gestures of their bodies, by a kind of natural language, common to all nations, which expresses itself through changes of countenance, glances of the eye, gestures and intonations which indicate a disposition and attitude—either to seek or to possess, to reject or to avoid. So it was that by frequently hearing words, in different phrases, I gradually identified the objects which the words stood for and, having formed my mouth to repeat these signs, I was thereby able to express my will. Thus I exchanged with those about me the verbal signs by which we express our wishes and advanced deeper into the stormy fellowship of human life, depending all the while upon the authority of my parents and the behest of my elders.

O my God! What miseries and mockeries did I then experience when it was impressed on me that obedience to my teachers was proper to my boyhood estate if I was to flourish in this world and distinguish myself in those tricks of speech which would gain honor for me among men, and deceitful riches! To this end I was sent to school to get learning, the value of which I knew not—wretch that I was. Yet if I was slow to learn, I was flogged. For this was deemed praiseworthy by our forefathers and many had passed before us in the same course, and thus had built up the precedent for the sorrowful road on which we too were compelled to travel, multiplying labor and sorrow upon the sons of Adam. About this time, O Lord, I observed men praying to thee, and I learned from them to conceive thee—after my capacity for understanding as it was then—to be some great Being, who, though not visible to our senses, was able to hear and help us. Thus as a boy I began to pray to thee, my Help and my Refuge, and, in calling on thee, broke the bands of my tongue. Small as I was, I prayed with no slight earnestness that I might not be beaten at school.[5] And when thou didst not heed me—for that would

5. Human relationships are described as "stormy" because conflict is ever present in all societies (even back then in Augustine's day).

have been giving me over to my folly—my elders and even my parents too, who wished me no ill, treated my stripes as a joke, though they were then a great and grievous ill to me.

Is there anyone, O Lord, with a spirit so great, who cleaves to thee with such steadfast affection (or is there even a kind of obtuseness that has the same effect)—is there any man who, by cleaving devoutly to thee, is endowed with so great a courage that he can regard indifferently those racks and hooks and other torture weapons from which men throughout the world pray so fervently to be spared; and can they scorn those who so greatly fear these torments, just as my parents were amused at the torments with which our teachers punished us boys? For we were no less afraid of our pains, nor did we beseech thee less to escape them. Yet, even so, we were sinning by writing or reading or studying less than our assigned lessons. For I did not, O Lord, lack memory or capacity, for, by thy will, I possessed enough for my age. However, my mind was absorbed only in play, and I was punished for this by those who were doing the same things themselves. But the idling of our elders is called business; the idling of boys, though quite like it, is punished by those same elders, and no one pities either the boys or the men.[6] For will any common sense observer agree that I was rightly punished as a boy for playing ball—just because this hindered me from learning more quickly those lessons by means of which, as a man, I could play at more shameful games? And did he by whom I was beaten do anything different? When he was worsted in some small controversy with a fellow teacher, he was more tormented by anger and envy than I was when beaten by a playmate in the ball game.[7]

And yet I sinned, O Lord my God, thou Ruler and Creator of all natural things—but of sins only the Ruler—I sinned, O Lord my God, in acting against the precepts of my parents and of those teachers. For this learning which they wished me to acquire—no matter what their motives were—I might have put to good account afterward. I disobeyed them, not because I had chosen a better way, but from a sheer love of

6. Augustine points out that success in school enables grown men to play "more shameful games," where they can afford expensive entertainment (shows and sports). Yet little boys are punished for playing games instead of doing their school work.

7. The goal of schooling was to make money and gain honor among men (very much as it is in secular schools today).

play. I loved the vanity of victory, and I loved to have my ears tickled with lying fables, which made them itch even more ardently, and a similar curiosity glowed more and more in my eyes for the shows and sports of my elders. Yet those who put on such shows are held in such high repute that almost all desire the same for their children. They are therefore willing to have them beaten, if their childhood games keep them from the studies by which their parents desire them to grow up to be able to give such shows.[8] Look down on these things with mercy, O Lord, and deliver us who now call upon thee; deliver those also who do not call upon thee, that they may call upon thee, and thou mayest deliver them.

Even as a boy I had heard of eternal life promised to us through the humility of the Lord our God, who came down to visit us in our pride, and I was signed with the sign of his cross, and was seasoned with his salt even from the womb of my mother, who greatly trusted in thee. Thou didst see, O Lord, how, once, while I was still a child, I was suddenly seized with stomach pains and was at the point of death—thou didst see, O my God, for even then thou wast my keeper, with what agitation and with what faith I solicited from the piety of my mother and from thy Church (which is the mother of us all) the baptism of thy Christ, my Lord and my God. The mother of my flesh was much perplexed, for, with a heart pure in thy faith, she was always in deep travail for my eternal salvation. If I had not quickly recovered, she would have provided forthwith for my initiation and washing by thy life-giving sacraments, confessing thee, O Lord Jesus, for the forgiveness of sins. So my cleansing was deferred, as if it were inevitable that, if I should live, I would be further polluted; and, further, because the guilt contracted by sin after baptism would be still greater and more perilous.[9] Thus, at that time, I "believed" along with my mother and the whole household, except my father. But he did not overcome the influence of my mother's piety in me, nor did he prevent my believing in Christ, although he had not yet believed in him. For it was her desire,

8. When Augustine began to pray, his big concern was the beatings he received from his teachers at school.

Romanesque baptismal font from Grötlingbo Church, Sweden

9. Baptism was delayed in some cases because of the mistaken notion that only sins committed prior to the baptism would be washed away.

O my God, that I should acknowledge thee as my Father rather than him. In this thou didst aid her to overcome her husband, to whom, though his superior, she yielded obedience. In this way she also yielded obedience to thee, who dost so command.

I ask thee, O my God, for I would gladly know if it be thy will, to what good end my baptism was deferred at that time? Was it indeed for my good that the reins were slackened, as it were, to encourage me in sin? Or, were they not slackened? If not, then why is it still dinned into our ears on all sides, "Let him alone, let him do as he pleases, for he is not yet baptized?" In the matter of bodily health, no one says, "Let him alone; let him be worse wounded; for he is not yet cured!" How much better, then, would it have been for me to have been cured at once—and if thereafter, through the diligent care of friends and myself, my soul's restored health had been kept safe in thy keeping, who gave it in the first place! This would have been far better, in truth. But how many and great the waves of temptation which appeared to hang over me as I grew out of childhood! These were foreseen by my mother, and she preferred that the unformed clay should be risked to them rather than the clay molded after Christ's image.

But in this time of childhood—which was far less dreaded for me than my adolescence—I had no love of learning, and hated to be driven to it. Yet I was driven to it just the same, and good was done for me, even though I did not do it well, for I would not have learned if I had not been forced to it. For no man does well against his will, even if what he does is a good thing. Neither did they who forced me do well, but the good that was done me came from thee, my God. For they did not care about the way in which I would use what they forced me to learn, and took it for granted that it was to satisfy the inordinate desires of a rich beggary and a shameful glory. But thou, Lord, by whom the hairs of our head are numbered, didst use for my good the error of all who pushed me on to study: but my error in not being willing to learn thou didst use for my punishment. And I—though so small a boy yet so great a sinner—was not punished without warrant. Thus by the instrumentality of those who did not do well, thou didst well for me; and by my own sin thou didst justly punish me. For it is even as thou hast ordained: that every inordinate affection brings on its own punishment.

But what were the causes for my strong dislike of Greek literature, which I studied from my boyhood? Even to this day I have not fully understood them. For Latin I loved exceedingly—not just the rudiments, but what the grammarians teach. For those beginner's lessons in reading, writing, and reckoning, I considered no less a burden and pain than Greek. Yet whence came this, unless from the sin and vanity of this life? For I was "but flesh, a wind that passeth away and cometh not again." Those first lessons were better, assuredly, because they were more certain, and through them I acquired, and still retain, the power of reading what I find written and of writing for myself what I will. In the other subjects, however, I was compelled to learn about the wanderings of a certain Aeneas, oblivious of my own wanderings, and to weep for Dido dead, who slew herself for love.[10] And all this while I bore with dry eyes my own wretched self dying to thee, O God, my life, in the midst of these things.

For what can be more wretched than the wretch who has no pity upon himself, who sheds tears over Dido, dead for the love of Aeneas, but who sheds no tears for his own death in not loving thee, O God, light of my heart, and bread of the inner mouth of my soul, O power that links together my mind with my inmost thoughts? I did not love thee, and thus committed fornication against thee. Those around me, also sinning, thus cried out: "Well done! Well done!" The friendship of this world is fornication against thee; and "Well done! Well done!" is cried until one feels ashamed not to show himself a man in this way. For my own condition I shed no tears, though I wept for Dido,[11] who "sought death at the sword's point," while I myself was seeking the lowest rung of thy cre-

Bust of Virgil from the Tomb of Virgil in Naples, Italy

10. Dido is the first queen of Carthage, who shows up in a play by Virgil. She kills herself by falling on a sword after she is abandoned by the man she loves, Aeneas.

11. Augustine is ashamed that his emotions were wrapped up in these Greek fictions, while he would not weep over his own sin.

ation, having forsaken thee; earth sinking back to earth again. And, if I had been forbidden to read these poems, I would have grieved that I was not allowed to read what grieved me. This sort of madness is considered more honorable and more fruitful learning than the beginner's course in which I learned to read and write.

But now, O my God, cry unto my soul, and let thy truth say to me: "Not so, not so! That first learning was far better." For, obviously, I would rather forget the wanderings of Aeneas, and all such things, than forget how to write and read. Still, over the entrance of the grammar school there hangs a veil. This is not so much the sign of a covering for a mystery as a curtain for error. Let them exclaim against me—those I no longer fear—while I confess to thee, my God, what my soul desires, and let me find some rest, for in blaming my own evil ways I may come to love thy holy ways. Neither let those cry out against me who buy and sell the baubles of literature. For if I ask them if it is true, as the poet says, that Aeneas once came to Carthage, the unlearned will reply that they do not know and the learned will deny that it is true. But if I ask with what letters the name Aeneas is written, all who have ever learned this will answer correctly, in accordance with the conventional understanding men have agreed upon as to these signs. Again, if I should ask which would cause the greatest inconvenience in our life, if it were forgotten: reading and writing, or these poetical fictions, who does not see what everyone would answer who had not entirely lost his own memory? I erred, then, when as a boy I preferred those vain studies to these more profitable[12] ones, or rather loved the one and hated the other. "One and one are two, two and two are four:" this was then a truly hateful song to me. But the wooden horse full of its armed soldiers, and the holocaust of Troy, and the spectral image of Creusa were all a most delightful—and vain—show!

But why, then, did I dislike Greek learning, which was full of such tales? For Homer was skillful in inventing such poetic fictions and is most sweetly wanton; yet when I was a boy, he

Depiction of Homer, British Museum

12. Young children back then and now seem to prefer fictional reading over useful things like reading, writing, and arithmetic.

was most disagreeable to me. I believe that Virgil would have the same effect on Greek boys as Homer did on me if they were forced to learn him. For the tedium of learning a foreign language mingled gall into the sweetness of those Grecian myths. For I did not understand a word of the language, and yet I was driven with threats and cruel punishments to learn it. There was also a time when, as an infant, I knew no Latin; but this I acquired without any fear or tormenting, but merely by being alert to the blandishments of my nurses, the jests of those who smiled on me, and the sportiveness of those who toyed with me. I learned all this, indeed, without being urged by any pressure of punishment, for my own heart urged me to bring forth its own fashioning, which I could not do except by learning words: not from those who taught me but those who talked to me, into whose ears I could pour forth whatever I could fashion. From this it is sufficiently clear that a free curiosity is more effective in learning than a discipline based on fear. Yet, by thy ordinance, O God, discipline is given to restrain the excesses of freedom; this ranges from the ferule of the schoolmaster to the trials of the martyr and has the effect of mingling for us a wholesome bitterness, which calls us back to thee from the poisonous pleasures that first drew us from thee.

Hear my prayer, O Lord; let not my soul faint under thy discipline, nor let me faint in confessing unto thee thy mercies, whereby thou hast saved me from all my most wicked ways till thou shouldst become sweet to me beyond all the allurements that I used to follow. Let me come to love thee wholly, and grasp thy hand with my whole heart that thou mayest deliver me from every temptation, even unto the last. And thus, O Lord, my King and my God, may all things useful that I learned as a boy now be offered in thy service—let it be that for thy service I now speak and write and reckon. For when I was learning vain things, thou didst impose thy discipline upon me: and thou hast forgiven me my sin of delighting in those vanities. In those studies I learned many a useful word, but these might have been learned in matters not so vain; and surely that is the safe way for youths to walk in.

But woe unto you, O torrent of human custom! Who shall stay your course? When will you ever run dry? How long will you carry down the sons of Eve into that vast and hideous ocean, which even those who have the Tree (for an ark) can scarcely pass over? Do I not read in you the stories of Jove the thunderer—and the adulterer? How could he be both? But so it says, and the sham thunder served as a cloak for him to play at real adultery. Yet which of our gowned masters will give a tempered hearing to a man trained in their own schools who cries out and says: "These were Homer's fictions; he transfers things human to the gods. I could have wished that he would transfer divine things to us." But it would have been more true if he said, "These are, indeed, his fictions, but he attributed divine attributes to sinful men, that crimes might not be accounted crimes, and that whoever committed such crimes might appear to imitate the celestial gods and not abandoned men."

13. Augustine calls the works of Homer "a torrent from hell," and he is aghast that people pay money to teach their children these things in the classical schools of the day.

And yet, O torrent of hell,[13] the sons of men are still cast into you, and they pay fees for learning all these things. And much is made of it when this goes on in the forum under the auspices of laws which give a salary over and above the fees. And you beat against your rocky shore and roar: "Here words may be learned; here you can attain the eloquence which is so necessary to persuade people to your way of thinking; so helpful in unfolding your opinions." Verily, they seem to argue that we should never have understood these words, "golden shower," "bosom," "intrigue," "highest heavens," and other

14. Jove (or Jupiter) was the chief god of pagan Rome — the god of thunder (and an adulterer). Flawed gods who committed adultery became an excuse for people who wanted to get away with the same sins.

such words, if Terence had not introduced a good-for-nothing youth upon the stage, setting up a picture of Jove[14] as his example of lewdness and telling the tale

"Of Jove's descending in a golden shower
 Into Danae's bosom. . . With a woman to intrigue."

See how he excites himself to lust, as if by a heavenly authority, when he says:

"Great Jove, Who shakes the highest heavens with his thunder; Shall I, poor mortal man, not do the same? I've done it, and with all my heart, I'm glad."

These words are not learned one whit more easily because of this vileness, but through them the vileness is more boldly perpetrated. I do not blame the words, for they are, as it were, choice and precious vessels, but I do deplore the wine of error which was poured out to us by teachers already drunk. And, unless we also drank we were beaten, without liberty of appeal to a sober judge. And yet, O my God, in whose presence I can now with security recall this, I learned these things willingly and with delight, and for it I was called a boy of good promise.[15]

Bear with me, O my God, while I speak a little of those talents, thy gifts, and of the follies on which I wasted them. For a lesson was given me that sufficiently disturbed my soul, for in it there was both hope of praise and fear of shame or stripes. The assignment was that I should declaim the words of Juno, as she raged and sorrowed that she could not "Bar off Italy From all the approaches of the Teucrian king."

I had learned that Juno had never uttered these words. Yet we were compelled to stray in the footsteps of these poetic fictions, and to turn into prose what the poet had said in verse. In the declamation, the boy won most applause who most strikingly reproduced the passions of anger and sorrow according to the "character" of the persons presented and who clothed it all in the most suitable language. What is it now to me, O my true Life, my God, that my declaiming was applauded above that of many of my classmates and fellow students? Actually, was not all that smoke and wind? Besides, was there nothing else on which I could have exercised my wit and tongue? Thy praise, O Lord, thy praises might have propped up the tendrils of my heart by thy Scriptures; and it would not have been dragged away by these empty trifles, a shameful prey to the spirits of the air. For there is more than one way in which men sacrifice to the fallen angels.[16]

15. Words are like vessels that can carry poison or milk. The Greek pagan literature used words to carry poison.

16. Pagan writings are mere trifles, whereas a Christian education should focus on the Scriptures. Pagan plays are a form of a sacrifice to the Devil.

But it was no wonder that I was thus carried toward vanity and was estranged from thee, O my God, when men were held up as models to me who, when relating a deed of theirs—not in itself evil—were covered with confusion if found guilty of a barbarism or a solecism; but who could tell of their own licentiousness and be applauded for it, so long as they did it in a full and ornate oration of well-chosen words. Thou seest all this, O Lord, and dost keep silence—"long-suffering, and plenteous in mercy and truth" as thou art. Wilt thou keep silence forever? Even now thou drawest from that vast deep the soul that seeks thee and thirsts after thy delight, whose "heart said unto thee, 'I have sought thy face; thy face, Lord, will I seek.'" For I was far from thy face in the dark shadows of passion. For it is not by our feet, nor by change of place, that we either turn from thee or return to thee. That younger son did not charter horses or chariots, or ships, or fly away on visible wings, or journey by walking so that in the far country he might prodigally waste all that thou didst give him when he set out. A kind Father when thou gavest; and kinder still when he returned destitute![17] To be wanton, that is to say, to be darkened in heart—this is to be far from thy face.

17. Reference to the Prodigal Son in Luke 15.

Look down, O Lord God, and see patiently, as thou art wont to do, how diligently the sons of men observe the conventional rules of letters and syllables, taught them by those who learned their letters beforehand, while they neglect the eternal rules of everlasting salvation taught by thee. They carry it so far that if he who practices or teaches the established rules of pronunciation should speak (contrary to grammatical usage) without aspirating the first syllable of "hominem" ["ominem," and thus make it "a 'uman being"], he will offend men more than if he, a human being, were to hate another human being contrary to thy commandments. It is as if he should feel that there is an enemy who could be more destructive to himself than that hatred which excites him against his fellow man; or that he could destroy him whom he hates more completely than he destroys his own soul by this same hatred.

Now, obviously, there is no knowledge of letters more innate than the writing of conscience—against doing unto another what one would not have done to himself.

How mysterious thou art, who "dwellest on high" in silence. O thou, the only great God, who by an unwearied law hurlest down the penalty of blindness to unlawful desire! When a man seeking the reputation of eloquence stands before a human judge, while a thronging multitude surrounds him, and inveighs against his enemy with the most fierce hatred, he takes most vigilant heed that his tongue does not slip in a grammatical error, for example, and say inter hominibus [instead of inter homines], but he takes no heed lest, in the fury of his spirit, he cut off a man from his fellow men [ex hominibus].[18]

These were the customs in the midst of which I was cast, an unhappy boy. This was the wrestling arena in which I was more fearful of perpetrating a barbarism than, having done so, of envying those who had not. These things I declare and confess to thee, my God. I was applauded by those whom I then thought it my whole duty to please, for I did not perceive the gulf of infamy wherein I was cast away from thy eyes.

For in thy eyes, what was more infamous than I was already, since I displeased even my own kind and deceived, with endless lies, my tutor, my masters and parents—all from a love of play, a craving for frivolous spectacles, a stage-struck restlessness to imitate what I saw in these shows? I pilfered from my parents' cellar and table, sometimes driven by gluttony, sometimes just to have something to give to other boys in exchange for their baubles, which they were prepared to sell even though they liked them as well as I.[19] Moreover, in this kind of play, I often sought dishonest victories, being myself conquered by the vain desire for pre-eminence. And what was I so unwilling to endure, and what was it that I censured so violently when I caught anyone, except the very things I did to others? And, when I was myself detected and censured, I preferred to quarrel rather than to yield. Is this the inno-

18. Academics make a big deal out of mispronouncing a word but could not care less about a man hating his brother.

19. Augustine's sins as a young boy included lying, stealing, pride, and gluttony.

cence of childhood? It is not, O Lord, it is not. I entreat thy mercy, O my God, for these same sins as we grow older are transferred from tutors and masters; they pass from nuts and balls and sparrows, to magistrates and kings, to gold and lands and slaves, just as the rod is succeeded by more severe chastisements. It was, then, the fact of humility in childhood that thou, O our King, didst approve as a symbol of humility when thou saidst, "Of such is the Kingdom of Heaven."

However, O Lord, to thee most excellent and most good, thou Architect and Governor of the universe, thanks would be due thee, O our God, even if thou hadst not willed that I should survive my boyhood. For I existed even then; I lived and felt and was solicitous about my own well-being—a trace of that most mysterious unity from whence I had my being. I kept watch, by my inner sense, over the integrity of my outer senses, and even in these trifles and also in my thoughts about trifles, I learned to take pleasure in truth. I was averse to being deceived; I had a vigorous memory; I was gifted with the power of speech, was softened by friendship, shunned sorrow, meanness, ignorance. Is not such an animated creature as this wonderful and praiseworthy? But all these are gifts of my God; I did not give them to myself. Moreover, they are good, and they all together constitute myself. Good, then, is he that made me, and he is my God; and before him will I rejoice exceedingly for every good gift which, even as a boy, I had. But herein lay my sin, that it was not in him, but in his creatures—myself and the rest—that I sought for pleasures, honors, and truths. And I fell thereby into sorrows, troubles, and errors. Thanks be to thee, my joy, my pride, my confidence, my God—thanks be to thee for thy gifts; but do thou preserve them in me. For thus wilt thou preserve me; and those things which thou hast given me shall be developed and perfected, and I myself shall be with thee, for from thee is my being.

BOOK II

I wish now to review in memory my past wickedness and the carnal corruptions of my soul—not because I still love them, but that I may love thee, O my God. For love of thy love I do this, recalling in the bitterness of self-examination my wicked ways, that thou mayest grow sweet to me, thou sweetness without deception! Thou sweetness happy and assured! Thus thou mayest gather me up out of those fragments in which I was torn to pieces, while I turned away from thee, O Unity, and lost myself among "the many." For as I became a youth, I longed to be satisfied with worldly things, and I dared to grow wild in a succession of various and shadowy loves. My form wasted away, and I became corrupt in thy eyes, yet I was still pleasing to my own eyes—and eager to please the eyes of men.

But what was it that delighted me save to love and to be loved? Still I did not keep the moderate way of the love of mind to mind—the bright path of friendship. Instead, the mists of passion steamed up out of the puddly concupiscence of the flesh, and the hot imagination of puberty, and they so obscured and overcast my heart that I was unable to distinguish pure affection from unholy desire.[1] Both boiled confusedly within me, and dragged my unstable youth down over the cliffs of unchaste desires and plunged me into a gulf of infamy. Thy anger had come upon me, and I knew it not. I had

1. Human friendships are always damaged by sinful thinking and sinful lusts, whether we admit it or not.

2. A "restless lassitude" is a restless weariness. Sin wears us out with its many demands.

been deafened by the clanking of the chains of my mortality, the punishment for my soul's pride, and I wandered farther from thee, and thou didst permit me to do so. I was tossed to and fro, and wasted, and poured out, and I boiled over in my fornications—and yet thou didst hold thy peace, O my tardy Joy! Thou didst still hold thy peace, and I wandered still farther from thee into more and yet more barren fields of sorrow, in proud dejection and restless lassitude.[2]

If only there had been someone to regulate my disorder and turn to my profit the fleeting beauties of the things around me, and to fix a bound to their sweetness, so that the tides of my youth might have spent themselves upon the shore of marriage! Then they might have been tranquilized and satisfied with having children, as thy law prescribes, O Lord—O thou who dost form the offspring of our death and art able also with a tender hand to blunt the thorns which were excluded from thy paradise! For thy omnipotence is not far from us even when we are far from thee. Now, on the other hand, I might have given more vigilant heed to the voice from the clouds: "Nevertheless, such shall have trouble in the flesh, but I spare you," and, "It is good for a man not to touch a woman," and, "He that is unmarried cares for the things that belong to the Lord, how he may please the Lord; but he that is married cares for the things that are of the world, how he may please his wife." I should have listened more attentively to these words, and, thus having been "made a eunuch for the Kingdom of Heaven's sake," I would have with greater happiness expected thy embraces.[3]

3. Augustine would have preferred to have lived a single celibate life than to have wasted his life in fornication. He spent many years in fornicating relationships with women, instead of getting married.

But, fool that I was, I foamed in my wickedness as the sea and, forsaking thee, followed the rushing of my own tide, and burst out of all thy bounds. But I did not escape thy scourges. For what mortal can do so? Thou wast always by me, mercifully angry and flavoring all my unlawful pleasures with bitter discontent, in order that I might seek pleasures free from discontent. But where could I find such pleasure save in thee, O Lord—save in thee, who dost teach us by sorrow, who woundest us to heal us, and dost kill us that we may not die apart from thee. Where was I, and how far was I exiled from the delights of thy house, in that sixteenth year of the age of my flesh, when the madness of lust held full sway in me—that madness which grants indulgence to human shamelessness, even though it is forbidden by thy laws—and I gave myself entirely to it?[4] Meanwhile, my family took no care to save me from ruin by marriage, for their sole care was that I should learn how to make a powerful speech and become a persuasive orator.

Now, in that year my studies were interrupted. I had come back from Madaura, a neighboring city where I had gone to study grammar and rhetoric; and the money for a further term at Carthage was being got together for me. This project was more a matter of my father's ambition than of his means, for he was only a poor citizen of Tagaste.

To whom am I narrating all this? Not to thee, O my God, but to my own kind in thy presence—to that small part of the human race who may chance to come upon these writings. And to what end? That I and all who read them may understand what depths there are from which we are to cry unto thee. For what is more surely heard in thy ear than a confessing heart and a faithful life?[5]

Who did not extol and praise my father, because he went quite beyond his means to supply his son with the necessary expenses for a far journey in the interest of his education? For many far richer citizens did not do so much for their children. Still, this same father troubled himself not at all as to how I was progressing toward thee nor how chaste I was, just so long as I was skillful in speaking—no matter how barren I was to thy tillage, O God, who art the one true and good Lord of my heart, which is thy field.

During that sixteenth year of my age, I lived with my parents, having a holiday from school for a time—this idleness imposed upon me by my parents' straitened finances. The thornbushes of lust grew rank about my head, and there

Landscape of Souk Ahkras, modern day Tagaste

was no hand to root them out. Indeed, when my father saw me one day at the baths and perceived that I was becoming a man, and was showing the signs of adolescence, he joyfully told my mother about it as if already looking forward to grandchildren, rejoicing in that sort of inebriation in which the world so often forgets thee, its Creator, and falls in love with thy creature instead of thee—the inebriation of that invisible wine of a perverted will which turns and bows down to infamy.[6] But in my mother's breast thou hadst already begun to build thy temple and the foundation of thy holy habitation— whereas my father was only a catechumen, and that but recently. She was, therefore, startled with a holy fear and trembling: for though I had not yet been baptized, she feared those crooked ways in which they walk who turn their backs to thee and not their faces.

Woe is me! Do I dare affirm that thou didst hold thy peace, O my God, while I wandered farther away from thee? Didst thou really then hold thy peace? Then whose words were they but thine which by my mother, thy faithful handmaid, thou didst pour into my ears? None of them, however, sank into my heart to make me do anything. She deplored and, as I remember, warned me privately with great solicitude, "not to commit fornication; but above all things never to defile another man's wife."[7] These appeared to me but womanish counsels, which I would have blushed to obey. Yet they were from thee, and I knew it not. I thought that thou wast silent and that it was only she who spoke. Yet it was through her that thou didst not keep silence toward me; and in rejecting her counsel I was rejecting thee—I, her son, "the son of thy handmaid, thy servant." But I did not realize this, and rushed on headlong with such blindness that, among my friends, I was ashamed to be less shameless than they, when I heard them boasting of their disgraceful exploits—yes, and glorying all the more the worse their baseness was. What is worse, I took pleasure in such exploits, not for the pleasure's sake only but mostly for praise. What is worthy of vituperation except vice itself? Yet I made

6. At this time, Augustine's father was not yet a full member of the church. He was a catechumen, under the instruction of the church before getting baptized.

7. Augustine's mother feared God and warned him of sexual sin.

myself out worse than I was, in order that I might not go lacking for praise. And when in anything I had not sinned as the worst ones in the group, I would still say that I had done what I had not done, in order not to appear contemptible because I was more innocent than they; and not to drop in their esteem because I was more chaste.

Behold with what companions I walked the streets of Babylon! I rolled in its mire and lolled about on it, as if on a bed of spices and precious ointments. And, drawing me more closely to the very center of that city, my invisible enemy trod me down and seduced me, for I was easy to seduce. My mother had already fled out of the midst of Babylon and was progressing, albeit slowly, toward its outskirts. For in counseling me to chastity, she did not bear in mind what her husband had told her about me. And although she knew that my passions were destructive even then and dangerous for the future, she did not think they should be restrained by the bonds of conjugal affection—if, indeed, they could not be cut away to the quick. She took no heed of this, for she was afraid lest a wife should prove a hindrance and a burden to my hopes. These were not her hopes of the world to come, which my mother had in thee, but the hope of learning,[8] which both my parents were too anxious that I should acquire—my father, because he had little or no thought of thee, and only vain thoughts for me; my mother, because she thought that the usual course of study would not only be no hindrance but actually a furtherance toward my eventual return to thee. This much I conjecture, recalling as well as I can the temperaments of my parents. Meantime, the reins of discipline were slackened on me, so that without the restraint of due severity, I might play at whatsoever I fancied, even to the point of dissoluteness. And in all this there was that mist which shut out from my sight the brightness of thy truth, O my God; and my iniquity bulged out, as it were, with fatness!

Theft is punished by thy law, O Lord, and by the law written in men's hearts, which not even ingrained wickedness can

8. Augustine's mother was still drawn to academic success as many mothers are today. She even discouraged marriage in favor of developing his career. This became the means by which Augustine was taken down the wrong pathway.

erase. For what thief will tolerate another thief stealing from him? Even a rich thief will not tolerate a poor thief who is driven to theft by want. Yet I had a desire to commit robbery, and did so, compelled to it by neither hunger nor poverty, but through a contempt for well-doing and a strong impulse to iniquity. For I pilfered something which I already had in sufficient measure, and of much better quality. I did not desire to enjoy what I stole, but only the theft and the sin itself.

There was a pear tree close to our own vineyard, heavily laden with fruit, which was not tempting either for its color or for its flavor. Late one night—having prolonged our games in the streets until then, as our bad habit was—a group of young scoundrels, and I among them, went to shake and rob this tree. We carried off a huge load of pears, not to eat ourselves, but to dump out to the hogs, after barely tasting some of them ourselves.[9] Doing this pleased us all the more because it was forbidden. Such was my heart, O God, such was my heart—which thou didst pity even in that bottomless pit. Behold, now let my heart confess to thee what it was seeking there, when I was being gratuitously wanton, having no inducement to evil but the evil itself. It was foul, and I loved it. I loved my own undoing. I loved my error—not that for which I erred but the error itself. A depraved soul, falling away from security in thee to destruction in itself, seeking nothing from the shameful deed but shame itself.

Now there is a comeliness in all beautiful bodies, and in gold and silver and all things. The sense of touch has its own power to please and the other senses find their proper objects in physical sensation. Worldly honor also has its own glory, and so do the powers to command and to overcome: and from these there springs up the desire for revenge. Yet, in seeking these pleasures, we must not depart from thee, O Lord, nor deviate from thy law. The life which we live here has its own peculiar attractiveness because it has a certain measure of comeliness of its own and a harmony with all these inferior values. The bond of human friendship has a sweetness of its

9. Augustine illustrates his rebellion and autonomy in this story. He stole the pears only for the thrill of stealing.

own, binding many souls together as one. Yet because of these values, sin is committed, because we have an inordinate preference for these goods of a lower order and neglect the better and the higher good—neglecting thee, O our Lord God, and thy truth and thy law. For these inferior values have their delights, but not at all equal to my God, who hath made them all. For in him do the righteous delight and he is the sweetness of the upright in heart."[10]

When, therefore, we inquire why a crime was committed, we do not accept the explanation unless it appears that there was the desire to obtain some of those values which we designate inferior, or else a fear of losing them. For truly they are beautiful and comely, though in comparison with the superior and celestial goods they are abject and contemptible. A man has murdered another man—what was his motive? Either he desired his wife or his property or else he would steal to support himself; or else he was afraid of losing something to him; or else, having been injured, he was burning to be revenged. Would a man commit murder without a motive, taking delight simply in the act of murder? Who would believe such a thing? Even for that savage and brutal man [Catiline],[11] of whom it was said that he was gratuitously wicked and cruel, there is still a motive assigned to his deeds. "Lest through idleness," he says, "hand or heart should grow inactive." And to what purpose? Why, even this: that, having once got possession of the city through his practice of his wicked ways, he might gain honors, empire, and wealth, and thus be exempt from the fear of the laws and from financial difficulties in supplying the needs of his family—and from the consciousness of his own wickedness. So it seems that even Catiline himself loved not his own villainies, but something else, and it was this that gave him the motive for his crimes.

What was it in you, O theft of mine, that I, poor wretch, doted on—you deed of darkness—in that sixteenth year of my age? Beautiful you were not, for you were a theft. But are you anything at all, so that I could analyze the case with you?

10. Worldly honor and physical pleasures are not bad in and of themselves. These things corrupt when we place them at a higher priority than God Himself, the source of all good.

11. Cataline was a Roman Senator of the first century BC, who attempted to overthrow the Roman Republic twice, and has been accused of many gross crimes by various historians. He was an opponent of Cicero, the famous Roman historian.

Those pears that we stole were fair to the sight because they were thy creation, O Beauty beyond compare, O Creator of all, O thou good God—God the highest good and my true good. Those pears were truly pleasant to the sight, but it was not for them that my miserable soul lusted, for I had an abundance of better pears. I stole those simply that I might steal, for, having stolen them, I threw them away. My sole gratification in them was my own sin, which I was pleased to enjoy; for, if any one of these pears entered my mouth, the only good flavor it had was my sin in eating it. And now, O Lord my God, I ask what it was in that theft of mine that caused me such delight; for behold it had no beauty of its own—certainly not the sort of beauty that exists in justice and wisdom, nor such as is in the mind, memory senses, and the animal life of man; nor yet the kind that is the glory and beauty of the stars in their courses; nor the beauty of the earth, or the sea—teeming with spawning life, replacing in birth that which dies and decays. Indeed, it did not have that false and shadowy beauty which attends the deceptions of vice.[12]

12. Sin is incredibly deceitful. Every virtue has a false imitation.

For thus we see pride wearing the mask of high-spiritedness, although only thou, O God, art high above all. Ambition seeks honor and glory, whereas only thou shouldst be honored above all, and glorified forever. The powerful man seeks to be feared, because of his cruelty; but who ought really to be feared but God only? What can be forced away or withdrawn out of his power—when or where or whither or by whom? The enticements of the wanton claim the name of love; and yet nothing is more enticing than thy love, nor is anything loved more healthfully than thy truth, bright and beautiful above all. Curiosity prompts a desire for knowledge, whereas it is only thou who knowest all things supremely. Indeed, ignorance and foolishness themselves go masked under the names of simplicity and innocence; yet there is no being that has true simplicity like thine, and none is innocent as thou art. Thus it is that by a sinner's own deeds he is himself harmed. Human sloth pretends to long for rest, but what sure rest is there save in the Lord? Luxury would fain be called plenty and abundance; but thou art the fullness and unfailing abundance of unfading joy. Prodigality presents a show of liberality; but thou art the most lavish giver of all good things. Covetousness desires to possess much; but thou art already the possessor of all things. Envy contends that its aim is for excellence; but what is so excellent as thou? Anger seeks revenge; but who avenges more justly than thou? Fear recoils at the unfamiliar and the sudden changes which threaten things beloved, and is wary for its own security; but what can happen that is unfamiliar or sudden to thee? Or who can deprive thee of what thou lovest? Where, really, is there unshaken security save with thee? Grief languishes for things lost in which desire had taken delight, because it wills to have nothing taken from it, just as nothing can be taken from thee.[13]

Thus the soul commits fornication when she is turned from thee, and seeks apart from thee what she cannot find pure and untainted until she returns to thee. All things thus imitate thee—but pervertedly—when they separate themselves far from thee and raise themselves up against thee. But, even in this act of perverse imitation, they acknowledge thee to be the Creator of all nature, and recognize that there is no place whither they can altogether separate themselves from thee. What was it, then, that I loved in that theft? And wherein was I imitating my Lord, even in a corrupted and perverted way? Did I wish, if only by gesture, to rebel against thy law, even though I had no power to do so actually— so that, even as a captive, I might produce a sort of counterfeit liberty, by doing with impunity deeds that were forbidden, in a deluded sense of omnipotence? Behold this servant of thine, fleeing from his Lord and following a shadow! O rottenness! O monstrousness of life and abyss of death! Could I find pleasure only in what was unlawful, and only because it was unlawful?"

"What shall I render unto the Lord" for the fact that while my memory recalls these things my soul no longer fears them? I will love thee, O Lord, and thank thee, and confess to

13. Everything is perverted when we turn away from God as our chief delight.

thy name, because thou hast put away from me such wicked and evil deeds. To thy grace I attribute it and to thy mercy, that thou hast melted away my sin as if it were ice. To thy grace also I attribute whatsoever of evil I did not commit—for what might I not have done, loving sin as I did, just for the sake of sinning? Yea, all the sins that I confess now to have been forgiven me, both those which I committed willfully and those which, by thy providence, I did not commit. What man is there who, when reflecting upon his own infirmity, dares to ascribe his chastity and innocence to his own powers, so that he should love thee less—as if he were in less need of thy mercy in which thou forgivest the transgressions of those that return to thee? As for that man who, when called by thee, obeyed thy voice and shunned those things which he here reads of me as I recall and confess them of myself, let him not despise me—for I, who was sick, have been healed by the same Physician by whose aid it was that he did not fall sick, or rather was less sick than I. And for this let him love thee just as much—indeed, all the more—since he sees me restored from such a great weakness of sin by the selfsame Saviour by whom he sees himself preserved from such a weakness.[14]

What profit did I, a wretched one, receive from those things which, when I remember them now, cause me shame—above all, from that theft, which I loved only for the theft's sake? And, as the theft itself was nothing, I was all the more wretched in that I loved it so. Yet by myself alone I would not have done it—I still recall how I felt about this then—I could not have done it alone. I loved it then because of the companionship of my accomplices with whom I did it.[15] I did not, therefore, love the theft alone—yet, indeed, it was only the theft that I loved, for the companionship was nothing. What is this paradox? Who is it that can explain it to me but God, who illumines my heart and searches out the dark corners thereof? What is it that has prompted my mind to inquire about it, to discuss and to reflect upon all this? For had I at that time loved the pears that I stole and wished to

14. We are all recipients of God's grace. Those preserved from gross sins were preserved by God's grace. Those forgiven by God are forgiven by the same grace of God.

15. The encouragement to sin on the part of friends marks a perversion of friendship. This is false friendship.

enjoy them, I might have done so alone, if I could have been satisfied with the mere act of theft by which my pleasure was served. Nor did I need to have that itching of my own passions inflamed by the encouragement of my accomplices. But since the pleasure I got was not from the pears, it was in the crime itself, enhanced by the companionship of my fellow sinners.

By what passion, then, was I animated? It was undoubtedly depraved and a great misfortune for me to feel it. But still, what was it? "Who can understand his errors?"

We laughed because our hearts were tickled at the thought of deceiving the owners, who had no idea of what we were doing and would have strenuously objected. Yet, again, why did I find such delight in doing this which I would not have done alone? Is it that no one readily laughs alone? No one does so readily; but still sometimes, when men are by themselves and no one else is about, a fit of laughter will overcome them when something very droll presents itself to their sense or mind. Yet alone I would not have done it—alone I could not have done it at all. Behold, my God, the lively review of my soul's career is laid bare before thee. I would not have committed that theft alone. My pleasure in it was not what I stole but, rather, the act of stealing. Nor would I have enjoyed doing it alone—indeed I would not have done it! O friendship all unfriendly! You strange seducer of the soul, who hungers for mischief from impulses of mirth and wantonness, who craves another's loss without any desire for one's own profit or revenge—so that, when they say, "Let's go, let's do it," we are ashamed not to be shameless. Who can unravel such a twisted and tangled knottiness? It is unclean. I hate to reflect upon it. I hate to look on it. But I do long for thee, O Righteousness and Innocence, so beautiful and comely to all virtuous eyes—I long for thee with an insatiable satiety. With thee is perfect rest, and life unchanging. He who enters into thee enters into the joy of his Lord, and shall have no fear and shall achieve excellence in the Excellent. I fell away from thee, O my God, and in my youth I wandered too far from thee, my true support. And I became to myself a wasteland.

✥ BOOK III

Ruins of Carthage

Roman Theater in Amman, Jordan

I came to Carthage, where a caldron of unholy loves was seething and bubbling all around me. I was not in love as yet, but I was in love with love; and, from a hidden hunger, I hated myself for not feeling more intensely a sense of hunger. I was looking for something to love, for I was in love with loving, and I hated security and a smooth way, free from snares. Within me I had a dearth of that inner food which is thyself, my God—although that dearth caused me no hunger. And I remained without any appetite for incorruptible food—not because I was already filled with it, but because the emptier I became the more I loathed it. Because of this my soul was unhealthy; and, full of sores, it exuded itself forth, itching to be scratched by scraping on the things of the senses. Yet, had these things no soul, they would certainly not inspire our love.[1]

To love and to be loved was sweet to me, and all the more when I gained the enjoyment of the body of the person I loved. Thus I polluted the spring of friendship with the filth of concupiscence and I dimmed its luster with the slime of lust.[2] Yet, foul and unclean as I was, I still craved, in excessive vanity, to be thought elegant and urbane. And I did fall precipitately into the love I was longing for. My God, my mercy, with how much bitterness didst thou, out of thy infinite goodness, flavor that sweetness for me! For I was not only beloved but also I secretly reached the climax of enjoyment; and yet I was joyfully bound with troublesome tics, so that I could be scourged

1. Augustine plays with paradoxes and self-contradictions throughout. He was hungry, and only God would satisfy that hunger, but he had no taste for God. He sought to fill himself with everything else and only became hungrier as a result.

2. Sexual sin gave a temporary fulfillment, but it would also destroy friendship and bring about more jealousy, anger, and strife into relationships.

with the burning iron rods of jealousy, suspicion, fear, anger, and strife.

Stage plays also captivated me, with their sights full of the images of my own miseries: fuel for my own fire. Now, why does a man like to be made sad by viewing doleful and tragic scenes, which he himself could not by any means endure? Yet, as a spectator, he wishes to experience from them a sense of grief, and in this very sense of grief his pleasure consists. What is this but wretched madness? For a man is more affected by these actions the more he is spuriously involved in these affections. Now, if he should suffer them in his own person, it is the custom to call this "misery." But when he suffers with another, then it is called "compassion." But what kind of compassion is it that arises from viewing fictitious and unreal sufferings? The spectator is not expected to aid the sufferer but merely to grieve for him. And the more he grieves the more he applauds the actor of these fictions. If the misfortunes of the characters—whether historical or entirely imaginary—are represented so as not to touch the feelings of the spectator, he goes away disgusted and complaining. But if his feelings are deeply touched, he sits it out attentively, and sheds tears of joy.[3]

3. Augustine critiques stage plays (tragedies). These things are entertaining when in real life they would be painful. He calls these stage plays "wretched madness."

Tears and sorrow, then, are loved. Surely every man desires to be joyful. And, though no one is willingly miserable, one may, nevertheless, be pleased to be merciful so that we love their sorrows because without them we should have nothing to pity. This also springs from that same vein of friendship. But whither does it go? Whither does it flow? Why does it run into that torrent of pitch which seethes forth those huge tides of loathsome lusts in which it is changed and altered past recognition, being diverted and corrupted from its celestial purity by its own will? Shall, then, compassion be repudiated? By no means! Let us, however, love the sorrows of others. But let us beware of uncleanness, O my soul, under the protection of my God, the God of our fathers, who is to be praised and exalted—let us beware of uncleanness. I have not yet ceased to have compassion. But in those days in the theaters I sympathized with lovers when they sinfully enjoyed one another, although this was done fictitiously in the play. And when they lost one another, I grieved with them, as if pitying them, and yet had delight in both grief and pity.[4] Nowadays I feel much more pity for one who delights in his wickedness than for one who counts himself unfortunate because he fails to obtain some harmful pleasure or suffers the loss of some miserable felicity. This, surely, is the truer compassion, but the sorrow I feel in it has no delight for me. For although he that grieves with the unhappy should be commended for his work of love, yet he who has the power of real compassion would still prefer that there be nothing for him to grieve about. For if good will were to be ill will—which it cannot be—only then could he who is truly and sincerely compassionate wish that there were some unhappy people so that he might commiserate them. Some grief may then be justified, but none of it loved. Thus it is that thou dost act, O Lord God, for thou lovest souls far more purely than we do and art more incorruptibly compassionate, although thou art never wounded by any sorrow. Now "who is sufficient for these things?"

But at that time, in my wretchedness, I loved to grieve; and I sought for things to grieve about. In another man's misery, even though it was feigned and impersonated on the stage, that performance of the actor pleased me best and attracted me most powerfully which moved me to tears.[5] What marvel then was it that an unhappy sheep, straying from thy flock and impatient of thy care, I became infected with a foul disease? This is the reason for my love of griefs: that they would not probe into me too deeply (for I did not love to suffer in myself such things as I loved to look at), and they were the sort of grief which came from hearing those fictions, which affected only the surface of my emotion. Still, just as if they had been poisoned fingernails, their scratching was followed by inflammation, swelling, putrefaction, and corruption.[6] Such was my life! But was it life, O my God?

4. We ought to have more compassion over the sinner who commits fornication than the man in the movie or stage play who loses the girlfriend with whom he has been fornicating.

5. For some reason, people delight in weeping over tragic scenes in films. They will return again and again to see these films. Augustine says we should not delight in sorrowing over these misfortunes.

6. Augustine sees this love of tragic stage plays as a sort of foul disease.

And still thy faithful mercy hovered over me from afar. In what unseemly iniquities did I wear myself out, following a sacrilegious curiosity, which, having deserted thee, then began to drag me down into the treacherous abyss, into the beguiling obedience of devils, to whom I made offerings of my wicked deeds. And still in all this thou didst not fail to scourge me. I dared, even while thy solemn rites were being celebrated inside the walls of thy church, to desire and to plan a project which merited death as its fruit. For this thou didst chastise me with grievous punishments, but nothing in comparison with my fault, O thou my greatest mercy, my God, my refuge from those terrible dangers in which I wandered with stiff neck, receding farther from thee, loving my own ways and not thine—loving a vagrant liberty!

Those studies I was then pursuing, generally accounted as respectable, were aimed at distinction in the courts of law—to excel in which, the more crafty I was, the more I should be praised. Such is the blindness of men that they even glory in their blindness. And by this time I had become a master in the School of Rhetoric, and I rejoiced proudly in this honor and became inflated with arrogance. Still I was relatively sedate, O Lord, as thou knowest, and had no share in the wreckings of "The Wreckers"[7] (for this stupid and diabolical name was regarded as the very badge of gallantry) among whom I lived with a sort of ashamed embarrassment that I was not even as they were. But I lived with them, and at times I was delighted with their friendship, even when I abhorred their acts (that is, their "wrecking") in which they insolently attacked the modesty of strangers, tormenting them by uncalled-for jeers, gratifying their mischievous mirth. Nothing could more nearly resemble the actions of devils than these fellows. By what name, therefore, could they be more aptly called than "wreckers?"— being themselves wrecked first, and altogether turned upside down. They were secretly mocked at and seduced by the deceiving spirits, in the very acts by which they amused themselves in jeering and horseplay at the expense of others.

7. While a young man teaching Rhetoric, Augustine apparently lived with delinquent young men he calls "Wreckers."

Among such as these, in that unstable period of my life, I studied the books of eloquence, for it was in eloquence that I was eager to be eminent, though from a reprehensible and vainglorious motive, and a delight in human vanity. In the ordinary course of study I came upon a certain book of Cicero's, whose language almost all admire, though not his heart. This particular book of his contains an exhortation to philosophy and was called Hortensius. Now it was this book which quite definitely changed my whole attitude and turned my prayers toward thee, O Lord, and gave me new hope and new desires.[8] Suddenly every vain hope became worthless to me, and with an incredible warmth of heart I yearned for an immortality of wisdom and began now to arise that I might return to thee. It was not to sharpen my tongue further that I made use of that book. I was now nineteen; my father had been dead two years, and my mother was providing the money for my study of rhetoric. What won me in it [i.e., the Hortensius] was not its style but its substance.[9]

How ardent was I then, my God, how ardent to fly from earthly things to thee! Nor did I know how thou wast even then dealing with me. For with thee is wisdom. In Greek the love of wisdom is called "philosophy," and it was with this love that that book inflamed me. There are some who seduce through philosophy, under a great, alluring, and honorable name, using it to color and adorn their own errors. And almost all who did this, in Cicero's own time and earlier, are censored and pointed out in his book. In it there is also manifest that most salutary admonition of thy Spirit, spoken by thy good and pious servant: "Beware lest any man spoil you through philosophy and vain deceit, after the tradition of men, after the rudiments of the world, and not after Christ: for in him all the fullness of the Godhead dwells bodily." Since at that time, as thou knowest, O Light of my heart, the words of the apostle were unknown to me, I was delighted with Cicero's exhortation, at least enough so that I was stimulated by it, and enkindled and inflamed to love, to seek, to obtain, to hold, and

8. *Hortensius,* written by Cicero, is no longer available. Augustine's treatment of it (and quotations) is the largest portion of the text still extant.

9. After reading *Hortensius*, Augustine was less enamored with man's opinions (with all of its errors) and sought the immortality of wisdom instead.

to embrace, not this or that sect, but wisdom itself, wherever it might be. Only this checked my ardor: that the name of Christ was not in it. For this name, by thy mercy, O Lord, this name of my Saviour thy Son, my tender heart had piously drunk in, deeply treasured even with my mother's milk. And whatsoever was lacking that name, no matter how erudite, polished, and truthful, did not quite take complete hold of me.[10]

I resolved, therefore, to direct my mind to the Holy Scriptures, that I might see what they were. And behold, I saw something not comprehended by the proud, not disclosed to children, something lowly in the hearing, but sublime in the doing, and veiled in mysteries. Yet I was not of the number of those who could enter into it or bend my neck to follow its steps. For then it was quite different from what I now feel. When I then turned toward the Scriptures, they appeared to me to be quite unworthy to be compared with the dignity of Tully.[11] For my inflated pride was repelled by their style, nor could the sharpness of my wit penetrate their inner meaning.[12] Truly they were of a sort to aid the growth of little ones, but I scorned to be a little one and, swollen with pride, I looked upon myself as fully grown.

Thus I fell among men, delirious in their pride, carnal and voluble, whose mouths were the snares of the devil—a trap made out of a mixture of the syllables of thy name and the names of our Lord Jesus Christ and of the Paraclete.[13] These names were never out of their mouths, but only as sound and the clatter of tongues, for their heart was empty of truth. Still they cried, "Truth, Truth," and were forever speaking the word to me. But the thing itself was not in them. Indeed, they spoke falsely not only of thee—who truly art the Truth—but also about the basic elements of this world, thy creation. And, indeed, I should have passed by the philosophers themselves even when they were speaking truth concerning thy creatures, for the sake of thy love, O Highest Good, and my Father, O Beauty of all things beautiful.

10. Augustine quickly clarifies that Cicero did not mention the name of Christ, and this checked his ardor for Greek philosophy. Cicero prompted him to return to the Scriptures taught by his mother (from the time he was a baby).

11. Tully is a shortened version of Cicero's middle name.

12. Augustine despised the wisdom of Scripture because he had been well indoctrinated into the pride of classical academics.

13. Paraclete – The Holy Spirit (or the Comforter sent to us by Christ).

O Truth, Truth, how inwardly even then did the marrow of my soul sigh for thee when, frequently and in manifold ways, in numerous and vast books, [the Manicheans][14] sounded out thy name though it was only a sound! And in these dishes—while I starved for thee—they served up to me, in thy stead, the sun and moon thy beauteous works—but still only thy works and not thyself; indeed, not even thy first work. For thy spiritual works came before these material creations, celestial and shining though they are. But I was hungering and thirsting, not even after those first works of thine, but after thyself the Truth, "with whom is no variableness, neither shadow of turning." Yet they still served me glowing fantasies in those dishes. And, truly, it would have been better to have loved this very sun—which at least is true to our sight—than those illusions of theirs which deceive the mind through the eye. And yet because I supposed the illusions to be from thee I fed on them—not with avidity, for thou didst not taste in my mouth as thou art, and thou wast not these empty fictions. Neither was I nourished by them, but was instead exhausted. Food in dreams appears like our food awake; yet the sleepers are not nourished by it, for they are asleep. But the fantasies of the Manicheans were not in any way like thee as thou hast spoken to me now. They were simply fantastic and false. In comparison to them the actual bodies which we see with our fleshly sight, both celestial and terrestrial, are far more certain. These true bodies even the beasts and birds perceive as well as we do and they are more certain than the images we form about them. And again, we do with more certainty form our conceptions about them than, from them, we go on by means of them to imagine of other greater and infinite bodies which have no existence. With such empty husks was I then fed, and yet was not fed.[15]

But thou, my Love, for whom I longed in order that I might be strong, neither art those bodies that we see in heaven nor art thou those which we do not see there, for thou hast created them all and yet thou reckonest them not among thy

14. Augustine begins his narration of his experience with the Manicheans (who attempted to impose a human-derived philosophy over Scripture). These religionists spoke of biblical names and subjects with their own ideas stuffed into them.

Marcus Cicero (106–43 BC), a Roman politician, lawyer, and orator

15. Augustine admits that these false ideas of the Manicheans did not satisfy. They further exhausted him in the blind search for truth in the maze of human error.

greatest works. How far, then, art thou from those fantasies of mine, fantasies of bodies which have no real being at all!

The images of those bodies which actually exist are far more certain than these fantasies. The bodies themselves are more certain than the images, yet even these thou art not. Thou art not even the soul, which is the life of bodies; and, clearly, the life of the body is better than the body itself. But thou art the life of souls, life of lives, having life in thyself, and never changing, O Life of my soul.

Where, then, wast thou and how far from me? Far, indeed, was I wandering away from thee, being barred even from the husks of those swine whom I fed with husks. For how much better were the fables of the grammarians and poets than these snares [of the Manicheans]! For verses and poems and "the flying Medea"[16] are still more profitable truly than these men's "five elements," with their various colors, answering to "the five caves of darkness" (none of which exist and yet in which they slay the one who believes in them). For verses and poems I can turn into food for the mind, for though I sang about "the flying Medea" I never believed it, but those other things [the fantasies of the Manicheans] I did believe. Woe, woe, by what steps I was dragged down to "the depths of hell"—toiling and fuming because of my lack of the truth, even when I was seeking after thee, my God! To thee I now confess it, for thou didst have mercy on me when I had not yet confessed it. I sought after thee, but not according to the understanding of the mind, by means of which thou hast willed that I should excel the beasts, but only after the guidance of my physical senses. Thou wast more inward to me than the most inward part of me; and higher than my highest reach. I came upon that brazen woman, devoid of prudence, who, in Solomon's obscure parable, sits at the door of the house on a seat and says, "Stolen waters are sweet, and bread eaten in secret is pleasant." This woman seduced me, because she found my soul outside its own door, dwelling on the sensations of my

16. False religions and false philosophies are worse than fictions. The Flying Medea is an enchantress or witch in Greek mythology that fled from Athens in a flying chariot.

flesh and ruminating on such food as I had swallowed through these physical senses.

For I was ignorant of that other reality, true Being. And so it was that I was subtly persuaded to agree with these foolish deceivers when they put their questions to me: "Whence comes evil?"[17] and, "Is God limited by a bodily shape, and has he hairs and nails?" and, "Are those patriarchs to be esteemed righteous who had many wives at one time, and who killed men and who sacrificed living creatures?"[18] In my ignorance I was much disturbed over these things and, though I was retreating from the truth, I appeared to myself to be going toward it, because I did not yet know that evil was nothing but a privation of good (that, indeed, it has no being); and how should I have seen this when the sight of my eyes went no farther than physical objects, and the sight of my mind reached no farther than to fantasms? And I did not know that God is a spirit who has no parts extended in length and breadth, whose being has no mass—for every mass is less in a part than in a whole—and if it be an infinite mass it must be less in such parts as are limited by a certain space than in its infinity. It cannot therefore be wholly everywhere as Spirit is, as God is. And I was entirely ignorant as to what is that principle within us by which we are like God, and which is rightly said in Scripture to be made "after God's image."

Nor did I know that true inner righteousness—which does not judge according to custom but by the measure of the most perfect law of God Almighty—by which the mores of various places and times were adapted to those places and times (though the law itself is the same always and everywhere, not one thing in one place and another in another). By this inner righteousness Abraham and Isaac, and Jacob and Moses and David, and all those commended by the mouth of God were righteous and were judged unrighteous only by foolish men who were judging by human judgment and gauging their judgment of the mores of the whole human race by the narrow norms of their own mores.[19] It is as if a man in an armory, not

17. Augustine defines evil as the "absence of good."

18. Atheists and ungodly philosophers still ask these same questions, thinking they can answer them satisfactorily themselves (when indeed they do not).

19. Immoral fornicators scoff at polygamy, but they are not defining their ethics by God's law. This is because people develop their ethical views by cultural norms (or mores).

knowing what piece goes on what part of the body, should put a greave on his head and a helmet on his shin and then complain because they did not fit. Or as if, on some holiday when afternoon business was forbidden, one were to grumble at not being allowed to go on selling as it had been lawful for him to do in the forenoon. Or, again, as if, in a house, he sees a servant handle something that the butler is not permitted to touch, or when something is done behind a stable that would be prohibited in a dining room, and then a person should be indignant that in one house and one family the same things are not allowed to every member of the household. Such is the case with those who cannot endure to hear that something was lawful for righteous men in former times that is not so now; or that God, for certain temporal reasons, commanded then one thing to them and another now to these: yet both would be serving the same righteous will. These people should see that in one man, one day, and one house, different things are fit for different members; and a thing that was formerly lawful may become, after a time, unlawful—and something allowed or commanded in one place that is justly prohibited and punished in another. Is justice, then, variable and changeable? No, but the times over which she presides are not all alike because they are different times. But men, whose days upon the earth are few, cannot by their own perception harmonize the causes of former ages and other nations, of which they had no experience, and compare them with these of which they do have experience; although in one and the same body, or day, or family, they can readily see that what is suitable for each member, season, part, and person may differ. To the one they take exception; to the other they submit.[20]

These things I did not know then, nor had I observed their import. They met my eyes on every side, and I did not see. I composed poems,"in which I was not free to place each foot just anywhere, but in one" meter one way, and in another meter another way, nor even in any one verse was the same foot allowed in all places. Yet the art by which I composed

20. Augustine argues that God allowed polygamy for a while in the Old Testament era. There is a permanence about the principles of God's law, but given different situations throughout time, God retains the right to adjust certain applications. Another example might be Cain, who married his sister. Later, in the book of Leviticus, God disallows these incestuous relationships.

did not have different principles for each of these different cases, but the same law throughout. Still I did not see how, by that righteousness to which good and holy men submitted, all those things that God had commanded were gathered, in a far more excellent and sublime way, into one moral order; and it did not vary in any essential respect, though it did not in varying times prescribe all things at once but, rather, distributed and prescribed what was proper for each. And, being blind, I blamed those pious fathers, not only for making use of present things as God had commanded and inspired them to do, but also for foreshadowing things to come, as God revealed it to them.

Can it ever, at any time or place, be unrighteous for a man to love God with all his heart, with all his soul, and with all his mind; and his neighbor as himself? Similarly, offenses against nature are everywhere and at all times to be held in detestation and should be punished. Such offenses, for example, were those of the Sodomites; and, even if all nations should commit[21] them, they would all be judged guilty of the same crime by the divine law, which has not made men so that they should ever abuse one another in that way. For the fellowship that should be between God and us is violated whenever that nature of which he is the author is polluted by perverted lust. But these offenses against customary morality are to be avoided according to the variety of such customs. Thus, what is agreed upon by convention, and confirmed by custom or the law of any city or nation, may not be violated at the lawless pleasure of any, whether citizen or stranger. For any part that is not consistent with its whole is unseemly. Nevertheless, when God commands anything contrary to the customs or compacts of any nation, even though it were never done by them before, it is to be done; and if it has been interrupted, it is to be restored; and if it has never been established, it is to be established. For it is lawful for a king, in the state over which he reigns, to command that which neither he himself nor anyone before him had commanded. And if it cannot be

21. There are some laws that are perpetually applicable and will never change. Among these laws Augustine includes loving God with heart, soul, mind, and strength. Also, he includes biblical laws against those offenses contrary to nature, such as that committed by the Sodomites. Augustine says these "should at all times be punished."

22. God's law governs nations. If a nation's customs oppose God's laws, those customs should be altered in accordance with God's law.

held to be inimical to the public interest to obey him—and, in truth, it would be inimical if he were not obeyed, since obedience to princes is a general compact of human society—how much more, then, ought we unhesitatingly to obey God, the Governor of all his creatures! For, just as among the authorities in human society, the greater authority is obeyed before the lesser, so also must God be above all.[22]

This applies as well to deeds of violence where there is a real desire to harm another, either by humiliating treatment or by injury. Either of these may be done for reasons of revenge, as one enemy against another, or in order to obtain some advantage over another, as in the case of the "highwayman and the traveler; else they may be done in order to avoid" some other evil, as in the case of one who fears another; or through envy as, for example, an unfortunate man harming a happy one just because he is happy; or they may be done by a prosperous man against someone whom he fears will become equal to himself or whose equality he resents. They may even be done for the mere pleasure in another man's pain, as the spectators of gladiatorial shows or the people who deride and mock at others. These are the major forms of iniquity that spring out of the lust of the flesh, and of the eye, and of power. Sometimes there is just one; sometimes two together; sometimes all of them at once. Thus we live, offending against the Three and the Seven, that harp of ten strings, thy Decalogue, O God most high and most sweet. But now how can offenses of vileness harm thee who canst not be defiled; or how can deeds of violence harm thee who canst not be harmed? Still thou dost punish these sins which men commit against themselves because, even when they sin against thee, they are also committing impiety against their own souls. Iniquity gives itself the lie, either by corrupting or by perverting that nature which thou hast made and ordained. And they do this by an immoderate use of lawful things; or by lustful desire for things forbidden, as "against nature;" or when they are guilty of sin by raging with heart and voice against thee, rebelling against thee, "kicking against the pricks;" or when they cast aside respect for human society and take audacious delight in conspiracies and feuds according to their private likes and dislikes.[23]

This is what happens whenever thou art forsaken, O Fountain of Life, who art the one and true Creator and Ruler of the universe. This is what happens when through self-willed pride a part is loved under the false assumption that it is the whole. Therefore, we must return to thee in humble piety and let thee purge us from our evil ways, and be merciful to those who confess their sins to thee, and hear the groanings of the prisoners and loosen us from those fetters which we have forged for ourselves. This thou wilt do, provided we do not raise up against thee the arrogance of a false freedom—for thus we lose all through craving more, by loving our own good more than thee, the common good of all.

But among all these vices and crimes and manifold iniquities, there are also the sins that are committed by men who are, on the whole, making progress toward the good. When these are judged rightly and after the rule of perfection, the sins are censored but the men are to be commended because they show the hope of bearing fruit, like the green shoot of the growing corn.[24] And there are some deeds that resemble vice and crime and yet are not sin because they offend neither thee, our Lord God, nor social custom. For example, when suitable reserves for hard times are provided, we cannot judge that this is done merely from a hoarding impulse. Or, again, when acts are punished by constituted authority for the sake of correction, we cannot judge that they are done merely out of a desire to inflict pain. Thus, many a deed which is disapproved in man's sight may be approved by thy testimony. And many a man who is praised by men is condemned—as thou art witness—because frequently the deed itself, the mind of the doer, and the hidden exigency of the situation all vary among themselves. But when, contrary to human expectation, thou commandest something unusual or unthought of—indeed, something thou mayest formerly have forbidden, about

23. Major forms of iniquity include murder for pragmatic reasons, revenge, covetousness, envy, and taking pleasure in pain suffered by others (gladiatorial games), etc.

24. The Ten Commandments are presented as the basic moral law of God.

25. Some men still commit sin, but they are being sanctified by the Holy Spirit of God. Some deeds may appear wrong but as judged by the laws of God are not sinful.

26. Augustine allows for punishment for the sake of correction (which may include corporal punishment on the part of parents).

27. Apparently, the Manicheans lost the Creator-creature distinction and found God in the creation. Augustine points out the silliness of the reasoning of these proud men.

28. Augustine's mother, Monica, weeps over her son, but she is comforted by a dream.

which thou mayest conceal the reason for thy command at that particular time; and even though it may be contrary to the ordinance of some society of men—who doubts but that it should be done because only that society of men is righteous which obeys thee?[25] But blessed are they who know what thou dost command. For all things done by those who obey thee either exhibit something necessary at that particular time or they foreshow things to come.[26]

But I was ignorant of all this, and so I mocked those holy servants and prophets of thine. Yet what did I gain by mocking them save to be mocked in turn by thee? Insensibly and little by little, I was led on to such follies as to believe that a fig tree wept when it was plucked and that the sap of the mother tree was tears. Notwithstanding this, if a fig was plucked, by not his own but another man's wickedness, some Manichean saint might eat it, digest it in his stomach, and breathe it out again in the form of angels. Indeed, in his prayers he would assuredly groan and sigh forth particles of God, although these particles of the most high and true God would have remained bound in that fig unless they had been set free by the teeth and belly of some "elect saint"! And, wretch that I was, I believed that more mercy was to be shown to the fruits of the earth than unto men, for whom these fruits were created. For, if a hungry man—who was not a Manichean—should beg for any food, the morsel that we gave to him would seem condemned, as it were, to capital punishment.[27]

And now thou didst "stretch forth thy hand from above" and didst draw up my soul out of that profound darkness [of Manicheism] because my mother, thy faithful one, wept to thee on my behalf more than mothers are accustomed to weep for the bodily deaths of their children. For by the light of the faith and spirit which she received from thee, she saw that I was dead. And thou didst hear her, O Lord, thou didst hear her and despised not her tears when, pouring down, they watered the earth under her eyes in every place where she prayed. Thou didst truly hear her.[28]

For what other source was there for that dream by which thou didst console her, so that she permitted me to live with her, to have my meals in the same house at the table which she had begun to avoid, even while she hated and detested the blasphemies of my error? In her dream she saw herself standing on a sort of wooden rule, and saw a bright youth approaching her, joyous and smiling at her, while she was grieving and bowed down with sorrow. But when he inquired of her the cause of her sorrow and daily weeping (not to learn from her, but to teach her, as is customary in visions), and when she answered that it was my soul's doom she was lamenting, he bade her rest content and told her to look and see that where she was there I was also. And when she looked she saw me standing near her on the same rule.

Whence came this vision unless it was that thy ears were inclined toward her heart? O thou Omnipotent Good, thou carest for every one of us as if thou didst care for him only, and so for all as if they were but one!

And what was the reason for this also, that, when she told me of this vision, and I tried to put this construction on it: "that she should not despair of being someday what I was," she replied immediately, without hesitation, "No; for it was not told me that 'where he is, there you shall be' but 'where you are, there he will be'?" I confess my remembrance of this to thee, O Lord, as far as I can recall it—and I have often mentioned it. Thy answer, given through my watchful mother, in the fact that she was not disturbed by the plausibility of my false interpretation but saw immediately what should have been seen—and which I certainly had not seen until she spoke—this answer moved me more deeply than the dream itself. Still, by that dream, the joy that was to come to that pious woman so long after was predicted long before, as a consolation for her present anguish.

Nearly nine years passed in which I wallowed in the mud of that deep pit and in the darkness of falsehood, striving often to rise, but being all the more heavily dashed down. But all that time this chaste, pious, and sober widow—such as thou dost love—was now more buoyed up with hope, though no less zealous in her weeping and mourning; and she did not cease to bewail my case before thee, in all the hours of her supplication. Her prayers entered thy presence, and yet thou didst allow me still to tumble and toss around in that darkness.

Meanwhile, thou gavest her yet another answer, as I remember—for I pass over many things, hastening on to those things which more strongly impel me to confess to thee—and many things I have simply forgotten. But thou gavest her then another answer, by a priest of thine, a certain bishop reared in thy Church and well versed in thy books. When that woman had begged him to agree to have some discussion with me, to refute my errors, to help me to unlearn evil and to learn the good[29]— for it was his habit to do this when he found people ready to receive it—he refused, very prudently, as I afterward realized. For he answered that I was still unteachable, being inflated with the novelty of that heresy, and that I had already perplexed divers inexperienced persons with vexatious questions,[30] as she herself had told him. "But let him alone for a time," he said, "only pray God for him. He will of his own accord, by reading, come to discover what an error it is and how great its impiety is." He went on to tell her at the same time how he himself, as a boy, had been given over to the Manicheans by his misguided mother and not only had read but had even copied out almost all their books. Yet he had come to see, without external argument or proof from anyone else, how much that sect was to be shunned—and had shunned it. When he had said this she was not satisfied, but repeated more earnestly her entreaties, and shed copious tears, still beseeching him to see and talk with me. Finally the bishop, a little vexed at her importunity, exclaimed, "Go your way; as you live, it cannot be that the son of these tears should perish." As she often told me afterward, she accepted this answer as though it were a voice from heaven.

29. The persistence of Monica, this godly widow, in prayers, tears, and pleadings for her son's salvation is truly remarkable — a tremendous example of piety for every Christian parent.

30. One Christian bishop or pastor refused to speak to Augustine because he was proud and unteachable.

✥ BOOK IV

During this period of nine years, from my nineteenth year to my twenty-eighth, I went astray and led others astray.[1] I was deceived and deceived others, in varied lustful projects - sometimes publicly, by the teaching of what men style "the liberal arts"; sometimes secretly, under the false guise of religion. In the one, I was proud of myself; in the other, superstitious; in all, vain! In my public life I was striving after the emptiness of popular fame, going so far as to seek theatrical applause, entering poetic contests, striving for the straw garlands and the vanity of theatricals and intemperate desires. In my private life I was seeking to be purged from these corruptions of ours by carrying food to those who were called "elect" and "holy," which, in the laboratory of their stomachs,[2] they should make into angels and gods for us, and by them we might be set free. These projects I followed out and practiced with my friends, who were both deceived with me and by me. Let the proud laugh at me, and those who have not yet been savingly cast down and stricken by thee, O my God. Nevertheless, I would confess to thee my shame to thy glory. Bear with me, I beseech thee, and give me the grace to retrace in my present memory the devious ways of my past errors and thus be able to "offer to thee the sacrifice of thanksgiving." For what am I to myself without thee but a guide to my own downfall? Or what am I, even at the best,

1. Augustine deceived others in two ways — by teaching a humanist classical education and by advocating a false religion. This went on for nine years.

2. Mani was influenced by Buddhist thought. Followers of Mani were divided into two groups — the "elect" monks and the lay people (called "hearers").

but one suckled on thy milk and feeding on thee, O Food that never perishes? What indeed is any man, seeing that he is but a man? Therefore, let the strong and the mighty laugh at us, but let us who are "poor and needy" confess to thee.

During those years I taught the art of rhetoric. Conquered by the desire for gain, I offered for sale speaking skills with which to conquer others. And yet, O Lord, thou knowest that I really preferred to have honest scholars (or what were esteemed as such) and, without tricks of speech, I taught these scholars the tricks of speech—not to be used against the life of the innocent, but sometimes to save the life of a guilty man. And thou, O God, didst see me from afar, stumbling on that slippery path and sending out some flashes of fidelity amid much smoke—guiding those who loved vanity and sought after lying, being myself their companion.

In those years I had a mistress, to whom I was not joined in lawful marriage.[3] She was a woman I had discovered in my wayward passion, void as it was of understanding, yet she was the only one; and I remained faithful to her and with her I discovered, by my own experience, what a great difference there is between the restraint of the marriage bond contracted with a view to having children and the compact of a lustful love, where children are born against the parents' will—although once they are born they compel our love.

3. Augustine did not marry the woman with whom he had relations. The relationship he says was based in lust.

I remember too that, when I decided to compete for a theatrical prize, some magician—I do not remember him now—asked me what I would give him to be certain to win. But I detested and abominated such filthy mysteries, and answered "that, even if the garland was of imperishable gold, I would still not permit a fly to be killed to win it for me." For he would have slain certain living creatures in his sacrifices, and by those honors would have invited the devils to help me. This evil thing I refused, but not out of a pure love of thee, O God of my heart, for I knew not how to love thee because I knew not how to conceive of anything beyond corporeal splendors. And does not a soul, sighing after such idle fictions, commit fornication against thee, trust in false things, and "feed on the winds?" But still I would not have sacrifices offered to devils on my behalf, though I was myself still offering them sacrifices of a sort by my own [Manichean] superstition. For what else is it "to feed on the winds" but to feed on the devils, that is, in our wanderings to become their sport and mockery?

And yet, without scruple, I consulted those other impostors, whom they call "astrologers" [mathematicos], because they used no sacrifices and invoked the aid of no spirit for their divinations.[4] Still, true Christian piety must necessarily reject and condemn their art. It is good to confess to thee and to say, "Have mercy on me; heal my soul; for I have sinned against thee"—not to abuse thy goodness as a license to sin, but to remember the words of the Lord, "Behold, you are made whole: sin no more, lest a worse thing befall you." All this wholesome advice [the astrologers] labor to destroy when they say, "The cause of your sin is inevitably fixed in the heavens," and, "This is the doing of Venus, or of Saturn, or of Mars"—all this in order that a man, who is only flesh and blood and proud corruption, may regard himself as blameless, while the Creator and Ordainer of heaven and the stars must bear the blame of our ills and misfortunes.[5] But who is this Creator but thou, our God, the sweetness and wellspring of righteousness, who renderest to every man according to his works and despisest not "a broken and a contrite heart?"

There was at that time a wise man, very skillful and quite famous in medicine. He was proconsul then, and with his own hand he placed on my distempered head the crown I had won in a rhetorical contest.

He did not do this as a physician, however; and for this distemper "only thou canst heal who resisteth the proud and giveth grace to the humble." But didst thou fail me in that old man, or forbear from healing my soul? Actually when I became better acquainted with him, I used to listen, rapt and eager, to his words; for, though he spoke in simple language, his conversation was replete with vivacity, life, and earnestness.

4. Augustine had a conscience against magicians or wizards conducting animal sacrifices, but he still went after astrology. Evidently the Christian Church had condemned astrology at that time.

5. Astrology assigns the cause of certain events (even sins) to the motions of the stars. This was supposed to relieve human responsibility for sins. However, Augustine says those who hold such a view end up blaming God.

He recognized from my own talk that I was given to books of the horoscope-casters, but he, in a kind and fatherly way, advised me to throw them away and not to spend idly on these vanities care and labor that might otherwise go into useful things. He said that he himself in his earlier years had studied the astrologers' art with a view to gaining his living by it as a profession. Since he had already understood Hippocrates,[6] he was fully qualified to understand this too. Yet, he had given it up and followed medicine for the simple reason that he had discovered astrology to be utterly false and, as a man of honest character, he was unwilling to gain his living by beguiling people. "But you," he said, "have the profession of rhetoric to support yourself by, so that you are following this delusion in free will and not necessity. All the more, therefore, you ought to believe me, since I worked at it to learn the art perfectly because I wished to gain my living by it." When I asked him to account for the fact that many true things are foretold by astrology, he answered me, reasonably enough, that the force of chance, diffused through the whole order of nature, brought these things about. For when a man, by accident, opens the leaves of some poet (who sang and intended something far different) a verse oftentimes turns out to be wondrously apposite to the reader's present business. "It is not to be wondered at," he continued, "if out of the human mind, by some higher instinct which does not know what goes on within itself, an answer should be arrived at, by chance and not art, which would fit both the business and the action of the inquirer."

And thus truly, either by him or through him, thou wast looking after me. And thou didst fix all this in my memory so that afterward I might search it out for myself.

But at that time, neither the proconsul nor my most dear Nebridius—a splendid youth and most circumspect, who scoffed at the whole business of divination—could persuade me to give it up, for the authority of the astrological authors influenced me more than they did. And, thus far, I had come upon no certain proof—such as I sought—by which it could

6. Hippocrates is known as the Father of Modern Medicine, a Greek physician who lived around 460 BC.

Hippocrates of Kos
(460 – c. 370 BC)

be shown without doubt that what had been truly foretold by those consulted came from accident or chance, and not from the art of the stargazers.

In those years, when I first began to teach rhetoric in my native town, I had gained a very dear friend, about my own age, who was associated with me in the same studies. Like myself, he was just rising up into the flower of youth. He had grown up with me from childhood and we had been both school fellows and playmates. But he was not then my friend, nor indeed ever became my friend, in the true sense of the term; for there is no true friendship save between those thou dost bind together and who cleave to thee by that love which is "shed abroad in our hearts through the Holy Spirit who is given to us." Still, it was a sweet friendship, being ripened by the zeal of common studies. Moreover, I had turned him away from the true faith[7]—which he had not soundly and thoroughly mastered as a youth—and turned him toward those superstitious and harmful fables which my mother mourned in me. With me this man went wandering off in error and my soul could not exist without him. But behold thou wast close behind thy fugitives—at once a God of vengeance and a Fountain of mercies, who dost turn us to thyself by ways that make us marvel. Thus, thou didst take that man out of this life when he had scarcely completed one whole year of friendship with me, sweeter to me than all the sweetness of my life thus far.

Who can show forth all thy praise for that which he has experienced in himself alone? What was it that thou didst do at that time, O my God; how unsearchable are the depths of thy judgments! For when, sore sick of a fever, he long lay unconscious in a death sweat and everyone despaired of his recovery, he was baptized without his knowledge. And I myself cared little, at the time, presuming that his soul would retain what it had taken from me rather than what was done to his unconscious body. It turned out, however, far differently, for he was revived and restored. Immediately, as soon as I could

7. Augustine had led this friend away from the true faith to Manicheanism.

talk to him—and I did this as soon as he was able, for I never left him and we hung on each other overmuch—I tried to jest with him, supposing that he also would jest in return about that baptism which he had received when his mind and senses were inactive, but which he had since learned that he had received. But he recoiled from me, as if I were his enemy, and, with a remarkable and unexpected freedom, he admonished me that, if I desired to continue as his friend, I must cease to say such things. Confounded and confused, I concealed my feelings till he should get well and his health recover enough to allow me to deal with him as I wished. But he was snatched away from my madness, that with thee he might be preserved for my consolation. A few days after, during my absence, the fever returned and he died.[8]

8. The young man was baptized into the Christian faith and agreed with it before he died.

My heart was utterly darkened by this sorrow and everywhere I looked I saw death. My native place was a torture room to me and my father's house a strange unhappiness. And all the things I had done with him—now that he was gone—became a frightful torment. My eyes sought him everywhere, but they did not see him; and I hated all places because he was not in them, because they could not say to me, "Look, he is coming," as they did when he was alive and absent. I became a hard riddle to myself, and I asked my soul why she was so downcast and why this disquieted me so sorely. But she did not know how to answer me. And if I said, "Hope thou in God,"[9] she very properly disobeyed me, because that dearest friend she had lost was as an actual man, both truer and better than the imagined deity she was ordered to put her hope in. Nothing but tears were sweet to me and they took my friend's place in my heart's desire.

9. Augustine refers to Psalm 42 in this section.

But now, O Lord, these things are past and time has healed my wound. Let me learn from thee, who art Truth, and put the ear of my heart to thy mouth, that thou mayest tell me why weeping should be so sweet to the unhappy. Hast thou—though omnipresent—dismissed our miseries from thy concern? Thou abidest in thyself while we are disquieted with trial after trial. Yet unless we wept in thy ears, there would be no hope for us remaining. How does it happen that such sweet fruit is plucked from the bitterness of life, from groans, tears, sighs, and lamentations? Is it the hope that thou wilt hear us that sweetens it? This is true in the case of prayer, for in a prayer there is a desire to approach thee. But is it also the case in grief for a lost love, and in the kind of sorrow that had then overwhelmed me? For I had neither a hope of his coming back to life, nor in all my tears did I seek this. I simply grieved and wept, for I was miserable and had lost my joy. Or is weeping a bitter thing that gives us pleasure because of our aversion to the things we once enjoyed and this only as long as we loathe them?[10]

But why do I speak of these things? Now is not the time to ask such questions, but rather to confess to thee. I was wretched; and every soul is wretched that is fettered in the friendship of mortal things—it is torn to pieces when it loses them, and then realizes the misery which it had even before it lost them. Thus it was at that time with me. I wept most bitterly, and found a rest in bitterness. I was wretched, and yet that wretched life I still held dearer than my friend.[11] For though I would willingly have changed it, I was still more unwilling to lose it than to have lost him. Indeed, I doubt whether I was willing to lose it, even for him—as they tell (unless it be fiction) of the friendship of Orestes and Pylades;[12] they would have gladly died for one another, or both together, because not to love together was worse than death to them. But a strange kind of feeling had come over me, quite different from this, for now it was wearisome to live and a fearful thing to die. I suppose that the more I loved him the more I hated and feared, as the most cruel enemy, that death which had robbed me of him. I even imagined that it would suddenly annihilate all men, since it had had such a power over him. This is the way I remember it was with me.

Look into my heart, O God! Behold and look deep within me, for I remember it well, O my Hope who cleansest me

10. Augustine wonders why weeping can be comforting.

11. In grief, Augustine begins to understand human misery.

12. Orestes and Pylades were cousins, but they were raised together, becoming best friends in Greek mythology.

13. Augustine is convicted of an unclean affection for his friend who died. Possibly an idolatrous friendship that refused to acknowledge God.

from the uncleanness of such affections, directing my eyes toward thee and plucking my feet out of the snare.[13] And I marveled that other mortals went on living since he whom I had loved as if he would never die was now dead. And I marveled all the more that I, who had been a second self to him, could go on living when he was dead. Someone spoke rightly of his friend as being "his soul's other half"—for I felt that my soul and his soul were but one soul in two bodies. Consequently, my life was now a horror to me because I did not want to live as a half self. But it may have been that I was afraid to die, lest he should then die wholly whom I had so greatly loved.

O madness that knows not how to love men as they should be loved! O foolish man that I was then, enduring with so much rebellion the lot of every man! Thus I fretted, sighed, wept, tormented myself, and took neither rest nor counsel, for I was dragging around my torn and bloody soul. It was impatient of my dragging it around, and yet I could not find a place to lay it down. Not in pleasant groves, nor in sport or song, nor in fragrant bowers, nor in magnificent banquetings, nor in the pleasures of the bed or the couch; not even in books or poetry did it find rest. All things looked gloomy, even the very light itself. Whatsoever was not what he was, was now repulsive and hateful, except my groans and tears, for in those alone I found a little rest. But when my soul left off weeping, a heavy burden of misery weighed me down. It should have been raised up to thee, O Lord, for thee to lighten and to lift. This I knew, but I was neither willing nor able to do; especially since, in my thoughts of thee, thou wast not thyself but only an empty fantasm. Thus my error was my god. If I tried to cast off my burden on this fantasm, that it might find rest there, it sank through the vacuum and came rushing down again upon me. Thus I remained to myself an unhappy lodging where I could neither stay nor leave. For where could my heart fly from my heart? Where could I fly from my own self? Where would I not follow myself? And yet I did flee from my native place so that my eyes would look for him less in a place where they were not accustomed to see him. Thus I left the town of Tagaste and returned to Carthage.[14]

Time never lapses, nor does it glide at leisure through our sense perceptions. It does strange things in the mind. Lo, time came and went from day to day, and by coming and going it brought to my mind other ideas and remembrances, and little by little they patched me up again with earlier kinds of pleasure and my sorrow yielded a bit to them. But yet there followed after this sorrow, not other sorrows just like it, but the causes of other sorrows. For why had that first sorrow so easily penetrated to the quick except that I had poured out my soul onto the dust, by loving a man as if he would never die who nevertheless had to die? What revived and refreshed me, more than anything else, was the consolation of other friends, with whom I went on loving the things I loved instead of thee.[15] This was a monstrous fable and a tedious lie which was corrupting my soul with its "itching ears" by its adulterous rubbing. And that fable would not die to me as often as one of my friends died. And there were other things in our companionship that took strong hold of my mind: to discourse and jest with him; to indulge in courteous exchanges; to read pleasant books together; to trifle together; to be earnest together; to differ at times without ill-humor, as a man might do with himself, and even through these infrequent dissensions to find zest in our more frequent agreements; sometimes teaching, sometimes being taught; longing for someone absent with impatience and welcoming the homecomer with joy. These and similar tokens of friendship, which spring spontaneously from the hearts of those who love and are loved in return—in countenance, tongue, eyes, and a thousand ingratiating gestures—were all so much fuel to melt our souls together, and out of the many made us one.

This is what we love in our friends, and we love it so much that a man's conscience accuses itself if he does not love one who loves him, or respond in love to love, seeking nothing from the other but the evidences of his love. This is the

14. Carthage is modern day Tunis, about 120 miles to the east of Tagaste (in modern day Algeria).

15. The things we do with friends and friendships are sometimes used as a distraction to keep ourselves from God.

source of our moaning when one dies—the gloom of sorrow, the steeping of the heart in tears, all sweetness turned to bitterness—and the feeling of death in the living, because of the loss of the life of the dying.

Blessed is he who loves thee, and who loves his friend in thee, and his enemy also, for thy sake; for he alone loses none dear to him, if all are dear in Him who cannot be lost. And who is this but our God: the God that created heaven and earth, and filled them because he created them by filling them up? None loses thee but he who leaves thee; and he who leaves thee, where does he go, or where can he flee but from thee well-pleased to thee offended? For where does he not find thy law fulfilled in his own punishment? "Thy law is the truth" and thou art Truth.[16]

16. All true love must flow from the love of God and love for God, or it is false love.

"Turn us again, O Lord God of Hosts, cause thy face to shine; and we shall be saved." For wherever the soul of man turns itself, unless toward thee, it is enmeshed in sorrows, even though it is surrounded by beautiful things outside thee and outside itself. For lovely things would simply not be unless they were from thee. They come to be and they pass away, and by coming they begin to be, and they grow toward perfection. Then, when perfect, they begin to wax old and perish, and, if all do not wax old, still all perish.[17] Therefore, when they rise and grow toward being, the more rapidly they grow to maturity, so also the more rapidly they hasten back toward nonbeing. This is the way of things. This is the lot thou hast given them, because they are part of things which do not all exist at the same time, but by passing away and succeeding each other they all make up the universe, of which they are all parts. For example, our speech is accomplished by sounds which signify meanings, but a meaning is not complete unless one word passes away, when it has sounded its part, so that the next may follow after it. Let my soul praise thee, in all these things, O God, the Creator of all; but let not my soul be stuck to these things by the glue of love, through the senses of the body. For they go where they were meant to go, that they may

17. Life is transient. As the flower of the field, so we are here today and gone tomorrow.

exist no longer. And they rend the soul with pestilent desires because she longs to be and yet loves to rest secure in the created things she loves. But in these things there is no resting place to be found. They do not abide. They flee away; and who is he who can follow them with his physical senses? Or who can grasp them, even when they are present? For our physical sense is slow because it is a physical sense and bears its own limitations in itself. The physical sense is quite sufficient for what it was made to do; but it is not sufficient to stay things from running their courses from the beginning appointed to the end appointed. For in thy word, by which they were created, they hear their appointed bound: "From there—to here!"[18]

Be not foolish, O my soul, and do not let the tumult of your vanity deafen the ear of your heart. Be attentive. The Word itself calls you to return, and with him is a place of unperturbed rest, where love is not forsaken unless it first forsakes. Behold, these things pass away that others may come to be in their place. Thus even this lowest level of unity may be made complete in all its parts. "But do I ever pass away?" asks the Word of God. Fix your habitation in him. O my soul, commit whatsoever you have to him. For at long last you are now becoming tired of deceit. Commit to truth whatever you have received from the truth, and you will lose nothing. What is decayed will flourish again; your diseases will be healed; your perishable parts shall be reshaped and renovated, and made whole again in you. And these perishable things will not carry you with them down to where they go when they perish, but shall stand and abide, and you with them, before God, who abides and continues forever.[19]

Why then, my perverse soul, do you go on following your flesh? Instead, let it be converted so as to follow you. Whatever you feel through it is but partial. You do not know the whole, of which sensations are but parts; and yet the parts delight you. But if my physical senses had been able to comprehend the whole—and had not as a part of their punishment received only a portion of the whole as their own province—you would

18. We want to find security in our things (toys, sports, food, and drink), but these things are more transient than the human soul.

19. Eternal life is ours when we receive God's truth, when we are in a relationship with God (because He abides and continues forever).

then desire that whatever exists in the present time should also pass away so that the whole might please you more. For what we speak, you also hear through physical sensation, and yet you would not wish that the syllables should remain. Instead, you wish them to fly past so that others may follow them, and the whole be heard. Thus it is always that when any single thing is composed of many parts which do not coexist simultaneously, the whole gives more delight than the parts could ever do perceived separately. But far better than all this is He who made it all. He is our God and he does not pass away, for there is nothing to take his place.

If physical objects please you, praise God for them, but turn back your love to their Creator, lest, in those things which please you, you displease him. If souls please you, let them be loved in God; for in themselves they are mutable, but in him firmly established—without him they would simply cease to exist. In him, then, let them be loved; and bring along to him with yourself as many souls as you can, and say to them: "Let us love him, for he himself created all these,[20] and he is not far away from them. For he did not create them, and then go away. They are of him and in him. Behold, there he is, wherever truth is known. He is within the inmost heart, yet the heart has wandered away from him. Return to your heart, O you transgressors, and hold fast to him who made you. Stand with him and you shall stand fast. Rest in him and you shall be at rest. Where do you go along these rugged paths? Where are you going? The good that you love is from him, and insofar as it is also for him, it is both good and pleasant. But it will rightly be turned to bitterness if whatever comes from him is not rightly loved and if he is deserted for the love of the creature. Why then will you wander farther and farther in these difficult and toilsome ways? There is no rest where you seek it. Seek what you seek; but remember that it is not where you seek it. You seek for a blessed life in the land of death. It is not there. For how can there be a blessed life where life itself is not?"

20. These are beautiful words here. Always enjoy physical things (friendship, toys, sports, food, and drink) by thanking God for them. Encourage others to return to Him and love Him!

But our very Life came down to earth and bore our death, and slew it with the very abundance of his own life. And, thundering, he called us to return to him into that secret place from which he came forth to us— coming first into the virginal womb, where the human creature, our mortal flesh, was joined to him that it might not be forever mortal—and came "as a bridegroom coming out his chamber, rejoicing as a strong man to run a race." For he did not delay, but ran through the world, crying out by words, deeds, death, life, descent, ascension—crying aloud to us to return to him. And he departed from our sight that we might return to our hearts and find him there. For he left us, and behold, he is here. He could not be with us long, yet he did not leave us. He went back to the place that he had never left, for "the world was made by him." In this world he was, and into this world he came, to save sinners. To him my soul confesses, and he heals it, because it had sinned against him. O sons of men, how long will you be so slow of heart? Even now after Life itself has come down to you, will you not ascend and live? But where will you climb if you are already on a pinnacle and have set your mouth against the heavens? First come down that you may climb up, climb up to God.[21] For you have fallen by trying to climb against him. Tell this to the souls you love that they may weep in the valley of tears, and so bring them along with you to God, because it is by his spirit that you speak thus to them, if, as you speak, you burn with the fire of love.[22]

These things I did not understand at that time, and I loved those inferior beauties, and I was sinking down to the very depths. And I said to my friends: "Do we love anything but the beautiful? What then is the beautiful? And what is beauty? What is it that allures and unites us to the things we love; for unless there were a grace and beauty in them, they could not possibly attract us to them?" And I reflected on this and saw that in the objects themselves there is a kind of beauty which comes from their forming a whole and another kind of beauty that comes from mutual fitness—as the harmony of

21. Man is proud by nature. He must come down before he can be taken up to Life and Glory.

22. This entire section is a wonderful testimony to Jesus Christ, the Son of God — His life, death, and resurrection.

one part of the body with its whole, or a shoe with a foot, and so on. And this idea sprang up in my mind out of my inmost heart, and I wrote some books—two or three, I think—On the Beautiful and the Fitting. Thou knowest them, O Lord; they have escaped my memory. I no longer have them; somehow they have been mislaid.

What was it, O Lord my God, that prompted me to dedicate these books to Hierius, an orator of Rome, a man I did not know by sight but whom I loved for his reputation of learning, in which he was famous— and also for some words of his that I had heard which had pleased me? But he pleased me more because he pleased others, who gave him high praise and expressed amazement that a Syrian, who had first studied Greek eloquence, should thereafter become so wonderful a Latin orator and also so well versed in philosophy. Thus a man we have never seen is commended and loved. Does a love like this come into the heart of the hearer from the mouth of him who sings the other's praise? Not so. Instead, one catches the spark of love from one who loves. This is why we love one who is praised when the eulogist is believed to give his praise from an unfeigned heart; that is, when he who loves him praises him.[23]

23. Augustine is deeply introspective. He finds that he is impressed with a man and loves a man because of his fame (and what the flaky opinions of men think of the man).

Thus it was that I loved men on the basis of other men's judgment, and not thine, O my God, in whom no man is deceived. But why is it that the feeling I had for such men was not like my feeling toward the renowned charioteer, or the great gladiatorial hunter, famed far and wide and popular with the mob? Actually, I admired the orator in a different and more serious fashion, as I would myself desire to be admired. For I did not want them to praise and love me as actors were praised and loved—although I myself praise and love them too. I would prefer being unknown than known in that way, or even being hated than loved that way. How are these various influences and divers sorts of loves distributed within one soul? What is it that I am in love with in another which, if I did not hate, I should neither detest nor repel from myself, seeing that we are equally men? For it does not follow that because the good horse is admired by a man who would not be that horse—even if he could—the same kind of admiration should be given to an actor, who shares our nature. Do I then love that in a man, which I also, a man, would hate to be? Man is himself a great deep. Thou dost number his very hairs, O Lord, and they do not fall to the ground without thee, and yet the hairs of his head are more readily numbered than are his affections and the movements of his heart.

But that orator whom I admired so much was the kind of man I wished myself to be. Thus I erred through a swelling pride and "was carried about with every wind," but through it all I was being piloted by thee, though most secretly. And how is it that I know—whence comes my confident confession to thee—that I loved him more because of the love of those who praised him than for the things they praised in him? Because if he had gone unpraised, and these same people had criticized him and had spoken the same things of him in a tone of scorn and disapproval, I should never have been kindled and provoked to love him. And yet his qualities would not have been different, nor would he have been different himself; only the appraisals of the spectators. See where the helpless soul lies prostrate that is not yet sustained by the stability of truth! Just as the breezes of speech blow from the breast of the opinionated, so also the soul is tossed this way and that, driven forward and backward, and the light is obscured to it and the truth not seen. And yet, there it is in front of us. And to me it was a great matter that both my literary work and my zest for learning should be known by that man. For if he approved them, I would be even more fond of him; but if he disapproved, this vain heart of mine, devoid of thy steadfastness, would have been offended. And so I meditated on the problem "of the beautiful and the fitting" and dedicated my essay on it to him. I regarded it admiringly, though no one else joined me in doing so.

24. Augustine is still thinking of his first books on the nature of beauty in creation. He is convicted that he had failed to recognize the God who is the Creator of this creation!

25. The Greeks taught that the Monad was the Source of Being, and the Dyad was the creation (physical and non-physical). The Dyad contains evil, murder, lust, and violence.

26. There is more than our physical being and emotions that are contaminated. Our minds and souls are born in sin as well.

But I had not seen how the main point in these great issues [concerning the nature of beauty] lay really in thy craftsmanship, O Omnipotent One, "who alone doest great wonders."[24] And so my mind ranged through the corporeal forms, and I defined and distinguished as "beautiful" that which is so in itself and as "fit" that which is beautiful in relation to some other thing. This argument I supported by corporeal examples. And I turned my attention to the nature of the mind, but the false opinions which I held concerning spiritual things prevented me from seeing the truth. Still, the very power of truth forced itself on my gaze, and I turned my throbbing soul away from incorporeal substance to qualities of line and color and shape, and, because I could not perceive these with my mind, I concluded that I could not perceive my mind. And since I loved the peace which is in virtue, and hated the discord which is in vice, I distinguished between the unity there is in virtue and the discord there is in vice. I conceived that unity consisted of the rational soul and the nature of truth and the highest good. But I imagined that in the disunity there was some kind of substance of irrational life and some kind of entity in the supreme evil. This evil I thought was not only a substance but real life as well, and yet I believed that it did not come from thee, O my God, from whom are all things. And the first I called a Monad, as if it were a soul without sex. The other I called a Dyad,[25] which showed itself in anger in deeds of violence, in deeds of passion and lust—but I did not know what I was talking about. For I had not understood nor had I been taught that evil is not a substance at all and that our soul is not that supreme and unchangeable good.

For just as in violent acts, if the emotion of the soul from whence the violent impulse springs is depraved and asserts itself insolently and mutinously—and just as in the acts of passion, if the affection of the soul which gives rise to carnal desires is unrestrained—so also, in the same way, errors and false opinions contaminate life if the rational soul itself is depraved.[26] Thus it was then with me, for I was ignorant that my soul had to be enlightened by another light, if it was to be partaker of the truth, since it is not itself the essence of truth. "For thou wilt light my lamp; the Lord my God will lighten my darkness"; and "of his fullness have we all received," for "that was the true Light that lighteth every man that cometh into the world"; for "in thee there is no variableness, neither shadow of turning."

But I pushed on toward thee, and was pressed back by thee that I might know the taste of death, for "thou resistest the proud." And what greater pride could there be for me than, with a marvelous madness, to assert myself to be that nature which thou art?[27] I was mutable—this much was clear enough to me because my very longing to become wise arose out of a wish to change from worse to better—yet I chose rather to think thee mutable than to think that I was not as thou art. For this reason I was thrust back; thou didst resist my fickle pride. Thus I went on imagining corporeal forms, and, since I was flesh I accused the flesh, and, since I was "a wind that passes away," I did not return to thee but went wandering and wandering on toward those things that have no being— neither in thee nor in me, nor in the body. These fancies were not created for me by thy truth but conceived by my own vain conceit out of sensory notions. And I used to ask thy faithful children—my own fellow citizens, from whom I stood unconsciously exiled—I used flippantly and foolishly to ask them, "Why, then, does the soul, which God created, err?"[28] But I would not allow anyone to ask me, "Why, then, does God err?" I preferred to contend that thy immutable substance was involved in error through necessity rather than admit that my own mutable substance had gone astray of its own free will and had fallen into error as its punishment.

I was about twenty-six or twenty-seven when I wrote those books, analyzing and reflecting upon those sensory images which clamored in the ears of my heart. I was straining those ears to hear thy inward melody, O sweet Truth, pondering on "the beautiful and the fitting" and longing to stay and

27. He reduced God to a changeable, man-like creation, in order that he might see himself as God.

28. Proud men will blame God for sin, rather than take responsibility for their own sinful choices.

Aristotle (384–322 BC), a Greek philosopher and pupil of Plato

29. Aristotle was a Greek Philosopher from the 4th century BC. His ten categories are the ten things that can be used as a subject or predicate in a sentence or a proposition.

hear thee, and to rejoice greatly at "the Bridegroom's voice." Yet I could not, for by the clamor of my own errors I was hurried outside myself, and by the weight of my own pride I was sinking ever lower. You did not "make me to hear joy and gladness," nor did the bones rejoice which were not yet humbled.

And what did it profit me that, when I was scarcely twenty years old, a book of Aristotle's entitled *The Ten Categories*[29] fell into my hands? On the very title of this I hung as on something great and divine, since my rhetoric master at Carthage and others who had reputations for learning were always referring to it with such swelling pride. I read it by myself and understood it. And what did it mean that when I discussed it with others they said that even with the assistance of tutors—who not only explained it orally, but drew many diagrams in the sand—they scarcely understood it and could tell me no more about it than I had acquired in the reading of it by myself alone? For the book appeared to me to speak plainly enough about substances, such as a man; and of their qualities, such as the shape of a man, his kind, his stature, how many feet high, and his family relationship, his status, when born, whether he is sitting or standing, is shod or armed, or is doing something or having something done to him—and all the innumerable things that are classified under these nine categories (of which I have given some examples) or under the chief category of substance.

What did all this profit me, since it actually hindered me when I imagined that whatever existed was comprehended within those ten categories? I tried to interpret them, O my God, so that even thy wonderful and unchangeable unity could be understood as subjected to thy own magnitude or beauty, as if they existed in thee as their Subject—as they do in corporeal bodies—whereas thou art thyself thy own magnitude and beauty. A body is not great or fair because it is a body, because, even if it were less great or less beautiful, it would still be a body. But my conception of thee was falsity, not truth. It was a figment of my own misery, not the stable ground of thy blessedness. For thou hadst commanded, and it was carried out in me, that the earth should bring forth briars and thorns for me, and that with heavy labor I should gain my bread.[30]

And what did it profit me that I could read and understand for myself all the books I could get in the so-called "liberal arts," when I was actually a worthless slave of wicked lust? I took delight in them, not knowing the real source of what it was in them that was true and certain. For I had my back toward the light, and my face toward the things on which the light falls, so that my face, which looked toward the illuminated things, was not itself illuminated. Whatever was written in any of the fields of rhetoric or logic, geometry, music, or arithmetic, I could understand without any great difficulty and without the instruction of another man. All this thou knowest, O Lord my God, because both quickness in understanding and acuteness in insight are thy gifts. Yet for such gifts I made no thank offering to thee. Therefore, my abilities served not my profit but rather my loss, since I went about trying to bring so large a part of my substance into my own power. And I did not store up my strength for thee, but went away from thee into the far country to prostitute my gifts in disordered appetite.[31] And what did these abilities profit me, if I did not put them to good use? I did not realize that those arts were understood with great difficulty, even by the studious and the intelligent, until I tried to explain them to others and discovered that even the most proficient in them followed my explanations all too slowly.[32]

And yet what did this profit me, since I still supposed that thou, O Lord God, the Truth, wert a bright and vast body and that I was a particle of that body? O perversity gone too far! But so it was with me. And I do not blush, O my God, to confess thy mercies to me in thy presence, or to call upon thee—any more than I did not blush when I openly avowed my blasphemies before men, and bayed, houndlike, against thee. What good was it for me that my nimble wit could run through those studies and disentangle all those knotty vol-

30. The trap of education is that we focus on the things on which the light falls (certain truths), but forget the source of the light itself — God.

31. Reference to the Prodigal Son who received gifts but wasted them in the "far country."

32. Far less intelligent people use their minds in a better way in that they stay in the Church and are nourished by the food of the Word of God.

umes, without help from a human teacher, since all the while I was erring so hatefully and with such sacrilege as far as the right substance of pious faith was concerned? And what kind of burden was it for thy little ones to have a far slower wit, since they did not use it to depart from thee, and since they remained in the nest of thy Church to become safely fledged and to nourish the wings of love by the food of a sound faith. O Lord our God, under the shadow of thy wings let us hope— defend us and support us. Thou wilt bear us up when we are little and even down to our gray hairs thou wilt carry us. For our stability, when it is in thee, is stability indeed; but when it is in ourselves, then it is all unstable. Our good lives forever with thee, and when we turn from thee with aversion, we fall into our own perversion. Let us now, O Lord, return that we be not overturned, because with thee our good lives without blemish—for our good is thee thyself. And we need not fear that we shall find no place to return to because we fell away from it. For, in our absence, our home—which is thy eternity—does not fall away.

❧ BOOK V

Accept this sacrifice of my confessions from the hand of my tongue. Thou didst form it and hast prompted it to praise thy name. Heal all my bones and let them say, "O Lord, who is like unto thee?" It is not that one who confesses to thee instructs thee as to what goes on within him. For the closed heart does not bar thy sight into it, nor does the hardness of our heart hold back thy hands, for thou canst soften it at will, either by mercy or in vengeance,[1] "and there is no one who can hide himself from thy heat." But let my soul praise thee, that it may love thee, and let it confess thy mercies to thee, that it may praise thee. Thy whole creation praises thee without ceasing: the spirit of man, by his own lips, by his own voice, lifted up to thee; animals and lifeless matter by the mouths of those who meditate upon them. Thus our souls may climb out of their weariness toward thee and lean on those things which thou hast created and pass through them to thee, who didst create them in a marvelous way. With thee, there is refreshment and true strength.

Let the restless and the unrighteous depart,[2] and flee away from thee. Even so, thou seest them and thy eye pierces through the shadows in which they run. For lo, they live in a world of beauty and yet are themselves most foul. And how have they harmed thee? Or in what way have they discredited thy power, which is just and perfect in its rule even to the last

1. God can soften a hard heart if He wills to do so, by His mercy or by His judgment.

2. The unrighteous are equated to the restless or those whose hearts are not at peace.

item in creation? Indeed, where would they fly when they fled from thy presence? Wouldst thou be unable to find them? But they fled that they might not see thee, who sawest them; that they might be blinded and stumble into thee. But thou forsakest nothing that thou hast made. The unrighteous stumble against thee that they may be justly plagued, fleeing from thy gentleness and colliding with thy justice, and falling on their own rough paths.[3] For in truth they do not know that thou art everywhere; that no place contains thee, and that only thou art near even to those who go farthest from thee. Let them, therefore, turn back and seek thee, because even if they have abandoned thee, their Creator, thou hast not abandoned thy creatures. Let them turn back and seek thee—and lo, thou art there in their hearts, there in the hearts of those who confess to thee. Let them cast themselves upon thee, and weep on thy bosom, after all their weary wanderings; and thou wilt gently wipe away their tears. And they weep the more and rejoice in their weeping, since thou, O Lord, art not a man of flesh and blood. Thou art the Lord, who canst remake what thou didst make and canst comfort them. And where was I when I was seeking thee? There thou wast, before me; but I had gone away, even from myself, and I could not find myself, much less thee.

3. The futility of running away from God.

Let me now lay bare in the sight of God the twenty-ninth year of my age. There had just come to Carthage a certain bishop of the Manicheans, Faustus by name, a great snare of the devil; and many were entangled by him through the charm of his eloquence. Now, even though I found this eloquence admirable, I was beginning to distinguish the charm of words from the truth of things, which I was eager to learn. Nor did I consider the dish as much as I did the kind of meat that their famous Faustus[4] served up to me in it. His fame had run before him, as one very skilled in an honorable learning and pre-eminently skilled in the liberal arts.

And as I had already read and stored up in memory many of the injunctions of the philosophers, I began to compare some of their doctrines with the tedious fables of the Mani-

Manichean priests depicted in a Chinese mural

4. Faustus lived in Mileve (modern Algeria), about 300 miles southwest of Carthage. He was a leader in the Manichean cult. Augustine later wrote a book against his teaching called *Contra Faustus*.

cheans;[5] and it struck me that the probability was on the side of the philosophers, whose power reached far enough to enable them to form a fair judgment of the world, even though they had not discovered the sovereign Lord of it all. For thou art great, O Lord, and thou hast respect unto the lowly, but the proud thou knowest afar off. Thou drawest near to none but the contrite in heart, and canst not be found by the proud, even if in their inquisitive skill they may number the stars and the sands, and map out the constellations, and trace the courses of the planets.[6]

For it is by the mind and the intelligence which thou gavest them that they investigate these things. They have discovered much; and have foretold, many years in advance, the day, the hour, and the extent of the eclipses of those luminaries, the sun and the moon. Their calculations did not fail, and it came to pass as they predicted. And they wrote down the rules they had discovered, so that to this day they may be read and from them may be calculated in what year and month and day and hour of the day, and at what quarter of its light, either the moon or the sun will be eclipsed, and it will come to pass just as predicted. And men who are ignorant in these matters marvel and are amazed; and those who understand them exult and are exalted. Both, by an impious pride, withdraw from thee and forsake thy light. They foretell an eclipse of the sun before it happens, but they do not see their own eclipse which is even now occurring. For they do not ask, as religious men should, what is the source of the intelligence by which they investigate these matters. Moreover, when they discover that thou didst make them, they do not give themselves up to thee that thou mightest preserve what thou hast made. Nor do they offer, as sacrifice to thee, what they have made of themselves. For they do not slaughter their own pride—as they do the sacrificial fowls—nor their own curiosities by which, like the fishes of the sea, they wander through the unknown paths of the deep. Nor do they curb their own extravagances as they do those of "the beasts of the field," so that thou, O Lord, "a consuming

5. Manicheanism failed to properly explain the world (falling short of observational science).

6. Humanist scientists often become proud in what they have learned. At this point, they were able to predict eclipses of the sun and moon (and this was a big deal to the scientists of the day).

fire," mayest burn up their mortal cares and renew them unto immortality.

They do not know the way which is thy word, by which thou didst create all the things that are and also the men who measure them, and the senses by which they perceive what they measure, and the intelligence whereby they discern the patterns of measure. Thus they know not that thy wisdom is not a matter of measure. But the Only Begotten hath been "made unto us wisdom, and righteousness, and sanctification" and hath been numbered among us and paid tribute to Caesar. And they do not know this "Way" by which they could descend from themselves to him in order to ascend through him to him. They did not know this "Way," and so they fancied themselves exalted to the stars and the shining heavens. And lo, they fell upon the earth, and "their foolish heart was darkened." They saw many true things about the creature but they do not seek with true piety for the Truth, the Architect of Creation, and hence they do not find him. Or, if they do find him, and know that he is God, they do not glorify him as God; neither are they thankful but become vain in their imagination, and say that they themselves are wise, and attribute to themselves what is thine. At the same time, with the most perverse blindness, they wish to attribute to thee their own quality—so that they load their lies on thee who art the Truth, "changing the glory of the incorruptible God for an image of corruptible man, and birds, and four-footed beasts, and creeping things." "They exchanged thy truth for a lie, and worshiped and served the creature rather than the Creator."[7]

7. Augustine finds that the Romans 1:18-32 description applies to societies that become proud in their scientific knowledge (a clear indictment of the modern world).

Yet I remembered many a true saying of the philosophers about the creation, and I saw the confirmation of their calculations in the orderly sequence of seasons and in the visible evidence of the stars. And I compared this with the doctrines of Mani, who in his voluminous folly wrote many books on these subjects. But I could not discover there any account, of either the solstices or the equinoxes, or the eclipses of the sun and moon, or anything of the sort that I had learned in the books of secular philosophy. But still I was ordered to believe, even where the ideas did not correspond with—even when they contradicted—the rational theories established by mathematics and my own eyes, but were very different.

Yet, O Lord God of Truth, is any man pleasing to thee because he knows these things? No, for surely that man is unhappy who knows these things and does not know thee. And that man is happy who knows thee, even though he does not know these things. He who knows both thee and these things is not the more blessed for his learning, for thou only art his blessing, if knowing thee as God he glorifies thee and gives thanks and does not become vain in his thoughts. For just as that man who knows how to possess a tree, and give thanks to thee for the use of it—although he may not know how many feet high it is or how wide it spreads—is better than the man who can measure it and count all its branches, but neither owns it nor knows or loves its Creator: just so is a faithful man who possesses the world's wealth as though he had nothing, and possesses all things through his union through thee, whom all things serve, even though he does not know the circlings of the Great Bear.[8] Just so it is foolish to doubt that this faithful man may truly be better than the one who can measure the heavens and number the stars and weigh the elements, but who is forgetful of thee "who hast set in order all things in number, weight, and measure."[9]

And who ordered this Mani to write about these things, knowledge of which is not necessary to piety? For thou hast said to man, "Behold, godliness is wisdom"—and of this he might have been ignorant, however perfectly he may have known these other things. Yet, since he did not know even these other things, and most impudently dared to teach them, it is clear that he had no knowledge of piety. For, even when we have a knowledge of this worldly lore, it is folly to make a profession of it, when piety comes from confession to thee. From piety, therefore, Mani had gone astray, and all his show of learning only enabled the truly learned to perceive, from his

8. The circlings of the Great Bear are the movements of the Ursa Major constellation, the third largest constellation visible to man.

9. Knowing God is more important and more blessed than knowing scientific facts. Enjoying the God who made the tree is way more important than knowing every scientific fact about the tree.

10. The Manichean heretics were proud in their ignorant teachings, claiming that the Holy Spirit had revealed these falsehoods to them. The problem lies in the pride and the claim of supernatural insight.

11. The point of this section: Mani did not know God, and he didn't know anything about science either . . . a cult leader entirely void of any viable knowledge.

ignorance of what they knew, how little he was to be trusted to make plain these more really difficult matters. For he did not aim to be lightly esteemed, but went around trying to persuade men that the Holy Spirit, the Comforter and Enricher of thy faithful ones, was personally resident in him with full authority.[10] And, therefore, when he was detected in manifest errors about the sky, the stars, the movements of the sun and moon, even though these things do not relate to religious doctrine, the impious presumption of the man became clearly evident; for he not only taught things about which he was ignorant but also perverted them,[11] and this with pride so foolish and mad that he sought to claim that his own utterances were as if they had been those of a divine person.

When I hear of a Christian brother, ignorant of these things, or in error concerning them, I can tolerate his uninformed opinion; and I do not see that any lack of knowledge as to the form or nature of this material creation can do him much harm, as long as he does not hold a belief in anything which is unworthy of thee, O Lord, the Creator of all. But if he thinks that his secular knowledge pertains to the essence of the doctrine of piety, or ventures to assert dogmatic opinions in matters in which he is ignorant—there lies the injury. And yet even a weakness such as this, in the infancy of our faith, is tolerated by our Mother Charity until the new man can grow up "unto a perfect man," and not be "carried away with every wind of doctrine."

But Mani had presumed to be at once the teacher, author, guide, and leader of all whom he could persuade to believe this, so that all who followed him believed that they were following not an ordinary man but thy Holy Spirit. And who would not judge that such great madness, when it once stood convicted of false teaching, should then be abhorred and utterly rejected? But I had not yet clearly decided whether the alternation of day and night, and of longer and shorter days and nights, and the eclipses of sun and moon, and whatever else I read about in other books could be explained consistently with his theories. If they could have been so explained, there would still have remained a doubt in my mind whether the theories were right or wrong. Yet I was prepared, on the strength of his reputed godliness, to rest my faith on his authority.

For almost the whole of the nine years that I listened with unsettled mind to the Manichean teaching I had been looking forward with unbounded eagerness to the arrival of this Faustus. For all the other members of the sect that I happened to meet, when they were unable to answer the questions I raised, always referred me to his coming. They promised that, in discussion with him, these and even greater difficulties, if I had them, would be quite easily and amply cleared away. When at last he did come, I found him to be a man of pleasant speech, who spoke of the very same things they themselves did, although more fluently and in a more agreeable style. But what profit was there to me in the elegance of my cupbearer, since he could not offer me the more precious draught for which I thirsted? My ears had already had their fill of such stuff, and now it did not seem any better because it was better expressed nor more true because it was dressed up in rhetoric; nor could I think the man's soul necessarily wise because his face was comely and his language eloquent. But they who extolled him to me were not competent judges. They thought him able and wise because his eloquence delighted them.[12] At the same time I realized that there is another kind of man who is suspicious even of truth itself, if it is expressed in smooth and flowing language. But thou, O my God, hadst already taught me in wonderful and marvelous ways, and therefore I believed—because it is true—that thou didst teach me and that beside thee there is no other teacher of truth, wherever truth shines forth. Already I had learned from thee that because a thing is eloquently expressed it should not be taken to be as necessarily true; nor because it is uttered with stammering lips should it be supposed false. Nor, again, is it necessarily true because rudely uttered, nor untrue because the language is brilliant. Wisdom and folly both are like meats that are wholesome

12. People are taken easily by eloquent speakers, smooth talkers, and crowd pleasers. They don't judge the content of what is being said all that much.

and unwholesome, and courtly or simple words are like town-made or rustic vessels—both kinds of food may be served in either kind of dish.

That eagerness, therefore, with which I had so long awaited this man, was in truth delighted with his action and feeling in a disputation, and with the fluent and apt words with which he clothed his ideas. I was delighted, therefore, and I joined with others—and even exceeded them—in exalting and praising him. Yet it was a source of annoyance to me that, in his lecture room, I was not allowed to introduce and raise any of those questions that troubled me, in a familiar exchange of discussion with him. As soon as I found an opportunity for this, and gained his ear at a time when it was not inconvenient for him to enter into a discussion with me and my friends, I laid before him some of my doubts. I discovered at once that he knew nothing of the liberal arts except grammar, and that only in an ordinary way. He had, however, read some of Tully's orations, a very few books of Seneca,[13] and some of the poets, and such few books of his own sect as were written in good Latin. With this meager learning and his daily practice in speaking, he had acquired a sort of eloquence which proved the more delightful and enticing because it was under the direction of a ready wit and a sort of native grace. Was this not even as I now recall it, O Lord my God, Judge of my conscience? My heart and my memory are laid open before thee, who wast even then guiding me by the secret impulse of thy providence and wast setting my shameful errors before my face so that I might see and hate them.

For as soon as it became plain to me that Faustus was ignorant in those arts in which I had believed him eminent, I began to despair of his being able to clarify and explain all these perplexities that troubled me—though I realized that such ignorance need not have affected the authenticity of his piety, if he had not been a Manichean. For their books are full of long fables about the sky and the stars, the sun and the moon; and I had ceased to believe him able to show me in any

13. Tully is another name for Cicero, the Roman Historian. Seneca was a Roman Stoic Philosopher, during the time of Nero. He was forced to commit suicide.

satisfactory fashion what I so ardently desired: whether the explanations contained in the Manichean books were better or at least as good as the mathematical explanations I had read elsewhere. But when I proposed that these subjects should be considered and discussed, he quite modestly did not dare to undertake the task, for he was aware that he had no knowledge of these things and was not ashamed to confess it.[14] For he was not one of those talkative people—from whom I had endured so much—who undertook to teach me what I wanted to know, and then said nothing. Faustus had a heart which, if not right toward thee, was at least not altogether false toward himself; for he was not ignorant of his own ignorance, and he did not choose to be entangled in a controversy from which he could not draw back or retire gracefully. For this I liked him all the more. For the modesty of an ingenious mind is a finer thing than the acquisition of that knowledge I desired; and this I found to be his attitude toward all abstruse and difficult questions.

Thus the zeal with which I had plunged into the Manichean system was checked, and I despaired even more of their other teachers, because Faustus who was so famous among them had turned out so poorly in the various matters that puzzled me. And so I began to occupy myself with him in the study of his own favorite pursuit, that of literature, in which I was already teaching a class as a professor of rhetoric among the young Carthaginian students. With Faustus then I read whatever he himself wished to read, or what I judged suitable to his bent of mind. But all my endeavors to make further progress in Manicheism came completely to an end through my acquaintance with that man. I did not wholly separate myself from them, but as one who had not yet found anything better I decided to content myself, for the time being, with what I had stumbled upon one way or another, until by chance something more desirable should present itself. Thus that Faustus who had entrapped so many to their death—though neither willing nor witting it—now began to loosen the snare

14. Faustus turned out to be more humble by admitting he didn't know anything about the scientific mathematical calculations.

15. Augustine sees God's hand in every part of his life as he works his way to God. His mother's prayers and tears play a part in this.

in which I had been caught. For thy hands, O my God, in the hidden design of thy providence did not desert my soul; and out of the blood of my mother's heart, through the tears that she poured out by day and by night, there was a sacrifice offered to thee for me, and by marvelous ways thou didst deal with me.[15] For it was thou, O my God, who didst it: for "the steps of a man are ordered by the Lord, and he shall choose his way." How shall we attain salvation without thy hand remaking what it had already made?

Thou didst so deal with me, therefore, that I was persuaded to go to Rome and teach there what I had been teaching at Carthage. And how I was persuaded to do this I will not omit to confess to thee, for in this also the profoundest workings of thy wisdom and thy constant mercy toward us must be pondered and acknowledged. I did not wish to go to Rome because of the richer fees and the higher dignity which my friends promised me there—though these considerations did affect my decision. My principal and almost sole motive was that I had been informed that the students there studied more quietly and were better kept under the control of stern discipline, so that they did not capriciously and impudently rush into the classroom of a teacher not their own—indeed, they were not admitted at all without the permission of the teacher. At Carthage, on the contrary, there was a shameful and intemperate license among the students. They burst in rudely and, with furious gestures, would disrupt the discipline which the teacher had established for the good of his pupils. Many

16. The rudeness of the students disrupting his classes in Carthage was upsetting to Augustine. And this made him want to move to Rome.

outrages they perpetrated with astounding effrontery,[16] things that would be punishable by law if they were not sustained by custom. Thus custom makes plain that such behavior is all the more worthless because it allows men to do what thy eternal law never will allow. They think that they act thus with impunity, though the very blindness with which they act is their punishment, and they suffer far greater harm than they inflict.

The manners that I would not adopt as a student I was compelled as a teacher to endure in others. And so I was glad to go where all who knew the situation assured me that such conduct was not allowed. But thou, "O my refuge and my portion in the land of the living," didst goad me thus at Carthage so that I might thereby be pulled away from it and change my worldly habitation for the preservation of my soul. At the same time, thou didst offer me at Rome an enticement, through the agency of men enchanted with this death-in-life—by their insane conduct in the one place and their empty promises in the other. To correct my wandering footsteps, thou didst secretly employ their perversity and my own. For those who disturbed my tranquillity were blinded by shameful madness and also those who allured me elsewhere had nothing better than the earth's cunning. And I who hated actual misery in the one place sought fictitious happiness in the other.

Thou knewest the cause of my going from one country to the other, O God, but thou didst not disclose it either to me or to my mother, who grieved deeply over my departure and followed me down to the sea. She clasped me tight in her embrace, willing either to keep me back or to go with me, but I deceived her, pretending that I had a friend whom I could not leave until he had a favorable wind to set sail.[17] Thus I lied to my mother—and such a mother!—and escaped. For this too thou didst mercifully pardon me—fool that I was—and didst preserve me from the waters of the sea for the water of thy grace; so that, when I was purified by that, the fountain of my mother's eyes, from which she had daily watered the ground for me as she prayed to thee, should be dried. And, since she refused to return without me, I persuaded her, with some difficulty, to remain that night in a place quite close to our ship, where there was a shrine in memory of the blessed Cyprian.[18] That night I slipped away secretly, and she remained to pray and weep. And what was it, O Lord, that she was asking of thee in such a flood of tears but that thou wouldst not allow me to sail? But thou, taking thy own secret counsel and noting the real point to her desire, didst not grant what she was then

17. He lied to his mother, acting as if he was saying goodbye to a friend who was sailing to Rome.

18. Cyprian was the Christian pastor at Carthage between AD 248 and 258.

asking in order to grant to her the thing that she had always been asking.

The wind blew and filled our sails, and the shore dropped out of sight. Wild with grief, she was there the next morning and filled thy ears with complaints and groans which thou didst disregard, although, at the very same time, thou wast using my longings as a means and wast hastening me on to the fulfillment of all longing. Thus the earthly part of her love to me was justly purged by the scourge of sorrow. Still, like all mothers—though even more than others—she loved to have me with her, and did not know what joy thou wast preparing for her through my going away. Not knowing this secret end, she wept and mourned and saw in her agony the inheritance of Eve—seeking in sorrow what she had brought forth in sorrow. And yet, after accusing me of perfidy and cruelty, she still continued her intercessions for me to thee. She returned to her own home, and I went on to Rome.

And lo, I was received in Rome by the scourge of bodily sickness; and I was very near to falling into hell, burdened with all the many and grievous sins I had committed against thee, myself, and others—all over and above that fetter of original sin whereby we all die in Adam. For thou hadst forgiven me none of these things in Christ, neither had he abolished by his cross the enmity that I had incurred from thee through my sins. For how could he do so by the crucifixion of a phantom, which was all I supposed him to be? The death of my soul was as real then as the death of his flesh appeared to me unreal. And the life of my soul was as false, because it was as unreal as the death of his flesh was real, though I believed it not.

My fever increased, and I was on the verge of passing away and perishing; for, if I had passed away then, where should I have gone but into the fiery torment which my misdeeds deserved, measured by the truth of thy rule? My mother knew nothing of this; yet, far away, she went on praying for me. And thou, present everywhere, didst hear her where she was and had pity on me where I was, so that I regained my

bodily health,[19] although I was still disordered in my sacrilegious heart. For that peril of death did not make me wish
to be baptized. I was even better when, as a lad, I entreated
baptism of my mother's devotion, as I have already related and
confessed. But now I had since increased in dishonor, and I
madly scoffed at all the purposes of thy medicine which would
not have allowed me, though a sinner such as I was, to die a
double death. Had my mother's heart been pierced with this
wound, it never could have been cured, for I cannot adequately
tell of the love she had for me, or how she still travailed for
me in the spirit with a far keener anguish than when she bore
me in the flesh.[20]

I cannot conceive, therefore, how she could have been
healed if my death (still in my sins) had pierced her inmost
love. Where, then, would have been all her earnest, frequent,
and ceaseless prayers to thee? Nowhere but with thee. But
couldst thou, O most merciful God, despise the "contrite and
humble heart" of that pure and prudent widow, who was so
constant in her alms, so gracious and attentive to thy saints,
never missing a visit to church twice a day, morning and evening[21]—and this not for vain gossiping, nor old wives' fables,
but in order that she might listen to thee in thy sermons, and
thou to her in her prayers? Couldst thou, by whose gifts she
was so inspired, despise and disregard the tears of such a one
without coming to her aid—those tears by which she entreated thee, not for gold or silver, and not for any changing or
fleeting good, but for the salvation of the soul of her son? By
no means, O Lord. It is certain that thou wast near and wast
hearing and wast carrying out the plan by which thou hadst
predetermined it should be done. Far be it from thee that thou
shouldst have deluded her in those visions and the answers she
had received from thee—some of which I have mentioned,
and others not—which she kept in her faithful heart, and, forever beseeching, urged them on thee as if they had thy own
signature. For thou, "because thy mercy endureth forever," hast

19. Augustine contracted a deathly illness, but Monica's prayers were effectual for him.

20. Monica's travail in her soul for Augustine's soul was worse than the birth pang she felt when she bore him.

21. The church was faithful in preaching sermons twice a day, every day! This was the way that the church used to disciple the nations.

so condescended to those whose debts thou hast pardoned that thou likewise dost become a debtor by thy promises.

Thou didst restore me then from that illness, and didst heal the son of thy handmaid in his body, that he might live for thee and that thou mightest endow him with a better and more certain health. After this, at Rome, I again joined those deluding and deluded "saints"; and not their "hearers" only, such as the man was in whose house I had fallen sick, but also with those whom they called "the elect." For it still seemed to me "that it is not we who sin, but some other nature sinned in us." And it gratified my pride to be beyond blame, and when I did anything wrong not to have to confess that I had done wrong[22]—"that thou mightest heal my soul because it had sinned against thee"—and I loved to excuse my soul and to accuse something else inside me (I knew not what) but which was not I. But, assuredly, it was I, and it was my impiety that had divided me against myself. That sin then was all the more incurable because I did not deem myself a sinner. It was an execrable iniquity, O God Omnipotent, that I would have preferred to have thee defeated in me, to my destruction, than to be defeated by thee to my salvation. Not yet, therefore, hadst thou set a watch upon my mouth and a door around my lips that my heart might not incline to evil speech, to make excuse for sin with men that work iniquity. And, therefore, I continued still in the company of their "elect."

But now, hopeless of gaining any profit from that false doctrine, I began to hold more loosely and negligently even to those points which I had decided to rest content with, if I could find nothing better. I was now half inclined to believe that those philosophers whom they call "The Academics" were wiser than the rest in holding that we ought to doubt everything,[23] and in maintaining that man does not have the power of comprehending any certain truth, for, although I had not yet understood their meaning, I was fully persuaded that they thought just as they are commonly reputed to do. And I did not fail openly to dissuade my host from his confidence which

22. He sticks with the Manicheans even though he was a little disillusioned with them. What attracted him was the false impression that he was not to blame for his own sin. Instead, Mani taught that there was some foreign nature that sins within him.

23. The Academics were skeptics, who taught to doubt everything.

I observed that he had in those fictions of which the works of Mani are full. For all this, I was still on terms of more intimate friendship with these people than with others who were not of their heresy. I did not indeed defend it with my former ardor; but my familiarity with that group—and there were many of them concealed in Rome at that time—made me slower to seek any other way. This was particularly easy since I had no hope of finding in thy Church the truth from which they had turned me aside, O Lord of heaven and earth, Creator of all things visible and invisible. And it still seemed to me most unseemly to believe that thou couldst have the form of human flesh and be bounded by the bodily shape of our limbs. And when I desired to meditate on my God, I did not know what to think of but a huge extended body—for what did not have bodily extension did not seem to me to exist—and this was the greatest and almost the sole cause of my unavoidable errors.[24]

And thus I also believed that evil was a similar kind of substance, and that it had its own hideous and deformed extended body—either in a dense form which they called the earth or in a thin and subtle form as, for example, the substance of the air, which they imagined as some malignant spirit penetrating that earth. And because my piety—such as it was—still compelled me to believe that the good God never created any evil substance, I formed the idea of two masses, one opposed to the other, both infinite but with the evil more contracted and the good more expansive. And from this diseased beginning, the other sacrileges followed after.[25]

For when my mind tried to turn back to the Catholic faith, I was cast down, since the Catholic faith was not what I judged it to be. And it seemed to me a greater piety to regard thee, my God—to whom I make confession of thy mercies—as infinite in all respects save that one: where the extended mass of evil stood opposed to thee, where I was compelled to confess that thou art finite—than if I should think that thou couldst be confined by the form of a human body on every side. And it seemed better to me to believe that no evil had

24. The major stumbling block for Augustine: He could not believe that God could have been immense, omnipresent (everywhere at once) yet not constitute a physical body extended in space (like you and me). Thus, he reduced God to something finite and physical.

25. The second error was that evil must have been a substance not created by God. This would have entailed two eternal substances – God (which is good) and Evil.

been created by thee—for in my ignorance evil appeared not only to be some kind of substance but a corporeal one at that. This was because I had, thus far, no conception of mind, except as a subtle body diffused throughout local spaces. This seemed better than to believe that anything could emanate from thee which had the character that I considered evil to be in its nature. And I believed that our Saviour himself also—thy Only Begotten—had been brought forth, as it were, for our salvation out of the mass of thy bright shining substance. So that I could believe nothing about him except what I was able to harmonize with these vain imaginations. I thought, therefore, that such a nature could not be born of the Virgin Mary without being mingled with the flesh, and I could not see how the divine substance, as I had conceived it, could be mingled thus without being contaminated. I was afraid, therefore, to believe that he had been born in the flesh, lest I should also be compelled to believe that he had been contaminated by the flesh.[26] Now will thy spiritual ones smile blandly and lovingly at me if they read these confessions. Yet such was I.

Furthermore, the things they censured in thy Scriptures I thought impossible to be defended. And yet, occasionally, I desired to confer on various matters with someone well learned in those books, to test what he thought of them. For already the words of one Elpidius,[27] who spoke and disputed face to face against these same Manicheans, had begun to impress me, even when I was at Carthage; because he brought forth things out of the Scriptures that were not easily withstood, to which their answers appeared to me feeble. One of their answers they did not give forth publicly, but only to us in private—when they said that the writings of the New Testament had been tampered with by unknown persons who desired to ingraft the Jewish law into the Christian faith. But they themselves never brought forward any uncorrupted copies. Still thinking in corporeal categories and very much ensnared and to some extent stifled, I was borne down by those conceptions of bodi-

26. He did not want to believe that Jesus Christ had human flesh, a physical body (born of the Virgin Mary). Manicheans believed physical flesh was evil.

27. Elpidius must have been a Christian that argued ably against the Manichean cult.

ly substance. I panted under this load for the air of thy truth, but I was not able to breathe it pure and undefiled.

I set about diligently to practice what I came to Rome to do—the teaching of rhetoric. The first task was to bring together in my home a few people to whom and through whom I had begun to be known. And lo, I then began to learn that other offenses were committed in Rome which I had not had to bear in Africa. Just as I had been told, those riotous disruptions by young blackguards were not practiced here. Yet, now, my friends told me, many of the Roman students—breakers of faith, who, for the love of money, set a small value on justice— would conspire together and suddenly transfer to another teacher, to evade paying their master's fees.[28] My heart hated such people, though not with a "perfect hatred"; for doubtless I hated them more because I was to suffer from them than on account of their own illicit acts. Still, such people are base indeed; they fornicate against thee, for they love the transitory mockeries of temporal things and the filthy gain which begrimes the hand that grabs it; they embrace the fleeting world and scorn thee, who abidest and invitest us to return to thee and who pardonest the prostituted human soul when it does return to thee. Now I hate such crooked and perverse men, although I love them if they will be corrected and come to prefer the learning they obtain to money and, above all, to prefer thee to such learning, O God, the truth and fullness of our positive good, and our most pure peace. But then the wish was stronger in me for my own sake not to suffer evil from them than was my desire that they should become good for thy sake.

When, therefore, the officials of Milan sent to Rome, to the prefect of the city, to ask that he provide them with a teacher of rhetoric for their city and to send him at the public expense, I applied for the job through those same persons, drunk with the Manichean vanities, to be freed from whom I was going away—though neither they nor I were aware of it at the time. They recommended that Symmachus,[29] who was

28. Rome had its own ethical problems. People would skip out of his classes without paying fees for the classes.

Early New Testament manuscript (c. 400–440)

29. Symmachus was prefect in Milan (300 miles north of Rome). He auditioned Augustine for a position as a teacher of rhetoric (working for the city).

30. God brought him to Milan in order to be discipled by Ambrose, a famous pastor (bishop) in that city.

One of the first churches in Milan, Basilica of San Lorenzo

31. Augustine is drawn first to Ambrose's presentation, his rhetorical style (not to the sermon content Ambrose preached).

then prefect, after he had proved me by audition, should appoint me.

And to Milan I came, to Ambrose the bishop, famed through the whole world as one of the best of men, thy devoted servant.[30] His eloquent discourse in those times abundantly provided thy people with the flour of thy wheat, the gladness of thy oil, and the sober intoxication of thy wine. To him I was led by thee without my knowledge, that by him I might be led to thee in full knowledge. That man of God received me as a father would, and welcomed my coming as a good bishop should. And I began to love him, of course, not at the first as a teacher of the truth, for I had entirely despaired of finding that in thy Church—but as a friendly man. And I studiously listened to him—though not with the right motive—as he preached to the people. I was trying to discover whether his eloquence came up to his reputation, and whether it flowed fuller or thinner than others said it did. And thus I hung on his words intently, but, as to his subject matter, I was only a careless and contemptuous listener.[31] I was delighted with the charm of his speech, which was more erudite, though less cheerful and soothing, than Faustus' style. As for subject matter, however, there could be no comparison, for the latter was wandering around in Manichean deceptions, while the former was teaching salvation most soundly. But "salvation is far from the wicked," such as I was then when I stood before him. Yet I was drawing nearer, gradually and unconsciously.

For, although I took no trouble to learn what he said, but only to hear how he said it—for this empty concern remained foremost with me as long as I despaired of finding a clear path from man to thee— yet, along with the eloquence I prized, there also came into my mind the ideas which I ignored; for I could not separate them. And, while I opened my heart to acknowledge how skillfully he spoke, there also came an awareness of how truly he spoke—but only gradually. First of all, his ideas had already begun to appear to me defensible; and the Catholic faith, for which I supposed that nothing could be said against the onslaught of the Manicheans, I now realized could be maintained without presumption. This was especially clear after I had heard one or two parts of the Old Testament explained allegorically—whereas before this, when I had interpreted them literally, they had "killed" me spiritually.[32] However, when many of these passages in those books were expounded to me thus, I came to blame my own despair for having believed that no reply could be given to those who hated and scoffed at the Law and the Prophets. Yet I did not see that this was reason enough to follow the Catholic way, just because it had learned advocates who could answer objections adequately and without absurdity. Nor could I see that what I had held to heretofore should now be condemned, because both sides were equally defensible. For that way did not appear to me yet vanquished; but neither did it seem yet victorious.

But now I earnestly bent my mind to require if there was possible any way to prove the Manicheans guilty of falsehood. If I could have conceived of a spiritual substance, all their strongholds would have collapsed and been cast out of my mind. But I could not. Still, concerning the body of this world, nature as a whole—now that I was able to consider and compare such things more and more—I now decided that the majority of the philosophers held the more probable views. So, in what I thought was the method of the Academics—doubting everything and fluctuating between all the options—I came to the conclusion that the Manicheans were to be abandoned. For I judged, even in that period of doubt, that I could not remain in a sect to which I preferred some of the philosophers. But I refused to commit the cure of my fainting soul to the philosophers, because they were without the saving name of Christ. I resolved, therefore, to become a catechumen in the Catholic Church[33]— which my parents had so much urged upon me—until something certain shone forth by which I might guide my course.[34]

32. Augustine especially liked the allegorical interpretation of Old Testament teaching (vs. the literal message that "killed" him spiritually).

33. The Greek philosophers forced him away from the Manicheans. But he was not convinced that the philosophers knew what they were talking about either. He finally becomes a catechumen in the church.

34. A catechumen is one who receives instruction from the church in preparation for baptism.

✵ BOOK VI

Hope from my youth, where wast thou to me and where hadst thou gone away? For hadst thou not created me and differentiated me from the beasts of the field and the birds of the air, making me wiser than they? And yet I was wandering about in a dark and slippery way, seeking thee outside myself and thus not finding the God of my heart. I had gone down into the depths of the sea and had lost faith, and had despaired of ever finding the truth.

By this time my mother had come to me, having mustered the courage of piety, following over sea and land, secure in thee through all the perils of the journey. For in the dangers of the voyage she comforted the sailors[1]—to whom the inexperienced voyagers, when alarmed, were accustomed to go for comfort—and assured them of a safe arrival because she had been so assured by thee in a vision.

She found me in deadly peril through my despair of ever finding the truth. But when I told her that I was now no longer a Manichean, though not yet a Catholic Christian, she did not leap for joy as if this were unexpected; for she had already been reassured about that part of my misery for which she had mourned me as one dead, but also as one who would be raised to thee. She had carried me out on the bier of her thoughts, that thou mightest say to the widow's son, "Young man, I say unto you, arise!" and then he would revive and begin to speak,

1. Monica was a woman of faith, even comforting the sailors on the journey across the sea to Rome.

Augustine and his mother Monica

2. Augustine refers to the raising of the son of the widow at Nain (Luke 7:11ff).

Ambrose (c. 340 – 4 April 397), bishop of Milan

3. Monica would submit herself willingly to the counsel of the elders (Pastor Ambrose).

4. Fresh in the memory of the church were the martyrs who gave their lives up for their Christian testimony. These small chapels were built to help people remember the stories of the martyrs (before people had access to books).

and thou wouldst deliver him to his mother.[2] Therefore, her heart was not agitated with any violent exultation when she heard that so great a part of what she daily entreated thee to do had actually already been done—that, though I had not yet grasped the truth, I was rescued from falsehood. Instead, she was fully confident that thou who hadst promised the whole would give her the rest, and thus most calmly, and with a fully confident heart, she replied to me that she believed, in Christ, that before she died she would see me a faithful Catholic. And she said no more than this to me. But to thee, O Fountain of mercy, she poured out still more frequent prayers and tears that thou wouldst hasten thy aid and enlighten my darkness, and she hurried all the more zealously to the church and hung upon the words of Ambrose,[3] praying for the fountain of water that springs up into everlasting life. For she loved that man as an angel of God, since she knew that it was by him that I had been brought thus far to that wavering state of agitation I was now in, through which she was fully persuaded I should pass from sickness to health, even though it would be after a still sharper convulsion which physicians call "the crisis."

So also my mother brought to certain oratories, erected in the memory of the saints,[4] offerings of porridge, bread, and wine—as had been her custom in Africa—and she was forbidden to do so by the doorkeeper [ostiarius]. And as soon as she learned that it was the bishop who had forbidden it, she acquiesced so devoutly and obediently that I myself marveled how readily she could bring herself to turn critic of her own customs, rather than question his prohibition. For winebibbing had not taken possession of her spirit, nor did the love of wine stimulate her to hate the truth, as it does too many, both male and female, who turn as sick at a hymn to sobriety as drunkards do at a draught of water. When she had brought her basket with the festive gifts, which she would taste first herself and give the rest away, she would never allow herself more than one little cup of wine, diluted according to her own temperate palate, which she would taste out of courtesy. And, if there were many oratories of departed saints that ought to be honored in the same way, she still carried around with her the same little cup, to be used everywhere. This became not only very much watered but also quite tepid with carrying it about. She would distribute it by small sips to those around, for she sought to stimulate their devotion, not pleasure.

But as soon as she found that this custom was forbidden by that famous preacher and most pious prelate, even to those who would use it in moderation, lest thereby it might be an occasion of gluttony for those who were already drunken (and also because these funeral memorials were very much like some of the superstitious practices of the pagans), she most willingly abstained from it. And, in place of a basket filled with fruits of the earth, she had learned to bring to the oratories of the martyrs a heart full of purer petitions, and to give all that she could to the poor—so that the Communion of the Lord's body might be rightly celebrated in those places where, after the example of his Passion, the martyrs had been sacrificed and crowned.[5] But yet it seems to me, O Lord my God—and my heart thinks of it this way in thy sight—that my mother would probably not have given way so easily to the rejection of this custom if it had been forbidden by another, whom she did not love as she did Ambrose. For, out of her concern for my salvation, she loved him most dearly; and he loved her truly, on account of her faithful religious life, in which she frequented the church with good works, "fervent in spirit." Thus he would, when he saw me, often burst forth into praise of her, congratulating me that I had such a mother—little knowing what a son she had in me, who was still a skeptic in all these matters and who could not conceive that the way of life could be found out.

Nor had I come yet to groan in my prayers that thou wouldst help me. My mind was wholly intent on knowledge and eager for disputation. Ambrose himself I esteemed a happy man, as the world counted happiness, because great personages held him in honor. Only his celibacy appeared to me a

5. The Lord's Supper was offered at these small chapels. Typically, collections for the poor were always taken when the Lord's Supper was celebrated.

painful burden. But what hope he cherished, what struggles he had against the temptations that beset his high station, what solace in adversity, and what savory joys thy bread possessed for the hidden mouth of his heart when feeding on it, I could neither conjecture nor experience.

Nor did he know my own frustrations, nor the pit of my danger. For I could not request of him what I wanted as I wanted it, because I was debarred from hearing and speaking to him by crowds of busy people to whose infirmities he devoted himself. And when he was not engaged with them—which was never for long at a time—he was either refreshing his body with necessary food or his mind with reading.

Now, as he read, his eyes glanced over the pages and his heart searched out the sense, but his voice and tongue were silent. Often when we came to his room—for no one was forbidden to enter, nor was it his custom that the arrival of visitors should be announced to him—we would see him thus reading to himself.[6] After we had sat for a long time in silence—for who would dare interrupt one so intent?—we would then depart, realizing that he was unwilling to be distracted in the little time he could gain for the recruiting of his mind, free from the clamor of other men's business. Perhaps he was fearful lest, if the author he was studying should express himself vaguely, some doubtful and attentive hearer would ask him to expound it or discuss some of the more abstruse questions, so that he could not get over as much material as he wished, if his time was occupied with others. And even a truer reason for his reading to himself might have been the care for preserving his voice, which was very easily weakened. Whatever his motive was in so doing, it was doubtless, in such a man, a good one.

But actually I could find no opportunity of putting the questions I desired to that holy oracle of thine in his heart, unless it was a matter which could be dealt with briefly. However, those surgings in me required that he should give me his full leisure so that I might pour them out to him; but I never found him so. I heard him, indeed, every Lord's Day, "rightly

6. Pastor Ambrose's office door was always wide open, but he was usually reading when they found him there.

dividing the word of truth" among the people. And I became all the more convinced that all those knots of crafty calumnies which those deceivers of ours had knit together against the divine books could be unraveled. I soon understood that the statement that man was made after the image of Him that created him was not understood by thy spiritual sons— whom thou hadst regenerated through the Catholic Mother[7] through grace—as if they believed and imagined that thou wert bounded by a human form, although what was the nature of a spiritual substance I had not the faintest or vaguest notion. Still rejoicing, I blushed that for so many years I had bayed, not against the Catholic faith, but against the fables of fleshly imagination. For I had been both impious and rash in this, that I had condemned by pronouncement what I ought to have learned by inquiry. For thou, O Most High, and most near, most secret, yet most present, who dost not have limbs, some of which are larger and some smaller, but who art wholly everywhere and nowhere in space, and art not shaped by some corporeal form: thou didst create man after thy own image and, see, he dwells in space, both head and feet.[8]

Since I could not then understand how this image of thine could subsist, I should have knocked on the door and propounded the doubt as to how it was to be believed, and not have insultingly opposed it as if it were actually believed. Therefore, my anxiety as to what I could retain as certain gnawed all the more sharply into my soul, and I felt quite ashamed because during the long time I had been deluded and deceived by the [Manichean] promises of certainties, I had, with childish petulance, prated of so many uncertainties as if they were certain. That they were falsehoods became apparent to me only afterward. However, I was certain that they were uncertain and since I had held them as certainly uncertain I had accused thy Catholic Church with a blind contentiousness.[9] I had not yet discovered that it taught the truth, but I now knew that it did not teach what I had so vehemently accused it of. In this respect, at least, I was confounded and

7. Augustine uses "catholic mother" to refer to the Church.

8. Augustine answers for himself the questions he had about the Christian faith.

9. Unbelieving thought cannot explain this world, and it is filled with self-contradictions. God's revelation does explain this world, albeit with incomprehensibilities (at points).

converted; and I rejoiced, O my God, that the one Church, the body of thy only Son—in which the name of Christ had been sealed upon me as an infant—did not relish these childish trifles and did not maintain in its sound doctrine any tenet that would involve pressing thee, the Creator of all, into space, which, however extended and immense, would still be bounded on all sides—like the shape of a human body.

I was also glad that the old Scriptures of the Law and the Prophets were laid before me to be read, not now with an eye to what had seemed absurd in them when formerly I censured thy holy ones for thinking thus, when they actually did not think in that way. And I listened with delight to Ambrose, in his sermons to the people, often recommending this text most diligently as a rule: "The letter kills, but the spirit gives life," while at the same time he drew aside the mystic veil and opened to view the spiritual meaning of what seemed to teach perverse doctrine if it were taken according to the letter. I found nothing in his teachings that offended me, though I could not yet know for certain whether what he taught was true. For all this time I restrained my heart from assenting to anything, fearing to fall headlong into error. Instead, by this hanging in suspense, I was being strangled. For my desire was to be as certain of invisible things as I was that seven and three are ten. I was not so deranged as to believe that this could not be comprehended, but my desire was to have other things as clear as this, whether they were physical objects, which were not present to my senses, or spiritual objects, which I did not know how to conceive of except in physical terms.[10]

If I could have believed, I might have been cured, and, with the sight of my soul cleared up, it might in some way have been directed toward thy truth, which always abides and fails in nothing. But, just as it happens that a man who has tried a bad physician fears to trust himself with a good one, so it was with the health of my soul, which could not be healed except by believing. But lest it should believe falsehoods, it refused to be cured, resisting thy hand, who hast prepared for us the medicines of faith and applied them to the maladies of the whole world, and endowed them with such great efficacy.

Still, from this time forward, I began to prefer the Catholic doctrine. I felt that it was with moderation and honesty that it commanded things to be believed that were not demonstrated—whether they could be demonstrated, but not to everyone, or whether they could not be demonstrated at all. This was far better than the method of the Manicheans, in which our credulity was mocked by an audacious promise of knowledge and then many fabulous and absurd things were forced upon believers because they were incapable of demonstration. After that, O Lord, little by little, with a gentle and most merciful hand, drawing and calming my heart, thou didst persuade me that, if I took into account the multitude of things I had never seen, nor been present when they were enacted—such as many of the events of secular history; and the numerous reports of places and cities which I had not seen; or such as my relations with many friends, or physicians, or with these men and those—that unless we should believe, we should do nothing at all in this life. Finally, I was impressed with what an unalterable assurance I believed which two people were my parents, though this was impossible for me to know otherwise than by hearsay.[10] By bringing all this into my consideration, thou didst persuade me that it was not the ones who believed thy books—which with so great authority thou hast established among nearly all nations—but those who did not believe them who were to be blamed. Moreover, those men were not to be listened to who would say to me, "How do you know that those Scriptures were imparted to mankind by the Spirit of the one and most true God?" For this was the point that was most of all to be believed, since no wranglings of blasphemous questions such as I had read in the books of the self-contradicting philosophers could once snatch from me the belief that thou dost exist—although what thou art I did not know—and that to thee belongs the governance of human affairs.[11]

10. We often believe something that cannot be proven by personal observation (that we were truly the natural children of a certain two parents).

11. Initially, Augustine came to believe two things — that God exists and that He governs all of human affairs (including governments).

This much I believed, some times more strongly than other times. But I always believed both that thou art and that thou hast a care for us, although I was ignorant both as to what should be thought about thy substance and as to which way led, or led back, to thee. Thus, since we are too weak by unaided reason to find out truth, and since, because of this, we need the authority of the Holy Writings, I had now begun to believe that thou wouldst not, under any circumstances, have given such eminent authority to those Scriptures throughout all lands if it had not been that through them thy will may be believed in and that thou mightest be sought. For, as to those passages in the Scripture which had heretofore appeared incongruous and offensive to me, now that I had heard several of them expounded reasonably, I could see that they were to be resolved by the mysteries of spiritual interpretation. The authority of Scripture seemed to me all the more revered and worthy of devout belief because, although it was visible for all to read, it reserved the full majesty of its secret wisdom within its spiritual profundity. While it stooped to all in the great plainness of its language and simplicity of style, it yet required the closest attention of the most serious minded—so that it

12. The Bible speaks to the simplest people, but it also carries the deepest and most profound doctrine.

might receive all into its common bosom,[12] and direct some few through its narrow passages toward thee, yet many more than would have been the case had there not been in it such a lofty authority, which nevertheless allured multitudes to its bosom by its holy humility. I continued to reflect upon these things, and thou wast with me. I sighed, and thou didst hear me. I vacillated, and thou guidedst me. I roamed the broad way of the world, and thou didst not desert me.

I was still eagerly aspiring to honors, money, and matrimony; and thou didst mock me. In pursuit of these ambitions I endured the most bitter hardships, in which thou wast being the more gracious the less thou wouldst allow anything that was not thee to grow sweet to me. Look into my heart, O Lord, whose prompting it is that I should recall all this, and confess it to thee. Now let my soul cleave to thee, now that thou hast freed her from that fast-sticking glue of death."

How wretched she was! And thou didst irritate her sore wound so that she might forsake all else and turn to thee—who art above all and without whom all things would be nothing at all—so that she should be converted and healed. How wretched I was at that time, and how thou didst deal with me so as to make me aware of my wretchedness,[13] I recall from the incident of the day on which I was preparing to recite a panegyric on the emperor. In it I was to deliver many a lie, and the lying was to be applauded by those who knew I was lying. My heart was agitated with this sense of guilt and it seethed with the fever of my uneasiness. For, while walking along one of the streets of Milan, I saw a poor beggar—with what I believe was a full belly—joking and hilarious. And I sighed and spoke to the friends around me of the many sorrows that flowed from our madness, because in spite of all our exertions—such as those I was then laboring in, dragging the burden of my unhappiness under the spur of ambition, and, by dragging it, increasing it at the same time—still and all we aimed only to attain that very happiness which this beggar had reached before us; and there was a grim chance that we should never attain it! For what he had obtained through a few coins, got by his begging, I was still scheming for by many a wretched and tortuous turning—namely, the joy of a passing felicity. He had not, indeed, gained true joy, but, at the same time, with all my ambitions, I was seeking one still more untrue. Anyhow, he was now joyous and I was anxious. He was free from care, and I was full of alarms.[14] Now, if anyone should inquire of me whether I should prefer to be merry or anxious, I would reply, "Merry." Again, if I had been asked whether I should prefer to be as he was or as I myself then was, I would have chosen to be myself; though I was beset with cares and alarms. But would not this have been a false choice? Was the contrast valid? Actually, I ought not to prefer myself to him because I happened to be more learned than he was; for I got no great

13. Speaking of his own heart, Augustine began to feel his own wretchedness.

14. Augustine was impressed with a beggar who was happy for one meal, yet he was unhappy for all of his wealth and success.

pleasure from my learning, but sought, rather, to please men by its exhibition—and this not to instruct, but only to please. Thus thou didst break my bones with the rod of thy correction.

Let my soul take its leave of those who say: "It makes a difference as to the object from which a man derives his joy. The beggar rejoiced in drunkenness; you longed to rejoice in glory." What glory, O Lord? The kind that is not in thee, for, just as his was no true joy, so was mine no true glory; but it turned my head all the more. He would get over his drunkenness that same night, but I had slept with mine many a night and risen again with it, and was to sleep again and rise again with it, I know not how many times. It does indeed make a difference as to the object from which a man's joy is gained. I know this is so, and I know that the joy of a faithful hope is incomparably beyond such vanity. Yet, at the same time, this beggar was beyond me, for he truly was the happier man—not only because he was thoroughly steeped in his mirth while I was torn to pieces with my cares, but because he had gotten his wine by giving good wishes to the passers-by while I was following after the ambition of my pride by lying. Much to this effect I said to my good companions, and I saw how readily they reacted pretty much as I did. Thus I found that it went ill with me; and I fretted, and doubled that very ill. And if any prosperity smiled upon me, I loathed to seize it, for almost before I could grasp it, it would fly away. [15]

15. He argues that the glory and praise of men is no more satisfying than drunkenness for a beggar.

Those of us who were living like friends together used to bemoan our lot in our common talk; but I discussed it with Alypius and Nebridius more especially and in very familiar terms. Alypius had been born in the same town as I; his parents were of the highest rank there, but he was a bit younger than I. He had studied under me when I first taught in our town, and then afterward at Carthage. He esteemed me highly because I appeared to him good and learned, and I esteemed him for his inborn love of virtue, which was uncommonly marked in a man so young. But in the whirlpool of Carthaginian fashion—where frivolous spectacles are hotly followed—he had been inveigled into the madness of the gladiatorial games. While he was miserably tossed about in this fad, I was teaching rhetoric there in a public school. At that time he was not attending my classes because of some ill feeling that had arisen between me and his father. I then came to discover how fatally he doted upon the circus, and I was deeply grieved, for he seemed likely to cast away his very great promise—if, indeed, he had not already done so.[16] Yet I had no means of advising him, or any way of reclaiming him through restraint, either by the kindness of a friend or by the authority of a teacher. For I imagined that his feelings toward me were the same as his father's. But this turned out not to be the case. Indeed, disregarding his father's will in the matter, he began to be friendly and to visit my lecture room, to listen for a while and then depart.

But it slipped my memory to try to deal with his problem, to prevent him from ruining his excellent mind in his blind and headstrong passion for frivolous sport. But thou, O Lord, who holdest the helm of all that thou hast created, thou hadst not forgotten him who was one day to be numbered among thy sons, a chief minister of thy sacrament.[17] And in order that his amendment might plainly be attributed to thee, thou broughtest it about through me while I knew nothing of it.

One day, when I was sitting in my accustomed place with my scholars before me, he came in, greeted me, sat himself down, and fixed his attention on the subject I was then discussing. It so happened that I had a passage in hand and, while I was interpreting it, a simile occurred to me, taken from the gladiatorial games. It struck me as relevant to make more pleasant and plain the point I wanted to convey by adding a biting gibe at those whom that madness had enthralled. Thou knowest, O our God, that I had no thought at that time of curing Alypius of that plague. But he took it to himself and thought that I would not have said it but for his sake. And what any other man would have taken as an occasion of offense against me, this worthy young man took as a reason for being

16. Augustine's friend Alypius was impressed with the gladiatorial games conducted in Carthage. This was a big concern for Augustine (even as an unbeliever).

17. Alypius eventually became a pastor of a Christian church.

18. Alypius came to the conviction that attending the gladiatorial games was "madness," after hearing Augustine speak on it.

offended at himself, and for loving me the more fervently.[18] Thou hast said it long ago and written in thy Book, "Rebuke a wise man, and he will love you." Now I had not rebuked him; but thou who canst make use of everything, both witting and unwitting, and in the order which thou thyself knowest to be best—and that order is right—thou madest my heart and tongue into burning coals with which thou mightest cauterize and cure the hopeful mind thus languishing. Let him be silent in thy praise who does not meditate on thy mercy, which rises up in my inmost parts to confess to thee. For after that speech Alypius rushed up out of that deep pit into which he had willfully plunged and in which he had been blinded by its miserable pleasures. And he roused his mind with a resolve to moderation. When he had done this, all the filth of the gladiatorial pleasures dropped away from him, and he went to them no more. Then he also prevailed upon his reluctant father to let him be my pupil. And, at the son's urging, the father at last consented. Thus Alypius began again to hear my lectures and became involved with me in the same superstition, loving in the Manicheans that outward display of ascetic discipline which he believed was true and unfeigned. It was, however, a senseless and seducing continence, which ensnared precious souls who were not able as yet to reach the height of true virtue, and who were easily beguiled with the veneer of what was only a shadowy and feigned virtue.

He had gone on to Rome before me to study law—which was the worldly way which his parents were forever urging him to pursue— and there he was carried away again with an incredible passion for the gladiatorial shows. For, although he had been utterly opposed to such spectacles and detested them, one day he met by chance a company of his acquaintances and fellow students returning from dinner; and, with a friendly violence, they drew him, resisting and objecting vehemently, into the amphitheater, on a day of those cruel and murderous shows. He protested to them: "Though you drag my body to that place and set me down there, you cannot force me to give my mind or lend my eyes to these shows. Thus I will be absent while present, and so overcome both you and them." When they heard this, they dragged him on in, probably interested to see whether he could do as he said. When they got to the arena, and had taken what seats they could get, the whole place became a tumult of inhuman frenzy. But Alypius kept his eyes closed and forbade his mind to roam abroad after such wickedness. Would that he had shut his ears also! For when one of the combatants fell in the fight, a mighty cry from the whole audience stirred him so strongly that, overcome by curiosity and still prepared (as he thought) to despise and rise superior to it no matter what it was, he opened his eyes and was struck with a deeper wound in his soul than the victim whom he desired to see had been in his body. Thus he fell more miserably than the one whose fall had raised that mighty clamor which had entered through his ears and unlocked his eyes to make way for the wounding and beating down of his soul, which was more audacious than truly valiant—also it was weaker because it presumed on its own strength when it ought to have depended on Thee. For, as soon as he saw the blood, he drank in with it a savage temper, and he did not turn away, but fixed his eyes on the bloody pastime, unwittingly drinking in the madness—delighted with the wicked contest and drunk with blood lust. He was now no longer the same man who came in, but was one of the mob he came into, a true companion of those who had brought him thither. Why need I say more? He looked, he shouted, he was excited, and he took away with him the madness that would stimulate him to come again: not only with those who first enticed him, but even without them; indeed, dragging in others besides.[19] And yet from all this, with a most powerful and most merciful hand, thou didst pluck him and taught him not to rest his confidence in himself but in thee—but not till long after.[20]

But this was all being stored up in his memory as medicine for the future. So also was that other incident when he

Ruins of ancient Rome

19. Alypius was drawn into the games again after moving to Rome. Once more, he became a great supporter of the games (even inviting others with him to watch).

20. Augustine interprets these circumstances of his friend as God's providential hand working in his friend's life.

was still studying under me at Carthage and was meditating at noonday in the market place on what he had to recite—as scholars usually have to do for practice—and thou didst allow him to be arrested by the police officers in the market place as a thief. I believe, O my God, that thou didst allow this for no other reason than that this man who was in the future to prove so great should now begin to learn that, in making just decisions, a man should not readily be condemned by other men with reckless credulity.

For as he was walking up and down alone before the judgment seat with his tablets and pen, lo, a young man—another one of the scholars, who was the real thief—secretly brought a hatchet and, without Alypius seeing him, got in as far as the leaden bars which protected the silversmith shop and began to hack away at the lead gratings. But when the noise of the hatchet was heard the silversmiths below began to call to each other in whispers and sent men to arrest whomsoever they should find. The thief heard their voices and ran away, leaving his hatchet because he was afraid to be caught with it. Now Alypius, who had not seen him come in, got a glimpse of him as he went out and noticed that he went off in great haste. Being curious to know the reasons, he went up to the place, where he found the hatchet, and stood wondering and pondering when, behold, those that were sent caught him alone, holding the hatchet which had made the noise which had startled them and brought them there. They seized him and dragged him away, gathering the tenants of the market place about them and boasting that they had caught a notorious thief. Thereupon he was led away to appear before the judge.

But this is as far as his lesson was to go. For immediately, O Lord, thou didst come to the rescue of his innocence, of which thou wast the sole witness. As he was being led off to prison or punishment, they were met by the master builder who had charge of the public buildings. The captors were especially glad to meet him because he had more than once suspected them of stealing the goods that had been lost out of the market place. Now, at last, they thought they could convince him who it was that had committed the thefts. But the custodian had often met Alypius at the house of a certain senator, whose receptions he used to attend. He recognized him at once and, taking his hand, led him apart from the throng,[21] inquired the cause of all the trouble, and learned what had occurred. He then commanded all the rabble still around—and very uproarious and full of threatenings they were—to come along with him, and they came to the house of the young man who had committed the deed. There, before the door, was a slave boy so young that he was not restrained from telling the whole story by fear of harming his master. And he had followed his master to the market place. Alypius recognized him, and whispered to the architect, who showed the boy the hatchet and asked whose it was. "Ours," he answered directly. And, being further questioned, he disclosed the whole affair. Thus the guilt was shifted to that household and the rabble, who had begun to triumph over Alypius, were shamed. And so he went away home, this man who was to be the future steward of thy Word and judge of so many causes in thy Church—a wiser and more experienced man.

I found him at Rome, and he was bound to me with the strongest possible ties, and he went with me to Milan, in order that he might not be separated from me, and also that he might obtain some law practice, for which he had qualified with a view to pleasing his parents more than himself. He had already sat three times as assessor, showing an integrity that seemed strange to many others, though he thought them strange who could prefer gold to integrity. His character had also been tested, not only by the bait of covetousness, but by the spur of fear. At Rome he was assessor to the secretary of the Italian Treasury. There was at that time a very powerful senator to whose favors many were indebted, and of whom many stood in fear. In his usual highhanded way he demanded to have a favor granted him that was forbidden by the laws. This Alypius resisted. A bribe was promised, but he scorned

21. God brought the right man into the case to help exonerate Alypius from the false charges.

it with all his heart. Threats were employed, but he trampled them underfoot—so that all men marveled at so rare a spirit, which neither coveted the friendship nor feared the enmity of a man at once so powerful and so widely known for his great resources of helping his friends and doing harm to his enemies.[22] Even the official whose counselor Alypius was—although he was unwilling that the favor should be granted—would not openly refuse the request, but passed the responsibility on to Alypius, alleging that he would not permit him to give his assent. And the truth was that even if the judge had agreed, Alypius would have simply left the court.

There was one matter, however, which appealed to his love of learning, in which he was very nearly led astray. He found out that he might have books copied for himself at praetorian rates [i.e., at public expense]. But his sense of justice prevailed, and he changed his mind for the better, thinking that the rule that forbade him was still more profitable than the privilege that his office would have allowed him. These are little things, but "he that is faithful in a little matter is faithful also in a great one." Nor can that possibly be void which was uttered by the mouth of Thy truth: "If, therefore, you have not been faithful in the unrighteous mammon, who will commit to your trust the true riches? And if you have not been faithful in that which is another man's, who shall give you that which is your own?" Such a man was Alypius, who clung to me at that time and who wavered in his purpose, just as I did, as to what course of life to follow.

Nebridius also had come to Milan for no other reason than that he might live with me in a most ardent search after truth and wisdom. He had left his native place near Carthage—and Carthage itself, where he usually lived—leaving behind his fine family estate, his house, and his mother, who would not follow him. Like me, he sighed; like me, he wavered; an ardent seeker after the true life and a most acute analyst of the most abstruse questions. So there were three begging mouths, sighing out their wants one to the other, and

22. Alypius was a man of great integrity and would not trade his integrity for anything. He refused a powerful Senator who asked him for a bribe.

waiting upon thee, that thou mightest give them their meat in due season. And in all the vexations with which thy mercy followed our worldly pursuits, we sought for the reason why we suffered so—and all was darkness! We turned away groaning and exclaiming, "How long shall these things be?" And this we often asked, yet for all our asking we did not relinquish them; for as yet we had not discovered anything certain which, when we gave those others up, we might grasp in their stead.

And I especially puzzled and wondered when I remembered how long a time had passed since my nineteenth year, in which I had first fallen in love with wisdom and had determined as soon as I could find her to abandon the empty hopes and mad delusions of vain desires. Behold, I was now getting close to thirty, still stuck fast in the same mire, still greedy of enjoying present goods which fly away and distract me; and I was still saying, "Tomorrow I shall discover it; behold, it will become plain, and I shall see it; behold, Faustus will come and explain everything." Or I would say: "O you mighty Academics, is there no certainty that man can grasp for the guidance of his life? No, let us search the more diligently, and let us not despair. See, the things in the Church's books that appeared so absurd to us before do not appear so now, and may be otherwise and honestly interpreted. I will set my feet upon that step where, as a child, my parents placed me, until the clear truth is discovered. But where and when shall it be sought? Ambrose has no leisure—we have no leisure to read. Where are we to find the books? How or where could I get hold of them? From whom could I borrow them? Let me set a schedule for my days and set apart certain hours for the health of the soul. A great hope has risen up in us, because the Catholic faith does not teach what we thought it did, and vainly accused it of. Its teachers hold it as an abomination to believe that God is limited by the form of a human body. And do I doubt that I should 'knock' in order for the rest also to be 'opened' unto me? My pupils take up the morning hours; what am I doing with the rest of the day? Why not do this? But, then, when am I to

23. Augustine had abandoned hope that the Manicheans or the Greek Academics could satisfy his aching mind. So, he committed to continue sitting on the steps of the Christian church.

24. By AD 400, the Christian faith had spread around the whole Roman world.

25. The values of the humanists of the day included prestige, a position of authority, a wife who brought money into the marriage, and the pursuit of wisdom.

visit my influential friends, whose favors I need? When am I to prepare the orations that I sell to the class? When would I get some recreation and relax my mind from the strain of work?[23]

"Perish everything and let us dismiss these idle triflings. Let me devote myself solely to the search for truth. This life is unhappy, death uncertain. If it comes upon me suddenly, in what state shall I go hence and where shall I learn what here I have neglected? Should I not indeed suffer the punishment of my negligence here? But suppose death cuts off and finishes all care and feeling. This too is a question that calls for inquiry. God forbid that it should be so. It is not without reason, it is not in vain, that the stately authority of the Christian faith has spread over the entire world,[24] and God would never have done such great things for us if the life of the soul perished with the death of the body. Why, therefore, do I delay in abandoning my hopes of this world and giving myself wholly to seek after God and the blessed life?

"But wait a moment. This life also is pleasant, and it has a sweetness of its own, not at all negligible. We must not abandon it lightly, for it would be shameful to lapse back into it again. See now, it is important to gain some post of honor. And what more should I desire? I have crowds of influential friends, if nothing else; and, if I push my claims, a governorship may be offered me, and a wife with some money, so that she would not be an added expense. This would be the height of my desire. Many men, who are great and worthy of imitation, have combined the pursuit of wisdom with a marriage life."[25]

While I talked about these things, and the winds of opinions veered about and tossed my heart hither and thither, time was slipping away. I delayed my conversion to the Lord; I postponed from day to day the life in thee, but I could not postpone the daily death in myself. I was enamored of a happy life, but I still feared to seek it in its own abode, and so I fled from it while I sought it. I thought I should be miserable if I were deprived of the embraces of a woman, and I never gave a thought to the medicine that thy mercy has provided for the healing of that infirmity, for I had never tried it. As for continence, I imagined that it depended on one's own strength, though I found no such strength in myself, for in my folly I knew not what is written, "None can be continent unless thou dost grant it." Certainly thou wouldst have given it, if I had beseeched thy ears with heartfelt groaning, and if I had cast my care upon thee with firm faith.[26]

Actually, it was Alypius who prevented me from marrying, urging that if I did so it would not be possible for us to live together and to have as much undistracted leisure in the love of wisdom as we had long desired. For he himself was so chaste that it was wonderful, all the more because in his early youth he had entered upon the path of promiscuity, but had not continued in it. Instead, feeling sorrow and disgust at it, he had lived from that time down to the present most continently. I quoted against him the examples of men who had been married and still lovers of wisdom, who had pleased God and had been loyal and affectionate to their friends. I fell far short of them in greatness of soul, and, enthralled with the disease of my carnality and its deadly sweetness, I dragged my chain along, fearing to be loosed of it. Thus I rejected the words of him who counseled me wisely, as if the hand that would have loosed the chain only hurt my wound.[27] Moreover, the serpent spoke to Alypius himself by me, weaving and lying in his path, by my tongue to catch him with pleasant snares in which his honorable and free feet might be entangled.

For he wondered that I, for whom he had such a great esteem, should be stuck so fast in the gluepot of pleasure as to maintain, whenever we discussed the subject, that I could not possibly live a celibate life. And when I urged in my defense against his accusing questions that the hasty and stolen delight, which he had tasted and now hardly remembered, and therefore too easily disparaged, was not to be compared with a settled acquaintance with it; and that, if to this stable acquaintance were added the honorable name of marriage, he would

26. Augustine did not believe he could live the celibate life. He would discover that he could do it by the power that God gave to him.

27. These men wanted to enjoy a woman occasionally but spend more time with their male friends and pursuing "wisdom." Alypius gave up on his life of fornication and was now living a celibate life.

not then be astonished at my inability to give it up—when I spoke thus, then he also began to wish to be married, not because he was overcome by the lust for such pleasures, but out of curiosity. For, he said, he longed to know what that could be without which my life, which he thought was so happy, seemed to me to be no life at all, but a punishment. For he who wore no chain was amazed at my slavery, and his amazement awoke the desire for experience, and from that he would have gone on to the experiment itself, and then perhaps he would have fallen into the very slavery that amazed him in me, since he was ready to enter into "a covenant with death," for "he that loves danger shall fall into it." [28]

28. The men agreed that marriage was better than a life of fornication. First Corinthians 7 does say, "It is better to marry than to burn."

Now, the question of conjugal honor in the ordering of a good married life and the bringing up of children interested us but slightly. What afflicted me most and what had made me already a slave to it was the habit of satisfying an insatiable lust; but Alypius was about to be enslaved by a merely curious wonder. This is the state we were in until thou, O Most High, who never forsakest our lowliness, didst take pity on our misery and didst come to our rescue in wonderful and secret ways.

Active efforts were made to get me a wife. I wooed; I was engaged; and my mother took the greatest pains in the matter. For her hope was that, when I was once married, I might be washed clean in health- giving baptism for which I was being daily prepared, as she joyfully saw, taking note that her desires and promises were being fulfilled in my faith. Yet, when, at my request and her own impulse, she called upon thee daily with strong, heartfelt cries, that thou wouldst, by a vision, disclose unto her a leading about my future marriage, thou wouldst not. She did, indeed, see certain vain and fantastic things, such as are conjured up by the strong preoccupation of the human spirit, and these she supposed had some reference to me. And she told me about them, but not with the confidence she usually had when thou hadst shown her anything. For she always said that she could distinguish, by a certain feeling impossible to describe, between thy revelations and the dreams of her own soul.[29] Yet the matter was pressed forward, and proposals were made for a girl who was as yet some two years too young to marry. And because she pleased me, I agreed to wait for her.[30]

Many in my band of friends, consulting about and abhorring the turbulent vexations of human life, had often considered and were now almost determined to undertake a peaceful life, away from the turmoil of men. This we thought could be obtained by bringing together what we severally owned and thus making of it a common household, so that in the sincerity of our friendship nothing should belong more to one than to the other; but all were to have one purse and the whole was to belong to each and to all. We thought that this group might consist of ten persons, some of whom were very rich—especially Romanianus, my fellow townsman, an intimate friend from childhood days. He had been brought up to the court on grave business matters and he was the most earnest of us all about the project and his voice was of great weight in commending it because his estate was far more ample than that of the others. We had resolved, also, that each year two of us should be managers and provide all that was needful, while the rest were left undisturbed. But when we began to reflect whether this would be permitted by our wives, which some of us had already and others hoped to have, the whole plan, so excellently framed, collapsed in our hands and was utterly wrecked and cast aside. From this we fell again into sighs and groans, and our steps followed the broad and beaten ways of the world; for many thoughts were in our hearts, but "Thy counsel standeth fast forever." In thy counsel thou didst mock ours, and didst prepare thy own plan, for it was thy purpose "to give us meat in due season, to open thy hand, and to fill our souls with blessing." Meanwhile my sins were being multiplied. My mistress was torn from my side as an impediment to my marriage, and my heart which clung to her was torn and wounded till it bled. And she went back to Africa, vowing to thee never to know any other man and leaving with me my natural son by her. But I, unhappy as I was, and weaker than a

29. Augustine's mother believed she received revelation from God and that she could distinguish between the prophetic insights and her own thoughts.

30. Now at 30 years of age, Augustine is preparing for marriage. The arrangement is made for a girl two years under marriage age (at least according to the custom of the day).

31. Augustine had a mistress with whom he was committing fornication and with whom he had a son. When he was set up for marriage, the woman was sent back to Africa. Then, he went out to find another mistress. Thus, he became even more wretched (in his own words).

32. Augustine still had a fear of death and judgment.

33. Epicurus was a Greek philosopher who lived around 300 BC. He taught that there was no after-life and no judgment. Epicurus would have "carried off the palm," or won Augustine's support and honor. But Augustine could not believe that the soul was mortal and would die upon the death of the body.

woman, could not bear the delay of the two years that should elapse before I could obtain the bride I sought. And so, since I was not a lover of wedlock so much as a slave of lust, I procured another mistress—not a wife, of course. Thus in bondage to a lasting habit, the disease of my soul might be nursed up and kept in its vigor or even increased until it reached the realm of matrimony. Nor indeed was the wound healed that had been caused by cutting away my former mistress; only it ceased to burn and throb, and began to fester, and was more dangerous because it was less painful.[31]

Thine be the praise; unto thee be the glory, O Fountain of mercies. I became more wretched and thou didst come nearer. Thy right hand was ever ready to pluck me out of the mire and to cleanse me, but I did not know it. Nor did anything call me back from a still deeper plunge into carnal pleasure except the fear of death and of thy future judgment,[32] which, amid all the waverings of my opinions, never faded from my breast. And I discussed with my friends, Alypius and Nebridius, the nature of good and evil, maintaining that, in my judgment, Epicurus would have carried off the palm if I had not believed what Epicurus[33] would not believe: that after death there remains a life for the soul, and places of recompense. And I demanded of them: "Suppose we are immortal and live in the enjoyment of perpetual bodily pleasure, and that without any fear of losing it—why, then, should we not be happy, or why should we search for anything else?" I did not know that this was in fact the root of my misery: that I was so fallen and blinded that I could not discern the light of virtue and of beauty which must be embraced for its own sake, which the eye of flesh cannot see, and only the inner vision can see. Nor did I, alas, consider the reason why I found delight in discussing these very perplexities, shameful as they were, with my friends. For I could not be happy without friends, even according to the notions of happiness I had then, and no matter how rich the store of my carnal pleasures might be. Yet of a truth I loved my friends for their own sakes, and felt that they in turn loved me for my own sake.[34]

O crooked ways! Woe to the audacious soul which hoped that by forsaking thee it would find some better thing! It tossed and turned, upon back and side and belly—but the bed is hard, and thou alone givest it rest. And lo, thou art near, and thou deliverest us from our wretched wanderings and establishest us in thy way, and thou comfortest us and sayest, "Run, I will carry you; yea, I will lead you home and then I will set you free."

34. Augustine's vanity was in his assuming that man can live with pleasures and be happy apart from God.

❖ BOOK VII

D ead now was that evil and shameful youth of mine, and I was passing into full manhood. As I increased in years, the worse was my vanity. For I could not conceive of any substance but the sort I could see with my own eyes. I no longer thought of thee, O God, by the analogy of a human body. Ever since I inclined my ear to philosophy I had avoided this error—and the truth on this point I rejoiced to find in the faith of our spiritual mother, thy Catholic Church.[1] Yet I could not see how else to conceive thee. And I, a man— and such a man!—sought to conceive thee, the sovereign and only true God. In my inmost heart, I believed that thou art incorruptible and inviolable and unchangeable, because— though I knew not how or why—I could still see plainly and without doubt that the corruptible is inferior to the incorruptible, the inviolable obviously superior to its opposite, and the unchangeable better than the changeable.

My heart cried out violently against all fantasms, and with this one clear certainty I endeavored to brush away the swarm of unclean flies that swarmed around the eyes of my mind. But behold they were scarcely scattered before they gathered again, buzzed against my face, and beclouded my vision. I no longer thought of God in the analogy of a human body, yet I was constrained to conceive thee to be some kind of body in space, either infused into the world, or infinitely diffused

1. Augustine spoke of the Christian Church as a spiritual mother.

beyond the world—and this was the incorruptible, inviolable, unchangeable substance, which I thought was better than the corruptible, the violable, and the changeable. For whatever I conceived to be deprived of the dimensions of space appeared to me to be nothing, absolutely nothing; not even a void, for if a body is taken out of space, or if space is emptied of all its contents (of earth, water, air, or heaven), yet it remains an empty space—a spacious nothing, as it were.[2]

Being thus gross-hearted and not clear even to myself, I then held that whatever had neither length nor breadth nor density nor solidity, and did not or could not receive such dimensions, was absolutely nothing. For at that time my mind dwelt only with ideas, which resembled the forms with which my eyes are still familiar, nor could I see that the act of thought, by which I formed those ideas, was itself immaterial, and yet it could not have formed them if it were not itself a measurable entity.[3]

So also I thought about thee, O Life of my life, as stretched out through infinite space, interpenetrating the whole mass of the world, reaching out beyond in all directions, to immensity without end; so that the earth should have thee, the heaven have thee, all things have thee, and all of them be limited in thee, while thou art placed nowhere at all. As the body of the air above the earth does not bar the passage of the light of the sun, so that the light penetrates it, not by bursting nor dividing, but filling it entirely, so I imagined that the body of heaven and air and sea, and even of the earth, was all open to thee and, in all its greatest parts as well as the smallest, was ready to receive thy presence by a secret inspiration which, from within or without all, orders all things thou hast created.[4] This was my conjecture, because I was unable to think of anything else; yet it was untrue. For in this way a greater part of the earth would contain a greater part of thee; a smaller part, a smaller fraction of thee. All things would be full of thee in such a sense that there would be more of thee in an elephant than in a sparrow, because one is larger than the other and fills a larger space.

2. Augustine was still a materialist. He could not conceive of God without a physical being. If God did not take up space, Augustine did not see how He could exist.

3. A classic argument against the materialist: our thoughts are a product of something material and immaterial.

4. Now Augustine thought of God as distributed about the universe. So, a larger percentage of God's being was present on the sun than on the earth (since the sun is quite a bit larger than the earth). Thus, God would be present to a greater degree on the sun than He would be on the earth.

And this would make the portions of thyself present in the several portions of the world in fragments, great to the great, small to the small. But thou art not such a one. But as yet thou hadst not enlightened my darkness.

But it was not sufficient for me, O Lord, to be able to oppose those deceived deceivers and those dumb orators—dumb because thy Word did not sound forth from them[5]—to oppose them with the answer which, in the old Carthaginian days, Nebridius used to propound, shaking all of us who heard it: "What could this imaginary people of darkness, which the Manicheans usually set up as an army opposed to thee, have done to thee if thou hadst declined the combat?" If they replied that it could have hurt thee, they would then have made thee violable and corruptible.[6] If, on the other hand, the dark could have done thee no harm, then there was no cause for any battle at all; there was less cause for a battle in which a part of thee, one of thy members, a child of thy own substance, should be mixed up with opposing powers, not of thy creation; and should be corrupted and deteriorated and changed by them from happiness into misery, so that it could not be delivered and cleansed without thy help. This offspring of thy substance was supposed to be the human soul to which thy Word—free, pure, and entire—could bring help when it was being enslaved, contaminated, and corrupted. But on their hypothesis that Word was itself corruptible because it is one and the same substance as the soul.[7]

And therefore if they admitted that thy nature—whatsoever thou art—is incorruptible, then all these assertions of theirs are false and should be rejected with horror. But if thy substance is corruptible, then this is self-evidently false and should be abhorred at first utterance. This line of argument, then, was enough against those deceivers who ought to be cast forth from a surfeited stomach[8]—for out of this dilemma they could find no way of escape without dreadful sacrilege of mind and tongue, when they think and speak such things about thee.

5. Now he sees the Manicheans were dumb (ignorant) because they refused to root their ideas in God's Word.

6. The Manicheans taught equal forces of light and darkness, good and evil, God and the demons. Augustine argues that if the evil forces could affect God, He would be corruptible (and thereby forfeit His divinity).

7. The Word is Christ. The Manicheans taught wrongly that Christ was corruptible because He came in human flesh and a human soul.

8. "To be cast forth from a sufeited stomach" — a nice way of saying these deceivers should be vomited out of our thinking.

But as yet, although I said and was firmly persuaded that thou our Lord, the true God, who madest not only our souls but our bodies as well—and not only our souls and bodies but all creatures and all things—wast free from stain and alteration and in no way mutable, yet I could not readily and clearly understand what was the cause of evil. Whatever it was, I realized that the question must be so analyzed as not to constrain me by any answer to believe that the immutable God was mutable, lest I should myself become the thing that I was seeking out. And so I pursued the search with a quiet mind, now in a confident feeling that what had been said by the Manicheans—and I shrank from them with my whole heart—could not be true. I now realized that when they asked what was the origin of evil their answer was dictated by a wicked pride, which would rather affirm that thy nature is capable of suffering evil than that their own nature is capable of doing it.

And I directed my attention to understand what I now was told, that free will is the cause of our doing evil[9] and that thy just judgment is the cause of our having to suffer from its consequences. But I could not see this clearly. So then, trying to draw the eye of my mind up out of that pit, I was plunged back into it again, and trying often was just as often plunged back down. But one thing lifted me up toward thy light: it was that I had come to know that I had a will as certainly as I knew that I had life. When, therefore, I willed or was unwilling to do something, I was utterly certain that it was none but myself who willed or was unwilling—and immediately I realized that there was the cause of my sin. I could see that what I did against my will I suffered rather than did; and I did not regard such actions as faults, but rather as punishments in which I might quickly confess that I was not unjustly punished, since I believed thee to be most just. Who was it that put this in me, and implanted in me the root of bitterness, in spite of the fact that I was altogether the handiwork of my most sweet God? If the devil is to blame, who made the devil himself? And if

9. Christians teach that man's free will is the source of evil and sin. God brings His righteous judgment upon this rebellion, and thereby His righteousness is held inviolable.

he was a good angel who by his own wicked will became the devil, how did there happen to be in him that wicked will by which he became a devil, since a good Creator made him wholly a good angel?[10] By these reflections was I again cast down and stultified. Yet I was not plunged into that hell of error— where no man confesses to thee—where I thought that thou didst suffer evil, rather than that men do it.

For in my struggle to solve the rest of my difficulties, I now assumed henceforth as settled truth that the incorruptible must be superior to the corruptible, and I did acknowledge that thou, whatever thou art, art incorruptible. For there never yet was, nor will be, a soul able to conceive of anything better than thee, who art the highest and best good. And since most truly and certainly the incorruptible is to be placed above the corruptible—as I now admit it—it followed that I could rise in my thoughts to something better than my God, if thou wert not incorruptible. When, therefore, I saw that the incorruptible was to be preferred to the corruptible, I saw then where I ought to seek thee, and where I should look for the source of evil: that is, the corruption by which thy substance can in no way be profaned. For it is obvious that corruption in no way injures our God, by no inclination, by no necessity, by no unforeseen chance—because he is our God, and what he wills is good, and he himself is that good. But to be corrupted is not good. Nor art thou compelled to do anything against thy will, since thy will is not greater than thy power. But it would have to be greater if thou thyself wert greater than thyself—for the will and power of God are God himself. And what can take thee by surprise, since thou knowest all, and there is no sort of nature but thou knowest it? And what more should we say about why that substance which God is cannot be corrupted; because if this were so it could not be God?[11]

And I kept seeking for an answer to the question, Whence is evil? And I sought it in an evil way, and I did not see the evil in my very search. I marshaled before the sight of my spirit all creation: all that we see of earth and sea and air and stars and

10. Augustine asks the most difficult question of all. Where did evil come from before Satan rebelled against God? This question concerning the ultimate source of evil bothered him very much.

11. Augustine works out the problem in his mind. He rests on certain givens. God must be more powerful than evil, and He cannot be corrupted by it.

trees and animals; and all that we do not see, the firmament of the sky above and all the angels and all spiritual things, for my imagination arranged these also, as if they were bodies, in this place or that. And I pictured to myself thy creation as one vast mass, composed of various kinds of bodies—some of which were actually bodies, some of those which I imagined spirits were like. I pictured this mass as vast—of course not in its full dimensions, for these I could not know—but as large as I could possibly think, still only finite on every side. But thou, O Lord, I imagined as environing the mass on every side and penetrating it, still infinite in every direction— as if there were a sea everywhere, and everywhere through measureless space nothing but an infinite sea; and it contained within itself some sort of sponge, huge but still finite, so that the sponge would in all its parts be filled from the immeasurable sea.[12]

Thus I conceived thy creation itself to be finite, and filled by thee, the infinite. And I said, "Behold God, and behold what God hath created!" God is good, yea, most mightily and incomparably better than all his works. But yet he who is good has created them good; behold how he encircles and fills them. Where, then, is evil, and whence does it come and how has it crept in? What is its root and what its seed? Has it no being at all? Why, then, do we fear and shun what has no being? Or if we fear it needlessly, then surely that fear is evil by which the heart is unnecessarily stabbed and tortured—and indeed a greater evil since we have nothing real to fear, and yet do fear. Therefore, either that is evil which we fear, or the act of fearing is in itself evil. But, then, whence does it come, since God who is good has made all these things good?[13] Indeed, he is the greatest and chiefest Good, and hath created these lesser goods; but both Creator and created are all good. Whence, then, is evil? Or, again, was there some evil matter out of which he made and formed and ordered it, but left something in his creation that he did not convert into good? But why should this be? Was he powerless to change the whole lump so that no evil would remain in it, if he is the Omnipotent?

12. He imagined that God was water and that He filled all mass in the universe like water fills a sponge.

"The Expulsion of Adam and Eve from Paradise," 1791, by artist Benjamin West

13. He iterates the problem of evil many different ways. How can God be both all-powerful and all-good and still allow evil to exist? This is the question over which atheists and humanist philosophers almost always stumble.

Finally, why would he make anything at all out of such stuff? Why did he not, rather, annihilate it by his same almighty power? Could evil exist contrary to his will? And if it were from eternity, why did he permit it to be nonexistent for unmeasured intervals of time in the past, and why, then, was he pleased to make something out of it after so long a time? Or, if he wished now all of a sudden to create something, would not an almighty being have chosen to annihilate this evil matter and live by himself—the perfect, true, sovereign, and infinite Good? Or, if it were not good that he who was good should not also be the framer and creator of what was good, then why was that evil matter not removed and brought to nothing, so that he might form good matter, out of which he might then create all things? For he would not be omnipotent if he were not able to create something good without being assisted by that matter which had not been created by himself.

Such perplexities I revolved in my wretched breast, overwhelmed with gnawing cares lest I die before I discovered the truth. And still the faith of thy Christ, our Lord and Saviour, as it was taught me by the Catholic Church, stuck fast in my heart. As yet it was unformed on many points and diverged from the rule of right doctrine, but my mind did not utterly lose it, and every day drank in more and more of it.[14]

By now I had also repudiated the lying divinations and impious absurdities of the astrologers. Let thy mercies, out of the depth of my soul, confess this to thee also, O my God. For thou, thou only (for who else is it who calls us back from the death of all errors except the Life which does not know how to die and the Wisdom which gives light to minds that need it, although it itself has no need of light—by which the whole universe is governed, even to the fluttering leaves of the trees?)—thou alone providedst also for my obstinacy with which I struggled against Vindicianus,[15] a sagacious old man, and Nebridius, that remarkably talented young man. The former declared vehemently and the latter frequently—though with some reservation—that no art existed by which we fore-

14. The teaching concerning Christ seems to have more of an effect on him . . . almost distracting him from the deeper philosophical questioning.

15. Vindicianus was an older man, a wise man who debunked astrology. He told Augustine that astrologers might get it right from time to time, but they're only working "the odds."

see future things. But men's surmises have oftentimes the help of chance, and out of many things which they foretold some came to pass unawares to the predictors, who lighted on the truth by making so many guesses.

And thou also providedst a friend for me, who was not a negligent consulter of the astrologers even though he was not thoroughly skilled in the art either—as I said, one who consulted them out of curiosity. He knew a good deal about it which, he said, he had heard from his father, and he never realized how far his ideas would help to overthrow my estimation of that art. His name was Firminus and he had received a liberal education and was a cultivated rhetorician. It so happened that he consulted me, as one very dear to him, as to what I thought about some affairs of his in which his worldly hopes had risen, viewed in the light of his so-called horoscope. Although I had now begun to learn in this matter toward Nebridius' opinion, I did not quite decline to speculate about the matter or to tell him what thoughts still came into my irresolute mind, although I did add that I was almost persuaded now that these were but empty and ridiculous follies. He then told me that his father had been very much interested in such books, and that he had a friend who was as much interested in them as he was himself.[16] They, in combined study and consultation, fanned the flame of their affection for this folly, going so far as to observe the moment when the dumb animals which belonged to their household gave birth to young, and then observed the position of the heavens with regard to them, so as to gather fresh evidence for this so-called art. Moreover, he reported that his father had told him that, at the same time his mother was about to give birth to him [Firminus], a female slave of a friend of his father's was also pregnant. This could not be hidden from her master, who kept records with the most diligent exactness of the birth dates even of his dogs. And so it happened to pass that—under the most careful observations, one for his wife and the other for his servant, with exact calculations of the

16. A fellow rhetorician (a man who mastered the art of speaking) spoke to Augustine about his commitment to the horoscope.

days, hours, and minutes—both women were delivered at the same moment, so that both were compelled to cast the self-same horoscope, down to the minute: the one for his son, the other for his young slave. For as soon as the women began to be in labor, they each sent word to the other as to what was happening in their respective houses and had messengers ready to dispatch to one another as soon as they had information of the actual birth—and each, of course, knew instantly the exact time. It turned out, Firminus said, that the messengers from the respective houses met one another at a point equidistant from either house, so that neither of them could discern any difference either in the position of the stars or any other of the most minute points.[17] And yet Firminus, born in a high estate in his parents' house, ran his course through the prosperous paths of this world, was increased in wealth, and elevated to honors. At the same time, the slave, the yoke of his condition being still unrelaxed, continued to serve his masters as Firminus, who knew him, was able to report.[18]

Upon hearing and believing these things related by so reliable a person all my resistance melted away. First, I endeavored to reclaim Firminus himself from his superstition by telling him that after inspecting his horoscope, I ought, if I could foretell truly, to have seen in it parents eminent among their neighbors, a noble family in its own city, a good birth, a proper education, and liberal learning. But if that servant had consulted me with the same horoscope, since he had the same one, I ought again to tell him likewise truly that I saw in it the lowliness of his origin, the abjectness of his condition, and everything else different and contrary to the former prediction. If, then, by casting up the same horoscopes I should, in order to speak the truth, make contrary analyses, or else speak falsely if I made identical readings, then surely it followed that whatever was truly foretold by the analysis of the horoscopes was not by art, but by chance. And whatever was said falsely was not from incompetence in the art, but from the error of chance.[19]

17. The slave child and the child in the prosperous family were born under the same horoscope, at the very same time. No clocks were available at the time, so the timing of births was measured by runners who met each other exactly half way between the two homes.

18. The horoscope did not dictate the success of the two children. Firminius was successful in life, and the slave child remained a slave.

19. Augustine points to the circumstances of the two boys' lives that dictated their future. Man is searching for ultimate causes for what happens in life. Astrology provides an otherworldly explanation without conceding to the sovereignty of God.

An opening being thus made in my darkness, I began to consider other implications involved here. Suppose that one of the fools—who followed such an occupation and whom I longed to assail, and to reduce to confusion—should urge against me that Firminus had given me false information, or that his father had informed him falsely. I then turned my thoughts to those that are born twins, who generally come out of the womb so near the one to the other that the short interval between them—whatever importance they may ascribe to it in the nature of things—cannot be noted by human observation or expressed in those tables which the astrologer uses to examine when he undertakes to pronounce the truth. But such pronouncements cannot be true. For looking into the same horoscopes, he must have foretold the same future for Esau and Jacob, whereas the same future did not turn out for them.[20] He must therefore speak falsely. If he is to speak truly, then he must read contrary predictions into the same horoscopes. But this would mean that it was not by art, but by chance, that he would speak truly.

20. Augustine also considers twins born at the same time who end up in vastly different situations. Jacob and Esau is the best biblical example of this.

For thou, O Lord, most righteous ruler of the universe,[21] dost work by a secret impulse—whether those who inquire or those inquired of know it or not—so that the inquirer may hear what, according to the secret merit of his soul, he ought to hear from the deeps of thy righteous judgment. Therefore let no man say to thee, "What is this?" or, "Why is that?" Let him not speak thus, for he is only a man.

21. Augustine finally concedes that God is the Ruler of the Universe.

By now, O my Helper, thou hadst freed me from those fetters. But still I inquired, "Whence is evil?"—and found no answer. But thou didst not allow me to be carried away from the faith by these fluctuations of thought. I still believed both that thou dost exist and that thy substance is immutable, and that thou dost care for and wilt judge all men, and that in Christ, thy Son our Lord, and the Holy Scriptures, which the authority of thy Catholic Church pressed on me, thou hast planned the way of man's salvation to that life which is to come after this death.[22]

22. Augustine confesses that God provides a way of salvation through Jesus Christ, the Son of God.

With these convictions safe and immovably settled in my mind, I eagerly inquired, "Whence is evil?" What torments did my travailing heart then endure! What sighs, O my God! Yet even then thy ears were open and I knew it not, and when in stillness I sought earnestly, those silent contritions of my soul were loud cries to thy mercy. No man knew, but thou knewest what I endured.[23] How little of it could I express in words to the ears of my dearest friends! How could the whole tumult of my soul, for which neither time nor speech was sufficient, come to them? Yet the whole of it went into thy ears, all of which I bellowed out in the anguish of my heart. My desire was before thee, and the light of my eyes was not with me; for it was within and I was without. Nor was that light in any place; but I still kept thinking only of things that are contained in a place, and could find among them no place to rest in. They did not receive me in such a way that I could say, "It is sufficient; it is well." Nor did they allow me to turn back to where it might be well enough with me. For I was higher than they, though lower than thou. Thou art my true joy if I depend upon thee, and thou hadst subjected to me what thou didst create lower than I. And this was the true mean and middle way of salvation for me, to continue in thy image and by serving thee have dominion over the body. But when I lifted myself proudly against thee, and "ran against the Lord, even against his neck, with the thick bosses of my buckler," even the lower things were placed above me and pressed down on me, so that there was no respite or breathing space.[24] They thrust on my sight on every side, in crowds and masses, and when I tried to think, the images of bodies obtruded themselves into my way back to thee, as if they would say to me, "Where are you going, unworthy and unclean one?" And all these had sprung out of my wound, for thou hadst humbled the haughty as one that is wounded. By my swelling pride I was separated from thee, and my bloated cheeks blinded my eyes.

But thou, O Lord, art forever the same, yet thou art not forever angry with us, for thou hast compassion on our dust

23. Augustine speaks of his sins of the flesh here, probably his fornication (and his pride). Because he did not submit to God, his lusts (and his bodily passions) had the rule over him.

24. Grief, conviction, and disturbance of heart is a good thing. It is merciful when God helps us to see our problem.

and ashes. It was pleasing in thy sight to reform my deformity, and by inward stings thou didst disturb me so that I was impatient until thou wert made clear to my inward sight. By the secret hand of thy healing my swelling was lessened, the disordered and darkened eyesight of my mind was from day to day made whole by the stinging salve of wholesome grief.

And first of all, willing to show me how thou dost "resist the proud, but give grace to the humble," and how mercifully thou hast made known to men the way of humility in that thy Word "was made flesh and dwelt among men," thou didst procure for me, through one inflated with the most monstrous pride, certain books of the Platonists, translated from Greek into Latin.[25] And therein I found, not indeed in the same words, but to the selfsame effect, enforced by many and various reasons that "in the beginning was the Word, and the Word was with God, and the Word was God. The same was in the beginning with God. All things were made by him; and without him was not anything made that was made." That which was made by him is "life, and the life was the light of men. And the light shined in darkness; and the darkness comprehended it not." Furthermore, I read that the soul of man, though it "bears witness to the light," yet itself "is not the light; but the Word of God, being God, is that true light that lights every man who comes into the world." And further, that "he was in the world, and the world was made by him, and the world knew him not." But that "he came unto his own, and his own received him not. And as many as received him, to them gave he power to become the sons of God, even to them that believed on his name"—this I did not find there.[26]

Similarly, I read there that God the Word was born "not of flesh nor of blood, nor of the will of man, nor the will of the flesh, but of God." But, that "the Word was made flesh, and dwelt among us"—I found this nowhere there. And I discovered in those books, expressed in many and various ways, that "the Son was in the form of God and thought it not robbery to be equal in God," for he was naturally of the

25. The books containing Platonist (Greek) philosophy were given to him by a very proud man. The classical learning tended to produce much pride. Augustine contrasts the teaching of Jesus with this proud Greek learning.

26. Augustine finds some correlation between Greek thought and John 1:1. But he also finds much in the subsequent verses of John 1 that are not to be found in Greek thought. He delineates this over the next few paragraphs.

same substance. But, that "he emptied himself and took upon himself the form of a servant, and was made in the likeness of men: and being found in fashion as a man, he humbled himself, and became obedient unto death, even the death of the cross. Wherefore God also hath highly exalted him" from the dead, "and given him a name above every name; that at the name of Jesus every knee should bow, of things in heaven, and things in earth, and things under the earth; and that every tongue should confess that Jesus Christ is Lord, to the glory of God the Father"—this those books have not. I read further in them that before all times and beyond all times, thy only Son remaineth unchangeably coeternal with thee, and that of his fullness all souls receive that they may be blessed, and that by participation in that wisdom which abides in them, they are renewed that they may be wise. But, that "in due time, Christ died for the ungodly" and that thou "sparedst not thy only Son, but deliveredst him up for us all"—this is not there. "For thou hast hid these things from the wise and prudent, and hast revealed them unto babes"; that they "that labor and are heavy laden" might "come unto him and he might refresh them" because he is "meek and lowly in heart." "The meek will he guide in judgment; and the meek will he teach his way; beholding our lowliness and our trouble and forgiving all our sins." But those who strut in the high boots of what they deem to be superior knowledge will not hear Him who says, "Learn of me, for I am meek and lowly in heart, and you shall find rest for your souls." Thus, though they know God, yet they do not glorify him as God, nor are they thankful. Therefore, they "become vain in their imaginations; their foolish heart is darkened, and professing themselves to be wise they become fools."

And, moreover, I also read there how "they changed the glory of thy incorruptible nature into idols and various images—into an image made like corruptible man and to birds and four-footed beasts, and creeping things": namely, into that Egyptian food for which Esau lost his birthright; so that thy first-born people worshiped the head of a four-footed

27. He speaks of robbing the Egyptians of their gold but refusing to take their idolatry and worship their idols made of gold. Augustine finds a little bit of truth from Greek Platonic thought (and likens this to robbing the Egyptians of their gold before the Israelites left Egypt).

28. Augustine's search for wisdom seems to have led him on a search "without." This is a wild goose chase towards cults, philosophers, demons, etc. When he returns to himself, he is now guided by God's wisdom and not man's wisdom.

29. God's knowledge is above and beyond us. It is only achievable by God communicating that knowledge to us. We cannot reach up to heaven to get it. He reaches down from heaven to bestow it upon us.

beast instead of thee, turning back in their hearts toward Egypt and prostrating thy image (their own soul) before the image of an ox that eats grass. These things I found there, but I fed not on them. For it pleased thee, O Lord, to take away the reproach of his minority from Jacob, that the elder should serve the younger and thou mightest call the Gentiles, and I had sought strenuously after that gold which thou didst allow thy people to take from Egypt, since wherever it was it was thine.[27] And thou saidst unto the Athenians by the mouth of thy apostle that in thee "we live and move and have our being," as one of their own poets had said. And truly these books came from there. But I did not set my mind on the idols of Egypt which they fashioned of gold, "changing the truth of God into a lie and worshiping and serving the creature more than the Creator."

And being admonished by these books to return into myself, I entered into my inward soul, guided by thee. This I could do because thou wast my helper. And I entered, and with the eye of my soul—such as it was—saw above the same eye of my soul and above my mind the Immutable Light.[28] It was not the common light, which all flesh can see; nor was it simply a greater one of the same sort, as if the light of day were to grow brighter and brighter, and flood all space. It was not like that light, but different, yea, very different from all earthly light whatever. Nor was it above my mind in the same way as oil is above water, or heaven above earth, but it was higher, because it made me, and I was below it, because I was made by it. He who knows the Truth knows that Light, and he who knows it knows eternity. Love knows it, O Eternal Truth and True Love and Beloved Eternity! Thou art my God, to whom I sigh both night and day. When I first knew thee, thou didst lift me up, that I might see that there was something to be seen, though I was not yet fit to see it.[29] And thou didst beat back the weakness of my sight, shining forth upon me thy dazzling beams of light, and I trembled with love and fear. I realized that I was far away from thee in the land of unlikeness, as if I heard thy voice from on high: "I am the food of strong men; grow and you shall feed on me; nor shall you change me, like the food of your flesh into yourself, but you shall be changed into my likeness." And I understood that thou chastenest man for his iniquity, and makest my soul to be eaten away as though by a spider. And I said, "Is Truth, therefore, nothing, because it is not diffused through space—neither finite nor infinite?" And thou didst cry to me from afar, "I am that I am." And I heard this, as things are heard in the heart, and there was no room for doubt. I should have more readily doubted that I am alive than that the Truth exists—the Truth which is "clearly seen, being understood by the things that are made."[30]

And I viewed all the other things that are beneath thee, and I realized that they are neither wholly real nor wholly unreal. They are real in so far as they come from thee; but they are unreal in so far as they are not what thou art. For that is truly real which remains immutable. It is good, then, for me to hold fast to God, for if I do not remain in him, neither shall I abide in myself; but he, remaining in himself, renews all things. And thou art the Lord my God, since thou standest in no need of my goodness.

And it was made clear to me that all things are good even if they are corrupted. They could not be corrupted if they were supremely good; but unless they were good they could not be corrupted. If they were supremely good, they would be incorruptible; if they were not good at all, there would be nothing in them to be corrupted.[31] For corruption harms; but unless it could diminish goodness, it could not harm. Either, then, corruption does not harm—which cannot be—or, as is certain, all that is corrupted is thereby deprived of good. But if they are deprived of all good, they will cease to be. For if they are at all and cannot be at all corrupted, they will become better, because they will remain incorruptible. Now what can be more monstrous than to maintain that by losing all good they have become better? If, then, they are deprived of all good, they will cease to exist. So long as they are, therefore, they are

Apostle Paul, preaching to the Athenians that in God "we live and move and have our being"

30. God's existence and truth's existence are more ultimate than our own existence. All existence derives from God, who is the ultimate source of all reality. Everything is doubtful if God does not exist. Such considerations were over-powering to the mind of Augustine.

31. What has been corrupted must have been good originally. A rotten apple must have been a good apple originally before it turned rotten.

32. Augustine establishes his definition of evil here. Evil has no substance. Evil is the corruption of something that was originally good.

good. Therefore, whatsoever is, is good. Evil, then, the origin of which I had been seeking, has no substance at all; for if it were a substance, it would be good.[32] For either it would be an incorruptible substance and so a supreme good, or a corruptible substance, which could not be corrupted unless it were good. I understood, therefore, and it was made clear to me that thou madest all things good, nor is there any substance at all not made by thee. And because all that thou madest is not equal, each by itself is good, and the sum of all of them is very good, for our God made all things very good.

To thee there is no such thing as evil, and even in thy whole creation taken as a whole, there is not; because there is nothing from beyond it that can burst in and destroy the order which thou hast appointed for it. But in the parts of creation, some things, because they do not harmonize with others, are considered evil. Yet those same things harmonize with others and are good, and in themselves are good. And all these things which do not harmonize with each other still harmonize with the inferior part of creation which we call the earth, having its own cloudy and windy sky of like nature with itself. Far be it from me, then, to say, "These things should not be." For if I could see nothing but these, I should indeed desire something better—but still I ought to praise thee, if only for these created things. For that thou art to be praised is shown from the fact that "earth, dragons, and all deeps; fire, and hail, snow and vapors, stormy winds fulfilling thy word; mountains, and all hills, fruitful trees, and all cedars; beasts and all cattle; creeping things, and flying fowl; things of the earth, and all people; princes, and all judges of the earth; both young men and maidens, old men and children," praise thy name! But seeing also that in heaven all thy angels praise thee, O God, praise thee in the heights, "and all thy hosts, sun and moon, all stars and light, the heavens of heavens, and the waters that are above the heavens,"[33] praise thy name—seeing this, I say, I no longer desire a better world, because my thought ranged over all, and with a sounder judgment I reflected that the things

33. God will be sure that all of His creation will praise Him. Augustine quotes Psalm 148.

above were better than those below, yet that all creation to-gether was better than the higher things alone.[34]

There is no health in those who find fault with any part of thy creation; as there was no health in me when I found fault with so many of thy works. And, because my soul dared not be displeased with my God, it would not allow that the things which displeased me were from thee.[35] Hence it had wandered into the notion of two substances, and could find no rest, but talked foolishly, And turning from that error, it had then made for itself a god extended through infinite space; and it thought this was thou and set it up in its heart, and it became once more the temple of its own idol, an abomination to thee. But thou didst soothe my brain, though I was unaware of it, and closed my eyes lest they should behold vanity; and thus I ceased from preoccupation with self by a little and my madness was lulled to sleep; and I awoke in thee, and beheld thee as the Infinite, but not in the way I had thought—and this vision was not derived from the flesh.

And I looked around at other things, and I saw that it was to thee that all of them owed their being, and that they were all finite in thee; yet they are in thee not as in a space, but because thou holdest all things in the hand of thy truth, and because all things are true in so far as they are; and because false-hood is nothing except the existence in thought of what does not exist in fact. And I saw that all things harmonize, not only in their places but also in their seasons. And I saw that thou, who alone art eternal, didst not begin to work after unnum-bered periods of time—because all ages, both those which are past and those which shall pass, neither go nor come except through thy working and abiding.

And I saw and found it no marvel that bread which is distasteful to an unhealthy palate is pleasant to a healthy one; or that the light, which is painful to sore eyes, is a delight to sound ones. Thy righteousness displeases the wicked, and they find even more fault with the viper and the little worm, which thou hast created good, fitting in as they do with the inferi-

34. Augustine sees that God's creation as a whole (in its entirety, to include the present state and the future state) is a good thing. All things will work together for good. Eventually, those things that appear not to create a good harmony will come to create a good harmony.

35. Augustine finally confesses that his conception of God was only an idol he had made in his own mind.

36. Evil is defined as the perversion of the will, a self destructive "casting out of its own intestines."

37. Augustine is slowly changing his perspective concerning God, but then he reverts back into his old ideas of God. He relies upon his own unstable mind that is changeable and uncertain — not a reliable means of determining what is true.

38. The changeable mind cannot be the source of Truth. The knowledge must come from above and beyond the changeable mind. Man obtains some knowledge from the nature around him (and it is an "unchangeable" truth), but then he quickly suppresses it in unrighteousness (Rom. 1). This is what Augustine testifies of himself here.

or parts of creation. The wicked themselves also fit in here, and proportionately more so as they become unlike thee—but they harmonize with the higher creation proportionately as they become like thee. And I asked what wickedness was, and I found that it was no substance, but a perversion of the will bent aside from thee, O God, the supreme substance, toward these lower things, casting away its inmost treasure and becoming bloated with external good.[36]

And I marveled that I now loved thee, and no fantasm in thy stead, and yet I was not stable enough to enjoy my God steadily. Instead I was transported to thee by thy beauty, and then presently torn away from thee by my own weight, sinking with grief into these lower things. This weight was carnal habit. But thy memory dwelt with me, and I never doubted in the least that there was One for me to cleave to; but I was not yet ready to cleave to thee firmly.[37] For the body which is corrupted presses down the soul, and the earthly dwelling weighs down the mind, which muses upon many things. My greatest certainty was that "the invisible things of thine from the creation of the world are clearly seen, being understood by the things that are made, even thy eternal power and Godhead." For when I inquired how it was that I could appreciate the beauty of bodies, both celestial and terrestrial; and what it was that supported me in making correct judgments about things mutable; and when I concluded, "This ought to be thus; this ought not"—then when I inquired how it was that I could make such judgments (since I did, in fact, make them), I realized that I had found the unchangeable and true eternity of truth above my changeable mind.[38]

And thus by degrees I was led upward from bodies to the soul which perceives them by means of the bodily senses, and from there on to the soul's inward faculty, to which the bodily senses report outward things—and this belongs even to the capacities of the beasts—and thence on up to the reasoning power, to whose judgment is referred the experience received from the bodily sense. And when this power of reason within me also found that it was changeable, it raised itself up to its own intellectual principle, and withdrew its thoughts from experience, abstracting itself from the contradictory throng of fantasms in order to seek for that light in which it was bathed. Then, without any doubting, it cried out that the unchangeable was better than the changeable. From this it follows that the mind somehow knew the unchangeable, for, unless it had known it in some fashion, it could have had no sure ground for preferring it to the changeable. And thus with the flash of a trembling glance, it arrived at that which is. And I saw thy invisibility [invisibilia tua] understood by means of the things that are made. But I was not able to sustain my gaze. My weakness was dashed back, and I lapsed again into my accustomed ways, carrying along with me nothing but a loving memory of my vision, and an appetite for what I had, as it were, smelled the odor of, but was not yet able to eat.

I sought, therefore, some way to acquire the strength sufficient to enjoy thee; but I did not find it until I embraced that "Mediator between God and man, the man Christ Jesus," "who is over all, God blessed forever," who came calling and saying, "I am the way, the truth, and the life," and mingling with our fleshly humanity the heavenly food I was unable to receive.[39] For "the Word was made flesh" in order that thy wisdom, by which thou didst create all things, might become milk for our infancy. And, as yet, I was not humble enough to hold the humble Jesus; nor did I understand what lesson his weakness was meant to teach us. For thy Word, the eternal Truth, far exalted above even the higher parts of thy creation, lifts his subjects up toward himself. But in this lower world, he built for himself a humble habitation of our own clay, so that he might pull down from themselves and win over to himself those whom he is to bring subject to him; lowering their pride and heightening their love, to the end that they might go on no farther in self-confidence—but rather should become weak, seeing at their feet the Deity made weak by sharing our

39. This is a powerful confession of the simple Christian faith. It was only when Augustine embraced the person of Jesus Christ, that He found Truth. The end of the quest for knowledge can only be found in a Person. We must humble ourselves before the One who humbled Himself, if we are to be saved and lifted up by this Christ.

coats of skin—so that they might cast themselves, exhausted, upon him and be uplifted by his rising.

But I thought otherwise. I saw in our Lord Christ only a man of eminent wisdom to whom no other man could be compared—especially because he was miraculously born of a virgin—sent to set us an example of despising worldly things for the attainment of immortality, and thus exhibiting his divine care for us. Because of this, I held that he had merited his great authority as leader. But concerning the mystery contained in "the Word was made flesh," I could not even form a notion.[40] From what I learned from what has been handed down to us in the books about him—that he ate, drank, slept, walked, rejoiced in spirit, was sad, and discoursed with his fellows—I realized that his flesh alone was not bound unto thy Word, but also that there was a bond with the human soul and body. Everyone knows this who knows the unchangeableness of thy Word, and this I knew by now, as far as I was able, and I had no doubts at all about it. For at one time to move the limbs by an act of will, at another time not; at one time to feel some emotion, at another time not; at one time to speak intelligibly through verbal signs, at another, not—these are all properties of a soul and mind subject to change. And if these things were falsely written about him, all the rest would risk the imputation of falsehood, and there would remain in those books no saving faith for the human race.

Therefore, because they were written truthfully, I acknowledged a perfect man to be in Christ—not the body of a man only, nor, in the body, an animal soul without a rational one as well, but a true man. And this man I held to be superior to all others,[41] not only because he was a form of the Truth, but also because of the great excellence and perfection of his human nature, due to his participation in wisdom.[42]

Alypius, on the other hand, supposed the Catholics to believe that God was so clothed with flesh that besides God and the flesh there was no soul in Christ, and he did not think that a human mind was ascribed to him.[43] And because he was ful-

40. Augustine accepted the virgin birth and the example of humility in Christ. But he still did not see Christ's divine nature.

41. At this time, Augustine held that Christ was only a "superior man."

42. Augustine reasons that the Word (the Truth) is changeless, but human nature is subject to change. So, there must be something additional about the personality of Christ beyond his human nature.

43. Augustine's friend, Alypius, gave way to the Apollinarian heresy that taught Christ did not possess a human soul (only a human body). There were many heresies concerning the nature of Christ running around at this time.

ly persuaded that the actions recorded of him could not have been performed except by a living rational creature, he moved the more slowly toward Christian faith. But when he later learned that this was the error of the Apollinarian heretics, he rejoiced in the Catholic faith and accepted it. For myself, I must confess that it was even later that I learned how in the sentence, "The Word was made flesh," the Catholic truth can be distinguished from the falsehood of Photinus. For the refutation of heretics makes the tenets of thy Church and sound doctrine to stand out boldly. "For there must also be heresies [factions] that those who are approved may be made manifest among the weak."

By having thus read the books of the Platonists, and having been taught by them to search for the incorporeal Truth,[44] I saw how thy invisible things are understood through the things that are made. And, even when I was thrown back, I still sensed what it was that the dullness of my soul would not allow me to contemplate. I was assured that thou wast, and wast infinite, though not diffused in finite space or infinity; that thou truly art, who art ever the same, varying neither in part nor motion; and that all things are from thee, as is proved by this sure cause alone: that they exist.

Of all this I was convinced, yet I was too weak to enjoy thee. I chattered away as if I were an expert; but if I had not sought thy Way in Christ our Saviour, my knowledge would have turned out to be not instruction but destruction. For now full of what was in fact my punishment, I had begun to desire to seem wise. I did not mourn my ignorance, but rather was puffed up with knowledge.[45] For where was that love which builds upon the foundation of humility, which is Jesus Christ? Or, when would these books[46] teach me this? I now believe that it was thy pleasure that I should fall upon these books before I studied thy Scriptures, that it might be impressed on my memory how I was affected by them; and then afterward, when I was subdued by thy Scriptures and when my wounds were touched by thy healing fingers, I might discern and dis-

44. Plato taught that there was an immaterial source of truth and reality, but he was blinded to the Truth.

45. Humanist education always puffs up, encouraging pride.

46. "These books" still refer to Platonist writings. They did great damage to his mind and soul, producing pride in him. These dangerous books could push young children raised in the church off the "solid ground of godliness."

47. We receive both the Truth and the power to understand and know the truth from God.

Paul the Apostle by Rembrandt (1657)

48. Augustine applies the war in Romans 7 to the unconverted man. He was still subject to the law of sin and "that ancient sinner" the Devil.

tinguish what a difference there is between presumption and confession[47]—between those who saw where they were to go even if they did not see the way, and the Way which leads, not only to the observing, but also the inhabiting of the blessed country. For had I first been molded in thy Holy Scriptures, and if thou hadst grown sweet to me through my familiar use of them, and if then I had afterward fallen on those volumes, they might have pushed me off the solid ground of godliness— or if I had stood firm in that wholesome disposition which I had there acquired, I might have thought that wisdom could be attained by the study of those [Platonist] books alone.

With great eagerness, then, I fastened upon the venerable writings of thy Spirit and principally upon the apostle Paul. I had thought that he sometimes contradicted himself and that the text of his teaching did not agree with the testimonies of the Law and the Prophets; but now all these doubts vanished away. And I saw that those pure words had but one face, and I learned to rejoice with trembling. So I began, and I found that whatever truth I had read [in the Platonists] was here combined with the exaltation of thy grace. Thus, he who sees must not glory as if he had not received, not only the things that he sees, but the very power of sight—for what does he have that he has not received as a gift? By this he is not only exhorted to see, but also to be cleansed, that he may grasp thee, who art ever the same; and thus he who cannot see thee afar off may yet enter upon the road that leads to reaching, seeing, and possessing thee. For although a man may "delight in the law of God after the inward man," what shall he do with that other "law in his members which wars against the law of his mind, and brings him into captivity under the law of sin, which is in his members?" Thou art righteous, O Lord; but we have sinned and committed iniquities, and have done wickedly. Thy hand has grown heavy upon us, and we are justly delivered over to that ancient sinner, the lord of death.[48] For he persuaded our wills to become like his will, by which he remained not in thy truth. What shall "wretched man" do? "Who shall deliver him from the body of this death," except thy grace through Jesus Christ our Lord; whom thou hast begotten, coeternal with thyself, and didst create in the beginning of thy ways—in whom the prince of this world found nothing worthy of death, yet he killed him—and so the handwriting which was all against us was blotted out?

The books of the Platonists tell nothing of this. Their pages do not contain the expression of this kind of godliness—the tears of confession, thy sacrifice, a troubled spirit, a broken and a contrite heart, the salvation of thy people, the espoused City, the earnest of the Holy Spirit, the cup of our redemption. In them, no man sings: "Shall not my soul be subject unto God, for from him comes my salvation?"[49] He is my God and my salvation, my defender; I shall no more be moved." In them, no one hears him calling, "Come unto me all you who labor." They scorn to learn of him because he is "meek and lowly of heart"; for "thou hast hidden those things from the wise and prudent, and hast revealed them unto babes." For it is one thing to see the land of peace from a wooded mountaintop: and fail to find the way thither—to attempt impassable ways in vain, opposed and waylaid by fugitives and deserters under their captain, the "lion" and "dragon"; but it is quite another thing to keep to the highway that leads thither, guarded by the hosts of the heavenly Emperor, on which there are no deserters from the heavenly army to rob the passers-by, for they shun it as a torment.[50] These thoughts sank wondrously into my heart, when I read that "least of thy apostles" and when I had considered all thy works and trembled.

49. The main problem with Greek classical teaching is pride. It eschews the meekness of Christ.

50. Man's wisdom and God's wisdom are contrasted here. Man's wisdom provides no clear highway to truth while God's highway is clear of obstacles.

✨ BOOK VIII

O my God, let me remember with gratitude and confess to thee thy mercies toward me. Let my bones be bathed in thy love, and let them say: "Lord, who is like unto thee? Thou hast broken my bonds in sunder,[1] I will offer unto thee the sacrifice of thanksgiving." And how thou didst break them I will declare, and all who worship thee shall say, when they hear these things: "Blessed be the Lord in heaven and earth, great and wonderful is his name."

Thy words had stuck fast in my breast, and I was hedged round about by thee on every side. Of thy eternal life I was now certain, although I had seen it "through a glass darkly." And I had been relieved of all doubt that there is an incorruptible substance and that it is the source of every other substance. Nor did I any longer crave greater certainty about thee, but rather greater steadfastness in thee.

But as for my temporal life, everything was uncertain, and my heart had to be purged of the old leaven. "The Way"—the Saviour himself— pleased me well, but as yet I was reluctant to pass through the strait gate.

And thou didst put it into my mind, and it seemed good in my own sight, to go to Simplicianus,[2] who appeared to me a faithful servant of thine, and thy grace shone forth in him. I had also been told that from his youth up he had lived in entire devotion to thee. He was already an old man, and because

1. This chapter will tell the story of Augustine's conversion — how the Lord broke the chains of human bondage to human reason and his own autonomous thinking.

2. Augustine sought discipleship from an old man named Simplicianus. He had been a faithful disciple of Christ all of his life.

of his great age, which he had passed in such a zealous discipleship in thy way, he appeared to me likely to have gained much wisdom—and, indeed, he had. From all his experience, I desired him to tell me—setting before him all my agitations—which would be the most fitting way for one who felt as I did to walk in thy way.

For I saw the Church full; and one man was going this way and another that. Still, I could not be satisfied with the life I was living in the world. Now, indeed, my passions had ceased to excite me as of old with hopes of honor and wealth, and it was a grievous burden to go on in such servitude. For, compared with thy sweetness and the beauty of thy house—which I loved—those things delighted me no longer. But I was still tightly bound by the love of women; nor did the apostle forbid me to marry, although he exhorted me to something better, wishing earnestly that all men were as he himself was.[3]

But I was weak and chose the easier way, and for this single reason my whole life was one of inner turbulence and listless indecision, because from so many influences I was compelled—even though unwilling—to agree to a married life which bound me hand and foot. I had heard from the mouth of Truth that "there are eunuchs who have made themselves eunuchs for the Kingdom of Heaven's sake" but, said he, "He that is able to receive it, let him receive it." Of a certainty, all men are vain who do not have the knowledge of God, or have not been able, from the good things that are seen, to find him who is good. But I was no longer fettered in that vanity. I had surmounted it, and from the united testimony of thy whole creation had found thee, our Creator, and thy Word—God with thee, and together with thee and the Holy Spirit, one God—by whom thou hast created all things. There is still another sort of wicked men, who "when they knew God, they glorified him not as God, neither were thankful." Into this also I had fallen,[4] but thy right hand held me up and bore me away, and thou didst place me where I might recover. For thou hast said to men, "Behold the fear of the Lord, this is wisdom," and,

3. Augustine had given up on the pursuit of worldly honor and wealth. But he still held on to a lifestyle of fornication at this time.

4. At this point, he had acknowledged God and the Trinity, but he still did not glorify God and he was not thankful to Him.

"Be not wise in your own eyes," because "they that profess themselves to be wise become fools." But I had now found the goodly pearl; and I ought to have sold all that I had and bought it—yet I hesitated.

I went, therefore, to Simplicianus, the spiritual father of Ambrose (then a bishop), whom Ambrose truly loved as a father. I recounted to him all the mazes of my wanderings, but when I mentioned to him that I had read certain books of the Platonists which Victorinus—formerly professor of rhetoric at Rome, who died a Christian, as I had been told—had translated into Latin, Simplicianus congratulated me that I had not fallen upon the writings of other philosophers, which were full of fallacies and deceit, "after the beggarly elements of this world," whereas in the Platonists, at every turn, the pathway led to belief in God and his Word.[5]

Then, to encourage me to copy the humility of Christ, which is hidden from the wise and revealed to babes, he told me about Victorinus himself, whom he had known intimately at Rome. And I cannot refrain from repeating what he told me about him. For it contains a glorious proof of thy grace, which ought to be confessed to thee: how that old man, most learned, most skilled in all the liberal arts; who had read, criticized, and explained so many of the writings of the philosophers; the teacher of so many noble senators; one who, as a mark of his distinguished service in office had both merited and obtained a statue in the Roman Forum—which men of this world esteem a great honor—this man who, up to an advanced age, had been a worshiper of idols, a communicant in the sacrilegious rites to which almost all the nobility of Rome were wedded; and who had inspired the people with the love of Osiris and

> "The dog Anubis, and a medley crew
> Of monster gods who 'gainst Neptune stand in arms
> 'Gainst Venus and Minerva, steel-clad Mars,"

whom Rome once conquered, and now worshiped;[6] all of which old Victorinus had with thundering eloquence defend-

Plotinus (AD 204–270), a Greek-speaking Platonic philosopher

5. Victorinus had translated the Greek Platonic works into Latin. Augustine believed that Plato was the philosopher that pointed out the "way" to the Christian faith. Plato did not confess the Christian God, but his writing seemed to acknowledge something of a need for an ultimate, invisible source of Truth and Reality.

6. Augustine mocks the Greek gods that "Rome once conquered." It is a great irony that people worship the gods they conquer!

ed for so many years— despite all this, he did not blush to become a child of thy Christ, a babe at thy font, bowing his neck to the yoke of humility and submitting his forehead to the ignominy of the cross.

O Lord, Lord, "who didst bow the heavens and didst descend, who didst touch the mountains and they smoked," by what means didst thou find thy way into that breast? He used to read the Holy Scriptures, as Simplicianus said, and thought out and studied all the Christian writings most studiously. He said to Simplicianus—not openly but secretly as a friend—"You must know that I am a Christian." To which Simplicianus replied, "I shall not believe it, nor shall I count you among the Christians, until I see you in the Church of Christ." Victorinus then asked, with mild mockery, "Is it then the walls that make Christians?" Thus he often would affirm that he was already a Christian, and as often Simplicianus made the same answer; and just as often his jest about the walls was repeated. He was fearful of offending his friends, proud demon worshipers, from the height of whose Babylonian dignity,[7] as from the tops of the cedars of Lebanon which the Lord had not yet broken down, he feared that a storm of enmity would descend upon him.[8]

7. Rome and its proud idolators, ungodly humanists, government leaders, and rhetoricians are compared to Babel. God always breaks these proud empires down.

But he steadily gained strength from reading and inquiry, and came to fear lest he should be denied by Christ before the holy angels if he now was afraid to confess him before men. Thus he came to appear to himself guilty of a great fault, in being ashamed of the sacraments of the humility of thy Word, when he was not ashamed of the sacrilegious rites of those proud demons, whose pride he had imitated and whose rites he had shared. From this he became bold-faced against vanity and shamefaced toward the truth. Thus, suddenly and unexpectedly, he said to Simplicianus—as he himself told me—"Let us go to the church; I wish to become a Christian." Simplicianus went with him, scarcely able to contain himself for joy. He was admitted to the first sacraments of instruction, and not long afterward gave in his name that he might re-

8. Old Simplicianus tells Augustine the interesting story of the rhetorician Victorinus. At first Victorinus was embarrassed to go to the Christian church, even though he professed faith in Christ.

ceive the baptism of regeneration. At this Rome marveled and the Church rejoiced. The proud saw and were enraged; they gnashed their teeth and melted away! But the Lord God was thy servant's hope and he paid no attention to their vanity and lying madness.[9]

Finally, when the hour arrived for him to make a public profession of his faith—which at Rome those who are about to enter into thy grace make from a platform in the full sight of the faithful people, in a set form of words learned by heart—the presbyters offered Victorinus the chance to make his profession more privately, for this was the custom for some who were likely to be afraid through bashfulness. But Victorinus chose rather to profess his salvation in the presence of the holy congregation. For there was no salvation in the rhetoric which he taught: yet he had professed that openly. Why, then, should he shrink from naming thy Word before the sheep of thy flock, when he had not shrunk from uttering his own words before the mad multitude?

So, then, when he ascended the platform to make his profession, everyone, as they recognized him, whispered his name one to the other, in tones of jubilation. Who was there among them that did not know him? And a low murmur ran through the mouths of all the rejoicing multitude: "Victorinus! Victorinus!" There was a sudden burst of exaltation at the sight of him, and suddenly they were hushed that they might hear him.[10] He pronounced the true faith with an excellent boldness, and all desired to take him to their very heart—indeed, by their love and joy they did take him to their heart. And they received him with loving and joyful hands.

O good God, what happens in a man to make him rejoice more at the salvation of a soul that has been despaired of and then delivered from greater danger than over one who has never lost hope, or never been in such imminent danger? For thou also, O most merciful Father, "dost rejoice more over one that repents than over ninety and nine just persons that need no repentance." And we listen with much delight when-

9. Finally, Victorinus agreed to be baptized and to attend the Christian church. He abandoned the proud world and joined the humble church. This caused great consternation in Rome.

10. It is an exciting moment when people who have criticized Christianity get saved and join the Christian church.

11. There is great joy in heaven when one sinner repents. There is nothing more joyful than to have a son who, being dead, is raised from the dead and restored to his father and mother.

12. In the purposes of God, we find great joy and great glory (perhaps the greatest glory) in the redemption of sinners who died and are raised to life again. Augustine provides many earthly examples of the joy that comes in relief and salvation.

13. There have been others who have been saved from even a darker and deeper pit, speaking from the world's perspective. For example, a man named Jeffrey Dahmer (a serial killer), considered the most evil man of the 1970s and 1980s, was radically saved and baptized in prison shortly before he was killed by another prisoner.

ever we hear how the lost sheep is brought home again on the shepherd's shoulders while the angels rejoice;[11] or when the piece of money is restored to its place in the treasury and the neighbors rejoice with the woman who found it. And the joy of the solemn festival of thy house constrains us to tears when it is read in thy house: about the younger son who "was dead and is alive again, was lost and is found." For it is thou who rejoicest both in us and in thy angels, who are holy through holy love. For thou art ever the same because thou knowest unchangeably all things which remain neither the same nor forever.[12]

What, then, happens in the soul when it takes more delight at finding or having restored to it the things it loves than if it had always possessed them? Indeed, many other things bear witness that this is so—all things are full of witnesses, crying out, "So it is." The commander triumphs in victory; yet he could not have conquered if he had not fought; and the greater the peril of the battle, the more the joy of the triumph. The storm tosses the voyagers, threatens shipwreck, and everyone turns pale in the presence of death. Then the sky and sea grow calm, and they rejoice as much as they had feared. A loved one is sick and his pulse indicates danger; all who desire his safety are themselves sick at heart; he recovers, though not able as yet to walk with his former strength; and there is more joy now than there was before when he walked sound and strong. Indeed, the very pleasures of human life—not only those which rush upon us unexpectedly and involuntarily, but also those which are voluntary and planned—men obtain by difficulties. There is no pleasure in caring and drinking unless the pains of hunger and thirst have preceded. Drunkards even eat certain salt meats in order to create a painful thirst—and when the drink allays this, it causes pleasure. It is also the custom that the affianced bride should not be immediately given in marriage so that the husband may not esteem her any less, whom as his betrothed he longed for.[13]

This can be seen in the case of base and dishonorable pleasure. But it is also apparent in pleasures that are permitted and lawful: in the sincerity of honest friendship; and in him who was dead and lived again, who had been lost and was found. The greater joy is everywhere preceded by the greater pain. What does this mean, O Lord my God, when thou art an everlasting joy to thyself, and some creatures about thee are ever rejoicing in thee? What does it mean that this portion of creation thus ebbs and flows, alternately in want and satiety? Is this their mode of being and is this all thou hast allotted to them: that, from the highest heaven to the lowest earth, from the beginning of the world to the end, from the angels to the worm, from the first movement to the last, thou wast assigning to all their proper places and their proper seasons—to all the kinds of good things and to all thy just works? Alas, how high thou art in the highest and how deep in the deepest! Thou never departest from us, and yet only with difficulty do we return to thee.

Go on, O Lord, and act: stir us up and call us back; inflame us and draw us to thee; stir us up and grow sweet to us; let us now love thee, let us run to thee. Are there not many men who, out of a deeper pit of darkness than that of Victorinus, return to thee—who draw near to thee and are illuminated by that light which gives those who receive it power from thee to become thy sons? But if they are less well-known, even those who know them rejoice less for them. For when many rejoice together the joy of each one is fuller, in that they warm one another, catch fire from each other; moreover, those who are well-known influence many toward salvation and take the lead with many to follow them. Therefore, even those who took the way before them rejoice over them greatly, because they do not rejoice over them alone. But it ought never to be that in thy tabernacle the persons of the rich should be welcome before the poor, or the nobly born before the rest—since "thou hast rather chosen the weak things of the world to confound the strong; and hast chosen the base things of the world and things that are despised, and the things that are not, in order to bring to nought the things that are." It was even "the least of the apostles" by whose tongue thou didst sound forth these words. And when Paulus the proconsul had his pride overcome by the onslaught of the apostle and he was made to pass under the easy yoke of thy Christ and became an officer of the great King, he also desired to be called Paul instead of Saul, his former name, in testimony to such a great victory. For the enemy is more overcome in one on whom he has a greater hold, and whom he has hold of more completely. But the proud he controls more readily through their concern about their rank and, through them, he controls more by means of their influence. The more, therefore, the world prized the heart of Victorinus (which the devil had held in an impregnable stronghold) and the tongue of Victorinus (that sharp, strong weapon with which the devil had slain so many), all the more exultingly should Thy sons rejoice because our King hath bound the strong man, and they saw his vessels taken from him and cleansed, and made fit for thy honor and "profitable to the Lord for every good work."[14]

Now when this man of thine, Simplicianus, told me the story of Victorinus, I was eager to imitate him. Indeed, this was Simplicianus' purpose in telling it to me. But when he went on to tell how, in the reign of the Emperor Julian, there was a law passed by which Christians were forbidden to teach literature and rhetoric; and how Victorinus, in ready obedience to the law, chose to abandon his "school of words" rather than thy Word, by which thou makest eloquent the tongues of the dumb—he appeared to me not so much brave as happy, because he had found a reason for giving his time wholly to thee.[15] For this was what I was longing to do; but as yet I was bound by the iron chain of my own will. The enemy held fast my will, and had made of it a chain, and had bound me tight with it. For out of the perverse will came lust, and the service of lust ended in habit, and habit, not resisted, became necessity. By these links, as it were, forged together—which is why

14. Augustine mentions Paul and Paulus the Proconsul (Acts 13:7, 12), both important men and proud men who came under the humble yoke of Jesus Christ. In some respects, it is a bigger "win" for the Lord when he humbles the proudest men and robs the strong man's house (Matt. 12:29).

15. The Roman Emperor Julian ruled from AD 361-363, and he passed a law prohibiting Christians from teaching literature and rhetoric. Victorinus was happy to give up the secular school to teach Christian rhetoric from the Word of God, a vastly different approach to education.

I called it "a chain"—a hard bondage held me in slavery. But that new will which had begun to spring up in me freely to worship thee and to enjoy thee, O my God, the only certain Joy, was not able as yet to overcome my former willfulness, made strong by long indulgence. Thus my two wills—the old and the new, the carnal and the spiritual—were in conflict within me; and by their discord they tore my soul apart.[16]

Thus I came to understand from my own experience what I had read, how "the flesh lusts against the Spirit, and the Spirit against the flesh." I truly lusted both ways, yet more in that which I approved in myself than in that which I disapproved in myself. For in the latter it was not now really I that was involved, because here I was rather an unwilling sufferer than a willing actor. And yet it was through me that habit had become an armed enemy against me, because I had willingly come to be what I unwillingly found myself to be.

Who, then, can with any justice speak against it, when just punishment follows the sinner? I had now no longer my accustomed excuse that, as yet, I hesitated to forsake the world and serve thee because my perception of the truth was uncertain. For now it was certain. But, still bound to the earth, I refused to be thy soldier; and was as much afraid of being freed from all entanglements as we ought to fear to be entangled.

Thus with the baggage of the world I was sweetly burdened, as one in slumber, and my musings on thee were like the efforts of those who desire to awake, but who are still overpowered with drowsiness and fall back into deep slumber.[17] And as no one wishes to sleep forever (for all men rightly count waking better)—yet a man will usually defer shaking off his drowsiness when there is a heavy lethargy in his limbs; and he is glad to sleep on even when his reason disapproves, and the hour for rising has struck—so was I assured that it was much better for me to give myself up to thy love than to go on yielding myself to my own lust. Thy love satisfied and vanquished me; my lust pleased and fettered me. I had no answer to thy calling to me, "Awake, you who sleep, and arise from the

16. Augustine was bound by a chain. His perverse will gave birth to lusts (for honor and wealth), and that lust created a habit over time, and his habitual lifestyle became impossible to break.

17. Augustine describes his "awakening" in these most interesting terms. He is becoming aware of his own regeneration (someone who desires to be awake but keeps falling back asleep).

dead, and Christ shall give you light." On all sides, thou didst show me that thy words are true, and I, convicted by the truth, had nothing at all to reply but the drawling and drowsy words: "Presently; see, presently. Leave me alone a little while." But "presently, presently," had no present; and my "leave me alone a little while" went on for a long while. In vain did I "delight in thy law in the inner man" while "another law in my members warred against the law of my mind and brought me into captivity to the law of sin which is in my members." For the law of sin is the tyranny of habit, by which the mind is drawn and held, even against its will. Yet it deserves to be so held because it so willingly falls into the habit. "O wretched man that I am! Who shall deliver me from the body of this death" but thy grace alone, through Jesus Christ our Lord?

And now I will tell and confess unto thy name, O Lord, my helper and my redeemer, how thou didst deliver me from the chain of sexual desire by which I was so tightly held, and from the slavery of worldly business. With increasing anxiety I was going about my usual affairs, and daily sighing to thee. I attended thy church as frequently as my business, under the burden of which I groaned, left me free to do so. Alypius was with me, disengaged at last from his legal post, after a third term as assessor, and now waiting for private clients to whom he might sell his legal advice as I sold the power of speaking (as if it could be supplied by teaching). But Nebridius had consented, for the sake of our friendship, to teach under Verecundus—a citizen of Milan and professor of grammar, and a very intimate friend of us all—who ardently desired, and by right of friendship demanded from us, the faithful aid he greatly needed. Nebridius was not drawn to this by any desire of gain—for he could have made much more out of his learning had he been so inclined—but as he was a most sweet and kindly friend, he was unwilling, out of respect for the duties of friendship, to slight our request. But in this he acted very discreetly, taking care not to become known to those persons who had great reputations in the world. Thus he avoided all distractions of mind, and reserved as many hours as possible to pursue or read or listen to discussions about wisdom.[18]

On a certain day, then, when Nebridius was away—for some reason I cannot remember—there came to visit Alypius and me at our house one Ponticianus, a fellow countryman of ours from Africa,[19] who held high office in the emperor's court. What he wanted with us I do not know; but we sat down to talk together, and it chanced that he noticed a book on a game table before us. He took it up, opened it, and, contrary to his expectation, found it to be the apostle Paul, for he imagined that it was one of my wearisome rhetoric textbooks. At this, he looked up at me with a smile and expressed his delight and wonder that he had so unexpectedly found this book and only this one, lying before my eyes; for he was indeed a Christian and a faithful one at that, and often he prostrated himself before thee, our God, in the church in constant daily prayer. When I had told him that I had given much attention to these writings, a conversation followed in which he spoke of Anthony, the Egyptian monk, whose name was in high repute among thy servants, although up to that time not familiar to me. When he learned this, he lingered on the topic, giving us an account of this eminent man, and marveling at our ignorance. We in turn were amazed to hear of thy wonderful works so fully manifested in recent times—almost in our own—occurring in the true faith and the Catholic Church. We all wondered—we, that these things were so great, and he, that we had never heard of them.

From this, his conversation turned to the multitudes in the monasteries and their manners so fragrant to thee, and to the teeming solitudes of the wilderness, of which we knew nothing at all. There was even a monastery at Milan, outside the city's walls, full of good brothers under the fostering care of Ambrose—and we were ignorant of it.[20] He went on with his story, and we listened intently and in silence. He then told us how, on a certain afternoon, at Trier, when the emperor was occupied watching the gladiatorial games, he and three

18. Nebridius was a teacher (helping in the school of Verecundus). He was a humble man who did not seek honor but spent many hours studying.

19. Ponticianus was a friend from Africa who came to visit. He had become a Christian and told Augustine and Alypius of the monk named Anthony. At this point, there were monasteries, but they were not common knowledge. So, a man devoted to Christian meditation and study was rare.

St. Anthony
(AD 251–356)

20. Ambrose had organized a monastery in Milan for young men who wanted a Christian discipleship instead of a pagan education.

comrades went out for a walk in the gardens close to the city walls. There, as they chanced to walk two by two, one strolled away with him, while the other two went on by themselves. As they rambled, these first two came upon a certain cottage where lived some of thy servants, some of the "poor in spirit" ("of such is the Kingdom of Heaven"), where they found the book in which was written the life of Anthony! One of them began to read it, to marvel and to be inflamed by it. While reading, he meditated on embracing just such a life, giving up his worldly employment to seek thee alone. These two belonged to the group of officials called "secret service agents." Then, suddenly being overwhelmed with a holy love and a sober shame and as if in anger with himself, he fixed his eyes on his friend, exclaiming: "Tell me, I beg you, what goal are we seeking in all these toils of ours? What is it that we desire? What is our motive in public service? Can our hopes in the court rise higher than to be 'friends of the emperor'? But how frail, how beset with peril, is that pride! Through what dangers must we climb to a greater danger? And when shall we succeed? But if I chose to become a friend of God, see, I can become one now."[21] Thus he spoke, and in the pangs of the travail of the new life he turned his eyes again onto the page and continued reading; he was inwardly changed, as thou didst see, and the world dropped away from his mind, as soon became plain to others. For as he read with a heart like a stormy sea, more than once he groaned. Finally he saw the better course, and resolved on it. Then, having become thy servant, he said to his friend: "Now I have broken loose from those hopes we had, and I am determined to serve God; and I enter into that service from this hour in this place. If you are reluctant to imitate me, do not oppose me." The other replied that he would continue bound in his friendship, to share in so great a service for so great a prize. So both became thine, and began to "build a tower," counting the cost—namely, of forsaking all that they had and following thee. Shortly after, Ponticianus and his companion, who had walked with him in the

21. Two men who worked for the Emperor are struck with the emptiness (and the danger) of human ambition — climbing the ranks, bucking for promotions in business and the government, etc. At that time, political miscalculations could end in your execution. So, it was dangerous to seek promotions in the Emperor's court.

other part of the garden, came in search of them to the same place, and having found them reminded them to return, as the day was declining. But the first two, making known to Ponticianus their resolution and purpose, and how a resolve had sprung up and become confirmed in them, entreated them not to take it ill if they refused to join themselves with them. But Ponticianus and his friend, although not changed from their former course, did nevertheless (as he told us) bewail themselves and congratulated their friends on their godliness, recommending themselves to their prayers. And with hearts inclining again toward earthly things, they returned to the palace. But the other two, setting their affections on heavenly things, remained in the cottage. Both of them had affianced brides who, when they heard of this, likewise dedicated their virginity to thee.[22]

Such was the story Ponticianus told. But while he was speaking, thou, O Lord, turned me toward myself, taking me from behind my back, where I had put myself while unwilling to exercise self-scrutiny. And now thou didst set me face to face with myself, that I might see how ugly I was, and how crooked and sordid, bespotted and ulcerous.[23] And I looked and I loathed myself; but whither to fly from myself I could not discover. And if I sought to turn my gaze away from myself, he would continue his narrative, and thou wouldst oppose me to myself and thrust me before my own eyes that I might discover my iniquity and hate it. I had known it, but acted as though I knew it not—I winked at it and forgot it.

But now, the more ardently I loved those whose wholesome affections I heard reported—that they had given themselves up wholly to thee to be cured—the more did I abhor myself when compared with them. For many of my years—perhaps twelve—had passed away since my nineteenth, when, upon the reading of Cicero's Hortensius, I was roused to a desire for wisdom. And here I was, still postponing the abandonment of this world's happiness to devote myself to the search. For not just the finding alone, but also the bare search for it, ought to

22. The two men decided to be celibate (to never get married and never be with a woman). There are certain times and places in which celibacy is actually preferred. We ought not to despise the choices of these men. Paul preferred celibacy in 1 Corinthians 7, "for the present distress." The battle with the world's sexual anarchy was intense, and the Roman Empire was about to collapse. Celibacy might have been a good choice for these men, who wanted to dedicate themselves to a discipleship program.

23. As these men committed to celibacy, this struck Augustine with deep conviction. He has already noted that marriage is not a sin. But it was his habit of fornication, his fourteen years of sexual sin, that gave him great cause for conviction. He felt the filthiness of it, the foulness of his condition.

have been preferred above the treasures and kingdoms of this world; better than all bodily pleasures, though they were to be had for the taking. But, wretched youth that I was—supremely wretched even in the very outset of my youth—I had entreated chastity of thee and had prayed, "Grant me chastity and continence, but not yet." For I was afraid lest thou shouldst hear me too soon, and too soon cure me of my disease of lust which I desired to have satisfied rather than extinguished. And I had wandered through perverse ways of godless superstition—not really sure of it, either, but preferring it to the other, which I did not seek in piety, but opposed in malice.[24]

24. Augustine is convicted of his insincerity of heart in his prayer, "Grant me sexual purity . . . but not yet!"

And I had thought that I delayed from day to day in rejecting those worldly hopes and following thee alone because there did not appear anything certain by which I could direct my course. And now the day had arrived in which I was laid bare to myself and my conscience was to chide me: "Where are you, O my tongue? You said indeed that you were not willing to cast off the baggage of vanity for uncertain truth. But behold now it is certain, and still that burden oppresses you. At the same time those who have not worn themselves out with searching for it as you have, nor spent ten years and more in thinking about it, have had their shoulders unburdened and have received wings to fly away." Thus was I inwardly confused, and mightily confounded with a horrible shame, while Ponticianus went ahead speaking such things. And when he had finished his story and the business he came for, he went his way. And then what did I not say to myself, within myself? With what scourges of rebuke did I not lash my soul to make it follow me, as I was struggling to go after thee? Yet it drew back. It refused. It would not make an effort. All its arguments were exhausted and confuted. Yet it resisted in sullen disquiet, fearing the cutting off of that habit by which it was being wasted to death, as if that were death itself.[25]

25. Augustine's mind rebukes his soul, but his soul refuses to listen. It is steadfastly bound to its sin.

Then, as this vehement quarrel, which I waged with my soul in the chamber of my heart, was raging inside my inner dwelling, agitated both in mind and countenance, I seized upon Alypius and exclaimed: "What is the matter with us? What is this? What did you hear? The uninstructed start up and take heaven, and we—with all our learning but so little heart—see where we wallow in flesh and blood! Because others have gone before us, are we ashamed to follow, and not rather ashamed at our not following?" I scarcely knew what I said, and in my excitement I flung away from him, while he gazed at me in silent astonishment. For I did not sound like myself: my face, eyes, color, tone expressed my meaning more clearly than my words.[26]

There was a little garden belonging to our lodging, of which we had the use—as of the whole house—for the master, our landlord, did not live there. The tempest in my breast hurried me out into this garden, where no one might interrupt the fiery struggle in which I was engaged with myself, until it came to the outcome that thou knewest though I did not. But I was mad for health, and dying for life; knowing what evil thing I was, but not knowing what good thing I was so shortly to become.

I fled into the garden, with Alypius following step by step; for I had no secret in which he did not share, and how could he leave me in such distress? We sat down, as far from the house as possible. I was greatly disturbed in spirit, angry at myself with a turbulent indignation because I had not entered thy will and covenant, O my God, while all my bones cried out to me to enter, extolling it to the skies. The way therein is not by ships or chariots or feet—indeed it was not as far as I had come from the house to the place where we were seated. For to go along that road and indeed to reach the goal is nothing else but the will to go. But it must be a strong and single will, not staggering and swaying about this way and that—a changeable, twisting, fluctuating will, wrestling with itself while one part falls as another rises.[27]

Finally, in the very fever of my indecision, I made many motions with my body; like men do when they will to act but cannot, either because they do not have the limbs or because

26. Augustine contrasts himself and Alypius to the "uninstructed" soldiers (the two men) who were willing to leave all to follow Christ (the true Wisdom). However, these educated men (Augustine and Alypius) refuse to follow Christ.

The Conversion of St. Augustine by Fra Angelico

27. Augustine testifies to a changing, fluctuating will (that does not indicate a regenerate heart).

their limbs are bound or weakened by disease, or incapacitated in some other way. Thus if I tore my hair, struck my forehead, or, entwining my fingers, clasped my knee, these I did because I willed it. But I might have willed it and still not have done it, if the nerves had not obeyed my will. Many things then I did, in which the will and power to do were not the same. Yet I did not do that one thing which seemed to me infinitely more desirable, which before long I should have power to will because shortly when I willed, I would will with a single will. For in this, the power of willing is the power of doing; and as yet I could not do it. Thus my body more readily obeyed the slightest wish of the soul in moving its limbs at the order of my mind than my soul obeyed itself to accomplish in the will alone its great resolve.

How can there be such a strange anomaly?[28] And why is it? Let thy mercy shine on me, that I may inquire and find an answer, amid the dark labyrinth of human punishment and in the darkest contritions of the sons of Adam. Whence such an anomaly? And why should it be? The mind commands the body, and the body obeys. The mind commands itself and is resisted. The mind commands the hand to be moved and there is such readiness that the command is scarcely distinguished from the obedience in act. Yet the mind is mind, and the hand is body. The mind commands the mind to will, and yet though it be itself it does not obey itself. Whence this strange anomaly and why should it be? I repeat: The will commands itself to will, and could not give the command unless it wills; yet what is commanded is not done. But actually the will does not will entirely; therefore it does not command entirely. For as far as it wills, it commands. And as far as it does not will, the thing commanded is not done. For the will commands that there be an act of will—not another, but itself. But it does not command entirely. Therefore, what is commanded does not happen; for if the will were whole and entire, it would not even command it to be, because it would already be. It is, therefore, no strange anomaly partly to will and partly to be

28. The mind commands the body and the body obeys. But, the mind knows what is the right thing to do but cannot control the will and the soul of the man (who has been corrupted by sin). He calls this a tremendous mystery. (It is the Romans 7:14ff phenomenon.)

unwilling. This is actually an infirmity of mind, which cannot wholly rise, while pressed down by habit, even though it is supported by the truth. And so there are two wills, because one of them is not whole, and what is present in this one is lacking in the other.

Let them perish from thy presence, O God, as vain talkers, and deceivers of the soul perish, who, when they observe that there are two wills in the act of deliberation, go on to affirm that there are two kinds of minds in us: one good, the other evil. They are indeed themselves evil when they hold these evil opinions—and they shall become good only when they come to hold the truth and consent to the truth that thy apostle may say to them: "You were formerly in darkness, but now are you in the light in the Lord." But they desired to be light, not "in the Lord," but in themselves. They conceived the nature of the soul to be the same as what God is, and thus have become a thicker darkness than they were; for in their dread arrogance they have gone farther away from thee, from thee "the true Light, that lights every man that comes into the world." Mark what you say and blush for shame; draw near to him and be enlightened, and your faces shall not be ashamed. While I was deliberating whether I would serve the Lord my God now, as I had long purposed to do, it was I who willed and it was also I who was unwilling. In either case, it was I. I neither willed with my whole will nor was I wholly unwilling. And so I was at war with myself and torn apart by myself.[29] And this strife was against my will; yet it did not show the presence of another mind, but the punishment of my own. Thus it was no more I who did it, but the sin that dwelt in me—the punishment of a sin freely committed by Adam, and I was a son of Adam.

For if there are as many opposing natures as there are opposing wills, there will not be two but many more. If any man is trying to decide whether he should go to their conventicle or to the theater, the Manicheans at once cry out, "See, here are two natures—one good, drawing this way, another bad, drawing back that way; for how else can you explain this

29. Augustine is insistent that there are not two wills — one good and the other evil within us. There is one will that is torn within the man who is convicted of his sin but still unregenerate.

indecision between conflicting wills?" But I reply that both impulses are bad—that which draws to them and that which draws back to the theater. But they do not believe that the will which draws to them can be anything but good. Suppose, then, that one of us should try to decide, and through the conflict of his two wills should waver whether he should go to the theater or to our Church. Would not those also waver about the answer here? For either they must confess, which they are unwilling to do, that the will that leads to our church is as good as that which carries their own adherents and those captivated by their mysteries; or else they must imagine that there are two evil natures and two evil minds in one man, both at war with each other, and then it will not be true what they say, that there is one good and another bad.[30] Else they must be converted to the truth, and no longer deny that when anyone deliberates there is one soul fluctuating between conflicting wills.

Let them no longer maintain that when they perceive two wills to be contending with each other in the same man the contest is between two opposing minds, of two opposing substances, from two opposing principles, the one good and the other bad. Thus, O true God, thou dost reprove and confute and convict them. For both wills may be bad: as when a man tries to decide whether he should kill a man by poison or by the sword; whether he should take possession of this field or that one belonging to someone else, when he cannot get both; whether he should squander his money to buy pleasure or hold onto his money through the motive of covetousness; whether he should go to the circus or to the theater, if both are open on the same day; or, whether he should take a third course, open at the same time, and rob another man's house; or, a fourth option, whether he should commit adultery, if he has the opportunity—all these things concurring in the same space of time and all being equally longed for, although impossible to do at one time.[31] For the mind is pulled four ways by four antagonistic wills—or even more, in view of the vast

30. The Manicheans teach two hearts and two wills. When people choose whether to go to a Manichean service or to the movie theater on a Sunday morning, the heart that wants to hang out with the Manicheans is the good heart. Augustine says both inclinations are bad (because one shouldn't go to either the Manichean service or to the movie theater). He points out that if someone is given two bad choices and wavers between them, the Manicheans would have to concede that there are two bad hearts within that person.

31. Augustine gives examples of how men choose between multiple sinful choices. He includes the theater and the circus (the coliseums) as both sinful choices.

range of human desires—but even the Manicheans do not affirm that there are these many different substances. The same principle applies as in the action of good wills. For I ask them, "Is it a good thing to have delight in reading the apostle, or is it a good thing to delight in a sober psalm, or is it a good thing to discourse on the gospel?" To each of these, they will answer, "It is good." But what, then, if all delight us equally and all at the same time? Do not different wills distract the mind when a man is trying to decide what he should choose? Yet they are all good, and are at variance with each other until one is chosen. When this is done the whole united will may go forward on a single track instead of remaining as it was before, divided in many ways. So also, when eternity attracts us from above, and the pleasure of earthly delight pulls us down from below, the soul does not will either the one or the other with all its force, but till it is the same soul that does not will this or that with a united will, and is therefore pulled apart with grievous perplexities, because for truth's sake it prefers this, but for custom's sake it does not lay that aside.[32]

32. Augustine wants to retain personal responsibility for the decisions the will makes (despite the conflicts that occur within the single will).

Thus I was sick and tormented, reproaching myself more bitterly than ever, rolling and writhing in my chain till it should be utterly broken. By now I was held but slightly, but still was held. And thou, O Lord, didst press upon me in my inmost heart with a severe mercy,[33] redoubling the lashes of fear and shame; lest I should again give way and that same slender remaining tie not be broken off, but recover strength and enchain me yet more securely.

33. It is God's "severe mercy" that brings a crushing conviction down upon us. This conviction will eventually produce a conversion of true faith and repentance.

I kept saying to myself, "See, let it be done now; let it be done now." And as I said this I all but came to a firm decision. I all but did it—yet I did not quite. Still I did not fall back to my old condition, but stood aside for a moment and drew breath. And I tried again, and lacked only a very little of reaching the resolve—and then somewhat less, and then all but touched and grasped it. Yet I still did not quite reach or touch or grasp the goal, because I hesitated to die to death and to live to life. And the worse way, to which I was habituated,

34. Augustine speaks of what was about to happen to him – he was going to become "another man," a "new creature" in Christ.

35. Augustine affirms again that it was the sin of fornication that had him bound more than anything else. These old mistresses were pulling on his sleeves.

36. Augustine combines chastity and continence (celibacy). This can be confusing but ought not to be conflated. Celibacy is a *FORM* of chastity. Marriage is a *FORM* of chastity (or purity) as well.

was stronger in me than the better, which I had not tried. And up to the very moment in which I was to become another man,[34] the nearer the moment approached, the greater horror did it strike in me. But it did not strike me back, nor turn me aside, but held me in suspense.

It was, in fact, my old mistresses, trifles of trifles and vanities of vanities, who still enthralled me.[35] They tugged at my fleshly garments and softly whispered: "Are you going to part with us? And from that moment will we never be with you any more? And from that moment will not this and that be forbidden you forever?" What were they suggesting to me in those words "this or that?" What is it they suggested, O my God? Let thy mercy guard the soul of thy servant from the vileness and the shame they did suggest! And now I scarcely heard them, for they were not openly showing themselves and opposing me face to face; but muttering, as it were, behind my back; and furtively plucking at me as I was leaving, trying to make me look back at them. Still they delayed me, so that I hesitated to break loose and shake myself free of them and leap over to the place to which I was being called—for unruly habit kept saying to me, "Do you think you can live without them?"

But now it said this very faintly; for in the direction I had set my face, and yet toward which I still trembled to go, the chaste dignity of continence appeared to me—cheerful but not wanton, modestly alluring me to come and doubt nothing, extending her holy hands, full of a multitude of good examples—to receive and embrace me. There were there so many young men and maidens, a multitude of youth and every age, grave widows and ancient virgins; and continence[36] herself in their midst: not barren, but a fruitful mother of children—her joys—by thee, O Lord, her husband. And she smiled on me with a challenging smile as if to say: "Can you not do what these young men and maidens can? Or can any of them do it of themselves, and not rather in the Lord their God? The Lord their God gave me to them. Why do you stand in your own strength, and so stand not? Cast yourself on him; fear not.[37] He will not flinch and you will not fall. Cast yourself on him without fear, for he will receive and heal you." And I blushed violently, for I still heard the muttering of those "trifles" and hung suspended. Again she seemed to speak: "Stop your ears against those unclean members of yours, that they may be mortified. They tell you of delights, but not according to the law of the Lord thy God." This struggle raging in my heart was nothing but the contest of self against self. And Alypius kept close beside me, and awaited in silence the outcome of my extraordinary agitation.

Now when deep reflection had drawn up out of the secret depths of my soul all my misery and had heaped it up before the sight of my heart, there arose a mighty storm, accompanied by a mighty rain of tears. That I might give way fully to my tears and lamentations, I stole away from Alypius, for it seemed to me that solitude was more appropriate for the business of weeping. I went far enough away that I could feel that even his presence was no restraint upon me. This was the way I felt at the time, and he realized it. I suppose I had said something before I started up and he noticed that the sound of my voice was choked with weeping. And so he stayed alone, where we had been sitting together, greatly astonished. I flung myself down under a fig tree—how I know not—and gave free course to my tears. The streams of my eyes gushed out an acceptable sacrifice to thee. And, not indeed in these words, but to this effect, I cried to thee: "And thou, O Lord, how long? How long, O Lord? Wilt thou be angry forever? Oh, remember not against us our former iniquities." For I felt that I was still enthralled by them. I sent up these sorrowful cries: "How long, how long? Tomorrow and tomorrow? Why not now? Why not this very hour make an end to my uncleanness?"[38]

I was saying these things and weeping in the most bitter contrition of my heart, when suddenly I heard the voice of a boy or a girl I know not which—coming from the neighboring house, chanting over and over again, "Pick it up, read it; pick it

37. Essential to the Christian faith — You cannot overcome sinful desire by yourself. It must happen "in the Lord your God."

38. Finally, Augustine falls on his face in tears and cries out for cleansing *and* forgiveness for his sexual uncleanness (and other sins).

39. The reading of the Word of God is the means of salvation. It is the power of the Word applied to the soul that matters. The young child's admonition has become a famous statement in Christian history: "Tolle Lege." Pick it up and read!

up, read it."[39] Immediately I ceased weeping and began most earnestly to think whether it was usual for children in some kind of game to sing such a song, but I could not remember ever having heard the like. So, damming the torrent of my tears, I got to my feet, for I could not but think that this was a divine command to open the Bible and read the first passage I should light upon. For I had heard how Anthony, accidentally coming into church while the gospel was being read, received the admonition as if what was read had been addressed to him: "Go and sell what you have and give it to the poor, and you shall have treasure in heaven; and come and follow me." By such an oracle he was forthwith converted to thee.

So I quickly returned to the bench where Alypius was sitting, for there I had put down the apostle's book when I had left there. I snatched it up, opened it, and in silence read the paragraph on which my eyes first fell: "Not in rioting and drunkenness, not in chambering and wantonness, not in strife and envying, but put on the Lord Jesus Christ, and make no provision for the flesh to fulfill the lusts thereof."[40] I wanted to read no further, nor did I need to. For instantly, as the sentence ended, there was infused in my heart something like the light of full certainty and all the gloom of doubt vanished away.

40. It was the verse from Romans that came directly from God into his mind and heart, and came with absolute certainty, and he believed.

Closing the book, then, and putting my finger or something else for a mark I began—now with a tranquil countenance—to tell it all to Alypius. And he in turn disclosed to me what had been going on in himself, of which I knew nothing. He asked to see what I had read. I showed him, and he looked on even further than I had read. I had not known what followed. But indeed it was this, "Him that is weak in the faith, receive." This he applied to himself, and told me so. By these words of warning he was strengthened, and by exercising his good resolution and purpose—all very much in keeping with his character, in which, in these respects, he was always far different from and better than I—he joined me in full commitment without any restless hesitation.

Then we went in to my mother, and told her what happened, to her great joy. We explained to her how it had occurred—and she leaped for joy triumphant; and she blessed thee, who art "able to do exceedingly abundantly above all that we ask or think." For she saw that thou hadst granted her far more than she had ever asked for in all her pitiful and doleful lamentations. For thou didst so convert me to thee that I sought neither a wife nor any other of this world's hopes, but set my feet on that rule of faith which so many years before thou hadst showed her in her dream about me. And so thou didst turn her grief into gladness more plentiful than she had ventured to desire, and dearer and purer than the desire she used to cherish of having grandchildren of my flesh.

PATRICK'S CONFESSIONS & BREASTPLATE

Patrick of Ireland
AD 450

AN INTRODUCTION TO THE TESTIMONY OF PATRICK

Of all the great Christians who ever lived, Patrick of Ireland was one of the most remarkable for his faith, courage, and humility. We know very little about Patrick; the bulk of our information comes from the autobiographical confession found in these several short pages. It is important to remember the era Patrick lived in. Rome was collapsing and civilizations built upon humanist ideals were falling apart. So Patrick, armed with nothing but the Word of God, took the Gospel to the "far ends of the earth"—a thoroughly pagan land filled with witchcraft, human sacrifice, slavery, demonism, and sexual confusion. Over the course of his life, thousands were baptized, and a church was established which would evangelize large portions of Europe during the next 500 years.

The Influence of Patrick over the Millennia

The church Patrick founded flourished for 800 years. Although it is now shrouded in mystery, its influence on Western Christianity—including any Christian reading these works in the 21st century—is incalculable. The Scotch-Irish Culdean church would function largely independent of Rome until the 12th century. In 1176, a young Patrick Murray from Scotland, speaking to the English church, claimed that the Scottish Culdean church had always been "catholic and free." Following is his quote in its entirety:

"Thou seekest to oppress thy mother the Church of Scotland, which from the beginning hath been catholique and free, and which brought thee, when thou wast straying in the wilderness of heathenism, into the safe-guard of the true faith, and way unto life, even unto Jesus Christ, the author of eternal rest. She did wash thy kings, and princes, and people, in the laver of holy baptism: she taught thee the commandments of God, and instructed thee in moral duties."

Bede, from England, wrote concerning the Irish monasteries of the 7th century: "There were at that time in Ireland many both of the nobility and of the middle classes of the English nation, who, having left their native island, had retired thither for the sake of reading God's word, or leading a more holy life. . . . All of whom the Irish receiving most warmly, supplied, not only with daily food, free of charge, but even with books to read, and masters to teach gratuitously."

What to Look for in Patrick's Confessions

There are many issues to discuss and debate within the Christian faith. But what Patrick presents in his Confession is what we would describe as the substantive "trunk" issues of the faith. If you were to picture the many perspectives of the Word of God as a large tree that has grown over the centuries, you would see many branches, both large and small, and a variety of leaves. People disagree on important issues and less important issues.

But back in the 5th century, Patrick was a simple man who took the basic Gospel to a simple, pagan nation that had never heard the Gospel before. This is the "trunk" of the Christian faith. Too often professing Christians learn a few finely developed theological points or some minor lessons from the Bible, but they fail to subscribe to the trunk issues that constitute the basic faith. By reading this simple Confession from an early Christian believer, you will find that the most important doctrines are put first. Later, you may grapple with the branch and leaf discussions and debates on Christian theology. But first, get your trunk in place.

CHAPTER I - KIDNAPPED

Ballintoy, Northern Ireland

I, Patrick, a sinner,[1] a most simple countryman, the least of all the faithful and most contemptible to many, had for father the deacon Calpurnius, son of the late Potitus, a priest, of the settlement of Bannavem Taburniae; he had a small villa nearby where I was taken captive. I was at that time about sixteen years of age. I did not, indeed, know the true God;[2] and I was taken into captivity in Ireland with many thousands of people, according to our deserts, for quite drawn away from God, we did not keep his precepts, nor were we obedient to our priests who used to remind us of our salvation. And the Lord brought down on us the fury of his being and scattered us among many nations, even to the ends

1. Patrick identifies himself first as a "sinner." His father was a deacon and his grandfather a priest (or pastor). As a young man, Patrick was not faithful to his father's God.

2. Apostasy is described as ignoring the pastors who remind us of our salvation *and* ignoring the precepts of God. Revelation 14:12 describes the Christian as one who keeps the faith of Jesus and keeps the commandments of God.

3. Patrick believes that the Irish slave raids came about because the early English church was not faithful to the Christian doctrine they had been taught.

4. Patrick's goal in these *Confessions* is to exalt the Lord and confess his wonders before all nations (Ps. 96:1-3).

5. This is the "Trunk" faith, the basic faith of these courageous Christian missionaries. This includes the doctrine of the Trinity, the resurrection, the sovereign reign of Christ, our hope of resurrection, and the adoption of sons into the family of God. Note: The resurrection of Christ is more central to the Gospel message in Patrick's mind than the death on the cross for man's sins.

of the earth, where I, in my smallness, am now to be found among foreigners.[3]

2. And there the Lord opened my mind to an awareness of my unbelief, in order that, even so late, I might remember my transgressions and turn with all my heart to the Lord my God, who had regard for my insignificance and pitied my youth and ignorance. And he watched over me before I knew him, and before I learned sense or even distinguished between good and evil, and he protected me, and consoled me as a father would his son.

3. Therefore, indeed, I cannot keep silent, nor would it be proper, so many favours and graces has the Lord deigned to bestow on me in the land of my captivity. For after chastisement from God, and recognizing him, our way to repay him is to exalt him and confess his wonders before every nation under heaven.[4]

4. For there is no other God, nor ever was before, nor shall be hereafter, but God the Father, unbegotten and without beginning, in whom all things began, whose are all things, as we have been taught; and his son Jesus Christ, who manifestly always existed with the Father, before the beginning of time in the spirit with the Father, indescribably begotten before all things, and all things visible and invisible were made by him. He was made man, conquered death and was received into Heaven, to the Father who gave him all power over every name in Heaven and on Earth and in Hell, so that every tongue should confess that Jesus Christ is Lord and God, in whom we believe. And we look to his imminent coming again, the judge of the living and the dead, who will render to each according to his deeds. And he poured out his Holy Spirit on us in abundance, the gift and pledge of immortality, which makes the believers and the obedient into sons of God and co-heirs of Christ who is revealed, and we worship one God in the Trinity of holy name.[5]

5. He himself said through the prophet: "Call upon me in the day of trouble; I will deliver you, and you shall glorify me."

And again: "It is right to reveal and publish abroad the works of God."

6. I am imperfect in many things, nevertheless I want my brethren and kinsfolk to know my nature so that they may be able to perceive my soul's desire.

7. I am not ignorant of what is said of my Lord in the Psalm: "You destroy those who speak a lie." And again: "A lying mouth deals death to the soul." And likewise the Lord says in the Gospel: "On the day of judgment men shall render account for every idle word they utter."

8. So it is that I should mightily fear, with terror and trembling, this judgment on the day when no one shall be able to steal away or hide, but each and all shall render account for even our smallest sins before the judgment seat of Christ the Lord.

9. And therefore for some time I have thought of writing, but I have hesitated until now, for truly, I feared to expose myself to the criticism of men, because I have not studied like others, who have assimilated both Law and the Holy Scriptures equally and have never changed their idiom since their infancy,[6] but instead were always learning it increasingly, to perfection, while my idiom and language have been translated into a foreign tongue. So it is easy to prove from a sample of my writing, my ability in rhetoric and the extent of my preparation and knowledge, for as it is said, "wisdom shall be recognized in speech, and in understanding, and in knowledge and in the learning of truth."

10. But why make excuses close to the truth, especially when now I am presuming to try to grasp in my old age what I did not gain in my youth because my sins prevented me from making what I had read my own? But who will believe me, even though I should say it again? A young man, almost a beardless boy, I was taken captive before I knew what I should desire and what I should shun. So, consequently, today I feel ashamed and I am mightily afraid to expose my ignorance, because, [not being] eloquent, and with a small vocabulary, I

6. Patrick is commending those who study both the Law (the Old Testament) and the Holy Scriptures (the New Testament) equally. Both constitute the basis of study for the disciples of Jesus Christ.

7. Patrick is well aware of his lack of learning. But he is humble, fearing of God, and grateful to God. These are the greatest and most important qualifications for any Christian teacher in the church. They are more essential than all others. That is why Christian students will study Patrick.

8. Patrick is in awe that God would use such "a nobody" as himself to bring about such awesome work in the history of mankind, in the history of Christian missions!

am unable to explain as the spirit is eager to do and as the soul and the mind indicate.[7]

11. But had it been given to me as to others, in gratitude I should not have kept silent, and if it should appear that I put myself before others, with my ignorance and my slower speech, in truth, it is written: "The tongue of the stammerers shall speak rapidly and distinctly."[8] How much harder must we try to attain it, we of whom it is said: "You are an epistle of Christ in greeting to the ends of the earth. . . written on your hearts, not with ink but with the Spirit of the living God." And again, the Spirit witnessed that the rustic life was created by the Most High.

12. I am, then, first of all, countrified, an exile, evidently unlearned, one who is not able to see into the future, but I know for certain, that before I was humbled I was like a stone lying in deep mire, and he that is mighty came and in his mercy raised me up and, indeed, lifted me high up and placed me on top of the wall. And from there I ought to shout out in gratitude to the Lord for his great favours in this world and for ever, that the mind of man cannot measure.

13. Therefore be amazed, you great and small who fear God, and you men of God, eloquent speakers, listen and contemplate. Who was it summoned me, a fool, from the midst of those who appear wise and learned in the law and powerful in rhetoric and in all things? Me, truly wretched in this world, he inspired before others that I could be—if I would—such a one who, with fear and reverence, and faithfully, without complaint, would come to the people to whom the love of Christ brought me and gave me in my lifetime, if I should be worthy, to serve them truly and with humility.

14. According, therefore, to the measure of one's faith in the Trinity, one should proceed without holding back from danger to make known the gift of God and everlasting consolation, to spread God's name everywhere with confidence and without fear, in order to leave behind, after my death, founda-

tions for my brethren and sons whom I baptized in the Lord in so many thousands.

15. And I was not worthy, nor was I such that the Lord should grant his humble servant this, that after hardships and such great trials, after captivity, after many years, he should give me so much favour in these people, a thing which in the time of my youth I neither hoped for nor imagined.[9]

9. Patrick's groundbreaking work produced thousands of baptized converts in Ireland. It was a tremendous foundation for one of the strongest churches in Christendom that would last for at least a thousand years.

CHAPTER II - ESCAPE FROM IRELAND

But after I reached Ireland I used to pasture the flock each day and I used to pray many times a day. More and more did the love of God, and my fear of him and faith increase,[1] and my spirit was moved so that in a day [I said] from one up to a hundred prayers, and in the night a like number; besides I used to stay out in the forests and on the mountain and I would wake up before daylight to pray in the snow, in icy coldness, in rain, and I used to feel neither ill nor any slothfulness, because, as I now see, the Spirit was burning in me at that time.

17. And it was there of course that one night in my sleep I heard a voice saying to me: "You do well to fast: soon you will depart for your home country." And again, a very short time later, there was a voice prophesying: "Behold, your ship is ready."[2] And it was not close by, but, as it happened, two hundred miles away, where I had never been nor knew any person. And shortly thereafter I turned about and fled from the man with whom I had been for six years,[3] and I came, by the power of God who directed my route to advantage (and I was afraid of nothing), until I reached that ship.

18. And on the same day that I arrived, the ship was setting out from the place, and I said that I had the wherewithal to sail with them; and the steersman was displeased and re-

1. The relationship of the believer to God involves three dispositions — fear, faith, and love. They are all three equally important. As an Irish slave, Patrick prayed up to 100 times per day and 100 times per night to God.

2. Patrick is known for extremely vivid dreams, in which God gives him direction. He does not equate this to the divine revelation of Scripture (in its inspired character). However, he still speaks of the dreams as God's direction for his life.

3. Patrick served as a slave for six years in what is now called Mayo County over on the west side of Ireland.

plied in anger, sharply: "By no means attempt to go with us." Hearing this I left them to go to the hut where I was staying, and on the way I began to pray, and before the prayer was finished I heard one of them shouting loudly after me: "Come quickly because the men are calling you." And immediately I went back to them and they started to say to me: "Come, because we are admitting you out of good faith; make friendship with us in any way you wish." (And so, on that day, I refused to suck the breasts of these men from fear of God, but nevertheless I had hopes that they would come to faith in Jesus Christ, because they were barbarians.)[4] And for this I continued with them, and forthwith we put to sea.

4. Patrick refused to engage in a pagan rite with these sailors because he says at this point he "feared God."

Sheep in Downpatrick, Northern Ireland (the town's Irish name "Dún Pádraig" means "Patrick's Stronghold")

19. And after three days we reached land, and for twenty-eight days journeyed through uninhabited country, and the food ran out and hunger overtook them; and one day the steersman began saying: "Why is it, Christian? You say your God is great and all-powerful; then why can you not pray for us? For we may perish of hunger; it is unlikely indeed that we shall ever see another human being." In fact, I said to them, confidently: "Be converted by faith with all your heart to my Lord God, because nothing is impossible for him, so that today he will send food for you on your road, until you be sated,

because everywhere he abounds." And with God's help this came to pass; and behold, a herd of swine appeared on the road before our eyes, and they slew many of them, and remained there for two nights, and the men were full of their meat and well restored, for many of them had fainted and would otherwise have been left half dead by the wayside. And after this they gave the utmost thanks to God, and I was esteemed in their eyes, and from that day they had food abundantly. They discovered wild honey, besides, and they offered a share to me, and one of them said: "It is a sacrifice." Thanks be to God, I tasted none of it. [5]

20. The very same night while I was sleeping Satan attacked me violently, as I will remember as long as I shall be in this body; and there fell on top of me as it were, a huge rock, and not one of my members had any force. But from whence did it come to me, ignorant in the spirit, to call upon "Helias?" And meanwhile I saw the sun rising in the sky, and while I was crying out "Helias, Helias" with all my might, lo, the brilliance of that sun fell upon me and immediately shook me free of all the weight;[6] and I believe that I was aided by Christ my Lord, and that his Spirit then was crying out for me, and I hope that it will be so in the day of my affliction, just as it says in the Gospel: "In that hour," the Lord declares, "it is not you who speaks but the Spirit of your Father speaking in you."

21. And a second time, after many years, I was taken captive. On the first night I accordingly remained with my captors, but I heard a divine prophecy, saying to me: "You shall be with them for two months." So it happened. On the sixtieth night the Lord delivered me from their hands.

22. On the journey he provided us with food and fire and dry weather every day, until on the tenth day we came upon people.[7] As I mentioned above, we had journeyed through an unpopulated country for twenty-eight days, and in fact the night that we came upon people we had no food.

23. And after a few years I was again in Britain with my parents [kinsfolk], and they welcomed me as a son, and asked

5. The Barbarians gave thanks to God, and then they offered the honey as a sacrifice. Patrick did not participate in the heathen "sacrifice." It was at this point, "food offered to idols," and he wouldn't touch it.

6. When attacked by Satan, he calls out to the "sun," which is a symbolic reference to the light of the world, Jesus Christ. Reference paragraphs 59 and 60, where Christ is referred to as "the true sun."

7. God provided food, fire, and dry weather for the entire journey back home.

me, in faith, that after the great tribulations I had endured I should not go anywhere else away from them. And, of course, there, in a vision of the night, I saw a man whose name was Victoricus coming as if from Ireland with innumerable letters, and he gave me one of them, and I read the beginning of the letter: "The Voice of the Irish"; and as I was reading the beginning of the letter I seemed at that moment to hear the voice of those who were beside the forest of Foclut which is near the western sea, and they were crying as if with one voice: "We beg you, holy youth, that you shall come and shall walk again among us." And I was stung intensely in my heart so that I could read no more, and thus I awoke. Thanks be to God, because after so many years the Lord bestowed on them according to their cry.

CHAPTER III - PATRICK'S CALL TO IRELAND

And another night—God knows, I do not, whether within me or beside me—most words which I heard and could not understand, except at the end of the speech it was represented thus: "He who gave his life for you, he it is who speaks within you." And thus I awoke, joyful.[1]

25. And on a second occasion I saw Him praying within me, and I was as it were, inside my own body, and I heard Him above me—that is, above my inner self. He was praying powerfully with sighs. And in the course of this I was astonished and wondering, and I pondered who it could be who was praying within me. But at the end of the prayer it was revealed to me that it was the Spirit. And so I awoke and remembered the Apostle's words: "Likewise the Spirit helps us in our weakness; for we know not how to pray as we ought. But the Spirit Himself intercedes for us with sighs too deep for utterance." And again: "The Lord our advocate intercedes for us."

26. And then I was attacked by a goodly number of my elders, who [brought up] my sins against my arduous episcopate. That day in particular I was mightily upset, and might have fallen here and for ever; but the Lord generously spared me, a convert, and an alien, for his name's sake, and he came powerfully to my assistance in that state of being trampled

1. Patrick's call to Ireland, he believes, comes from Jesus Christ Himself. "He who gave his life for you" is a reference to Jesus.

down. I pray God that it shall not be held against them as a sin that I fell truly into disgrace and scandal.

27. They brought up against me after thirty years an occurrence I had confessed before becoming a deacon. On account of the anxiety in my sorrowful mind, I laid before my close friend what I had perpetrated on a day—nay, rather in one hour—in my boyhood because I was not yet proof against sin. God knows—I do not—whether I was fifteen years old at the time, and I did not then believe in the living God, nor had I believed, since my infancy; but I remained in death and unbelief until I was severely rebuked, and in truth I was humbled every day by hunger and nakedness.[2]

28. On the other hand, I did not proceed to Ireland of my own accord until I was almost giving up, but through this I was corrected by the Lord, and he prepared me so that today I should be what was once far from me, in order that I should have the care of—or rather, I should be concerned for—the salvation of others, when at that time, still, I was only concerned for myself.

29. Therefore, on that day when I was rebuked, as I have just mentioned, I saw in a vision of the night a document before my face, without honour, and meanwhile I heard a divine prophecy, saying to me: "We have seen with displeasure the face of the chosen one divested of [his good] name." And he did not say, "You have seen with displeasure," but "We have seen with displeasure" (as if He included Himself). He said then: "He who touches you, touches the apple of my eye."

30. For that reason, I give thanks to him who strengthened me in all things, so that I should not be hindered in my setting out and also in my work which I was taught by Christ my Lord; but more, from that state of affairs I felt, within me, no little courage, and vindicated my faith before God and man.

31. Hence, therefore, I say boldly that my conscience is clear now and hereafter. God is my witness that I have not lied in these words to you.

2. There is no hint as to the sin that Patrick sinned when he was 15 years old. It was quite heinous according to those who were opposing his pastorate (when he was 30 years old). God, in His mercy, wiped the sin away and would not allow any evidence of it to slip into the annals of history.

Ruins of Monasterboice, founded in the 5th century in Ireland

because of him we deserved to hear such a prophecy. The one to whom I entrusted my soul! And I found out from a goodly number of brethren, before the case was made in my defense (in which I did not take part, nor was I in Britain, nor was it pleaded by me), that in my absence he would fight in my behalf. Besides, he told me himself: "See, the rank of bishop goes to you"—of which I was not worthy. But how did it come to him, shortly afterwards, to disgrace me publicly, in the presence of all, good and bad, because previously, gladly and of his own free will, he pardoned me, as did the Lord, who is greater than all?[3]

3. Patrick tells of his "close friend" who betrayed him by sharing with the other pastors/ bishops what Patrick had told him in private.

4. Patrick is very conscious of the indwelling of the Holy Spirit and believes this is what has preserved him from evil.

5. Patrick acknowledges God's sovereign working in him along the way. God works in us to will and to do of His good pleasure. Patrick also realizes God's fore ordination, purposing to call Patrick and others to be heralds of the Gospel. Patrick has the true Christian spirit, thanking God always, whether we receive good or bad circumstances.
It is not unusual for Christians to consider themselves living in the "last days." Patrick is anxious to see the Gospel preached through ALL nations.

33. I have said enough. But all the same, I ought not to conceal God's gift which he lavished on us in the land of my captivity, for then I sought him resolutely, and I found him there, and he preserved me from all evils (as I believe) through the in-dwelling of his Spirit, which works in me to this day.[4] Again, boldly, but God knows, if this had been made known to me by man, I might, perhaps, have kept silent for the love of Christ.

34. Thus I give untiring thanks to God who kept me faithful in the day of my temptation, so that today I may confidently offer my soul as a living sacrifice for Christ my Lord; who am I, Lord? Or, rather, what is my calling? That you appeared to me in so great a divine quality, so that today among the barbarians I might constantly exalt and magnify your name in whatever place I should be, and not only in good fortune, but even in affliction? So that whatever befalls me, be it good or bad, I should accept it equally, and give thanks always to God who revealed to me that I might trust in him, implicitly and forever, and who will encourage me so that, ignorant, and in the last days, I may dare to undertake so devout and so wonderful a work; so that I might imitate one of those whom, once, long ago, the Lord already pre-ordained to be heralds of his Gospel to witness to all peoples to the ends of the earth. So are we seeing, and so it is fulfilled; behold, we are witnesses because the Gospel has been preached as far as the places beyond which no man lives.[5]

❈ CHAPTER IV - PATRICK'S MINISTRY

But it is tedious to describe in detail all my labours one by one. I will tell briefly how most holy God frequently delivered me, from slavery, and from the twelve trials with which my soul was threatened, from man traps as well, and from things I am not able to put into words. I would not cause offence to readers, but I have God as witness who knew all things even before they happened that, though I was a poor, ignorant waif, still he gave me abundant warnings through divine prophecy.[1]

36. Whence came to me this wisdom which was not my own, I who neither knew the number of days nor had knowledge of God? Whence came the so great and so healthful gift of knowing or rather loving God,[2] though I should lose homeland and family?

37. And many gifts were offered to me with weeping and tears, and I offended them [the donors], and also went against the wishes of a good number of my elders; but guided by God, I neither agreed with them nor deferred to them,[3] not by my own grace but by God who is victorious in me and withstands them all, so that I might come to the Irish people to preach the Gospel and endure insults from unbelievers; that I might hear scandal of my travels, and endure many persecutions to the extent of prison;[4] and so that I might give up my free birthright for the advantage of others, and if I should be wor-

1. Patrick suffered nightmarish trials that he fears would be an offense to his readers. Supernatural prophetic revelations preserved his life at points.

2. The highest blessing a man can ever experience — to know and love God.

3. Patrick was not controlled by money and power.

4. Patrick's persecutions included imprisonment at times. A man who is willing to give up his life for Christ is best suited for this misssionary work.

thy, I am ready [to give] even my life without hesitation; and most willingly for His name. And I choose to devote it to him even unto death, if God grant it to me.

38. I am greatly God's debtor, because he granted me so much grace, that through me many people would be reborn in God, and soon after confirmed,[5] and that clergy would be ordained everywhere for them, the masses lately come to belief, whom the Lord drew from the ends of the earth, just as he once promised through his prophets: "To you shall the nations come from the ends of the earth, and shall say, 'Our fathers have inherited naught but lies, worthless things in which there is no profit.'" And again: "I have set you to be a light for the Gentiles that you may bring salvation to the uttermost ends of the earth."

39. And I wish to wait then for his promise which is never unfulfilled, just as it is promised in the Gospel: "Many shall come from east and west and shall sit at table with Abraham and Isaac and Jacob." Just as we believe that believers will come from all the world.[6]

40. So for that reason one should, in fact, fish well and diligently, just as the Lord foretells and teaches, saying, "Follow me, and I will make you fishers of men," and, again, through the prophets: "'Behold, I am sending forth many fishers and hunters,' says the Lord," et cetera. So it behooved us to spread our nets, that a vast multitude and throng might be caught for God, and so there might be clergy everywhere who baptized and exhorted a needy and desirous people. Just as the Lord says in the Gospel, admonishing and instructing: "Go therefore and make disciples of all nations, baptizing them in the name of the Father and of the Son and of the Holy Spirit, teaching them to observe all that I have commanded you; and lo, I am with you always to the end of time." And again he says: "Go forth into the world and preach the Gospel to all creation. He who believes and is baptized shall be saved; but he who does not believe shall be condemned." And again: "This Gospel of the Kingdom shall be preached throughout the whole world

5. Patrick saw true regenerations among these barbarian tribes. Then he helped them through a "confirmation." Effectively, the confirmation is ongoing discipleship work that makes certain of their regeneration.

6. Patrick has a good grasp on Scripture, both Old and New Testaments. These passages refer to God's purposes to reach the Gentiles and the whole world with the Gospel of the Kingdom.

as a witness to all nations; and then the end of the world shall come."[7] And likewise the Lord foretells through the prophet: "And it shall come to pass in the last days (sayeth the Lord) that I will pour out my spirit upon all flesh, and your sons and daughters shall prophesy, and your young men shall see visions and your old men shall dream dreams; yea, and on my menservants and my maidservants in those days I will pour out my Spirit and they shall prophesy." And in Hosea he says: "Those who are not my people I will call my people, and those not beloved I will call my beloved, and in the very place where it was said to them, 'You are not my people,' they will be called 'Sons of the living God.'"

41. So, how is it that in Ireland, where they never had any knowledge of God but, always, until now, cherished idols and unclean things, they are lately become a people of the Lord, and are called children of God; the sons of the Irish [Scotti] and the daughters of the chieftains are to be seen as monks and virgins of Christ.[8]

42. And there was, besides, a most beautiful, blessed, native-born noble Irish [Scotta] woman of adult age whom I baptized; and a few days later she had reason to come to us to intimate that she had received a prophecy from a divine messenger [who] advised her that she should become a virgin of Christ and she would draw nearer to God. Thanks be to God, six days from then, opportunely and most eagerly, she took the course that all virgins of God take, not with their fathers' consent but enduring the persecutions and deceitful hindrances of their parents. Notwithstanding that, their number increases, (we do not know the number of them that are so reborn) besides the widows, and those who practice self-denial. Those who are kept in slavery suffer the most. They endure terrors and constant threats, but the Lord has given grace to many of his handmaidens, for even though they are forbidden to do so, still they resolutely follow his example.[9]

43. So it is that even if I should wish to separate from them in order to go to Britain, and most willingly was I pre-

7. Two parts of the great commission are practiced here. First, they baptize, and then they teach and admonish. The early missionaries did not require a profession of faith first, as some require today.

8. Ireland was a place of idolatry, demon-worship, human sacrifice, and much sexual sin. Patrick summarizes their problems as idolatry and uncleanness. Now Ireland has become a people of the Lord.

9. Some women dedicated themselves to the service of the Lord in the church as celibate. They did not get married. Some made this choice even against the wishes of their parents.

*Mt. Croagh Patrick
in Ireland*

10. Patrick longs to visit his brothers and family members in Britain and Gaul, but he is called to this mission. He refuses to take a vacation. Some of the most effective missionaries have dedicated their lives to the task and have refused to take vacations or furloughs.

11. Patrick admits to the attacks of the flesh and the Devil. He admits to an imperfect life but sees that he has grown in love for God and the fear of God over the years — an honest, humble, and encouraging testimony.

pared to go to my homeland and kinsfolk—and not only there, but as far as Gaul to visit the brethren there, so that I might see the faces of the holy ones of my Lord, God knows how strongly I desired this—I am bound by the Spirit, who witnessed to me that if I did so he would mark me out as guilty, and I fear to waste the labour that I began, and not I, but Christ the Lord, who commanded me to come to be with them for the rest of my life, if the Lord shall will it and shield me from every evil, so that I may not sin before him.[10]

44. So I hope that I did as I ought, but I do not trust myself as long as I am in this mortal body, for he is strong who strives daily to turn me away from the faith and true holiness to which I aspire until the end of my life for Christ my Lord, but the hostile flesh is always dragging one down to death, that is, to unlawful attractions. And I know in part why I did not lead a perfect life like other believers, but I confess to my Lord and do not blush in his sight, because I am not lying; from the time when I came to know him in my youth, the love of God and fear of him increased in me, and right up until now, by God's favour, I have kept the faith.[11]

45. What is more, let anyone laugh and taunt if he so wishes. I am not keeping silent, nor am I hiding the signs and wonders that were shown to me by the Lord many years before they happened, [he] who knew everything, even before the beginning of time.

46. Thus, I should give thanks unceasingly to God, who frequently forgave my folly and my negligence, in more than one instance so as not to be violently angry with me, who am placed as his helper, and I did not easily assent to what had been revealed to me, as the Spirit was urging; and the Lord took pity on me thousands upon thousands of times, because he saw within me that I was prepared, but that I was ignorant of what to do in view of my situation; because many were trying to prevent this mission. They were talking among themselves behind my back, and saying: "Why is this fellow throwing himself into danger among enemies who know not

God?" Not from malice, but having no liking for it; likewise, as I myself can testify, they perceived my rusticity. And I was not quick to recognize the grace that was then in me; I now know that I should have done so earlier.[12]

47. Now I have put it frankly to my brethren and co-workers, who have believed me because of what I have foretold and still foretell to strengthen and reinforce your faith.[13] I wish only that you, too, would make greater and better efforts. This will be my pride, for "a wise son makes a proud father."

48. You know, as God does, how I went about among you from my youth in the faith of truth and in sincerity of heart. As well as to the heathen among whom I live, I have shown them trust and always show them trust. God knows I did not cheat any one of them, nor consider it, for the sake of God and his Church, lest I arouse them and [bring about] persecution for them and for all of us, and lest the Lord's name be blasphemed because of me, for it is written: "Woe to the men through whom the name of the Lord is blasphemed."

49. For even though I am ignorant in all things, nevertheless I attempted to safeguard some and myself also. And I gave back again to my Christian brethren and the virgins of Christ and the holy women the small unasked for gifts that they used to give me or some of their ornaments which they used to throw on the altar. And they would be offended with me because I did this. But in the hope of eternity, I safeguarded myself carefully in all things, so that they might not cheat me of my office of service on any pretext of dishonesty, and so that I should not in the smallest way provide any occasion for defamation or disparagement on the part of unbelievers.[14]

50. What is more, when I baptized so many thousands of people, did I hope for even half a jot from any of them? [If so] tell me, and I will give it back to you. And when the Lord ordained clergy everywhere by my humble means, and I freely conferred office on them, if I asked any of them anywhere even for the price of one shoe, say so to my face and I will give it back.

12. Patrick acknowledges his reluctance to act on the call, especially with all the naysayers around him. He is thankful that God was patient with him, but he wishes he had recognized the grace of God working in him earlier on in his ministry.

13. Patrick wants to encourage the faith of his brothers through his prophetic gift. Apparently, Patrick claims to have had some ability to foretell future events.

14. Patrick was especially careful with money and material gifts. He returned some of the gifts that the brothers and sisters gave to him.

51. More, I spent for you so that they would receive me. And I went about among you, and everywhere for your sake, in danger, and as far as the outermost regions beyond which no one lived, and where no one had ever penetrated before, to baptize or to ordain clergy or to confirm people. Conscientiously and gladly I did all this work by God's gift for your salvation.

52. From time to time I gave rewards to the kings, as well as making payments to their sons who travel with me; notwithstanding which, they seized me with my companions, and that day most avidly desired to kill me.[15] But my time had not yet come. They plundered everything they found on us anyway, and fettered me in irons; and on the fourteenth day the Lord freed me from their power, and whatever they had of ours was given back to us for the sake of God on account of the indispensable friends whom we had made before.

53. Also you know from experience how much I was paying to those who were administering justice in all the regions, which I visited often. I estimate truly that I distributed to them not less than the price of fifteen men, in order that you should enjoy my company and I enjoy yours, always, in God. I do not regret this nor do I regard it as enough. I am paying out still and I shall pay out more. The Lord has the power to grant me that I may soon spend my own self, for your souls.

54. Behold, I call on God as my witness upon my soul that I am not lying; nor would I write to you for it to be an occasion for flattery or selfishness, nor hoping for honour from any one of you.[16] Sufficient is the honour which is not yet seen, but in which the heart has confidence. He who made the promise is faithful; he never lies.

55. But I see that even here and now, I have been exalted beyond measure by the Lord, and I was not worthy that he should grant me this, while I know most certainly that poverty and failure suit me better than wealth and delight (but Christ the Lord was poor for our sakes); I certainly am wretched and unfortunate; even if I wanted wealth I have no resources, nor

15. Patrick was forced to pay "rewards" or fees to kings and tribal leaders. He paid "the price of 15 men" in total. Value was measured by the cost of a single male slave. In today's money, this would have amounted to $100,000–$300,000. He would have been willing to pay anything to be able to preach the Gospel in these regions of the world (that had never heard the Good News).

16. Patrick has no interest in the honor of man. He does not wish to boast of his own accomplishments. He is only interested in the honor that comes from God, in glory.

is it my own estimation of myself, for daily I expect to be murdered or betrayed or reduced to slavery if the occasion arises.[17] But I fear nothing, because of the promises of Heaven; for I have cast myself into the hands of Almighty God, who reigns everywhere. As the prophet says: "Cast your burden on the Lord and he will sustain you."

17. Wealth has no value to him because his life is constantly threatened with murder, betrayal, and slavery.

CHAPTER V -
PATRICK'S CONFESSION

Behold now I commend my soul to God who is most faithful and for whom I perform my mission in obscurity, but he is no respecter of persons and he chose me for this service that I might be one of the least of his ministers.

57. For which reason I should make return for all that he returns me. But what should I say, or what should I promise to my Lord, for I, alone, can do nothing unless he himself vouchsafe it to me.[1] But let him search my heart and [my] nature, for I crave enough for it, even too much, and I am ready for him to grant me that I drink of his chalice,[2] as he has granted to others who love him.

58. Therefore may it never befall me to be separated by my God from his people whom he has won in this most remote land. I pray God that he gives me perseverance, and that he will deign that I should be a faithful witness for his sake right up to the time of my passing.

59. And if at any time I managed anything of good for the sake of my God whom I love, I beg of him that he grant it to me to shed my blood for his name with proselytes and captives, even should I be left unburied, or even were my wretched body to be torn limb from limb by dogs or savage beasts, or were it to be devoured by the birds of the air, I think, most surely, were this to have happened to me, I had saved both my soul and my body.[3] For beyond any doubt on that day we shall

1. We can give nothing to God but what he has first given to us. It is all of grace.

2. To drink of his chalice may be a reference to the final wedding feast, awaiting the saints in glory.

3. Here is a very passionate confession of his dedication to the missionary work. Especially important is the confident confession concerning the final resurrection of the body.

4. Patrick opposes the worship of the sun by claiming Christ as the one who commands the sun to rise.

5. The Christian is defined as the one who believes in Christ, worships Christ, and serves Christ. This is the one who will abide forever.

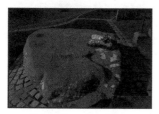

Patrick's gravesite in Down Cathedral

6. The reason for the mission to Ireland was to share the Gospel and the promises of God.

7. The Christian is defined again as the one who believes in and fears God.

8. His last point — All is of grace; all that he ever did that was of any good was a gift from God — what a powerful testimony.

rise again in the brightness of the sun, that is, in the glory of Christ Jesus our Redeemer, as children of the living God and co-heirs of Christ, made in his image; for we shall reign through him and for him and in him.

60. For the sun we see rises each day for us at [his] command, but it will never reign, neither will its splendor last, but all who worship it will come wretchedly to punishment.[4] We, on the other hand, shall not die, who believe in and worship the true sun, Christ, who will never die, no more shall he die who has done Christ's will, but will abide for ever just as Christ abides for ever, who reigns with God the Father Almighty and with the Holy Spirit before the beginning of time and now and for ever and ever. Amen.[5]

61. Behold over and over again I would briefly set out the words of my confession. I testify in truthfulness and gladness of heart before God and his holy angels that I never had any reason, except the Gospel and his promises, ever to have returned to that nation from which I had previously escaped with difficulty.[6]

62. But I entreat those who believe in and fear God,[7] whoever deigns to examine or receive this document composed by the obviously unlearned sinner Patrick in Ireland, that nobody shall ever ascribe to my ignorance any trivial thing that I achieved or may have expounded that was pleasing to God, but accept and truly believe that it would have been the gift of God. And this is my confession before I die.[8]

PATRICK'S BREASTPLATE

I arise today
Through a mighty strength, the invocation of the Trinity,
Through the belief in the threeness,
Through the confession of the oneness
Of the Creator of Creation.

I arise today
Through the strength of Christ's birth with his
baptism,
Through the strength of his crucifixion with his burial,
Through the strength of his resurrection with
his ascension,
Through the strength of his descent for the Judgment Day.

I arise today
Through the strength of the love of Cherubim,
In obedience of angels,
In the service of archangels,
In hope of resurrection to meet with reward,
In prayers of patriarchs,
In predictions of prophets,
In preaching of apostles,
In faith of confessors,
In innocence of holy virgins,
In deeds of righteous men.

I arise today
Through the strength of heaven:
Light of sun,
Radiance of moon,
Splendor of fire,
Speed of lightning,
Swiftness of wind,
Depth of sea,
Stability of earth,
Firmness of rock.

I arise today
Through God's strength to pilot me:
God's might to uphold me,
God's wisdom to guide me,
God's eye to look before me,
God's ear to hear me,
God's word to speak for me,
God's hand to guard me,
God's way to lie before me,
God's shield to protect me,
God's host to save me
From snares of demons,
From temptations of vices,
From everyone who shall wish me ill,
Afar and anear,
Alone and in multitude.

I summon today all these powers between me and
those evils,
Against every cruel merciless power that may oppose my body and soul,
Against incantations of false prophets,
Against black laws of pagandom,
Against false laws of heretics,
Against craft of idolatry,
Against spells of witches and smiths and wizards,
Against every knowledge that corrupts man's body and soul.

Christ to shield me today
Against poison, against burning,
Against drowning, against wounding,
So that there may come to me abundance of reward.
Christ with me,
Christ before me, Christ behind me,
Christ in me,
Christ beneath me, Christ above me,
Christ on my right, Christ on my left,
Christ when I lie down, Christ when I sit down, Christ when I arise,
Christ in the heart of every man who thinks of me,
Christ in the mouth of everyone who speaks of me,
Christ in every eye that sees me,
Christ in every ear that hears me.

I arise today
Through a mighty strength,
the invocation of the Trinity,
Through belief in the threeness,
Through confession of the oneness
Of the Creator of Creation.

HISTORY OF THE REFORMATION OF RELIGION WITHIN THE REALM OF SCOTLAND

John Knox
AD 1571

Abridged & Edited by Joshua Schwisow

AN INTRODUCTION TO THE TESTIMONY OF JOHN KNOX

Scotland was a wild country in John Knox's day. Its people were unlearned, and its clergy was both unlearned and corrupt. When Reformers arose in Scotland, calling for those who would hear the Word of God to worship God in purity and truth, resistance came from many directions. There was no such thing as a purely intellectual or spiritual debate; livelihoods, political power, and freedom were all at stake. Governments were allied with churches: France was Roman Catholic, England was Protestant. Governments inevitably rely on religion to unite a people and make them governable as one country; England and France fought over religious and cultural influence in Scotland. Scotland itself was split between the commoners, who were being awakened in greater numbers to the truth of God's Word, and some of the nobility, who still derived their influence from their relationships with the Roman Church and the Queen. The Priests', Cardinals', and Bishops' money and power came from the belief that the head of the church was in Rome. Against this, the Reformers sought to purify their land from the Catholic Church's idolatry, superstition, and corruption. However, some Reformers just wanted to get their hands on lands belonging to the Catholic Church. This is the complex world in which God used

John Knox to lead His people to see His Word with clarity, and to speak the truth to the worldly powers in the name of Jesus Christ.

The following excerpts cover seven selections from John Knox's *History of the Reformation in Scotland*, which in its entirety covers the years 1528-1564. John Knox, being one of the principal players in that Reformation, wrote about himself in the third person voice. The first two selections include Knox as a follower of the George Wishart (who became a martyr), the events surrounding Knox's calling to the ministry, and his capture and slavery in a French galley. The last four selections cover Knox's interaction with Mary, Queen of Scots, in which he spoke the Word of God to a Queen who defied it.

John Knox saw that God is the King of all, and the Word of God speaks to all areas of life. Knox feared God and only God, and so he lived boldly and sacrificially. At his funeral, the eulogy contained these poignant words, "Here lies one who neither flattered nor feared any flesh."

JOHN KNOX AS A FOLLOWER OF GEORGE WISHART

FROM THE REFORMATION IN SCOTLAND (BOOK I, CHAPTER III)

From George Wishart's arrival in Scotland in 1544 to his martyrdom in March 1546, and the retributory murder of Cardinal Beaton two months later

In the midst of all the calamities that came upon this Realm after the defection of the Governor, the Earl of Arran, from Christ Jesus, Master George Wishart came to Scotland, that Blessed Martyr of God, in the year of God 1544.[1] He was a man of such graces as before were never heard within this Realm, yes, and are rare to be found yet in any man, notwithstanding the great light of God that since his days has shined upon us. He was singularly learned, as well in all godly knowledge as in all honest human science. Also he was so clearly illuminated with the Spirit of Prophecy,[2] that he saw not only things pertaining to himself, but also such things as some towns and the whole Realm afterwards felt, which he forespoke, not in secret, but in the audience of many.

1. The original text of John Knox's *History of the Refomation in Scotland* was written between 1559 and 1571. For a complete text, see the version reprinted by the Banner of Truth Trust. This edition was first edited by Charles J. Guthrie, first published in 1898. It has been updated and modernized by Joshua Schwisow for this publication.

2. Wishart was well educated, he had godly knowledge, and he had a Gift of Prophecy. This refers to the ability to lay out an appropriate message that spoke powerfully to the present situation — apples of gold on platters of silver (Prov. 25:11).

3. George Wishart (AD 1513–1546) preached for only two years in Montrose, Ayr, Perth, Edinburgh, Leith, and Haddington before he was martyred. He was hanged and his body was burned on March 1, 1546.

4. Ayr is on the Southwest coast of Scotland (about 25 miles from Glasgow).

5. The Archbishop of Glasgow came down to Ayr to see what Wishart was doing. He barred Wishart from the church building.

6. The Archbishop's sermon was pretty worthless, as Wishart had predicted.

7. The tabernacle in the Church of Mauchline was probably a collection of idolatrous imagery.

8. Reformers would preach three-hour sermons, and modern churches get complaints if the sermons exceed 45 minutes.

The beginning of his teaching was in Montrose.[3] At Ayr,[4] Gawin Dunbar, the Archbishop of Glasgow, by instigation of Cardinal Beaton, came with his gatherings to make resistance to Master George, and did first occupy the Kirk [the church].[5] The Earl of Glencairn returned with his friends to the town with diligence, and so did various gentlemen of Kyle. When all were assembled, it was concluded that they would have the Kirk. At that, Master George utterly resisted, saying 'Let him alone! His sermon will not much hurt. Let us go to the Market Cross.' And so they did, where Master George made so notable a sermon, that the very enemies themselves were confounded. The Archbishop preached to his bodyguards and to some old bosses of the town. The sum of all his sermon was: 'They say that we should preach! Why not? Better late thrive than never thrive! Keep us still for your Bishops, and we shall provide better the next time.' This was the beginning and the end of the Archbishop's sermon, who with haste departed the town, but did not return again to fulfill his promise.[6]

Master George was asked to come to the Kirk of Mauchline, as he did.

But the Sheriff of Ayr fortified the Kirk for the preservation of a tabernacle[7] that was there, beautiful to the eye. Some zealous men of the parish, among whom was Hugh Campbell of Kinyeancleuch who was offended that they should be debarred from their Parish Kirk, sought to enter by force. But Master George took Hugh Campbell aside, and said to him: 'Brother, Christ Jesus is as potent upon the fields as in the kirk. He Himself preached more often in the desert, at the seaside, and in other places judged profane, than He did in the Temple of Jerusalem. It is the Word of Peace that God sends by me. The blood of no man shall be shed this day for the preaching of it.' So, he withdrew with the rest of the people and he came to a dike in a moor edge, upon the south-west side of Mauchline, upon which he ascended, the multitude standing and sitting about him. God gave a day that was pleasing and hot; and he continued to preach for more than three hours.[8] In that sermon God used him so mightily, that one of the wicked men in that country, Laurence Rankin, Laird (Lord) of Sheill, was converted. The tears ran from his eyes in such abundance, that all men were in awe. His conversion was without hypocrisy; for his life and conversation witnessed it in all times to come.

Portrait of George Wishart

While this faithful servant of God was occupied in Kyle, word rose that the plague of pestilence had risen in Dundee, which began within four days after Master George's preaching was suppressed; and the plague was so aggressive, that it almost passed credibility, to hear what number departed every twenty-four hours.[9] This certainty being understood, Master George left Kyle, and that with the regret of many. But no request could make him remain. His reason was, 'They are now in trouble, and they need comfort. Perhaps this Hand of God will make them magnify and reverence that Word which before, because of the fear of men, they set at a light price.'

Coming to Dundee, the joy of the Faithful was exceedingly great.[10] Master George delayed no time, but gave indication that he would preach; and, because most of the people were either sick, or else were in company with those that were sick, he chose the head of the East Port of the town for his preaching place; and the people sat or stood within, and the sick and infected within the Port. The text on which his first sermon was made was from the Hundred and Seventh Psalm: 'He sent His Word and healed them'; and with this joined these words, 'It is neither herb nor plaster, O Lord, but Your Word heals all!' In this sermon, he most comfortably implored the people concerning the dignity and utility of God's Word; the punishment that comes for contempt of the Word; the promptness of God's Mercy to such as truly turn to Him; yes, the great happiness of those whom God takes from this misery, even in His own gentle visitation, which the malice of men can neither lengthen nor impair.[11] By this sermon he so raised up the hearts of all that heard him, that they did not fear death, but judged more happy those that should depart, than those who should remain behind; considering that they

9. A severe plague came to Dundee, and a number of people died in just 24 hours.

10. Wishart returns to Dundee to minister.

11. Wishart's sermon included the authority of God's Word (central to the Reformation), warnings of punishment for those who reject God's Word, and the Mercy of God to those who turn back to Him.

*Portrait of
Cardinal Beaton*

12. The Roman Catholic Cardinal was above the Archbishop in the hierarchy. Cardinal Beaton is referred to as the Devil's own son. He hired an assassin to murder George Wishart, revealing the tremendous evil character of the Roman Church at this time.

*Modern-day
Haddington, Scotland*

13. Wishart defended the life of the man who would have killed him.

do not know if they should have such a comforter with them at all times. He visited them that day into the late hours, and comforted them as he could. And he ministered all things necessary to those that might need meat or drink; and because of this the Town was wondrously benevolent; because the poor were no more neglected than were the rich.

While he was spending his life to comfort the afflicted, the Devil ceased not to stir up his own son, Cardinal Beaton. He bribed by money a desperate Priest named Sir John Wighton, to slay Master George,[12] who did not look to himself in all things as carefully as worldly men would have done. On a day when the sermon was ended, and the people were departing, and since no man was suspecting danger, and therefore not watching out for Master George, the Priest stood waiting at the foot of the steps, his gown loose, and his drawn knife in his hand under his gown. Master George, who was most sharp of eye and judgment, noted his presence, and as he came near, he said, 'My friend, what would you do?' At that he clapped his hand upon the Priest's hand, where the knife was, and took it from him. The Priest being disconcerted, fell down at his feet, and openly confessed the truth. A noise then began to rise and it came to the ears of the sick. They cried:

'Deliver the traitor to us, or else we will take him by force'; and they forced their way in through the gate. But Master George took him in his arms and said: 'Whoever troubles him shall trouble me. He has hurt me in nothing, but he has done great comfort both to you and to me in that he has let us understand what we may fear. In times to come, we will watch better.' So he appeased the people and saved the life of him that sought his.[13]

Near the end of the Christmas season, Master George Wishart went to Haddington. The first night he stayed within the town. The second night he stayed at Lethington, the Laird of Lethington [Sir Richard Maitland, Secretary Lethington's father] was most civil, though not persuaded in religion. The day following, before Master George passed to the sermon, there came to him a boy with a letter from the West Land, which he received and read. He had been called for by John Knox, who had waited upon him carefully from the time he came to Lothian; with whom he began to enter into conversation saying, 'that he wearied of the world, for he perceived that men had begun to be weary of God.'

John Knox, wondering that he desired to keep any time before the sermon, for that was never his accustomed use before, said: 'Sir, the time of sermon approaches; I will leave you for the present time to your meditation'; and so left him. Master George paced up and down behind the High Altar for more than half an hour:[14] his weary countenance declaring the grief and disquietude of his mind. At last he entered the pulpit, but the audience was small. He was going to have implored the people of the Second Table of the Law; but instead in that sermon he spoke very little of that, but began on this manner:—

14. John Knox is with Wishart in Haddington. Wishart's last sermon in Haddington was prepared 30 minutes before it was delivered.

'O Lord, how long will it be that Your Holy Word will be despised, and men will not regard their own salvation? I have heard of you, Haddington, that you would have attended to see many vain miracles, even two or three thousand people; and now, to hear the Messenger of the Eternal God, the town or parish is not even one hundred people! Sore and fearful shall the plagues be that will ensue due to your contempt! With fire and sword you will be plagued! Yes, Haddington, strangers will possess you, and you, the present inhabitants, will either in bondage serve your enemies, or else you will be chased from your homes; and this will take place because you have not known, nor will not know, the time of God's merciful visitation.'[15]

In such vehemency and threatening continued that servant of God for almost an hour and a half, in which he declared all the plagues that ensued, as plainly as after our eyes saw them performed. In the end he said: 'I have forgotten myself and the matter that I should have implored; but let these my last words that concern public preaching remain in

15. A prophetic statement concerning God's judgment over the city of Haddington.

16. The 90 minute sermon included prophetic words that were fulfilled, including "all the plagues" mentioned. Important applications from the sermon included the fear of God and works of mercy, critical for all true believers.

your minds until God send you new comfort.' After saying this, he made a short paraphrase upon the second table of the Law, with an exhortation to patience, to the fear of God, and to the works of mercy;[16] and then ended the sermon, as if he was making his last testament. The message declared that the Spirit of Truth and of True Judgment were both in his heart and mouth; for that same night he was apprehended, before midnight, in the House of Ormiston, by the Earl Bothwell, who was hired by Cardinal Beaton in exchange for money.

The manner of Master George Wishart's imprisonment was this: —Departing from Haddington, he said good night, as if it was his last to all his acquaintances, especially from Hugh Douglas of Longniddry. John Knox desired to go with him, Master George said: 'No, return to your pupils, and God bless you. One is sufficient for a sacrifice.' He then ordered a two-handed sword, which commonly was carried with him, to be taken from John Knox who obeyed, albeit unwillingly, and returned with Hugh Douglas.[17] Master George accompanied the Laird of Ormiston, John Sandilands of Calder, younger, the Laird of Brunestane, and others, with their servants and passed on foot—for it was a vehement frost—to Ormiston. After supper, he spoke comfortably of the death of God's chosen children, and cheerfully said, 'I think that I desire earnestly to sleep'; and 'Will we sing a Psalm?' So he appointed the fifty-first Psalm, which began thus in Scottish meter:— 'Have mercy on me now, good Lord, After Your great mercy, My sinful life does bring me remorse, Which sin has greatly grieved You.'[18] This being ended he passed to his chamber, and, sooner than his normal practice, went to bed with these words, 'God grant quiet rest.'

17. Wishart seemed to be strongly aware of his imminent death as he encouraged John Knox to leave him. "One is sufficient for a sacrifice" — famous words.

18. They sang a psalm before they went to bed. Psalm-singing was always basic to the Scottish church.

Before midnight, the place was surrounded so that none could escape to make it known. At the first word, Master George said, 'Open the gates. The Blessed Will of my God be done!' The Earl of Bothwell called for the Landowner, and said: 'It was but vain to make him hold his house; for the Governor and the Cardinal with all their power were coming'—

indeed, the Cardinal was at Elphinstone Tower, not even a mile away—'but if he would deliver the man to him, he would promise upon his honor, that by the power of the Cardinal, he would not do him any harm or damage.' At this promise, made in the presence of God, and hands struck by both the parties for observation of the promise, Master George was delivered to the hands of the Earl Bothwell.[19] He was carried first to Edinburgh, and after that brought back for the sake of appearance to the house of Hailes again, which was the principal place that then the Earl of Bothwell had in Lothian. But, as gold and women have corrupted all worldly and fleshly men from the beginning, so the Earl was also corrupted. He made some resistance at first, by reason of his promise. But an effeminate man cannot long withstand the assaults of a gracious Queen; and so was the servant of God transported to Edinburgh Castle, and afterwards to the Sea-Tower of St. Andrews.[20]

In the meantime at Ormiston the Lairds of Calder, Brunestane, and Ormiston kept a good countenance, and implored the gentlemen to drink, and to prepare their horses until they might be ready to ride with them. Brunestane then went, first secretly, then by speed of foot, to Ormiston Wood, and then to Drundallon, and so escaped. The other two were put into the Castle of Edinburgh, where Calder remained until his bond of support to the Cardinal was the means of his deliverance. Ormiston freed himself by leaping the wall of the Castle, between ten hours and eleven before noon; and so breaking free, he escaped prison, which he had unjustly suffered.[21]

If we interlace merriness with serious matters, pardon us, good Reader, for this fact is so notable that it deserves retelling:— The Cardinal Beaton was known to be proud; and Gawin Dunbar, Archbishop of Glasgow, was known to be a glorious fool. Yet, because he had been the King's Master Tutor, he was Chancellor of Scotland. The Cardinal being in the town of Glasgow, and the Archbishop in the Castle, questions

19. The Earl of Bothwell arrested George Wishart with the promise that nobody would harm the man. Of course, they would break their promises.

20. Money and sex (gold and women) corrupt rich men like the Earl of Bothwell. The man had no character, even called "effeminate" by John Knox in this account. So, Wishart was taken to Edinburgh.

21. The three lords that supported George Wishart go away from the arresting troop. Calder compromised his faith by agreeing with the Cardinal. The other two (Lords of Ormiston and Brunestane) managed to escape the party.

arose about bearing their crosses. The Cardinal alleged, by reason of his Cardinalship, and because he was Legatus Natus, and Primate within Scotland in the Kingdom of the Antichrist, that he should have the pre-eminence, and that his cross should not only go before, but also that it only should be carried wherever he was. The Archbishop lacked no reasons for maintaining his glory. 'He was an Archbishop in his own diocese, and in his own Cathedral seat and church, and therefore he ought not give place to any other man. The power of the Cardinal was derived from Rome, and pertained but to his own person and not to his bishopric; for it might be that his successor should not be Cardinal. But his dignity was connected with his office, and pertained to all that ever should be Archbishops of Glasgow.' So that the Doctors of Divinity of both the Prelates might resolve these doubts, the decision was made as you shall hear. Coming forth or going in—all is one—at the Choir Door of Glasgow Kirk, there begins striving for position between the two cross-bearers. From glooming, they come to shouldering; from shouldering, they go to buffets, and from dry blows to fists and fistcuffing. Then, for charity's sake, they cry, Dispersit, dedit pauperibus, and discuss which of the crosses was finest metal, which staff was the strongest, and which cross-bearer could best defend his master's pre-eminence; and that there should be no superiority in that behalf, to the ground go both of the crosses. Then there began no little brawl, but yet a merry game. Vestments were rent; tippets were torn, crowns were broken, and long gowns might have been seen wantonly thrown from the one wall to the other. Many of them lacked beards. That was the more pity; therefore they could not buckle each other by the beard as bold men would have done. But woe on the bodyguards that did not their duty! Had the one part of them countered the other, then all had gone right. But the Sanctuary, we suppose, saved the lives of many. How merrily so ever this be written, it was bitter jesting to the Cardinal and his Court. It was more than irregularity. Yes, it might well have been judged treason to the

Woodcut depicting the martyrdom of George Wishart

Son of Perdition, the Pope's own person; and yet the other, in his folly as proud as a peacock, would let the Cardinal know that he was a Bishop when the other was but Beaton, before he got the Abbey of Aberbrothock [Arbroath].[22]

This enmity was judged deadly, and without hope of reconciliation. But the blood of the innocent servant of God, Master George Wishart, buried in oblivion the whole feud; for the Archbishop of Glasgow was the first to whom the Cardinal wrote, telling what was done, and earnestly craving that he would assist with his presence and counsel how such an enemy to their Estate might be suppressed. At that the other was not slow, but kept the appointed time, sat next to the Cardinal, voted and subscribed first in the rank, and lay over the East Blockhouse [tower] with the Cardinal till the Martyr of God was consumed by fire.[23]

This we must note, that as all these beasts consented in heart to the slaughter of that innocent, so did they approve it with their presence, having the whole artillery of the Castle of St. Andrews bent towards the place of execution,[24] which was near the Castle, ready to shoot if any would have made defense or rescue of God's Servant.

The Bishops, with their accomplices, condemned this innocent man to be burnt as a heretic, thinking truly, that they should give a good sacrifice to God, conformable to the saying of Jesus Christ in the Gospel of St. John, Chapter 16: 'They shall excommunicate you; yes, and the time shall come, that he which kills you shall think that he has done a good service to God.'

The prayer of Master George Wishart: 'O Immortal God! How long will You allow the great cruelty of the ungodly to exercise their fury upon Your servants, which do extend Your Word in this world? . . . O Lord, we know surely that Your true servants must suffer for Your name's sake, persecution, affliction, and troubles in this present life, which is but a shadow, as You have shown unto us by Your Prophets and Apostles.[25] Yet we desire You, Merciful Father, that You would

22. John Knox gives a tongue-in-cheek rendition of the squabble between the Cardinal and the Archbishop over who gets to carry the cross into the towns. Apparently, the two men actually engaged in a knock-down, drag-out fight over the ridiculous matter.

23. The Devil had his way with the corrupt church in Scotland at this time, with both the Archbishop and the Cardinal consenting to Wishart's hanging and burning.

24. The wicked usually gain unity in their opposition to God's true saints. This they did by joining forces against George Wishart.

25. Jesus' statement in John 16 has truly come to pass at various times in Church history. Most of the martyrdoms in the 12th century onwards came about by religious men who thought they were doing God a favor. This illustrates the very dark and deep deception of the Devil.

26. One of Wishart's last prayers is for the church, specifically that God's people would hear the Word preached.

conserve, defend, and help Your congregation, which You have chosen before the beginning of the world, and give them Your grace to hear Your Word, and to be Your true servants in this present life.'[26]

At this, they caused the common people to be removed, whose desire was always to hear that innocent man speak. The Sons of Darkness then pronounced their definitive sentence, not having respect for the judgment of God. When all was done and said, my Lord Cardinal caused his tormentors to pass again with the meek lamb into the Castle, until such time as fire was made ready. When he had come into the Castle, there came Friar Scott and his mate, saying: 'Sir, you must make your confession unto us.' He answered: 'I will make no confession unto you. Go fetch me the man that preached this day, and I will make my confession unto him.' Then they sent for the Sub-Prior of the Abbey, Dean John Winram, but what he said in this confession I cannot show.[27]

27. Wishart made a final confession of his sin before a sub-prior (a rather lowly position in the church). God's people always humbly confess their sins, right to the end of their lives.

When the fire was made ready, and the gallows, at the west part of the Castle of St. Andrews near the Priory [a religious house governed by a prior], my Lord Cardinal, fearing that Master George should have been taken away by his friends, commanded to direct all of the artillery of the Castle right against the place of execution, and commanded all his gunners to stand beside their guns, until such time as he was burned. They bound Master George's hands behind his back, and led him forth with their soldiers from the Castle, to the place of their cruel and wicked execution.

As he came forth through the Castle Gate, there were certain beggars who met him, asking of him alms for God's sake. To whom he answered: 'My hands are bound and thus I cannot give you alms. But the merciful Lord, of His kindness and abundant grace, that feeds all men, promises to give you all that is necessary, both unto your bodies and souls.' Then afterward he met two false fiends—I should say Friars—saying: 'Master George, pray to Our Lady, that she may be a mediator for you to her Son.' To whom he answered meekly: 'Cease!

Do not tempt me, my brothers.' After this, he was led to the fire, with a rope about his neck, and a chain of iron around the middle of his body.

When he came to the fire, he sat down upon his knees, and rose up again; and three times said these words: 'O, Savior of the World, have mercy upon me! Father of Heaven, I commend my spirit into Your holy hands.'[28] Then he turned to the people and said: 'I implore you Christian Brothers and Sisters, do not be offended at the Word of God, for the affliction and torments which you see prepared for me. But I exhort you, love the Word of God and suffer patiently, and with a comfortable heart, for the Word's sake, which is your undoubted salvation and everlasting comfort. Moreover, I urge you, tell my brothers and sisters, which have heard me often, that they should not cease to learn the Word of God because of persecutions in the world, which I taught unto them, because these persecutions do not last. Show them that my doctrine was no wives' fables, after the constitutions made by men. If I had taught men's doctrine, I would have gotten greater thanks by men. But for the true Gospel, which was given to me by the Grace of God, I suffer this day by men, not sorrowfully, but with a glad heart and mind.[29] For this cause I was sent, that I should suffer this fire for Christ's sake. Consider and behold my countenance. You shall not see me change my color! This grim fire I do not fear: and so I pray you to do, if any persecution come unto you for the Word's sake; do not fear those that slay the body, and afterward have no power to slay the soul. Some have said I taught that the soul of man should sleep until the Last Day; but I know surely that my soul shall dine with my Savior this night, before it be six hours, for whom I suffer this.'[30]

Then he prayed for them which accused him, saying: 'I implore You, Father of Heaven, forgive them that have any ignorance, or else of any evil mind, have forged lies concerning me. I forgive them with all my heart. I implore Christ to forgive them that have condemned me to death this day

28. Wishart kneels and prays for mercy three times before his death.

29. Wishart's message to the people is to revere the Word of God, receive the Word of God, and be willing to suffer for the Word of God.

30. Wishart also rejects the "soul sleep" doctrine. He truly believes, with the Apostle Paul, "to be absent from the body is to be present with the Lord."

31. His last prayer is a prayer of forgiveness. He forgives his persecutors, and he asks God to forgive his persecutors (as Jesus did on the cross). He desires the pastors and bishops would learn the Word of God and would repent of their sins (or they will face the judgment of God).

32. His last words were to forgive the man who executed him, and he kissed the man (in a remarkable act of compassion and mercy).

33. A synod of priests and bishops is held, and Knox refers to them as "Baal's shaven sort." The priests would shave their heads and their beards, and Knox saw them as priests of Baal.

34. The powerful Earl of Angus didn't like the Cardinal, but he didn't like the Reformers either. He was friends with Catholic France, and he felt he had the Queen in his grasp. He was a proud and powerful man.

ignorantly.'[31] Last of all, he said to the people on this manner: 'I implore you, Brothers and Sisters, to exhort your Prelates to the learning of the Word of God, that they may be ashamed to do evil, and learn to do good. If they will not convert themselves from their wicked errors, there shall hastily come upon them the Wrath of God, which they shall not avoid.'

He said many faithful words during this time, taking no heed of the cruel torments prepared for him. Last of all, the hangman, his tormentor, upon his knees, said: 'Sir, I pray you, forgive me, for I am not guilty of your death.'.

To whom he answered: 'Come near to me.' When he had come to him, he kissed his cheek, and said: 'Behold! here is a token that I forgive you. Do your office!'[32] Then, the trumpet sounded and he was put upon the gallows and hanged, and there burnt to powder. When the people saw the great tormenting of that innocent man, they did not withhold from compassionate mourning and complaining of the innocent lamb's slaughter.

After the death of this Blessed Martyr of God, the people began to speak plainly, to damn and detest the cruelty that was used. Yes, men of great birth, estimation, and honor, at open tables, declared that the blood of Master George should be revenged, or else it should cost a life.

After Easter, the Cardinal came to Edinburgh, to hold the Synod, as the Papists term their unhappy assembly of Baal's shaven sort.[33] It was rumored that something was planned against the Cardinal by the Earl of Angus, whom he mortally hated, and whose destruction he sought. But it failed; and he only rejoiced and said: 'Eat and be glad, my soul, for you have great riches laid up in store for many days!' Also he said: 'Tush! A fig for the feud, and a button for the bragging of all heretics in Scotland! Is not my Lord Governor mine? Witness his eldest son in pledge at my table! Have I not the Queen at my own devotion? Is not France my friend, and I a friend to France? What danger should I fear?'[34]

Thus, in vanity, the carnal Cardinal delighted himself a little before his death. He had devised to cut off those who were planning against him. He was slain upon the Saturday, and he had appointed the whole Gentlemen of Fife to meet him at Falkland the Monday after. His treasonable purpose was this:—that Norman Leslie, Sheriff of Fife and heir-apparent to his father, the Earl of Rothes, John Leslie, father's brother to Norman Leslie, the Lairds of Grange, elder and younger, Sir James Learmonth of Dairsie, Provost of St. Andrews, and the faithful Laird of Raith, should either have been slain, or else taken, and after used at his pleasure.[35]

Many purposes were devised as to how that wicked man might have been taken away. But all failed till Friday the 28th May 1546, when the Norman already spoken of came at night to St. Andrews. William Kirkcaldy of Grange, younger, arrived in the town first. Last came John Leslie, who was the most suspected.

Early on the Saturday morning they were in various companies in the Abbey Kirkyard not very far from the Castle.

The Cardinal, wakened with the shouts, asked from his window, 'What is this noise?' It was answered that Norman Leslie had taken his Castle. When he understood, he ran to the back gate; but, perceiving the passage to be occupied, he returned quickly to his chamber, took his two-handed sword, and made his chamber-child cast chests and other impediments against the door. In the meantime came John Leslie unto it and bid open.

The Cardinal. 'Who calls?'

Leslie. 'My name is Leslie.'

The Cardinal. 'Is that Norman?'

Leslie. 'No, my name is John.'

The Cardinal. 'I will see Norman. He is my friend.'

Leslie. 'Content yourself with those who are here. You shall not get any others.'

There was also with John, James Melvin, a man familiarly acquainted with Master George Wishart, and Peter Carmi-

35. There were many dangerous political conflicts in the work. The Cardinal was hoping to arrest or kill some of the powerful lords in the land, and they were hoping to kill him.

chael, a stout Gentleman. In the meantime, while they forced the door, the Cardinal hid a box of gold under coals that were laid in a secret corner. He then asked, 'Will you save my life?'

Leslie. 'It may be that we will.'

The Cardinal. 'No. Swear to me by God's Wounds, and I shall open the door.'

Leslie. 'That which you said is unsaid. Fire! Fire!'

The door was very stiff; and so they brought a grate full of burning coals. When this was perceived, the Cardinal or his chamber-child—it is uncertain who—opened the door; and the Cardinal sat down in a chair, and cried: 'I am a priest! I am a priest! You will not slay me!' John Leslie, according to his former vows, struck him first once or twice, and so did Peter. But James Melvin, a man by nature most gentle and most modest, perceiving them both in anger, took them aside and said: 'This judgment of God, although it be secret, ought to be done with greater gravity.' He presented unto him the point of the sword and said: 'Repent of your former wicked life, especially of the shedding of the blood of that notable instrument of God, Master George Wishart, which, although the flame of fire consumed him before men, yet it cries vengeance upon you;[36] and we are sent from God to revenge it. Here, before my God, I protest that neither the hatred of your person, nor the love of your riches, nor the fear of any trouble that you could have done to me in particular, moved or moves me to strike you, but only because you have been and remain an obstinate enemy to Christ Jesus and His Holy Gospel.'[37]

So Melvin struck the Cardinal twice or three times through with a stabbing sword; and he fell, with no word heard out of his mouth, except 'I am a priest! I am a priest![38] All is gone.'

36. These magistrates (Lords) saw the Cardinal as a murderer who needed to be held to account for his driving the arrest and murder of Wishart. In the end, Melvin called the Cardinal an "enemy to Christ Jesus and His holy Gospel."

37. James Melvin offered an opportunity for the Cardinal to repent, especially of the arrest and the shedding of innocent blood (of the martyr, George Wishart).

38. The civil war was on. And . . . it was the Lords of Grange and a man named James Melvin that eventually killed the Cardinal. These were "lower magistrates" who saw themselves as qualified to address the lawless tyranny imposed by the higher magistrates. The doctrine of interposition had worked strongly in the Western world since the time of the Magna Carta (when the lords threw off the tyranny of King John in AD 1300).

JOHN KNOX'S CALLING TO MINISTRY

FROM THE REFORMATION IN SCOTLAND (BOOK I, CHAPTER IV)

From the entry of John Knox into the Castle of St. Andrews on 10th of April 1547, to his liberation from the French Galleys in 1550

Woodcut portrait of John Knox

At Easter, 1547, John Knox came to the castle of St. Andrews, who, being wearied from going place to place, due to the persecution that came upon him by the Archbishop of St. Andrews [Cardinal Beaton's successor, John Hamilton], Knox was determined to leave Scotland, and to visit the Schools of Germany. He had no pleasure in England, because, though the Pope's name was suppressed, yet his laws and corruptions remained in full force.[1] But he had the care of some Gentlemen's children, who in certain years past he had nourished in godliness; and their fathers requested him to go to St. Andrews, that he himself might have the benefit of the Castle, and their children the benefit of his doctrine. So he came to St. Andrews, having in his company Francis Douglas of Longniddry, George his brother, and Alexander Cockburn, eldest son to the Laird of Ormiston, and he began to teach them as was his normal custom. Besides the Grammar, and other authors, he read to them a Catechism,

1. John Knox was persecuted out of Scotland and fled to Germany for a while. The Reformation in England was too weak. England had rejected the Pope but had more or less retained the same church system.

2. John Knox begins his ministry as a discipler for young men. He taught them the Catechism and the Gospel of John (as his curriculum).

3. The chaplain of the garrison at St. Andrews, a man named John Rough, was insistent on calling John Knox to the preaching ministry. St. Andrews is in Fife, Scotland. It was the ecclesiastical center of Scotland for many centuries, and the place where Cardinal Beaton was killed. St. Andrews became the location of the first Protestant church in Scotland.

*Ruins of
St. Andrews Castle*

which he caused them to recite publicly in the Parish Kirk of St. Andrews. He also read to them the Gospel of John,[2] proceeding where he had left off at his departing from Longniddry, where his residence was before; and that lecture he read in the Chapel, within the Castle, at a certain hour. Those who lived there, especially Master Henry Balnaves and John Rough the preacher, perceiving the manner of his doctrine, began earnestly to request that he would take the work of preaching in that Kirk upon himself.[3] But he utterly refused, alleging that 'He would not run where God has not called him': meaning that he would do nothing without a lawful vocation [calling].

After Knox had said this, they discussed amongst themselves in council with Sir David Lyndsay of the Mount and they concluded they would give a call to John Knox, and that they would do so publicly by the mouth of their preacher. So upon a certain day, John Rough preached a sermon of the Election of Ministers speaking of what power the congregation had over any man in whom they saw the gifts of God, and how dangerous it was to refuse the voice of those who desire to be instructed. These and other topics having been declared, John Rough, the preacher, directed his words to John Knox, saying: 'Brother, you shall not be offended, albeit that I speak to you that which I have in charge, even from all those here present:—In the name of God, and of His Son Jesus Christ, and in the name of these that presently call you by my mouth, I charge you, that you refuse not this holy vocation, but, as you seek the Glory of God, the increase of Christ and His Kingdom, the edification of your brothers, and the comfort of me, oppressed by many labors, that you take upon yourself the public office of preaching, even as you look to avoid God's heavy displeasure, and desire that He shall multiply His graces upon you.' In the end, he said to those present: 'Was not this your charge to me? Do you not approve this vocation?' They answered, 'It was; and we approve it.'

At this, John Knox was humbled and burst forth in most abundant tears, and went to his chamber. His countenance and behavior, from that day until the day he was compelled to present himself to the public work of preaching, did sufficiently declare the grief and trouble of his heart; for no man saw any sign of cheerfulness in him, nor did he have the pleasure to accompany any man for many days.

What impelled him to enter into the public work of preaching, besides the vocation, was:—Dean John Annan, Principal of St. Leonard's College, a rotten Papist, had long troubled John Rough in his preaching.[4] John Knox had fortified the doctrine of the preacher by his pen, and had broken down all the defenses of Dean John and compelled him to flee to his last refuge, that is, to the Authority of the Church. 'That authority,' said he, 'damns all Lutherans and heretics. Therefore we do not need to dispute any further.' John Knox answered: 'Before we defend ourselves or you can sufficiently convict us, we must define the Church, as it is taught to us in God's Scriptures. We must discern the Immaculate Spouse of Jesus Christ from the Mother of Confusion, Spiritual Babylon, lest we embrace with imprudence a harlot instead of the chaste spouse,—yes, to speak in plain words, lest we submit ourselves to Satan,[5] thinking that we submit ourselves to Jesus Christ. As for your Roman Kirk, it is now corrupted along with its authority and this is where your hope of victory stands. I no longer doubt that it is the synagogue of Satan, and the head of that church, called the Pope, is that Man of Sin of whom the Apostle speaks. Just as Jesus Christ suffered by the procurement of the visible Church of Jerusalem. Yes, I offer myself, by word or writing, to prove the Roman Church of today further degenerate from the purity which was in the days of the Apostles, than was the Church of the Jews from the ordinance given by Moses, when they consented to the innocent death of Jesus Christ.'[6]

John Knox spoke these words in open audience, in the Parish Church of St. Andrews, after Dean John Annan had spoken what pleased him, and had refused to dispute. The people, hearing the offer, cried with one consent: 'We cannot

4. Knox was first motivated to enter the pulpit to counter Dean John Annan, at St. Leonard's College.

5. The early Reformers used harsh language to describe the Roman Church — a harlot and a synagogue of Satan. The church was in worse condition than the Jews who put the Lord Jesus Christ to death.

6. Knox disagreed with Annan on the definition of the Church, holding the definition of the Church to the Scriptures. Annan held John Knox to be wrong according to the tradition and teaching of the church (not the Scriptures).

all read your writings, but we may all hear your preaching. Therefore we urge you in the Name of God that you will let us hear the probation of that which he has affirmed. If it is true, we have been miserably deceived.'

The next Sunday was appointed for John Knox, to express his mind in the public preaching place. With the day approaching, he took the text written in Daniel, the Seventh Chapter, 24th and 25th verses, beginning thus: 'Another king shall rise after them, and he shall be unlike the first, and he shall subdue three kings, and shall speak words against the Most High, and shall consume the Saints of the Most High, and think that he may change times and laws, and they shall be given into his hands, until a time, and times, and dividing of times.'

He then began to describe the lives of various Popes, and the lives of all the shavelings. He plainly proved that their doctrine and laws were directly opposed to the doctrine and laws of God the Father, and of Christ Jesus His Son.[7] This he proved by comparing the doctrine of Justification expressed in the Scriptures—which teaches that 'man is justified by faith only,' and that 'the blood of Jesus Christ cleanses us from all our sins'—and the doctrine of the Papists, which attributes justification to the works of the Law, yes, to the works of man's intervention, as Pilgrimages, Pardons, and other such baggage.[8]

At the end he said: 'If any here say'—and there were present for the University, Master John Major, Dean of the Faculty of Theology, the Sub-Prior, John Winram, and many Canons, with some Friars of both orders— 'that I have taught that Scripture, Doctor, or History, is different than it is written, let them come to me with sufficient witnesses; and, by conference, I shall let them see, not only the original where my testimonies are written, but I shall prove that the writers meant as I have spoken.'

Of this sermon, which was the first that John Knox ever spoke in public, there were various rumors. Some said: 'Lop off the branches of the Papistry, but he strikes at the root also, to

7. Knox's first sermon addressed both the doctrine and the laws (the teaching and the practices) of the Roman Church as all anti-Scriptural.

8. Knox taught the doctrine of Justification by Faith alone, against the Roman Catholic doctrine of justification by the works of the Law. Roman Catholic doctrine teaches that pilgrimages, pardons, etc. are needed for forgiveness and a right standing with God.

destroy the whole.' Others said: 'If the Doctors and Esteemed Teachers do not defend the Pope and his authority, which in their own presence is so manifestly challenged, the Devil have my part of him, and of his laws also!' Others said: 'Master George Wishart never spoke so plainly; and yet he was burnt. Even so will John Knox be as well.' In the end, others said: 'The tyranny of the Cardinal did not make his cause any better, though neither did the suffering of God's servant make his cause worse. Therefore we would counsel you and them, to provide better defenses than fire and sword; for otherwise you may be disappointed. Men now have other eyes than they had then.'[9] James Forsyth gave this answer, the Laird of Nydie, a man fervent and upright in religion.

The bastard Bishop, who was not yet execrated—consecrated, they call it—wrote to the Sub-Prior of St. Andrews, who, sede vacante, was Vicar-General, that 'he was amazed that he allowed such heretical and schismatic doctrine to be taught, and that he did not oppose the teaching of this doctrine.'[10] At this rebuke there was a convention of Grey and Black Friars appointed, with the Sub-Prior, Dean John Winram, in St. Leonards' Yards, and they first called John Rough, and they read certain Articles to him; and after that John Knox was called for. The cause of their convention, and why they were called, was expanded and the Articles were read, which were these:—

I. 'No mortal man can be the Head of the Church.'

II. 'The Pope is an Antichrist; and so is no member of Christ's mystical body.'

III. 'Man may neither make nor devise a religion that is acceptable to God: but man is bound to observe and keep the religion that from God is received, without chopping or changing thereof.'

IV. 'The Sacraments of the New Testament ought to be ministered as they were instituted by Christ Jesus, and practiced by His Apostles. Nothing ought to be added unto them; nothing ought to be diminished from them.'

9. Some thought John Knox went too far in his teachings. Some thought Knox would be burned at the stake. But most concluded that it wasn't worth persecuting John Knox because persecution would only strengthen the cause of the Reformation.

10. A bastard bishop speaks to an illegitimate bishop that has no right to pastor the church. This "Vicar General" called for somebody to rein Knox in.

V. 'The Mass is abominable idolatry, blasphemous to the Death of Christ, and a profanation of the Lord's Supper.'

VI. 'There is no Purgatory, in which the souls of men can either be pained or purged after this life. Heaven resteth to the faithful, and hell to the reprobate and unthankful.'

VII. 'Praying for the dead is vain, and to the dead is idolatry.'

VIII. 'There are no Bishops, except they preach by themselves, without any substitute.'

IX. 'By God's law, the teinds [tithes] do not appertain of necessity to the Churchman.'

The Sub-Prior. 'The strangeness of these Articles, which are summaries of your doctrine, has moved us to call for you to hear your own answers.'

John Knox. 'I, for my part, praise my God that I see so honorable and apparently so modest and quiet a hearing. It is long since I have heard that you [Winram] are not ignorant of the Truth. Therefore I must implore you in the name of God, and I appeal to your conscience before that Supreme Judge, that if you think any Article there expressed is contrary to the Truth of God, that you oppose yourself plainly to it, and that you do not allow the people to be deceived by it. But, if in your conscience you know the doctrine to be true, then I urge your support for it; that by your authority the people may be moved to believe the Truth, since many doubt because of our youth.'[11]

For Purgatory, Alexander Arbuckle, a Grey Friar, had no better proof but the authority of Virgil in his Sixth book of Aeneid;[12] and the pains of it to him was an evil wife![13] John Knox answered this and many other things as he himself witnessed in a Treatise that he wrote in the Galleys, containing the sum of his doctrine and the confession of his faith, and sent to his familiars in Scotland.

After this, the Friars did not have any heart for further disputation. They invented another shift, which seemed to proceed from godliness. It was this. Every learned man in the Abbey, and in the University, should preach in the Parish Kirk.

11. These articles are probably fair representations of what John Knox was teaching. John Knox did not argue with them but rather urged support for them (among the leaders).

12. This Roman Catholic friar tried to argue from the words of a pagan historian to bolster the doctrine of purgatory. Virgil was a Roman poet who wrote Roman history in poetry. Virgil is the guide for Dante through hell and purgatory in *The Divine Comedy*.

13. This friar likened the pains of purgatory to being married to a bad wife.

The Sub-Prior began, followed by the Official called Master John Spittal, Rector of the University—sermons penned to offend no man!—followed by all the rest in their ranks.[14] So John Knox smelled out their plot, and in his sermons which he preached on the week-days, he prayed to God that they should be as busy in preaching when there should be more need of it than there was at that time. 'Although,' said he, 'I praise God that Christ Jesus is preached, and that nothing is said publicly against the doctrine that you have heard. If in my absence they should speak anything which in my presence they do not, I urge that you suspend your judgment until it pleases God for you to hear me again.'

God so assisted His weak soldier and so blessed his labors, that not only all those of the Castle, but also a great number of the town of St. Andrews, openly professed, by participation of the Lord's Table in the same purity that now it is ministered in the churches of Scotland, that same doctrine that he had taught unto them.

Among these people was he that now either rules or else misrules Scotland: Sir James Balfour, sometimes called Master James of Pittendriech, son of Balfour of Mountquhanie, the chief and principal Protestant that was then to be found in this Realm. We write this because we have heard that Master James alleges that he was never part of our religion, but that he was brought up in Martin Luther's opinion of the Sacrament, and therefore he cannot share in the Lord's Supper with us! But his own conscience, and two hundred witnesses besides, knows that he lies;[15] and that he was one of the men that would have given his life, if men might credit his words, for defense of the doctrine that John Knox taught. But, it is no great wonder that those that never were of us—as Mountquhanie's sons have shown themselves to be—depart from us. It is proper and natural that the children follow the father! Let the godly beware of that race and their offspring; for if there is either fear of God or love of virtue in them more than the

14. The friars decided not to prosecute John Knox but to provide a variety of preachers at the Parish church. Preaching occurred on a daily basis. This is unusual today but not so much during times of reformation.

15. James Balfour pretended to be a Protestant for a while but turned out to be a reprobate (or a false brother in the church).

present advantage persuades them, men of judgment are deceived; but to return to our History.

The Priests and Bishops, enraged at these proceedings in St. Andrews, ran now to the Governor, to the Queen, and to the whole Council, and there were may complaints and cries that were heard, 'What are we doing? Shall you suffer this whole Realm to be infected with pernicious doctrine? The Queen and the Seigneur D'Oysel [the French Ambassador] comforted them, and willed them to be quiet and promised that they should see a remedy before it was too late. And this was proven indeed; because on the next to last day of June, one-hundred and twenty French galleys appeared in the sight of the Castle of St. Andrews. They appeared with a well-provided army, the likes which had never been seen in that Firth before.[16]

This treasonable means had been set up the Governor, the Archbishop of St. Andrews, the Queen, and Monsieur D'Oysel, under their Appointment.[17]

But, to excuse their treason, eight days before, they had presented an Absolution, as sent from Rome, containing, after the aggravation of the crime, this clause, Remittimus Irremissibile, that is, 'We remit the crime that cannot be remitted.' This was considered by the most of the company that was in the Castle when the Castle of St. Andrews was required to be delivered; and an answer was given, 'That the Governor and Council of the Realm had promised to them a sufficient and assured absolution did not appear to be the case. Therefore they could not deliver the House, neither, they thought, that any reasonable man would require them to do so, considering that the promise was not kept to them.'

The next day, after the galleys arrived, they summoned the Castle of St. Andrews, but they were denied. Because they knew that they were not magistrates in Scotland, they prepared for a siege. First, they began to assault by sea, and shot for two days. In this they did not gain either advantage or honor; for they broke down the slates of houses, but neither

16. The Queen, the Archbishop of St. Andrews, and others called on the French to bomb the castle (where John Knox preached). This would have been seen as a treasonous act by any nation. The Queen had attempted a siege on the fortress in October of 1546 and then called on the aid of French warships (which occurred in July of 1547).

17. The lords who had supported the taking of St. Andrews included: Norman Leslie (Master of Rothes), James Kirkcaldy of Grange, Master Henry Balnaves, and Captain John Borthwick killed man, nor did harm to any wall. And this is the way that the Castle handled them, that Sancta Barbara, the gunners' goddess, did not help them at all; for they lost many of their rowers, chained in the galleys, and some soldiers, both by sea and land. Furthermore, a galley that approached closer than the rest, was so damaged by cannons and other artillery, that she would have drowned, were it not that the rest given to her in time by drawing her first to the West Sands, beyond the shot of the Castle, and then to Dundee, where they remained until the Governor came to them, with the rest of the French faction.

The siege by land was confirmed the nineteenth day of July. The trenches were cast; and artillery was planted on the Abbey Kirk, and on St. Salvator's College, which so harmed the Castle, that they could not they keep their Block-houses, the Sea-Tower, nor the West Wall; as men were slain in all these places by great artillery. Yes, they mounted the artillery high upon the Abbey Kirk, that they might discover the ground of the Court of the Castle in various places. Moreover, within the Castle was the pestilence, and various people within died, which frightened some within more than the external force. John Knox was of another judgment, for he always said, 'That their corrupt life could not escape the punishment of God';[18] and that was his continual declaration, from the time that he was called to preach. When they triumphed—the first twenty days they had many prosperous chances—he lamented, and always said, 'They did not see what he saw.' When they bragged of the force and thickness of their walls, he said, 'They will be but egg-shells.' When they boasted, 'England will rescue us,' he said, 'You will not see them; but you will be delivered into your enemy's hands, and will be carried to a strange country.'

On the next to last day of July, at night, the artillery was planted for the battery; fourteen cannons, and four were Cannons Royal, called Double Cannons, besides other pieces. The battery began at four in the morning; and before ten hours

18. John Knox was dismayed by the corrupt life lived by the Scots at St. Andrews and had warned them of God's judgment from the time he started preaching there.

of the day had passed, the whole south quarter, between the Fore Tower and the East Block-house, was made assailable. The lower passage was condemned, with various slain in it, and the East Block-house was shut off from the rest of the place, between ten and eleven hours. A shower of rain fell, that continued for nearly an hour and such great amounts of rain was not often seen. It was so vehement that no man was able to abide within the house; and the cannons were left alone. Some within the Castle were of the judgment that the men should have gone out, and put all in the hands of God. But because William Kirkcaldy was communing with Leo Strozzi, the Prior of Capua [the French Admiral], who had the Commission of that journey from the King of France, nothing was arranged; and so the terms were made, and the Castle was surrendered on Saturday, the last of July [1547].

The headings of the Appointment were: 'That the lives of all within the Castle should be saved, both English and Scottish; that they should be safely transported to France; and in case, on the conditions to be offered them by the King of France, if they could not be content to remain in service and freedom there, they would be safely transported at the expense of the King of France, to whatever country they would require, other than Scotland.' They would have nothing to do with the Governor, nor with any Scotsman; for they had all betrayed them as traitors. 'Which,' said the Laird of Grange—a man simple and of most stout courage—'I am assured God will revenge, before too long.'

The galleys, being well furnished with the spoil of the Castle, after a certain amount of days, returned to France.[19] Escaping a great danger—for they all struck upon the back of the sands—they arrived first at Fécamp, and then passed up the Water of Sequane [Seine], and lay before Rouen; where the principal gentlemen, who looked for freedom, were dispersed and put in various prisons. The rest were left in the galleys and were miserably treated there. These things were done at Rouen despite the promises made; but Princes have no fi-

19. Terms of surrender allowed the lords to be transported to any country they would like outside of Scotland. Immediately, the French broke the terms of the truce and took everybody to France.

delity beyond what is to their own advantage. Then the galleys departed to Nantes, in Bartainzie [Britany], where, upon the waters of Loire, they stayed the whole winter.

Among those in the galleys was Master James Balfour and his two brothers, David and Gilbert, men without God.[20] We write this because we hear that Master James denies that he had anything to do with the Castle of St. Andrews, or that he was ever in the French galleys.[21] Then the joy of the Papists both of Scotland and of France was made perfect; for this was their song of triumph—

'Priests content you now! Priests content you now!

For Norman and his company have filled the galleys full.'

The Pope wrote letters to the King of France and to the Governor of Scotland, thanking them heartily for working to revenge the death of his kind creature, David Beaton, the Cardinal of Scotland; desiring them to continue in their severity, so that such things would not be attempted again. All those that there were apprehended in the Castle were damned to perpetual prison; and so the ungodly judged that after this Christ Jesus should never triumph in Scotland.

One thing we cannot pass by. There was sent a famous clerk from Scotland—laugh not, reader!—Master John Hamilton of Milburn, with credit to the King of France, and to the Cardinal of Lorraine. Yet he knew neither French nor Latin, and some say his Scottish tongue was not very good! The content of his negotiation was, that those of the Castle should be severely handled. In this request he was heard with favor, and was dispatched from the Court of France with letters, and great credit, which that famous clerk forgot by the way; because as he was passing up to the Craig of Dumbarton, before his letters were delivered, he broke his neck; and so God took away a proud, ignorant enemy.[22]

This winter, in the time of Christen Masse, was the Castle of Home recovered from the English, by the negligence of the Captain named Sir Edward Dudley.

20. Norman Leslie was imprisoned in Cherbourg in Normandy (France). John Knox, David, Gilbert, and James Balfour were put in the French galleys.

21. A typical French galley ship was manned by 250 rowers, 50-100 sailors, and 50-100 soldiers (25 pairs of oars with five men on each oar). They would carry one big 24-36 pounder gun, and two smaller 4-12 pounders.

22. A certain clerk of the court by the name of John Hamilton brought a message to the French court, requesting that the Protestants should be badly treated. On his return, the man broke his neck and died. The French communique never reached the Scottish court.

23. Sir John Melville was one of the few lords that supported the Protestant cause.

24. The Bishop of Saint Andrews, referred to here as the man who sought Melville's execution, was the Roman Catholic, Archbishop John Hamilton. He conspired with his brother to kill the King Regent, James Stuart, Earl of Moray (a tremendous historical scandal). This "bishop" had three children by his "mistress." The corruption in the Catholic Church was thorough by this time.

25. The Protestants, William Kirkcaldy, Peter Carmichael, and others, refused to participate in the Mass while they were under arrest by the French.

This winter, Sir John Melville, the Laird of Raith, suffered innocently,[23] and after that was betrayed because he wrote a letter to his son, John Melville, who was then in England, which was alleged to have been found in the house of Ormiston; but many suspected the cunning and craft of Ringzeane (Ninian) Cockburn, now called Captain Ringzaine, to whom the letter was delivered. But however it was, these cruel beasts, the Bishop of St. Andrews and the Abbot of Dunfermline, did not cease until the head of the noble man was taken from him;[24] especially because he was known to be the one that genuinely favored the truth of God's Word, and was a great friend of those who had been in the Castle of St. Andrews, of whose deliverance and of God's wondrous working with them during the time of their bondage, we must now speak, lest, in suppressing such a notable work of God, we might justly be accused of ingratitude.

The principals being put in several houses, great labor was made to make them have a good opinion of the Mass. They pressed Norman Leslie, the Laird of Grange, and David Monypenny, the Laird of Pitmilly, who were in the Castle of Scherisburgh [Cherbourg] that they would come to Mass with the Captain.[25] They answered: 'The Captain has power over our bodies; but he has no power to command our conscience.' The Captain replied: 'That he had power to compel them to go where he went.' They answered: 'We would not refuse to go any lawful place with you; but to do anything that is against our conscience, we will not, neither for you, nor for the King.' The Captain said: 'Will you not go to the Mass?' They answered: 'No; and if you compel us, we will displease you more; for we will so conduct ourselves there, that all those present will know that we despise it.'

These same answers, and some even sharper, they gave to the Captain, William Kirkcaldy, Peter Carmichael, and those who were with them in Mont St. Michael in Normandy. They said: 'They would not only hear Mass every day, but they would help to say it; provided they might stick the priests!'

Master Henry Balnaves, who was in the Castle of Rouen, was most sharply assaulted out of all of them. Because he was judged to be learned—as he was, and is, indeed—therefore learned men were appointed to persuade him. He had many conflicts with them; but God so assisted him, that they departed confounded, and he, by the power of God's Spirit, remained constant in the truth and profession of the same, without any wavering or declining to idolatry. In the prison he wrote a most profitable Treatise of Justification.[26]

At certain times the Mass was said in the galleys, or else heard upon the shore, and those that were in the galleys were threatened with torments if they would not give reverence to the Mass. But they could never make the poorest of that company to give reverence to that idol. Even on Saturday at night when they sang their Salve Regina, all of the Scottishmen put on their caps, their hoods, or anything that they had to cover their heads;[27] and when others were compelled to kiss a painted board, which they called 'Notre Dame,' they were not forced after one time; for this was what happened:—

Soon after their arrival at Nantes, their great Salve was sung, and a glorious painted Lady was brought in to be kissed, and, among others, it was presented to one of the Scottishmen who was chained. He gently said: 'Do not trouble me. Such an idol is accursed; therefore I will not touch it.' The Patron [Skipper] and the Arguesyn [Lieutenant], with two other officers, having the chief charge of such matters, said, 'You will handle it'; and they violently thrust it to his face, and put it between his hands. As he held the idol, he looked about himself and then cast it into the river, and said: 'Let our lady now save herself. She is light enough; let her learn to swim!' After that no Scotsman had to deal with that idolatry!

These are things that appear to be of no great importance. Yet, if we rightly consider them, they express the same obedience that God required of His people Israel, when they were to be carried to Babylon. He gave a charge to them, that when they should see the Babylonians worship their gods of gold,

26. This was the second time Henry Balnaves had been arrested. He had supported a law that would have allowed the reading of Scripture in the common language. Now, he was imprisoned in Normandy (France), and he could not return to Scotland for 11 years! During this time he wrote a book on Justification by Faith. This stalwart Protestant refused to bow to an idol or participate in the Mass during all of this time!

27. The Protestant men in the galleys refused to sing French Catholic hymns ("Salve Regina") and would not remove their caps to show reverence while the songs were sung.

28. Knox compares his captivity to the Babylonian captivity, and the Roman Catholic idols with the Babylonian gods.

silver, metal, and wood, they were to say: 'The gods that have not made the Heaven and the Earth shall perish from the Heaven and the Earth.'[28]

We now proceed in our narrative: Master James Balfour and John Knox were in one galley, and since they were well acquainted, Master James would often ask Knox's judgment as to whether he thought that they should ever be delivered? Knox's answer was, from the day they entered into the galleys, 'God will deliver us from this bondage, to His glory, even in this life.' Lying between Dundee and St. Andrews, the second time the galleys returned to Scotland, John Knox was so extremely sick that few believed he would survive, Master James told him to look to the land, and asked him if he knew it; and he answered, 'Yes; I know it well. I see the steeple of that place where God first in public opened my mouth to His glory, and I am fully persuaded, no matter how weak I now appear, I will not depart this life until my tongue shall glorify His Holy Name in the same place.'[29] Master William Kirkaldy, then of Grange, younger, Peter Carmichael, Robert and William Leslie, who were together in Mont St. Michel, wrote to John Knox, asking counsel, 'If they might break from their prison in good conscience?' Knox answered them, 'If they did not spill the blood of any for deliverance, they might set themselves free. But to shed any man's blood for their freedom, Knox would never consent to.'[30] Knox added further to his counsel saying, 'I am assured that God will deliver you, and the rest of your company, even in the eyes of the world; but not by such means as you have looked for, that is, by the force of friends, or by your own labors.' By this he affirmed that God would so work in their deliverance that the praise should resound to His glory only. He willed every one to take the occasion that God offered them, providing that they did nothing against God's express commandments. He was even more earnest in giving his counsel, because the old Laird of Grange and others resisted their attempts of escape, fearing that the escape of others should be an occasion for their own worse treatment.

29. Though James Balfour was not a Christian, he still relied on John Knox for his prophetic wisdom.

30. John Knox was careful not to advocate the killing of anybody to gain their freedom. He was convinced that God would deliver them in a miraculous way, which would give much glory to God. Others were too fearful to escape, and this John Knox also resisted.

To this John Knox answered: 'Such fear proceeds not from God's Spirit, but only from a blind love of self. No good purpose can be held back that is in the hands and power of God.' And he added: 'In one instant God delivered all that company into the hands of unfaithful men, but He will not deliver them in the same way. Some He will deliver by one means, and others must abide for a season upon His good pleasure.'

In the end they embraced this counsel given by Knox. On the Kings' Even [5th January 1549], when Frenchmen commonly use to drink liberally, the previously mentioned four persons had the help and conducting of a boy of the House. They bound all those that were in the Castle in Mont St. Michel, put them in various houses, locked the doors on them, took the keys from the Captain, and departed, without doing harm to anyone, and without touching anything that belonged to the King, the Captain, or the House.

A great search was made through the whole country for them. But it was God's good pleasure to arrange that they escaped the hands of the faithless, although with many difficulties and great pain and poverty. The French boy left them, and took with him their small treasure. So, having neither money nor knowledge of the country, and fearing that the boy should discover them—as he did—they decided to divide themselves, and to change their garments. The two brothers, William and Robert Leslie came to Rouen. These men have now become enemies to Christ Jesus and to all virtue, and especially Robert.[31] William Kirkaldy and Peter Carmichael, disguised in beggars' garments, came to Le Conquet, in Brittany, and in twelve or thirteen weeks they travelled as poor mariners, from port to port until at length they got a French ship, and landed in the West, and then came to England, where they met John Knox, who that same winter was delivered with Alexander Clerk of Balbirnie in his company.[32]

31. Kirkaldy, Carmichael, and William and Robert Leslie (Norman Leslie's sons) escaped. The Leslie brothers turned against the Protestant faith, not unusual when the church goes through trial and tribulation.

32. John Knox and Alexander Clerk also escaped around the same time frame.

JOHN KNOX'S FIRST INTERVIEW WITH MARY, QUEEN OF SCOTS

FROM THE REFORMATION IN SCOTLAND (BOOK IV, CHAPTER I) PREFACE TO BOOK IV

Chapter 1: from the Return to Scotland of Mary "Queen of Scots," on August 1561, to Her first Interview with John Knox at Holyrood on 26th August 1561

In the former Books, Gentle Reader, you may clearly see how greatly God has performed, in these last and wicked days,[1] as well as in the ages before us, the promises made to the Servants of God by the Prophet Isaiah, 'They that wait upon the Lord shall renew their strength; they shall lift up on wings like eagles: they shall run and not be weary; they shall walk, and not faint.'

What was our force? What was our number? What wisdom or worldly policy was in us, to have been brought to a good end and so great an enterprise?—our very enemies can bear witness. Yet in how great purity did God establish among us His True Religion, both in doctrine as in ceremonies! Both the doctrine taught by our Ministers, and the Administration of the sacraments used in our churches, we are bold to affirm that there is no realm today upon the face of the earth that has them in greater purity.[2] Yes, we must speak the truth, no matter who we offend, that there is no realm that has them in greater purity. All others—however sincere the doctrine may be—retain in their Churches, and in their Ministers, some footsteps of Antichrist, and some remnant of Papistry; but we give all

1. John Knox saw these as the "last days" as did Patrick in his *Confessions*.

2. Knox saw that Scotland had been blessed with the strongest doctrine and practice throughout the land of any reforming countries. England retained much Catholicism and reverted back and forth (esp. with the Stuarts). France never reformed. Switzerland was a mix, depending on the canton. Scotland became a hotbed for revival, missionary agencies, etc. for hundreds of years thereafter. The Reformation is virtually dead now, but the effects of Knox's work were obvious.

3. The Reformers referred to the Pope as the Anti-Christ or the Man of Sin — difficult language today. This was common terminology then, especially after millions of men and women had been subjected to severe persecutions at the hands of the Catholic Church for centuries.

4. Essential Reformation teaching. The trappings and institutionalization of the Catholic Church over the ages had obscured the true doctrine and practice of the New Testament church. The goal of every reforming church is to try to understand and return to the basic elements of the New Testament church revealed in Acts 2 and throughout the New Testament.

5. Murderers and adulterers sometimes take political leadership in the various nations. This is fairly normal even in our day.

praise to God alone! We have nothing within our Churches that ever flowed from that Man of Sin.[3] We acknowledge this to be the strength given to us by God, because we did not consider ourselves wise in our own eyes, but, understanding our own wisdom to be but foolishness before the Lord our God, we laid it aside, and followed only that which we found approved by God.[4]

In this point our enemies could never cause us to faint, for our First Petition was, 'That the true face of the Primitive and Apostolic Church should be brought back again to the eyes and knowledge of men.' In that point, our God has strengthened us until the work was finished, as the world may see.

Why does this miserable dispersion of God's people come within this Realm, this day, 1566, in May? What is the cause that the just are now compelled to keep silence, good men are banished, murderers and such as are known unworthy of the common society bear the whole regiment and power within this realm?[5] We answer that because suddenly all of us declined from the purity of God's Word, and began to follow the world; and to again shake hands with the devil, and with idolatry, as in this Fourth Book we will hear. The troubles of the Kirk within Scotland flowed from the Courtiers that seemed to profess the Gospel.

While Papists were so confounded, that none within the Realm dared to acknowledge or declare the hearing or saying of Mass, than the thieves of Liddesdale would confess their theft in the presence of an upright judge, there were Protestants found that were not ashamed to ask at tables and other open places, 'Why may not the Queen have her own Mass, and the form of her religion? How can that hurt our own religion?' And from these two—'Why' and 'What'— at length this affirmation came, 'The Queen's Mass and her Priests we will maintain. This hand and this blade shall fight in their defense!'

The Truth of God was almost forgotten; and from this fountain: that flesh and blood was and is preferred over God and to His messengers rebuking vice and vanity;[6] from this all of our misery has proceeded. For just as before, although the Ministers have to beg, the guard and the men of war are served! Though the blood of Ministers is spilt, it is the Queen's Servants that did it! Although Masses be multiplied in all areas of the Realm, who can stop the Queen's subjects to live in the Queen's religion? Although innocent men are imprisoned, it is the Queen's pleasure as she is offended at such men![7] Although, under pretence of justice, innocents are cruelly murdered, the Lord's people will weep, but the Queen's mind must be satisfied! Nobles of the Realm, Barons, and Councilors are banished, their estates forfeited and given to others and their lives are unjustly pursued. The Queen has lost her trusty servant Davy [David Rizzio]: he was dear to her; and therefore, for her honor's sake, she must show severity to revenge his death![8]

Yet some know that she has plainly planned to wreck the true religion within this Realm;[9] that she has made her promise to the Roman Antichrist; and that she has taken money from him to uphold his pomp within this Realm; yet will they let the people understand, that the Queen will establish Religion, and provide all things orderly, if she was once delivered.

If such dealings, which are common among our Protestants, are not preferring flesh and blood to God, to His truth, to justice, to religion, and to the liberty of this oppressed realm, let the world judge. The plagues that were threatened have been present and yet the rest approach. And yet, who from the heart cries 'I have offended the Lord and He knows; in You only is the trust of the oppressed; for vain is the help of man?' But now we return to our History.

The nineteenth day of August, the year of God 1561, between the seventh and eighth hour before noon, Mary, Queen of Scotland, then a widow, arrived at Leith with two galleys of France. In her company, besides her gentlewomen, called the Maries [Mary Fleming, Mary Seton, Mary Beaton, and Mary Livingstone], were her three uncles, Claude de Lorraine, the

6. False believers were also a problem for them. These are people who profess faith because it is culturally acceptable, but they turn out to be false to their profession.

7. The major concern was that the Queen (Mary of Scots) wanted to remain a Catholic, while the rest of the country was moving towards reformation.

8. The political intrigue, the killings of certain key political leaders like David Rizzio, resulted in more murders in the realm. Innocent pastors who would preach the Word against the sins of the day (addressing the Queen's sins as well) would lose their lives.

9. The Queen was committed to obliterating the Protestant religion, so the situation was touch-and-go for the Reformers during these years.

Duke d'Aumale, Francis de Lorraine, the Grand Prior, and René de Lorraine, Marquis d'Elbœuf. Seigneur de Damville, son to the Constable of France, accompanied her also with other gentlemen of inferior condition, along with servants and officers.

The very face of heaven at the time of her arrival, clearly spoke of what sort of comfort was brought into this country with her, namely, sorrow, darkness, and all impiety.[10] In the memory of man, that day of the year, was never seen a more sorrowful face of the sky. Besides the immoderate wet, and corruption of the air, the mist was so thick and so dark, that it would be difficult for a man to see another even at a short distance. The sun did not shine two days before, or the two days after. God gave us this forewarning but many were still blind to it.

At the sound of the cannons that the galleys shot, the multitude being announced, happy was the person that might first be in the presence of the Queen! The Protestants were not the slowest and they were not to be blamed. Because the Palace of Holyroodhouse was not thoroughly put in order in that her coming was more sudden than many had expected—she remained in Leith until it was near evening, and then she returned. On the way, between Leith and the Abbey, she met the rebels of the Crafts, of whom we spoke before, namely, those that had violated the authority of the Magistrates, and had besieged the Provost. But, because she was sufficiently instructed that all they did was done in spite of the Protestant Religion, they were easily pardoned.[11] Fires of joy were set forth all night, and a company of the most honest, with instruments of music, and with musicians, gave their salutations at her chamber window. She liked the melody; and she had the musicians play the same music many nights after the first.

With great diligence the Lords came to her from all quarters. And so nothing happened but mirth and quietness until the next Sunday, which was the 24th of August. Then preparation began to be made for that idol, the Mass, to be said in the

---

10. Mary Queen of Scots had married Francis II, King of France in 1558 (and the King died two years later). As Queen of France, she had pushed hard for the persecution of the Huguenot Protestant Christians in France. She had encouraged the torture and burning of Christians. And now she had returned to Scotland. It was a sad day in Scotland when she returned.

11. Mary quickly forgave the Catholic rebels called the "Crafts," who had stirred up anarchy in the land.

Chapel of Holyroodhouse,[12] which pierced the hearts of all. The godly began to be bold; and men began to openly speak.

'Will that idol be allowed again to take place within this Realm? It will not.' The Lord Lyndsay—then but Master—with the Gentlemen of Fife and others, plainly cried in the courtyard, 'The idolater Priest will die the death, according to God's law.' The one that carried in the candle was greatly afraid; but the Lord James Stewart, the man whom all the godly most respected, took upon himself the task of guarding the Chapel Door. His best excuse was, that he would stop all Scotsmen to enter in to the Mass. But it is sufficiently known that the door was kept that none should have the courage to trouble the Priest, who, after the Mass, was committed to the protection of Lord John Stewart, Prior of Coldingham, and Lord Robert Stewart, Abbot of Holyroodhouse the Queen's natural brothers, who then were both Protestants, and who would partake at the Table of the Lord. Between these two was the Priest escorted to his chamber.

The godly departed with great grief of heart, and at afternoon they came to the Abbey in great numbers, and they gave plain indication that they could not abide to see the land polluted with idolatry, which God by His power had previously purged. When this was understood, complaint after complaint began to arise. The old loose characters, and others that long had served in the Court, and had no remission of sins, except by the Mass, cried, 'We would go to France without delay; we could not live without the Mass.' The Queen's uncles made the same declaration. And what blessing it would be if God had ridden the land of that crowd together with the Mass forever for then Scotland would have been rid of an unprofitable burden of devouring strangers, and of the curse of God that has stricken, and yet will strike, for all of this idolatry!

The Council assembled and disputation occurred concerning the next remedy. Political heads were sent to the Gentlemen and those of a similar persuasion: 'Why will you chase our Sovereign from us? She will return angry to her galleys,

12. Mary instituted Catholic Mass in her private chambers, causing a great deal of consternation for the Protestants. Every government commits itself to a certain faith and issues laws on the basis of that faith. We are always interested in the faith to which our leaders profess.

Holyrood Palace

*Portrait of Mary,
Queen of Scots*

13. John Knox believed that God paid attention to our politics and the practices of our leaders. This fear of God expressed by pastors from the pulpits is essential. Pastors like this are usually mocked for this kind of sermon, as in the case of John Knox here.

14. Instead of backing down on what he said, John Knox says he repents of not being severe enough in his sermons.

and what then will all the Realms say of us? May we not put up with her for a little while? We do not doubt that she will leave it. If we were not assured that she might be won, we would be as great enemies to her Mass as you should be. Her uncles will depart; and then we will rule all at our pleasure. With these and other similar persuasions the fervency of the Brothers was quenched.

The next Sunday [31st August 1561], John Knox, who was attacking the idolatry, showed what terrible plagues God had placed on realms and nations for such idolatry. Knox added: 'One Mass is more fearful to me than ten thousand armed enemies landing in any part of the Realm to suppress the whole Religion. In our God there is strength to resist and confound multitudes if we honestly depend upon Him, and this we have already experienced. But when we join hands with idolatry, both God's peaceful presence and comfortable defense leaves us, and what will then become of us? I fear that experience will teach us leading to the grief of many.'[13]

At these words the guilders of the Court mocked, and plainly said—

'Such fear was no point of their faith. It was not the point of his text, and it was a very untimely admonition.' But we heard John Knox, in the audience of the same men, recite the same words again in the midst of troubles. In the audience of many, he asked God's mercy that he was not more vehement and upright in the suppressing of that idol in the beginning. 'Although I spoke that which offended some, and to this day they see and feel it to be true, yet I did not do what I might have done. God had not only given me knowledge and a tongue to make the impiety of that idol known, but He had given me credit with many who could have executed God's judgments, if I would only have consented to that.[14] But I desired that common tranquility, and I was so reluctant to offend those of whom I had a good opinion of, that in secret discussion with earnest and zealous men, I exerted myself to mitigate and to slacken the fervency that God had kindled in others, than to animate or encourage them to put their hands to the Lord's work. In this I genuinely acknowledge myself to have acted most wickedly, and from the bottom of my heart ask of my God grace and pardon.' Many heard these words that John Knox spoke in public places, in the month of December, the year of God 1565. But we now return from where we have digressed.

Whether it was by the counsel of others, or of Queen Mary's own desire, we do not know which, the Queen spoke with John Knox at Holyrood and had a long disputation with him with no others present except the Lord James Stewart, while two gentlewomen stood in the other end of the house.

The Queen accused John Knox of raising some of her subjects against her mother and against herself; that he had written a book against her just authority,—she meant the treatise against the Regiment of Women[15]—which she caused the most learned in Europe to write against; and that he was the cause of great sedition and great slaughter in England; and that it was said to her, that all which he did was by sorcery.

To this John Knox answered: 'Madam, may it please Your Majesty patiently to hear my simple answers? First, if to teach the Truth of God in sincerity, if to rebuke idolatry and to teach a people to worship God according to His Word, is to raise subjects against their Princes, then I cannot be excused; for it has pleased God of His Mercy to make me one among many to make known to this Realm the vanity of the Papal Religion, and the deceit, pride, and tyranny of that Roman Antichrist. But, Madam, if the true knowledge of God and His right worshipping are the chief causes that must move men from their heart to obey their just Princes,[16] as it is most certain they are, where can I be accused?

'And, concerning that Book which seems to so highly offend Your Majesty, it is most certain that I wrote it, and I am content that all the learned of the world judge it. I hear that an Englishman has written against it, but I have not read him. If he has sufficiently disproved my reasons, and estab-

15. The Queen requested a meeting with John Knox. She was particularly concerned about a book he wrote called *A Trumpet Blast Against the Monstrous Regiment of Women*. Knox believed that nations led by women are subjected to the curse of God.

16. John Knox argues that when pastors teach a right knowledge of God and a right worship of God, the end result will be less revolt against kings and queens and more peaceful submission to lawful authorities.

17. Knox felt his position on women in the office of magistrate had not received a serious challenge.

lished his contrary propositions with as evident testimonies as I have done mine, I will not be stubborn, but will confess my error and ignorance. But to this hour I have considered, and still consider, myself alone to be more than able to sustain the things affirmed in my work, than any ten in Europe will be able to refute it.'[17]

Queen Mary. 'You think then that I have no just authority?'

John Knox. 'Please Your Majesty, learned men in all ages have had their judgments free. They have most commonly disagreed from the common judgment of the world. They have also published, both with pen and tongue, and yet they themselves have lived in common society with others, and have dealt patiently with the errors and imperfections, which they could not change. Plato, the philosopher, wrote his book of The Commonwealth, in which he damns many things that then were maintained in the world, and he urged for many things to be reformed.[18] Yet, he lived under such policies as then were universally received, without further troubling anyone. Even so, Madam, I am content to do this same thing in uprightness of heart and with the testimony of a good conscience. I have communicated my judgment to the world. If the Realm finds no inconvenience from the government of a woman, that which they approve I will not further disallow aside from my own opinion, but will be as content to live under Your Grace as Paul was to live under Nero.[19] My hope is this, that so long as you do not defile your hands with the blood of the Saints of God, against that wicked Jezebel of England.' (Queen Mary Tudor).

Queen Mary. 'But do you speak of women in general?'

John Knox. 'This is true, Madam. Yet it appeared to me that wisdom should persuade Your Grace, never to raise trouble for that, which to this day has not troubled Your Majesty, neither in person nor yet in authority. In recent years many things, which before were considered stable, have been called into doubt; and they have even been plainly attacked. Yet, Madam, I am assured that neither Protestant nor Papist will

18. Knox insists he has the right to maintain a different perspective and press for a reforming agenda. Even the pagan philosopher Plato advocated an agenda that was not in line with the present order of things.

19. He is content to live under bad political leaders, as Paul had to live under Nero.

be able to prove, that any such question was made in public or in secret by me. Now, Madam, if I had intended to trouble your estate because you are a woman, I would have chosen a time more convenient for that purpose, than I can do now, when your own presence is within the realm.

'But now, Madam, to answer the other two accusations: I heartily praise my God through Jesus Christ, if Satan, the enemy of mankind, and the wicked of the world, have no other crimes to lay to my charge, than those that the very world itself knows to be false and vain. I lived in England for five years. The places I lived were Berwick, where I stayed two years; and two years in Newcastle; and a year in London. Now, Madam, if any man is able to prove that there was either battle, sedition, or mutiny while I was in these places, I will confess that I myself am guilty and the shedder of blood. I am not ashamed, Madam, to affirm that God has so blessed my weak labors, that in Berwick—where there used to be slaughter due to quarrels among soldiers—there was great peace the entire time that I remained there, as there is this day in Edinburgh. And where they slander me of magic, sorcery, or of any other art forbidden by God, I have witnesses, besides my own conscience—all congregations that have ever heard me—to how I spoke against such arts and against those that use such impiety.'[20]

Queen Mary. 'But yet you have taught the people to receive another religion than their Princes can allow. How can that doctrine be of God since God commands subjects to obey their Princes?'[21]

John Knox. 'Madam, since right religion takes neither its original strength nor authority from worldly princes, but from the Eternal God alone, so the subjects are not bound to frame their religion according to the appetites of their princes. Princes are often the most ignorant of all others in God's true religion, as we may read in the Histories, both before the death of Christ Jesus and after. If all the seed of Abraham was of the religion of Pharaoh, to whom they were long subjects,

20. Knox addresses the other two charges against him — that he is accused of stirring up sedition and sorcery.

21. Mary asks him if he is encouraging rebellion against civil authority when he opposes the official religion of the land.

22. Knox answers that there have been many (if not most) godly men who have opposed the official religion of the land (e.g. the Israelites under Pharaoh, Daniel under the Persians, the Apostles under the pagan Romans).

23. Mary now wants to know if Knox would approve violent resistance against magistrates who oppose his religion and on what basis might he approve it.

I ask you, Madam, what religion should there have been in the world? Or, if all men in the days of the Apostles were of the religion of the Roman Emperors, what religion should there have been upon the face of the earth? Daniel and his fellows were subjects to Nebuchadnezzar and to Darius, and yet, Madam, they would not be of their religion; for the three children said: "We make it known unto you, O King, that we will not worship your Gods." Daniel also did pray publicly to his God against the expressed commandment of the King. And so Madam, you may perceive that subjects are not bound to the religion of their princes, although they are commanded to give them obedience.'[22]

Queen Mary. 'Yes, but none of these men raised the sword against their princes.'

John Knox. 'Yet, Madam, you cannot deny that they resisted, for those who obey not the commandments that are given, in some way resist.'

Queen Mary. 'But yet, they did not resist by the sword?'

John Knox. 'Madam, God had not given them the power and the means.'

Queen Mary. 'Do you think subjects who have the power, may resist their princes?'[23]

John Knox. 'If their princes exceed their bounds, Madam, no doubt they may be resisted, even by force. For there is neither greater honor, nor greater obedience, to be given to kings or princes, than God has commanded to be given to father and mother. But the father may be stricken with a frenzy, in which he would slay his children. If the children arise, join themselves together, apprehend the father, take the sword from him, bind his hands, and keep him in prison until his frenzy is past, do you think, Madam, that the children have done anything wrong? This is also the case, Madam, with princes that would murder the children of God that are subjects to them. Their blind zeal is nothing but a very mad frenzy, and therefore, to take the sword from them, to bind their hands, and to cast them into prison until they be brought to a more sober mind, is no disobedience against princes, but just obedience, because it agrees with the will of God.'[24]

At these words, the Queen was amazed. Her countenance was altered, so that Lord James began to implore her and to demand, 'What has offended you, Madam?'

At length she said to John Knox: 'Well then, I perceive that my subjects will obey you, and not me. They will do what they believe is right, and not what I command; and so I must be subject to them, and not they to me.'

John Knox. 'God forbid that ever I command any to obey me, or yet to set subjects at liberty to do what pleases them! My goal is that both princes and subjects obey God. Madam, do not think that wrong is done you, when you are called to be subject to God. It is He that subjects people under princes, and causes obedience to be given to them. Yes, God desires that Kings be foster-fathers to His Church, and commands Queens to be nurses to His people. This subjection, Madam, to God, and to His troubled Church, is the greatest dignity that flesh can have upon the face of the earth; for it shall carry them to everlasting glory.'[25]

Queen Mary. 'Yes, but you are not the Kirk that I will nourish. I will defend the Kirk of Rome, for it is, I think, the true Kirk of God.'

John Knox. 'Your will, Madam, is no reason for this belief; neither does your thought make that Roman harlot to be the true and immaculate spouse of Jesus Christ. Do not be amazed, Madam, that I call Rome a harlot; for that Church is altogether polluted with all kinds of spiritual fornication, both in doctrine and in practice. Yes, Madam, I offer myself to prove, that the Church of the Jews which crucified Christ Jesus, was not as degenerate from the ordinances which God gave by Moses and Aaron to his people, when they manifestly denied the Son of God, as the Church of Rome has declined, and more than five hundred years has declined, from the purity of that religion which the Apostles taught and established.'[26]

Queen Mary. 'My conscience does not say so.'

24. Knox claims that subjects can bind back a magistrate who is dangerous, such that he is bound to kill his subjects over these matters.

25. Mary now reduces it to a power struggle between herself and Knox (and his political alliances). Knox responds that there should be no power struggle if everybody submitted to God's law first.

26. Knox reiterates that the church of Rome is more degenerate than the Jews in the time of Christ (who still clung to some of the ordinances that God gave by Moses). He dates the decline of the Western Church from roughly AD 1000.

John Knox. 'Conscience, Madam, requires knowledge, and I fear that you do not have the right knowledge.'

Queen Mary. 'I have both heard and read.'

John Knox. 'Madam, so did the Jews who crucified Christ Jesus; they read both the Law and the Prophets, and heard them interpreted. Have you heard any teach outside of those that the Pope and his Cardinals have allowed? You may be assured that they will not allow anyone to speak and to offend their own estate.'

Queen Mary. 'You interpret the Scriptures in one manner, and they interpret it in another manner. Who should I believe? Who will be the judge?'

27. Mary thinks it is all a matter of interpretation. But Knox encourages her to read the Word of God for herself. He believes that the Scriptures are plain.

John Knox. 'You will believe God who plainly speaks in His Word;[27] and if anyone teaches beyond that Word, you should not believe them. The Word of God is plain in itself. If there appear any obscurity in one place, the Holy Spirit, who is never contrary to Himself, explains the same doctrine more clearly in other places; so that there can be no doubt except for those who remain stubbornly ignorant.

'Consider one of the chief points, Madam, which today is a controversy between the Papists and us. The Papists have boldly affirmed that the Mass is the ordinance of God, and the institution of Jesus Christ, and a sacrifice for the sins of the living and the dead. We deny each of these propositions. We affirm that the Mass, as it is now practiced, is nothing but the invention of man, and, therefore, is an abomination before God, and it is not a sacrifice that God commanded. Now, Madam, who will judge between us and the Papists? Neither of the parties should be believed simply due to their witness. Instead, let them prove their affirmations by the plain words of the Book of God. What our Master Jesus Christ did, we know by His Evangelists; what the priest does at Mass, the world sees. Now, does not the Word of God plainly assure us, that Christ Jesus neither said Mass, nor did He command Mass to be said, at His Last Supper, seeing that no such thing as their Mass is mentioned in all of Holy Scripture?'

Queen Mary. 'You are too hard for me, but if they (priests) were here, they would answer you.'

John Knox. 'Madam, would that God bring the most learned Papist in Europe, one that you would most believe, were present with Your Grace to sustain the argument; and that you would patiently abide to hear the matter reasoned to the end! Then, I do not doubt, Madam, that you would hear the vanity of Papal Religion, and how little basis it has within the Word of God.'[28]

Queen Mary. 'Well, you may get that chance sooner than you believe.'

John Knox. 'Assuredly, if I ever get that in my life, I will get it sooner than I believe. The ignorant Papists cannot patiently reason, and the learned and crafty Papist will never come into your audience, Madam, to have the basis of their religion searched out. They know that they are never able to sustain an argument, except by using fire and sword and their own laws to be judges.'

Queen Mary. 'So you say; but I cannot believe that.'

John Knox. 'It has been this way to this day. How often have the Papists in this and other Realms been asked to come to the conference, and yet it could never be obtained, unless they themselves were admitted as Judges. Therefore, Madam, I must say again that they dare never dispute unless they themselves are both judge and disputant. If you will let me see the contrary, I will grant myself to have been deceived in that regard.'

With this, the Queen was called to dinner, because it was the afternoon. While departing, John Knox said to her: 'I pray to God, Madam, that you may be as blessed within the Commonwealth of Scotland, if it is the pleasure of God, as Deborah was in the Commonwealth of Israel.'[29]

There were various opinions on this conference. The Papists resented the meeting and feared that which they did not need to fear. The godly, thinking at least that the Queen would have heard the preaching, rejoiced; but they were all utterly

28. Knox challenges the "most learned" papist to a debate. He says they are sloppy in their reasoning and easy to answer.

29. Knox indicated that he could offer a blessing for a female civil leader at the end of the discussion (when he brought up Deborah as one who was blessed in Israel). Perhaps he is backing off the hard line he took in his *Trumpet Blast*.

30. Knox did not trust the Queen. He believed she had a proud mind, a deceitful approach, and a hard heart.

deceived, for she continued in her Masses, and despised and quietly mocked all exhortation Some asked John Knox, what he thought of the Queen? 'If there is not in her,' said Knox, 'a proud mind, a crafty wit, and a hard heart against God and His truth, my judgment fails me.'[30]

JOHN KNOX'S SECOND INTERVIEW WITH MARY, QUEEN OF SCOTS

FROM THE REFORMATION IN SCOTLAND (BOOK IV, CHAPTER III)

At Holyrood on 15th December 1562

The Queen returned to Edinburgh, and then was joyful and danced; for her friends began to triumph in France. The certainty of this came to the ears of John Knox, for there were some that showed to him, from time to time, the state of things. Amongst others, he was assured that the Queen had danced excessively until after midnight, because she had received letters that persecution had begun again in France,[1] and that her uncles were beginning to trouble the whole Realm of France. Upon occasion of this text, 'And now understand, O you Kings, and be learned, you that judge the earth,' he began to challenge the ignorance, the vanity, and the malice of princes that were raised against all virtue, and against all those in whom hatred of vice and love of virtue appeared.

When this report was made to the Queen, John Knox was sent for. Master Alexander Cockburn, eldest son of John Cockburn of Ormiston, who had been his student, and was very familiar with him, was the messenger, who gave him

1. The Huguenots were French Christians (Protestants) who had been persecuted from as early as 1534. While Mary Queen of Scots was married to Francis II, she had encouraged the torture and burning of Huguenots.

Modern day city of Edinburgh

Queen was in her bedchamber, and with her, besides the Ladies and the common servants, were the Lord James [the Earl of Moray], the Earl of Morton, Secretary Lethington, and some of the guard that had made the report. He was called and accused as one that had irreverently spoken of the Queen, and that strived to bring her into hatred and contempt of the people, and that he had exceeded the bounds of his text.[2] Upon these three heads, the Queen made a long oration. John Knox answered as follows:—

'Madam, this is often the just retribution which God gives to the stubborn of the world. Because they will not hear God speaking to the comfort of the penitent, and for the amendment of the wicked, they are often compelled to hear the false reports of others, to their greater displeasure. I do not doubt that it came to the ears of proud Herod, that our Master Christ Jesus called him a fox; but they told him not how

2. Accusations towards preachers who "exceed the bound of their texts" is pretty common. When preachers begin to preach against specific sins of the day and make certain "prophetic" applications (especially as it applies to civil magistrates), people will complain that they are going beyond the Bible or the Gospel message.

odious a thing it was before God to murder an innocent, as he had lately done, causing him to behead John the Baptist, to reward the dancing of a harlot's daughter. Madam, if the reporters of my words had been honest men, they would have reported my words, and also the circumstances of these words. But, because they would have credit in Court, and since they lack virtue they must have something to please Your Majesty, even if it were but flattery and lies. For, Madam, if your own ears had heard the whole matter that I implored; if there is any sparkle of the Spirit of God in you, yes, of honesty or wisdom, you could not justly have been offended by anything that I spoke. And because you have heard their report, please let me rehearse mine.

'After, Madam, I had declared the dignity of kings, the honor in which God has placed them, and the obedience that is due to them, being God's Lieutenants, I demanded this question,—What account shall most Princes make before that Supreme Judge, whose authority they so shamefully abuse? While murderers, oppressors, and criminals dare be bold to present themselves before Kings, while the poor saints of God are banished, what shall we say, but that the Devil has taken possession in the Throne of God, which ought to be fearful to all evildoers, and a refuge to the innocent who are oppressed. How else can it be? Princes despise God's law; they will not understand his statutes or Holy ordinances. They are more excited in fiddling and dancing than in reading or hearing God's Most Blessed Word; and fiddlers and flatterers are more precious in their eyes than men of wisdom and gravity, who by wholesome admonition might beat down in them some part of that pride in which we all are born, but in which Princes take deep root by wicked education.[3]

'Of dancing, Madam, I said, that although in Scripture I find no praise of it, and in profane writers, it is termed the gesture of those that are in frenzy rather than sober men; yet do I not utterly condemn it, providing that two vices be avoided. The former is that the principal vocation of those that use

3. Knox reviews his sermon with the Queen. 1. He encouraged honor and obedience to kings (for the congregation he was preaching to). 2. Princes will have to give account for their wicked abuse of innocent people. They reward murderers (Planned Parenthood–in our day), and they persecute innocent Christians. Knox refers to Romans 13. Evildoers should fear the rulers. 3. The root problem is that our political rulers despise God's laws. 4. Princes are more interested in entertainment — dancing and fiddling — than in going to hear the preaching of the Word. This is true of a great percentage of our modern people today. 5. The princes become proud by their educational programs. This is typical for humanist forms of education.

the exercise be not neglected for the pleasure of dancing. Secondly, that they do not dance for the pleasure they take in the persecution of God's people.[4] If any man, Madam, will say that I spoke more, let him presently accuse me. I think I have not only touched the sum of what I spoke, but the very words as I spoke them.' Many that stood by bore witness with John Knox that he had recited the very words that he had spoken publicly.

The Queen looked at some of the reporters, and said: 'Your words are sharp enough as you have spoken them; but yet they were told to me in another manner. I know that my uncles and you are not of one religion, and therefore I cannot blame you, although you have no good opinion of them. But if you hear anything of me that is negative concerning you, come to me and tell me, and I will hear you.'[5]

'Madam,' said he, 'I am assured that your uncles are enemies to God, and to His Son Jesus Christ; and that for maintenance of their own pomp, they spill the blood of many innocents. Therefore, I am assured that their endeavors will have no better success than others have had that have tried the same in the past. But as for you, Madam, I would be glad to do all I could to Your Grace's contentment, provided I do not exceed the bounds of my vocation. I am called, Madam, to a public function within the Church of God, and I am appointed by God to rebuke the sins and vices of all. I am not appointed to come to every man in particular to show him his offence; because that labor would be infinite. If Your Grace would frequent the public sermons, then I do not doubt that you will fully understand both what I like and dislike, both in Your Majesty as in all others. Or, if Your Grace will assign to me a certain day and hour when it will please you to hear the substance of the doctrine which is presented in public to the Churches of this Realm, I will most gladly await upon Your Grace's pleasure, as to the time and place. But to wait upon your chamber-door, and then to have no further liberty but to whisper my mind in Your Grace's ear, or to tell you what

4. Knox clarified that he does not completely oppose dancing, as long as (1) we don't shirk our work responsibilities for this entertainment, and (2) we don't dance for joy over the persecution of God's people (which is what he suspects the Queen had been doing).

5. The Queen acts as if she is the reconciler between her uncles (Catholics who rule in France) and John Knox.

others think and speak of you, neither will my conscience nor the vocation to which God has called me to allow it.[6]

John Knox departed with a reasonable merry countenance; and at this some Papists who were offended, said: 'He is not afraid.' When John Knox heard this, he answered: 'Why should the pleasing face of a gentlewoman frighten me? I have looked in the faces of many angry men, and yet have not been afraid above measure.'[7] And so he left the Queen and the Court for that time.

6. Knox assures the Queen that these her uncles (who live in France) are enemies of God, for they have killed innocent Huguenots. He invites her to listen to his sermons if she wants the straight scoop on what he speaks publicly.

7. John Knox demonstrated a lack of the fear of man. This is remarkable given that these kings and queens would take away people's lives at a whim.

JOHN KNOX'S THIRD INTERVIEW WITH MARY, QUEEN OF SCOTS

FROM THE REFORMATION IN SCOTLAND (BOOK IV, CHAPTER IV)

At Lochleven on 13th and 14th April 1563

The Papists at that Easter, 1563, in various parts of the Realm, had erected that idol, the Mass. The brothers, universally offended, and seeing that the Queen, by her Proclamations, mocked them, determined to use their own hands, and to punish this, for an example to others. Some Priests in the West Land were arrested, and suggestion was made to others, as to the Abbot of Crossraguel, the Parson of Sanquhar, and such, that they should neither complain to Queen nor Council, but, by another means they should execute the punishment that God has appointed to idolaters in His law, wherever they should be apprehended.[1]

The Queen attacked the Brother's freedom of speech, but she could not change it because they were of one mind, to maintain the Truth of God and to suppress idolatry. Therefore she began to invent a new craft. She sent for John Knox to come to her at Lochleven, and she disputed with him ear-

[1] A fairly harsh application of Old Testament law is advocated for the punishment of idolatry (especially when the Mass is interpreted as an idolatrous practice). The lower magistrates may very well have been contemplating execution or exile.

2. The Queen's purpose for this meeting was to gain support from Knox to persuade the gentlemen in Western Scotland to forbear on the attempts to stop the Mass there.

nestly for two hours before her supper, that he would be the instrument to persuade the people, and principally the Gentlemen of the West, not to put hands to punish any man for engaging themselves in religious activities as it pleased them.[2] The other, perceiving her craftiness, willed Her Grace to punish criminals according to the laws, and he dared to promise quietness on the part of all them that professed the Lord Jesus within Scotland. But if Her Majesty thought to elude the laws, he feared some would let the Papists understand that, without punishment, they should not be allowed to so manifestly offend God's Majesty.

'Will you,' said she, 'allow that they should take my sword in their hand?'

'The Sword of Justice,' said he, 'Madam, is God's, and is given to princes and rulers for one purpose. If they transgress, sparing the wicked and oppressing innocents, their subjects, who execute judgment in the fear of God, where God has commanded, do not offend at all. Neither do those sin who bridle Kings from striking innocent men in their rage. The examples are evident:—Samuel did not fear to slay Agag, the fat and delicate King of Amalek, whom King Saul had saved.[3] In this case I would earnestly implore Your Majesty to take good counsel, and that Your Grace should let the Papists understand that their attempts will not go unpunished. It will be profitable to Your Majesty to consider what it is that Your Grace's subjects look to receive of Your Majesty, and what it is that you ought to do to them by mutual contract. They are bound to obey you, but only in God: you are bound to keep laws for them. You desire their service; they desire your protection and defense against evildoers. Now, Madam, if you deny your duty to them, who especially desire that you punish criminals, do you think you will receive full obedience from them? I fear, Madam, you shall not.'

3. Knox is not opposed to the civil magistrate in the Western part of Scotland prosecuting men who break the law of the land (which at that time did not allow for a public practice of the Mass). He tells the Queen not to interfere with the magistrates and speaks of Samuel's severe treatment of King Agag (as a just executor of God's law).

At this, the Queen, being somewhat offended, went to supper. John Knox left her, informed the Earl of Moray of the whole discussion, and departed, with the purpose of returning

Lochleven Castle

But before the sunrise, two messengers were directed to him—Wat Melville was one—commanding him not to depart until he spoke with the Queen's Majesty. He met her at the hawking, west of Kinross. Whether it was the night's sleep or a deep masquerade locked in her breast that made her forget her former anger, wise men may doubt; but there she never said a word about the previous matter, but began with various other subjects, such as the offering of a ring to her by the Lord Ruthven.

Queen Mary. 'I cannot love Lord Ruthven, for I know him to use sorcery; and yet he is part of my private council.'[4]

John Knox. 'Who blames Your Grace about this matter?'

Queen Mary. 'Lethington is the reason.'

John Knox. 'That man is presently absent, Madam, and therefore I will not speak anything on his behalf.'

Queen Mary. 'I understand that you are appointed to go to Dumfries, for the election of a Superintendent to be established in that country?'

John Knox. 'Yes. Those quarters have great need, and some of the Gentlemen require it.'

4. Now the Queen confides with him concerning her personal matters. Apparently, a Lord Ruthven had offered to marry the Queen. Ruthven actually organized the murder of David Rizzio (the Queen's private secretary). Rumors had it that Rizzio's relationship with the Queen was something beyond platonic.

Queen Mary. 'But I hear that the Bishop of Athens would be Superintendent?'

John Knox. 'He is one, Madam, that is in the election.'

Queen Mary. 'If you knew him as well as I do, you would never promote him to that office, nor yet to any other within your Kirk.'

John Knox. 'What he has been, Madam, I neither know, nor will I inquire. In time of darkness, what could we do but grope, and go wrong, even as darkness carried us? But if he does not fear God now, he deceives many more than me. And yet, Madam, I am assured that God will not suffer His Church to be so far deceived as that an unworthy man will be elected, where free election is, and the Spirit of God is earnestly called upon to decide between the two.'[5]

Queen Mary. 'Well, do as you will, but that man is a dangerous man.'

And in this the Queen was not deceived: for the Bishop of Athens had corrupted most of the Gentlemen not only to nominate him, but also to elect him; which being perceived by John Knox the Commissioner; he delayed the election, and so the Bishop's plans were frustrated.[6] Yet he was very friendly with John Knox both at house and at table.

When the Queen had spoken long with John Knox, and with Knox all the while wanting to be dismissed, she said, 'I have one of the greatest matters that has happened since I came into this Realm, to tell to you, and I must have your help with it.' And she began to make a long discourse about her sister, the Countess of Argyle, and how she was not as circumspect as the Queen wanted her to be.

Queen Mary. 'Yet, my Lord her husband, whom I love, implores her in many things in a dishonest and ungodly manner, as I think you yourself would require.'

John Knox. 'Madam, I have been troubled with that matter before. Once I put such an end to it and that was before Your Grace's arrival—that both she and her friends seemed fully contented. She herself promised before her friends, that she

5. Knox is careful not to take sides in the dangerous politics in the court of Queen Mary

6. There are free elections for church offices (something the Protestants introduced). The Queen turned out to be right on the character of the Bishop of Athens.

should never complain to anyone until I should first understand the controversy by her own mouth, or else by an assured messenger. I now have heard nothing of her part; and therefore I think there is nothing but agreement.'

Queen Mary. 'Well it is worse than you believe. But do this much for my sake, to once again to put them at unity. If she does not behave herself as she ought to do, she will find no favor from me. But, either way, do not let my Lord know that I have requested you in this matter. I would be very sorry to offend him in that or any other thing. And now, concerning our reasoning last night, I promise to do as you required. I will summon all the offenders; and you will know that I minister justice.'[7]

John Knox. 'I am assured then that you will please God and enjoy rest and tranquility within your Realm; which to Your Majesty is more profitable than all the Pope's power can be.'

And then they departed.

This conference we have inserted to let the world see how deeply Mary, Queen of Scotland, can conceal a matter; and how she could cause men to think that she bore no indignation for any controversy in religion, while yet in her heart there was nothing but venom and destruction, as it appeared shortly after.

7. The Queen is attempting to draw John Knox into the political wranglings, and she might be prodding into some of the counseling he is doing as a pastor.

JOHN KNOX'S FOURTH INTERVIEW WITH MARY, QUEEN OF SCOTS

FROM THE REFORMATION IN SCOTLAND (BOOK IV, CHAPTER V)

John Knox preaching (stained glass in St. Giles, Edinburgh)

In the progress of this corruption, and before the Parliament dissolved, John Knox, preached sermon before the Nobility.[1] He began to enter into a deep discourse on God's mercies which that Realm had felt, and of that ingratitude which he saw almost in the whole multitude, whom God had marvelously delivered from the bondage and tyranny both of body and soul. 'And now, my Lords,' he said, 'I praise my God, through Jesus Christ, that in your own presence I may pour forth the sorrows of my heart. Yes, you shall be witnesses, if I shall make any lie in things that have taken place. From the beginning of God's mighty working within this Realm, I have been with you in your most desperate temptations. Ask your own consciences, and let them answer you before God, if I—not I, but God's Spirit by me—in your greatest extremity ever exhorted you to not depend upon your God, and in His name promised you victory and preservation from your enemies, if you would only depend upon His protection, and prefer His glory to your own lives and worldly commodities. In your most extreme dangers I have been with you. St. Johnestoun, Cupar Muir, and the Crags of Edinburgh, are yet recent in my

1. It was not unusual for preachers to deliver sermons before parliaments, legislatures, and house of the lords. This is highly unusual today because we live in a secular age that has turned radically against Jesus Christ in all of its institutions (especially the schools and the universities).

2. John Knox points out that He was willing to take every risk to preach the Word of God and depend upon God to defend him. He pointed out that the lords were lacking in courage and would skip town when things became difficult.

3. The lords seemed to fear the Queen more than they feared God.

4. The Parliament of 1560 abolished the control of the Roman Catholic Church over Scotland. It set the church and the nation free from the highly centralized political control of the Pope. They also ratified and adopted a new Confession of Faith that was drafted by six preachers, John Knox, John Row, John Winram, John Spottiswoode, John Willock, and John Douglas. Some people were apparently questioning the legitimacy of this parliament.

heart; yes, that dark and sorrowful night, in which all of you, my Lords, with shame and fear left this town, is yet in my mind. God forbid that ever I forget it! What was my exhortation to you, and what is fallen in vain of all that ever God promised to you by my mouth, you yourselves yet live to testify. Not one of you, against whom death and destruction were threatened, perished in that danger. And how many of your enemies has God plagued before your eyes! Shall this be the thankfulness that you shall render to your God, to betray His cause, when you have it in your own hands to establish it as you please?[2]

'You say the Queen will not agree with us! Ask of her that which by God's Word you may justly require, and if she will not agree with you in God, you are not bound to agree with her in the Devil![3] Let her plainly understand your minds, and do not retreat from your former courage in God, and He shall prosper you in your endeavors. But I can see nothing but a recoiling from Christ Jesus, so that the man that first and most speedily flees from Christ's standard, considers himself most happy. Yes, I hear that some say, "We have nothing of our Religion established," neither by Law or Parliament! Although such malicious words can neither hurt the Truth of God, nor can it hurt us, yet the speaker, for his treason against God that he has committed, and against this poor Commonwealth, deserves the gallows. For our Religion being commanded and established by God, is accepted within this Realm in public Parliament. If they say that the Parliament of 1560 was not a true Parliament, we must, and will say, and also prove, that that Parliament was as lawful as any that passed before it within this Realm.[4] Yes, if the King then living [Francis II] was King of Scotland and France, and the Queen now in this Realm is the lawful Queen of Scotland, that Parliament cannot be denied.

'Now, my Lords, to conclude my discourse, I hear of the Queen's marriage. Dukes, brethren to Emperors, and Kings, strive all for the best game; but this, my Lords, will I say—

note the day, and bear witness after—whenever the Nobility of Scotland professing the Lord Jesus, consent that an infidel— and all the Papists are infidels—shall be head to our Sovereign, you are doing as much as you can to banish Christ Jesus from this Realm. You will bring God's vengeance upon the country, a plague upon yourselves, and you will do favor to your Sovereign.'

John Knox's words and his manner of speaking were judged intolerable. Papists and Protestants were both offended; yes, his friends even disdained him.[5] Parasites and flatterers posted to the Court to give advertisement that Knox had spoken against the Queen's proposed marriage with Don Carlos,[6] son of Philip II of Spain.[7] The Provost of Lincluden, Robert Douglas of Drumlanrig by surname, gave the charge that John Knox should present himself before the Queen; which he did soon after dinner. The Lord Ochiltree, and various people of the Faithful, kept him company to the Abbey of Holyroodhouse; but none saw the Queen with him in the Cabinet except John Erskine of Dun, then Superintendent of Angus and Mearns. The Queen in vehement anger began to cry out, that no Prince was handled as she had been.

Queen Mary. 'I have dealt with you in all your rigorous manner of speaking, both against myself and against my uncles [the Duke of Guise and the Cardinal of Lorraine]. Yes, I have sought your favor by all possible means. I offered to you presence and audience whenever it pleased you to admonish me; and yet I cannot be rid of you! I vow to God, I will be revenged!'[8]

With these words, scarcely could Marna, her secret chamber boy, get napkins to keep her eyes dry from the tears; and the howling, besides womanly weeping, slowed her speech. John Knox patiently dealt with all of this, and when he had opportunity, answered:—

John Knox. 'It is true, Madam, Your Grace and I have been together at various controversies, in which I never perceived Your Grace to be offended at me. But, when it pleases God to

5. Everybody was offended by this sermon — Roman Catholics and Christian Protestants both. John Knox was never out to curry favor with political-minded men. Preachers must preach their conscience as bound by the Word of God, no matter what the political fall-out may be.

6. Phillip II, Emperor of Spain, led the inquisition, torturing and killing 10,000s of innocent people in the Netherlands and Spain. Now, Queen Mary wanted to marry his son, Don Carlos.

7. Knox encouraged the lords to oppose the marriage of the Queen to a Roman Catholic. At that time, the lords had some political sway over the Queen, and Knox was encouraging them to exercise it.

8. Queen Mary was very angry at John Knox, the preacher of righteousness who called these wicked leaders to account.

9. Knox admitted that it was the preaching that offended her, but he would not back off from his strong words in the pulpit.

10. Knox said that his business was not politics. His business was to preach the Gospel, which calls for two things — faith and repentance. These are both crucial elements that will appear in EVERY true preaching ministry. Repentance is a change of mind towards God and a turning away from sin (the breaking of the law of God). Faith is to believe in Jesus Christ as Savior and Lord.

deliver you from that bondage of darkness and error in which you have been nourished for the lack of true doctrine, Your Majesty will find the liberty of my tongue not offensive at all. Outside the preaching place, Madam, I think few have occasion to be offended by me. There, Madam, I am not master of myself, but must obey Him who commands me to speak plain, and to flatter no flesh upon the face of the earth.'[9]

Queen Mary. 'But what business do you have with my marriage?'

John Knox. 'If it pleases Your Majesty patiently to hear me, I shall show the truth in plain words. I grant Your Grace offered to me was more than I ever required; but my answer was then, as it is now, that God has not sent me to wait upon the courts of Princes, nor upon the chambers of Ladies; but I am sent to preach the Gospel of Jesus Christ, to those who will hear it. It has two parts—Repentance and Faith.[10] Now, Madam, in preaching Repentance, it is of necessity that the sins of men be so noted, that they may know where they offend God. But most of your Nobility are so addicted to your affections, that neither God's Word, nor yet their Commonwealth, are rightly regarded. Therefore, it is right for me to speak, that they may know their duty.'

Queen Mary. 'What business do you have with my marriage? Or what are you within this Commonwealth?'

John Knox. 'A subject related to the other, Madam, and although I am neither Earl, Lord, nor Baron within it, yet God has made me—despite how low I am in your eyes—a profitable member within the Realm. Yes, Madam, it is my position to forewarn of things that may hurt it, if I foresee them, more than it is the job of any of the Nobility; for both my vocation and my conscience require plainness in my speech. Therefore, Madam, to you I also say that which I spoke in public places:—Whenever the Nobility of this Realm will consent that you be subject to an unfaithful husband, they do effectively renounce Christ, they banish His truth from them, they betray the freedom of this Realm, and they shall in the end do no favor to yourself.'[11]

At these words, howling was heard, and tears might have been seen in greater abundance than the matter required. John Erskine of Dun, a man of meek and gentle spirit, stood beside, and tried what he could to mitigate her anger. He gave to her many pleasing words of her beauty, of her excellence, and how all the Princes of Europe would be glad to seek her favor. But all that was to cast oil on the flaming fire. John Knox stood still, without any change of countenance for a while; while the Queen gave place to her inordinate passion.

In the end he said: 'Madam, in God's presence I speak. I never delight in the weeping of any of God's creatures. Yes, I can scarcely well abide the tears of my own boys when my own hand corrects them; much less can I rejoice in Your Majesty's weeping.[12] But, seeing that I have offered to you no just occasion to be offended, but have spoken the truth, as my vocation require of me, I must stand on this position, though unwillingly. I must speak these things to Your Majesty's ears, rather than hurt my conscience, or betray my Commonwealth through my silence.'

At this the Queen was more offended, and commanded John Knox to be dismissed from the Cabinet, and to wait in the Chamber as long as she desired. The Laird of Dun lingered, and Lord John Stewart, Prior of Coldingham [the Queen's brother] came into the Cabinet, and they both remained with her for about one hour. John Knox stood in the Chamber, as one whom men had never seen—so all were afraid—except that the Lord Ochiltree kept him company. Therefore he began to talk with the ladies who were sitting there in all their gorgeous apparel; and seeing this, he merrily said, 'O fair Ladies! How pleasing is this life of yours, if it should ever abide, and then in the end that we might pass to Heaven with all of this apparel! But this death will come, whether we will or not! And when death has laid his hands on us, the foul worms will be busy with our flesh no matter how fair and how tender; and

11. John Knox lists the problems with a marriage between Queen Mary and the son of King Phillip II of Spain: 1. The nobility would banish the truth of God's Word. 2. These men would destroy religious freedom for true Christians in Scotland. 3. This arrangement would not be good for Queen Mary either.

12. Knox says he does not enjoy watching people cry. When he disciplines his own sons and they turn to crying, he does not find any "delight" in it.

Don Carlos of Spain by Alonso Sánchez Coello (1564)

13. John Knox warned the women in the court who took delight in vanities that they would not look so beautiful when the worms consume their bodies in the grave. This would not be the "politically correct" thing to say! Good preachers will always give us this perspective of life and death, heaven and hell, a perspective of eternity.

the silly soul, I fear, will be so feeble, that it can neither carry with it gold, ornaments, silver, pearl nor precious stones!' In this way he spoke to the company of women![13] He passed the time until the Laird of Dun commanded him to depart to his house until his presence was requested again.

The Queen would have had the judgment of the Lords of the Articles, if such manner of speaking did not deserve punishment. But she was counseled to desist; and so that storm of anger disappeared from her countenance, but not in her heart.

GRACE ABOUNDING TO THE CHIEF OF SINNERS

John Bunyan
AD 1666

AN INTRODUCTION TO THE TESTIMONY OF JOHN BUNYAN

Speaking of John Bunyan, John Owen, the greatest of the English Puritans, said he would "gladly exchange all his learning for Bunyan's power of touching men's hearts." Truly a giant among Christian writers in history, John Bunyan never attended college, barely obtaining any education at all as a child. Yet his influence over four hundred years of Protestant Christianity is practically unmatched by any other great Christian writer. His works have been translated into over two hundred languages.

John Bunyan's writings are picturesque, robust, deeply emotional, plain, and profound. Such literature speaks across generations. Hardly any of his writings bear such witness to the inward raging within the human soul as his own testimony, *Grace Abounding to the Chief of Sinners.* Here we witness, blow-by-blow, a man who thinks and feels deeply and who is, by God's infinitely good and wise providence, subjected to the most severe spiritual attacks of the evil one.

Bunyan wrote this book in 1666 during his first imprisonment in the Bedford Jail. It was during his second imprisonment in 1678 that he wrote his most famous work, *The Pilgrim's Progress.* For the purposes of this compendium of great autobiographical narratives, we have selected a slightly modernized edition of *Grace Abounding* for the Christian student.

Grace Abounding to the Chief of Sinners

In a faithful account of the life of John Bunyan, or
a brief relation of the exceeding mercy of God in Christ
to him; namely, in taking him out of the dunghill, and
converting him to the faith of His blessed Son,
JESUS CHRIST.
Here is also
particularly showed, what sight of, and what trouble he had for sin; and also what various temptations
he met with; and how God hath carried him through
them. Corrected and much enlarged by the author, for
the benefit of the tempted and dejected Christian.
By JOHN BUNYAN.
LONDON,
Published by George Larkin, 1666.
John Bunyan wrote this book
while still in Bedford Prison.
It was first published in 1666, the
year of the Fire of London.

❋ PREFACE

Children, grace be with you, Amen. I having been taken from you in presence, and so tied up,[1] that I cannot perform that duty which God has given me for you, for your further edifying and building up in faith and holiness, etc., so that you may see my soul has fatherly care and desire after your spiritual and everlasting welfare; I now once again, as before, from the top of Shenir and Hermon, so now from the lions' dens, from the mountains of the leopards (Song of Sol. 4:8), do look yet after you all, greatly longing to see your safe arrival into the desired haven.

I thank God upon every remembrance of you; and rejoice, even while I stick between the teeth of the lions in the wilderness, at the grace, and mercy, and knowledge of Christ our Savior, which God has bestowed upon you, with abundance of faith and love. Your hungerings and thirstings also after further acquaintance with the Father, in His Son; your tenderness of heart, your trembling at sin, your sober and holy deportment also, before both God and men, is great refreshment to me; 'For ye are my glory and joy' (1 Thess. 2:20).[2]

I have sent you here enclosed, a drop of that honey, that I have taken out of the carcass of a lion (Judg. 14:5-9). I have eaten from it myself also, and am much refreshed by this. (Temptations, when we meet them at first, are as the lion that roared upon Samson; but if we overcome them, the next time

1. The book was written for his congregation, while he was incarcerated in the Bedford jail. John Bunyan was a Baptist pastor, caught in the persecutions that Charles II brought upon the dissenting churches (those that did not want to be part of the Church of England). It was around this time that 2,000 Puritan pastors were discharged from their pastorates and forced into hiding (if they wanted to continue in ministry). Many were arrested and suffered and died in jail during these years.

2. What delights a pastor most is to hear that his congregation trembles at sin, fears God, loves God, and knows God.

we see them, we shall find a nest of honey within them.) The Philistines do not understand me. It is something of a relation of the work of God upon my own soul, even from the very first, till now; wherein you may perceive my castings down, and raisings up; for he wounds, and his hands make whole. It is written in the Scripture (Isa. 38:19), "The father to the children shall make known the truth of God." Yes, it was for this reason I lay so long at Sinai (Deut. 4:10, 11), to see the fire, and the cloud, and the darkness, that I might fear the Lord all the days of my life upon earth, and tell of his wondrous works to my children (Ps. 78:3-5).[3]

3. By reviewing his previous battles, he and others will receive great encouragement. The trials are not pleasant at the time. But when the lion is dead and bees make honey in his carcass, we can enjoy the honey. This is the encouragement we get when we review the grace that God bestowed on us as we faced these trials.

Moses (Num. 33:1, 2) wrote of the journeyings of the children of Israel, from Egypt to the land of Canaan; and commanded also, to remember their forty years' travel in the wilderness. "Thou shalt remember all the way which the Lord thy God led thee these forty years in the wilderness, to humble thee, and to prove thee, to know what was in thine heart, whether thou wouldest keep his commandments, or no" (Deut. 8:2). Therefore this I have endeavored to do; and not only so, but to publish it also; that, if God will, others may be put in remembrance of what He has done for their souls, by reading of His work upon me.

It is profitable for Christians to be often calling to mind the very beginnings of grace with their souls. "It is a night to be much observed unto the Lord for bringing them out from the land of Egypt: this is that night of the Lord to be observed of all the children of Israel in their generations" (Ex. 12:42). "O my God," saith David (Ps. 42:6), "my soul is cast down within me; therefore will I remember thee from the land of Jordan, and of the Hermonites, from the hill Mizar." He remembered also the lion and the bear, when he went to fight with the giant of Gath (1 Sam. 17:36, 37).[4]

4. Another benefit to a testimony like this: It is a monument of remembrance to God's mighty works. David, Moses, and Paul would do the same thing, sharing the testimonies of God's mighty works in their lives.

It was Paul's accustomed manner (Acts 22), and that even when his life was in danger (Acts 24), always to open, before his judges, the manner of his conversion: he would think of that day, and that hour, in the which he first did meet with grace, for he found it a support unto him. When God had brought the children of Israel through the Red Sea, far into the wilderness, yet they must turn quite about thither again, to remember the drowning of their enemies there (Num.14:25). For though they sang His praise before, yet "they soon forgat his works" (Ps. 106:11-13).

In this discourse of mine you may see much; much, I say, of the grace of God towards me. I thank God I can count it much, for it was above my sins and Satan's temptations too. I can remember my fears, and doubts, and sad months with comfort; they are as the head of Goliath in my hand.[5] There was nothing to David like Goliath's sword, even that sword that should have been sheathed in his bowels; for the very sight and remembrance of that preached forth God's deliverance to him. Oh, the remembrance of my great sins, of my great temptations, and of my great fears of perishing for ever! They bring afresh into my mind the remembrance of my great help, my great support from heaven, and the great grace that God extended to such a wretch as I.

My dear children, call to mind the former days, and the years of ancient times: remember also your songs in the night; and commune with your own heart (Ps. 77:5-12). Yes, look diligently, and leave no corner unsearched, for there is treasure hidden, even the treasure of your first and second experience of the grace of God toward you. Remember, I say, the word that first laid hold upon you; remember your terrors of conscience, and fear of death and hell; remember also your tears and prayers to God; how you sighed under every hedge for mercy. Do you have a hill Mizar to remember? Have you forgotten the milk house, the stable, the barn, and the like, where God visited your soul? Remember also the Word—the Word, I say, upon which the Lord has caused you to hope. If you have sinned against light; if you are tempted to blaspheme; if you are down in despair; if you think God fights against you; or if heaven is hidden from your eyes, remember it was this way with your father,[6] but out of them all the Lord delivered me.

5. Bunyan likens his doubts and sins to Goliath, the giant whom David fought in the Valley of Elam.

6. "Your father" speaks of John Bunyan — their father in the faith, their pastor.

I could have made my discourse longer, of my temptations and troubles for sin; as also of the merciful kindness and working of God with my soul. I could also have stepped into a style much higher than this in which I have here discoursed, and could have adorned all things more than here I have seemed to do, but I dare not do that. God did not play in convincing me, the devil did not play in tempting me, neither did I play when I sunk as into a bottomless pit, when the pangs of hell caught hold upon me; therefore I may not play in my relating of them, but I must be plain and simple, and lay down the thing as it was. He that likes it, let him receive it; and he that does not, let him produce something better. Farewell.

My dear children, the milk and honey are beyond this wilderness, God be merciful to you, and grant that you do not be slothful to go in to possess the land.[7]

7. Bunyan had a gift for writing and could have used more flowery prose. He chooses not to because he does not want to lose the seriousness, the gravitas, and the realness of his experience and God's truth that ministered to him.

CHAPTER I – BEGINNINGS OF GOD'S WORKINGS

In telling you of the way God so mercifully worked upon my soul, it will perhaps not be amiss if in the first place I tell you a little bit about my background and the way I was brought up; for then the goodness of God toward me will be the more evident.

I came from a family that had a very low station in life. My father's house was one of the most despised of all the families of the land. So I cannot, as some others can, boast of noble blood and the high-born state. But even so I magnify God because it was from this background that He called me to partake of the grace and life that is in Christ.[1]

Notwithstanding the poverty of my parents, it pleased God to put into their hearts that I should go to school to learn both reading and writing. I learned about as well as other children did from poor homes; though I must confess to my shame that I soon lost what I learned, long before the Lord did His gracious work of conversion upon my soul.

During the years that I was without God, I followed along the course of the world, the spirit that "now worketh in the children of disobedience" (Ephesians 2:2). It was my delight to be taken captive by the devil at his will (2 Timothy 2:26), being filled with all unrighteousness, which worked so strongly within me that I had but few equals for cursing, swearing, lying, and blaspheming the holy name of God.[2]

1. Bunyan was a tinker, which means he traveled about repairing pots and pans. It is a wonder that God chooses "the foolish things of the world to confound the wise." A man of such ignominious background becomes one of the most influential Christians of the last five hundred years.

2. Bunyan was especially given to swearing, lying, and cursing. He counts himself one of the worst men in the community where he was raised.

3. As a 9–10 year old child, he was convicted of his sins, but suppressed it by running headlong into more sins, lusts, and pleasures.

The Town of Bedford, England

I became so settled and rooted in these things that they became a sort of second nature to me. This offended the Lord so much that even in my childhood He scared me with fearful dreams and visions. For often after I had spent a day in sin, I was greatly afflicted while asleep with a feeling of the presence of devils and wicked spirits who, as I then thought, were trying to carry me off with them, and I could not get rid of them.[3]

It was also during these years that I was greatly troubled with the thoughts of the fearful torments of hell fire. I feared that it would be my lot to be among those devils and hellish fiends who are bound there with the chains and bonds of darkness, waiting for the judgment.

When I was a child of only nine or ten years old, these things so distressed my soul that, even in the midst of my many sports and other childish activities and among my thoughtless play fellows, I was often very much depressed and afflicted in my mind with these thoughts; yet I could not let go of my sins. I was so overcome with despair that I would never see Heaven, that I often wished that either there were no Hell, or if there were that I could be a devil, for I supposed that it would be better to be a tormentor rather than to be tormented myself.

After a while these terrible dreams stopped and I soon forgot them, for my evil pleasures quickly cut off any memory of them as if they had never been. And then, with more greediness than ever, I let loose the reins of my lust and delighted in all transgressions against the law of God; so I was the ringleader in all manner of vice and ungodliness until my marriage. But, if it were not for a miracle of grace, I would not only have perished by a stroke of eternal justice, but would also have laid myself open to shame and disgrace before the face of the whole world.

During these times, thoughts of God were very unpleasant to me. I could neither endure such thoughts myself, nor could I stand it if any others had such thoughts; and whenever I saw someone reading Christian books, I felt as though he were in prison. Then I said to God, "Depart from me for

I desire not a knowledge of thy ways" (Job 21:14). By this time I was free from everything good. Heaven and Hell were both out of sight and out of mind; as for being saved or being damned, I cared not in the least. Oh Lord, You know my life and what it was like; my ways are not hidden from You.[4]

And yet how well I remember that although I could sin with the greatest delight and ease, even then if I saw anyone doing wrong, who claimed to be a Christian, it made my spirit tremble. I remember one time in particular, when I was at my worst, and I heard someone swear who was thought to be a religious man, it plunged my spirits into the greatest depression and made my heart ache.

But God did not utterly leave me, but kept following along behind me. He did not at this time make me feel how wicked I was, but instead sent strokes of judgment mixed with mercy. Once I fell into a creek and almost drowned. Another time I fell out of a boat into Bedford River, but His mercy preserved me. Still another time, I went out into a field with my friends and an adder crawled over the road; and I struck it over the back with my stick. When I had stunned it I forced open its mouth with my stick and pulled out the sting with my fingers. If it had not been for God's mercy upon me, I might have brought myself to a sudden end with this foolishness.

Something else happened that I have often thought of with thanksgiving. When I was a soldier,[5] I was sent out along with some others to a certain place to besiege it; but just as I was ready to go, someone asked to go in my place; and as he stood sentry duty, he was shot in the head with a musket bullet and died.

These, as I have said, were some of God's judgments and mercies. But none of these things awakened my soul to righteousness, so I kept on sinning and grew more and more rebellious against God and careless of my own salvation.[6]

Soon after this I married, and, in the providence of God, my wife had a brother and mother who were godly people. At the time we married, my wife and I were as poor as poor

4. Bunyan intersperses prayers (as in Augustine's *Confessions*). "Oh Lord, You know my life. . . "

5. Bunyan served in the army under Oliver Cromwell.

6. Life-threatening circumstances in his early years (at least three related here) did not awaken him from the slumbers of his soul.

could be—not having even so much as a dish or a spoon or any other household items between the two of us. Yet she did have two books, *The Plain Man's Pathway to Heaven* and *The Practice of Piety*,[7] which her father had left her when he died. I read those books sometimes, and I found some things in them that pleased me, though they did not convict me of my sin. She often told me what a godly man her father was, how he would scold and punish all that was wrong—both in his own house and also among his neighbors—and what a strict and holy life he lived throughout his days, both in word and deed.

So these books, although they did not reach my heart to awaken it concerning its sad and sinful state, did make me want to reform my vicious life, and I began to fall in very eagerly with the religion of the times. I went to church twice a day on Sundays,[8] and while there I was very devout, talking and singing just as the others did, yet all the while keeping my wicked life. And I was so filled with superstition that I had the greatest devotion to anything belonging to the church—the priest, the clerk, the vestments, the service and everything else. I counted all things holy that were in the church and thought that the priest and clerks must be especially happy and especially blessed because they were the servants, as I then thought, of God. This feeling grew so strong within me that whenever I saw a priest, no matter how sordid or debauched his life might be, I would find my spirit bowing down to reverence him. I felt that for the great love that I had for them—because I supposed that they were the ministers of God—I could have lain down at their feet. Their name, their clothing and their work fascinated and bewitched me.[9]

7. *The Plain Man's Pathway* was written by Arthur Dent, an early Puritan who ministered in Essex in the later 16th century. Lewis Bayly, author of *The Practice of Piety,* was a Puritan and a chaplain for King James I.

8. It was as common for Englishmen to attend church twice on Sunday as it is common today for men to watch football and baseball games on Sundays.

9. Unbelievers like the superficial elements of religion. They like to believe that they have satisfied the gods with a bit of perfunctory religious exercise.

After I had been that way quite a while, another thought came into my mind, and that was as to whether or not we were descended from the Israelites.[10] I had found in the Scriptures that the Israelites were the special people of God, so I thought that if I were one of this race my soul would indeed be happy. I longed to know the answer to this question but couldn't figure out how to find out. At last I asked my father about it and he told me no, that we were not. So my spirit fell again and so remained.

All this was happening while I was not even aware of the danger and evil of sin! I never considered that sin would damn me,[11] no matter what religion I followed, unless I was found in Christ. I never even thought about whether there was such a Person or not. Thus, a man wanders blindly, for he knows not the way to the city of God (Ecclesiastes 10:15).

But one day it happened that, among the various sermons our parson preached, his subject was "The Sabbath Day," and the evil of breaking it either with work or sports or in any other way. Then my conscience began to prick me and I thought that he had preached this sermon on purpose to show me my evil ways. That was the first time I can remember that I felt guilty and very burdened, for the moment at least, and I went home when the sermon was ended with a great depression upon my spirit.[12]

For a little while this made me bitter against my former pleasures, but it didn't last very long. Before I had had a good dinner, the trouble began to go off my mind and my heart returned to its old course. Oh, how glad I was that the fire was put out so that I might sin again without worrying about it! And so, after my dinner, I shook the sermon out of my mind and returned with great delight to my usual custom of sports that afternoon.

But the same day, as I was in the middle of a game of "cat"[13] and had just struck one blow, and was about to strike the second time, a voice darted from Heaven into my soul and

10. Unbelievers also tend to migrate towards weird cults as Augustine did with the Manicheans. This is very common in Western nations today with their proliferation of cults — always a market for them among the unbelieving populace. British Israelitism is still around today — the belief that the lost tribes of Israel ended up in Great Britain.

11. The problem of course is that people are avoiding the core problem — their sin.

12. It is still common for people to ignore the Sabbath Day (the Lord's Day) by playing sports or working on Sunday.

13. The game of "Cat" was an early version of baseball. The cat (a piece of wood) is placed on the ground, struck at one end to propel it upward, and then slammed with the stick as far as possible. The batter then runs the bases before the fielder retrieves the cat and throws it back to home base.

said, "Will you leave your sins and go to Heaven, or keep your sins and go to Hell?"

I was immeasurably surprised, and leaving my "cat" upon the ground I looked up to Heaven. I felt as though I could almost see the Lord Jesus looking down upon me with hot displeasure, as though He were severely threatening me with some terrible punishment for this and other ungodly practices.[14]

14. Bunyan was convicted of his insensitivity to his sins.

This thought had no sooner come into my mind, when suddenly this conclusion fastened on my spirit (for my sins were suddenly very much before me again) that I had been such a great sinner that now it was too late for me to think about Heaven; for Christ would not forgive men nor pardon my transgressions. Then, while I was thinking about this and fearing that it might be so, I felt my heart sink in despair, concluding it was too late; and so I decided that I might as well go on in sin. I decided that I would be miserable if I left my sins and miserable if I followed them; and, if I were going to be damned anyway, I might as well be damned for many sins as be damned for a few.[15]

15. Bunyan commits two sins here — refusing to believe that God's gift of forgiveness could be effectual for him and his commitment to plunge back into sin with as much force as he could muster.

So there I stood in the middle of my play, in front of all the others, but I told them nothing. Having decided this, I returned desperately to my sports again; and I well remember that presently such a despair took hold of my soul that I was persuaded that I could never again be happy except for whatever happiness I could get out of my sin. Heaven was already gone—I must not think any more about that—so I found an increasing desire to take my fill of sin and to taste the sweetness of it. I made as much haste as I could to fill my belly with its delicacies, lest I should die before I had my desires, for that was the thing that I most greatly feared. I do not lie. These were really my desires and I wanted them with all my heart. May the good Lord whose mercy is unsearchable forgive my transgressions. I am confident that this temptation of the Devil is more common among the poor creatures around us than many are aware of. They have concluded that there is no hope for them because they have loved sin; therefore, after sin they will go (Jeremiah 2:25; 18:12).

And so I went on in sin, but was disturbed because it never seemed to satisfy me. This went on for about a month or more. Then one day as I was standing at a neighbor's shop window, cursing and swearing in my usual way, the neighbor's wife was sitting inside and heard me. Although she was a very loose and ungodly wretch, she protested because I swore and cursed so much. She said she trembled to hear me. She told me that I was the ungodliest fellow for swearing that she ever heard in all her life, and that by doing this I was going to spoil all the young people in the whole town if they got into my company.

At this reproof I was silenced and put to secret shame.[16] I stood there with my head hanging down and wishing that I might be a little child again and that my father might teach me to speak without this wicked swearing. I thought, "I'm so accustomed to it now it is useless to think of reforming, for I could never do it." But—how it happened I do not know— from this time forward I stopped my swearing to such an extent that it was a great wonder to me to see it happen. Whereas formerly I put one oath before what I said and another behind it, to make my words have authority, now without swearing, I could speak better and more pleasantly than ever before. But all this time I knew not Jesus Christ, nor did I leave my sports and play.

Soon after this I fell into company with a poor man who called himself a Christian. He talked very pleasantly about the Scriptures and about religion. Liking what he said, I found my Bible and began to take quite a bit of pleasure in reading it, especially the historical parts. As for Paul's letters and other parts of Scripture like that, I couldn't understand them at all. I was still ignorant of my own nature and of the desire and ability of Jesus Christ to save us.

16. Bunyan was corrected by an immoral woman (for his bad language), and he was shamed into changing his ways. This, he says, did not constitute salvation.

CHAPTER II – AN OUTWARD CHANGE OF LIFE

So I began some outward reformation, both in my speech and life, and decided to try to keep the Ten Commandments as a way of getting to Heaven. I tried hard and thought I did pretty well sometimes in keeping them, and at such times I was quite pleased with myself.[1] But now and then I would break one and it worried my conscience so that I could hardly sleep. Then I would repent and say that I was sorry for it and promise God to do better next time, and I would begin to feel hopeful again—for I thought that at such times I was pleasing God as well as any man in England.

1. Bunyan attempts a salvation by works approach for a while. This was the next form of false religion he played with.

I continued this way for about a year, and all this time our neighbors took me to be very godly and marveled greatly to see so much change in my life and actions. Indeed, there was a great change, though I knew not Christ nor His grace nor faith nor hope; but as I have since learned, if I had died then my situation would have been most fearful.

Bedford River

As I say, my neighbors were amazed at this great conversion from rebel profanity to something like a moral life and a sober man. So now they began to praise me and to speak well of me both to my face and behind my back. Now I was, as they said, a godly man. Now I had become honest. And how pleased I was when I heard them say these things about me for, although I was still nothing but a poor painted hypocrite,

2. "Ringing" the bells in the church was a form of music. An impoverished people did not have access to musical instruments as we do today.

3. In a day where there were no fast cars and heavy objects flying around, the church bells were the heaviest objects that might have easily killed somebody. Our lives are always in God's hands, and we are always one breath away from death.

4. John Bunyan hoped that his giving up dancing would merit a right relationship with God.

I loved to be talked about as one who was truly godly. I was proud of my godliness and indeed I did everything I could to be well-spoken of. And so I continued for a year or more.

Now I must tell you that before this time I used to have a great delight in ringing,[2] but my conscience now began to be tender and I thought that this was something I ought not to do. I forced myself to quit; yet my mind still hankered for this, and so I would go to the steeple-house and look on, though I dared not ring myself. I decided this was not right either, but still I forced myself to stay and look on. But then I began to think, "What if one of the bells should fall?" So I stood under a main beam that lay across the steeple under the bells, thinking that I would be safe there. But then I thought: "What if the bell fell with a swing? It might hit the wall first and then rebound upon me and kill me anyway."[3] This made me stand in the steeple door, and now I thought I was surely safe enough. If the bell should fall, I could slip out behind the thick walls and so be preserved.

After this, I still would go to see them ring, but would not go any farther than the steeple door. Then it came into my head: "What if the steeple itself should fall?" This thought so shook my mind that I dared no longer stand even in the steeple door, but was forced to flee for fear the steeple would fall upon my head.

Another thing was my dancing. It was a full year before I could finally leave that. But all this time, when I thought that I was keeping this or that commandment, or when I did something good, I had a fine feeling and thought that now God will surely be pleased with me; I thought no one in England could please God better than I.[4]

But, poor wretch that I was, all this time I was ignorant of Jesus Christ and was trying to establish my own righteousness, and would have perished thereby if God had not been merciful to me.

Then on a certain day, in the good providence of God, I had to make a trip to Bedford for my work; and in one of the streets of that town I came to a place where there were three or four poor women sitting in a door in the sun talking about the things of God. Since I was now willing to listen to such discussion, I came close to hear what they were saying—I was now myself a brisk talker in matters of religion—but they were far above my reach. Their talk was about a new birth, a work of God in their hearts, and how they were sure that they had been born as helpless sinners. They talked about the way that God had visited their souls with His love in the Lord Jesus, and spoke of the particular words and promises that had helped and comforted and supported them against the temptations of the Devil. What's more, they talked about particular temptations they had from Satan, and told each other how God had helped them.

They also talked about their evil hearts and their unbelief and their goodness. It seemed to me that they spoke with such pleasure of the Bible, and they had so much grace in all that they said, that they had found a new sort of world; they were people that could not be compared with anyone else (Numbers 23:9).[5]

Now my heart began to shake for I saw that all my thoughts about religion and salvation had never once considered the question of the new birth. I began to realize that I knew nothing about the comfort and the promise that this might give, nor about the deceitfulness and treachery of my own wicked heart. As for my secret evil thoughts, I had never taken any notice of them; I did not even recognize Satan's temptations and certainly did not know how they could be resisted.

After I had listened a while and thought about what they said, I left them and went my way. My heart was still with them, for I was greatly affected by their words because I was convinced by them that I did not have what would make me a truly godly man, and I was convinced that those who were truly godly were really happy and blessed.

5. These Christian women seemed different to Bunyan. Their lives were marked by godliness: they loved God's Word, they realized the New Birth, they were sensitive to Satan's temptations, and they appreciated the love of Jesus Christ.

6. Two things were happening to Bunyan at this time as the Holy Spirit worked on him. He was convicted of the truth of the Bible, and he became more reflective on the truth he had heard in the past.

7. The friend from his past was known for his foul mouth and his fornication. The friend was enslaved to his sins.

8. The Ranters were a cult that developed during this time of upheaval in England. They were extremely heretical — pantheistic and antinomian (radically licentious). They denied the authority of Scripture and all church leadership. Laurence Clarkson was one of their leaders, who taught that only the commandment "Thou shalt not murder" was worth keeping.

So I made it my business to go there often and be in the company of these poor people, for I could not stay away; and the more I was there, the more I realized the seriousness of my own condition. I still remember quite clearly how two things were happening to me that surprised me very much, especially considering how blind, ignorant, and ungodly I had been just before. The first of these two things was a very great tenderness which caused me to be deeply convicted that whatever they told me from the Bible was true; the other was that my mind kept turning back to the things they had told me and to all other good things that I had ever heard or read about.[6]

Now my mind was like a horse-leech, sucking at a vein and stuffed full but still crying out, "Give, give" (Proverbs 30:15). It was so fixed on eternity and the things concerning the kingdom of Heaven—though I knew very little yet about them—that neither pleasure nor profit nor persuasion nor threat could make me let go my hold. I say this with shame, but it is certainly true, that it was then as difficult for me to take my mind from Heaven and bring it down to earth as it has since been very often to get it away from earth and up to Heaven.

There is one thing I must tell you about now. There was a young man in our town whom I used to feel closer to than anyone else; but he was terribly wicked with his cursing, swearing, and whoring;[7] so I shook him off and quit his company. About three months afterward I met him going along the road and asked him how he was getting along. His reply was full of curses, and he told me that he was well. "But, Harry," I said, "why do you curse and swear like this? What will become of you if you die in this condition?" He answered me in great anger, "What would the Devil do for company if it were not for such as I?"

About this time I came across some books by the Ranters,[8] which were thought very highly of by several old Christians I knew. I read some of these but was not able to decide very much about them, so I thought— seeing that I was not able to judge whether they were good or not—I would pray fervently and say, "Oh Lord, I am a fool and not able to tell truth from error. Lord, don't leave me in my blindness. Don't let me wrongly approve or condemn this doctrine. If it is of God, do not let me despise it, and if it is of the Devil, do not let me embrace it. Lord, I lay my soul at Your feet concerning this matter. Do not let me be deceived, I humbly beseech Thee."

All this time I had one very close spiritual companion and that was the poor man I spoke of before. But about this time, he became a Ranter and gave himself up to every manner of sin; he would deny that there was a God, angel or spirit, and would laugh at all my attempts to keep him sober.

When I rebuked his wickedness, he only laughed the more, and said that he had tried all religions and had never hit the right one until now. So I turned aside from these cursed principles and became as great a stranger to him as I had before been his friend.

This man was not my only temptation. Because of my job, I frequently had to go out into the country where I happened to meet several people who, although formerly very strict in religious matters, had now been drawn away by the Ranters. They would tell me about the evil things that they were doing in the darkness. For they had become perfect, they said, and so they could do whatever they wanted and it would not be sin! These were terrible temptations to me, very suitable to my lusts, since I was only a young man.[9] God, who had designed me for better things, kept me in the fear of His name and did not suffer me to accept such cursed principles. Blessed be God who put it into my heart to cry out to Him to be kept and directed and to distrust my own wisdom; for I have seen the effect of that prayer right up to the present time, in His preserving me, not only from these particular areas, but also from those that have come up since.

Cutaway of a church bell

9. Bunyan had the privilege of witnessing the many demonic ploys that deceive mankind. He watched his own friends and acquaintances taken by weird cults. This can be rather intimidating if not frightening. He cried out to God to direct him in the proper way. Only God can preserve us from deception within us and around us.

✺ CHAPTER III – INTERNAL WRESTLINGS

The Bible was precious to me in those days and I began to look at it with new eyes. The letters of the apostle Paul were especially sweet to me. It seemed as though I were never out of the Bible, but I was always either reading it or thinking about it. While I was reading, I came upon this passage: "To one is given by the Spirit the word of wisdom; to another the word of knowledge by the same Spirit; to another faith" (I Corinthians 12:8–9). I know now, of course, that this is talking about an extraordinary kind of faith, but at that time I thought that it meant ordinary faith that other Christians had. I thought about this a long time and could not tell what to do. Sometimes I questioned whether I had any faith at all, but I did not want to decide that I had none, for if I did that, I thought that I would then forever be a castaway from God.

I decided that though I was but an ignorant sot, and did not have those blessed gifts of knowledge and understanding that other people had, I was not altogether faithless, even though I did not quite know what faith was. For it had been shown to me (by Satan, I have since learned) that those who decide they have no faith have no hope forever.[1]

1. Faith is basic to salvation. Some people may have faith but lose assurance that they have faith at points.

2. John Bunyan is very aware of the Devil's existence and his methods. The Tempter takes advantage of those who are ignorant of Scripture and those who are not grounded in the truth.

And so I would not admit to myself the true state of affairs in my soul. But God did not let me continue to heal myself and thus destroy my soul.

He made me keep on searching until I knew for sure whether I actually did have faith or not. And always, there were running through my mind these questions: Do I really lack faith? How can I tell whether or not I have faith? I saw quite clearly that if I had none, I was sure to perish forever.

And so at last I faced the question squarely and was willing to test myself as to whether or not I had faith. But I was so ignorant that I no more knew how to find out than I would know how to begin some new and strange piece of work which I had never seen done before nor thought about.

Up until now, I had not talked to anyone about this but had only thought about it myself. While I was trying to think how to begin, the Tempter came in with his lies to tell me that there was no way for me to know whether I had faith until I had tried to work some miracles, and he brought to my mind Scriptures that seemed to make this idea logical.[2] One day, as I was going along between the towns of Elstow and Bedford, the temptation was hot upon me to try to do a miracle to see if I had faith. The miracle was that I would say to the puddles to dry up and to the dry spots in the road that they should be puddles. But just as I was about to speak the thought came into my mind that I had better go over under a hedge nearby and pray first that God would make me able. But when I had decided to pray, the terrible thought came that if I prayed and then tried and nothing happened, it would be very clear that I had no faith and would forever be lost. So I decided that I would not force the issue but would wait a while before trying.[3]

3. The essence of faith is not working miracles. The essence of faith is to believe that God exists and that He is a rewarder of those who diligently seek Him (Heb. 11:6). It is to believe on the Lord Jesus Christ and that God has raised Him from the dead.

Now I was at a great loss to know what to think, for if only those who could do such miracles had faith, I was certainly never likely to have it. So I was caught between the Devil's temptation and my own ignorance, and I was so perplexed that I simply didn't know what to do.[4]

4. The test of the existence of faith in a person is not miracle working either. The test of the existence of faith is seen in the person's life (James 2:18ff).

It was about this time that I had sort of a vision of the wonderful state of happiness that these poor people at Bedford were in. I saw them as if they were on the sunny side of a high mountain and were there refreshing themselves in the pleasant sun, while I was shivering and shrinking in the cold with frost, snow, and dark clouds all about me. It seemed that there was between me and them a high wall that went all around the mountain. How I wanted to get through that wall so that I could enjoy myself there in the heat of the sun as they were doing!

Again and again I tried to find a way to get through the wall, but for a long time I could find no entrance until finally I saw a tiny doorway. I tried to go through, but it was so narrow that all my efforts were in vain. At last, after a great struggle, I did get my head through, and after that, by squeezing myself along, my shoulders followed, and finally my whole body. Then I was very glad and went and sat down in the midst of them and was comforted with the light and the heat of their sun.[5]

The mountain was the Church of the living God. The sun that shown upon it was the shining from God's merciful face. The wall was the Bible that separated between the Christians and the world. The door was Jesus Christ who is the way to God the Father (John 14:6; Matthew 7:14). The fact that this door was so narrow that I could hardly get in showed me that no one could enter into this life but those who were in real earnest and left the wicked world behind them. For there is room here only for body and soul and, not for a body, soul, and a load of sin.

This vision and its meaning bore down upon my spirits for many days, during which I saw what a forlorn and sad condition I was in.[6] Yet at the same time I prayed much, both at home and at work. Both in the house and in the field, I lifted my heart up to God, repeating the cry of David in Psalm 25, "O bring thou me out of my distresses!" for I still didn't know what to do.

Woodcut portrait of John Bunyan

5. Bunyan meditated on this allegory for a while, but it is not clear that he acted on it, entered through the door, and believed in Christ (at this moment).

6. An unhealthy questioning into God's election can lead to discouragement. We are to respond to His commands (to believe in Christ), not worry about whether we are among the elect.

I could not yet begin to feel any assurance that I had faith in Christ, but instead I began to have fresh doubts about the possibility of my future happiness. Was I among the elect? What if the day of grace had already passed and gone?

These two questions worried me a great deal. I was determined to find my way to Heaven and to glory and yet the question of election terribly discouraged me, and sometimes it seemed as though all the strength of my body had been taken away by the force and the power of this terrible question. One Scripture especially seemed to trample upon all my hopes: "It is not of him that willeth, nor of him that runneth, but of God that showeth mercy" (Romans 9:16).

I didn't know what to do with this Scripture, for I saw quite clearly that unless God had chosen me as one upon whom He could have mercy, I could wish and hope and work until my heart broke, but it would do me no good. So I kept asking myself, "How can I tell if I am elected?" "What if I am not?" "What then?"

"Oh, Lord," I thought, "what if I am not among the elect?"

"You probably aren't," said the Tempter.

"But it may be that I am," I thought.

"Well," said Satan, "you may as well forget about it. If you are not chosen of God, there's no hope of your being saved, for 'it is not of him that willeth, nor of him that runneth, but of God that showeth mercy.'"

I was at the end of my wits over these things, not knowing what to say or how to answer. In fact, I didn't realize that it was Satan who was tempting me, but thought it was my own good thinking that brought up this question. I agreed perfectly with the idea that only the elect could have eternal life; my question was whether I was one of them.

And so for several days I was in the greatest perplexity and often ready to give up. But one day after many weeks of depression over this matter—as I was finally giving up the ghost of all my hopes of ever attaining life—there came into my mind a single sentence: "Look at the generations of old and see: did ever any trust in the Lord and was confounded?"[7]

This mightily encouraged my soul.[8] At that very instant it became clear to me that if I began at the beginning of Genesis and read to the end of Revelation, I would not find a single person who had trusted in the Lord and had been rejected. So, I went to my Bible to see if this were so, for I knew that my Bible would surely tell me. It was a great strength and comfort to my spirit, as though it actually talked with me.

I looked and looked, but I couldn't find this verse. Then I asked first one good man and then another if he knew where it could be found in the Bible, but they knew of no such sentence. I wondered why this sentence should come to me so suddenly with so much comfort and stay with me, and yet no one else could find it—but I never doubted that it was in the Bible. I kept looking for about a year and still couldn't find the place, until at last I found it in one of the apocryphal books, Ecclesiasticus 2:11.[9] At first this bothered me considerably because it was not in the Bible itself; but since this sentence was a summary of many promises that are actually in the Bible, I decided that it was my duty to take comfort from it. And I blessed God for leading me to this conclusion, for it helped me a lot, and that particular sentence still often shines before my face.

It was after this that other doubts came strongly upon me. How did I know that the day of grace had not already gone? How did I know that it was not too late for me? I could remember that one day I was out in the country walking along and thinking about this a lot. The Tempter aggravated my trouble by telling me that these good people of Bedford were already converted, that they were all that God had saved in this part of the country, and that I had come too late, for these had received the blessing before I came.

This brought me into great distress, for I thought it very likely that this was the situation. I was crushed as I thought of the long years I had spent in sin, and often cried out, "Oh

7. Ecclesiasticus 2:10 reads "Look at the generations of old, and see; did ever any trust in the Lord, and was confounded? or did any abide in his fear, and was forsaken? or whom did he ever despise, that called upon him?"

8. It is promises based on Scripture that feed Bunyan's soul and lift him out of the malaise of discouragement.

9. The Protestants have rejected the book of Ecclesiasticus as part of the canon of Scripture. It is considered apocryphal.

that I had listened sooner! If only I had turned to God seven years ago!" It made me angry with myself to think that I had no more wit than to trifle away my time until my soul and Heaven were lost.

After a long time, I was hardly able to go on because of this fear. As I was out walking one day and was just about at the same place where I received my other encouragement, these words broke in upon my mind: "Compel them to come in, that my house may be filled. . . and yet there is room" (Luke 14:23, 22). The words "and yet there is room" were sweet words to me, for truly I thought that the Lord Jesus had me in mind when He said this,[10] and that He knew the time would come when I would be filled with the fear that there was no place left for me in His kingdom. And so He spoke this word and left it upon the record so that I could find it and get help from it against this vile temptation. This I at that time fully believed.

I went on quite a while in the light and encouragement of these words, and they were especially a comfort to me when I thought that the Lord Jesus had spoken them on purpose for my sake.

10. Faith receives the Word as God's word spoken directly to "me." The Word of God needs to speak louder in our minds than the voice of the Devil (who speaks lies).

CHAPTER IV – TEMPTATIONS TO DOUBT

After this there were plenty of temptations to go back again into sin: temptations from Satan, from my own heart, and from my godless friends. But I thank God that these were allayed by a clear understanding of death and the day of judgment which were ever before me. I would often think about Nebuchadnezzar to whom God had given so much and yet, I thought, if this great man had everything in the world, one hour in hell-fire would make him forget all. This thought was a great help to me.

About this time I noticed something in the Bible that interested me about the animals that were called clean and unclean under the Mosaic laws. I thought of these animals as being types of men: the clean animals were types of those men who were the children of God; the unclean ones were the children of the Wicked One. When I read that the clean beasts "chewed the cud," I thought that this meant that we are to feed upon the Word of God. They also "parted," and I decided this meant that if we are to be saved, we must part with the ways of ungodly men.[1] As I read further, I noticed that if we chew the cud as the hare does, but we walk with claws as a dog or parted hoof like a swine, we are still unclean. Or, if we part the hoof like the swine but do not chew cud as the sheep do, we are also unclean. I thought that the hare was a type of those

1. Bunyan was always quick to draw allegories. This time, he draws them from the description of the clean animals in the Old Testament. The clean animals chewed the cud (meditated on the Word of God) and parted the hoof (would come out from the world and be separate.)

that talk about the Word and yet walk in the ways of sin; that the swine was like a person that parts with his outward sin, but still does not have the Word of faith, without which there can be no salvation, no matter how devout a person may be (Deuteronomy 14). I found out from reading the Word that those who are to be glorified with Christ in another world must be called by Him here. They must know the comforts of His Spirit down here as a preparation for that future rest in the house of glory, which is in Heaven above.

And so now again, I was in distress not knowing what to do because I feared that I was not among those whom He had called. If I am not called, I thought, who then can help me? But I now began to love those words that spoke about a Christian's being called, as when the Lord said to one, "Follow me," and to another, "Come after me." And oh, how I wished that He would say this to me too! How gladly would I have come![2]

2. God calls all men everywhere to repentance. What we need are ears to hear that call. Christ (Wisdom) cries out to us. He calls us. Those who read the Scriptures with ears of faith recognize the call is personal.

I cannot express in words my longings and my cryings out to Christ to call me. This went on for quite a while; I was eager to be converted to Jesus Christ and I could see that being converted would put me into such a glorious state that I could never be content without a share in it. If it could have been gotten for gold, what would I not have given for it! If I had the whole world, I would have given it ten thousand times over for this, that my soul might be converted.

And now how lovely in my eyes was everyone I thought to be converted! They shone and walked like people who carried the feel of Heaven upon them. I could see how the lot was fallen to them in pleasant places and they had a goodly heritage (Psalm 16:6).

The verse that really made me sick was one in St. Mark concerning Christ: "He goeth up into a mountain, and calleth unto him whom he would and they came unto him" (Mark 3:13).

This Scripture made me faint with fear and yet it also kindled fire in my soul. I feared that Christ would have no liking for me, for He called only "those whom he would." But the great glory of those who are called so inflamed my heart that I could not read of any of those whom Christ had called without wishing: Oh, that I had been in their clothes; Oh, that I had been born Peter, or John. Would that I had been there and heard Him when He called them. How I would have cried out, "O Lord, call me too!" But I feared that He would not.

And the Lord let me go on this way for many months and showed me nothing more, neither that I was already called nor that I might be called later on. But at last, after much time spent and many groans to God, there came to me this thought: "I will cleanse their blood that I have not cleansed: for the Lord dwelleth in Zion" (Joel 3:21). These words, I felt, were sent to encourage me to keep waiting upon God, and they seemed to say that if I were not already converted, yet the time might come.

It was about this time that I began to tell these poor people in Bedford about my situation. When they knew about it they talked to Mr. Gifford about me and he came and talked to me and seemed to be hopeful for me, though I think there was actually little reason for this. He invited me to his house where I could hear him talk with others about the way God had dealt with their souls. But from all this I still received no certainty, and from that time I began to see more clearly the terrible condition of my wicked heart. Now I began to recognize sin, wicked thoughts within me which I had not noticed before. Meanwhile, my desire for Heaven and eternal life began to fade and I found that, whereas my soul was full of longing for God, I now began to hanker after every foolish thing.

Now, I thought, I am growing worse and worse; now I am farther from conversion than ever before. So again I became terribly discouraged. I did not believe that Christ loved me. I could not see Him, nor hear Him, nor feel Him, nor enjoy any of His things. I was driven with the tempest and my heart wanted to be unclean.[3]

Plaque: "IN THIS HOUSE JOHN BUNYAN SOUGHT SPIRITUAL HELP FROM JOHN GIFFORD IN THE 1650'S"

3. By the law comes the knowledge of sin and conviction of sin. Bunyan begins to see a clearer picture of his own sin and defilement.

Sometimes I would tell my condition to the people of God and they would pity me and tell me of the promises, but they might as well have told me to reach the sun with my fingers as to rely upon these promises, for all sense and feeling was against it. I saw that I had a heart that insisted upon sin; therefore I must be condemned.

I have often thought since that I was somewhat like the child whom the father brought to Christ, and while he was on the way to Him, the Devil threw him down and tore him so that he lay wallowing and foaming (Luke 9:42 and Mark 9:20).

4. Bunyan sees that he was resisting Christ at this time.

In those days I sometimes found my heart so shut against the Lord and His Word that it seemed as though my shoulder were to the door to keep Him out,[4] and all the while I was crying out with many a bitter sigh, "Good Lord, break it open; Lord, break these gates of brass and cut these bars of iron asunder!" (Psalm 107:16). And sometimes there seemed to come a word of peace from the Lord: "I girded thee though thou hast not known me" (Isaiah 45:5).

But all this while, I had never been more tender of conscience against sinning, and would smart at every touch of evil. I could hardly talk for fear I would somehow say the wrong thing. I found myself in a miry bog that shook if I so much as stirred and it seemed I had been abandoned there by God and Christ and the Spirit and all good things.[5]

5. It is the agony of conviction, the "spirit of bondage again to fear," that Bunyan is experiencing here. These were very uncomfortable years for him. The agony of soul this man felt over the years is truly a remarkable element of his testimony.

But I did notice this, that although I had been such a great sinner before turning to God, yet God never seemed to charge me as guilty for the sins that I had done while I was ignorant. He did show me though, that I was lost if I did not have life, because of the sins I had done. I understood perfectly well that I needed to be presented without fault before God and that this could only be done by Jesus Christ.

But the sin and pollution I was born with—that was my great plague and affliction. I was more loathsome in my own eyes than a toad, and I thought that I was the same way in God's eyes. I could see that sin and corruption came out of my heart as naturally as water bubbled out of a fountain. I thought that everyone else had a better heart than mine, and that none but the Devil himself could equal me for inward wickedness and pollution of mind. And so it was that I fell again into the deepest despair because of my vileness, for I concluded that this condition I was in could not be true if I were in a state of grace. I am surely forsaken of God and given up to the Devil, I thought. And thus I continued for many years.

During this period there were two things that made me wonder. The first was when I saw old people hunting after the things of this life as if they would live forever; the other was when I saw Christians crushed by outward losses as of a husband, wife, or child. "Lord," I thought, "if they work so hard and shed so many tears for the things of this present life, how I am to be pitied and prayed for, for my soul is dying, my soul is being damned. If my soul were in good condition and I were sure of it, oh, how rich would I think myself, blessed with but bread and water! I would count these but small afflictions and bear them as little burdens, 'but a wounded spirit, who can bear?'"[6]

And although I was so troubled with the realization of my own wickedness, I was afraid to let go of this sense of guilt, for I found that unless guilt on one's conscience were taken off in the right way—that is, through the blood of Christ—a man would grow worse because he was no longer troubled about his sin.[7] And so whenever I felt this sense of sin disappearing, I would strive for it again by thinking of the punishment of sin in hell-fire. I would cry, "Lord, do not let this sense of guiltiness go away except it be through the blood of Christ and the application of Your mercy through Him to my soul"—for that Bible verse lay heavily upon me: "Without shedding of blood is no remission" (Hebrews 9:22). What frightened me was that I had seen some people who, while under the wounds of conscience, would cry and pray, but now they felt at ease about their trouble—though they had received no pardon for sin—and did not seem to care how they lost their feeling of guilt as

6. Bunyan is seeing the eternal perspective. Earthly losses and gains are nothing in comparison to eternal losses and gains. What shall a man profit if he gain the whole world and lose his own soul?

7. Some are convicted of their sins for a while, and then become more hardened in their sins later. These stories do produce the fear of God in the soul. When Ananias and Sapphira were killed in Acts 5, "great fear came upon all the church."

long as they got it off their minds. And since they'd gotten rid of it the wrong way, they had become harder and blinder and more wicked than before. It made me afraid and made me cry out to God that it might not be so with me.

And now I was sorry that God had made me, for I feared that I had been cast aside, and I counted an unconverted man the saddest of all creatures.

I did not think it was possible that I could ever have enough goodness in my heart even to thank God that He had made me a man, though I knew that man is the most noble of all creatures, although by sin he has made himself the lowest. I was glad for the beasts, birds, and fishes, for they did not have a sinful nature and were not subject to the wrath of God. They were not to go to hell-fire after death, and I would have been glad if I had been one of them.

❈ CHAPTER V – FAITH

But at last there came the comforting time. I heard a sermon from the Song of Solomon (4:1): "Behold, thou art fair, my love; behold, thou art fair." From this text the preacher came to these conclusions: (1) That the Church, and so every saved soul, is the object of Christ's love. (2) Christ's love is without a cause. (3) Christ's love has been hated by the world. (4) Christ's love continues when those He loves are under temptation and seeming destruction. (5) Christ's love lasts to the end.

It was only when he came to his fourth point that I got something out of the sermon. He said that the saved soul is Christ's love even when tempted and deserted and so the poor tempted soul needs still to remember these two words: "my love."[1]

On the way home, I kept thinking about these things and I well remember saying in my heart: "What is the use of thinking about these two words?" But this question had no sooner passed through my mind than the two words began to kindle in my spirit. "Thou art my love," something kept saying to me and must have repeated it twenty times. As these words continued, they became stronger and warmer and began to make me look up, but I was still between hope and fear and replied in my heart: "But is it true? But is it true?" And then

1. It is hard to identify the exact moment of a man's conversion or regeneration. We take this to be the point of Bunyan's conversion, when he heard this sermon on Song of Solomon 4:1.

2. God's Word comes audibly to John Bunyan throughout this narrative. There is nothing in terms of extra-scriptural revelation here, but Bunyan makes prophetic application to himself from the Word of God (an actual text) conveyed to him with force.

3. Maturity in faith demands watchfulness and prayer.

4. Bunyan enjoyed peace after his conversion for forty days before the major storm hit.

that sentence came to me, "He. . . wist not that it was true which was done by the angel" (Acts 12:9).[2]

Then I began to receive the word that had over and over made this joyful sound within my soul: "Thou art my love, and nothing shall separate thee from my love." And now at last my heart was full of comfort and hope and now I could believe that my sins would be forgiven. Yes, I was now so taken up with the love and mercy of God that I remember wondering how I could contain it till I got home. I felt that I could have spoken of His love and mercy to me even to the very crows that sat upon the plowed lands as I went by, had they been capable of understanding me. And so I said in my soul with much gladness, "I am sure that I will never forget this experience forty years from now." But alas! Within less than forty days I began to question everything again.[3]

Yet there were times when I was helped to believe that this had been a true manifestation of grace to my soul, even though I had lost much of the feeling of it. It was about a week or two after this that I began to think a lot about the Scripture: "Simon, Simon, behold, Satan hath desired to have you" (Luke 22:31). Sometimes it would sound so loud within me that once I remember I turned around thinking that someone had called to me from a great distance away. As I look back on it now, I think that this word came to stir me up to prayer and watchfulness and to tell me that a cloud and a storm were coming down upon me, but I did not understand it.

And if I remember rightly, that time it called so loudly to me was the last time I heard it. I can still hear these words, "Simon, Simon," as they sounded in my ears. Although that was not my name, it made me suddenly look behind me, believing that the one calling so loudly meant me.

But I was so foolish and ignorant that I did not understand the reason why this happened, though all too soon I was able to see that it was sent from Heaven as an alarm to awaken me to prepare for what was coming. But right then I only wondered what it was all about.[4]

CHAPTER VI – THE GREAT STORM

About a month later, "the great storm" arrived and mauled me twenty times worse than anything I had met with before. It came stealing in upon me, first from one side and then from another. First, all my comfort was taken from me and darkness seized upon me. After this, whole floods of blasphemies against God and Christ and the Scriptures seemed to pour into my spirit, to my great confusion and astonishment. These blasphemous thoughts also stirred up questions in me against the very being of God and His only beloved Son, whether there were really a God or Christ and whether the Holy Scriptures might not be just fables and cunning stories, rather than the holy and pure Word of God.[1]

The Tempter also struck me heavily with this question, "How can you tell that the Turks may not have as good Scriptures to prove their Mohammed as the Saviour as we have to prove our Jesus?" Was it possible to think that the many ten thousands in many countries and kingdoms should be without the knowledge of the right way to Heaven (if there were indeed a Heaven) and that we who lived in one little corner of the earth should alone be blessed with this knowledge? Everyone thinks his own religion is right, whether he is a Jew or a Mohammedan or a pagan, and what if all our faith in Christ and the Scriptures were just our imagination?[2]

1. There is no question that John Bunyan was used mightily by God, but men like this are often subject to the most ferocious Satanic attacks.

2. He received doubtful thoughts from the Devil. These caused him major consternation.

3. The Devil can make suggestions in our minds, and we mistake it for our own thoughts. This may have been what John Bunyan was experiencing.

4. The repetition and force by which these suggestions came to him appears to be very strong. Being a young Christian, he was unfamiliar with resisting the Devil. This was new territory for him.

5. The Devil also seemed to be tempting him where he was once most given to sin — blasphemy and swearing.

Sometimes I tried to argue against these thoughts and to think of some of the things that the blessed Paul had said against them. But these thoughts of Paul were eaten up by the very arguments within me.[3] For though we made so much of Paul and of his words, how could I tell but that he might have been a very subtle and cunning man, or might have been badly deceived or even have deliberately tried to mislead and destroy his fellow men?

These suggestions gripped my spirit with their number, continuance, and fiery force. I felt nothing else but these from morning to night, and I concluded that God had in very wrath against my soul given me up to them to be carried away with them as with a mighty whirlwind.[4]

I still felt that there was something in me that refused to go along with these terrible thoughts, because of the distaste that they gave to my spirit. But all such hopeful thoughts were soon drowned out. I often found my mind suddenly begin to curse and to swear, or to speak some grievous thing against God, or Christ, His Son, or against the Scriptures.

Now I thought, "Surely I am possessed of the Devil." And at other times I thought I had become insane, for instead of lauding and magnifying God, when I heard Him spoken of, there would come some horrible blasphemous thought that would bolt out of my heart against Him.[5]

These things sank me into a very deep despair, for I concluded that such things could not possibly be found among those that loved God. I often compared myself with a child who had been kidnapped and carried away from friend and country, kicking and screaming. Kick I did, and also shriek and cry, and yet I was bound in the wings of the temptation and the wind carried me away. I thought also of Saul and of the evil spirit that possessed him, and I greatly feared that my condition was the same as his (1 Samuel 16:14).

During those days, when I heard others talk of the sin against the Holy Spirit, the Tempter would make me want to sin that sin, and want it so much that I felt as though I could never be quiet until I had committed it. If the sin were by speaking some word against the Holy Spirit, then my mouth seemed ready to speak that word whether I would let it or not. The temptation was so strong upon me that often I pressed my hands under my chin to hold my mouth from opening; at other times I leaped head down into some mudhole to keep my mouth from speaking.

And now once again I felt that everything that God had made was better off than I was. I would gladly have exchanged my life for the life of a dog or a horse. They have no souls to perish as mine is likely to do, and added to all my sorrow, I did not seem even to desire deliverance any more. And that Scripture tore at my soul in the midst of these other distractions: "The wicked are like the troubled sea, when it cannot rest, whose waters cast up mire and dirt. There is no peace, saith my God, to the wicked" (Isaiah 57:20–21). Now my heart became exceedingly hard. I could not weep, nor did I desire to. Others could mourn and lament their sins and could rejoice and bless God for Jesus Christ; others could quietly talk of the Word of God; I only was caught in the tempest, and get out of it I could not.

This temptation lasted for about a year[6] and all this time I had to give up Bible reading and prayer, for it was then that I was most distressed with these blasphemies. There would be sudden thoughts to question all that I read. Or again, my mind would be strangely snatched away that I could not remember so much as the sentence that I had just completed.

I was also greatly troubled when I attempted to pray during this time. Sometimes I have felt Satan behind me, pulling my clothes. He would also continually be at me in the time of prayer to "get it done, break off, make haste, you have prayed enough, stay no longer." Sometimes also he would cast his wicked thoughts into my mind; for instance, that I ought to pray to him.

And when my thoughts wandered away, and I tried to fix them upon God, then the Tempter with great force presented

6. This attack lasted for an entire year. That the Devil would put so much time into tempting this man of God is truly extraordinary.

to my heart and fancy the form of a bush or a bull—that I could pray to one of them. And he so got hold of my mind that it was as if I could think of nothing else or pray to nothing else but to these.

Yet there were times, too, when I had some strong feelings of the presence of God and of the reality and truth of His gospel. And at such times, my heart poured itself out with inexpressible groanings. My whole soul was in every word. I cried out with terrible pangs of pain to God that He would be merciful to me, but it was no good. I thought at once that God merely mocked at these prayers, saying as the holy angels listened, "This poor simple wretch keeps after Me as though I had nothing else to do with My mercy but to give it to such a one as he. Alas, poor soul, how you are fooled! It is not for such as you to have favor with the Highest."

Then the Tempter came upon me also with such discouragement as this: "You are very anxious for mercy, but I will cool you off. This frame of mind will not last forever, you know. Many others have been as warmhearted as you are, but I have quenched their zeal."[7] Then he would set before my mind the name of someone who had fallen away and I would become afraid that I would do so too. I was glad when these thoughts came to my mind, because I said to myself that they would make me watchful and careful. But then Satan replied, "I may be too hard and clever for you. I will cool you off little by little so that you will scarcely notice it. And what do I care though it take seven years to chill your heart, if I can do it at last? Continual rocking will lull a crying child to sleep. I will play it carefully and I will have my end at last. Though you be full of zeal at present, I can pull you from the fire. I shall have you cold before very long."

These ideas brought me into a terrible state of mind, for I knew that I was not fit for death now and feared that the longer I lived the more unfit I would be. In time I would forget everything, even the remembrance of the evil of sin, the worth of Heaven and the need I had of the blood of Christ

7. Watching others fall away from a profession of faith can be very discouraging and create doubts concerning ourselves.

to wash me. I thank Christ Jesus these things did not make me stop crying to God, but rather increased it. After a while a good word came to my mind: "I am persuaded, that neither death, nor life, nor angels, nor principalities, nor powers, nor things present, nor things to come, nor height, nor depth, nor any other creature, shall be able to separate us from the love of God, which is in Christ Jesus our Lord" (Romans 8:38–39). So now I hoped that long life would not destroy me, nor make me miss Heaven.

Another help I had during this temptation, even though it was a support that I doubted, was in Jeremiah, chapter 3: that although we have spoken and done as evilly as we could, yet we may cry unto God, "My Father, Thou art the guide of my youth," and may return unto Him.[8]

Then one time I had the sweet words from 2 Corinthians 5:21: "For he hath made him to be sin for us, who knew no sin; that we might be made the righteousness of God in him." I remember that one day as I was sitting in a neighbor's house, very sad at the thought of my many blasphemies, I was saying to myself, "How in the world could one who has been so vile as I ever inherit eternal life?" Then suddenly there came that word to me: "What shall we then say to these things? If God be for us, who can be against us?" (Romans 8:31). This was also a help to me: "Because I live, ye shall live also" (John 14:19). But these words were but hints and tiny visits. Even though very sweet when present, they never lasted. Suddenly they were gone again.

But afterward the Lord showed Himself to me more fully and graciously. He not only delivered me from the guilt that lay upon my conscience because of these blasphemies, but also removed the temptation, and I was put into my right mind again even as other Christians.[9]

8. True faith cries out even louder and more insistently during these times of trial — and this proves that Bunyan was a believer during this time.

9. The Word comforted him again and again as he reached out by faith and applied it to himself.

✴ CHAPTER VII – DELIVERANCE

I remember that one day as I was thinking about the wickedness and the blasphemy of my heart, and considering the anger against God that was within me, the Scripture came into my mind which says that he hath "made peace through the blood of his cross" (Colossians 1:20). And by this I was made to see again and again that God and my soul were friends because of His blood. Yes, I saw that the justice of God and my sinful soul could embrace and kiss each other through His blood. This was a good day to me; I hope I shall never forget it.

Another time, as I sat by the fire in my house thinking about my wretchedness, the Lord gave me this precious word: "Forasmuch then as the children are partakers of flesh and blood, he also himself likewise took part of the same; that through death he might destroy him that had the power of death, that is, the devil; and deliver them who through fear of death were all their lifetime subject to bondage" (Hebrews 2:14–15). I thought that the glory of these words was so great that I was going to faint as I sat there—not with grief and trouble but with joy and peace.[1]

At this time I sat under the ministry of dear Mr. Gifford,[2] whose doctrine, by God's grace, was exactly what I needed. This man made it his business to deliver the people of God from all those false securities upon which they tend to rest.

1. The Word has an even more powerful impression on Bunyan.

2. John Gifford was a former Royalist army officer turned pastor.

He told us to pay special heed not to accept any truth just upon blind trust. Instead, to cry mightily to God so that God would convince us of the reality of it and immerse us in it by His own Spirit in the holy Word. "For," he said, "when temptation comes strongly upon you, if you have not received these things with evidence from Heaven, you will soon find that you do not have that help and strength to resist that you thought you did."[3]

3. His pastor, Mr. Gifford, taught him the need for the Spirit to impress the truths deep into the soul. This Bunyan felt was the thing lacking when he faced his first onslaught of temptation.

This was just what my soul needed. I had found out by sad experience the truth of these words. So I prayed to God that in nothing related to His glory and my own eternal happiness would I be without the confirmation from Heaven that I needed. Now I clearly saw the difference between human notions and revelation from God; also the difference between a faith that is pretended and that which comes as a result of a man's being born into it by God (Matthew 16:15–17; 1 John 5:1).

And now my soul was led along by God from truth to truth, all the way from the birth of the Son of God to His ascension and second coming from Heaven to judge the world.

The great God was indeed very good to me, for I do not remember a single thing that He did not reveal to me when I cried unto him about it. Step by step I was led into every part of the gospel. It was as though I had seen Him grow up, from the cradle to the cross; I saw how gently He gave Himself to be hanged there and nailed upon it for my sins and wicked doings, and I remembered that He was ordained for the slaughter (1 Peter 1:20).

4. Bunyan is particularly taken by the life, death, and resurrection of Christ — which is the core of the Gospel message.

And then I considered the truth of His resurrection and could almost see Him leap out of the grave's mouth, for joy that He was risen again and had conquered over our dreadful foes (John 20:17). And I have also, in the Spirit, seen Him sitting there on the right hand of God the Father for me, and have seen the manner of His coming from Heaven to judge the world with glory (Acts 1:9–10, 7:56, 10:42; Hebrews 7:24; Revelation 1:18; 1 Thessalonians 4:16–18).[4]

Once I had been troubled to know whether the Lord Jesus was truly man as well as God, and truly God as well as man. In those days, no matter what people said, unless I had it with evidence from Heaven, I did not believe.[5] But at last Revelation 5:6 relieved my mind: "And I beheld, and, lo, in the midst of the throne and of the four beasts, and in the midst of the elders, stood a Lamb." That phrase "in the midst of the throne" is what did it! There, I said to myself, is the Godhead. And "in the midst of the elders"—there is the Manhood. What a glorious thought this was! Such sweet satisfaction it gave me. This other Scripture helped me much in this too: "Unto us a child is born, unto us a son is given: and the government shall be upon his shoulder: and his name shall be called Wonderful, Counsellor, The mighty God, The everlasting Father, The Prince of Peace" (Isaiah 9:6).

Besides these teachings, the Lord also made use of errors to confirm me in the truth. One about the Word of God; the other, about the guilt of sin. They were:

(1) That the Holy Scriptures were not the Word of God.

(2) That every man in the world had the spirit of Christ, grace, faith, etc.

(3) That Christ Jesus had not satisfied divine justice for the sins of the people when He was crucified.

(4) That Christ's flesh and blood were in the saints.

(5) That the bodies of the good and bad that are buried shall not rise again.

(6) That the resurrection is past with good men already.

(7) That Jesus, who was crucified between two thieves of Calvary, was not ascended above the starry heavens.

(8) That this same Jesus who died by the hands of the Jews would not come again at the last day and as man judge all nations.

I was driven to a more careful search of the Scriptures.[6]

It would take too long to tell in detail how God helped me and how He opened His words to me and made them shine before me, and caused them to dwell with me and talk

5. Bunyan said he needed confirmation from heaven to believe the doctrine of the two natures of Christ — that Christ has a human nature and a divine nature. The picture of Christ standing in the middle of God's throne and in the middle of the elders in Revelation 5:6 convinced him. Bunyan seemed to learn from vivid pictures, illustrations, and parables more than others.

6. Apparently, there were many different odd teachings relating to biblical subjects that were bandied about at that time. Bunyan spent time studying Scripture so as to address each of these strange ideas.

7. Bunyan was encouraged by Scripture through a two fold process:
1. He was subjected to temptations, doubts, and tremendous guilt for his sins.
2. He would read encouraging passages from the Word that would bear greater meaning and relevance to him.

8. Luther's *Commentary on Galatians* was very influential for many reformers and those who led the Protestant Reformation.

9. The law of Moses can add to our temptations if we do not receive the law in the context of grace. We cease from sin (breaking God's law) as we are under the influence of grace, rather than under the force of law (Rom. 6:14).

with me and comfort me over and over. But I will say only that this is the way He dealt with me: First, He allowed me to be afflicted with temptations about these truths, and then revealed them to me. Sometimes, for instance, I would be under a great burden of guilt for my sins and crushed to the ground by them. Then the Lord would show me the death of Christ and so sprinkle my conscience with His blood that, where the moment before the law raged against me, now suddenly there would be rest and peace and the love of God through Christ.[7]

How I longed for the day to come when I would see Him whose head was crowned with thorns, whose face was spit upon, whose body was broken, and whose soul was made an offering for my sin. Whereas, before I lay continually trembling at the mouth of Hell, now I felt that I had gotten so far back from it that I could not even see it any more. And how I wished that I could be eighty years old and die quickly so that my soul might go to rest.

But before I had finally gotten out of these temptations, I began to long greatly to see the experience of some godly men of former years, who had lived perhaps hundreds of years before I was born. Well, after I had talked to the Lord about this, He caused to come into my hands one day a book of Martin's—his *Commentary on Galatians*.[8] It was so old that it was ready to fall to pieces. I was very pleased that such an old book had fallen into my hands, and when I had read only a little I found my own condition was handled in such detail by this book as though I had written it. This made me marvel, for I realized that this man could not know anything of the Christians of my day, but was writing and speaking the experience of those of other years.

Martin Luther discussed carefully the rise of temptations such as blasphemy, desperation, and such like. He showed that the law of Moses, as well as the Devil and death and Hell, had a very great hand in bringing them about. At first this seemed very strange to me, but after thinking about it and watching my own experience, I found that it was indeed true.[9] I don't wish to go into other particulars at this time, except to say that (except for the Bible) I prefer this book of Martin Luther's on Galatians above all the books that I have ever seen. It is most useful for a wounded conscience.

Portrait of Martin Luther by Lucas Cranach the Elder (1528)

Now I found, or at least I thought I had, that I really loved Christ dearly. I thought that my soul would cling to Him forever and that my love for Him would remain as fire, but I quickly found out that my great love was all too little and that I who had, as I thought, such a burning love to Christ could let Him go again for a trifle. God knows how to abase us and show us our pride. Soon after this, my love was tried for this very purpose.

CHAPTER VIII – THROUGH THE VALLEY OF THE SHADOW OF DEATH

After the Lord had so graciously delivered me from terrible temptations and had given me such consolation and such blessed evidence that He loved me, the Tempter came upon me again, this time with even more terrible temptation than before.

This time the temptation was to part with Christ in exchange for the things of this life.[1] This temptation lay strongly upon me for an entire year and followed me so continually that I was not rid of it a single day, sometimes not one hour for many days together, except when I was asleep.

I was sure that those who were once really in Christ could never lose Him forever—for "the land shall not be sold for ever: for the land is mine," saith God (Leviticus 25:23). Yet, it was a constant grievance to me to think that I would have even one thought within me against a Christ who had done all that He had done for me; I had almost no other thoughts about Him except blasphemies, and neither my hating these thoughts nor my resisting them helped in the least to keep them away. No matter what I thought or did, they were still there. When I ate my food, when I stooped to pick up a pin, when I chopped a stick of wood or looked at this or that, the

1. This temptation was to prefer worldly things to Christ. The temptation pressed on him for another full year.

temptation would come: "Sell Christ for this, or sell Christ for that; sell Him, sell Him."

Sometimes these words would run through my thoughts a hundred times together: "Sell Him, sell Him." And for whole hours at a time I have been forced to stand guard, leaning and forcing my spirit against it for fear that before I was aware of what was happening, some wicked thought might arise in my heart that would consent to this temptation. Sometimes the tempter would make me believe that I had consented to it, and then I would be as though tortured upon a rack for whole days together.[2]

This temptation scared me very much because as I have said, I was afraid that I might be overcome by it. And I fought so hard against it with my mind that my body too, would go into motion, by way of pushing or thrusting with my hands or elbows. As fast as the destroyer said "Sell Him," I would answer, "I will not, I will not, I will not; No, not for millions and millions and millions of worlds." I said this because I was afraid I would set too low a value on Him, and I was so confused and upset that I scarcely knew where I was or how to be quiet again.

During this time, I could not eat food peacefully, but as soon as I sat down at the table, I had to go away and pray. I had to leave my food immediately but it was the Devil who was tempting me to do it by his counterfeit holiness. I would say to him, "I am eating now, let me finish first." "No," he would say, "You must do it now, or you will displease God, or despise Christ." I imagined that these must be impulses from God and that if I did not follow them I would be denying God.[3]

To be brief: one morning as I lay on my bed, I was, as at many other times, fiercely assaulted with this temptation to sell Christ. The wicked suggestion ran through my mind as fast as a man could speak: "Sell Him, sell Him, sell Him, sell Him, sell Him." As usual, my mind answered: "No, not for thousands, thousands, thousands, thousands." Twenty times together I repeated it, but at last after great struggle I felt this

2. Demonic temptations can be as torturous to the Christian as physical torture on the rack. The rack is a reference to a device used by the Inquisition to stretch arms and legs to the point of breaking.

3. The Devil was tempting him to think that there were certain things he must do to prove his love for Christ.

thought pass through my heart: "Let Him go if He will,"[4] and my heart agreed.

And, suddenly, Satan had won the battle and down I fell, as a bird that is shot from the top of a tree, into mighty guilt and fearful despair. Getting out of my bed, I went out into the field with as heavy a heart as a mortal man could ever have. There for about two hours I was like a man bereft of life and past all recovery, bound over to eternal punishment.

This is the Scripture that seized my soul: "Profane person, as Esau, who for one morsel of meat sold his birthright. For ye know how that afterward, when he would have inherited the blessing, he was rejected: for he found no place of repentance, though he sought it carefully with tears" (Hebrews 12:16–17).

Now I was bound over to the judgment to come. There was nothing for all the years ahead but damnation.

Months went by, and the sound of that verse concerning Esau went continually through my mind. But about ten or eleven o'clock one morning as I was walking along under a hedge, full of sorrow and guilt, and thinking of this sad thing that had happened to me, suddenly this sentence came rushing in upon me: "The blood of Christ remits all guilt." Suddenly, I stopped and made a stand in my spirit and this wonderful verse took hold upon me: "The blood of Jesus Christ his Son cleanseth us from all sin" (1 John 1:7).[5]

Peace began to steal into my soul and I thought I could see the Tempter stealing away as though ashamed of what he had done. At the same time, I began to see that my sin when compared to the blood of Christ was no more than a clod or stone in this vast, wide field where I stood. This encouraged me greatly for two or three hours, during which time also I thought I saw by faith the Son of God suffering for my sins. But because this feeling did not last, I soon sank back in my spirit in exceeding guilt again.

But it was chiefly that Scripture about Esau selling his birthright that lay all day long on my mind. When I tried to think of some other Scripture for relief, that one sentence

4. Note: "Let Him go if He will" hinges Christ's departure on His will (not man's will). Thankfully, we are more held by Christ (and His will) than we hold to Christ.

5. The voice of Scripture should come to us louder than the voice of the Devil. And it did when Bunyan was encouraged by 1 John 1:7.

6. Immature Christians quickly lose the force of the Word. It is only when the Word abides in them that they overcome the evil one (1 John 2:14), and this is the test of the mature "young man" in Christ.

would sound within me: "For ye know how that afterward, when he would have inherited the blessing. . . he found no place of repentance, though he sought it carefully with tears."[6]

Once in a while I had a sense of peace from the verse in Luke 22:32—"I have prayed for thee, that thy faith fail not"— but it did not last, and when I thought about it I could see no reason why there should be grace for me who had sinned as much as I had. So I was torn apart for many days together.

Then I began with sad and careful heart to consider the nature and largeness of my sin and to search the Word of God to see if I could find anywhere a promise that would give me any relief. I began to consider, He shall be forgiven, "wherewith soever they shall blaspheme" (Mark 3:28). At first thought, it seemed that this contained a glorious promise for the pardon of such high offenses as mine. But as I thought more about it, I decided it probably was talking about those who had sinned before they had come to Christ, but did not apply to one who had received light and mercy, and then afterward had slighted Christ as I had done.

7. There is great terror in the heart of the one who greatly desires forgiveness of sins but does not believe he has it.

This made me fear that my sin was the unpardonable one of which it says, "He that shall blaspheme against the Holy Ghost hath never forgiveness, but is in danger of eternal damnation" (Mark 3:29). And that verse from Hebrews seemed to confirm this terrible thought: "For ye know how that afterward, when he would have inherited the blessing, he was rejected: for he found no place of repentance, though he sought it carefully with tears."[7] And this is the word that stuck with me.[8]

And now I was both a burden and a terror to myself. I was weary of life and afraid to die. How gladly I would have been anyone but myself, anything but a man, and in any condition but my own! It came to me frequently that it was impossible for me to be forgiven and to be saved from the wrath to come.

8. The sin of blasphemy against the Holy Spirit is called the unpardonable sin. Ascribing the works of the Holy Spirit to the Devil would be an example of the unpardonable sin. It is a thorough rejection of the Holy Spirit of God. Those who are concerned they have sinned the unpardonable sin most likely have not committed it. Only the hardest of hearts would do such a thing.

I began to think back and to wish a thousand times over that the day was yet to come when I would be tempted with some particular sin; and I became fiercely indignant against the sin, and said to myself that I would rather be torn in pieces than to consent to such a thing. But alas! these wishes and resolves were now too late to help me, for I felt that God had let me go, and I thought: O that it might be as Job said, "As in months past, as in the days when God preserved me" (Job 29:2).

And then I began to compare my sins with those of others, to see if I could find any of those who were saved who had done as I had done. So I considered David's adultery and murder, and found them to be terrible crimes indeed. They had been committed after he had received light and grace. Yet I saw that his transgressions were only against the Law of Moses; but mine were against the Gospel, against the Mediator Himself; I had sold my Saviour.

And so again I felt as though I were being racked upon the wheel. Oh, why did it have to be this particular sin that I had sinned? How this thought whipped and stung!

"What!" thought I, "Is there but one sin that is unpardonable? Only one sin that lays the soul outside the reach of God's mercy? And must I be guilty of that one? Is there but one sin among so many millions of sins for which there is no forgiveness—and must I commit this one?" These things would so break my spirit that I thought at times that I had lost my mind. No one can ever know the terror of those days but myself.

After this I began to consider Peter's sin in denying his Master. This seemed to come closest to mine of any that I could find. He had denied his Saviour as I had after he had received light and mercy, and after he had been warned. I also considered that he did it more than once and with times to consider in between. But although I put all these circumstances together to try if possible to find some help, yet I soon saw that this sin of Peter's was only a denial of his Master; mine was a selling of my Saviour. It seemed to me that my situation was closer to that of Judas than to either David or Peter.[9]

9. Bunyan believed his sin came closest to Judas' sin of betraying Christ (vs. David's sin or Peter's sin).

10. A son of perdition is a reprobate who has turned away from the truth (permanently). The term is used by Christ for Judas.

11. Bunyan acknowledged that God is in control over all tempting situations.

Here again my torment flamed out. I was ground down and crushed when I considered how God preserved others while He let me fall into the snare. I could easily see that God was keeping them even though they were wicked, and would not let them, as He had let me, become a son of perdition.[10]

How I loved to see the way God did preserve His people! How safely they walked whom God had hedged in! They were within His care and special providence, even though they were fully as bad as I was by nature. Because He loved them He would not let them fall outside the range of His mercy, but He would not preserve me nor keep me. He had let me fall because I was a reprobate.[11] Those wonderful places in the Scriptures that speak of God's keeping His people shone out like the sun—but not to comfort me—for they showed me the blessed state and heritage of those whom the Lord had blessed.

I saw that God had His hand in all the things that overtook His elect, and He had His hand also in all their temptations to sin against Him. He would leave them for a little while to take up with these temptations; not so that they would be destroyed, but that they would be humbled. It was not to put them beyond His mercy, but to put them in the place to receive it. What love, what care, what kindness and mercy I saw God mixing in with the most severe and dreadful of His ways with His people. He let David, Hezekiah, Solomon, Peter, and others fall, but He would not let them fall into the unpardonable sin or into Hell. Of course, all these thoughts added sorrow and horror to me. I guessed that as all things worked together for the best for these who were called according to His purpose, so all things worked together for my damage and my eternal overthrow.

After that I began to compare my sin with that of Judas in the hope that I might find that mine was different, for I knew that his was truly unpardonable. And I thought that if it would differ from his, even by the breadth of a hair, what a happy condition mine would be. I discovered that Judas sinned intentionally, but my sin was despite my praying and striving against it; his was committed with serious deliberation; mine was done in a fearful hurry.[12]

And so this consideration of Judas' sin was for a while at least of some relief to me, for I saw that I had not transgressed as fully as he had. But this hope was quickly gone again, for I realized that there might be more ways than one to commit this unpardonable sin, and so this terrible iniquity of mine might be one that could never be forgiven.

I was terribly ashamed to be so much like Judas, and I thought how loathsome I would be to all the saints at the judgment day. I could hardly look at a man I believed had a good conscience, but that I would feel my heart tremble while in his presence. What a glory it must be to walk with God, and what a mercy to have a good conscience before Him.

About this time I tried to content myself by listening to false doctrines: that there would be no judgment day; that we would not rise again; that sin is not as terrible as we have thought. "Even if these things are really true," the Tempter said, "yet it is easier, for the moment at least, not to believe them if you are going to perish anyway. There is no use tormenting yourself about it beforehand. Drive the thoughts out of your mind by believing what the atheists and Ranters do."

I see from this that Satan will use any means to keep the soul from Christ.[13] He is frightened when someone has an awakened spirit. His kingdom is false security, blindness, darkness, and error.

It was hard now to pray because darkness and despair were swallowing me up. "It is too late, I am lost, God hath let me fall—not to my correction, but to my condemnation. My sin is unpardonable."

About this time I came upon a book that told the dreadful story of the miserable Francis Spira.[14]

This book was to my troubled spirit like salt rubbed into a fresh wound—every sentence in that book, every groan of that man. One sentence of his was particularly frightful: "Man knows the beginning of sin, but who can tell where it will

12. He began to see that his sin was committed after all his prayer and striving against it. Whether Bunyan had actually sinned by saying "Let Him go if He will" is still questionable. At the very least, it seems that it was a lapse of faith, and he should have confessed it as such. Obviously, Bunyan had a very tender conscience on these matters.

13. Satan does not give up on his goods readily (as the strong man in Jesus' words). He goes after a man like Bunyan, newly converted.

14. Francis Spira was a well known Protestant Italian, who later recanted. He regretted his recantation and some believe he committed suicide or died by starving himself.

end?" For whole days at a time it caused my mind to shake and totter under the sense of the dreadful judgment of God that I was sure was upon me. And I felt such heat at my stomach, by reason of my terror, that it felt as though my breast bone would split apart; then I thought of that which was written concerning Judas, who by falling headlong burst asunder "and all his bowels gushed out" (Acts 1:18).

But this was the mark that God set on Cain; continual fear and trembling under the heavy load of guilt that he had charged upon him for the blood of his brother Abel. So I could not stand, nor walk, nor lie quietly.

Sometimes that saying would come into my mind, "Thou hast received gifts. . . for the rebellious" (Psalm 68:18). Why, I thought, surely that would include me. I once loved Him, feared Him, served Him, but now I am a rebel; He has gifts for rebels, then why not for me? I tried hard to take hold of this hope but I could not do it.[15]

15. Sinning against "the Gospel" is not so much different from sinning against "the law." Those who sin in spite of the revelation they have received heighten the seriousness of it.

Then I decided to consider my sins against the sins of all the rest of the saints. Although mine were bigger than those of anyone else, yet if all theirs should be put together and mine is no larger than all, then surely there is hope. The blood that has virtue enough in it to wash away all theirs, has virtue enough in it to wash away all mine, even though mine should be as big as all theirs together.

I thought of the sins of David and Solomon, of Manasseh, of Peter, and the other great offenders, and tried to show myself that their sins were even greater than they really were. I argued to myself that David shed blood to cover his adultery, and that this murder was done in a deliberate way, so that his sin was very great. But then I thought that these were but sins against the Law, not directly against the Saviour as mine were.

Then I thought about Solomon and how he sinned in loving strange women, in falling away to their idols and in building them temples, even after he had light and had received great mercy in his old age. But again I came to the same conclusion: my sin was far worse in selling my Saviour than Solomon's sin against the Law.

I considered also the sins of Manasseh who built altars for idols in the house of the Lord, and used enchantments and wizards with familiar spirits, who burned his children in the fire sacrificed to devils and made the streets of Jerusalem run down with the blood of innocence. But then I said to myself: "These are not of the same nature as your sins. You have parted with Jesus. You have sold your Saviour."

This one consideration seemed larger than the sins of the whole world. All of them together were not equal to mine.

Now I began to flee from God as from the face of a dreadful Judge, for "It is a fearful thing to fall into the hands of the living God" (Hebrews 10:31). But by His grace there came occasionally calling after me these words: "I have blotted out, as a thick cloud, thy transgressions, and, as a cloud, thy sins: return unto me; for I have redeemed thee" (Isaiah 44:22).

And this would make me stop a little, and as it were look over my shoulder to see if I could discern that the God of grace were following me with a pardon in His hand. But no sooner would I do this than there came again the awful realization of Esau's rejection: "He found no place of repentance, though he sought it carefully with tears."[16]

One day while walking back and forth in the shop of a Christian, I was thinking of my sad and terrible condition, lamenting for this great sin which I had committed, and praying that if this sin of mine were different from that against the Holy Ghost the Lord would show it to me. Suddenly there was the noise of wind rushing in through the window upon me, very pleasant, and I seemed to hear a voice saying to me, "Did you ever refuse to be justified by the blood of Christ?" In one moment my whole life was open before me and I was made to see that I had never willingly refused Him. So my heart answered with groans, "No, this I have never refused." Then there fell with great power that word of God upon me: "See that ye refuse not him that speaketh" (Hebrews 12:25).

16. Christians are sometimes rightly concerned about the sincerity of their repentance and their confession of sin (as Esau's repentance was not genuine). When Christians confess and then return to their sin with enthusiasm, they should re-examine the sincerity of their confessions. Do they really have any grief and hatred for their sins? In Bunyan's case, his hatred of his sin only grows with each successive temptation and demonic attack.

17. The Word of God must speak louder in our minds than the howling of the tumultuous thoughts and demonic suggestions in our minds. Bunyan was encouraged by Hebrews 12:25. He did not refuse to listen to the blood of Jesus Christ that speaks louder than the blood of Abel.

This word made a strange seizure upon my spirit; it brought light with it and commanded a silence in my heart of all those tumultuous thoughts that were there before like masterless hell-hounds, roaring and bellowing, and making a hideous noise within me. It showed me also that Jesus Christ had yet a word of grace and mercy for me, and that He had not, as I feared, forsaken me and cast off my soul. And it seemed to me that this was a kind of threatening of me if I did not venture my salvation upon the Son of God notwithstanding my sins and the terribleness of them.[17]

I do not know what actually happened, though twenty years have now gone by for me to think about it. I thought then what I hesitate to say now— that that sudden rushing wind was as if an angel had come upon me, but I will not try to say until we learn all things at the day of judgment. But I will say this: it brought about a great calm in my soul and persuaded me that there might be hope. It showed me what the unpardonable sin was and that my soul still had the blessed privilege of fleeing to Jesus Christ for mercy.[18] I certainly do not base my salvation upon this experience, but upon the promise that the Lord Jesus gave me. I have spoken of this strange situation very reluctantly, but since I am in this book unfolding the secret things of my life, I thought it might not be wrong to say this much about it.[19]

18. Bunyan was truly concerned that he had offended Jesus. There was no doubt in his mind that Jesus Christ was a real Person and really died on the cross for those who would believe in Him.

The glory of this experience lasted for three or four days, and then I began to lose my trust again and to enter again into despair.

19. Evidently, Bunyan must have been 30 years old when he went through this trial (in 1658–1659).

My life was now hanging in doubt before me and I did not know which way I should tip. My soul was ever anxious to cast itself at the foot of grace by prayer. I found it hard to pray to Christ for mercy, because of the way that I had sinned against Him so vilely. How could I ever look Him in the face again? How ashamed I was to pray for mercy when I had thrust it away from me such a little while before. But I saw that there was only one thing for me to do—go to Him and humble myself and beg that, because of His wonderful mercy, He would pity me and have mercy upon my wretched, sinful soul.

But when the Tempter saw what I was going to do, he told me that I should not pray to God; that it would do no good since I had rejected the Mediator by whom all prayers would be acceptable to the Father. "To pray now," he said, "seeing that God has cast you off, will offend Him more than ever before."

He said, "God has been weary of you now for thirty years, because you are none of His. Your bawlings in His ears have been no pleasant voice to Him; that is why He let you sin this sin, so that you might be cut off—and now will you still try to pray?" So the Devil spoke, and reminded me of what Moses said to the children of Israel—that because they would not go up to possess the land when God told them to, forever after they were barred out from it, even though they might pray much with tears.[20]

In another place (Exodus 21:14), it tells of the man who had sinned deliberately and was to be dragged away from God's altar to die, even as Joab was slain by King Solomon when he tried to find shelter there (1 Kings 2:28–34). And yet, I thought to myself, I can but die—it will be no worse with me than it is already. And so I came to Him, although with such great difficulty, because of that saying about Esau which seemed to sit at my heart like a flaming sword to keep me away from the tree of life, lest I should taste thereof and live. Oh, who knows how hard a thing it sometimes is to come to God in prayer?

I was anxious too, that others would pray for me, but I feared that God would give them little heart to do it. In fact, I trembled with fear that soon someone who had tried to pray for me would tell me (as God said once to the prophet concerning the children of Israel), "Pray not thou for this people"[21] (Jeremiah 11:4). I feared that the Lord had rejected me as He had rejected them. I thought that perhaps He had whis-

20. Bunyan keeps bringing up examples of hardened souls like Judas or the children of Judah who were stubborn and vehemently opposed to Jeremiah's teaching (in the final days of the Southern Kingdom). We do not get the impression that Bunyan is such a hardened soul.

21. Bunyan even trembled in the presence of other Christians as the elders of Bethlehem trembled in Samuel's presence (1 Sam. 16:4).

pered this to some already, but they were afraid to tell me for fear that it might be so. Then I would indeed be beside myself.

But about this time I did speak to an old Christian about my situation and told him that I was afraid I had sinned the sin against the Holy Ghost. He told me that he thought so too. So I had but cold comfort. But talking a little more with him I found that, although he was a good man, he had not had very much combat with the Devil.[22] So I went back to God again as well as I could, still pleading for mercy.

And now the Tempter mocked me in my misery, saying that since I had parted from the Lord Jesus and provoked Him to displeasure, the only thing to do was to pray that God the Father would be the Mediator between the Son and me, that we might be reconciled again. Then that Scripture seized upon me which says, "He is of one mind, and who can turn Him?" I saw at once that it would be easier to persuade Him to make a new world or a new Bible than to listen to such a prayer as that. I remembered that "Neither is there salvation in any other: for there is none other name under heaven given among men, whereby we must be saved" (Acts 4:12).

Now the most wonderful words of the gospel were the greatest torment to me. Nothing so afflicted me as the thoughts of Jesus Christ, the remembrance of a Saviour, because I had cast Him off. Every thought of His grace, love, goodness, kindness, gentleness, meekness, comforts, and consolations went through my soul like a sword. This is the One, I kept saying to myself, from whom I have parted and whom I have slighted, despised, and abused. This is the Saviour who loved sinners so much that He washed them from their sins in His own precious blood. But you have no part in Him, because you have said in your heart, "Let Him go if He will." Oh, it is a terrible thing to be destroyed by the grace and mercy of God; to have the Lamb, the Saviour, turn Lion and Destroyer (Revelation 6). I also trembled, as I have already said, at the sight of the saints of God who greatly loved Him and made it their business to walk carefully before Him. Their words

22. There is a naiveté about the work of the Devil in many churches, and it usually isn't productive to ask counsel of those who have never spent much time combatting the Devil.

and actions and all their expressions of tenderness and fear to sin against their precious Saviour condemned me. The dread of them was upon me, and I trembled at God's Samuels (1 Samuel 16:4).

Now the Tempter began a new attack by telling me that Christ pitied me and was sorry for my loss, but He was helpless to save me from my sins, for they were not the kind for which He had bled and died. These things may sound ridiculous, but to me they were terrible torments. Every one of them increased my misery. It was not that I felt He was not great enough or that His grace and salvation had already been used up on others, but that because of His faithfulness to His threatenings, He could not extend His mercy to me. So all these fears arose from my steadfast belief in the truth of the Word of God and from my being misinformed as to the nature of my sin.[23]

This thought—that I was guilty of a sin for which He did not die—so tied me up that I did not know what to do. How I wished that He would come and die again. How I wished that the work of man's redemption was yet to be completed. How I would then entreat Him to count this sin among the rest for which He would die. But this Scripture would strike me down as dead: "Christ being raised from the dead dieth no more; death hath no more dominion over him" (Romans 6:9).

By these strange and unusual assaults of the Tempter, my soul was like a broken vessel driven with the winds and tossed headlong into despair. I was as the man who had his dwelling among the tombs with the dead, who was always crying out and cutting himself with stones (Mark 5:2–5). Desperation will not comfort him. But out of this experience I did get a deeper realization of the fact that the Scriptures were the Word of God. I cannot express how clearly I now saw and felt the steadiness of Him who is the Rock of man's salvation. What He said could not be unsaid. I saw that sin called "the unpardonable sin" might drive the soul beyond the help

23. Bunyan is too open to the tempting thoughts of the Devil. These were crazy suggestions and had no backing in Scripture. At this point, he is not rooted in the Truth of God's Word, and he is too given to the sway of the Devil.

24. Christ died for every kind of sin, except for blasphemy against the Holy Spirit. No other exceptions.

25. Reference 1 John 5:16-17. It is helpful when another voice, another brother reminds us that "this is not a sin unto death." This means that it is a sin from which we may be delivered.

of Christ, but woe unto him who is thus driven, for the Word would shut him out.[24]

One day I walked to a neighboring town and sat down upon a bench along the street. I was in deep thought about the terrible state into which my sins had brought me. While I was musing, I lifted my head and thought I saw the sun shining in the heavens begin to hate to give me light, that the very stones in the street and tiles on the houses bent themselves against me. I saw how much happier every creature was as compared with myself, and in bitterness of my spirit I said to myself, with a terrible sigh, "How can God comfort such a wretch as I?" I had no sooner said that when it came to me as an echo answers a voice, "This sin is not unto death."[25]

CHAPTER IX – HOPE BREAKS THROUGH

Suddenly, it was as if I had been raised out of the grave, and I cried out, "Lord, where did You ever find such a wonderful word as this?" The power and sweetness and light and glory of this unexpected word was marvelous to me. Now for a while, I was out of doubt. *If this sin is not unto death*, I thought, *then it is pardonable. I know from this that God is encouraging me to come to Christ for mercy, and that He stands there with open arms to receive me as well as others.* No one who has not gone through this understands what relief came to my soul. The terrible storm was ended, and I now seemed to stand upon the same ground as other sinners and to have as much right to the Word and to prayer as any of them.[1]

But oh, how Satan thrashed about to bring me down again! But he could not do it, not that day nor most of the next, for the sentence that I had heard stood like a wall against my back. But toward the evening of the next day I felt the power of this Word begin to leave me and to withdraw its support, and so I returned to my old fears again.

The next day at evening, although under great fear, I went to seek the Lord, and I cried out to Him with strong cries, "Oh Lord, I beseech Thee, show me that Thou hast loved me with everlasting love" (Jeremiah 31:3). I had no sooner said

1. Repentance comes about by a true sense of sin and a turning away from sin with an apprehension of God's mercy. Bunyan has truly apprehended God's mercy, and this is greatly encouraging to him.

2. Bunyan is hearing the voice of God THROUGH Scripture. It is God's Word directed towards him.

3. Esau's false repentance from Hebrews 12:16-17 comes back to bother Bunyan. Esau did not truly repent of his sin. He rather only regretted the loss of the birthright and the attendant material blessings that would have come through the inheritance from Isaac.

4. Bunyan associates a fatherly fear/reverence with love. Certainly, a proper fear of God will lead to love for God.

this than there returned sweetly to me, like an echo, "I have loved thee with an everlasting love."[2]

Now I went to bed in quietness, and when I awoke the next morning the assurance was still fresh on my soul, and I believed it. A hundred times the tempter sought to break my peace. Oh, the conflicts that I met with now! As I strove to hold to this good word, that concerning Esau would fly in my face like lightning.[3] Sometimes I would be up and down twenty times in one hour, yet God helped me and kept my heart upon this word from which I had much sweetness and hope for several days together. I felt that he would surely pardon me, for it seemed to me that he was saying, "I loved you while you were committing this sin, I loved you before, I love you still, and I will love you forever."

I saw that my sin was a particularly filthy one and knew that I had horribly abused the holy Son of God. I felt a great love and pity for Him and I yearned toward Him, for I saw He was still my Friend and was rewarding me good for evil. My affection for Him burned so strongly within me that I was full of hot desire that He revenge Himself upon me for the abuse that I had done him. To speak now as I thought then, I felt that if I had a thousand gallons of blood within my veins, I would freely have spilt it all at the feet of my Lord.

Another good word came to me at this time: "If thou, Lord, shouldest mark iniquities, O Lord, who shall stand? But there is forgiveness with thee, that thou mayest be feared" (Psalm 130:3–4). These were good words to me, especially the part that says there is forgiveness with the Lord so that He might be feared. As I understood it, this meant that he forgave us so that we could love Him. It seemed that the great God set such a high esteem upon the love of His poor creatures that he would rather pardon their transgression than go without their love.[4]

I was refreshed and sustained by Ezekiel 16:63: "they be ashamed and confounded, and never open their mouths any more because of their shame, when I am pacified toward them for all that they have done, saith the Lord God." And so it was that my soul was set at liberty—forever, I felt—from being afflicted with my guilt as I had been so terribly before. But later I began to be full of despondence again, fearing that, in spite of all the peace I had enjoyed, I might be fooling myself and might still be destroyed finally. For I felt very strongly that no matter what comfort and peace I might feel, if the Scriptures did not concur, then all my feelings would be of no use. "The Scripture cannot be broken" (John 10:35).

So I went over the ground again to see whether one who had sinned as I had might still trust in the Lord, and at this time there came into my mind: "For it is impossible for those who were once enlightened, and have tasted of the heavenly gift, and were made partakers of the Holy Ghost, and have tasted the good word of God, and the powers of the world to come, if they shall fall away, to renew them again unto repentance" (Hebrews 6:4–6). "For if we sin willfully after that we have received the knowledge of the truth, there remaineth no more sacrifice for sins, but a certain fearful looking for of judgment and fiery indignation, which shall devour the adversaries" (Hebrews 10:26–27).

There was Esau "who for one morsel of meat sold his birthright. For ye know how that afterward, when he would have inherited the blessing, he was rejected: for he found no place of repentance, though he sought it carefully with tears" (Hebrews 12:16–17).[5]

And now it seemed that there was no promise of the gospel that was left for me anywhere in the Bible, and I kept thinking of Hosea 9:1—"Rejoice not, O Israel, for joy, as other people." There was surely plenty of cause for those to rejoice who belonged to Jesus; but as for me, I had cut myself off by my sins and there remained neither foothold nor handhold among all the promises in the precious Word of God. I felt like a child who had fallen into a pond; he might struggle around in the water, yet, because he can find no hold for foot or hand, he must die at last. As soon as this fresh assault from

5. Bunyan is especially bothered by all of the difficult passages that speak of the reprobate. This is the apostate that turns his back on the Gospel, usually because of his attraction to the world (Demas, Judas, Esau, and others being examples of this). Tender consciences easily misapply these passages to themselves.

6. Incredibly, Bunyan faces another two-and-a-half years of Satanic attacks and doubts concerning his own salvation.

Satan had taken its grip upon my soul, this Scripture came into my heart: "The vision is for many days" (Daniel 10:14). Indeed, I found that that is just what happened, for I could not find peace again for almost two and a half years.[6] Actually, these words were of some encouragement to me, for I felt that many days are not forever. They will some time have an end. I was glad that it was only for a limited time, even though long. But these thoughts didn't help too much, for I could not keep my mind thinking along these lines.

At this time I felt encouraged to prayer, but the Tempter again laughed at me, suggesting that the mercy of God and the blood of Christ were certainly not for me and could not help my sin, so prayer would be in vain. Yet, even so, I decided to pray. "But," said the Tempter, "your sin is unpardonable."

"Well," I replied, "I will pray anyway."

"It will do you no good," he said.

"Still," I replied, "I will pray."

So I went to prayer and said, "Lord, Satan tells me that your mercy and Christ's blood are not sufficient to save my soul. Lord, shall I honor You by believing that You can and will? Or shall I honor Satan by believing that You cannot and will not? Lord, I want to honor You by believing that You can and will."

As I was thus praying, this Scripture fastened on my heart: "O. . . great is thy faith" (Matthew 15:28). This came to me as sharply and suddenly as though someone had slapped me on the back while I was there on my knees, yet I was not able to believe that this was a prayer of faith until almost six months later. I just couldn't believe it. So I went around still in the jaws of desperation, mourning up and down in this sad condition.[7]

7. Bunyan is setting the Devil's word against God's Word and holding to God's truth. This is the right thing to do when the Devil tempts with his deceptions.

There was nothing that I longed for more than to find out once and for all if there was any hope for me or not. Then these words came rolling into my mind: "Will the Lord cast off for ever? And will he be favourable no more? Is His mercy clean gone forever? Doth his promise fail for evermore? Hath God forgotten to be gracious? hath he in anger shut up his tender mercies?" (Psalm 77:7–9). All the while these questions from the Word were running through my mind, I felt that the very fact that they were questions indicated that He surely had not cast off forever but would be favorable; that His promise had not failed; that He had not forgotten to be gracious nor would He in anger shut up His tender mercies from me. There was another Scripture that came to mind about the same time— though I don't remember just what it was—which also made me feel that God's mercy might not be quite gone.

Another time, while I was desperately debating the question as to whether the blood of Christ was sufficient to save my soul, the doubt continued from morning until about seven or eight at night. When I was quite worn out with my fears, suddenly the words "He is able" came into my heart. It seemed that these words were spoken aloud to me, and all fear was knocked out of me for at least a day; I had never had more certainty in my life.

Then as I was again at prayer and trembling under fear that no Word of God could help me, the words came upon me, "My grace is sufficient," and I felt hopeful. And yet, just about two weeks before I had been reading this very verse, and at that time I thought that it was of no help nor comfort to me at all. In fact I threw down the Book with impatience for I thought it was not large enough for me. But again it seemed as if this verse had arms of grace so wide that it could not only enclose me but many more besides.[8]

I was sustained by these words, through many more conflicts, for about seven or eight weeks. During that time my peace was in it and out, sometimes twenty times a day. Now a bit of comfort, and then suddenly much trouble; now some peace, but before I could go a few hundred feet, I would become as full of fear and guilt as ever a heart could hold. And this was not only now and then, but for that entire seven weeks. This verse about the sufficiency of grace and that one about Esau's parting with his birthright were like scales

8. Importantly, Bunyan does not give up in his struggles. He goes for two weeks with no comfort from the Word, but eventually the Word from which he gained no comfort does ring true and comforts his soul.

9. Was there anybody who struggled for so many years, tossed to and fro for so long, and was attacked by the Devil so relentlessly as John Bunyan?

10. God is merciful to Bunyan, bringing His Word with a special force into the mind of the poor man — three times repeating "My grace is sufficient for you."

weighing back and forth in my mind; sometimes one end would be uppermost and sometimes the other.[9]

I kept on praying that God would show me the complete answer. I knew now that there was a possibility of grace for me, but I could not go further. My first question was answered; there was hope, and God was still merciful. But the second question—was there hope for me?—was still unanswered.

One day, in a meeting of God's people, I was full of sadness and terror, for my fears were strong upon me again. Suddenly, there broke in upon me this word, "My grace is sufficient for thee, My grace is sufficient for thee, My grace is sufficient for thee." Three times it came. The word was a mighty one for me.[10]

At this time my understanding was enlightened, and I felt as though I had seen the Lord Jesus looking down from Heaven right through the roof, directing His words right to me. This sent me home mourning, for it broke my heart, filled me with joy, and laid me low as the dust. Of course, this glory and refreshment did not last long, but it did continue for several weeks. Then, as usual, the other word concerning Esau came back to me, and there came again that up-and-down experience of now peace and now terror.

Thus I went on for several weeks, sometimes comforted, sometimes tormented. Sometimes I would say to myself, "Why, how many Scriptures are there against me? There are only three or four, and cannot God overlook these and save me?" One day I remember wondering what would happen if some verse of terror, such as the one about Esau, should come into my heart at the same moment that there came one of promise and peace. I began to long that this would happen and desired of God that it might be.

Well, about two or three days afterward, that is exactly what happened. Both folded in upon me at the same time and worked and struggled strongly in me for a while. But at last, the one about Esau's birthright left and the one about the sufficiency of grace prevailed with peace and joy. Then this

Scripture came in upon me: "Mercy rejoiceth against judgment" (James 2:13).

This Scripture also helped me: "And him that cometh to me I will in no wise cast out" (John 6:37). Oh, the comfort that I had through this word, "in no wise." Satan tried hard to pull this promise away from me, saying that Christ did not mean me and that He spoke of sinners who had not done the same thing that I had. But I would answer him, "Satan, there is no exception in these words. 'Him that comes' means any 'him.'" As I look back on this experience, I remember that Satan never once put this further question to me: "But do you come aright?" And I think the reason was that he was afraid I would be reminded that to come aright was to come as I was, a vile and ungodly sinner, and to cast myself at the feet of mercy. If ever Satan and I strove about anything in the Bible, it was over this word from the Gospel of John. And God be praised, I overcame him and got sweetness from the verse.[11]

Notwithstanding all these helps and the blessed words of grace, there were still times of great distress of conscience. And the words concerning Esau would again make me fear. I could never quite get rid of it, and every day it would come in upon me. So now I went to work another way. I would try to find hope by looking squarely at what I had done, examining every part of the situation, and seeing exactly where it left me. When I had done this, I found that I had clearly left the Lord Jesus Christ to His choice as to whether He would be my Saviour or not; for these were the wicked words I had said: "Let Him go if He will." But this Scripture gave me much hope because the Lord Jesus said, "I will never leave thee, nor forsake thee" (Hebrews 13:5). "O Lord," I said, "but I have left You."

Yet the answer came again, "But I will not leave thee." For this I thanked God.[12]

But I was terribly afraid that He would leave me, and I found it hard to trust Him because I had offended Him so much.[13] I saw that I was like Joseph's brothers who felt so guilty

11. Bunyan holds Jesus to his promise in John 6:37. The believer must claim the promises of God.

12. Bunyan learns how to overcome the Devil by the right use of Scripture. Satan is very good at the wrong use of Scripture, as he used the Esau passage against Bunyan many times.

13. Bunyan honestly considers his sin and discovers that he had left the choice up to the Lord as to whether He would withdraw His presence from him.

14. Joseph was gracious to his brothers, though his brothers suspected his graciousness was insincere. We must never suspect this of Christ.

because of what they had done to Joseph that they were often afraid their brother would despise them (Genesis 50:15–17).[14]

The Scripture that helped most was in Joshua 20, where it speaks of the slayer who was to flee for refuge. If the avenger of blood pursued the slayer, Moses said that the elders of the city of refuge should not deliver the slayer into his hands because he had killed his neighbor accidentally, not deliberately, and had not hated him. O bless God for this word! I was convinced that I was a slayer and that the avenger of blood pursued me. Did I have a right to enter the city of refuge? I could not if I had shed blood willfully. But one who happened to kill someone without spite or grudge or malice could enter in.

So I decided that I could enter. I had not hated Him. I had prayed unto Him and was tender toward Him, hating to sin against Him. And I had labored hard for twelve months to keep from committing this wickedness in spite of the terrible temptations that there had been. Yes, I surely had a right to enter this city, and the elders—the apostles—were not to deliver me up. This was a wonderful comfort to me and gave me much ground of hope.

Yet there still remained one question, and that was whether it was possible for anyone who had sinned the unpardonable sin to be able to have any hope. No, he could not for these reasons: First, because he who has thus sinned is debarred from a share in the blood of Christ; second, because he is debarred a share in the promise of life, he shall never be forgiven, "neither in this world, neither in the world to come" (Matthew 12:32); third, because the Son of God excludes him from a share in His prayers, being forever ashamed to own him before His holy Father and the blessed angels in Heaven (Mark 8:38).[15]

15. Satan wants us to doubt our faith, our love, and our commitment to Christ. This is how he shakes the believer's assurance. By the Spirit's help, we ascertain that we really do believe and that we really do love Jesus. This is what is happening to John Bunyan.

When I had considered this carefully, and realized that the Lord had surely been comforting me, even after my sin, then I felt that at last I could look more carefully at those terrible Scriptures which had frightened me so much, and which until now I had not dared to think about. Now I began to come close to them, to read them, to think about them, and to weigh them.[16]

And when I did, I found they were not as terrible as I had thought. First I looked at the sixth chapter of Hebrews, trembling for fear that it would strike me down. But when I considered it, I found that it was talking about those who completely left the Lord and absolutely denied the gospel and the remission of sins through Christ. It was with these people in mind that the apostle began his argument in verses 1, 2, and 3. Then I found that the falling away it was talking about was of an open kind, in the view of all the world, in such a way as to "put Christ to an open shame." I found that those he was talking about were forever kept in blindness, hardness, and impenitence—it is impossible that they should be renewed again to repentance. And so I saw clearly, to God's everlasting praise, that my sin was not the one that he was talking about there.[17]

Then I turned to Hebrews 10 and found that the willful sin it mentions there is not just any willful sin, but it is the particular one of disowning Christ and His commandments.[18] This also must be done openly before two or three witnesses. This sin cannot be committed unless one walks directly against the working of God in his heart, which is trying to persuade him against doing it. The Lord knows that though my sin was terrible, it was not the same as this, which these verses were talking about.

And then at last I came to Hebrews 12:17. It almost killed me to look at this verse, but now I saw that Esau's sin was not a hasty thought, but a deliberate one (Genesis 25). Second, it was a public and open action—at least it was known to his brother—and this made his sin more terrible than it otherwise would have been. Third, he continued to slight his birthright—"He did eat and drink, and rose up, and went his way: thus Esau despised his birthright." Even twenty years later, he still despised it, for he said, "I have enough, my brother; keep that thou hast unto thyself" (Genesis 33:9).[19]

16. Now he analyzes the difficult passages. He agrees that the one who blasphemes the Holy Spirit (Matt. 12:32) cannot be forgiven of his sin ever. While some fit into this horrible category, Bunyan does not.

17. He looks at the Hebrews 6 apostates. They were once professing believers, but now they mock Jesus and hold him in contempt. John Bunyan never did this. The minute he sinned, he was not hardened in his sin. He was rather distraught over it.

18. He analyzes another difficult passage, Hebrews 10:26-29, very carefully. This speaks of an ongoing pattern of sin that continues in a willful manner. It is a lifestyle of rebellion and also a contempt for the atoning blood of Jesus Christ.

19. Esau did not care for the birthright (which represented covenant membership and would have symbolized regeneration). He was upset that he lost the blessing. He didn't seek after a changed heart and life: however, he did want to go to heaven.

I had, as you know, been greatly troubled and horribly depressed by the fact that Esau sought a place of repentance and could not find it. But now I saw that it was because he had lost the blessing, not because he lost the birthright. This is clear from the apostles, and is made clear by Esau himself, for he said, "He took away my birthright; and behold, now he hath taken away my blessing" (Genesis 27:36).

Then I went to the New Testament to see what it had to say about Esau's sin. It appeared that the birthright was a symbol of regeneration and that the blessing was a symbol of our eternal inheritance. There are many in this day of grace and mercy who despise Christ who is the birthright to heaven, and yet at the judgment day will cry as loudly as Esau did, "Lord, Lord, open unto us." But God the Father will not repent, but will say, "I have blessed these others and they shall indeed be blessed. But as for you, 'Depart from me, all ye workers of iniquity'" (Genesis 27:34; Luke 13:25–27).

I saw that it was proper to understand the Scriptures in this way, that doing so was in accordance with other Scriptures and not against them, and I was greatly encouraged and comforted.

And now there remained only the end portion of the tempest. The thunder was gone now, and only some small drops remained that now and then would fall upon me. But since my former fright was so very sore and deep, I was like those who have been scarred with fire. I thought that every little touch would hurt my tender conscience.

20. The believer's righteousness is that imputed to him by Jesus. Our salvation does not depend on the degree of our sanctification or the amount of good works we do. This is comforting to the believer who has both good days and bad days.

One day, as I was passing into the field, suddenly this sentence fell upon my soul: "Thy righteousness is in heaven." And I thought that I could see Jesus Christ at God's right hand. Yes, there indeed was my righteousness so that wherever I was or whatever I was doing, God could not say about me that I did not have righteousness, for it was standing there before Him.[20]

I also saw that it was not my good feelings that made my righteousness better, and that my bad feelings did not make my righteousness worse, for my righteousness was Jesus Christ Himself, "the same yesterday, and today, and forever" (Hebrews 13:8).

Now indeed the chains fell off my legs; I was loosened from my afflictions and irons. My temptations also fled away so that from that time forward those dreadful Scriptures terrified me no more. Now I went home rejoicing because of the grace and love of God, and went to my Bible to look up where the verse was found that said, "Thy righteousness is in heaven." But I could not find it. And so my heart began to sink again until suddenly, there came to my remembrance 1 Corinthians 1:30—"Who of God is made unto us wisdom, and righteousness, and sanctification, and redemption." From this, I saw that the other sentence was also true.

I lived here sweetly at peace with God through Christ for a long time. There was nothing but Christ before my eyes. I was not thinking of Him now as concerning His blood, His burial or His resurrection, but I was thinking of Christ Himself, sitting on the right hand of God in Heaven.[21]

I gloried to see His exaltation, and the wonders of His benefits which He bestowed so readily. I saw that all those graces of God, that belonged to me, but which I showed so little, were like those few coins that rich men used to carry in their purses while their gold was in their trunks at home. I saw that my gold was in my trunk at Home—in Christ, my Lord and Saviour. Now Christ was all—all my righteousness, all my sanctification, and all my redemption.[22]

Moreover, the Lord also led me into the mystery of union with the Son of God, and I saw that I was joined to Him, that I was flesh of His flesh and bone of His bone. And if He and I were one, then His righteousness was mine, His merits mine, His victory also mine. Now I could see myself in Heaven and earth at the same time; in Heaven by my Christ, my Head, my Righteousness and my Life; and on earth by my own body.[23]

I saw that we fulfilled the law by Him, died by Him, rose from the dead by Him, got the victory over sin, death, the

21. The reality of the risen, living Christ on the right hand of the Father is the object of the Christian's faith. This was the Apostles' message to the nations (through the book of Acts).

22. First Corinthians 1:30 teaches that Jesus is our wisdom, righteousness, sanctification, and redemption.

23. This association with Christ in His death, burial, and resurrection is the basis for our victory over sin (cf. Rom 6:14).

devil and Hell by Him. When He died, we died, and so it was also with His resurrection: "After two days will He revive us: in the third day he will raise us up, and we shall live in his sight" (Hosea 6:2). This is now fulfilled as the Son of Man sits down on "the right hand of the Majesty in the heavens;" as it says in Ephesians, He "hath raised us up together, and made us sit together in heavenly places in Christ Jesus" (Ephesians 2:6). Oh, praise the Lord for all such Scriptures!

I have given you a taste of the sorrow and affliction my soul went through, and of the sweet and blessed comfort that came to me afterward. And now, before I go any further, I will tell you what I believe was the cause of this temptation, and also why it was good for my soul.

The causes seem to me to be two in particular. The first was that when delivered from an earlier temptation, I did not pray to God to keep me from later temptations. I prayed a great deal before this trial seized me, but I only prayed for the removal of present troubles and for fresh discoveries of His love in Christ, which I saw afterward was not enough to do. I should also have prayed that the great God would keep me from the evil that was before me.[24]

I became deeply aware of this as I read the prayer of David, who when he was in a state of present joy before the Lord, prayed that God would hold him back from sin and temptation to come. "Then," he said, "shall I be upright, and I shall be innocent from the great transgression" (Psalm 19:13). Another verse along this same line that I want particularly to mention is Hebrews 4:16: "Let us therefore come boldly unto the throne of grace, that we may obtain mercy, and find grace to help in time of need." This I had not done, and so I was permitted to sin and fall, because I had not done Matthew 26:41. This truth means so much to me right up to this present day that I dare not, when I come before the Lord, get off my knees until I have entreated Him for help and mercy against the temptations that are to come. I plead with you, dear reader, that you also learn through my negligence and my afflictions

24. Bunyan provides the causes for his falling so hard into the last temptation. The first cause was that he did not pray "Lead us not into temptation but deliver us from evil" continually, as Jesus instructed us to pray in the Lord's Prayer.

that went on for days and months and years, so that you will beware.

The second cause of this temptation was that I had tempted God, and this is the way it came about. It was at a time when my wife was great with child, but before her time had come to be delivered. And yet, great pains came upon her just as though she were in labor and would be delivered of her child. It was at this very time that I had been so strongly tempted to question the existence of God. So as my wife lay there crying, I said, but with all secrecy, only thinking it in my heart, "Lord, if you will remove these pains from my wife, so that she will not be troubled any more with them tonight, then I will know that You can understand the most secret thoughts of the heart."[25]

I had no sooner said this in my heart than the pains were taken from her and she fell into a deep sleep, and so continued until morning. I greatly marveled at this, not knowing what to think, but after I had lain awake a long time and she cried no more, I fell asleep. When I awoke in the morning, I remembered what I had said in my heart and what the Lord had done, and this was a great astonishment to me for many weeks afterward.

It was about a year and a half afterward that there went through my wicked heart that terrible thought about which I have spoken when I said, "Let Christ go if He will." When the terrible guilt of that thought was upon me for so long, it was made the more severe as I remembered that other secret thought concerning my wife, and my conscience cried out, "Now you know that God knows the most secret thoughts of your heart, and knows that you thought: 'Let Christ go if He will.'"

And now I thought of the Scriptures that told about Gideon and how he tempted God with his fleece, both wet and dry, when he should have believed and ventured out upon God's commands; and so afterward, the Lord tried him by sending him against an innumerable enemy. So it was also

25. The second cause was his tempting God while his wife was suffering in labor with his child.

with me, and justly so, for I should have believed His Word and not have imposed a check upon the all-seeingness of God.

I will tell you some of the advantages that I gained through this temptation. First, it made me so much aware of the blessedness and glory of God and of His beloved Son.

26. Bunyan also reviews the blessings he received through the temptation. Firstly, he came to appreciate the glory of God and the blessedness of His Son. He had a vision of the holiness of God, the compassion of Jesus, and the preciousness of Christ.

In the earlier temptation, my trouble was unbelief, blasphemy, hardness of heart, and questions about the being of God and of Christ, about the truth of the Word, and the certainty of the world to come. Then my problem was atheism, but now it was quite different. In this second great temptation, God and Christ were continually before me though, of course, not in the way of comfort, but in dread and fear. The glory of the holiness of God broke me to pieces and the compassion of Christ did the same; I thought of Him as a Christ I had lost and rejected, and the memory of what I had done was as the continual breaking of my bones.[26]

The Scriptures also became very wonderful to me. I saw that the truths of them were keys of the kingdom of Heaven. Those favored by the Scriptures inherited bliss, and those opposed and condemned by the Scriptures must perish forevermore. That word, "for the Scriptures cannot be broken," broke my heart, and so did that other one, "Whose soever sins ye remit, they are remitted unto them; and whose soever sins ye retain, they are retained" (John 20:23). One sentence of Scripture terrified me more than an army of 40,000 men that might come against me.[27]

27. Secondly, Bunyan came to appreciate the value, the authority, and the absolute truthfulness of Scripture. He came to revere Scripture to the highest degree.

This temptation also helped me to see more clearly than ever before the nature of the promises of God. As I lay there trembling under the mighty hand of God, I was continually torn by the thundering of His justice against me. It made my heart exceedingly watchful so that with great fearfulness I turned every page and carefully considered every sentence and all of its implications.[28]

28. Thirdly, he learned never to pass over a promise in Scripture lightly. He clung to it with all his might.

I learned too, from this temptation, to discontinue my former foolish practice of trying to put out of mind the words of promise that might come. Now, like a sinking man, I caught at all I saw, even though they might not be for me. Formerly, I thought that I might not meddle with the promise, but now there was no time to wait, for the avenger of blood was too close upon me.

Now I caught at any word, even though I feared I had no right to it, and even leaped into the bosom of that promise that I feared shut its heart against me. Now, also, I tried to take the words as God had laid them down without trying to explain away a single syllable of them. I began to realize that God had a bigger mouth to speak with than I had a heart to understand. I realized also that He had not spoken His words hastily, but with infinite wisdom and judgment and in very truth and faithfulness. In my great agony, I would flounce toward the promise as the horses in the mire do toward sound ground. I was almost out of my wits through fear, and yet struggled on toward the promise: "Him that cometh to me I will in no wise cast out" (John 6:37).

Trying to reach the promise, it would seem to me as if the Lord were thrusting at me with a flaming sword to keep me away. Then I would think of Esther, who went to the king, and of Benhadad's servants who went, with ropes upon their heads, to their enemies for mercy. There was the woman of Canaan also, who was not daunted though called a dog by Christ, and the man who went to borrow bread at midnight. These were great encouragements to me.[29]

Before this temptation, I had never seen such heights and depths in grace and love and mercy as I saw afterward. Great sins draw out great grace, and where guilt is most terrible and fierce, there the mercy of God in Christ, when it is finally revealed to the soul, appears the highest. When Job had passed through his captivity, he had "twice as much as he had before" (Job 42:10). I pray to God that what happened to me may make others fear to offend lest they also be made to bear the iron yoke as I did.

And I would add that two or three times, at about the time that I was delivered from this temptation, I had such

29. Esther and the Canaanite woman were most encouraging to him for their persistence and faith. They were willing to venture out and risk their lives in order to save themselves and their families.

30. Fourthly, Bunyan learned the heights and depths of God's grace, love, and mercy.

an amazing understanding of the divine grace of God that I could hardly bear up under it. It was so out of measure that if it had stayed upon me, I do think it would have made me incapable for business.[30]

And now I want to tell you of a few of the Lord's other dealings with me at various times, and of some of the other temptations I met. I will begin with what happened to me when I first joined in fellowship with the people of God in Bedford. I was admitted by them into the fellowship of the Lord's Supper, and that Scripture, "This do in remembrance of me" (Luke 22:19), was made very precious to me. By it, the Lord came down upon my conscience with the discovery of His death for my sins. But it was not long before it happened, when I was partaking of the ordinance, that there came fierce temptations to blaspheme the ordinance and to wish some deadly thing to those that were eating of it. To keep myself from consenting to these wicked and fearful thoughts, I had, as it were, to lean myself mightily against them, crying out to God to keep me from such blasphemies, and to bless the cup and bread to those who were drinking from it. I have since thought that the reason for this temptation was because I did not come with sufficient reverence to the table to partake thereof.[31]

31. The Devil seems to take advantage of irreverence. Bunyan does not think he was approaching the Lord's Table with enough reverence.

This kept on for nine months and would neither rest nor ease, but at last the Lord came in upon my soul with that same Scripture He had used before. After that, I was usually able to partake of the blessed ordinance with great comfort and, I trust, discerned therein the Lord's body broken for my sin and His precious blood shed for my transgressions.

32. Consumption is tuberculosis. Symptoms are chronic cough, fever, and night sweats. Many would die of this bacterial disease in previous centuries.

Another time I seemed to be getting consumption[32] and along during the springtime I was suddenly and violently seized with so much weakness that I thought I would not live. Once again I gave myself up to a serious examination of my state and my prospects for the future. For, blessed be the name of God, I have been enabled at all times to keep my interest in the life to come clearly before my eyes, especially in the day of affliction.

But I had no sooner begun to recall to mind my experiences of the goodness of God, than there came flocking into my mind also the remembrance of an innumerable number of sins, especially my coldness of heart, my weariness in doing good, and my lack of love for God, His ways, and His people. And along with them came this question: Are these the signs of a man who has been blessed of God?

Now my sickness was doubled, for now I was sick in my inward man, my soul clogged with guilt, and my experiences of God's goodness were quite taken out of mind as though they had never existed. Now my soul was tossed between these two conclusions: live I must not; die I dare not. And so I gave up all for lost.[33] But just then as I was walking up and down in the house, in the most dreadful state of mind, this word of God took hold upon my heart: Ye are "justified freely by His grace through the redemption that is in Christ Jesus"[34] (Romans 3:24). Oh, what a turn this made upon me! Oh, what a sudden change it made!

It was as though I had awakened out of a nightmare. Now God seemed to be saying to me: "Sinner, you think that I cannot save your soul because of your sins; behold my Son is here, and I look upon Him and not on you, and I shall deal with you according as I am pleased with Him." By this I was made to understand that God can justify a sinner at any time by looking upon Christ and imputing His benefits to him.

Then also, this Scripture came upon my spirit with great power: "Not by works of righteousness which we have done, but according to his mercy he saved us" (Titus 3:5; 2 Timothy 1:9). Now I was walking on air, for I saw myself within the arms of grace and mercy and, whereas before I was afraid to die, now I cried out, "Let me die." Now death was lovely and beautiful in my sight, for I saw that we will never really live until we have come to the other world. This life, I saw, was but a slumber in comparison with that above. It was at this time

33. The Devil comes upon us in our weakest moments, even physical weakness. Be ready with the Word of God upon every assault of the Devil.

34. Justification is the judicial declaration God pronounces upon a sinner. He declares us righteous because of the righteousness of His Son imputed to us and received by faith alone. John Bunyan realizes that God declares a sinner righteous because of His Son's righteousness. He is looking upon His Son's righteousness and putting that righteousness to our account. Bunyan finds this very encouraging.

also, that I saw more in these three words than I shall ever be able to express: "Heirs of God" (Romans 8:17). God Himself is the portion of the saints. This I saw and wondered at, but I cannot explain what it meant to me.

Another time I was very weak and ill, and again the Tempter was there. I find he is most present to assault the soul when it begins to approach the grave. That was his opportunity and he worked hard to hide from me my experiences of God's goodness and set before me the terrors of death and the judgment of God, and, through my fear that I would be lost if I died, I was as one dead before death came. It was as if I were already descending into the pit. But then, just as I was in the midst of these fears, the words of the angel carrying Lazarus into Abraham's bosom darted in upon me, and I felt that it would be even so with me when I left this world.[35] This thought wonderfully revived my spirits and helped me to have hope again in God. And after I had thought about this for a while, the words fell with great weight upon my mind: "O death, where is thy sting? O grave, where is thy victory?" (1 Corinthians 15:55). At once I became well both in body and in mind; my sickness vanished, and I walked comfortably in my work for God again. Another time, when I had been getting along well in spiritual things, suddenly there fell upon me a great cloud of darkness, which so hid from me the things of God in Christ that it seemed as though I had never known about them in all my life. My soul was seized in a spiritual paralysis such that I could not stir after grace and the life that is in Christ. It was as if my hands and feet were bound with chains.

I had remained in this condition for three or four days when, as I was sitting by the fire, this word suddenly struck into my heart[36]: I must go to Jesus. At that moment the darkness and atheism fled away and the blessed things of Heaven came into my view. I cried out to my wife, "Is there such a Scripture as this: 'I must go to Jesus'?" She said she did not know, so I sat there trying to think if I could remember such

35. The words of the angel carrying Lazarus into Abraham's bosom are not recorded.

36. Note: The subsequent trials last only 3-4 days.

a place. I had been sitting there two or three minutes when there came bolting in upon me, "and to an innumerable company of angels" and all the twelfth chapter of Hebrews about Mount Sion, especially the phrase from verse 22, along with these words in verse 24, "And to Jesus."[37]

That night was one that I shall long remember. Christ was so precious to my soul that I could scarcely lie in my bed for joy and peace and triumph through Christ. The glory of it did not continue, but Hebrews 12:22–24 was a blessed Scripture to me for many days after that. The words are these, "Ye are come unto Mount Sion, and unto the city of the living God: the heavenly Jerusalem, and to an innumerable company of angels, to the general assembly and church of the firstborn, which are written in heaven, and to God the Judge of all, and to the spirits of just men made perfect, and to Jesus the mediator of the new covenant, and to the blood of sprinkling, that speaketh better things than that of Abel." Through this sentence the Lord led me over and over first to this word and then to that and showed me wonderful glory in every one of them. These words have often refreshed my spirit. Blessed be God for having mercy on me!

37. It is interesting that the passage in Hebrews 12:17 concerning Esau was Bunyan's greatest affliction, but in the end the reference to Christ in Hebrews 12:22-24 became his greatest comfort.

THE AUTHOR'S CALL TO THE WORK OF THE MINISTRY

A nd now, while telling you about my experiences, I will put in a word or two about preaching the Word and of God's dealings in calling me to this work.

I had been awake to the Lord for five or six years, having seen the great worth of Jesus Christ our Lord, and my need for Him, and having been enabled to trust my soul to Him. Some of the saints who had good judgment and holiness of life seemed to feel that God had counted me worthy to understand the blessed Word and that He had given me some measure of ability to express helpfully to others what I saw in it. So they asked me to speak a word of exhortation to them in one of the meetings.

At first this seemed to be an impossible thing for me to do, but they kept at it. I finally consented and spoke twice to small meetings of Christians only, but with much weakness and infirmity. So I tested my gift among them, and it seemed as I spoke that they were being given a blessing. Afterward many told me, in the sight of the great God, that they were helped and comforted. They gave thanks to the Father of mercies for this gift He had given to me.

Afterward, when some of them occasionally went into the country to teach, they asked me to go with them. I did, and I

1. Sometime around 1656 (when Bunyan was 28 years old), he began an itinerant preaching ministry in the surrounding countryside around Bedford (about 50 miles north of London).

2. It is a good thing to surround an ordination of a pastor with prayer and fasting.

3. He was still going through some of his internal struggles when he began his preaching ministry.

spoke sometimes, and began occasionally to speak in a more public way also. And these others also received the Word with rejoicing and said that their souls were edified.[1]

The church continued to feel that I should preach, and so after solemn prayer to the Lord with fasting,[2] I was ordained to regular public preaching of the Word among those who believed and also to those who had not yet received the faith. About this time I began to feel in my heart a great desire to preach to the unsaved, not for the desire of glorifying myself, for at that time I was particularly being afflicted with the fiery darts of the Devil concerning my eternal state.[3]

I could not be at rest unless I was exercising this gift of preaching, and I was pressed forward into it not only by a constant desire of the brethren, but also by Paul's statement to the Corinthians, "I beseech you, brethren, (ye know the house of Stephanas, that it is the firstfruits of Achaia, and that they have addicted themselves to the ministry of the saints,) that ye submit yourselves unto such, and to every one that helpeth with us, and laboreth" (1 Corinthians 16:15–16).

I could see from this text that the Holy Ghost never intended that men who had gifts and abilities should bury them in the earth, but rather He commanded and stirred up such people to the exercise of their gift and sent out to the work those who were able and ready. "They have addicted themselves to the ministry of the saints." This Scripture continually ran in my mind to encourage me during those days and strengthen me in my work for God. I was also encouraged from several other scriptures, giving examples of the godly (Acts 8:4; Acts 18:24–25; 1 Peter 4:10; Romans 12:6), and so, although I was the most unworthy of all the saints, I set upon this work. Though trembling, I used my gift to preach the blessed gospel in proportion to my faith as God had showed me in the holy Word of truth. When the word got around that I was doing this, people came in by hundreds from all over to hear the Word preached.

I thank God that he gave me great concern and pity for their souls. This made me labor with great earnestness to hold out to them such a message that, if God would bless it, would awaken their consciences.[4] And the Lord answered my request, for I had not preached long before some began to be touched by the message and to be greatly afflicted in their minds because of the greatness of their sins and of their need of Jesus Christ.

At first I could hardly believe that God would speak through me to the heart of anyone, and I still counted myself unworthy. Yet those who were quickened through my preaching loved me and had a particular respect for me. Although I insisted that it was not because of what I had said, still they publicly declared that it was so. They, in fact, blessed God for me, unworthy wretch though I was, and counted me as God's instrument who showed them the way of salvation.

And when I saw that they were beginning to live differently as well as speak differently, and that their hearts were eagerly pressing after the knowledge of Christ, and rejoicing that God sent me to them, then I began to conclude that it must be so that God had blessed His work through me. And then came the Word of God to my heart with such sweet refreshment: "The blessing of him that was ready to perish came upon me: and I caused the widow's heart to sing for joy" (Job 29:13).[5]

And so I rejoiced. Yes, the tears of those whom God awakened by my preaching were my solace and my encouragement.[6] I thought of the verses: "Who is he that maketh me glad, but the same which is made sorry by me?" (2 Corinthians 2:2) and, "If I be not an apostle to others, yet doubtless I am to you; for the seal of mine apostleship are ye in the Lord" (1 Corinthians 9:2). In my preaching of the Word I noticed that the Lord led me to begin where His Word begins with sinners; that is, to condemn all flesh and to state clearly that the curse of God is upon all men as they come into the world because of sin.[7] And this part of my work I fulfilled easily, for

4. Bunyan's major motivation was a concern and pity for souls. He wanted to preach the Gospel.

5. A small revival happened as people would come by the hundreds to hear the preaching, and they would be greatly convicted by the message.

6. The true test of a revival — lives were changed.

7. Good preaching begins with the terrors of the law and the curse of God upon all mankind. People must hear the bad news before they are prepared to hear the good news.

the terrors of the Law and the guilt of my transgressions lay heavy on my conscience. I preached what I felt, even that under which my own poor soul groaned and trembled.

Indeed, I was as one sent to them from the dead. I went myself in chains, preached to them in chains, and had in my own conscience that fire which I pleaded with them to beware of. I can honestly say that many a time as I have gone to preach I have been full of guilt and terror right up to the pulpit door, and there it has been taken off and I have been at liberty until my work was done. Then immediately, before I could get down the pulpit stairs, it was upon me as bad as before. Yet God carried me on, but surely with a strong hand.

I went on this way for two years, crying out against men's sins and their fearful state because of them. After this, the Lord came in upon my soul with the sure peace and comfort that there was blessed grace to me.

8. Bunyan's second approach to preaching included more of a demonstration of the goodness of Jesus Christ. He went after false supports, every approach men resort to that prevent them from coming to Christ.

So now I changed my preaching, for still I preached what I myself saw and felt. Now I tried to show everyone the wonderful Jesus Christ in all His offices, relationships, and benefits to the world, and tried to point out and condemn and remove all those false supports on which the world leans and by which it perishes. And I preached along these lines about as long as I had on the other.[8]

9. Bunyan's third emphasis was union with Christ.

After this, God led me into something of the mystery of the union of Christ, so I showed them that.[9] When I had traveled through these three chief points of the Word of God during a five-year period, I came into my present situation, having been cast into prison—where I have now been five years longer—in order to confirm the truth by way of suffering, just as I before confirmed it by testifying to it through preaching.

In all my preaching, thank God, my heart has earnestly cried out to God to make the Word effectual to the salvation of souls, for I have been fearful that the enemy would take the Word away from the conscience and so it would be unfruitful.[10] I have tried to speak the Word so that a particular person might realize himself guilty of a particular sin.

And after I have preached, my heart has been full of concern to think that the Word might now fall as rain on stony places, and I have often cried out from my heart, "Oh, that those who have heard me speak today will but see as I do what sin, death, hell, and the curse of God really are, and that they might understand the grace and love and mercy of God, that it is through Christ to men no matter in what condition they are, even if they are His enemies!" And I often told the Lord that if I were killed before their eyes and it would be a means to awaken them and confirm them in the truth, I would gladly have that done. Especially when I have spoken of the life that is in Christ without works, it has sometimes seemed as if an angel of God were standing behind me to encourage me. With great power and with heavenly evidence upon my own soul, I have been laboring to unfold this wonderful doctrine, to demonstrate it and to fasten it upon the consciences of my hearers. For this doctrine seemed to me not only to be true, but more than true!

When I first went to preach the Word in other places, the regular preachers everywhere opened up against me. I was convinced that I should not return railing for railing, but I wanted to see how many of these carnal Christians[11] could be convinced of their miserable state as they trusted in the Law, and of their need of Christ and of His great worth. For I thought, that shall "answer for me in time to come," when they shall be for my hire before their face (Genesis 30:33).

As to controversies among the saints, I never cared to meddle with such things. My work was to preach with all earnestness the word of faith and the remission of sin by the death and sufferings of Jesus. The other things I let alone, because I saw that they brought strife and that God had neither commanded that we do or not do them. My work ran in another channel and I stuck to that alone.[12]

10. Bunyan's passion is seen in preaching. He would be willing to be killed in front of the congregation if he could get his message across. Human methods, however, won't save anybody without the working of the Spirit of God in the hard hearts of men and women.

11. Opposition came from what he called "carnal Christians" or the regular preachers in the churches.

12. He avoided controversies over minor issues. He was not interested in sectarian battles. He wanted to get the major point across. We are sinners, and we need Christ to save us from our sins.

I never dared to use other men's thoughts and sermons (Romans 15:18), though I do not condemn those who do. But as for me, I have found that what I have been taught by the Word and by the Spirit of Christ, that I could speak boldly, with my conscience vindicating all that I said. Although I will not give more details at this time, I will say that my experience has more interest in that text of Scripture—Galatians 1:11–12—than many are aware of. In other words, the Lord Himself has taught me a great deal.

When, as sometimes happened, those who were awakened by my ministry afterward fell back into sin, I can truly say that their loss was more terrible to me than if my own children, begotten of my own body, had gone to their graves. I think I can say this without any offense to the Lord, that nothing has ever hurt me so much unless it was the fear of the loss of the salvation of my own soul.[13] I have thought of myself as having great possessions in those places where my children were born. I felt that I was more blessed and honored of God by this than if He had made me the emperor of the Christian world, or the Lord of all the glory of the whole earth, without having this glory of doing God's excellent work. Wonderful indeed are such verses as these: "He which converteth the sinner from the error of his way shall save a soul from death!" (James 5:20). "The fruits of the righteous is a tree of life; and he that winneth souls is wise" (Proverbs 11:30). "They that be wise shall shine as the brightness of the firmament; and they that turn many to righteousness as the stars forever and ever" (Daniel 12:3). "For what is our hope, or joy, or crown of rejoicing? Are not even ye in the presence of our Lord Jesus Christ at his coming? for ye are our glory and joy" (1 Thessalonians 2:19–20).

I have noticed that when there is a particular work I am to do for God, there has come over my spirit ahead of time a great desire to go and preach at a certain place. I have often noticed too that particular names have been strongly set upon my heart, names of people I knew, and I cried out for their salvation. And these were the very souls who were given to

13. Ministry yields great joy when souls are converted and great pain when some who we think are converted slip back into the life of sin. This double-edged sword holds much pain and much delight.

me as a result of my ministry at that place when I went to preach. Sometimes I have noticed that a word cast in, by the way, has done more than all the rest of the sermon. Sometimes when I thought I had done the least, then it developed that the most had been accomplished; and at other times when I thought I had really gotten hold of them, I found I had fished for nothing.[14]

But I have also observed that where there has been a work to do with sinners, there the Devil has begun to roar in the hearts and by the mouths of his servants.[15] And sometimes when the wicked world has been most disturbed, then the most souls have been awakened by the Word. I could give you illustrations, but I forbear.

I was anxious in fulfilling my ministry to get into the darkest places of the country, among those who were farthest from God. This was not because I was afraid to show my gospel to those who already had some instruction, but because that is the way my spirit leans. Like Paul, "so have I strived to preach the gospel, not where Christ was named, lest I should build upon another man's foundation" (Romans 15:20).

In my preaching, I have actually been in real pain, travailing to bring forth children to God, and I have never been satisfied unless there has been some fruit. If not, it made no difference who complimented me, but if I were fruitful I did not care who might condemn me.[16] I have often thought of that verse: "Lo, children are an heritage of the Lord: and the fruit of the womb is his reward. As arrows are in the hand of a mighty man; so are children of the youth. Happy is the man that hath his quiver full of them: they shall not be ashamed, but they shall speak with the enemies in the gate" (Psalm 127:3–5).

It never pleased me to see people merely drinking in opinions if they were ignorant of Christ and the value of His salvation. When I saw sound conviction for sin, especially the sin of unbelief, and saw hearts set on fire to be saved by Christ, those were the souls I counted blessed.[17]

14. God's Spirit surprises us in ministry, doing work when and where we least expect it.

15. The Devil's roaring refers to the persecution that happens when the Gospel begins to make an impact.

16. Bunyan's highest priority was fruit, not the compliments or condemnation of men. This is a good distinction to draw in ministry. What really matters is the fruit of a pious, God-worshiping people.

17. He does not look for people agreeing with a theological persuasion. He wanted to see conviction of sin and people running to Christ for salvation.

18. Temptations for preachers are multitudinous. Discouragement is common (after almost every sermon). Satan can attack a man while he preaches in order to disorient him.

19. A preacher must be willing to confess his own weaknesses as he preaches. He preaches at himself as well as everybody else.

20. Samson brought the house down upon himself and all the Philistines at the end of his life – a terrific metaphor for preaching against sin.

21. Pride is another temptation for preachers and leaders in the church. God uses the horrific trials Bunyan faced to keep him humble. Thank God for these things. Pride is a terrible, terrible plight for any church leader.

But in this work, as in any other, I had my different temptations. Sometimes I would suffer from discouragement, fearing that I would not be of any help to anyone and that I would not even be able to speak sense to the people. At such times, I have had a strange faintness seize me. At other times, when I have been preaching, I have been violently assaulted with thoughts of blasphemy before the congregation. At times, I have been speaking with clearness and great liberty when suddenly everything would go blank and I would not know what to say or how to finish.[18]

Again, there have been times when I have been about to preach on some searching portion of the Word, and I have found the Tempter suggesting, "What! Will you preach this? This condemns you. Your own soul is guilty of this; you must not preach on it. If you do, you must leave a door open for you to escape from the guilt of what you will say. If you preach like this, you will lay that guilt upon your own soul and you will never be able to get out from under it."

I've been kept from consenting to these horrid suggestions and instead have, like Samson, preached against sin and transgression wherever I found it, even though it did bring guilt upon my own conscience.[19] "Let me die," I thought, "with the Philistines" (Judges 16:30)[20]—rather than deal corruptly with the blessed Word of God. Thou that teachest another, teachest thou not thyself? It is far better to bring oneself under condemnation by plain preaching to others, than to save yourself by imprisoning the truth in unrighteousness. Blessed be God for His help also in this.

I have often found in this blessed work of Christ that I have been tempted to pride, but the Lord in His precious mercy has, for the most part, kept me from giving way to such a thing. Every day I have been able to see the evil of my own heart and my head has hung down with shame despite the gifts and the attainments that He has given to me. So I feel that this thorn in the flesh is the very mercy of God to me (2 Corinthians 12:7–9).[21]

I have also had the Word come to me with some sharp, piercing sentence concerning the perishing of the soul notwithstanding the gifts God has given. For instance: "Though I speak with the tongues of men and of angels, and have not charity, I am become as sounding brass, or a tinkling cymbal" (1 Corinthians 13:1).

A tinkling cymbal is a musical instrument with which a skillful player can make heart-inflaming melody, so that all who hear him play can scarcely keep from dancing. Yet the cymbal does not contain life, and the music does not come out of it except by the ability of the one who plays upon it. The instrument can be crushed and thrown away, even though in the past wonderfully sweet music has been played upon it.

So are all those who have gifts but do not have saving grace. They are in the hands of Christ as the cymbal was in the hand of David.[22] As David could use the cymbal in the service of God to lift up the hearts of the worshipers, so Christ can use gifted men to affect the souls of the people in His Church, yet when He has finished using them, He can hang them up without life, even though they are sounding cymbals.[23]

Such considerations were a sledge hammer upon the head of pride and the desire of vainglory. *What!* thought I, *shall I be proud because I am a sounding brass? Is it such a great thing to be a fiddle? Does not the person who has the least of the life of God in him have more than these instruments?* Besides, I remembered that these instruments would vanish away, though love would never die. So I concluded that a little grace, a little love, a little of the true fear of God are better than all the gifts. I am convinced that it is possible for an ignorant soul who can scarcely give a right answer to have a thousand times more grace, and to be more in the love and the favor of the Lord, than some who have marvelous gifts and can deliver themselves like angels.[24]

I perceived that although gifts are good to accomplish the task they are designed for—the edification of others—yet they are empty and without power to save the soul unless God is

22. Musical instruments are worthless until somebody very talented plays them. So, the preacher is of little use unless the Spirit of God is working through him.

23. Gifts of speaking and preaching are nowhere near as crucial to the Christian as the gift of love, faith, and real fear of God. A man who demonstrates fear of God and love for God and others in teaching is far ahead of the most talented speaker.

24. Every talented preacher is not necessarily converted by definition.

25. The preacher must rely on the grace of God and walk humbly before God always.

26. Seek grace over the gift (of speaking and preaching). This grace is the grace of being loved, apprehending that love, and loving others as Christ loved us.

27. The preacher is a man almost always beset by attacks from the evil one. Even before the internet came around, good men of God were falsely accused of many things. Bunyan was accused of being a witch, a Jesuit, a highwayman, and even an adulterer. The attitude of the godly man is to just keep moving ahead and let God sort it out at the final judgment.

using them. And having gifts is no sign of the man's relationship to God. This also made me see that gifts are dangerous things, not in themselves, but because of those evils of pride and vainglory that attend them. Blown up with the applause of ill-advised Christians, the poor creatures who possess these gifts can easily fall into the condemnation of the Devil.

I saw that he who has these gifts needs to be led into an understanding of the nature of them—that they do not prove that he is in a saved condition— lest he rely on them and so fall short of the grace of God.

He needs to learn to walk humbly with God, to be little in his own eyes, and to remember that his gifts are not his own—they belong to the Church. By them he is made a servant of the Church; he must give at the last an account of his stewardship unto the Lord Jesus; and it will be a wonderful thing if he can give a good account.[25]

Gifts are desirable, but great grace and small gifts are better than great gifts and no grace. The Bible does not say that the Lord gives gifts and glory, but that He gives grace and glory. Blessed is everyone to whom the Lord gives true grace, for that is a certain forerunner of glory.[26]

When Satan saw that this temptation would not do what he had hoped— overthrow my ministry, making it ineffectual—he tried another way. He stirred up the minds of the ignorant and malicious to load me with slanders and reproaches. All that the Devil could devise and invent was whirled up and down the country against me, the Devil thinking that in this way he could make me abandon the ministry.

It began to be rumored that I was a witch, a Jesuit, a highwayman, and so on.[27]

To all this I only say that God knows I am innocent. As for my accusers, let them prepare to meet me before the judgment seat of the Son of God. There they shall answer for all these things they have said against me and for all the rest of their iniquities unless—as I pray with all my heart—God gives them repentance.

It was reported against me with the greatest certainty that I had my mistresses, my whores, and my bastards. But I can glory in these slanders cast upon me by the Devil because if the world did not deal wickedly with me, I would wonder whether I were really a child of God. "Blessed are ye," said the Lord Jesus, "when men shall revile you, and persecute you, and shall say all manner of evil against you falsely, for my sake. Rejoice, and be exceeding glad: for great is your reward in heaven: for so persecuted they the prophets, which were before you" (Matthew 5:11–12).

These would not have bothered me if there had been twenty times more of them than there were. I have a good conscience, and they shall be ashamed who speak evil of me and falsely accuse my good conversation in Christ.

Now then, what shall I say about those who have thus bespattered me? Shall I threaten them? Shall I flatter them? Shall I entreat them to hold their tongues? No, not I. Except for the fact that it makes them ripe for damnation that say these things, they could keep on at it. I would bind these slanders to me as an ornament. It is part of my Christian profession to be vilified, slandered, reproached, and reviled. Since these things are not true, I rejoice in reproaches for Christ's sake.

Now I would like to call attention to how foolish those people are who accuse me of having other women. Let them make the fullest inquiry that they can. They will find no woman in Heaven or earth or Hell who can say that at any time, in any place, by day or night, I have been dishonorable with her.

My foes have missed their mark in trying to shoot me with this charge. I am simply not the man. I hope that they themselves are as guiltless as I am in this matter. If all the fornicators and adulterers in England were hanged by the neck till they were dead, John Bunyan, the object of their envy, would still be alive and well. Except for my wife, I have not the slightest interest in women, and do not even know that they exist except by their clothing, their children, or what is said about them.

And I praise God and admire His wisdom that He has made me shy of women, right from the time of my conversion until now. Those who know me best would be my witnesses that it is a rare thing to see me talking pleasantly to a woman. I abhor conversation with them. I cannot stand their company. I seldom so much as touch a woman's hand for I think these things are not wise.[28] When I have seen good men kiss women at the end of a visit, I have at times made objection to it. When they have answered that it was but a piece of civility, I told them that it is not good. Some have told me that the holy kiss is scriptural, but then I have asked them why they tend to kiss those who are beautiful and let the ill-favored go. And so, no matter how wise these things have been in the eyes of others, they have been wrong to me.

And now I call not only upon men but upon angels to say if I have been guilty of having any other woman except my wife. Yes, I call God Himself for a record upon my soul that in these things I am innocent. It is not that I have been kept from these things because of any goodness that is in me, but because God has been merciful to me and has kept me. And I pray that He will always keep me, not only from this, but from every evil way and work and preserve me to His heavenly kingdom. Amen.

The result of Satan's work to make me vile among my countrymen— and if possible, to make my preaching useless—was to add to my long and tedious imprisonment, so that I would be frightened from my service for Christ, and the world made afraid to hear me preach. Of these things I will give a brief account now.[29]

28. John Bunyan is careful to vindicate himself on the charge of adultery. A pastor must maintain a good reputation (1 Tim. 3:1-6) and defend that reputation when he must. Bunyan admits to being shy around women. His efforts to avoid all reproach may have been overkill — "I cannot stand their company. I seldom so much as touch a woman's hand. . . ." In a day where accusations fly and fornication is common, a pastor in the church may have to be overly careful when in the presence of a woman not his wife.

29. Bunyan interprets Satan's strategy to be two-fold: (1) imprison him so that he would not be able to preach, and (2) make the world afraid to associate with somebody who is being persecuted by the civil magistrate.

A BRIEF ACCOUNT OF THE AUTHOR'S IMPRISONMENT

After I had been a Christian for a long time and had been preaching for about five years, I was arrested at a meeting of good people in the country, among whom, if they had let me alone, I would have preached that day. They took me away from among them and before a justice. I offered security to appear at the next session, but he threw me into jail because those who were ready to make up the bond for me would not agree to be bound that I would preach no more to the people.

At the next session, I was indicted as one who had encouraged unlawful assemblies and non-conformance to the national worship of the Church of England. The judges thought that my plain dealing with them was proof enough, and sentenced me to life imprisonment because I refused to conform.[1]

John Bunyan writing in prison

1. If Bunyan would have agreed not to preach, he would have been released.

2. The monarchy (of the Stuarts) was restored in 1660, four years after Bunyan began to preach. Immediately, the little Bedford congregation could no longer meet at the Anglican church in town, so they moved off to a farm house in the country. He was accused of violating the Conventicle Act of 1593, which provided a three month sentence for those participating in a meeting with more than five people attending (that was not organized by the parish church). Things were bound to get difficult for the non-conformists (like Bunyan). Two years later, the Act of Uniformity would require all preachers to be ordained by an Anglican bishop. Also, the Book of Common Prayer would be required for all church services. Bunyan would remain in jail for 12 years.

3. The benefits of prison have been the study of God's Word. The Scriptures became very plain to Bunyan as he meditated upon them in the prison. His relationship with Christ became more real — sharing in the fellowship of Jesus' sufferings (as Paul put it).

So I was again given to the jailer and sent to prison, where I have now lain for these twelve years, waiting to see what God would let these men do with me.[2]

In this condition I have found much contentment through grace, so there have been many turnings and goings upon my heart from the Lord, from Satan, and from my own corruption. After all these things—glory be to Jesus Christ—I have also received much instruction and understanding. I will not speak at length of these things, but will give you at least a hint or two that may stir up the godly to bless God and to pray for me, and to take encouragement, should they find themselves in need of it, not to fear what man can do unto them.

I have never in all my life had so much of the Word of God opened up so plainly to me before. Those Scriptures that I saw nothing particular in before have been made in this place to shine upon me. Also, Jesus Christ was never more real to me than now; here I have seen and felt Him indeed. That "we have not followed cunningly devised fables" (2 Peter 1:16), and that God raised Christ "from the dead, and gave him glory; that your faith and hope might be in God" have been blessed portions to me in this my imprisonment.[3]

I would also say that John 14:1–4, John 16:33, Colossians 3:3–4, and Hebrews 12:22–24 have been great refreshments to me here. Sometimes when they have been much upon my heart, I have been able to laugh at destruction and to fear neither the horse nor his rider. I have had sweet sights in this place of the forgiveness of my sins, and of my being with Jesus in another world. Oh, how I long for Mount Zion, the heavenly Jerusalem, the innumerable company of angels, God the Judge of all, the spirits of just men made perfect, and Jesus (Hebrews 12:22–24). How sweet these have been to me in this place. I have seen things here that I am sure I will never in all the world be able to express. And I have seen the truth in this Scripture: "Whom having not seen, ye love; in whom, though now ye see him not, yet believing, ye rejoice with joy unspeakable and full of glory" (1 Peter 1:8).[4]

I never knew before what it really was for God to stand beside me at all times. As soon as fears have presented themselves, so have supports and encouragements. Sometimes when I have been startled by my shadow, being so full of fear, God has been very tender to me and has not suffered me to be molested by Satan, but has given me one Scripture after another to strengthen me against it all. I have often said, "Were it lawful, I could pray for greater trouble, for the greater comfort's sake" (Ecclesiastes 7:14; 2 Corinthians 1:5).

Before I came to prison, I saw what was coming, and two things were particularly heavy upon my heart.

The first was how I would be able to encounter death if that should be my portion. Colossians 1:11 helped me greatly at this point to pray to God to be "strengthened with all might, according to his glorious power, unto all patience and longsuffering with joyfulness."[5] For at least a year before I was in prison, I could scarcely go to prayer without this sentence thrusting itself into my mind and persuading me that if I would ever have to go through long suffering, I would need much patience especially if I were to endure it joyfully.

The second thing that bothered me was what would happen to my wife and family. Concerning this, this Scripture helped me: "But we had the sentence of death in ourselves, that we should not trust in ourselves, but in God which raiseth the dead" (2 Corinthians 1:9). By this Scripture I was made to see that if ever I must suffer properly, I must first pass the sentence of death upon everything that can be in this life; even to reckon myself, my wife, my children, my health, my enjoyments, and all, as dead to me; and myself, as dead to them.[6]

I saw, moreover, as Paul said, that the way not to faint is to "look not at the things which are seen, but at the things which are not seen: for the things which are seen are temporal; but the things which are not seen are eternal" (2 Corinthians 4:18). I reasoned that if I prepare only for imprisonment, then

4. God provides very strong comfort (and thereby a strong sense of his presence) during these times of severe persecution.

5. Two challenges faced him as he came to the jail. First, he was concerned about how he would die. He wanted to suffer and die joyfully. This prayer was answered.

6. The second challenge Bunyan faced was his concern for his wife and children. He had to come to the conclusion that he must die to his family since he was apart from them. Everything would be made right at the resurrection. He had to take the eternal view of his sufferings. He expected the worst — death and a martyrdom — and this helped him immensely.

I am whipped, and if I prepare myself for these, then I am not fit for banishment. If I decide that I could stand banishment, then if I am killed, I would be surprised. So I saw that the best way to go through sufferings is to trust in God through Christ concerning the world to come and to expect the worst down here, to count the grave as my house, to make my bed in darkness.

This helped, but I am a man with many weaknesses. Parting with my wife and poor children has often been to me like pulling the flesh from my bones, not only because of all that they mean to me, but also because I have thought so much of many hardships, miseries and wants that they were likely to meet, were I taken from them; especially my poor blind child, who was nearer my heart than all of the others. Oh, the thoughts that went through my mind of the hardship I thought my poor blind one might undergo which would break my heart![7]

Poor child, I thought, *what sorrows you are likely to have as your portion in this world. You will probably be beaten and have to beg and suffer hunger, cold, nakedness and a thousand calamities, though I cannot endure the thought of even the wind blowing against you. But I must venture you all with God, though it cuts to the heart to leave you.* I saw that I was as a man who was pulling down his house upon the head of his wife and children, yet I thought, *I must do it, I must do it.* And now I thought about those two milch kine that were to carry the ark of God into another country, while leaving their calves behind them (1 Samuel 6:10).[8]

Three things especially helped me along about this time. The first was the consideration of these Scriptures: "Leave thy fatherless children, I will preserve them alive; and let thy widows trust in me." And again, "The Lord said, Verily it shall be well with thy remnant; verily I will cause the enemy to entreat thee well in the time of evil" (Jeremiah 49:11; 15:11).[9]

The second thing was that I felt that if I should venture all for God, then I would be hiring God to take care of all

John Bunyan in Prison

7. Bunyan was especially concerned for his blind child.

8. Three things encouraged Bunyan in the separation from his family. First, he considered the promise that God would care for the fatherless.

9. The second thing that encouraged Bunyan as he was separated from his family was God's loyalty to him. Surely, as Bunyan was loyal and faithful, would God be less so?

my concerns. But if I forsook Him for fear of any trouble that would come to me or mine, then I would be deserting my faith. In that case, those things which I was so concerned about would not be nearly so safe under my own care while denying God as if they were left at God's feet while I stood for Him.

And that Scripture also fastened itself upon me where Christ prays against Judas, that God would disappoint him in his selfish thoughts which moved him to sell his Master. Please read carefully Psalm 109:6–20.

Another thing that greatly moved me was the dread of the torments of Hell, which I was sure that those must partake of who, for fear of the cross, shrink from doing their duty in Christ. I thought also of the glory that is prepared for those who stand in faith, love, and patience. These things, I say, have helped me when the thoughts of the misery that would come upon both myself and mine because of my love for Christ assaulted me.[10]

When I have been afraid that I might be banished, then I have thought of that Scripture: "They were stoned, they were sawn asunder, were tempted, were slain with the sword: they wandered about in sheepskins and goatskins; being destitute, afflicted, tormented; (of whom the world was not worthy)" (Hebrews 11:37–38). I have also thought of that saying: "The Holy Ghost witnesseth in every city. . . that bonds and afflictions abide me" (Acts 20:23). I have often imagined what it would be like to be banished; how such people are exposed to hunger, to cold, to perils, to nakedness, to enemies and a thousand calamities, and at last they die in a ditch like poor and desolate sheep. But I thank God that until now I have not been greatly moved by these fears but have rather more sought after God because of them.

Let me tell you about an interesting thing that happened. I was once in a particularly sad condition for many weeks. I was only a young prisoner at the time and not acquainted with the laws, and I thought that it was probable that my impris-

10. The third encouragement was a view of heaven and hell. To deny Christ before men is not for the Christian.

onment would end at the gallows. All this time, Satan was beating upon me and saying, "If you are going to die, what will happen to you if you are not enjoying the things of God and have no evidence from your feelings that you are going to Heaven?" Indeed, at this time all the things of God seemed to be hidden from my soul.

This bothered me terribly at first, for I thought that in my present condition, I was not fit to die. If I were so frightened that I would fall off as I was climbing up the ladder to the gallows, I would give much occasion to the enemy to reproach the way of God and the fearfulness of His people. I was ashamed to think that I might die with a pale face and tottering knees. So I prayed to God that He would comfort me and give me strength for whatever He called upon me to do; but no comfort appeared and all was as dark as before. At this time I was so obsessed with the thought of death that I often felt myself standing on the ladder with a rope about my neck. Only this was of some encouragement to me, that I might have a last opportunity to speak to a large multitude which I thought would come to see me die. And I thought: If this must be, and God will convert even one soul by my last words, I will not count my life as thrown away.[11]

And still the Tempter kept following me around, saying, "Where are you going when you die? What will become of you? What evidence have you for Heaven and glory and an inheritance among those who are sanctified?" So it was that I was tossed about for many weeks and knew not what to do. But at last this consideration fell with great weight upon me, that it was for the Word and way of God that I was in this condition; wherefore, I was engaged not to flinch a hair's breadth from it.

I decided also that God might choose whether He would give me comfort now or at the hour of death, but I had no choice as to whether to hold to my profession or not. I was bound, but He was free. It was my duty to stand up for His Word, whether He would ever look upon me with mercy to

11. Bunyan was bothered for a while with the premonition of the gallows — that he would be hung. He was concerned that he might be fearful, faithless, and bear a terrible testimony in his martyrdom. He was encouraged by the thought that this would be a last opportunity to preach the Gospel to a large crowd.

save me at the last or not. I will go on, I said to myself, and venture my eternal state with Christ, whether I feel it here or not. If God does not give me joy, thought I, then I will leap off the ladder blindfolded into eternity, sink or swim, come Heaven, come Hell. Lord Jesus, if You will catch me, do; if not, I will venture for Your name anyway.

I had no sooner resolved this than I thought of that word: "Doth Job fear God for naught?" It was as if the Accuser had said, "Lord, Job is not an upright man. He is serving You for what he can get out of it. You have given him everything he wants, but if You put forth Your hand against him and take away all that he has, then he will curse You to Your face." Well, I thought, then it must be the sign of an upright soul that is on its way to Heaven to desire to serve God when all is taken from him. The truly godly man will serve God for nothing rather than giving up. Blessed be God! Then I began to hope that I did indeed have an upright heart, for I was resolved, God giving me strength, never to deny my Lord though I got nothing at all for my pains; and as I was thinking about this God put into my mind Psalm 44:12–26.

Now my heart became full of comfort, and I would not have missed this trial for a great deal. I am still comforted every time I think of it and I will bless God forever for what He has taught me out of this experience. There are of course, many more of God's dealings with me, but of the spoils won in battle these have I dedicated to maintain the house of God (1 Chronicles 26:27).[12]

12. He committed himself to stand up for God's Word and cast himself on the mercy of Jesus.

✂ CONCLUSION

Of all the temptations that I have ever met with in my life, the worst is to question the being of God and the truth of His gospel, and that is the hardest to bear. When this temptation comes, it takes away my girdle form me and removes the foundation from under my feet. I have often thought of that word: "If the foundations be destroyed, what can the righteous do?" (Psalm 11:3).

Sometimes when I have sinned and have looked for a great chastening from the hand of God, instead I have made new discoveries of His grace. Sometimes when I have been experiencing the peace of God, I have thought that I was a fool for ever sinking down under trouble. Then again, sometimes when I have been in the midst of the trouble, I have wondered whether I ought to let myself be comforted, for both these things have been a blessing to me.

It seemed very strange to me that though God sometimes visits my soul with wonderfully blessed things, yet sometime afterwards, for hours at a time, I have been filled with such darkness that I could not even remember what the comfort was that had refreshed me before.

Sometimes I have gotten so much out of my Bible that I could hardly stand it. At other times the whole Bible has been as dry as a stick to me; or rather my heart has been so dead and dry to it, that I could not get the least drop of refreshment out of it though I looked everywhere for it.

Of all fears, those are best that are made by the blood of Christ; and of all joy, the sweetest is that which is mixed with mourning over Christ.

I find to this day seven evils in my heart:

(1) Inclining to unbelief.

(2) Suddenly to forget the love and mercy that Christ has shown to me.

(3) A leaning toward the works of the Law.

(4) Wanderings and coldness in prayer.

(5) To forget to watch for my prayers to be answered.

(6) Apt to murmur because I have no more, and yet ready to abuse what I have.

(7) I can do none of those things which God commands me, but my sins keep interfering. "When I would do good, evil is present with me" (Romans 7:21).

These are seven things that continually oppress me and yet I see that God in His wisdom has given them to me for my good.

All of these things mentioned above—

(1) Make me abhor myself.

(2) Keep me from trusting my own heart.

(3) Convince me of the insufficiency of all inherent righteousness.

(4) Show me the necessity of flying to Jesus.

(5) Press me to pray unto God.

(6) Show me the need I have to watch and to be sober.

(7) Provoke me to pray unto God through Christ, to help me and carry me through this world.

THE
AUTOBIOGRAPHY OF
JOHN G. PATON

John G. Paton
AD 1891

AN INTRODUCTION TO THE TESTIMONY OF JOHN PATON
The Story of John G. Paton

Throughout the past two thousand years, Christ's kingdom has expanded around the globe and the Christian Church has been formed on every continent. While the 19th and 20th century represented the collapse of the faith in Europe and America, there were still tremendous breakthroughs on the part of the Church as it continued its assault on the gates of hell around the world. What the early church accomplished in a pagan Roman empire and what Patrick did in the heathen land of Ireland are patterns we witness again in the autobiography of John G. Paton. During the latter half of the 19th century, under the steadfast and courageous work of men like Paton, entire island chains—where Satanic worship, cannibalism, and widow-killing were common practices—became citadels of Christian charity and faith.

Paton's is a story of suffering, persecution, and martyrdom. It is the Christian story of love, forgiveness, and relentless faith in the promise of Christ: "I will be with you even unto the end of the world." It is the story of the kingdom of Christ.

You will find three worldviews in conflict in this story: the polytheist pagans, the Western materialist slave-traders, and the self-sacrificing Christian missionaries. Sadly, as paganism died in these countries, Western materialism eventually captured the hearts of the natives and seven demons of even worse character wreaked their havoc. Nevertheless, the influence of Christian missionaries is undeniable even to this day, with Christian churches planted throughout much of Asia, Africa, and the South Pacific.

The most important facet of this story is the life of a Christian man whose faith rooted itself in a Christian heritage that was generations deep. The greatest men have great fathers in the faith, men of vision and wholehearted commitment to the kingdom of God. If there is an example in history of a father that lived the biblical vision for fatherhood and impacted the kingdom through the generations, this is it. When the hearts of the fathers turn to the sons, and the sons to the fathers, you can be sure that a reformation of New Testament proportions is happening (Mal. 4:6). Indeed, this is the normative pattern for the building of the kingdom, exemplified in the life of John G. Paton.

I pray that this story will inspire millions of young people to take their own parents' vision for the kingdom of God, applying a generational leverage in the expansion of that kingdom. This is especially relevant to a nation that has cast its heritage of faith aside and is in the throes of generational apostasy.

CHAPTER I – THE HOME LIFE
A.D. 1824-1834. Age 1-10

What I write here is for the glory of God. For more than twenty years have I been urged to record my story as a missionary of the Cross; but always till now, in my sixty-fourth year,[1] my heart has shrunk from the task, as savoring too much of self. Latterly, the conviction has been borne home to me that if there be much in my experience which the Church of God ought to know, it would be pride on my part, and not humility, to let it die with me. I lift my pen, therefore, with that motive supreme in my heart; and, so far as memory and entries in my note-books and letters of my own and of other friends serve or help my sincere desire to be truthful and fair, the following chapters will present a faithful picture of the life through which the Lord has led me. If it bows any of my readers under as deep and certain a confidence as mine, that in "God's hand our breath is, and His are all our ways," my task will not be fruitless in the Great Day.

I was born in a cottage on the farm of Braehead, in the parish of Kirkmahoe, near Dumfries,[2] in the south of Scotland, on the 24th May, 1824. My father, James Paton, was a stocking manufacturer in a small way; and he and his young wife, Janet Jardine Rogerson, lived on terms of warm personal friendship with the "gentleman farmer," so they gave me his name, John Gibson;[3] and the curly-haired child of the cottage was soon

1. John G. Paton was born May 24, 1824. This autobiography would have been written around 1886.

2. Dumfries is located in southern Scotland near the English border.

A cottage in Torthorwald

3. John Gibson Paton was named after the landlord (in his honor).

4. The loss of family businesses, "well-cultivated plots," and the rise of the Industrial Revolution constitute a real loss to the nation. Family economies were replaced by large corporations in the 19th century. This produced many problems for family life, faith, and culture in the years that followed. The loss was practically "irreparable."

5. Paton's family moved four miles north of Dumfries to Tothorwald when he was five years old.

6. A cooper is a maker of barrels and casks.

able to toddle across to the mansion, and became a great pet of the lady there. More than once, in my many journeyings, have I met with one or another, in some way connected with that family, and heard little incidents not needing to be repeated here, showing how beautiful and tender and altogether human was the relationship in those days betwixt the landlord and the cottars on his estate. On my last visit to Scotland, sixty years after, I drove to Braehead in company with my youngest brother James and my cousin David—the latter born the same week as I, and the former nearly twenty years my junior—and we found no cottage, nor trace of a cottage, but amused ourselves by supposing that we could discover by the rising of the grassy mound, the outline where the foundations once had been! Of ten thousand homes in Scotland, once sweet and beautiful, each a little possible Paradise in its own well-cultivated plot, this is true today; and where are the healthy, happy peasant boys and girls that such homes bred and reared? They are sweltering and struggling for existence in our towns and cities. I am told that this must be—that it is all the result of economic laws; but I confess to a deepening conviction that it need not be, and that the loss to the nation as a whole is vital, if not irreparable.[4]

While yet a mere child, five years or so of age, my parents took me to a new home in the ancient village of Torthorwald,[5] about four and a quarter miles north from Dumfries, on the road to Lockerbie. At that time, about 1830, Torthorwald was a busy and thriving village, and comparatively populous, with its cottars and crofters, large farmers and small farmers, weavers and shoemakers, doggers and coopers,[6] blacksmiths and tailors. Fifty-five years later, when I last visited the scenes of my youth, the village proper was literally extinct, except for five thatched cottages where the lingering patriarchs were permitted to die slowly away, when they too would be swept into the large farms, and their garden plots ploughed over, like sixty or seventy others that had been obliterated! Of course the Village Smithy still survives, but its sparks are few and fading, the great cultivators patronizing rather the towns. The Meal Mill still grinds away, but nothing like what it did when every villager bought or cultivated his few acres of corn, and every crofter[7] and farmer in the parish sent all his grist to the mill. The Grocer's Shop still recalls the well-known name of Robert Henderson; but so few are the mouths now to be fed, that his warm-hearted wife and universal favorite, the very heroine of our village life, "Jean Grier," is retiring from it in disgust, and leaving it to her son-in-law, declaring that "these Tory landlords and their big farms hae driven our folks a' awa, and spoiled the Schule and the Shop, the Kirk and the Mill." And verily the School is robbed of its children, and the Parish Church of its worshippers, when five families only are reared where twenty once flourished! Political economy may curse me, if it will; but I heard with grim satisfaction that this system of large farming, which extinguishes our village homes, and sends our peasantry to rear their children in lanes and alleys, in attics and cellars of populous towns, was proving ruinous at length to the landlords and factors, who had in many cases cruelly forced it on an unwilling people for mere selfish gain.[8]

The Villagers of my early days—the agricultural servants, or occasional laborers, the tradesmen, the small farmers—were, generally speaking, a very industrious and thoroughly independent race of people.[9] Hard workers they had to be, else they would starve; yet they were keen debaters on all affairs both in Church and State, and sometimes in the "smiddy"[10] of the "kiln," sometimes in a happy knot on the "village green" or on the road to the "kirk" or the "market," the questions that were tearing the mighty world beyond were fought over again by secluded peasants with amazing passion and bright intelligence.

From the Bank Hill, close above our village, and accessible in a walk of fifteen minutes, a view opens to the eye which, despite several easily understood prejudices of mine that may discount any opinion that I offer, still appears to me well

7. A crofter is a tenant farmer who works a small plot of land. The family economy has survived here and there in the 21st century, but it is rare.

8. The landowners raised the rents to exorbitant levels in order to use the lands for their own benefits in the 19th century. This pushed the poorer people into the large cities. Paton attributes this to "selfish gain." While technology contributed greatly to the Industrial Revolution, one cannot discount the condition of the hearts of men.

9. The family economies were happy with their independence, although they might not have been wealthy. They had their small family businesses, and they were free from the hierarchy of corporate management. Very rare today.

10. "Smiddy" is the Scottish reference to the blacksmith that worked iron and steel in the kilns.

11. The Parish School operated by the local church. Children were taught in Christian schools exclusively in Paton's early years. The Western world had not been thoroughly secularized as it has been in the 20th and 21st centuries.

12. "Days of blood and border foray" refer to the Scottish battles for independence against England (under Robert the Bruce and William Wallace).

13. After the duel between Robert the Bruce and Red Comyn in the Greyfriars Church of Dumfries, Kirkpatrick was known for returning to the scene to make sure that Comyn was dead. Comyn was known for his double-dealings with the King of England during the wars between Scotland and England (as Scotland fought for its independence).

14. Mt. Criffel outside of Dumfries is 1,870 feet in elevation at its peak.

worth seeing amongst all the beauties of Scotland. At your feet lay a thriving village, every cottage sitting in its own plot of garden, and sending up its blue cloud of "peat reek," which never somehow seemed to pollute the blessed air; and after all has been said or sung, a beautifully situated village of healthy and happy homes for God's children is surely the finest feature in every landscape! There nestled the Manse amongst its ancient trees, sometimes wisely, sometimes foolishly tenanted, but still the "man's-house," the man of God's house, when such can be found for it. There, close by, the Parish School, where rich and poor met together on equal terms, as God's children; and we learned that brains and character make the only aristocracy worth mentioning.[11] Yonder, amid its graves the Village Church; and there, on its little natural hill, at the end of the village, rises the old valley of the Nith, and telling of days of blood and Border foray.[12] It was one of the many castles of the Kirkpatricks, and its enormous and imperishable walls seem worthy of him who wrote the legend of his family in the blood of the Red Comyn, stabbed in the Greyfriars Church of Dumfries, when he smote an extra blow to that of Bruce, and cried, "I mak' siccar" (sure). Beyond, betwixt you and the Nith, crawls the slow-creeping Lochar towards the Solway, through miles and miles of moss and heather—the nearest realization that I ever beheld of a "stagnant stream."[13] Looking from the Bank Hill on a summer day, Dumfries with its spires shone so conspicuous that you could have believed it not more than two miles away; the splendid sweeping vale through which Nith rolls to Solway, lay all before the naked eye, beautiful with village spires, mansion houses, and white shining farms; the Galloway hills, gloomy and far-tumbling, bounded the forward view, while to the left rose Criffel, cloud-capped and majestic;[14] then the white sands of Solway, with tides swifter than horsemen; and finally the eye rested joyfully upon the hills of Cumberland,

and noticed with glee the blue curling smoke from its villages on the southern Solway shores.[15] Four miles behind you lie the ruins of the Castle of the Bruce,[16] within the domains of his own Royal Burgh of Lochmaben; a few miles in front, the still beautiful and amazing remains of Caerlaverock Castle, famous in many a Border story; all around you, scattered throughout the dale of Nith, memories or other ruins of other baronial "keeps," rich in suggestion to the peasant fancy! Traditions lost nothing in bulk, or in graphic force, as they were retold for the thousandth time by village patriarchs around the kindly peat fire, with the younger rustics gaping round. A high spirit of patriotism, and a certain glorious delight in daring enterprises, was part of our common heritage.

There, amid this wholesome and breezy village life, our dear parents found their home for the long period of forty years. There too were born to them eight additional children, making in all a family of five sons and six daughters. Theirs was the first of the thatched cottages on the left, past the "miller's house," going up the "village gate," with a small garden in front of it, and a large garden across the road; and it is one of the few still lingering to show to a new generation what the homes of their fathers were. The architect who planned that cottage had no ideas of art, but a fine eye for durability![17] It consists at present of three, but originally of four, pairs of "oak couples" (Scottice *kipples*) planted like solid trees in the ground at equal intervals, and gently sloped inwards till they meet or are "coupled" at the ridge, this coupling being managed not by rusty iron, but by great solid pins of oak. A roof of oaken wattles was laid across these, till within eleven or twelve feet of the ground, and from the ground upwards a stone wall was raised, as perpendicular as was found practicable, towards these overhang-wattles, this wall being roughly "pointed" with sand and clay and lime. Now into and upon the roof was woven and intertwisted a covering of thatch, that defied all winds and weathers, and that made the cottage marvelously cozy—being renewed year by year, and never allowed

15. The Solway Coast is about 15 miles south of Dumfries, where Paton was raised.

16. The Castle of Bruce, referring to Robert the Bruce (who won the Scottish War for Independence at Bannockburn in AD 1312).

Modern day Dumfries

17. The Paton cottage was 400 years old, built to last! The thatched roof was repaired on an annual basis.

18. Peat reek is the smoke from the burning peat. Peat is decayed plant growth found in bogs and marshes — dried and used for fire.

to remain in disrepair at any season. But the beauty of the construction was and is its durability, or rather the permanence of its oaken ribs! There they stand, after probably not less than four centuries, japanned with "peat reek"[18] till they are literally shining, so hard that no ordinary nail can be driven into them, and perfectly capable of service for four centuries more on the same conditions. The walls are quite modern, having all been rebuilt in my father's time, except only the few great foundation boulders, piled around the oaken couples; and parts of the roofing also may plead guilty to having found its way thither only in recent days; but the architect's one idea survives, baffling time and change–the ribs and rafters of oak.

Our home consisted of a "but" and a "ben" and a "mid room," or chamber, called the "closet." The one end was my mother's domain, and served all the purposes of dining-room and kitchen and parlor, besides containing two large wooden erections, called by our Scotch peasantry "box beds"; not holes in the wall, as in cities, but grand, big, airy beds, adorned with many-colored counterpanes, and hung with natty curtains, showing the skill of the mistress of the house. The other end was my father's workshop, filled with five or six "stocking-frames," whirring with the constant action of five or six pairs of busy hands and feet, and producing right genuine hosiery for the merchants at Hawick and Dumfries. The "closet" was a very small apartment betwixt the other two, having room only for a bed, a little table and a chair, with a diminutive window shedding diminutive light on the scene. This was the Sanctuary of that cottage home. Thither daily, and oftentimes a day, generally after each meal, we saw our father retire, and "shut to the door"; and we children got to understand by a sort of spiritual instinct (for the thing was too sacred to be talked about) that prayers were being poured out there for us, as of old by the High Priest within the veil in the Most Holy Place. We occasionally heard the pathetic echoes of a trembling voice pleading as if for life, and we learned to slip out and in past that door on tiptoe, not to disturb the holy colloquy. The outside world might not know, but we knew, whence came that happy light as of a new-born smile that always was dawning on my father's face: it was a reflection from the Divine Presence, in the consciousness of which he lived. Never, in temple or cathedral, on mountain or in glen, can I hope to feel that the Lord God is more near, more visibly walking and talking with men, than under that humble cottage roof of thatch and oaken wattles. Though everything else in religion were by some unthinkable catastrophe to be swept out of memory, or blotted from my understanding, my soul would wander back to those early scenes, and shut itself up once again in that Sanctuary Closet, and, hearing still the echoes of those cries to God, would hurl back all doubt with the victorious appeal, "He walked with God, why may not I?"[19]

A few notes had better here be given as to our "Forebears," the kind of stock from which my father and mother sprang. My father's mother, Janet Murray, claimed to be descended from a Galloway family that fought and suffered for Christ's Crown and Covenant in Scotland's "killing time," and was herself a woman of a pronouncedly religious development.[20] Her husband, our grandfather, William Paton, had passed through a roving and romantic career, before he settled down to be a douce deacon of the weavers of Dumfries, like his father before him.

Forced by a press-gang to serve on board a British Man-of-war, he was taken prisoner by the French, and thereafter placed under Paul Jones, the pirate of the seas, and bore to his dying day the mark of a slash from the captain's sword across his shoulder for some slight disrespect or offense. Determining with two others to escape, the three were hotly pursued by Paul Jones's men. One, who could swim but little, was shot, and had to be cut adrift by the other two, who in the darkness swam into a cave and managed to evade for two nights and a day the rage of their pursuers. My grandfather, being young and gentle and yellow-haired, persuaded some kind heart to rig him out in female attire, and in this costume escaped the

19. Paton's father, James, was the epitome of the Psalm 112:1 and Psalm 128:1 man — a godly man, a God-fearing man, a God-worshiping man, a man of deep piety. Paton describes him best as a man who "walked with God."

20. Paton's paternal grandmother had descended from the famous Covenanters who suffered greatly under Charles II and James II during what they called "the Killing Time" (between 1661 and 1681). Author Daniel Defoe estimated a total of 18,000 martyrs died under the persecution.

attentions of the press-gang more than once; till, after many hardships, he bargained with the captain of a coal sloop to stow him away amongst his black diamonds; and thus, in due time, he found his way home to Dumfries, where he tackled bravely and wisely the duties of husband, father, and citizen for the remainder of his days. The smack of the sea about the stories of his youth gave zest to the talks round their quiet fireside, and that, again, was seasoned by the warm Evangelical spirit of his Covenanting wife, her lips "dropping grace."

Of their children, two reproduced the disposition of their father, and three that of their mother.[21] William took to the soldier's career, and died in Spain; May, the only daughter, gave her heart and hand to John Wood, a jolly and gallant Englishman, who fought at Waterloo, and lived to see his hundredth birthday. John, James, and Spiers learned the stocking manufacturing business of their fathers, and also followed their mother's piety—becoming from early teens at once pronounced and consistent disciples of the Lord.

On the other side, my mother, Janet Rogerson, had for parents a father and mother of the Annandale stock. William Rogerson, her father, was one of many brothers, all men of uncommon strength and great force of character, quite worthy of the Border Rievers of an earlier day. Indeed, it was in some such way that he secured his wife, though the dear old lady in after days was chary[22] about telling the story. She was a girl of good position, the ward of two unscrupulous uncles who had charge of her small estate, near Langholm; and while attending some boarding school she fell devotedly in love with the tall, fair-haired, gallant young blacksmith, William Rogerson. Her guardians, doubtless very properly, objected to the "connection"; but our young Lochinvar, with his six or seven stalwart brothers and other trusty "lads," all mounted, and with some ready tools in case of need, went boldly and claimed his bride, and she, willingly mounting at his side, was borne off in the light of open day, joyously married, and took possession of her "but and ben,"[23] as the mistress of the blacksmith's castle.

21. Two of his four uncles and aunts (on his father's side) embraced their mother's faith, as was also true of his father.

22. "Chary" is Scottish for cautious.

23. "But and Ben" refer to the outer and inner part of a house (respectively).

The uncles had it out with him, however, in another way. While he was enjoying his honeymoon, and careless of mere mundane affairs, they managed to dispose of all the property of their ward, and make good their escape with the proceeds to the New World. Having heard a rumor of some such sale, our young blacksmith on horseback just reached the scene in time to see the last article—a Family Bible—put up for auction. This he claimed, or purchased, or seized, in name of the heiress—but that was all that she ever inherited! It was used devoutly by her till her dying day, and was adorned with the record of her own marriage and of the birth of a large and happy family, whom by-and-by God gave to her.[24]

Janet Jardine bowed her neck to the self-chosen yoke, with the light of a supreme affection in her heart, and showed in her gentler ways, her love of books, her fine accomplishments with the needle, and her general air of ladyhood, that her lot had once been cast in easier, but not necessarily happier, ways. Her blacksmith lover proved not unworthy of his lady bride, and in old age found for her a quiet and modest home, the fruit of years of toil and hopeful thrift, their own little property, in which they rested and waited a happy end. Amongst those who at last wept by her grave stood, amidst many sons and daughters, her son the Rev. James J. Rogerson, clergyman of the Church of England,[25] who, for many years thereafter, and till quite recently, was spared to occupy a distinguished position at ancient Shrewsbury and has left behind him there an honored and beloved name.

One thing else, beautiful in its pathos, I must record of that dear old lady. Her son, Walter, had gone forth from her, in prosecution of his calling, had corresponded with her from various counties in England, and then had suddenly disappeared; and no sign came to her, whether he was dead or alive. The mother-heart in her clung to the hope of his return; every night she prayed for that happy event, and before closing the door, threw it wide open, and peered into the darkness with a cry, "Come hame, my boy Walter, your mither wearies sair";

24. His mother's mother had an inheritance, but it was stolen by her two uncles (and they took everything to America). The only thing she salvaged was the Family Bible.

25. His uncle on his mother's side was a clergyman for the Church of England — Rev. James J. Rogerson.

and every morning, at early break of day, for a period of more than twenty years, she toddled up from her cottage door, at Johnsfield, Lockerbie, to a little round hill, called the "Corbie Dykes," and, gazing with tear-filled eyes towards the south for the form of her returning boy, prayed the Lord God to keep him safe and restore him to her yet again. Always, as I think upon that scene, my heart finds consolation in reflecting that if not here, then for certain there, such deathless longing love will be rewarded, and, rushing into long-delayed embrace, will exclaim—"Was lost and is found."

From such a home came our mother, Janet Jardine Rogerson, a bright-hearted, high-spirited, patient-toiling, and altogether heroic little woman; who, for about forty-three years, made and kept such a wholesome, independent, God-fearing, and self-reliant life for her family of five sons and six daughters, as constrains me, when I look back on it now, in the light of all I have since seen and known of others far differently situated, almost to worship her memory. She had gone with her high spirits and breezy disposition to gladden as their companion, the quiet abode of some grand or great-grand-uncle and aunt, familiarly named in all that Dalswinton neighborhood, "Old Adam and Eve." Their house was on the outskirts of the moor, and life for the young girl there had not probably too much excitement. But one thing had arrested her attention. She had noticed that a young stocking-maker from the "Brig End," James Paton, the son of William and Janet there, was in the habit of stealing alone into the quiet wood, book in hand, day after day, at certain hours, as if for private study and meditation. It was a very excusable curiosity that led the young bright heart of the girl to watch him devoutly reading and hear him reverently reciting (though she knew not then, it was Ralph Erskine's *Gospel Sonnets*,[26] which he could say by heart sixty years afterwards, as he lay on his bed of death); and finally that curiosity awed itself into a holy respect, when she saw him lay aside his broad Scotch bonnet, kneel down under the sheltering wings of some tree, and pour out all his

26. Ralph Erskine's father was a Covenanter pastor who was persecuted for his faith, and Ralph carried on the ministry himself between 1709 and 1752. He is known for his "Gospel Sonnets."

soul in daily prayers to God.[27] As yet they had never spoken. What spirit moved her, let lovers tell—was it all devotion, or was it a touch of unconscious love kindling in her towards the yellow-haired and thoughtful youth? Or was there a stroke of mischief, of that teasing, which so often opens up the door to the most serious step in all our lives? Anyhow, one day she slipped in quietly, stole away his bonnet, and hung it on a branch near by, while his trance of devotion made him oblivious of all around; then, from a safe retreat, she watched and enjoyed his perplexity in seeking for and finding it! A second day this was repeated; but his manifest disturbance of mind, and his long pondering with the bonnet in hand, as if almost alarmed, seemed to touch another chord in her heart—that chord of pity which is so often the prelude of love, that finer pity that grieves to wound anything nobler or tenderer than ourselves. Next day, when he came to his accustomed place of prayer, a little card was pinned against the tree just where he knelt, and on it these words:

"She who stole away your bonnet is ashamed of what she did; she has a great respect for you, and asks you to pray for her, that she may become as good a Christian as you."

Staring long at that writing, he forgot Ralph Erskine for one day! Taking down the card, and wondering who the writer could be, he was abusing himself for his stupidity in not suspecting that some one had discovered his retreat and removed his bonnet, instead of wondering whether angels had been there during his prayer—when, suddenly raising his eyes, he saw in front of old Adam's cottage, though a lane amongst the trees, the passing of another kind of angel, swinging a milk-pail in her hand and merrily singing some snatch of old Scottish song. He knew, in that moment, by a Divine instinct, as infallible as any voice that ever came to seer of old, that she was the angel visitor that had stolen in upon his retreat— that bright-faced, clever-witted niece of old Adam and Eve, to whom he had never yet spoken, but whose praises he had often heard said and sung— "Wee Jen." I am afraid he did pray

27. Even as a young man, Paton's father was devoted to prayer. This godliness seemed to attract young Janet to him.

28. James Paton made public profession of faith at 17 years of age. Not much is said about his "conversion."

29. Scotland's First Reformation came by men like George Wishart and John Knox in the 1550s and 1560s. The second wave of Reformation came by way of men like David Dickson, John Livingstone, Robert Bruce, and Alexander Henderson between 1610 and 1638. It was a period of extraordinary spiritual refreshing and ended with the Solemn League and Covenant made with King Charles I (restoring Presbyterianism, in which local churches are ruled by elders).

"for her," in more senses than one, that afternoon; at any rate, more than a Scotch bonnet was very effectually stolen; a good heart and true was there virtually bestowed, and the trust was never regretted on either side, and never betrayed.

Often and often, in the genial and beautiful hours of the autumntide of their long life, have I heard my dear father tease "Jen" about her maidenly intentions in the stealing of that bonnet; and often have heard her quick mother-wit in the happy retort, that had his motives for coming to that retreat been altogether and exclusively pious, he would probably have found his way to the other side of the wood, but that men who prowled about the Garden of Eden ran the risk of meeting some day with a daughter of Eve!

Somewhere in or about his seventeenth year, my father passed through a crisis of religious experience; and from that day he openly and very decidedly followed the Lord Jesus.[28] His parents had belonged to one of the older branches of what is now called the United Presbyterian Church; but my father, having made an independent study of the Scotch Worthies, the Cloud of Witnesses, the Testimonies, and the Confession of Faith, resolved to cast in his lot with the oldest of all the Scotch Churches, the Reformed Presbyterian, as most nearly representing the Covenanters and the attainments of both the first and second Reformations in Scotland.[29]

This choice he deliberately made, and sincerely and intelligently adhered to; and was able at all times to give strong and clear reasons from Bible and from history for the principles he upheld.[30] Still his sympathies and votes always went with the more progressive party in that ancient Church. He held it to be right that Cameronians, like other citizens, should exercise the municipal and political franchise, and he adhered to the "Majority Synod," which has since been incorporated with the Free Church of Scotland.[31] While glorying in the Psalms, he rejoiced to sing other hymns and spiritual songs (thanks to Ralph Erskine's *Sonnets*, perhaps, for that!) from his earliest days, at least everywhere except in the ordinary Public Worship; and long before he died, though he still held the Psalms to be supreme, he had learned to hear with glowing delight vast congregations singing the hymns of modern days, had learned joyfully to join in these songs of Zion, and was heard often to confess his belief that God had greatly owned and blessed the ministry of song in the service of the Gospel.[32]

30. James Paton shifted churches from the more liberal United Presbyterian Church to the Reformed Presbyterian Church of Scotland. This group started in 1690, refusing to take part in the established Church of Scotland. There are only five churches left in Scotland as part of the denomination (250 members as of 2016). The distinction of this church is that they are committed to the Solemn League and Covenant that was adopted by the Scottish church in 1638. Charles II reneged on the covenant when he took the throne in 1660.

31. Many of the Reformed Presbyterians joined the Free Church of Scotland in 1876.

32. Reformed Presbyterians tend to be "exclusive psalmists." This means they only sing the 150 Psalms found in Scripture during public worship. Evidently, James Paton was willing to sing both the Psalms and the hymns.

33. Apparently, James Paton's father only held a weekly time of family worship on Sundays. James preferred a daily morning AND evening worship time. As a 17-year-old young man, James Paton began leading family worship in his father's home. This is a mark of healthy faith in a Christian home. It is very rare today, but very seldom does the faith survive from generation to generation without a daily piety and a daily worship.

34. James Paton continued the practice of twice-a-day family worship for sixty years!

35. Family worship is usually a mix of Bible reading, singing, and prayer.

36. John Paton has immense respect for his father. It's hard to find a son who would so honor his father's legacy as this.

Besides his independent choice of a Church for himself there was one other mark and fruit of his early religious decision, which looks even fairer through all these years. Family Worship had heretofore been held only on Sabbath Day in his father's house; but the young Christian, entering into conference with his sympathizing mother, managed to get the household persuaded that there ought to be daily morning and evening prayer and reading of the Bible and holy singing. This the more readily, as he himself agreed to take part regularly in the same, and so relieve the old warrior of what might have proved for him too arduous spiritual toils! And so began in his seventeenth year that blessed custom of Family Prayer, morning and evening,[33] which my father practiced probably without one single avoidable omission till he lay on his deathbed, seventy-seven years of age;[34] when ever to the last day of his life, a portion of Scripture was read, and his voice was heard softly joining in the Psalm, and his lips breathed the morning and evening Prayer—falling in sweet benediction on the heads of all his children, far away many of them over all the earth, but all meeting him there at the Throne of Grace. None of us can remember that any day ever passed unhallowed thus; no hurry for market, no rush to business, no arrival of friends or guests, no trouble or sorrow, no joy or excitement, ever prevented at least our kneeling around the family altar, while the High Priest led our prayers to God, and offered himself and his children there.[35] And blessed to others, as well as to ourselves, was the light of such example![36] I have heard that, in long after-years, the worst woman in the village of Torthorwald, then leading an immoral life, but since changed by the grace of God, was known to declare, that the only thing that kept her from despair and from the Hell of the suicide, was when in the dark winter nights she crept close up underneath my father's window, and heard him pleading in Family Worship that God would convert "the sinner from the error of wicked ways, and polish him as a jewel for the Redeemer's crown." "I felt," said she, "that I was a burden on that good man's heart, and I knew that God would not disappoint him. That thought kept me out of Hell, and at last led me to the only Saviour."[37]

My father had a strong desire to be a Minister of the Gospel, but when he finally saw that God's will had marked out for him another lot, he reconciled himself by entering with his own soul into this solemn vow—that if God gave him sons, he would consecrate them unreservedly to the Ministry of Christ, if the Lord saw fit to accept the offering, and open up their way. It may be enough here to say that he lived to see three of us entering upon and not unblessed in the Holy Office—myself, the eldest born; my brother Walter, several years my junior; and my brother James, the youngest of eleven, the Benjamin of the flock.[38]

Our place of worship was the Reformed Presbyterian Church at Dumfries, under the ministry, during most of these days, of Rev. John McDermid—a genuine, solemn, lovable Covenanter, who cherished towards my father a warm respect, that deepened into apostolic affection when the yellow hair turned snow-white and both of them grew patriarchal in their years. The Minister, indeed, was translated to a Glasgow charge; but that rather exalted than suspended their mutual love. Dumfries was four miles fully from our Torthorwald home; but the tradition is that during all these forty years my father was only thrice prevented from attending the worship of God—once by snow, so deep that he was baffled and had to return; once by ice on the road, so dangerous that he was forced to crawl back up the Roucan Brae on his hands and knees, after having descended it so far with many falls; and once by the terrible outbreak of cholera at Dumfries. All intercourse betwixt the town and the surrounding villages, during that awful visitation, was publicly prohibited; and the farmers and villagers, suspecting that no cholera would make my father stay at home on Sabbath, sent a deputation to my mother on the Saturday evening, and urged her to restrain his

37. An amazing story of a wicked woman contemplating suicide who was saved by the testimony of James Paton and his faithful, godly piety.

38. Three sons — John, Walter, and James Jr. — became preachers or pastors of churches (in accord with their father's heartfelt desires).

39. James Paton only missed church three times in 40 years — walking four miles each direction (two to three hours of walking)!

40. There was real spiritual interest in the sermons.

41. Sunday evenings would involve more Bible Readings and Catechisms. Paton recommends catechism as a good means of teaching the foundations of the faith to children.

devotions for once! That, however, was needless; as, where the life of others was at stake, his very devotion came to their aid.[39]

Each of us, from very early days, considered it no penalty, but a great joy, to go with our father to the church; the four miles were a treat to our young spirits, the company by the way was a fresh incitement, and occasionally some of the wonders of city-life rewarded our eager eyes. A few other pious men and women, of the best Evangelical type, went from the same parish to one or other favorite Minister at Dumfries; and when these God-fearing peasants "forgathered" in the way to or from the House of God, we youngsters had sometimes rare glimpses of what Christian talk may be and ought to be. They went to the church, full of beautiful expectancy of spirit—their souls were on the outlook for God; they returned from the church, ready and even anxious to exchange ideas as to what they had heard and received of the things of life. I have to bear my testimony that religion was presented to us with a great deal of intellectual freshness, and that it did not repel us, but kindled our spiritual interest. The talks which we heard were, however, genuine; not the make-believe of religious conversation, but the sincere outcome of their own personalities. That, perhaps, makes all the difference betwixt talk that attracts and talk that drives away.[40]

We had, too, special Bible Readings on the Lord's Day evening—mother and children and visitors reading in turns, with fresh and interesting question, answer, and exposition, all tending to impress us with the infinite grace of a God of love and mercy in the great gift of His dear Son Jesus, our Saviour. The Shorter Catechism was gone through regularly, each answering the question asked, till the whole had been explained, and its foundation in Scripture shown by the proof-texts adduced. It has been an amazing thing to me, occasionally to meet with men who blamed this "catechizing" for giving them a distaste to religion; every one in all our circle thinks and feels exactly the opposite. It laid the solid rock-foundations of our religious life.[41] After-years have given to these questions and their answers a deeper or a modified meaning, but none of us has ever once even dreamed of wishing that we had been otherwise trained. Of course, if the parents are not devout, sincere, and affectionate—if the whole affair on both sides is taskwork, or worse, hypocritical and false—results must be very different indeed![42]

Oh, I can remember those happy Sabbath evenings; no blinds down, and shutters up, to keep out the sun from us, as some scandalously affirm; but a holy, happy, entirely human day, for a Christian father, mother and children to spend. How my father would parade across and across our flag-floor, telling over the substance of the day's sermons to our dear mother, who, because of the great distance and because of her many living "encumbrances," got very seldom indeed to the church, but gladly embraced every chance, when there was prospect or promise of a "lift" either way from some friendly gig![43] How he would entice us to help him to recall some idea or other, praising us when we got the length of "taking notes" and reading them over on our return; how he would turn the talk ever so naturally to some Bible story of some Martyr reminiscence, or some happy allusion to the *Pilgrim's Progress*![44] And then it was quite a contest, which of us would get reading aloud, while all the rest listened, and father added here and there a happy thought, or illustration, or anecdote. Others must write and say what they will, and as they feel; but so must I. There were eleven of us brought up in a home like that; and never one of the eleven, boy or girl, man or woman, has been heard, or ever will be heard, saying that Sabbath was dull and wearisome for us, or suggesting that we have heard of or seen any way more likely than that for making the Day of the Lord bright and blessed alike for parents and for children.

42. True devotion to God, sincerity, and affection are essential for godly parenting. Without this children become embittered against the fake faith some parents will attempt to share with their children. This fake faith is common today.

43. Apparently, Mrs. Paton would often not make it to church due to physical problems.

44. Most families had copies of John Bunyan's *Pilgrim's Progress* in the 18th and 19th centuries, sometimes their only book outside of the Bible.

45. Sabbatarians (people who were very strict on keeping the Sabbath, forbidding all work and play) had the reputation of being austere — making Sunday a dull and wearisome day. This is the way Laura Ingalls Wilder describes the day when she was raised in the 1880s and 1890s (in her books, *Little House on the Prairie* and *Farmer Boy*). Wilder writes, "The whole afternoon they sat in the drowsy warm dining-room. Mother read the Bible. . . Almanzo just sat. He had to. He was not allowed to do anything else, for Sunday was not a day for working or playing. It was a day for going to church and sitting still." Truly godly families would actually enjoy the day of worship because there was love for the Lord and a love for each other.

46. There was very little use of the "rod" or severe discipline in the home. It was a home ruled by prayer and love. These priorities are key.

But God help the homes where these things are done by force and not by love![45]

The very discipline through which our father passed us was a kind of religion in itself. If anything really serious required to be punished, he retired first to his "closet" for prayer, and we boys got to understand that he was laying the whole matter before God; and that was the severest part of the punishment for me to bear! I could have defied any amount of mere penalty, but this spoke to my conscience as a message from God. We loved him all the more, when we saw how much it cost him to punish us; and, in truth, he had never very much of that kind of work to do upon any one of all the eleven—we were ruled by love far more than by fear.[46]

As I must, however, leave the story of my father's life—much more worthy, in many ways, of being written than my own—I may here mention that his long and upright life made him a great favorite in all religious circles far and near within the neighborhood, that at sick-beds and at funerals he was constantly sent for and much appreciated, and that this appreciation greatly increased, instead of diminishing, when years whitened his long, flowing locks,[47] and gave him an apostolic beauty; till finally, for the last twelve years or so of his life, he became by appointment a sort of Rural Missionary for the four nearest parishes, and spent his autumn in literally sowing the good seed of the Kingdom as a Colporteur of the Tract and Book Society of Scotland. His success in this work, for a rural locality, was beyond all belief. Within a radius of five miles he was known in every home, welcomed by the children, respected by the servants, longed for eagerly by the sick and aged. He gloried in showing off the beautiful Bibles and other precious books, which he sold in amazing numbers. He sang sweet Psalms beside the sick, and prayed like the voice of God at their dying beds. He went cheerily from farm to farm, from cot to cot; and when he wearied on the moorland roads, he refreshed his soul by reciting aloud one of Ralph Erskine's *Sonnets*, or crooning to the birds one of David's Psalms.[48] His happy partner, our beloved mother, died in 1865, and he himself in 1868, having reached his seventy-seventh year, an altogether beautiful and noble episode of human existence having been enacted, amid the humblest surroundings of a Scottish peasant's home, through the influence of their united love by the grace of God; and in this world, or in any world, all their children will rise up at mention of their names and call them blessed![49]

47. The long, flowing locks refer to his father's hair. As can be ascertained by the picture of John G. Paton, these men were hairy men — big beards and lots of hair. It was by no means a feminine look. The Bible (1 Cor. 11:14) does not want men to have a feminine hairdo (the Greek word is "Koma"). This speaks to the treating of hair as an ornament and does not primarily refer to length. The verse does not give some hard and fast rule concerning hair length.

48. Though James Paton was not a pastor, his service to the kingdom was powerful in distributing Bibles and tracts, praying with the sick and dying, and so forth.

49. Call her blessed — reference to Proverbs 31:28.

CHAPTER II – SCHOOL AND EARLY COLLEGE DAYS
A.D. 1834 -1847. Age 10-23

In my boyhood, Torthorwald had one of the grand old typical Parish Schools of Scotland; where the rich and the poor met together in perfect equality; where Bible and Catechism were taught as zealously as grammar and geography;[1] and where capable lads from the humblest of cottages were prepared in Latin and Mathematics and Greek to go straight from their Village class to the University bench. Besides, at that time, an accomplished pedagogue of the name of Smith, a learned man of more than local fame, had added a Boarding House to the ordinary School, and had attracted some of the better class gentlemen and farmers' sons from the surrounding country; so that Torthorwald, under his régime, reached the zenith of its educational fame. In this School I was initiated into the mystery of letters, and all my brothers and sisters after me, though some of them under other masters than mine—my youngest brother James, trained there under a master named William Lithgow, going direct from the Village School to the University of Glasgow in his fourteenth year!

My teacher punished severely—rather, I should say, savagely—especially for lessons badly prepared. Yet, that he was in some respects kindly and tender-hearted, I had the best of reasons to know. Seeing me not so "braw" as the well-to-do fellows of my year, and taking a warm interest in me as a pupil, he, concluding probably that new suits were not so

1. The schools still incorporated the Bible and catechism into the daily routine, as zealously as grammar and geography. This was well before the modern world turned away from God to humanism, and the schools led the way.

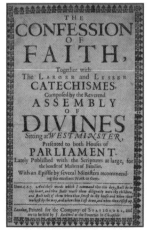

Title page of a 1658 printing of the Westminster Standards

easily got in my home as in some of the rest, planned a happy and kind-hearted surprise—a sort of acknowledged school prize. One evening, when my father was "taking the books," and pouring out his heart in Family Worship, the door of our house gently opened on the latch, and gently closed again. After prayer, on rushing to the door, I found a parcel containing a new suit of warm and excellent clothes—seeing which my mother said that "God had sent them to me, and I should thankfully receive them as from His hand, whoever might have brought them." Appearing in them at school next morning, the teacher cheerily saluted and complemented me on my "braws." I innocently told him how they came and what my mother said; and he laughingly replied:

"John, whenever you need anything after this just tell your father to 'tak' the Book,' and God will send it in answer to prayer!"

Years passed by before I came to know, what the reader has already guessed, that the good-hearted schoolmaster's hand lifted the latch that evening during my father's prayers.

All his influence, however, was marred by occasional bursts of fierce and ungovernable temper, amounting to savagery.[2] His favoritism, too, was sometimes disheartening—as when I won a Latin prize for an exercise by the verdict of the second master, yet it was withheld from me, and prizes were bestowed without merit on other and especially wealthier boys; so at least I imagined, and it cooled my ambition to excel. Favoritism might be borne, but not mere brutality when passion mastered him. Once, after having flogged me unjustly, on my return only at my mother's entreaty, he ran at me again, kicked me, and I fled in pain and terror from his presence, rushing home. When his passion subsided, he came to my parents, apologized, and pled with me to return; but all in vain—nothing would induce me to resume my studies there. Undoubtedly at that time I had a great thirst for education, and a retentive memory, which made all lessons comparatively

2. The discipline could be harsh in the schools. The Bible does not oppose discipline (Heb. 12:6-9, Prov. 13:24). As God disciplines us out of love, Christian fathers must discipline out of love, not hatred. This teacher, Mr. Smith, seems to have had an anger problem, which he took out on the children.

easy; and, as no other school was within my reach, it was a great loss that my heart shrank from this teacher.

Though still under twelve years of age, I started to learn my father's trade, in which I made surprising progress.[3] We wrought from six in the morning till ten at night, with an hour at dinner-time and half an hour at breakfast and again at supper. These spare moments every day I devoutly spent on my books, chiefly in the rudiments of Latin and Greek; for I had given my soul to God, and was resolved to aim at being a Missionary of the Cross, or a Minister of the Gospel. Yet I gladly testify that what I learned of the stocking frame was not thrown away; the facility of using tools, and of watching and keeping the machinery in order, came to be of great value to me in the Foreign Mission field.[4]

How much my father's prayers at this time impressed me I can never explain, nor could any stranger understand. When, on his knees and all of us kneeling around him in Family Worship, he poured out his whole soul with tears for the conversion of the Heathen World to the service of Jesus, and for every personal and domestic need, we all felt as if in the presence of the living Saviour, and learned to know and love Him as our Divine Friend. As we rose from our knees, I used to look at the light on my father's face, and wish I were like him in spirit—hoping that, in answer to his prayers, I might be privileged and prepared to carry the blessed Gospel to some portion of the Heathen World.

One incident of this time I must record here, because of the lasting impression made upon my religious life. Our family, like all others of peasant rank in the land, were plunged into deep distress, and felt the pinch severely, through the failure of the potato, the badness of other crops, and the ransom-price of food. Our father had gone off with work to Hawick, and would return next evening with money and supplies; but meantime the meal barrel ran low, and our dear mother, too proud and too sensitive to let any one know, or to ask aid from any quarter, coaxed us all to rest, assuring us that she had told God

3. At 11 years of age, John G. Paton quit school. In those days, there was no compulsory attendance law that forced children to attend school (and abandon the family economy entirely). It was a day of comparable freedom for families.

4. He continued to be homeschooled while he worked 16-hour days with his father. Practical eduction (in a craft) is equally important to academic education. This is the piece largely missing today for 95% of our youth.

everything, and that He would send us plenty in the morning. Next day, with the carrier from Lockerbie came a present from her father, who, knowing nothing of her circumstances or of this special trial, had been moved of God to send at that particular nick of time a love-offering to his daughter, such as they still send to each other in those kindly Scottish shires—a bag of new potatoes, a stone of the first ground meal or flour, or the earliest homemade cheese of the season—which largely supplied all our need. My mother, seeing our surprise at such an answer to her prayers, took us around her knees, thanked God for His goodness, and said to us:

"O my children, love your Heavenly Father, tell Him in faith and prayer all your needs, and He will supply your wants so far as it shall be for your good and His glory."[5]

Perhaps, amidst all their struggles in rearing a family of eleven, this was the hardest time they ever had, and the only time they ever felt the actual pinch of hunger; for the little that they had was marvelously blessed of God, and was not less marvelously utilized by that noble mother of ours, whose high spirit, side by side with her humble and gracious piety, made us, under God, what we are today.[6]

I saved as much at my trade as enabled me to go for six weeks to Dumfries Academy; this awoke in me again the hunger for learning, and I resolved to give up that trade and turn to something that might be made helpful to the prosecution of my education. An engagement was secured with the Sappers and Miners, who were mapping and measuring the county of Dumfries in connection with the Ordnance Survey of Scotland. The office hours were from 9 a.m. till 4 p.m.; and though my walk from home was above four miles every morning, and the same by return in the evening, I found much spare time for private study, both on the way to and from my work and also after hours. Instead of spending the mid-day hour with the rest, at football and other games, I stole away to a quiet spot on the banks of the Nith, and there pored over my book, all alone. Our lieutenant, unknown to me, had ob-

5. These paragraphs constitute the most remarkable picture of a father's piety and vision found anywhere in the history of the Church. What tremendous influence a father bears on those whom he disciples. This is where the commitment for missions formed in the heart of John G. Paton, as he watched his father on his knees and heard him crying out for the salvation of natives in far-off lands.

6. His mother's faith is also related here, another strong influence upon him.

served this from his house on the other side of the stream, and after a time called me into his office and inquired what I was studying. I told him the whole truth as to my position and my desires. After conferring with some of the other officials there, he summoned me again, and in their presence promised me promotion in the service, and special training in Woolwich at the Government's expense, on condition that I would sign an engagement for seven years. Thanking him most gratefully for his kind offer, I agreed to bind myself for three years or four, but not for seven.

Excitedly he said, "Why? Will you refuse an offer that many gentlemen's sons would be proud of?"

I said, "My life is given to another Master, so I cannot engage for seven years."

He asked sharply, "To whom?"

I replied, "To the Lord Jesus; and I want to prepare as soon as possible for His service in the proclaiming of the Gospel."

In great anger he sprang across the room, called the pay-master and exclaimed, "Accept my offer, or you are dismissed on the spot!"

I answered, "I am extremely sorry if you do so, but to bind myself for seven years would probably frustrate the purpose of my life; and though I am greatly obliged to you, I cannot make such an engagement."

His anger made him unwilling or unable to comprehend my difficulty; the drawing instruments were delivered up, I received my pay, and departed, without further parley.[7] The men, both over me and beside me, were mostly Roman Catholics, and their talk was the most profane I had ever heard.[8] Few of them spoke at any time without larding their language with oaths, and I was thankful to get away from hearing their shocking speech. But to me personally both officers and men had been extremely kind, for which, on leaving, I thanked them all very cordially, and they looked not a little surprised—as if unused to such recognitions!

7. Young John Paton received his first persecution at the hands of Roman Catholics (the men who were in charge of the surveying company). They dismissed him when they found out he was studying for the ministry.

8. The profane language would be a violation of the third commandment, common among unbelievers.

Hearing how I had been treated, and why, Mr. Maxwell, the Rector of Dumfries Academy, offered to let me attend all classes there, free of charge so long as I cared to remain; but that, in lack of means of support, was for the time impossible, as I would not and could not be a burden on my dear father, but was determined rather to help him in educating the rest. I went therefore to what was known as the Lamb Fair at Lockerbie, and for the first time in my life took a "fee" for the harvest. On arriving at the field when shearing and mowing began, the farmer asked me to bind a sheaf; when I had done so, he seized it by the band, and it fell to pieces! Instead of disheartening me, however, he gave me a careful lesson how to bind; and the second that I bound did not collapse when shaken, and the third he pitched across the field, and on finding that it still remained firm, he cried to me cheerily:

"Right now, my lad; go ahead!"

It was hard work for me at first, and my hands got very sore; but, being willing and determined, I soon got into the way of it, and kept up with the best of them. The male harvesters were told off to sleep in a large hayloft, the beds being arranged all along the side, like barracks. Many of the fellows were rough and boisterous; and I suppose my look showed that I hesitated in mingling with them, for the quick eye and kind heart of the farmer's wife prompted her to suggest that I, being so much younger than the rest, might sleep with her son George in the house—an offer, oh, how gratefully accepted! A beautiful new steading had recently been built for them; and during certain days, or portions of days, while waiting for the grain to ripen or to dry, I planned and laid out an ornamental garden in front of it, which gave great satisfaction—a taste inherited from my mother, with her joy in flowers and garden plots. They gave me, on leaving, a handsome present, as well as my fee, for I had got on very pleasantly with them all. This experience, too, came to be valuable to me,[9] when, in long-after days, and far other lands, Mission buildings had to be erected,

9. Every practical experience he had was of great value to his later labors on the mission field. No preparation is wasted in a young man's life.

and garden and field cropped and cultivated without the aid of a single European hand.[10]

Before going to my first harvesting, I had applied for a situation in Glasgow, apparently exactly suited for my case; but I had little or no hope of ever hearing of it further. An offer of £50 per annum[11] was made by the West Campbell Street Reformed Presbyterian Congregation, then under the good and noble Dr. Bates, for a young man to act as district visitor and tract distributor, especially amongst the absentees from the Sabbath School; with the privilege of receiving one year's training at the Free Church Normal Seminary, that he might qualify himself for teaching, and thereby push forward to the Holy Ministry. The candidates, along with their application and certificates, were to send an essay on some subject, of their own composition, and in their own handwriting. I sent in two long poems on the Covenanters, which must have exceedingly amused them, as I had not learned to write even decent prose. But, much to my surprise, immediately on the close of the harvesting experience, a letter arrived, intimating that I, along with another young man, had been put upon the short leet, and that both were requested to appear in Glasgow on a given day and compete for the appointment.

Two days thereafter I started out from my quiet country home on the road to Glasgow. Literally "on the road," for from Torthorwald to Kilmarnock—about forty miles[12]—had to be done on foot, and thence to Glasgow by rail. Railways in those days were as yet few, and coach-traveling was far beyond my purse. A small bundle contained my Bible and all my personal belongings. Thus was I launched upon the ocean of life. I thought on One who says, "I know thy poverty, but thou art rich."

My dear father walked with me the first six miles of the way. His counsels and tears and heavenly conversation on that parting journey are fresh in my heart as if it had been but yesterday; and tears are on my cheeks as freely now as then, whenever memory steals me away to the scene. For the last half mile

10. He worked for a farmer for a wage. Previously, he had worked in the fields as a volunteer laborer (probably on his family farm).

11. In the mid-1800s, common laborers would receive about 50 pounds per year, and engineers would receive closer to 110 pounds per year. This was not an exorbitant amount of money, but surely John G. Paton would have appreciated it.

12. Evidently, this family walked almost everywhere (too poor to afford a horse and carriage). He had to walk 40 miles to a train station — at least three full days of walking.

or so we walked on together in almost unbroken silence—my father, as was often his custom, carrying hat in hand, while his long, flowing yellow hair (then yellow, but in later years white as snow) streamed like a girl's down his shoulders. His lips kept moving in silent prayers for me; and his tears fell fast when our eyes met each other in looks of which all speech was vain! We halted on reaching the appointed parting-place; he grasped my hand firmly for a minute in silence, and then solemnly and affectionately said:

"God bless you, my son! Your father's God prosper you, and keep you from all evil!"

Unable to say more, his lips kept moving in silent prayer; in tears we embraced, and parted. I ran off as fast as I could; and, when about to turn a corner in the road where he would lose sight of me, I looked back and saw him still standing with head uncovered where I had left him—gazing after me. Waving my hat in adieu, I was round the corner and out of sight in an instant. But my heart was too full and sore to carry me farther, so I darted into the side of the road and wept for a time. Then, rising up cautiously, I climbed the dyke to see if he yet stood where I had left him; and just at that moment I caught a glimpse of him climbing the dyke and looking out for me! He did not see me, and after he had gazed eagerly in my direction for a while he got down, set his face towards home, and began to return—his head still uncovered, and his heart, I felt sure, still rising in prayers for me. I watched through blinding tears, till his form faded from my gaze; and then, hastening on my way, vowed deeply and oft, by the help of God, to live and act so as never to grieve or dishonor such a father and mother as He had given me. The appearance of my father, when we parted—his advice, prayers, and tears—the road, the dyke, the climbing up on it and then walking away, head uncovered—have often, often, all through life, risen vividly before my mind, and do so now while I am writing, as if it had been but an hour ago. In my earlier years particularly, when exposed to many temptations, his parting form rose before me as that of a guardian angel.[13] It is no Pharisaism, but deep gratitude, which makes me here testify that the memory of that scene not only helped, by God's grace, to keep me pure from the prevailing sins, but also stimulated me in all my studies, that I might not fall short of his hopes, and in all my Christian duties, that I might faithfully follow his shining example.[14]

I reached Glasgow on the third day, having slept one night at Thornhill, and another at New Cumnock; and having needed, owing to the kindness of acquaintances upon whom I called by the way, to spend only three halfpence of my modest funds. Safely arrived, but weary, I secured a humble room for my lodging, for which I had to pay one shilling and sixpence per week. Buoyant and full of hope and looking up to God for guidance, I appeared at the appointed hour before the examiners, as did also the other candidate; and they having carefully gone through their work, asked us to retire. When recalled, they informed us that they had great difficulty in choosing, and suggested that the one of us might withdraw in favor of the other, or that both might submit to a more testing examination. Neither seemed inclined to give it up, both were willing for a second examination; but the patrons made another suggestion. They had only £50 per annum to give; but if we would agree to divide it betwixt us, and go into one lodging, we might both be able to struggle through, they would pay our entrance fees at the Free Normal Seminary,[15] and provide us with the books required; and perhaps they might be able to add a little to the sum promised to each of us. By dividing the mission work appointed, and each taking only the half, more time also might be secured for our studies. Though the two candidates had never seen each other before, we at once accepted this proposal, and got on famously together, never having had a dispute on anything of common interest throughout our whole career.

As our fellow-students at the Normal were all far advanced beyond us in their education, we found it killing work, and had to grind away incessantly, late and early. Both of us,

13. His father's care for him kept him from prevailing sins later in his life.

14. Paton's relationship with his father and his father's love for him are powerfully expressed in this section. Beautiful story here.

Dumfries Free Church in Dumfries, Scotland

15. The Free Normal Seminary was a teaching college founded by the Free Church of Scotland. The Free Church was formed in 1843 as a break away from the Church of Scotland. They were protesting the state control of the church.

before the year closed, broke down in health; partly by hard study, but principally, perhaps, for lack of nourishing diet. A severe cough seized upon me; I began spitting blood, and a doctor ordered me at once home to the country and forbade all attempts at study. My heart sank; it was a dreadful disappointment, and to me a bitter trial. Soon after, my companion, though apparently much stronger than I, was similarly seized. He, however, never entirely recovered, though for some years he taught in a humble school; and long ago he fell asleep in Jesus, a devoted and honored Christian man.

16. John Paton starts his teaching career at a small school near his parents' home.

I, on the other hand, after a short rest, nourished by the hill air of Torthorwald and by the new milk of our family cow, was ere long at work again. Renting a house, I began to teach a small school at Girvan,[16] and gradually but completely recovered my health.

Having saved £10 by my teaching, I returned to Glasgow, and was enrolled as a student at the College; but before the session was finished my money was exhausted—I had lent some to a poor student, who failed to repay me—and only nine shillings remained in my purse. There was no one from whom to borrow, had I been willing; I had been disappointed in attempting to secure private tuition; and no course seemed open for me, except to pay what little I owed, give up my College career, and seek for teaching or other work in the country. I wrote a letter to my father and mother, informing them of my circumstances; that I was leaving Glasgow in quest of work, and that they would not hear from me again till I had found a suitable situation. I told them that if otherwise unsuccessful, I should fall back on my own trade, though I shrank from that as not tending to advance my education;[17] but that they might rest assured I would do nothing to dishonor them or my own Christian profession. Having read that letter over again through many tears, I said—I cannot send that, for it will grieve my darling parents; and therefore, leaving it on the table, I locked my room door and ran out to find a place where I might sell my precious books, and hold on a few weeks longer.

17. Paton's objective is to seek training for the ministry, so to leave college would hamper that goal.

But, as I stood on the opposite side and wondered whether these folks in a shop with the three golden balls would care to have a poor student's books, and as I hesitated, knowing how much I needed them for my studies, conscience smote me as if for doing a guilty thing; I imagined that the people were watching me like one about to commit a theft; and I made off from the scene at full speed, with a feeling of intense shame at having dreamed of such a thing! Passing through one short street into another, I marched on mechanically; but the Lord God of my father was guiding my steps, all unknown to me.

A certain notice in a window, into which I had probably never in my life looked before, here caught my eye, to this effect—"Teacher wanted, Maryhill Free Church school; apply at the Manse." A coach or bus was just passing, when I turned round; I leapt into it, saw the Minister, arranged to undertake the School, returned to Glasgow, paid my landlady's lodging score, tore up that letter to my parents and wrote another full of cheer and hope; and early next morning entered the School and began a tough and trying job. The Minister warned me that the School was a wreck, and had been broken up chiefly by coarse and bad characters from mills and coal-pits, who attended the evening classes. They had abused several masters in succession; and, laying a thick and heavy cane on the desk, he said:

"Use that freely, or you will never keep order here!"

I put it aside into the drawer of my desk, saying, "That will be my last resource."

There were very few scholars for the first week—about eighteen in the Day School and twenty in the Night School.[18] The clerk of the mill, a good young fellow, came to the evening classes, avowedly to learn book-keeping, but privately he said he had come to save me from personal injury.

The following week, a young man and a young woman began to attend the Night School, who showed from the first moment that they were bent on mischief. On my repeated appeals for quiet and order, they became the more boisterous, and

18. Church-sponsored schools were intended for the poorer people in the area. The night school was made up of young adults, and the day school made up of a range of ages.

gave great merriment to a few of the scholars present. I finally urged the young man, a tall, powerful fellow, to be quiet or at once to leave, declaring that at all hazards I must and would have perfect order; but he only mocked at me, and assumed a fighting attitude. Quietly locking the door and putting the key in my pocket, I turned to my desk, armed myself with the cane, and dared any one at his peril to interfere betwixt us. It was a rough struggle—he smashing at me clumsily with his fists, I with quick movements evading and dealing him blow after blow with the heavy cane for several rounds—till at length he crouched down at his desk, exhausted and beaten,[19] and I ordered him to turn to his book, which he did in sulky silence. Going to my desk, I addressed them and asked them to inform all who wished to come to the School—That if they came for education, everything would be heartily done that it was in my power to do; but that any who wished for mischief had better stay away, as I was determined to conquer, not to be conquered, and to secure order and silence, whatever it might cost. Further, I assured them that that cane would not again be lifted by me, if kindness and forbearance on my part could possibly gain the day, as I wished to rule by love and not by terror.[20] But this young man knew he was in the wrong, and it was that which had made him weak against me, though every way stronger far than I. Yet I would be his friend and helper, if he was willing to be friendly with me, the same as if this night had never been. At these words a dead silence fell on the School: every one buried face diligently in book; and the evening closed in uncommon quiet and order.

Next morning, two of the bigger boys at the Day School, instead of taking their seats like the rest, got in under the gallery where coals and lumber were kept, and made a great noise as if dog and cat were worrying each other. Pleading with them only increased the uproar; so I locked the doors, laid past the keys, and proceeded with the morning's work. Half an hour before the mid-day rest, I began singing a hymn, and marched the children round as if to leave; then the two young rascals

19. Violence at the hands of students was not unusual in the 19th century. Other authors like Laura Ingalls Wilder relate similarly violent conditions for teachers in the schools.

20. Paton provides a firmness in discipline that is unusual in our day. He does emphasize his commitment to rule by "love not by terror."

came out, and, walking in front, sang boisterously. Seizing the first boy by the collar, I made him stagger into the middle of the floor, and, dragging the other beside him, I raised my heavy cane and dared them to move. Ordering the children to resume their seats, I appointed them a jury to hear the case and to pass sentence. The two were found guilty, and awarded a severe lashing. I proposed, as this was their first offence, and as I only used the cane for a last resource, to forego all punishment, if they apologized and promised to be attentive and obedient in the future. They both heartily did so, and became my favourite scholars. Next evening I had little difficulty, as the worst characters did not at once return, guessing that they had got a bit of lion in the new "dominie," that was more likely to subdue than to be subdued.

On the following day, the parents of some children, getting alarmed by the rumors of these exploits, waited on me accompanied by the Minister, and said their children were terrified to come. I said that no *child* had been beaten by me, but that I insisted upon order and obedience; I reminded the Minister that of my immediate predecessors three had suffered from these rowdies in the evening class—one actually going wrong in the mind over the worry, another losing his health and dying, and the third leaving in disgust; and finally I declared that I must either be master, at whatever cost, or leave the School. From that time perfect order was established, and the School flourished apace. During next week, many of the worst characters returned to their class work in the evening; but thence forward the behavior of all towards me was admirable. The attendance grew, till the School became crowded, both during the day and at night. During the mid-day hour even, I had a large class of young women who came to improve themselves in writing and arithmetic. By and by the cane became a forgotten implement; the sorrow and pain which I showed as to badly-done lessons, or anything blameworthy, proved the far more effectual penalty.

The School Committee had promised me at least ten shillings per week, and guaranteed to make up any deficit if the fees fell short of that sum; but if the income from fees exceeded that sum, all was to be mine. Affairs went on prosperously for a season; indeed, too much so for my selfish interest. The Committee took advantage of the large attendance and better repute of the School, to secure the services of a master of the highest grade. The parents of many of the children offered to take and seat a hall, if I would remain, but I knew too well that I had neither education nor experience to compete with an accomplished teacher.[21] Their children, however, got up a testimonial and subscription, which was presented to me on the day before I left and this I valued chiefly because the presentation was made by the young fellows who at first behaved so badly, but were now my devoted friends.

Once more I committed my future to the Lord God of my father, assured that in my very heart I was willing and anxious to serve Him and to follow the blessed Saviour, yet feeling keenly that intense darkness had again enclosed my path.

21. After Paton grew the school to a larger size, the Committee felt they could afford a more well-educated teacher, and Paton lost his job.

CHAPTER III – IN GLASGOW CITY MISSION
A.D. 1847-1856. Age 23-32

Before undertaking the Maryhill School, I had applied to be taken on as an agent in the Glasgow City Mission;[1] and the night before I had to leave Maryhill, I received a letter from Rev. Thomas Caie, the superintendent of the said Mission, saying that the directors had kept their eyes on me ever since my application, and requesting, as they understood I was leaving the School, that I would appear before them the next morning, and have my qualifications for becoming a Missionary examined into. Praising God, I went off at once, passed the examination successfully, and was appointed to spend two hours that afternoon and the following Monday in visitation with two of the directors, calling at every house in a low district of the town, and conversing with all the characters encountered there as to their eternal welfare. I had also to preach a "trial" discourse in a Mission meeting, where a deputation of directors would be present, the following evening being Sunday; and on Wednesday evening they met again to hear their report and to accept or reject me.

All this had come upon me so unexpectedly, that I almost anticipated failure; but looking up for help I went through with it, and on the fifth day after leaving the School they called me before a meeting of directors, and informed me that

1. By God's good providence, Paton was immediately accepted into the Glasgow City Mission upon his dismissal from the school. This was much more in line with his future calling. Young men should take note of the path taken by Paton towards his calling. Each successive step draws him closer to what God has for him, and each step is preparatory for that calling.

2. Pastor William Symington (1795–1862) was an influential pastor in Glasgow. He had a strong, optimistic eschatology, which affected missions in the 19th century in an important way. Symington's most famous book is *Messiah the Prince: The Mediatorial Dominion of Jesus Christ*. Symington was a huge advocate of home missions, foreign missions, and the distribution of Bibles. Of course, this would influence John G. Paton's thinking as well.

3. This on-the-street training in evangelism was crucial for Paton's future missionary work. He learned a special boldness and forwardness and a passion for souls.

I had passed my trials most successfully, and that the reports were so favorable that they had unanimously resolved to receive me at once as one of their City Missionaries.

It was further explained that one of their number, Matthew Fairley, Esq., an elder in Dr. Symington's[2] congregation, had guaranteed the half of my salary for two years, the other half to be met by the resources of the Mission voluntarily contributed—the whole salary at that time amounting to £40 per annum. The district allocated to me was one especially needful and trying, that had never been thus heretofore occupied, in and around the Green Street of Calton, and I was enjoined to enter upon my duties at once. After receiving many good and kind counsels from these good and kind men, one of them in prayer very solemnly dedicated me and my work to the Lord; and several of them were appointed to introduce me to my district, taking a day each by turns, and to assist me in making arrangements for the on-carrying of the work. Deeply solemnized with the responsibilities of my new office, I left that meeting praising God for all His undeserved mercies, and seeing most clearly His gracious hand in all the way by which He had led me, and the trials by which He had prepared me for this sphere of service. Man proposes—God disposes.

Most of these directors were men of God, adapted and qualified for this special work, and very helpful in counsel as they went with me from day to day, introducing me to my district, and seeing the character and surroundings of the people dwelling there. Looking back upon these Mission experiences, I have ever felt that they were, to me and many others, a good and profitable training of students for the office of the Ministry, preparing us to deal with men of every shade and thought and character, and to lead them to the knowledge and service of the Lord Jesus.[3]

I found the district a very degraded one. Many families said they had never been visited by any Minister; and many were lapsed professors of religion who had attended no church for ten, sixteen, or twenty years, and said they had never been called upon by any Christian visitor. In it were congregated many avowed infidels, Romanists, and drunkards[4]—living together, and associated for evil, but apparently without any effective counteracting influence. In many of its closes and courts sin and vice walked about openly—naked and not ashamed. We were expected to spend four hours daily in visiting from house to house, holding kitchen prayer meetings amongst those visited, calling them together also in the evenings for worship or instruction, and trying by all means to do whatever good was possible amongst them.[5] And the only place in the whole district available for a Sabbath evening Evangelistic Service was a hay-loft, under which a cow-feeder kept a large number of cows, and which was reached by an outside rickety wood stair.

After nearly a year's hard work, I had only six or seven non-church-goers, who had been led to attend regularly there, besides about the same number who met on a week evening in the ground-floor of a house kindly granted for the purpose by a poor and industrious but ill-used Irishwoman. She supported her family by keeping a little shop, and selling coals. Her husband was a powerful man—a good worker, but a hard drinker; and, like too many others addicted to intemperance, he abused and beat her, and pawned and drank everything he could get hold of. She, amid many prayers and tears, bore everything patiently, and strove to bring up her only daughter in the fear of God. We exerted, by God's blessing, a good influence upon him through our meetings. He became a Total Abstainer, gave up his evil ways, and attended Church regularly with his wife. As his interest increased, he tried to bring others also to the meetings, and urged them to become Abstainers. His wife became a center of help and of good influence in all the district, as she kindly invited all and welcomed them to the meeting in her house, and my work grew every day more hopeful.[6]

Seeing, however, that one year's hard work showed such small results, the directors proposed to remove me to another

4. The mission field was made up of infidels (atheists), Romanists (Roman Catholics), and drunkards.

5. John G. Paton did not let the grass grow under his feet. He arranged Bible studies and prayer meetings every day of the week.

6. Growing churches are always looking for opportunities to serve both physical and spiritual needs at the same time. This can happen through schools. These churches learn to adapt their services and their meetings to the needs of the neighborhoods.

7. Reformed Presbyterians have always taken singing seriously. They usually sing without accompaniment and train their members to sing well (and to sing in parts).

8. Communicants' Class would prepare new believers (sometimes young people) for church membership (so as they could take the Lord's Supper). Presbyterian churches use the Westminster Shorter Catechism as a teaching tool, so as to be sure that the new members are well rooted in biblical truth.

9. The Industrial Revolution would work single women and single men seven days a week. Churches would try innovative means to provide evangelism, schools, and church meetings to accommodate them.

district, as in their estimation the non-church-goers in Green Street were unassailable by ordinary means. I pleaded for six months' longer trial, as I had gained the confidence of many of the poor people there, and had an invincible faith that the good seed sown would soon bear blessed fruit. To this the directors kindly agreed. At our next meeting I informed those present that, if we could not draw out more of the non-church-goers to attend the services, I should be removed to another part of the city. Each one there and then agreed to bring another to our next meeting. Both our meetings at once doubled their attendance. Henceforth Meeting and Class were both too large for any house that was available for us in the whole of our district. We instituted a Bible Class, a Singing Class,[7] a Communicants' Class,[8] and a Total Abstinence Society; and, in addition to the usual meetings, we opened two prayer-meetings specially for the Calton division of the Glasgow Police—one at a suitable hour for the men on day duty, and another for those on night duty.[9] The men got up a Mutual Improvement Society and Singing Class also amongst themselves, weekly, on another evening. My work now occupied every evening in the week; and I had two meetings every Sabbath. By God's blessing they all prospered, and gave evidence of such fruits as showed that the Lord was working there for good by our humble instrumentality.

The kind cowfeeder had to inform us—and he did it with much genuine sorrow—that at a given date he would require the hay-loft, which was our place of meeting; and as no other suitable house or hall could be got, the poor people and I feared the extinction of our work. On hearing this the ostlers and other servants of Menzies, the coach-hirer, who had extensive premises near our place of meeting, of their own accord asked and obtained liberty to clear out a hay-loft of theirs that was seldom in use, and resolved, at their own expense, to erect an outside wooden stair for the convenience of the people. This becoming known, and being much talked of, caused great joy in the district, arrested general attention, and increased the interest of our work. But I saw that, however generous, it could be at the best only another temporary arrangement, and that the premises might again at any moment be required. After prayer I therefore laid the whole case before my good and great-hearted friend, Thomas Binnie, Sen., Monteith Row, and he, after inquiring into all the circumstances, secured a good site for a Mission Hall in a piece of unoccupied ground near our old hay-loft, on which he proposed to build suitable premises at his own expense.

At that very time however, a commodious block of buildings, that had been Church, Schools, Manse, etc., came into the market. Mr. Binnie persuaded Dr. Symington's congregation, Great Hamilton Street, in connection with which my Mission was carried on, to purchase the whole property for Mission purposes. Its situation at the foot of Green Street gave it a control of the district where my work lay; and so the Church was given to me in which to conduct all my meetings, while the other Halls were adapted as Schools for poor girls and boys, where they were educated by a proper master, and were largely supplied with books, clothing, and sometimes even food, by the ladies of the congregation. The purchasing and using of these buildings for an Evangelistic and Educational Mission became a blessing—a very conspicuous blessing—to that district in the Calton of Glasgow; and the blessing still perpetuates itself not only in the old premises, now used for an Industrial School, but still more in the beautiful and spacious Mission Halls, erected immediately in front of the old, and consecrated to the work of the Lord in that poor and crowded and clamant portion of the city.

Availing myself of the increased facilities, my work was all reorganized. On Sabbath morning, at seven o'clock, I had one of the most deeply interesting and fruitful of all my Classes for the study of the Bible. It was attended by from seventy to a hundred of the very poorest young women and grown-up lads of the whole district. They had nothing to put on except their ordinary work-day clothes—all without bonnets, some

Glasgow University in the 1890s

Presbyterian Church in Glasgow, Scotland

10. Alexander Smith Paterson wrote an introduction to the Shorter Catechism, published in 1848.

without shoes. Beautiful was it to mark how the poorest began to improve in personal appearance immediately after they came to our Class; how they gradually got shoes and one bit of clothing after another, to enable them to attend our other Meetings, and then to go to Church; and, above all, how eagerly they sought to bring others with them, taking a deep personal interest in all the work of the Mission. Long after they themselves could appear in excellent dress, many of them still continued to attend in their working clothes, and to bring other and poorer girls with them to that Morning Class, and thereby helped to improve and elevate their companions.

My delight in that Bible Class was among the purest joys in all my life, and the results were amongst the most certain and precious of all my Ministry. Yet it was not made successful without unceasing pains and prayers. What would my younger brethren in the Ministry, or in the Mission, think of starting out at six o'clock every Sunday morning, running from street to street for an hour, knocking at the doors and rousing the careless, and thus getting together, and keeping together, their Bible Class? This was what I did at first; but, in course of time, a band of voluntary visitors belonging to the Class took charge of all the irregulars, the indifferents, and the new-comers, and thereby not only relieved and assisted me, but vastly increased their own personal interest in the work, and became warmly attached to each other.

I had also a very large Bible Class—a sort of Bible-Reading—on Monday night, attended by all, of both sexes and of any age, who cared to come or had any interest in the Mission. Wednesday evening, again, was devoted to a prayer-meeting for all; and the attendance often more than half-filled the Church. There I usually took up some book of Holy Scripture and read and lectured right through, practically expounding and applying it. On Thursday I held a Communicants' Class, intended for the more careful instruction of all who wished to become full members of the Church. Our constant text-book was Paterson on the Shorter Catechism[10] (Nelson and

Sons), than which I have never seen a better compendium of the doctrines of Holy Scripture. Each being thus trained for a season, received from me, if found worthy, a letter to the Minister of any Protestant Church which he or she felt inclined to join. In this way great numbers became active and useful communicants in the surrounding congregations; and eight young lads of humble circumstances educated themselves for the Ministry of the Church—most of them getting their first lessons in Latin and Greek from my very poor stock of the same! Friday evening was occupied with a Singing Class, teaching Church music, and practicing for our Sabbath meetings. On Saturday evening we held our Total Abstinence meeting, at which the members themselves took a principal part, in readings, addresses, recitations, singing hymns, etc.

Great good resulted from this Total Abstinence work. Many adults took and kept the pledge, thereby greatly increasing the comfort and happiness of their homes. Many were led to attend the Church on the Lord's Day, who had formerly spent it in rioting and drinking. But, above all, it trained the young to fear the very name of Intoxicating Drink, and to hate and keep far away from everything that led to intemperance. From observation, at an early age I became convinced that mere Temperance Societies were a failure, and that Total Abstinence, by the grace of God, was the only sure preventive as well as remedy. What was temperance in one man was drunkenness in another; and all the drunkards came, not from those who practiced total abstinence, but from those who practiced temperance. I had seen *temperance* men drinking wine in the presence of others who drank to excess, and never could see how they felt themselves clear of blame; and I had known Ministers and others, once strong temperance advocates, fall through this so-called "moderation," and become drunkards. Therefore it has all my life appeared to me beyond dispute, in reference to intoxicants of every kind, that the only rational temperance is Total Abstinence from them as beverages,[11] and the use of them exclusively as drugs,[12] and then only with

11. John G. Paton saw the devastation that alcohol had brought to the inner city. This no doubt encouraged him to the position of Total Abstinence from alcohol. Such a position was common among conservative Christians in the 19th century.

12. His position is that alcohol could be used for a drug — the Proverbs speak of "strong drink for the dying" (Prov. 31:6).

13. The Reformed Presbyterian Church of North America now allows its members and leaders to drink alcohol, but still holds that abstinence from alcohol is a "fitting choice." By the 1880s, all members and leaders in the denomination were prohibited from drinking alcohol. The denomination supported the 18th Amendment to the U.S. Constitution, and the Prohibition movement of the early 20th century.

14. The Bible forbids excess, idolatry, and the lack of gratefulness. These are the root sins that have corrupted man again and again. A man can abstain from alcohol and tobacco and still give way to excess, idolatry, and a lack of gratefulness. Sometimes, fasting and self-denial is the key to repentance in these areas. Reference 1 Corinthians 6:12 and Romans 14:6.

15. Paton was especially insistent that church leaders should totally abstain. His concern was that they would (1) slip into drunkenness themselves, or (2) offend the weaker brother and tempt him to drink to excess.

extreme caution, as they are deceptive and deleterious poisons of the most debasing and demoralising kind. I found also, that when I tried to reclaim a drunkard, or caution any one as to intemperate habits, one of the first questions was:

"Are you a pledged Abstainer yourself?"

By being enabled to reply decidedly, "Yes, I am," the mouth of the objector was closed; and that gave me a hundred-fold more influence with him than if I had had to confess that I was only "temperate." For the good of others, and for the increase of their personal influence as the servants of Christ, I would plead with every Minister and Missionary, every Office-bearer and Sabbath-school Teacher, every one who wishes to work for the Lord Jesus in the Family, the Church, and the World, to be a Total Abstainer from all intoxicating drinks as common beverages.[13]

I would add my testimony also against the use of tobacco, which injures and leads many astray, especially lads and young men, and which never can be required by any person in ordinary health. But I would not be understood to regard the evils that flow from it as deserving to be mentioned in comparison with the unutterable woes and miseries of intemperance. To be protected, however, from suspicion and from evil, all the followers of our Lord Jesus should in self-denial (how small!) and in consecration to His service,[14] be pledged Abstainers from both of these selfish indulgences, which are certainly injurious to many, which are no ornament to any character, and which can be no help in well-doing. Praise God for the many who are now so pledged! Happy day for poor Humanity, when all the Lord's people adopt this self-denying ordinance for the good of the race![15]

Not boastfully, but gratefully, let me record that my Classes and Meetings were now attended by such numbers that they were amongst the largest and most successful that the City Mission had ever known; and by God's blessing I was enabled to develop them into a regular, warmly-attached, and intelligent Congregation. My work, however exacting, was full of joy to me. From five to six hundred people were in usual weekly attendance;[16] consisting exclusively of poor working persons, and largely of the humbler class of mill-workers. So soon as their circumstances improved, they were constantly removing to more respectable and healthy localities, and got to be scattered over all the city. But wherever they went, I visited them regularly to prevent their falling away, and held by them till I got them interested in some Church near where they had gone to live. On my return, many years after, from the Foreign Mission field, there was scarcely a congregation in any part of the city where some one did not warmly salute me with the cry, "Don't you remember me?" And then, after greetings, came the well-remembered name of one or other member of my old Bible Class.

Such toils left me but small time for private studies. The City Missionary was required to spend four hours daily in visitation-work; but often I had to spend double that time, day after day, in order to overtake what was laid upon me. About eight or ten of my most devoted young men, and double that number of young women, whom I had trained to become Visitors and Tract Distributors, greatly strengthened my hands. Each of the young men by himself, and the young women two by two, had charge of a portion of a street, which was visited by them regularly twice every month.[17] At a monthly meeting of all our Workers, reports were given in, changes were noted, and all matters brought under review were attended to. Besides, if any note or message were left at my lodging, or any case of sickness or want reported, it was looked after by me without delay. Several Christian gentlemen, mill-owners and other employers in the Calton, Mile-end, and Bridgeton of Glasgow, were so interested in my work that they kindly offered to give employment to every deserving person recommended by me, and that relieved much distress and greatly increased my influence for good.[18]

Almost the only enemies I had were the keepers of Public-Houses, whose trade had been injured by the Total Ab-

16. Paton's ministry expanded to 500 persons involved in his network of ministries.

17. Paton's organizational skills played in strongly. The committees, the meetings, and the teamwork were all important to the Presbyterian methodology.

18. Paton kept his meetings to teaching, singing, and prayer — no other frills.

stinence Society. Besides the Saturday night meetings all the year round, we held, in summer evenings and on Saturday afternoons, Evangelistic and Total Abstinence services in the open air. We met in Thomson's Lane, a short and broad street, not open for the traffic of conveyances, and admirably situated for our purposes. Our pulpit was formed by the top of an outside stair, leading to the second flat of a house in the middle of the lane. Prominent Christian workers took part with us in delivering addresses; and intimation through my Classes usually secured good audiences; and the hearty singing of hymns by my Mission Choir gave zest and joy to the whole proceedings. Of other so-called "attractions" we had none, and needed none, save the sincere proclamation of the Good Tidings from God to men!

On one occasion, it becoming known that we had arranged for a special Saturday afternoon Temperance demonstration, a deputation of Publicans complained beforehand to the Captain of the Police—that our meetings were interfering with their legitimate trade. He heard their complaints to send officers to watch the meeting, prevent any disturbance, and take in charge all offenders, but declined to prohibit the meetings till he received their reports. The Captain, a pious Wesleyan, who was in full sympathy with us and our work, informed me of the complaints made, and intimated that his men would be present; but I was just to conduct the meeting as usual, and he would guarantee that strict justice would be done. The Publicans having announced amongst their sympathizers that the Police were to break up and prevent our meeting and take the conductors in charge, a very large crowd assembled, both friendly and unfriendly, for the Publicans[19] and their hangers-on were there "to see the fun," and to help in "baiting" the Missionary. Punctually, I ascended the stone stair, accompanied by another Missionary who was also to deliver an address, and announced our opening hymn. As we sang, a company of Police appeared, and were quietly located here and there among the crowd, the sergeant himself tak-

19. "Publicans" — a reference to the tax collectors in Jesus' day, who were most concerned with their material wealth.

ing his post close by the platform, whence the whole assembly could be scanned. Our enemies were jubilant, and signals were passed betwixt them and their friends, as if the time had come to provoke a row. Before the hymn was finished, Captain Baker himself, to the infinite surprise of friend and foe alike, joined us on the platform, devoutly listened to all that was said, and waited till the close. The Publicans could not for very shame leave, while he was there at their suggestion and request, though they had wit enough to perceive that his presence had frustrated all their sinister plans. They had to hear our addresses and prayers and hymns; they had to listen to the intimation of our future meetings. When all had quietly dispersed, the Captain warmly congratulated us on our large and well-conducted congregation, and hoped that great good would result from our efforts. This opposition also the Lord overruled to increase our influence, and to give point and publicity to our assaults upon the kingdom of Satan.[20]

Though disappointed thus, some of the Publicans resolved to have revenge. On the following Saturday evening, when a large meeting was being addressed in our Green Street Church, which had to be entered by a great iron gateway, a spirit merchant ran his van in front of the gate, so that the people could not leave the Church without its removal. Hearing this, I sent two of my young men to draw it aside and clear the way. The Publicans, watching near by in league with two policemen, pounced upon the young men whenever they seized the shafts, and gave them in charge for removing his property. On hearing that the young men were being marched to the Police Office, I ran after them and asked what was their offence? They replied that they were in charge for injuring the spirit merchant's property; and the officers tartly informed me that if I further interfered I should be taken too. I replied, that as the young men only did what was necessary, and at my request, I would go with them to prison.[21]

The cry now went through the street, that the Publicans were sending the Missionary and his young men to the Police

20. Any kingdom work is going to stir up opposition. Satan does not appreciate the robbing of his house.

21. God often places men or women in high position (such as Daniel, Joseph, or Esther) who may defend God's people when necessary. This is what we see happening at the police station (with John G. Paton and his two men).

Office, and a huge mob rushed together to rescue us; but I earnestly entreated them not to raise disturbance, but allow us quietly to pass on. At the Office, it appeared as if the lieutenant on duty and the men under him were all in sympathy with the Publicans. He took down in writing all their allegations, but would not listen to us. At this stage a handsomely dressed and dignified gentleman came forward and said, "What bail is required?"

A few sharp words passed; another and apparently higher officer entered, and took part of the colloquy. I could only hear the gentleman protest, in authoritative tones, the policemen having been quietly asked some questions, "I know this whole case, I will expose it to the bottom; expect me here to stand by the Missionary and these young men on Monday morning."

Before I could collect my wits to thank him, and before I quite understood what was going on, he disappeared; and the superior officer turned to us and intimated in a very respectful manner that the charge had been withdrawn, and that I and my friends were at liberty. I never found out exactly who the gentleman was that befriended us; but from the manner in which he asserted himself and was listened to, I saw that he was a Citizen well known in official quarters. From that day our work progressed without further open opposition; and many, who had been slaves of intemperance, were not only reformed but became fervent workers in the Total Abstinence cause.

Though Intemperance was the main cause of poverty, suffering, misery, and vice in that district of Glasgow, I had also considerable opposition from Romanists and Infidels, many of whom met in clubs, where they drank together, and gloried in their wickedness and in leading other young men astray.[22] Against these I prepared and delivered lectures, at the close of which "discussion" was invited and allowed; but I fear they did little good. These men embraced the opportunity of airing their absurdities, or sowing the seeds of corruption in those whom otherwise they could never have reached, while their

22. Although materialism, atheism, and agnosticism are the official religions of most Western countries today, this was not so in the mid-19th century. By this time, the influence of David Hume, Ralph Waldo Emerson, Jeremy Bentham, John Stuart Mill, Charles Darwin, and Karl Marx was just beginning to take root.

own hearts and minds were fast shut against all conviction or light.

One infidel Lecturer in the district became very ill. His wife called me in to visit him. I found him possessed of a Circulating Library of infidel books, by which he sought to pervert unwary minds. Though he talked and lectured much against the Gospel, he did not at all really understand its message. He had read the Bible, but only to find food there for ridicule. Now supposed to be dying, he confessed that his mind was full of terror as to the Future. After several visits and frequent conversations and prayers, he became genuinely and deeply interested, drank in God's message of salvation, and cried aloud with many tears for pardon and peace. He bitterly lamented the evil he had done, and called in all the infidel literature that he had in circulation, with the purpose of destroying it. He began to speak solemnly to any of his companions that came to see him, telling them what he had found in the Lord Jesus. At his request I bought and brought to him a Bible, which he received with great joy, saying, "This is the book for me now"; and adding, "Since you were here last, I gathered together all my infidel books; my wife locked the door till she and my daughter tore them to pieces, and I struck the light that reduced the pile to ashes."

As long as he lived, this man was unwearied and unflinching in testifying, to all that crossed his path, how much Jesus Christ had been to his heart and soul; and he died in the possession of a full and blessed hope.

Another Infidel, whose wife was a Roman Catholic, also became unwell, and gradually sank under great suffering and agony. His blasphemies against God were known and shuddered at by all the neighbors. His wife pled with me to visit him. She refused, at my suggestion, to call her own priest, so I accompanied her at last. The man refused to hear one word about spiritual things, and foamed with rage. He even spat at me, when I mentioned the name of Jesus. "The natural receiveth not the things of the Spirit of God; for they are foolishness unto him!" There is a "wisdom" which is at best earthly, and at worst "sensual and devilish." I visited the poor man daily, but his enmity to God and his sufferings together seemed to drive him mad. Towards the end I pleaded with him even then to look to the Lord Jesus, and asked if I might pray with him? With all his remaining strength he shouted at me, "Pray for me to the devil!"

Reminding him how he had always denied that there was any devil, I suggested that he must surely believe in one now, else he would scarcely make such a request, even in mockery. In great rage he cried, "Yes, I believe there is a devil, and a God, and a just God too; but I have hated Him in life, and I hate Him in death!"

With these awful words he wriggled into Eternity; but his shocking death produced a very serious impression for good, especially amongst young men, in the district where his character was known.[23]

How different was the case of that Doctor who also had been an unbeliever as well as a drunkard! Highly educated, skilful, and gifted above most in his profession, he was taken into consultation for specially dangerous cases, whenever they could find him tolerably sober. After one of his excessive "bouts" he had a dreadful attack of *delirium tremens*. At one time wife and watchers had a fierce struggle to dash from his lips a draught of prussic acid; at another, they detected the silver-hafted lancet concealed in the band of his shirt, as he lay down, to bleed himself to death.[24] His aunt came and pleaded with me to visit him. My heart bled for his poor young wife and two beautiful little children. Visiting him twice daily, and sometimes even more frequently, I found the way somehow into his heart, and he would do almost anything for me and longed for my visits. When again the fit of self-destruction seized him, they sent for me; he held out his hand eagerly, and grasping mine said, "Put all these people out of the room, remain you with me; I will be quiet, I will do everything you ask!"

23. The spiritual nature of atheism, the hatred for God that simmers in the heart, becomes obvious at points with the infidel or apostate (especially as they near death). This story of the infidel's death provides frightening insight into the horrors of rebellion and the judgment that follows.

24. The doctor attempted suicide several times and had a real problem with drunkenness.

I got them all to leave, but whispered to one in passing to "keep near the door."

Alone I sat beside him, my hand in his, and kept up a quiet conversation for several hours. After we had talked of everything that I could think of, and it was now far into the morning, I said, "If you had a Bible here, we might read a chapter, verse about."

He said dreamily, "There was once a Bible above yon press; if you can get up to it, you might find it there yet."

Getting it, dusting it, and laying it on a small table which I drew near to the sofa on which we sat, we read there and then a chapter together. After this I said, :Now, shall we pray?"

He replied heartily, "Yes."

I having removed the little table, we kneeled down together at the sofa; and after a solemn pause I whispered, "You pray first."

He replied, "I curse, I cannot pray; would you have me curse God to His face?"

I answered, "You promised to do all that I asked; you must pray, or try to pray, and let me hear that you cannot."

He said, "I cannot curse God on my knees; let me stand, and I will curse Him; I cannot pray."

I gently held him on his knees, saying, "Just try to pray, and let me hear you cannot."

Instantly he cried out, "O Lord, Thou knowest I cannot pray," and was going to say something dreadful as he strove to rise up. But I took up gently the words he had uttered as if they had been my own and continued the prayer, pleading for him and his dear ones as we knelt there together, till he showed that he was completely subdued and lying low at the feet of God. On rising from our knees he was manifestly greatly impressed, and I said, "Now, as I must be at College by daybreak and must return to my lodging for my books and an hour's rest, will do you one thing more for me before I go?"

"Yes," was his reply.

25. The man was in spiritual bondage and could not pray. This was the substance of John Paton's prayer for him — that God would enable him to pray.

26. It is customary in Presbyterian churches for the children to be baptized when the father makes a profession of faith and is received into membership in the church.

27. *I Lay My Sins on Jesus* was Horatius Bonar's first hymn, written in 1843.

"Then," said I, "it is long since you had a refreshing sleep; now, will you lie down, and I will sit by you till you fall asleep?"

He lay down, and was soon fast asleep. After commending him to the care and blessing of the Lord, I quietly slipped out, and his wife returned to watch by his side. When I came back later in the day, after my Classes were over, he, on hearing my foot and voice, came to meet me, and clasping me in his arms, cried, "Thank God, I can pray now! I rose this morning refreshed from sleep, and prayed with my wife and children for the first time in my life; and now I shall do so every day, and serve God while I live, who hath dealt in so great mercy with me!"[25]

After delightful conversation, he promised to go with me to Dr. Symington's church on Sabbath Day; there he took sittings beside me; at next half-yearly Communion he and his wife were received into membership, and their children were baptized;[26] and from that day till his death he led a devoted and most useful Christian life. He now sleeps in Jesus; and I do believe I shall meet him in Glory as a trophy of redeeming grace and love!

In my Mission district I was the witness of many joyful departures to be with Jesus—I do not like to name them "deaths" at all. They left us rejoicing in the bright assurance that nothing present or to come "could ever separate them or us from the love of God which is in Christ Jesus our Lord." Many examples might be given; but I can find room for only one. John Sim, a dear little boy, was carried away by consumption. His child-heart seemed to be filled with joy about seeing Jesus. His simple prattle, mingled with deep questionings, arrested not only his young companions, but pierced the hearts of some careless sinners who heard him, and greatly refreshed the faith of God's dear people. It was the very pathos of song incarnated to hear the weak quaver of his dying voice sing out—

"I lay my sins on Jesus,
The spotless Lamb of God."[27]

Shortly before his decease he said to his parents, "I am going soon to be with Jesus; but I sometimes fear that I may not see you there."

"Why so, my child?" said his weeping mother.

"Because," he answered, "if you were set upon going to Heaven and seeing Jesus there, you would pray about it, and sing about it; you would talk about Jesus to others, and tell them of that happy meeting with Him in Glory. All this my dear Sabbath School teacher taught me, and she will meet me there.[28] Now why did not you, my father and mother, tell me all these things about Jesus, if you are going to meet Him too?" Their tears fell fast over their dying child; and he little knew, in his unthinking eighth year, what a message from God had pierced their souls through his innocent words.

One day an aunt from the country visited his mother, and their talk had run in channels for which the child no longer felt any interest. On my sitting down beside him, he said, "Sit you down and talk with me about Jesus; I am tired hearing so much talk about everything else but Jesus; I am going soon to be with Him. Oh, do tell me everything you know or have ever heard about Jesus, the spotless Lamb of God!"

At last the child literally longed to be away, not for rest, or freedom from pain—for of that he had very little—but, as he himself always put it, "to see Jesus." And, after all, that was the wisdom of the heart, however he learned it. Eternal life, here or hereafter, is just the vision of Jesus.

Amongst many of the Roman Catholics in my Mission district, also, I was very kindly received, and allowed even to read the Scriptures and to pray. At length, however, a young woman who professed to be converted by my Classes and Meetings brought things to a crisis betwixt them and me. She had renounced her former faith, was living in a Protestant family, and looked to me as her pastor and teacher. One night, a closed carriage, with two men and women, was sent from a Nunnery in Clyde Street, to take her and her little sister with them. She refused, and declined all authority on their part, de-

28. Little John Sims was profoundly influenced by his Sunday School teacher, and apparently his parents were not interested in the things of the Lord.

29. The Roman Catholics in this case functioned as a cult might function by not allowing members to act freely and make their own decisions.

claring that she was now a Protestant by her own free choice. During this altercation, a message had been sent for me. On arriving, I found the house filled with a noisy crowd. Before them all, she appealed to me for protection from these her enemies. The Romanists, becoming enraged, jostled me into a corner of the room, and there enclosed me. The two women pulled her out of bed by force, for the girl had been sick, and began to dress her, but she fainted among their hands.[29]

I called out, "Do not murder the poor girl! Get her water, quick, quick!" and leaving my hat on the table, I rushed through amongst them, as if in search of water, and they let me pass. Knowing that the house had only one door, I quickly slipped the key from within, shut and locked the door outside, and with the key in my hand ran to the Police Office.

Having secured two constables to protect the girl and take the would-be captors into custody, I returned, opened the door, and found, alas! That these constables were themselves Roman Catholics, and at once set about frustrating me and assisting their own friends. The poor sick girl was supported by the arms into the carriage; the policemen cleared the way through the crowd; and before I could force my way through the obstructions in the house, the conveyance was already starting. I appealed and shouted to the crowds to protect the girl, and seize and take the whole party to the Police Office. A gentleman in the crowd took my part and said to a big Highland policeman in the street, "Mac, I commit that conveyance and party to you on a criminal charge, before witnesses; you will if they escape."

The driver lashing at his horse to get away, Mac drew his baton and struck, when the driver leapt down to the street on the opposite side, and threw the reins in the policeman's face. Thereupon our stalwart friend at once mounted the box, and drove straight for the Police Office. On arriving there, we discovered that only the women were inside with the sick girl—the men having escaped in the scuffle and the crush. What proved more disappointing was that the lieutenant on

duty happened to be a Papist, who, after hearing our statement and conferring with the parties in the conveyance, returned, and said:

"Her friends are taking her to a comfortable home; you
have no right to interfere, and I have let them go." He further
refused to hear the grounds of our complaint, and ordered the
police to clear the Office.

Next morning, a false and foolish account of the whole
affair appeared in the Newspapers, condemnatory of the Mission and of myself; a meeting of the directors was summoned,
and the Superintendent came to my lodging to take me before them. Having heard all, and questioned and cross-ques-
tioned me, they resolved to prosecute the abductors of the
girl. The Nunnery authorities confessed that the little sister
was with them, but denied that the other had been taken in
there, or that they knew anything of her case. Though the girl
was sought for carefully by the Police, and by all the members
of my Class, for nearly a fortnight, no trace of her or of the
coachman or of any of the parties could be discovered; till one
day from a cellar, through a grated window, she called to one
of my Class girls passing by, and begged her to run and let me
know that she was confined there. At once, the directors of the
City Mission were informed by me, and Police were sent to
rescue her; but on examining that house they found that she
had been again removed. The occupiers denied all knowledge
of where she had gone, or who had taken her away from their
lodging. All other efforts failed to find her, till she was left at
the Poor House door, far gone in dropsy,[30] and soon after died
in that last refuge of the destitute and forsaken.

Anonymous letters were now sent, threatening my life;
and I was publicly cursed from the altar by the priests in Ab-
ercromby Street Chapel. The directors of the Mission, fearing violence, advised me to leave Glasgow for a short holiday,
and even offered to arrange for my being taken for work in
Edinburgh for a year, that the fanatical passions of the Irish
Papists might have time to subside. But I refused to leave my

30. Dropsy is an older
term for edema or the
accumulation of excess
fluids in the body.

31. The animus towards John G. Paton from the Catholics constituted a threat to his life. Paton's courage in the face of danger would characterize his life. Later, deadly threats came again and again by the cannibals on the islands.

32. The Roman Catholic Church is not as much known for its tyranny today as in previous centuries. The Inquisitions are long past. Nonetheless, doctrines that do not allow for assurance of salvation or that impose fear on the people, requiring subjugation to systems of confessions and indulgences, really do constitute a tyranny.

33. The Presbyterian Church is ruled by elders who sit on a session with the pastor. The pastor is known as a teaching elder, and the others are ruling elders. John G. Paton became a ruling elder in his early thirties. His father served as a ruling elder as well.

work. I went on conducting it all as in the past. The worst thing that happened was, that on rushing one day past a row of houses occupied exclusively by Papists, a stone thrown from one of them cut me severely above the eye, and I fell stunned and bleeding. When I recovered and scrambled to my feet, no person of course that could be suspected was to be seen! The doctor having dressed the wound, it rapidly healed, and after a short confinement I resumed my work and my studies without any further serious annoyance. Attempts were made more than once, in these Papist closes, and I believe by the Papists themselves, to pour pails of boiling water on my head, over windows and down dark stairs, but in every case I marvelously escaped;[31] and as I would not turn coward, their malice tired itself out, and they ultimately left me entirely at peace. Is not this a feature of the lower Irish, and especially Popish population? Let them see that bullying makes you afraid, and they will brutally and cruelly misuse you; but defy them fearlessly, or take them by the nose, and they will crouch like whelps beneath your feet. Is there anything in their religion that accounts for this? Is it not a system of alternating tyranny on the one part, and terror, abject terror, on the other?[32]

About this same time there was an election of Elders for Dr. Symington's congregation, and I was by an almost unanimous vote chosen for that office. For years now I had been attached to them as City Missionary for their district, and many friends urged me to accept the eldership, as likely to increase my usefulness, and give me varied experience for my future work. My dear father, also, himself an Elder in the congregation at Dumfries, advised me similarly; and though very young, comparatively, for such a post, I did accept the office, and continued to act as an Elder and member of Dr. Symington's Kirk Session till by-and-by I was ordained as a Missionary to the New Hebrides—where the great lot of my life had been cast by the Lord, as yet unknown to me.[33]

All through my City Mission period, I was painfully carrying on my studies, first at the University of Glasgow, and thereafter at the Reformed Presbyterian Divinity Hall; and also medical classes at the Andersonian College. With the exception of one session, when failure of health broke me down, I struggled patiently on through ten years. The work was hard and most exacting; and if I never attained the scholarship for which I thirsted—being but poorly grounded in my younger days—I yet had much of the blessed Master's presence in all my efforts, which many better scholars sorely lacked; and I was sustained by the lofty aim which burned all these years bright within my soul, namely—to be qualified as a preacher of the Gospel of Christ to be owned and used by Him for the salvation of perishing men.[34]

34. Over the course of ten years, Paton took an undergraduate degree, a seminary degree (at Reformed Presbyterian Divinity Hall), and some medical training (which would be helpful for someone on the mission field).

CHAPTER IV – FOREIGN MISSION CLAIMS

A.D. 1856-1857. Age 32-33

Happy in my work as I felt through these ten years, and successful by the blessing of God, yet I continually heard, and chiefly during my last years in the Divinity Hall, the wail of the perishing Heathen in the South Seas; and I saw that few were caring for them, while I well knew that many would be ready to take up my work in Calton, and carry it forward perhaps with more efficiency than myself. Without revealing the state of my mind to any person, this was the supreme subject of my daily meditation and prayer; and this also led me to enter upon those medical studies, in which I purposed taking the full course; but at the close of my third year, an incident occurred, which led me at once to offer myself for the Foreign Mission field.

Streets of Glasgow

The Reformed Presbyterian Church of Scotland, in which I had been brought up, had been advertising for another Missionary to join the Rev. John Inglis in his grand work on the New Hebrides.[1] Dr. Bates, the excellent convener of the Heathen Missions Committee, was deeply grieved, because for two years their appeal had failed. At length, the Synod, after much prayer and consultation, felt the claims of the Heathen so gently pressed upon them by the Lord's repeated calls, that they resolved to cast lots, to discover whether God would thus

1. The Reformed Presbyterian missionary Pastor John Inglis had reached the mission field in the New Hebrides (on the island of Aneityum) in 1852. He served there for 24 years.

select any Minister to be relieved from his home-charge, and designated as a Missionary to the South Seas. Each member of Synod, as I was informed, agreed to hand in, after solemn appeal to God, the names of the three best qualified in his esteem for such a work, and he who had the clear majority was to be loosed from his congregation, and to proceed to the Mission field—or the first and second highest, if two could be secured. Hearing this debate, and feeling an intense interest in these most unusual proceedings, I remember yet the hushed solemnity of the prayer before the names were handed in. I remember the strained silence that held the Assembly while the scrutiners retired to examine the papers; and I remember how tears blinded my eyes when they returned to announce that the result was so indecisive, that it was clear that the Lord had not in that way provided a Missionary. The cause was once again solemnly laid before God in prayer, and a cloud of sadness appeared to fall over all the Synod.

The Lord kept saying within me, "Since none better qualified can be got, rise and offer yourself!" Almost overpowering was the impulse to answer aloud, "Here am I, send me." But I was dreadfully afraid of mistaking my mere human emotions for the will of God. So I resolved to make it a subject of close deliberation and prayer for a few days longer, and to look at the proposal from every possible aspect. Besides, I was keenly solicitous about the effect upon the hundreds of young people and others, now attached to all my Classes and Meetings; and yet I felt a growing assurance that this was the call of God to His servant, and that He who was willing to employ me in the work abroad, was both able and willing to provide for the on-carrying of my work at home. The wail and the claims of the Heathen were constantly sounding in my ears. I saw them perishing for lack of the knowledge of the true God[2] and His Son Jesus, while my Green Street people had the open Bible and all the means of grace within easy reach, which, if they rejected, they did so willfully, and at their own peril.[3] None seemed prepared for the Heathen field; many were capable

2. Our fundamental goal in Christian ministry is that people would know the true God and Jesus Christ whom he has sent (John 17:3).

3. Paton saw that the Western nations had far more access to the Word of God than these far-off heathen nations.

*Erromango, Dillon's Bay by Thomas Bent (1858), martyrdom site of
John Williams, first missionary to the New Hebrides*

as my literary and divinity training, had specially qualified me
in some ways for the Foreign field, and from every aspect at
which I could look the whole facts in the face, the voice within me sounded like a voice from God.

It was under good Dr. Bates of West Campbell Street that
I had begun my career in Glasgow—receiving £25 per annum
for district visitation in connection with his Congregation,
along with instruction under Mr. Hislop and his staff in the
Free Church Normal Seminary—and oh, how Dr. Bates did
rejoice, and even weep for joy, when I called on him, and offered myself for the New Hebrides Mission! I returned to my
lodging with a lighter heart than I had for sometime enjoyed,
feeling that nothing so clears the vision, and lifts up the life,
as a decision to move forward in what you know to be entirely
the will of the Lord. I said to my fellow-student, Joseph Copeland, who had chummed with me all through our course at

college, "I have been away signing my banishment" (a rather trifling way of talk for such an occasion). "I have offered myself as a Missionary for the New Hebrides."

After a long and silent meditation, in which he seemed lost in far-wandering thoughts, his answer was, "If they will accept of me, I am also resolved to go!"

I said, "Will you write the Convener to that effect, or let me do so?"

He replied, "You may."

A few minutes later his letter of offer was in the post-office. Next morning Dr. Bates called upon us, early, and after a long conversation, commended us and our future work to the Lord God in fervent prayer.

This fellow student, Mr. Joseph Copeland, had also for some time been a very successful City Missionary in the Camlachie district, while attending along with me at the Divinity Hall. The leading of God, whereby we both resolved at the same time to give ourselves to the Foreign Mission field, was wholly unexpected by us, as we had never once spoken to each other about going abroad. At a meeting of the Foreign Missions Committee, held immediately thereafter, both were, after due deliberation, formally accepted, on condition that we passed successfully the usual examinations required of candidates for the Ministry. And for the next twelve months we were placed under a special committee for advice as to medical experience, acquaintance with the rudiments of trades, and anything else which might be thought useful to us in the Foreign field.[4]

When it became known that I was preparing to go abroad as Missionary, nearly all were dead against the proposal, except Dr. Bates and my fellow-student. My dear father and mother, however, when I consulted them, characteristically replied, "that they had long since given me away to the Lord, and in this matter also would leave me to God's disposal." From other quarters we were besieged with the strongest opposition on all sides. Even Dr. Symington, one of my professors in divinity,

4. The Presbyterians have a fairly robust systems of exams for men who want to be pastors or missionaries. These exams often take about a year for men to get through.

and the beloved Minister in connection with whose congregation I had wrought so long as a City Missionary, and in whose Kirk Session I had for years sat as an Elder, repeatedly urged me to remain at home. He argued, that "Green Street Church was doubtless the sphere for which God had given me peculiar qualifications, and in which He had so largely blessed my labors; that if I left those now attending my Classes and Meetings, they might be scattered and many of them would probably fall away; that I was leaving certainty for uncertainty—work in which God had made me greatly useful, for work in which I might fail to be useful, and only throw away my life among the Cannibals."[5]

To his arguments I replied, "that my mind was finally resolved; that, though I loved my work and my people, yet I felt that I could leave them to the care of Jesus, who would soon provide them a better pastor than I; and that, with regard to my life amongst the Cannibals, as I had only once to die, I was content to leave the time and place and means in the hand of God who had already marvelously preserved me when visiting cholera patients and the fever-stricken poor;[6] on that score I had positively no further concern, having left it all absolutely to the Lord, whom I sought to serve and honor, whether in life or by death."

The house connected with my Green Street Church was now offered to me for a Manse, and any reasonable salary that I cared to ask (as against the promised £120 per annum for the far-off and dangerous New Hebrides), on condition that I would remain at home.[7] I cannot honestly say that such offers or opposing influences proved a heavy trial to me; they rather tended to confirm my determination that the path of duty was to go abroad.

Amongst many who sought to deter me, was one dear old Christian gentleman, whose crowning argument always was, "The cannibals! you will be eaten by cannibals!" At last I replied, "Mr. Dickson, you are advanced in years now, and your own prospect is soon to be laid in the grave, there to be eaten

5. Dr. Symington discouraged Paton from taking on the foreign missionary work, especially since Paton proved himself so strong in the City Mission work. Paton was an elder in the church (with the session) where Dr. Symington served as pastor.

6. Paton had already risked his life visiting patients in the inner-city who had come down with cholera (a highly-infectious bacterial infection in the small intestine).

7. He was offered a Manse (a house where he could live) and any salary he suggested if he would stay and minister in Glasgow.

by worms, I confess to you, that if I can but live and die serving and honoring the Lord Jesus, it will make no difference to me whether I am eaten by cannibals or by worms; and in the Great Day my resurrection body will arise as fair as yours in the likeness of our risen Redeemer."[8]

The old gentleman, raising his hands in a deprecating attitude, left the room exclaiming, "After that I have nothing more to say!"

My dear Green Street people grieved excessively at the thought of my leaving them, and daily pleaded with me to remain. Indeed, the opposition was so strong from nearly all, and many of them warm Christian friends, that I was sorely tempted to question whether I was carrying out the Divine will, or only some headstrong wish of my own. This also caused me much anxiety, and drove me close to God in prayer. But again every doubt would vanish, when I clearly saw that all at home had free access to the Bible and the means of grace, with Gospel light shining all around them, while the poor Heathen were perishing, without even the chance of knowing all God's love and mercy to men.[9] But conscience said louder and clearer every day, "Leave all these results with Jesus your Lord, who said, 'Go ye into all the world, preach the Gospel to every creature, and lo! I am with you alway.'" These words kept ringing in my ears; these were our marching orders.[10]

Some retorted upon me, "There are Heathen at home; let us seek and save, first of all, the lost ones perishing at our doors." This I felt to be most true, and an appalling fact; but I unfailingly observed that those who made this retort neglected these Home Heathen themselves; and so the objection, as from them, lost all its power. They would ungrudgingly spend more on a fashionable party at dinner or tea, on concert or ball or theatre, or on some ostentatious display, or worldly and selfish indulgence, ten times more, perhaps in a single day, than they would give in a year, or in half a lifetime, for the conversion of the whole Heathen World, either at home or abroad. Objections from all such people must, of course, always count

8. Paton doesn't care if his body is eaten by cannibals or worms; the important thing is that the body will be resurrected at the last day anyway! He is living in the reality of the resurrection.

9. There is so much light available in some nations, while there is almost complete darkness in other nations. John Paton is motivated by the desire to proclaim God's love and mercy to these nations.

10. There seems to be a reticence among some Christians to sacrifice and suffer for Christ. They seek a convenient life, but this is not what Paton was seeking.

for nothing among men to whom spiritual things are realities. For these people themselves—I do, and always did, only pity them, as God's stewards making such a miserable use of time and money entrusted in their care.

On meeting, however, with so many obstructing influences, I again laid the whole matter before my dear parents, and their reply was to this effect: "Heretofore we feared to bias you, but now we must tell you why we praise God for the decision to which you have been led. Your father's heart was set upon being a Minister, but other claims forced him to give it up! When you were given to them, your father and mother laid you upon the altar, their first-born, to be consecrated, if God saw fit, as a Missionary of the Cross; and it has been their constant prayer that you might be prepared, qualified, and led to this very decision; and we pray with all our heart that the Lord may accept your offering, long spare you, and give you many souls from the Heathen World for your hire." From that moment, every doubt as to my path of duty forever vanished. I saw the hand of God very visibly, not only preparing me for, but now leading me to, the Foreign Mission field.[11]

Well did I know that the sympathy and prayers of my dear parents were warmly with me in all my studies and in all my Mission work; but for my education they could of course, give me no money help. All through, on the contrary, it was my pride and joy to help them, being the eldest in a family of eleven; though I here most gladly and gratefully record that all my brothers and sisters, as they grew up and began to earn a living, took their full share in this same blessed privilege. First, I assisted them to purchase the family cow, without whose invaluable aid my ever-memorable mother never could have reared and fed her numerous flock; then, I paid them for the house-rent and the cow's grass on the Bank Hill, till some of the others were more able, and relieved me by paying these in my stead; and finally, I helped to pay the school-fees and to provide clothing for the younger ones—in short, I gave, and gladly, what could possibly be saved out of my City Mis-

11. Now the vision of a father and mother (from his birth) came to bear on Paton's life. He was consecrated to be a missionary, and this was the answer to many of his father's prayers. This was absolute confirmation for Paton.

12. Paton helped with his parent's expenses as the eldest son. But, the other siblings were now able to pitch in and help. Paton shared out of his minimal income of 40 pounds per year. This was less than a common day laborer earned in a year.

13. Paton was able to pay for his own education without racking up any debt (or taking on government handouts).

14. Paton's integrity is further seen in his commitment to settle a debt imposed on his grandfather by an unprincipled landlord.

sion salary of £40 ultimately advanced to £45 per annum.[12] Self-educated thus, and without the help of one shilling from any other source, readers will easily imagine that I had many a staggering difficulty to overcome in my long curriculum in Arts, Divinity, and Medicine; but God so guided me, and blessed all my little arrangements, that I never incurred one farthing of personal debt.[13]

There was, however, a heavy burden always pressing upon me, and crushing my spirit from the day I left my home, which had been thus incurred. The late owner of the Dalswinton estate allowed, as a prize, the cottager who had the tidiest house and the most beautiful flower garden to sit rent-free. For several years in succession, my old seafaring grandfather won this prize, partly by his own handy skill, partly by his wife's joy in flowers. Unfortunately no clearance receipt had been asked for or given for these rents—the proprietor and his cottars treating each other as friends, rather than as men of business. The new heir, unexpectedly succeeding, found himself in need of money, and threatened prosecution for such rents as arrears. The money had to be borrowed. A money-lending lawyer gave it at usurious interest, on condition of my father also becoming responsible for interest and principal. This burden hung like a millstone around my grandfather's neck till the day of his death; and it then became suspended round my father's neck alone. The lawyer, on hearing of my giving up trade and entering upon study, threatened to prosecute my father for the capital, unless my name were given along with his for security. Every shilling that I or any of our family could save, all through these ten years, went to pay off that interest and gradually to reduce the capital; and this burden we managed, amongst us, to extinguish just on the eve of my departure for the South Seas.[14] Indeed, one of the purest joys connected with that time was that I received my first foreign Mission salary and outfit money in advance, and could send home a sum sufficient to wipe out the last penny of a claim by that money-lender or by any one else against my beloved parents, in connection with the noble struggle they had made in rearing so large a family in sternly-noble Scottish independence. And that joy was hallowed by the knowledge that my other brothers and sisters were now both willing and able to do more than all that would in future be required—for we stuck to each other and to the old folks like burs, and had all things "in common," as a family in Christ—and I knew that never again, howsoever long they might be spared through the peaceful autumn of life, would the dear old father and mother lack any joy or comfort that the willing hands and loving hearts of all their children could singly or unitedly provide. For all this I did praise the Lord! It consoled me beyond description, in parting from them, probably forever, in this world at least.[15]

The Directors of Glasgow City Mission, along with the Great Hamilton Street congregation, had made every effort to find a suitable successor to me in my Green Street work, but in vain. Despairing of success, as no inexperienced worker could with any hope undertake it, Rev. Mr. Caie, the superintendent, felt moved to appeal to my brother Walter—then in a good business situation in the city, who had been of late closely associated with me in all my undertakings—if he would not come to the rescue, devote himself to the Mission, and prepare for the Holy Ministry. My brother resigned a good position and excellent prospects in the business world, set himself to carry forward the Green Street Mission, and did so with abundant energy and manifest blessing, persevered in his studies despite a long-continued illness, and became an honored Minister of the Gospel, in the Reformed Presbyterian Church first of all, and thereafter in the Free Church of Scotland.

On my brother withdrawing from Green Street, God provided for the district a devoted young Minister, admirably adapted for the work, Rev. John Edgar, M.A., who succeeded in drawing together such a body of people that they hived off and built a new church in Landressy Street, which is now, by amalgamation, known as the Barrowfield Free Church of Glasgow.[16] For that fruit too, while giving all praise to other

15. Paton felt a great deal of responsibility to his parents — this is a tremendous example of a man who honored his father and mother in their old age as Jesus taught us to do (Matt. 15:1-6).

16. At first, Paton's brother, Walter, took over the Green Street Mission. Then, it was passed on to a Rev. John Edgar. This mission work eventually formed its own local church. John Paton's work in Glasgow really did bear good fruit over time.

devoted workers, we bless God as we trace the history of the Green Street Mission. Let him that soweth and him that reapeth rejoice unfeignedly together! The spirit of the old Green Street workers lives on too, as I have already said, in the new Halls erected close thereby; and in no more conspicuously than in the son of my staunch patron and friend, another Thomas Binnie, who in Foundry Boy meetings and otherwise devotes the consecrated leisure of a busy and prosperous life to the direct personal service of his Lord and Master. The blessing of Jehovah God be ever upon that place, and upon all who there seek to win their fellows to the love and service of Jesus Christ.

When I left Glasgow, many of the young men and women of my Classes would, if it had been possible, have gone with me, to live and die among the Heathen. Though chiefly working girls and lads in trades and mills, their deep interest led them to unite their pennies and sixpences, and to buy web after web of calico, print, and woolen stuffs, which they themselves shaped and sewed into dresses for the women, and kilts and pants for men, on the New Hebrides. This continued to be repeated year after year, long after I had left them; and to this day no box from Glasgow goes to the New Hebrides Mission which does not contain article after article from one or other of the old Green Street hands.[17] I do certainly anticipate that, when they and I meet in Glory, those days in which we learned the joy of Christian service in the Green Street Mission Halls will form no unwelcome theme of holy and happy converse.

What able and devoted Minister of the Gospel, Dr. Bates, the Convener of the Heathen Missions, had taken the deepest and most fatherly interest in all our preparations. On the morning of our final examinations he was confined to bed with sickness, yet could not be content without sending his daughter to wait in the adjoining room near the Presbytery House, to learn the result, and instantly to carry him word. When she, hurrying home, informed him that we both had passed suc-

17. The Green Street Mission would continue to draw together their few resources to make clothes for the natives of the New Hebrides.

cessfully, and that the day of our ordinations as Missionaries to the New Hebrides had been appointed, the apostolic old man praised God for the glad tidings, and said his work was now done, and that he could now depart in peace having seen two devoted men set apart to preach the Gospel to these dark and bloody Islands, in answer to his prayers and tears for many a day. Thereafter he rapidly sank, and soon fell asleep in Jesus. He was from the first a very precious friend to me, one of the most ablest Ministers our Church ever had, by far the warmest advocate of her Foreign Missions and altogether a most attractive, white-souled, and noble specimens of an ambassador for Christ, beseeching men to be reconciled to God.[18]

18. Dr. Stewart Bates preached a sermon to the Synod of the Reformed Presbyterian Church in 1828 on the importance of Christian missions that seems to have been the beginning of the denomination's missions committee. Apparently, Dr. Bates spearheaded the Missions effort until he died in 1856.

❧ CHAPTER V –
THE NEW HEBRIDES
A.D. 1857-1858. Age 33-34

O n the first of December 1857—being then in my thirty-third year—the other Missionary-designate and I were "licensed" as preachers of the Gospel. Thereafter we spent four months in visiting and addressing nearly every Congregation and Sabbath School in the Reformed Presbyterian Church of Scotland, that the people might see us and know us, and thereby take a personal interest in our work. That idea was certainly excellent, and might well be adapted to the larger churches, by allocating one Missionary to each Province or to so many Presbyteries, sending him to address these, and training them to regard him as their Missionary and his work as theirs. On the 23rd March, 1858, in Dr. Symington's church, Glasgow, in presence of a mighty crowd, and after a magnificent sermon on "Come over and help us," we were solemnly ordained as Ministers of the Gospel, and set apart as Missionaries to the New Hebrides. On the 16th April of the same year, we left the Tail of the Bank at Greenock, and set sail in the *Clutha* for the Foreign Mission field.[1]

Our voyage to Melbourne was rather tedious, but ended prosperously, under Captain Broadfoot, a kindly, brave-hearted Scot, who did everything that was possible for our comfort. He himself led the singing on board at Worship, which was

1. Paton set out on his voyage with his wife and a fellow missionary (and friend from college), Joseph Copeland.

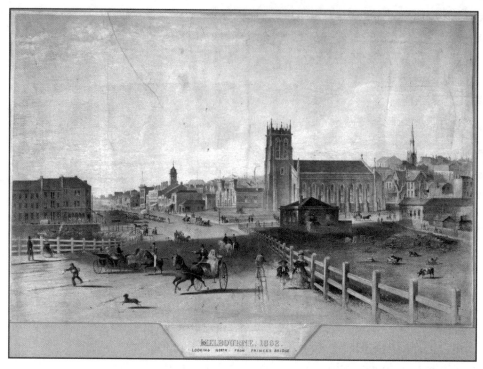

Melbourne in 1862

2. Paton organizes daily worship and Bible studies on the ship, something all pastors and missionaries will do.

3. Melbourne became a mission base for Paton. He was buried in a church yard in Melbourne, Australia almost 50 years later.

4. Geelong is about 25 miles west of Melbourne — a port city.

both the crew and the passengers, at times and places approved of by the Captain in which there was great joy.[2] Nearly thirty years after, when I returned the second time to Scotland, a gentleman of good position, and the father of a large family in the West, saluted me warmly at the close of one of my meetings, and reminded me that he was my precentor [facilitator] in the Bible Class on board the *Clutha*! It was gratifying to hear him say that he had never forgotten the scene and the lessons there.

Arriving at Melbourne,[3] we were welcomed by Rev. Mr. Moor, Mr. and Mrs. Samuel Wilson, and Mr. Wright, all Reformed Presbyterians from Geelong. Mr. Wilson's two children, Jessie and Donald, had been under our care during the voyage; and my young wife and I went with them for a few days on a visit to Geelong,[4] while Mr. Copeland remained on board the *Clutha* to look after our boxes and to watch for any opportunity of reaching our destination on the Islands. He heard that an American ship, the *Frances P. Sage*, was sailing from Melbourne to Penang; and the Captain agreed to land us on Aneityum, New Hebrides, with our two boats and fifty boxes, for £100. We got on board on the 12th August, but such a gale blew that we did not sail till the 17th. On the *Clutha* all was quiet, and good order prevailed; in the *F. P. Sage* all was noise and profanity. The Captain said he kept his second mate for the purpose of swearing at the men and knocking them about. The voyage was most disagreeable to all of us, but fortunately it lasted only twelve days. On the 29th we were close up to Aneityum; but the Captain refused to land us, even in his boats; some of us suspecting that his men were so badly used that had they got on shore they would never have returned to him! In any case he had beforehand secured his £100.[5]

He lay off the island till a trader's boat pulled across to see what we wanted, and by it we sent a note to Dr. Geddie, one of the Missionaries there. Early next morning, Monday, he arrived in his boat, accompanied by Mr. Mathieson, a newly arrived Missionary from Nova Scotia; bringing also Captain Andersen in the small Mission schooner, the *John Knox*,[6] and a large Mission boat called the *Columbia*, well manned with crews of able and willing Natives. Our fifty boxes were soon on board the *John Knox*, the *Columbia*, and our own boats—all being heavily loaded and built up, except those that had to be used in pulling the others ashore. Dr. Geddie, Mr. Mathieson, Mrs. Paton, and I were perched among the boxes on the *John Knox*, and had to hold on as best we could. On sheering off from the *F. P. Sage*, one of her davits[7] caught and broke the mainmast of the little John Knox by the deck; and I saved my wife from being crushed to death by its fall, through managing to swing her instantaneously aside in an apparently impossible manner. It did graze Mr. Mathieson, but he was not hurt. The *John Knox*, already overloaded, was thus quite disabled; we were about ten miles at sea, and in imminent danger; but the

5. Many of the trading ships were populated by men who were extremely unprincipled and were more bothersome to the missionaries than the natives (in many cases). They held to a materialistic worldview. They did not fear God or worship the true and living God.

6. The schooner, *John Knox*, was named after the Scottish Reformer.

7. The davit (a crane) was used for lowering smaller boats into the water.

8. Tanna was the most dangerous of the islands, although the first missionary to the New Hebrides, John Williams, was martyred on Erromango in 1839.

9. Dr. Inglis was the Reformed Presbyterian missionary who had gone ahead of Paton in 1852 (5 years earlier).

Tanna Island

captain of the *F. P. Sage* heartlessly sailed away, and left us to struggle with our fate.

We drifted steadily in the direction of Tanna, an island of cannibals, where our goods would have been plundered and all of us cooked and eaten.[8] Dr. Geddie's boat and mine had the *John Knox* in tow; and Mr. Copeland, with a crew of Natives, was struggling hard with his boat to pull the *Columbia* and her load towards Aneityum. As God mercifully ordered it, though we had a stiff trade wind to pull against, we had a comparatively calm sea; yet we drifted still to leeward, till Dr. Inglis[9] going round to the harbor in his boat, as he had heard of our arrival, saw us far at sea, and hastened to our rescue. All the boats now, with their willing Native crews, got fastened to our schooner, and to our great joy she began to move ahead. After pulling for hours and hours, under the scorching rays of a tropical sun, we were all safely landed on shore at Aneityum, about six o'clock in the evening of 30th August, just four months and fourteen days since we sailed from Greenock. We got a hearty welcome from the Missionaries' wives, Mrs. Geddie, Mrs. Inglis, and Mrs. Mathieson, and from all our new friends, the Christian Natives of Aneityum; and the great danger in which both life and property had been placed at the close of our voyage, made us praise God all the more that He had brought us to this quiet resting-place, around which lay the Islands of the New Hebrides, to which our eager hearts had looked forward, and into which we entered now in the name of the Lord.

Mr. Copeland, Mrs. Paton, and I went round the island to Dr. Inglis's Station, where we were most cordially received and entertained by his dear lady, and by the Christian Natives there. As he was making several additions to his house at that time, we received for the next few weeks our first practical and valuable training in Mission house-building, as well as in higher matters. Soon after, a meeting was called to consult about our settlement, and, by the advice and with the concurrence of all, Mr. and Mrs. Mathieson from Nova Scotia were located on the south side of Tanna, at Umairarekar, and Mrs. Paton and I at Port Resolution, on the same island. At first it was agreed that Mr. Copeland should be placed along with us; but owing to the weakly state of Mrs. Mathieson's health, it was afterwards resolved that, for a time at least, Mr. Copeland should live at either Station as might seem most suitable or most requisite. Till the close of the sailing season, his time was spent chiefly in the *John Knox*, helping Captain Anderson in loading and disloading the wood and house-building materials betwixt Aneityum and Tanna; while I was occupied chiefly with the house-building and preparatory arrangements.[10]

Dr. Inglis and a number of his most energetic Natives accompanied us to Kwamera, Tanna. There we purchased a site for Mission House and Church, and laid a stone foundation, and advanced as far as practicable the erection of a dwelling for Mr. and Mrs. Mathieson. Thence we proceeded to Port Resolution, Tanna, and similarly purchased a site, and advanced, to a forward stage, the house which Mrs. Paton and I were to occupy on our settlement there. Lime for plastering had to be burned in kilns from the coral rocks; and thatch, for roofing with sugar-cane leaf, had to be prepared by the Natives at both Stations before our return; for which, as for all else, a price was duly agreed upon, and was scrupulously paid. Unfortunately we learned, when too late, that both houses were too near the shore, exposed to unwholesome miasma,[11] and productive of the dreaded fever and ague—the most virulent and insidious enemy to all Europeans in those Southern Seas.

At both Stations, but especially at Port Resolution, we found the Natives in a very excited and unsettled state. Threatened wars kept them in constant terror—war betwixt distant tribes or adjoining villages, or nearest neighbors. The Chiefs, at both Stations, willingly sold sites for houses, and appeared to desire Missionaries to live amongst them; but perhaps it was with an eye to axes, knives, fishhooks, blankets, and clothing, which they got in payment, or hoped for in plunder, rather than from any thirst for the Gospel, as they were all Savages

Efate, Vanuatu

10. It was decided that the Mathiesons (from Nova Scotia) and the Patons would attempt mission work on Tanna, the dangerous island. Mr. Copeland would help with both families. The island of Tanna is about 12 miles wide and 25 miles long. James Cook was the first Westerner to visit the island in August, 1774 (attracted by the light of a volcano at the center of the island). To this day, the island remains the least Christianized.

11. The miasma theory of disease held that diseases were spread by bad air, rather than germs carried by mosquitos, etc.

12. "Nonce," defined as "a single occasion."

13. The tribes were almost in a continual state of warfare. Romans 1 speaks of the depths to which humans go when they pervert their sexuality and become idolatrous. This was a perfect description of the people in Tanna (and in Western nations today).

14. The conditions were even more horrifying than the inner city of Glasgow. Paton's heart enlarged, and he learned to love these people as well and throw himself into the work with as much energy and eagerness as he had exercised in Scotland.

15. It is interesting that the character of the island (and willingness to accept the Gospel) was completely different on Aneityum (only 50 miles away)!

and Cannibals. They warily declined to promise protection to the Mission families and the Teachers; but they said they would not themselves do any harm, though they could not say what the Inland people might do—not a bad specimen of diplomacy, leaving an open door for any future emergency, and neither better nor worse than the methods by which the civilized European nations make and break their treaties in peace and war! Such promises meant, and were intended to mean, nothing. The Natives, both on Tanna, and on my second home at Aniwa, believed that they had kept their promise, if they inflicted no injury with their own hands, even though they had hired others to do so. No Heathen there could be trusted one step beyond what appeared to be his own self-interest for the nonce;[12] and nothing conceivable was too base or cruel to be done, if it only served his turn. The "depths of Satan," outlined in the first chapter of the Romans, were uncovered there before our eyes in the daily life of the people, without veil and without excuse.[13]

My first impressions drove me, I must confess, to the verge of utter dismay. On beholding these Natives in their paint and nakedness and misery, my heart was as full of horror as of pity. Had I given up my much-beloved work and my dear people in Glasgow, with so many delightful associations, to consecrate my life to these degraded creatures? Was it possible to teach them right and wrong, to Christianize, or even to civilize them? But that was only a passing feeling; I soon got as deeply interested in them, and in all that tended to advance them, and to lead them to the knowledge and love of Jesus, as ever I had been in my work at Glasgow.[14] We were surprised and delighted at the remarkable change produced on the Natives of Aneityum through the instrumentality of Drs. Geddie and Inglis in so short a time; and we hoped, by prayerful perseverance in the use of similar means, to see the same work of God repeated on Tanna.[15] Besides, the wonderful and blessed work done by Mrs. Inglis and Mrs. Geddie, at their Stations, filled our wives with the buoyant hope of being instruments in the hand of God to produce an equally benefi-cent change amongst the savage women of Tanna. Mrs. Paton had been left with Mrs. Inglis to learn all she could from her of Mission work on the Islands, till I returned with Dr. Inglis from the house-building operations on Tanna; during which period Mr. and Mrs. Mathieson were also being instructed by Dr. and Mrs. Geddie.

To the Tannese, Dr. Inglis and I were objects of curiosi-ty and fear; they came crowding to gaze on our wooden and lime-plastered house; they chattered incessantly with each other, and left the scene day after day with undisguised and increasing wonderment. Possibly they thought us rather mad than wise!

Party after party of armed men going and coming in a state of great excitement, we were informed that war was on foot; but our Aneityumese Teachers were told to assure us that the Harbor people would only act on the defensive, and that no one would molest us at our work. One day two hostile tribes met near our Station; high words arose, and old feuds were revived. The Inland people withdrew; but the Harbor people, false to their promises, flew to arms and rushed past us in pursuit of their enemies. The discharge of muskets in the adjoining bush, and the horrid yells of the savages, soon informed us that they were engaged in deadly fights. Ex-citement and terror were on every countenance; armed men rushed about in every direction, with feathers in their twisted hair—with faces painted red, black, and white, and some, one cheek black, the other red, others, the brow white, the chin blue—in fact, any color and on any part—the more grotesque and savage-looking, the higher the art! Some of the women ran with their children to places of safety; but even then we saw other girls and women, on the shore close by, chewing sugar-cane and chaffering[16] and laughing, as if their fathers and brothers had been engaged in a country dance, instead of a bloody conflict.[17]

16. "Chaffering," de-fined as "haggling over a price."

17. Life was cheap on Tanna, and the women seemed indifferent about their husbands or brothers dying.

In the afternoon, as the sounds of the muskets and the yelling of the warriors came unpleasantly near to us, Dr. Inglis, leaning against a post for a little while in silent prayer, looked on us and said, "The walls of Jerusalem were built in troublous times, and why not the Mission House on Tanna? But let us rest for this day, and pray for these poor Heathen."

We retired to a Native house that had been temporarily granted to us for rest, and there pled before God for them all. The noise and the discharge of muskets gradually receded, as if the Inland people were retiring; and towards evening the people around us returned to their villages. We were afterwards informed that five or six men had been shot dead; that their bodies had been carried by the conquerors from the field of battle, and cooked and eaten that very night at a boiling spring near the head of the bay, less than a mile from the spot where my house was being built. We had also a more graphic illustration of the surroundings into which we had come, through Dr. Inglis's Aneityum boy, who accompanied us as cook. When our tea was wanted next morning, the boy could not be found. After a while of great anxiety on our part, he returned, saying, "Missi, this is a dark land. The people of this land do dark works. At the boiling spring they have cooked and feasted upon the slain. They have washed the blood into the water; they have bathed there, polluting everything. I cannot get pure water to make your tea. What shall I do?"[18]

Dr. Inglis told him that he must try for water elsewhere, till the rains came and cleansed away the pollution; and that meanwhile, instead of tea, we would drink from the cocoanut, as they had often done before. The lad was quite relieved. It not a little astonished us, however, to see that his mind regarded their killing and eating each other as a thing scarcely to be noticed, but that it was horrible that they should spoil the water! How much are even our deepest instincts the creatures of mere circumstances! I, if trained like him, would probably have felt like him.

18. Here is Paton's first encounter with cannibalism — horrifying to a Christian culture, but less so to a culture that has warmed up to things like vampirism, human sacrifice, and the like.

Next evening, as we sat talking about the people, and the dark scenes around us, the quiet of the night was broken by a wild wailing cry from the villages around, long-continued and unearthly. We were informed that one of the wounded men, carried home from the battle, had just died; and that they had strangled his widow to death, that her spirit might accompany him to the other world, and be his servant there, as she had been here.[19] Now their dead bodies were laid side by side, ready to be buried in the sea. Our hearts sank to think of all this happening within ear-shot, and that we knew it not! Every new scene, every fresh incident, set more clearly before us the benighted condition and shocking cruelties of these Heathen people, and we longed to be able to speak to them of Jesus and the love of God. We eagerly tried to pick up every word of their language, that we might, in their own tongue, unfold to them the knowledge of the true God and of salvation from all these sins through Jesus Christ.

Dr. Inglis and I, with the help of the Natives from Aneityum, having accomplished all that could be done for lack of lime and sawn wood to finish the new Mission House on Tanna, made an agreement with the Natives for knives, calico, and axes to burn lime and prepare other things for our return. We then hastened back to Aneityum, that we might, if possible, get ready for settling on Tanna before the Rainy Season set in. That was rapidly approaching, and with it discomfort and unhealth to Europeans throughout all the Pacific Isles.

19. Widow killing upon a husband's death is very common with pagan tribes. People in India would practice *sati* (widow burning) for many generations until Christians put a stop to it.

CHAPTER VI – LIFE AND DEATH ON TANNA
A.D. 1858-1859. Age 34-35

Our small Missionary schooner, the *John Knox*, having no accommodation for lady passengers, and little for anybody else except the discomfort of lying on deck, we took advantage of a trader to convey us from Aneityum to Tanna. The Captain kindly offered to take us and about thirty casks and boxes to Port Resolution for £5, which we gladly accepted. After a few hours' sailing we were all safely landed on Tanna on the 5th November, 1858.[1] Dr. Geddie went for a fortnight to Umairarekar, now known as Kwamera, on the south side of Tanna, to assist in the settlement of Mr. and Mrs. Mathieson, and to help in making their house habitable and comfortable. Mr. Copeland, Mrs. Paton, and I were left at Port Resolution, to finish the building of our house there, and work our way into the good will of the Natives as best we could.

On landing, we found the people to be literally naked and painted Savages; they were at least as destitute of clothing as Adam and Eve after the fall, when they sewed fig-leaves for a girdle, and even more so, for the women wore only a tiny apron of grass, in some cases shaped like a skirt or girdle, the men an indescribable affair like a pouch or bag, and the children absolutely nothing whatever.[2]

At first they came in crowds to look at us, and at everything we did or had. We knew nothing of their language; we

1. At this point, they have been on the islands for 2 1/2 months.

2. This is an excellent example of a pioneering mission work (performed many times in history, but recorded in great detail for us by John G. Paton).

could not speak a single word to them, nor they to us. We looked at them, they at us; we smiled and nodded, and made signs to each other; this was our first meeting and parting. One day I observed two men, the one lifting up one of our articles to the other, and saying, "Nungsi nari enu?"

I concluded that he was asking, "What is this?" Instantly, lifting a piece of wood, I said, "Nungsi nari enu?"

They smiled and spoke to each other. I understood them to be saying, "He has got hold of our language now." Then they told me their name for the thing which I had pointed to. I found that they understood my question, What is this? or, What is that? and that I could now get from them the name of every visible or tangible thing around us! We carefully noted down every name they gave us, spelling all phonetically, and also every strange sound we heard from them; thereafter, by painstaking comparison of different circumstances, we tried to ascertain their meanings, testing our own guess by again cross-questioning the Natives. One day I saw two men approaching, when one, who was a stranger, pointed to me with his finger, and said, "Se nangin?"

Concluding that he was asking my name, I pointed to one of them with my finger, and looking at the other, inquired, "Se nangin?"

They smiled, and gave me their names. We were now able to get the names of persons and things, and so our ears got familiarized with the distinctive sounds of their language; and being always keenly on the alert, we made extraordinary progress in attempting bits of conversation and in reducing their speech for the first time to a written form—for the New Hebrideans had no literature, and not even the rudiments of an alphabet. I used to hire some of the more intelligent lads and men to sit and talk with us, and answer our questions about names and sounds; but they so often deceived us, and we, doubtless, misunderstood them so often, that this course was not satisfactory, till after we had gained some knowledge of their language and its construction, and they themselves had become interested in helping us. Amongst our most interesting helpers, and most trustworthy, were two aged chiefs—Nowa and Nouka[3]—in many respects two of Nature's noblest gentlemen, kind at heart to all, and distinguished by a certain native dignity of bearing. But they were both under the leadership of the war-chief Miaki,[4] a kind of devil-king over many villages and tribes. He and his brother were the recognized leaders in all deeds of darkness: they gloried in blood shedding, and in war, and in cannibalism; and they could always command a following of desperate men, who lived in and about their own village, and who were prepared to go anywhere and do anything at Miaki's will.

The Tannese had hosts of stone idols, charms, and sacred objects, which they abjectly feared, and in which they devoutly believed. They were given up to countless superstitions, and firmly glued to their dark heathen practices. Their worship was entirely a service of fear, its aim being to propitiate this or that Evil Spirit, to prevent calamity or to secure revenge. They deified their chiefs, like the Romans of old, so that almost every village or tribe had its own Sacred Man, and some of them had many. They exercised an extraordinary influence for evil, these village or tribal priests, and were believed to have the disposal of life and death through their sacred ceremonies, not only in their own tribe, but over all the Islands. Sacred men and women, wizards and witches, received presents regularly to influence the gods, and to remove sickness, or to cause it by the *Nahak*, i.e. incantation over remains of food, or the skin of fruit, such as banana, which the person has eaten on whom they wish to operate. They also worshiped the spirits of departed ancestors and heroes, through their material idols of wood and stone, but chiefly of stone. They feared these spirits and sought their aid; especially seeking to propitiate those who presided over war and peace, famine and plenty, health and sickness, destruction and prosperity, life and death. Their whole worship was one of slavish fear; and, so far as ever I could learn, they had no idea of a God of mercy or grace.[5]

3. Nowa and Nouka were chiefs under Miaki.

4. Miaki is the Georgewar-chief, a recognized leader over much of Tanna. Bad leaders cast a pall over an entire country.

5. Here are the characteristic sins of these people:
1. They worshiped idols, and their demons kept them in abject fear and superstition (based on false ideas).
2. They turned their chiefs (their government leaders) into gods.
3. They practiced witchcraft in an attempt to satiate or control the demon world.
4. They worshiped the spirits of departed ancestors as the Japanese do (and many other pagan peoples).

6. The most pagan tribes that are isolated from all civilizations still believe in some form of deity or deities. Although all creation points to God, these pagans would rather worship the gods of their own making. They worship the creature more than the Creator (including fingernails).

7. This references Roman Catholics who seem to gravitate towards idolatry with their beads, holy water, and relics.

8. The priests maintain some secrecy concerning religious practices. Thus, the people are kept ignorant concerning the darkness that is upheld in the religions. He references freemasonry, secret societies that do not reveal their true religious commitments until the members have advanced to the higher levels. The Christian faith is never kept in secret. Only demonic religious systems require secrecy. The Christian faith involves historical events that were "not done in a corner" (Acts 26:26).

Let me here give my testimony on a matter of some importance—that among these Islands, if anywhere men might be found destitute of the faculty of worship, men absolutely without idols, if such men exist under the face of the sky. Everything seemed to favor such a discovery; but the New Hebrides, on the contrary, are full of gods. The Natives, destitute of the knowledge of the true God, are ceaselessly groping after Him, if perchance they may find Him. Not finding Him, and not being able to live without some sort of God, they have made idols of almost everything: trees and groves, rocks and stones, springs and streams, insects and beasts, men and departed spirits, relics such as hair and finger nails,[6] the heavenly bodies and the volcanoes; in fact every being and every thing within the range of vision or of knowledge has been appealed to by them as God—clearly proving that the instincts of Humanity, however degraded, prompt man to worship and lean upon some Being or Power outside himself, and greater than himself, in whom he lives and moves and has his being, and without the knowledge of whom his soul cannot find its true rest or its eternal life. Imperfect acquaintance with the language and customs of certain tribes may easily have led early discoverers to proclaim that they have no sense of worship and no idols, because nothing of the kind is visible on the surface. But there is a sort of freemasonry in Heathen Religions; they have mysterious customs and symbols, which none even amongst themselves understand, except the priests and Sacred Men. It pays these men to keep their devotees in the dark—and how much more to deceive a passing inquirer! Nor need we hold up our hands in surprise at this; it pays also nearer home to pretend and to perpetuate a mystery about beads and crucifixes, holy water and relics[7]—a state of mind not so very far removed from that of the South Sea islander, not disproving but rather strongly proving that, whether savage or civilized, man must either know the true God, or must find an idol to put in His place.[8]

Further, these very facts—that they did worship something, that they believed in spirits of ancestors and heroes, and that they cherished many legends regarding those whom they had never seen, and handed these down to their children—and the fact that they had ideas about the invisible world and its inhabitants, made it not so hard as some might suppose to convey to their minds, once their language and modes of thought were understood, some clear ideal of Jehovah God as the great uncreated Spirit Father, who Himself created and sustains all that is.[9] It could not, however, be done offhand, or by a few airy lessons. The whole heart and soul and life had to be put into the enterprise. The idea that man disobeyed God, and was a fallen and sinful creature—the idea that this Jesus so lived and died and rose from the dead as to take away man's sin, and make it possible for men to return to God, and to be made into the very likeness of His Son Jesus—and the idea that this Jesus will at death receive to the mansions of Glory every creature under heaven that loves and tries to follow Him[10]—these ideas had to be woven into their spiritual consciousness, had to become the very warp and woof of their religion. But it could be done—that we believed because they were men, not beasts; it had been done—that we saw in the converts on Aneityum; and our hearts rose to the task with quenchless hope!

The Tannese called Heaven by the name Aneai, and we afterwards discovered that this was the name of the highest and most beautifully situated village on the island. Their best bit of Earth was to them the symbol and type of Heaven; their Canaan, too, was a kind of prophecy of another country, even a heavenly Canaan. The fact that they had an Aneai, a promised land, opening their minds naturally to our idea of the promised land of the future, the Aneai of the Gospel hope and faith. The universal craving to know the greater and more powerful gods, and to have them on their side, led them, whenever we could speak their language, to listen eagerly to all our stories about the Jehovah God and His Son Jesus, and all

9. Common ground is found (even with the pagans) in that they had a sense of deity, a sense of the eternal — something beyond this life.

10. A good summary here — the Christian message includes a message about God as Creator, a message on sin, and a message on the life, the death, and the resurrection of Jesus Christ.

11. Reference John 3:20, "For every one that doeth evil hateth the light, neither cometh to the light, lest his deeds should be reproved."

12. They loved to hear of the great and powerful God, but it was the message of repentance that they rejected. They did not want to repent of their idolatry and their heathen customs.

13. The translation of the Bible into the native language was essential for Protestant missions and resulted in much stronger discipleship (than what the Roman Catholics had accomplished in previous centuries).

14. Fotuna is a tiny island 60 miles to the east of Tanna. Joseph Copeland lived there from 1856 to 1866. The island has a population of 535, and the islanders are still known for their hymn-singing and gospel-singing groups.

the mighty works recorded in the Bible. But when we began to teach them that, in order to serve this Almighty and living Jehovah God, they must cast aside all their idols and leave off every heathen custom and vice, they rose in anger and cruelty against us, they persecuted every one that was friendly to the Mission, and passed us through the dreadful experiences to be hereafter recorded. It was the old battle of History; light had attacked darkness in its very stronghold, and it almost seemed for a season that the light would be finally eclipsed,[11] and that God's day would never dawn on Tanna.[12]

My companion Missionary, Mr. Copeland, had to go to Aneityum and take charge of Dr. Inglis's Station, during the absence of that distinguished Missionary and his devoted wife, while carrying through the press at home the first complete Aneityumese New Testament. He succeeded admirably in taking up and carrying forward all their work, and gave vital assistance in translating the Old Testament into the language of Aneityum, for his was an exact and scholarly mind.[13] After their return, he similarly occupied the station of Dr. Geddie on another part of the same island, while he sought reinvigoration in Nova Scotia on a well-merited furlough. Thereafter, he was placed on the island of Fotuna;[14] and there, with Mrs. Copeland, he labored devotedly and zealously, till at last she died and his own health gave way to such an extent as compelled him to retire from the Mission field. He found congenial employment in editing, with great acceptance, the *Sydney Presbyterian Witness*, and thereby still furthering the cause of the Gospel and of Missions.

A glance backwards over the story of the Gospel in the New Hebrides may help to bring my readers into touch with the events that are to follow. The ever-famous names of Williams and Harris are associated with the earliest efforts to introduce Christianity amongst this group of islands in the South Pacific Seas. John Williams and his young Missionary companion Harris, under the auspices of the London Missionary Society, landed on Erromanga on the 30th of November, 1839. Alas, within a few minutes of their touching land, both were clubbed to death; and the savages proceeded to cook and feast upon their bodies.[15] Thus were the New Hebrides baptized with the blood of Martyrs; and Christ thereby told the whole Christian world that He claimed these Islands as His own. His cross must yet be lifted up, where the blood of His saints has been poured forth in His name! The poor Heathen knew not that they had slain their best friends; but tears and prayers ascended for them from all Christian souls, wherever the story of the martyrdom on Erromanga was read or heard.

Again, therefore, in 1842, the London Missionary Society sent out Messrs. Turner and Nisbet to pierce this kingdom of Satan. They placed their standard on our chosen island of Tanna, the nearest to Erromanga. In less than seven months, however, their persecution by the savages became so dreadful, that we see them in a boat trying to escape by night with bare life. Out on that dangerous sea they would certainly have been lost, but the Ever-Merciful drove them back to land, and sent next morning a whaling vessel, which, contrary to custom, called there, and just in the nick of time. They, with all goods that could be rescued, were got safely on board, and sailed for Samoa.[16] Say not their plans and prayers were baffled; for God heard and abundantly blessed them there, beyond all their dreams. Dr. Turner has been specially used of God for educating many Native Teachers and Missionaries, and in translating and publishing edition after edition of the Bible, besides giving them many other educational and religious books in their own language—blessed work, in which, while I am writing these words, he and his gifted wife are still honorably and fruitfully engaged in the holy autumn of their days.

After these things, the London Missionary Society again and again placed Samoan Native Teachers on one or other island of the New Hebrides; but their unhealthiness, compared with the more wholesome Samoa or Rarotonga, so afflicted them with the dreaded ague and fever, besides what they en-

15. In December of 2009, Williams' descendants made the journey to Erromanga, where they received apologies from the descendants of the cannibals who had killed the missionary 170 years earlier. The President of Vanuatu (the New Hebrides) told the BBC that they felt the nation may be suffering a curse because of the way they treated the early missionaries. Iolu Johnson Abil was quoted in the news story from the BBC, "Since we claim to be a Christian country it is very important that we have a reconciliation like this." Nations always remember Christian martyrs, for hundreds of years, even thousands of years in some cases.

16. George Turner and Henry Nisbet were sent out by the London Missionary Society to the New Hebrides, but again, were driven out by unfriendly natives. They eventually ministered in Samoa with great success.

dured from the inhospitable savages themselves, that no effective Mission work had been accomplished there till at last the Presbyterian Missionaries were led to enter upon the scene. Christianity had no foothold anywhere on the New Hebrides, unless it were in the memory and the blood of the Martyrs of Erromanga.

The Rev. John Geddie and his wife, from Nova Scotia, were landed on Aneityum, the most southerly island of the New Hebrides, in 1848; and the Rev. John Inglis and his wife, from Scotland, were landed on the other side of the same island, in 1852. An agent for the London Missionary Society, the Rev. T. Powell, accompanied Dr. Geddie for about a year, to advise as to his settlement and to assist in opening up the work. Marvelous as it may seem, the Natives on Aneityum, showed interest in the Missionaries from the very first, and listened to their teachings; so that in a few years Dr. Inglis and Dr. Geddie saw about 3,500 savages throwing away their idols,[17] renouncing their Heathen customs, and avowing themselves to be worshipers of the true Jehovah God. Slowly, yet progressively, they unlearned their Heathenism; surely and hopefully they learned Christianity and civilization. In course of time a simple form of Family Worship was introduced into and observed by every household on the island;[18] God's blessing was asked on every meal; peace and public order were secured; and property was perfectly safe under the sanctifying and civilizing Gospel of Christ. And by-and-by these Missionaries lived to see the whole Bible, which they and Mr. Copeland had so painfully translated, placed in the hands of the Aneityumese by the aid of the British and Foreign Bible Society—that noblest handmaid of every Missionary enterprise. But how was this accomplished? As a boon of charity? Listen! When these Missionaries "came to this Island, there were no Christians there; when they left it, there were no Heathens."

Further, these poor Aneityumese, having glimpses of the Word of God, determined to have a Holy Bible in their own mother tongue, wherein before no book or page ever had been

---

17. Instant success for the Geddies and Inglises — 3,500 natives renounced their idols.

18. Family worship is basic to rooting the faith and discipling these little nations. If families will perpetuate the faith generation by generation, there must be attention paid to Deuteronomy 6:7-9 and Ephesians 6:4. The early missionaries to Hawaii and other places were very careful to teach parents to read the Bible and pray every day with their children.

written in the history of their race. The consecrated brain and hand of their Missionaries kept toiling day and night in translating the book of God; and the willing hands and feet of the Natives kept toiling through fifteen long but unwearying years, planting and preparing arrowroot to pay the £1,200 required to be laid out in the printing and publishing of the book. Year after year the arrowroot, too sacred to be used for their daily food, was set apart as the Lord's portion; the Missionaries sent it to Australia and Scotland, where it was sold by private friends, and the whole proceeds consecrated to this purpose. On the completion of the great undertaking by the Bible Society, it was found that the Natives had earned as much as to pay every penny of the outlay; and their first Bibles went out to them, purchased with the consecrated toils of fifteen years![19] Some of our friends may think that the sum was large; but I know, from experience, that if such a difficult job had been carried through the press and so bound by any other printing establishment, the expense would have been greater far. One book of Scripture, printed by me in Melbourne for the Aniwans at a later day, under the auspices of the Bible Society too, cost eight shillings per leaf, and that was the cheapest style; and this the Aniwans also paid for by dedicating their arrowroot[20] to God.

Let those who lightly esteem their Bibles think on those things. Eight shillings for every leaf, or the labor and proceeds of fifteen years for the Bible entire, did not appear to these poor converted savages too much to pay for that Word of God, which had sent to them the Missionaries, which had revealed to them the grace of God in Christ, and which had opened their eyes to the wonders and glories of redeeming love! They had felt, and we had observed, that in all lands and amongst all branches of the human family, the Holy Bible is, wheresoever received and obeyed, the power of God unto salvation; it had lifted them out of savagery, and set them at the feet of the Lord Jesus. Oh that the pleasure seeking men and women of the world could only taste and feel the real joy of those who

19. The native believers were not to rely upon outside charity. They used arrowroot to pay the 1,200 pounds required for publishing the Bible. They worked and saved for 15 years for their Bibles.

20. Arrowroot is a starch, good for people with dietary restrictions. It was used in the Victorian era to make puddings, cakes, biscuits, hot sauces, and jellies.

The Landing at Tana one of the New Hebrides by William Hodges

know and love the true God—a heritage which the world and all that pertains thereto cannot give to them, but which the poorest and humblest followers of Jesus inherit and enjoy!

My first house on Tanna was on the old site occupied by Turner and Nisbet, near the shore, for obvious reasons, and only a few feet above tide-mark. So was that of Mr. Mathieson, handy for materials as goods being landed, and, as we imagined, close to the healthy breezes of the sea. Alas! we had to learn by sad experience, like our brethren in all untried Mission fields. The sites proved to be hot-beds for Fever and Ague, mine especially; and much of this might have been escaped by building on the higher ground, and in the sweep of the refreshing trade-winds. For all this, however, no one was to blame; everything was done for the best, according to the knowledge then possessed. Our house was sheltered behind by an abrupt hill about two hundred feet high, which gave the site a feeling of coziness. It was surrounded and much shaded, by beautiful breadfruit trees, and very large cocoanut trees; too largely beautiful, indeed, for they shut out many a healthy breeze that we sorely needed! There was a long swamp at the head of the bay, and, the ground at the other end on which our house stood being scarcely raised perceptibly higher, the malaria almost constantly enveloped us. Once, after a smart attack of the fever, an intelligent Chief said to me, "Missi, if you stay here, you will soon die! No Tanna man sleeps so low down as you do, in this damp weather, or he too would die. We sleep on the high ground, and the trade-wind keeps us well. You must go and sleep on the hill, and then you will have better health."[21]

I at once resolved to remove my house to higher ground, at the earliest practicable moment; heavy though the undertaking would necessarily be, it seemed our only hope of being able to live on the island. Alas, for one of us, it was already too late!

My dear young wife, Mary Ann Robson—daughter of Peter Robson, Esquire, a well known and highly-esteemed gentleman, at Coldstream on the Borders—and I were landed on Tanna on the 5th November, 1858, in excellent health and full of all tender and holy hopes. On the 12th February, 1859, she was confined of a son; for two days or so both mother and child seemed to prosper, and our island-exile thrilled with joy! But the greatest of sorrows was treading hard upon the heels of that joy! My darling's strength showed no signs of rallying. She had an attack of ague[22] and fever a few days before; on the third day or so thereafter, it returned, and attacked her every second day with increasing severity for a fortnight. Diarrhea ensued, and symptoms of pneumonia, with slight delirium at intervals; and then in a moment, altogether unexpectedly, she died on the 3rd March.[23] To crown my sorrows, and complete my loneliness, the dear baby-boy, whom we had named after her father, Peter Robert Robson, was taken from me after one week's sickness, on the 20th March. Let those who have ever passed through any similar darkness as of midnight feel for me; as for all others, it would be more than vain to try to paint my sorrows!

I knew then, when too late, that our work had been entered on too near the beginning of the rainy season. We were

21. The problem was the mosquito, breeding in the swamps (spreading malaria). The sea breezes would not have done much for them one way or the other. No doubt the rainy season added to the population of mosquitos.

22. Ague is probably malaria, involving fever and uncontrollable shaking.

23. Paton's wife survived four months on Tanna and passed away soon after the birth of her son.

both, however, healthy and hearty; and I daily pushed on with the house, making things hourly more comfortable, in the hope that long lives were before us both, to be spent for Jesus in seeking the salvation of the perishing Heathen. Oh, the vain yet bitter regrets, that my dear wife had not been left on Aneityum till after the unhealthy Rainy Season! But no one advised this course; and she, high-spirited, full of buoyant hope, and afraid of being left behind me, or of me being left without her on Tanna,[24] refused to allow the thing to be suggested. In our mutual inexperience, and with our hearts aglow for the work of our lives, we incurred this risk which should never have been incurred; and I only refer to the matter thus, in the hope that others may take warning.

Stunned by that dreadful loss, in entering upon this field of labor to which the Lord had Himself so evidently led me, my reason seemed for a time almost to give way. Ague and fever, too, laid a depressing and weakening hand upon me, continuously recurring, and reaching oftentimes the very height of its worst burning stages. But I was never altogether forsaken. The ever-merciful Lord sustained me, to lay the precious dust of my beloved Ones in the same quiet grave, dug for them close by at the end of the house; in all of which last offices my own hands, despite breaking heart, had to take the principal share! I built the grave round and round with coral blocks, and covered the top with beautiful white coral, broken small as gravel; and that spot became my sacred and much-frequented shrine, during all the following months and years when I labored on for the salvation of these savage Islanders amidst difficulties, dangers, and deaths. Whensoever Tanna turns to the Lord, and is won for Christ, men in after-days will find the memory of that spot still green—where with ceaseless prayers and tears I claimed that land for God in which I had "buried my dead" with faith and hope. But for Jesus, and the fellowship He vouchsafed me there, I must have gone mad and died beside that lonely grave![25]

24. Tanna was the most difficult island and stood against the Gospel for a long time.

25. Heart-rending trials and tribulations pave the way in missionary work like this.

The organ of the Church to which we belonged, *The Reformed Presbyterian Magazine*, published the following words of condolence: "In regard to the death of Mrs. Paton one feeling of grief and regret will fill the hearts of all who knew her. To add a sentence to the singularly just and graceful tribute Mr. Inglis pays to the memory of the deceased, would only mar its pathos and effect. Such language, from one accustomed to weigh carefully every word he pens, bespeaks at once the rare excellences of her that is gone, as well as the heavy loss our Mission and our Church have sustained in her death. Her parents, who gave her by a double baptism to the Lord, have this consolation, that her death may exert a more elevating and sanctifying influence for good, than the longest life of many ordinary Christians. Deep sympathy with Mr. Paton will pervade the church, in the sore trial with which he has been visited."

Dr. Inglis, my brother Missionary on Aneityum, wrote to *The Reformed Presbyterian Magazine*: "I trust all those who shed tears of sorrow on account of her early death will be enabled in the exercise of faith and resignation to say, 'The Will of the Lord be done; the Lord gave and the Lord hath taken away: blessed be the Name of the Lord!'[26] I need not say how deeply we sympathize with her bereaved parents, as well as with her sorrowing husband. By her death the Mission has sustained a heavy loss. We were greatly pleased with Mrs. Paton during the period of our short intercourse with her. Her mind, naturally vigorous, had been cultivated by a superior education. She was full of Missionary spirit, and took a deep interest in the Native women. This was seen further, when she went to Tanna, where, in less than three months, she had collected a class of eight females, who came regularly to her to receive instruction.[27] There was about her a maturity of thought, a solidity of character, a loftiness of aim and purpose, rarely found in one so young. Trained up in the fear of the Lord from childhood, like another Mary she had evidently chosen that good part, which is never taken away from those

26. Dr. Inglis quotes Job 1:21.

27. Mrs. Paton had developed a Bible study for eight native women upon arriving at Tanna.

possessed of it. When she left this island, she had to all human appearance a long career of usefulness and happiness on Earth before her, but the Lord has appointed otherwise. She has gone, as we trust, to her rest and her reward. The Lord has said to her as He said to David, 'Thou didst well in that it was in thine heart to build a House for My Name.' Let us watch and pray, for our Lord cometh as a thief in the night."

The Missionaries assembled at Tanna, on April 27th, 1859, passed the following resolution: "That this meeting deeply and sincerely sympathizes with Mr. Paton in the heavy and trying bereavement with which the Lord has seen meet to visit him in the death of his beloved wife and child; and the Missionaries record their sense of the loss this Mission has sustained, in the early, sudden, and unexpected death of Mrs. Paton. Her earnest Christian character, her devoted Missionary spirit, her excellent education, her kind and obliging disposition, and the influence she was fast acquiring over the Natives, excited expectations of great future usefulness. That they express their heartfelt sympathy with the parents and other relatives of the deceased; that they recommend Mr. Paton to pay a visit to Aneityum for the benefit of his health; that they commend him to the tender mercies of Him who was sent to comfort all who mourn; and that they regard this striking dispensation of God's providence as a loud call to themselves, to be more in earnest in attending to the sate of their own souls, and more diligent in pressing the concerns of eternity on the minds of others."

Soon after her death, the good Bishop Selwyn called at Port Resolution, Tanna, in his Mission Ship. He came on shore to visit me, accompanied by the Rev. J. O. Patteson. They had met Mrs. Paton on Aneityum in the previous year soon after our arrival, and, as she was then the picture of perfect health, they also felt her loss very keenly. Standing with me beside the grave of mother and child, I weeping aloud on his one hand, and Patteson—afterward the Martyr Bishop of Kakupu—sobbing silently on the other, the godly Bishop Selwyn poured out his heart to God amidst sobs and tears, during which he laid his hands on my head, and invoked Heaven's richest consolations and blessings on me and my trying labors.[28] The virtue of that kind of Episcopal consecration I did and do most warmly appreciate! They urged me by many appeals to take a trip with them round the Islands, as my life was daily in great danger from the Savages; they generously offered to convey me directly to Aneityum, or wherever I wished to go. I greatly needed rest and change. But, with a heart full of gratitude to them, I yet resolved to remain, feeling that I was at the post of duty where God had placed me; and besides, fearing that if I left once the Natives would not let me land again on returning to their island, I determined to hold on as long as possible, though feeling very weak and suffering badly from ague.

Sorrow and love make me linger a little to quote these extracts, printed in The Reformed Presbyterian Magazine for January 1860, from Mrs. Paton's last letter to her friends at home. It is dated from Port Resolution, Tanna, 28th December, 1858.

"My Dear Father, Mother, and Sisters:

"When I wrote last, we were just about to leave Aneityum for Tanna, the sphere of our future labors. One can have no idea of the dark and degraded state of these poor Heathen, unless really living amongst them. Still we trust that the cloud which has so long enveloped Tanna will soon be rolled away, and the light of the Sun of Righteousness irradiate this dark land. We have been here about two months, and so far the people among whom we live appear to be friendly. A numerous priesthood reside in the neighborhood of the Volcano, from whom we anticipate much opposition, as they know that wherever the Missionary gains a footing among the people, their influence is lost. The Tannese are very avaricious. If one renders the least assistance, he demands a most exorbitant pay; indeed, we can hardly satisfy them. We have a number of male, but very few female visitors, the latter being just slaves to do all the work.[29] The men disfigure their faces with red

28. Bishop George Selwyn (from New Zealand) and Rev. John Patteson were some of the most well-known missionaries in the South Pacific, representing the Anglican Church. Patteson was martyred in the Solomon Islands twelve years after this meeting.

29. The last letter from Mrs. Paton to her family describes the Tannese. They are avaricious (greedy or covetous). Typical to pagan societies, the women do all the work (while the men engage in tribal warfare and trade the women around).

and black paint, and always carry spears and clubs. At first I was quite shocked with their appearance, but one soon becomes accustomed to such sights. They likewise possess powder and muskets—guns and tobacco being the chief objects of their ambition. Indeed, such is their degraded condition that, were not the power and grace of God all-sufficient, one might almost despair of ever making any impression on them. All the Natives are in a state of entire nudity, with this exception, that females wear short petticoats made of grass. Young girls are very fond of beads, and sometimes have their necks quite covered with them. They likewise bore holes in the ear, from which they suspend large rolls (circles) of tortoise shell. Two or three little girls come about me, whom I am teaching to sew and sing; but no great good can be accomplished till we master their language. We have picked up a good many words, and I trust, with the blessing of God, will soon be able to speak to them of things pertaining to their everlasting peace.

"Port Resolution is a most beautiful Bay. I have never seen such a lovely spot. Indeed, everything around delights the eye, and 'only man is vile.'[30] Our house is at the head of the Bay, on the foundation of Dr. Turner's, from which he had to fly fifteen years ago. The sea, at full tide, comes within a few yards of the door. Mr. Copeland is staying with us now. During the Rainy Season, he is to be sometimes with us, and at other times with Mr. Mathieson, who is in delicate health. The thermometer averages from 80-85 degrees. The Rainy Season having now set in, it is not likely we will have any opportunity of sending or receiving letters for three or four months. I am wearying very much to hear from you. I can hardly realize that nine months have rolled away since I left bonny Scotia! How many changes will take place before I again revisit it! Both my husband and I are in excellent health, and though the heat feels oppressive, we like the climate very well. A Happy New Year to you all, and many happy returns! I am writing hurriedly, as a vessel has called, and leaves tomorrow morning. I expect to get

30. "Only man is vile" comes from Reginald Heber's famous hymn, "From Greenland's Icy Mountains."

all the news when you write, for my interest in and affection for home and home-folks haven't in the least abated.

"Now I must conclude; with love to you all and to all my companions, believe me ever your loving daughter and sister,

"Mary Ann Paton."

Her last words were, "Oh, that my dear mother were here! She is a good woman, my mother, a jewel of a woman."

Then, observing Mr. Copeland near by, she said, "Oh, Mr. Copeland, I did not know you were there! You must not think that I regret coming here, and leaving my mother. If I had the same thing to do over again, I would do it with far more pleasure, yes, with all my heart. Oh no! I do not regret leaving home and friends, though at the time I felt it keenly."

Soon after this, looking up and putting her hand in mine, she said—

"J.C. wrote to our Janet saying, that young Christians under their first impressions thought they could do anything or make any sacrifice for Jesus, and he asked if she believed it, for he did not think they could, when tested; but Janet wrote back that she believed they could, and" (added she with great emphasis) "I believe it is true!"

In a moment, altogether unexpectedly, she fell asleep in Jesus, with these words on her lips. "Not lost, only gone before to be forever with the Lord"[31]—my heart keeps saying or singing to itself from that hour till now.

Ever since the day of our happy marriage, a strange presentiment possessed my heart that I should lose her soon and suddenly. Perhaps I am not the first who has wrestled through such unworthy forebodings—that that which was so precious and blessed was about to be withdrawn! Our short united life had been cloudless and happy; I felt her loss beyond all conception or description, in that dark land. It was very difficult to be resigned, left alone, and in sorrowful circumstance; but feeling immovably assured that my God and Father was too wise and loving to err in anything that He does or permits, I looked up to the Lord for help, and struggled on in His

31. Mrs. Paton dies in faith-filled testimonies. Her last words before she died were, "Only gone before to be forever with the Lord."

32. The priority is for us to love Christ and serve Him here, whether we are in comfort or in severe trial (as Paton experienced in losing his wife).

work.[32] I do not pretend to see through the mystery of such visitations—wherein God calls away the young, the promising, and those sorely needed for His service here; but this I do know and feel, that, in the light of such dispensations, it becomes us all to love and serve our blessed Lord Jesus so that we may be ready at His call for death and Eternity.

CHAPTER VII – MISSION LEAVES FROM TANNA
A.D. 1859 -1860. Age 35-36

In the first letter, sent jointly by Mr. Copeland and myself from Tanna to the Church at home, the following statements occur:

"We found the Tannese to be painted Savages, enveloped in all the superstition and wickedness of Heathenism. All the men and children go in a state of nudity. The older women wear grass skirts, and the young women and girls, grass or leaf aprons like Eve in Eden. They are exceedingly ignorant, vicious, and bigoted, and almost void of natural affection. Instead of the inhabitants of Port Resolution being improved by coming in contact with white men they are rendered much worse; for they have learned all their vices but none of their virtues—if such are possessed by the pioneer traders among such races! The Sandal-wood[1] Traders are as a class the most godless of men, whose cruelty and wickedness make us ashamed to own them as our countrymen. By them the poor defenseless Natives are oppressed and robbed on every hand;[2] and if they offer the slightest resistance, they are ruthlessly silenced by the musket or revolver.

1. Sandalwood is a heavy, yellow wood with an odor that hangs on for many more years than other species of wood. It is found in India, the South Pacific, Australia, Bangladesh, and Nepal. Sandalwood oil is especially desired for fragrance and cosmetics (and incense).

2. The Sandalwood traders robbed, murdered, and enslaved the natives — shameful treatment of these people at the hands of the white, materialist traders.

3. There were three worldviews operating during the 19th century mission work: (1) the Western materialists and apostate Christians, (2) the pagan animists, and (3) the Christian missionaries. Sadly, the Western materialists in many cases were more successful with their "evangelism" and did a great deal to worsen the natives (and harden them against the Christian Gospel).

4. Christian missionaries are always challenged with this question: Shall they play along with the cheating, the systems of bribes, and the fraudulent practices carried on by the natives and government officials? Some missionaries resist it, in order not to support the natives in their sin. They do so at their own peril. In this case, John G. Paton was forced to make three payments for the same piece of property.

Few months here pass without some of them being so shot, and, instead of their murderers feeling ashamed, they boast of how they dispatch them.[3] Such treatment keeps the Natives always burning under a desire for revenge, so that it is a wonder any white man is allowed to come among them. Indeed, all Traders here are able to maintain their position only by revolvers and rifles; but we hope a better state of affairs is at hand for Tanna."

The novelty of our being among them soon passed away, and they began to show their avarice and deceitfulness in every possible way. The Chiefs united and refused to give us the half of the small piece of land which had been purchased, on which to build our Mission House, and when we attempted to fence in the part they had left to us, they "tabooed" it, i.e. threatened our Teachers and us with death if we proceeded further with the work. This they did by placing certain reeds stuck into the ground here and there around our house, which our Aneityumese servants at once knew the meaning of, and warned us of our danger; so we left off making the fence, that we might if possible evade all offense. They then divided the few breadfruit and cocoanut trees on the ground amongst themselves, or demanded such payment for these trees as we did not possess, and threatened revenge on us if the trees were injured by any person. They now became so unreasonable and offensive, and our dangers so increased, as to make our residence amongst them extremely trying. At this time a vessel called; I bought from the Captain the things for payment which they demanded; on receiving it, they lifted the Taboo, and for a little season appeared to be friendly again. This was the third payment they had got for that site, and to yield was teaching them a cruel lesson; all this we felt and clearly saw, but they had by some means to be conciliated, if possible, and our lives had to be saved, if that could be done without dishonor to the Christian name.[4]

After these events, a few weeks of dry weather began to tell against the growth of their yams and bananas. The drought was instantly ascribed to us and our God. The Natives far and near were summoned to consider the matter in public assembly. Next day, Nouka, the high chief, and Miaki, the war-chief, his nephew, came to inform us that two powerful Chiefs had openly declared in that assembly that if the Harbor people did not at once kill us or compel us to leave the island they would, unless the rain came plentifully in the meantime, summon all the Inland people and murder both our Chiefs and us. The friendly Chiefs said, "Pray to your Jehovah God for rain, and do not go far beyond your door for a time; we are all in greatest danger, and if war breaks out we fear we cannot protect you."[5]

But this friendliness was all pretense; they themselves, being Sacred Men, professed to have the power of sending or withholding rain, and tried to fix the blame of their discomfiture on us. The rage of the poor ignorant Heathen was thereby fed against us. The Ever-Merciful, however, again interposed on our behalf. On the following Sabbath, just when we were assembling for Worship, rain began to fall, and in great abundance. The whole inhabitants believed, apparently, that it was sent to save us in answer to our prayers; so they met again, and resolved to allow us to remain on Tanna. Alas! on the other hand, the continuous and heavy rains brought much sickness and fever in their train, and again their Sacred Men pointed to us as the cause. Hurricane winds also blew and injured their fruits and fruit-trees—another opportunity for our enemies to lay the blame of everything upon the Missionaries and their Jehovah God! The trial and the danger daily grew, of living among a people so dreadfully benighted by superstition, and so easily swayed by prejudice and passion.

On Sabbath afternoon, the 6th of January, 1860, in a severe gale, we were surprised to see a large Sydney vessel come to anchor in the Harbor at Port Resolution, right opposite our house. Though wind and sea were both dangerously high, the Captain and all hands, as we were afterwards informed, coolly went to sleep. Gradually, but quite perceptibly, the vessel was allowed to drift as if by deliberate intention, till she struck on

5. Deceit, covetousness, and random acts of violence define these depraved tribes. All-in-all this makes for a very dangerous world.

6. The traders, as always, were wicked men and served only to further set the natives against the missionaries.

7. Besides killing in war, the natives also engaged in human sacrifice, and they would eat of the sacrifice. This is not unusual for pagan countries in the history of Christian missions.

8. The natives would even dig up the buried dead and consume their flesh — terrible barbarism at its very worst.

the beach at the head of the Bay, and there was soon broken up and became a total wreck. For this also the ignorant Natives gave us credit,[6] as for everything uncommon or disagreeable on Tanna; but we were ever conscious that our Lord Jesus was near us, and all trials that lead us to cling closer in fellowship with our Saviour are really blessings in disguise. The Captain of that vessel, known to us only as "Big Hays," and his wife, said to be the wife of a man in Sydney who had run away with him, and his like-minded crew became by their shocking conduct a horrible curse to our poor Islanders, and greatly embittered the feeling against us. They were armed with deadly weapons, and did their wicked will amongst our Natives, who durst not attack so large a party of desperate and well-armed men. But they were white people, and so were the Missionaries; to the savage mind that was enough, and revenge would be taken upon the first white faces, however innocent, who came within their power.

The Natives of Tanna were well-nigh constantly at war amongst themselves, every man doing that which was right in his own eyes, and almost every quarrel ending in an appeal to arms. Besides many battles far inland, one was fought beside our houses and several around the Harbor. In these conflicts many men were bruised with clubs and wounded with arrows, but few lives were lost, considering the savage uproar and frenzy of the scene. In one case, of which we obtained certain information, seven men were killed in an engagement; and, according to Tannese custom, the warriors and their friends feasted on them at the close of the fray,[7] the widows of the slain being also strangled to death, and similarly disposed of. Besides those who fell in war, the Natives living in our quarter had killed and feasted on eight persons, usually, in sacrificial rites.

It is said that the habitual Cannibal's desire for human flesh becomes so horrible that he has been known to disinter and feast upon those recently buried.[8] Two cases of this revolting barbarism were reported as having occurred amongst the villagers living near us. On another occasion the great chief Nouka took seriously unwell, and his people sacrificed three women for his recovery! All such cruel and horrifying practices, however, they tried to conceal from us; and many must have perished in this way of whom we, though living at their doors, were never permitted to hear.

Amongst the Heathen, in the New Hebrides, and especially on Tanna, woman is the down-trodden slave of man. She is kept working hard, and bears all the heavier burdens, while he walks by her side with musket, club, or spear. If she offends him, he beats or abuses her at pleasure. A savage gave his poor wife a severe beating in front of our house and just before our eyes, while in vain we strove to prevent it. Such scenes were so common that no one thought of interfering. Even if the woman died in his hands, or immediately thereafter, neighbors took little notice, if any at all.[9] And their children were so little cared for, that my constant wonder was how any of them survived at all! As soon as they are able to knock about, they are left practically to care for themselves; hence the very small affection they show towards their parents, which results in the aged who are unable to work being neglected, starved to death, and sometimes even more directly and violently destroyed.[10]

A Heathen boy's education consists in being taught to aim skillfully with the bow, throw the spear faultlessly at a mark, to wield powerfully the club and tomahawk, and to shoot well with musket and revolver when these can be obtained. He accompanies his father and brothers in all the wars and preparations for war, and is diligently initiated into all their cruelties and lusts, as the very prerequisite of his being regarded and acknowledged to be a man and a warrior. The girls have, with their mother and sisters, to toil and slave in the village plantations, to prepare all the materials for fencing these around, to bear every burden, and to be knocked about at will by the men and boys.

Oh, how sad and degraded is the position of Woman where the teaching of Christ is unknown, or disregarded

9. Men could beat their wives to death, at will — no criminal penalties at all. Christianity has produced a better situation for women in every culture. In their journeys across America in the early 19th century, Lewis and Clark found the Native American women treated very cruelly. The women did most of the work, even rowing the canoes while the men saved their strength for warfare and sexual exploits.

10. Pagan societies eventually work towards euthanasia for the inconvenient elderly. Life is cheap to them. Modern pagan societies develop more acceptable terms for euthanasia like "doctor-assisted suicide."

11. A right view of Christian missions and the history of the world would find that the Lord Jesus Christ has made a powerful impact on the entire world, and all its institutions over 2000 years! Speaking of Christ, David writes in Psalm 72: "Kings shall fall down before Him; all nations shall serve Him. For He will deliver the needy when he cries, the poor also, and him who has no helper. He will spare the poor and needy, and will save the souls of the needy. He will redeem their life from oppression and violence; and precious shall be their blood in His sight."

12. Tanna was a slow-going work. Twenty-four miles of walking in one day would have taken at least eight hours.

though known! It is the Christ of the Bible, it is His Spirit entering into humanity, that has lifted Woman, and made her the helpmate and the friend of Man, not his toy or his slave.[11]

To the best of our observation, the Heathen, though vaguely following some division of the week into seven days, spent the Sabbath on Tanna much the same as their other days were spent even when some were led to give up manual labors on that day, they spent it, like too many Christians elsewhere, in visiting friends and in selfish pleasures, on feasting and drinking. After we had been about one year on the island, we had a morning Church Service, attended by about ten Chiefs and as many women and children belonging to them; though, once the Service was over, they paid no more attention to the Lord's Day. On some of the more Northern Islands of the group, the Heathen had a sacred day. Twice, sailing with the *Dayspring*, we cast anchor at an Island, but could not see a single Native till next day, when one who could speak broken English informed us that none of the people had been seen moving about because they were "keeping their Sunday." A number of the Tannese spoke a little English, but they were the worst and most treacherous characters of all. They had imbibed the profane Trader's language and his hatred of Missionaries and their work; and these, added to their own Heathen prejudices, made them the most troublesome and dangerous of men.

After the Sabbath Morning Service we used to walk many miles, visiting all the villages within reach, even before we had got so much of their language as to be able to speak freely to the people. Sometimes we made a circuit amongst them, ten or twelve miles away and as many back again.[12] We tried to talk a little to all who were willing to listen; and we conducted the Worship of Jehovah, wherever we could find two or three disposed to gather together and to sit or kneel beside us. It was to flesh and blood weary work, and in many ways disheartening—no responsive faces and hearts there to cheer us on and lift us up into fellowship with the Lord! But it helped us to see the people, and to get acquainted with the districts around; it also secured for us very considerable audiences, except when they were engaged in war.

No real progress could be made in imparting to them spiritual knowledge, till we had attained some familiarity with their language. By finding out, as before recorded, the Tannese for "What is this?" and "What is his or her name?" we got the names of things and people, and made amazing progress towards mutual intelligence. We soon found out that there were two distinct languages spoken in and around Port Resolution; but we confined ourselves to that which was understood as far as the other Mission Station; and, by God's help and great diligence, we were able ere long to speak to them of sin and salvation through Jesus Christ

Twelve Aneityumese Teachers were at this time living on Tanna, but they had no Schools, and no Books in Tannese, for that language had never yet been reduced to forms that could be printed. The work of the Teachers, besides telling to the people around all that they could regarding Christ and the Christian religion, found its highest value in presenting through their own spirit and character a nobler type of life than any that Heathenism could show.[13]

When a Missionary arrives, the Teacher's first duty is to help him in house-building, fencing, and the many manual and other toils required in organizing the new Station, besides accompanying him on the inland journeys, assisting him in regard to the language as far as possible, and in general furthering the cause. But in altogether virgin soil like that of Tanna, the Aneityumese Teacher, or one from any other island, had the language to acquire first of all, not less than the European Missionary, and was therefore of little use except for manual labor, and that too had to be carried on by signs much more than by words. Not only has every island its own tongue, differing widely from and unintelligible to all the others, but even the people on one side of an island could not sometimes understand or converse with the people on the opposite side

13. The missionaries were assisted by natives from Aneityum, twelve Christian teachers who had come to Christ under the work of the Inglises.

14. The effect of the Tower of Babel was quite strong on these tiny tribes, who would not speak the language of another tribe that resided a mere 10-20 miles distant. The cultural decentralization that came when God confused the tongues is quite impressive (Gen. 11:1-9).

15. Laudanum is a tincture containing 10% opium.

16. Excessive alcohol aids the tribes in their irrational drive towards war and destruction.

of the same. This rendered our work in the New Hebrides not only exceptionally difficult, but its progressive movement distressingly slow.[14]

Word had reached Tanna, that, in a quarrel with Sandal-wooders, the Erromangans had murdered three white men and a number of Natives in their employment, in revenge for the white men's shamefully entreating and murdering the Erromangans. On Tanna all such news were reported and talked over, when the Chiefs and their men of war met for their evening repast—an event that generally wound up with drinking *Kava*, which first produced intoxication like whisky and then stupefaction like a dose of laudanum.[15] Excited by the rumors from Erromanga, they had drunk more than usual, and lay about their Village Drinking-Hall—a helpless host. Enemies from an inland tribe stealthily drew near, and discharged their muskets amongst them in the dark, killing one man, and so, according to their custom, war was known to be declared.[16]

Early next morning, Miaki, the war-chief, dispatched his herald to sound the Conch and summon the people to battle. He made the Harbor and all the country resound with it for six miles around, and the savage hordes gathered to the call. Putting our trust in God, we quietly resolved to attend as usual to our work and await the result. Excitement and terror drove the Natives hither and thither. One man close to us being nearly killed, his friends assembled in great force, and with clubs and spears, tomahawks and muskets, drove the offending tribe more than a mile into the bush. They, in turn, being reinforced, drove their enemies back again to the beach. There, seated within hearing distance, they carried on a grand sort of barbarous-Homeric scolding match, and exhausted their rage in javelins of reproach. A great relief seemed thereby to ensue, for the rival Chiefs thereon approached our house and entreated me to dress their wounds! I did so, and appealed to them for peace, and got their promise to let that conflict come to an end. Alas, for the passing influence of such appeals—for I learned shortly after this, on my return from Aneityum, where I had gone for a fortnight to recruit from the effects of an almost three months' continuance of recurring ague and fever,[17] that eight of the Harbor people had been murdered near our house at Port Resolution. The Natives got into a dreadfully unsettled state, each one wondering in terror who would be the next to fall.

About the time of my dear wife's death, our brother Missionary, Mr. Mathieson, also became exceedingly unwell. His delicate frame fast gave way, and brought with it weakness of the mind as well; and he was removed to Aneityum apparently in a dying condition. These sad visitations had a bad effect on the natives, owing to their wild superstitions about the cause of death and sickness. We had reason to fear that they would even interfere with the precious grave, over which we kept careful watch for a season; but God mercifully restrained them. Unfortunately, however, one of my Aneityumese Teachers who had gone round to Mr. Mathieson's Station took ill and died there, and this rekindled all their prejudices. He, poor fellow, before death said, "I shall not again return to Port Resolution, or see my dear Missi; but tell him that I die happy, for I love Jesus much, and I am going to Jesus!"

Hearing these things, the natives insolently demanded me to tell them the cause of his death, and of Mr. Mathieson's trouble, and of the other deaths.[18] Other reasoning or explanation being to them useless, I turned the tables, and demanded them to tell me why all this trouble and death had overtaken us in their land, and whether they themselves were not the cause of it all? Strange to say, this simple question turned the whole current of their speculations. They held meeting after meeting to discuss it for several days, and returned the message, "We do not blame you, and you must not blame us, for causing these troubles and deaths; but we believe that a Bushman must have got hold of a portion of something we had eaten, and must have thrown it to the great Evil Spirit in the volcano, thereby bringing all these troubles and curses."

17. Paton spent two weeks in Aneityum to recover from malaria.

18. Pagans work overtime trying to identify a cause for a particular death, blaming it on a certain action. Christians are cautious about assigning specific causes to a death, outside of the fact that God has inscrutable, higher purposes for the timing of deaths.

Another Chief vindicated himself and others thus: "Kara-panamun, the Aurumanu or great Evil Spirit of Tanna, whom we all fear and worship, is causing these troubles; for he knows that if we become worshipers of your Jehovah God, we cannot continue to fear him, or present him with the best of every-thing, as our forefathers have always done; he is angry at you and at us all."

The fear of the deaths and troubles being ascribed to them silenced their talk against us for a season; but very little made them either friends or foes, as the next event will too painfully show.

Nowhat, an old Chief of the highest rank from Aneityum, who spoke Tannese and was much respected by the natives all round the south side of Tanna, came on a visit to our is-land. After returning home, he became very ill and died in a few days. The deluded Tannese, hearing of his death, ascribed it to me and the Worship, and resolved to burn our house and property, and either murder the whole Mission party, or compel us to leave the island. Nowhat's brother was sent from Aneityum to talk to the Tannese and conciliate them, but unfortunately he could not speak the language well; and the Aneityumese Teachers felt their lives to be at this time in such danger that they durst not accompany him as interpreters, while I, on the other hand, did not understand his language, nor he, mine. Within two days after landing, he had a severe attack of ague and fever; and, though the vessel he came in remained eight days, he was prostrated all the time, so that his well-intentioned visit did us much harm. The Tannese became furious. This was proof positive that we were the cause of all their sickness and death![19] Inland and all along the weather side of the island, when far enough away from us, they said that the natives were enjoying excellent health. Meeting after meeting was held; exciting speeches were delivered; and feasts were given, for which it was said that several women were sacrificed, cooked and eaten—such being the bonds by which they entered into covenant with each other for life or death.

19. Apparently, Paton's side of the island must have been a very bad location for mosquitos and the spreading of malaria or dengue fever. Both the Chief from Aneityum and his brother contracted the disease. The natives associated it with Paton's presence on the island.

On the morning of the following Sabbath, we heard what were said to be the dying shrieks of two woman sacrifices;[20] but we went not near—we had no power to save them, and the savages only waited such a chance of sacrificing us too. Soon after, three women came running to the Mission House, and in tears implored us to try and protect them from being killed by their husbands. Alas, we could only plead for them, the Tannese and Aneityumese Teachers warning us that if we even pled we would be instantly murdered, as the men were raging mad with the thirst of blood. At another time, eight inland girls came running to us and sat in front of our house all day, saying they were afraid to go home, as the men were fighting with their women and killing them. At night-fall, however, the poor creatures withdrew, we knew not to what fate.

The inhabitants for miles around united in seeking our destruction, but God put it into even savage hearts to save us. Old Nowar, the Chief under whom we lived, and the Chief next under him, Arkurat, set themselves to rescue us. Along with Manuman and Sirawia they opposed every plan in the public assembly for taking our lives. Some of their people also remained friendly to us, and by the help of our Aneityumese Teachers, warned us of danger and protected our lives. Determined not to be baffled, a meeting of all our enemies on the island was summoned, and it was publicly resolved that a band of men be selected and enjoined to kill the whole of those friendly to the Mission, old Nowar among the rest, and not only to murder the Mission party, but also a trader who had lately landed to live there, that no one might be left to give information to the white men or bring punishment on the Islanders. Frenzy of excitement prevailed, and the blood-fiend seemed to override the whole assembly; when, under an impulse that surely came from the Lord of Pity, one great warrior Chief who had hitherto kept silent, rose, swung aloft a mighty club, and smashing it earthwards, cried aloud, "The man that kills Missi must first kill me—the men that kill the Mission

20. The sacrifice of women and the murder of women at the hands of their husbands must have been very common. The demon world seems to have had a strong hold on these people for hundreds of years.

Teachers must first kill me and my people—for we shall stand by them and defend them till death."

Instantaneously, another Chief thundered in with the same declaration; and the great assembly broke up in dismay. All the more remarkable was this deliverance, as these two Chiefs lived nearly four miles inland, and, as reputed disease makers and Sacred Men, were regarded as amongst our bitterest enemies. It had happened that, a brother of the former Chief having been wounded in battle, I had dressed his wounds and he recovered, for which perhaps he now favored us. But I do not put very much value on that consideration; for too clearly did our dear Lord Jesus interpose directly on our behalf that day. I and my defenseless company had spent it in anxious prayers and tears; and our hearts overflowed with gratitude to the Saviour who rescued us from the lions' jaws.[21]

21. Paton sees the hand of God rescuing him and his people. This is a reference to Daniel in the Lions' Den, where they are saved from "the lions' jaws."

The excitement did not at once subside, men continuing to club and beat the women for the smallest offence. At every opportunity I denounced their conduct and rebuked them severely—especially one wretch, who beat his wife just in front of our house as well as one of the women who tried to protect her. On the following day, he returned with an armed band, and threatened our lives; but I stood up in front of their weapons, and firmly condemned their conduct, telling that man particularly that his conduct was bad and cowardly. At length his wrath gave way; he grounded his club in a penitent mood, and promised to refrain from such evil ways.

22. Paton shows great courage in standing against sin and evil, specifically the beating of a wife. Taking the higher moral ground is critical for God's men. He must be willing to stand against the sins of the day, and call men and women to repentance.

Leaving all consequences to the disposal of my Lord, I determined to make an unflinching stand against wife-beating and widow-strangling, feeling confident that even their natural conscience would be on my side. I accordingly pled with all who were in power to unite and put down these shocking and disgraceful customs.[22]

At length ten Chiefs entered into an agreement not to allow any more beating of wives or strangling of widows, and to forbid all common labor on the Lord's day;[23] but alas, except for purposes of war or other wickedness, the influence of the Chiefs on Tanna was comparatively small. One Chief boldly declared, "If we did not beat our women, they would never work; they would not fear and obey us; but when we have beaten, and killed, and feasted on two or three, the rest are all very quiet and good for a long time to come!"

I tried to show him how cruel it was, besides that it made them unable for work, and that kindness would have a much better effect; but he promptly assured me that Tannese women "could not understand kindness." For the sake of teaching by example, my Aneityumese Teachers and I used to go a mile or two inland on the principal pathway, along with the Teachers' wives, and there cutting and carrying home a heavy load of firewood for myself and each of the men, while we gave only a small burden to each of the women. Meeting many Tanna-men by the way, I used to explain to them that this was how Christians helped and treated their wives and sisters, and then they loved their husbands and were strong to work at home; and that as men were made stronger, they were intended to bear the heavier burdens, and especially in all labors out of doors. Our habits and practices had thus as much to do as, perhaps more than, all our appeals, in leading them to glimpses of the life to which the Lord Jesus was calling them.[24]

Another war-burst, that caused immense consternation, passed over with only two or three deaths; and I succeeded in obtaining the consent of twenty Chiefs to fight no more except on the defensive[25]—a covenant to which, for a considerable time, they strictly adhered, in the midst of fierce provocations. But to gain any such end, the masses of the people must be educated to the point of desiring it. The few cannot, in such circumstances, act up to it, without laying themselves open to be downtrodden and swept away by the savages around.

23. Part of discipling the nations and teaching them to observe the commandments of Jesus (Matt. 28:18-20) involves pressing the civil government for the very basics of justice. Paton's first impact on the civil magistrate on the islands is found when he gets a few chiefs to agree to (1) stop beating wives, (2) stop strangling widows, and (3) forbid common labor on the Lord's Day (Sunday). However, anarchy seems to be the rule of the day, and the chiefs had little power over the people.

24. Paton attempted to set a good example for the natives (with the Aneityumese Teachers) in treating women with kindness and respect.

25. Paton also worked on teaching them a biblical view of warfare — only defensive warfare allowed.

About this time, several men, afraid or ashamed by day, came to me regularly by night for conversation and instruction. Having seen the doors of the Mission House made fast and the windows blinded so that they could not be observed, they continued with me for many hours, asking all strange questions about the new Religion and its laws. I remember one Chief particularly, who came often, saying to me, "I would be an Awfuaki man (i.e. a Christian) were it not that all the rest would laugh at me; that I could not stand!"

"Almost persuaded"—before you blame him, remember how many in Christian lands and amid greater privileges live and die without ever passing beyond that stage.[26]

26. After two years into the mission, there was very little progress.

The wife of one of those Chiefs died, and he resolved to imitate a Christian burial. Having purchased white calico from a Trader, he came to me for some tape which the Trader could not supply, and told me that he was going to dress the body as he had seen my dear wife's dressed, and lay her also in a similar grave. He declined my offer to attend the funeral and to pray with them, as in that case many of the villagers would not attend. He wanted all the people to be present, to see and to hear, as it was the first funeral of the kind ever celebrated among the Tannese; and my friend Nowar the Chief had promised to conduct a Service and offer prayer to Jehovah before all the Heathen. It moved me to many strange emotions, this Christian burial, conducted by a Heathen and in the presence of Heathens, with an appeal to the true and living God by a man as yet darkly groping among idols and superstitions. Many were the wondering questions from time to time addressed to me. The idea of a resurrection from the dead was that which most keenly interested these Natives, and called forth all their powers of inquiry and argument. Thus the waves of hope and fear swept alternately across our lives; but we embraced every possible opportunity of telling them the story of the life and death of Jesus, in the strong hope that God would spare us yet to bring the benighted Heathen to the knowledge of the true salvation, and to love and serve the only Saviour.[27]

27. Paton's goal remained to teach these souls the Gospel story of Jesus Christ in His death and resurrection.

Confessedly, however, it was uphill, weary, and trying work. For one thing, these Tannese were terribly dishonest; and when there was any special sickness, or excitement from any cause, their bad feeling towards the Worship was displayed by the more insolent way in which they carried off whatever they could seize. When I opposed them, the club or tomahawk, the musket or kawas (i.e. killing-stone), being instantly raised, intimated that my life would be taken, if I resisted. Their skill in stealing on the sly was phenomenal! If an article fell, or was seen on the floor, a Tanna-man would neatly cover it with his foot, while looking you frankly in the face, and, having fixed it by his toes or by bending in his great toe like a thumb to hold it, would walk off with it, assuming the most innocent look in the world. In this way, a knife, a pair of scissors or any smaller article, would at once disappear. Another fellow would deftly stick something out of sight amongst the whipcord plaits of his hair, another would conceal it underneath his naked arm, while yet another would shamelessly lift what he coveted and openly carry it away.[28]

28. Stealing and lying remain chief sins amongst these people.

With most of them, however, the shame was not in the theft, but in doing it so clumsily that they were discovered! Once, after continuous rain and a hot damp atmosphere, when the sun shone out I put my bedclothes on a rope to dry. I stood at hand watching, as also the wives of two Teachers, for things were mysteriously disappearing almost under our very eyes. Suddenly, Miaki, who with his war-companions had been watching us unobserved, came rushing to me breathless and alone, crying, "Missi, come in, quick, quick! I want to tell you something and to get your advice!"

He ran into my house, and I followed; but before he had got into his story, we heard the two women crying out, "Missi, Missi, come quick! Miaki's men are stealing your sheets and blankets!"

I ran at once, but all were gone into the bush, and with them my sheets and blankets. Miaki for a moment looked abashed, as I charged him with deceiving me just to give his men their opportunity. But he soon rose to the occasion. He wrought himself into a towering rage at them, flourished his huge club and smashed the bushes all around, shouting to me, "Thus will I smash these fellows, and compel them to return your clothes."

Perhaps he hoped to move me to intercede for his men, and to prevent bloodshed, as he knew that I always did, even to my own loss; but I resisted all his tricks, and urged him to return these articles at once if there were any honor or honesty in him or his men. Of course, he left me but to share the plunder! He kept out of my way for a considerable time, which showed a small glimmering of conscience somewhere; and when I tackled him on the subject, at our first meeting, he declared he was unable to get the articles back, which of course showed the lying spirit, amongst them everywhere applauded—for a lie that succeeded, or seemed to succeed, was in their esteem a crowning virtue.

One dark night, I heard them amongst my fowls. These I had purchased from them for knives and calico; and they now stole them all away, dead or alive. Had I interfered, they would have gloried in the chance to club or shoot me in the dark, when no one could exactly say who had done the deed. Several of the few goats, which I had for milk, were also killed or driven away; indeed, all the injury that was possible was done to me, short of taking away my life, and that was now frequently attempted.[29] Having no fires or fireplaces in my Mission House, such being not required there—though sometimes a fire would have been invaluable for drying our bedclothes in the rainy season—we had a house near by in which all our food was cooked, and there, under lock and key, we secured all our cooking utensils, pots, dishes, etc. One night that too was broken into, and everything was stolen. In consternation, I appealed to the Chief, telling him what had been done. He also flew into a great rage, and vowed vengeance on the thieves, saying that he would compel them to return everything. But, of course, nothing was returned; the thief could not be found!

29. Paton faced frequent attempts on his life.

I, unable to live without something in which to boil water, at length offered a blanket to any one that would bring back my kettle. Miaki himself, after much professed difficulty, returned it minus the lid—that, he said, probably fishing for a higher bribe, could not be got at any price, being at the other side of the island in a tribe over which he had no control! In the circumstances, I was glad to get kettle minus lid—realizing how life itself may depend on so small a luxury![30]

One morning, the Tannese, rushing towards me in great excitement, cried, "Missi, Missi, there is a God, or a ship on fire, or something of fear, coming over the sea! We see no flames, but it smokes like a volcano. Is it a Spirit, a God, or a ship on fire? What is it? What is it?"

One party after another followed in quick succession, shouting the same questions in great alarm, to which I replied, "I cannot go at once; I must dress first in my best clothes; it will likely be one of Queen Victoria's Men-of-war, coming to ask of me if your conduct is good or bad, if you are stealing my property, or threatening my life, or how you are using me?"

They pled with me to go and see it; but I made much fuss about dressing, and getting ready to meet the great Chief on the vessel, and would not go with them. The two principal Chiefs now came running and asked, "Missi, will it be a ship of war?"[31]

I called to them, "I think it will; but I have no time to speak to you now, I must get on my best clothes!"

They said, "Missi, only tell us, will he ask you if we have been stealing your things?"

I answered, "I expect he will."

They asked, "And will you tell him?"

I said, "I must tell him the truth; if he asks, I will tell him."

They then cried out, "Oh, Missi, tell him not! Everything shall be brought back to you at once, and no one will be allowed again to steal from you."

30. Boiling water was essential for survival under conditions like these. Thus, Paton needed his kettle returned to him.

31. The British Man-of-war was a sailing ship armed with cannon. These tribes understood superior military power.

Then said I, "Be quick! Everything must be returned before he comes. Away, away! and let me get ready to meet the great Chief on the Man-of-war."

Hitherto, no thief could ever be found, and no Chief had power to cause anything to be restored to me; but now, in an incredibly brief space of time, one came running to the Mission House with a pot, another with a pan, another with a blanket, others with knives, forks, plates, and all sorts of stolen property. The Chiefs called me to receive these things, but I replied, "Lay them all down at the door, bring everything together quickly; I have no time to speak with you!"

I delayed my toilet, enjoying mischievously the magical effect of an approaching vessel that might bring penalty to thieves. At last the Chiefs, running in breathless haste, called out to me, "Missi, Missi, do tell us, is the stolen property all here?"

Of course I could not tell, but, running out, I looked on the promiscuous heap of my belongings, and said, "I don't see the lid of the kettle there yet!"

One Chief said, "No, Missi, for it is on the other side of the island; but tell him not, I have sent for it, and it will be here tomorrow."

I answered, "I am glad you have brought back so much; and now, if you three Chiefs, Nauka, Miaki, and Nowar, do not run away when he comes, he will not likely punish you; but, if you and your people run away, he will ask me why you are afraid, and I will be forced to tell him! Keep near me and you are all safe; only there must be no more stealing from me."[32]

32. Paton took advantage of this military protection as best as he could (without resorting to any violence).

They said, "We are in black fear, but we will keep near you, and our bad conduct to you is done."

The charm and joy of that morning are fresh to me still, when H.M.S. *Cordelia*, Captain Vernon, steamed into our lovely Harbor. The Commander, having heard rumor of my dangers on Tanna, kindly came on shore as soon as the ship cast anchor, with two boats, and a number of his officers and men, so far armed. He was dressed in splendid uniform, being a tall and handsome man, and he and his attendants made a grand and imposing show. On seeing Captain Vernon's boat nearing the shore, and the men glittering in gold lace and arms, Miaki the Chief left my side on the beach and rushed towards his village. I concluded that he had run for it through terror, but he had other and more civilized intentions in his Heathen head! Having obtained, from some trader or visitor in previous days, a soldier's old red coat, he had resolved to rise to the occasion and appear in his best before the Captain and his men. As I was shaking hands with them and welcoming them to Tanna, Miaki returned with the short red coat on, buttoned tightly round his otherwise naked body; and, surmounted by his ugly painted face and long whipcords of twisted hair, it completely spoiled any appearance that he might otherwise have had of savage freedom, and made him look a dirty and insignificant creature.

The Captain was talking to me, his men stood in order near by—to my eyes, oh how charming a glimpse of Home life!—when Miaki marched up and took his place most consequentially at my side. He felt himself the most important personage in the scene, and with an attempt at haughty dignity he began to survey the visitors. All eyes were fixed on the impudent little man, and the Captain asked, "What sort of a character is this?"

I replied, "This is Miaki, our great war Chief"; and whispered to the Captain to be on his guard, as this man knew a little English, and might understand or misunderstand just enough to make it afterwards dangerous to me.

The Captain only muttered, "The contemptible creature!" But such words were far enough beyond Miaki's vocabulary, so he looked on and grinned complacently.

At last he said, "Missi, this great Chief whom Queen Victoria has sent to visit you in her Man-of-war, cannot go over the whole of this island so as to be seen by all our people; and I wish you to ask him if he will stand by a tree, and allow me to put a spear on the ground at his heel, and we will make a nick in it at the top of his head, and the spear will be sent round the island to let all the people see how tall this great man is!" They were delighted at the good Captain agreeing to their simple request; and that spear was exhibited to thousands, as the vessel, her Commander, officers, and men, were afterwards talked of round and round the island.

Captain Vernon[33] was extremely kind, and offered to do anything in his power for me, thus left alone on the island amongst such savages; but, as my main difficulties were connected with my spiritual work amongst them, rousing up their cruel prejudices, I did not see his kindness could effectually interpose. At his suggestion, however, I sent a general invitation to all the Chiefs within reach, to meet the Captain next morning at my house. True to their instincts of suspicion and fear, they dispatched all their women and children to the beach on the opposite side of the island, beyond reach of danger, and next morning my house was crowded with armed men, manifestly much afraid. Punctually at the hour appointed, 10 a.m., the Captain came on shore; and soon thereafter twenty Chiefs were seated with him in my house. He very kindly spent about an hour, giving them wise counsels and warning them against outrages on strangers, all calculated to secure our safety and advance the interests of our Mission work.[34] He then invited all the Chiefs to go on board and see his vessel. They were taken to see the Armory, and the sight of the big guns running so easily on rails vastly astonished them. He then placed them round us on deck and showed them two shells discharged towards the ocean, at which, as they burst and fell far off, splash–splashing into the water, the terror of the Natives visibly increased. But, when he sent a large ball crashing through a cocoanut grove, breaking the trees like straws and cutting its way clear and swift, they were quite dumfounded and pled to be again set safely on shore. After receiving each some small gift, however, they were reconciled to the situation, and returned immensely interested in all that they had seen. Doubt-

33. Commander Charles Egerton Harcourt-Vernon sailed in the H.M.S. *Cordelia*, an 11-gun sloop launched in 1856.

34. Isaiah 49:23 is realized when the civil government actually protects missionaries who are trying to build the Church. "And kings shall be thy nursing fathers, and their queens thy nursing mothers: they shall bow down to thee with their face toward the earth, and lick up the dust of thy feet; and thou shalt know that I am the LORD: for they shall not be ashamed that wait for me."

less many a wild romance was spun by these savage heads, in trying to describe and hand down to others the wonders of the fire-god of the sea, and the Captain of the great white Queen. How easily it all lends itself to the service of poetry and myth!

About this time also, the London Missionary Society's ship, the *John Williams*, visited me, having on board the Rev. Messrs. Turner, Inglis, Baker, and Macfarlan. They urged me to go with them on a three weeks' trip round the Islands, as I had lately suffered much from fever and ague, and was greatly reduced by it. But a party of Bush Natives had killed one of our Harbor people the week before, and sadly bruised several others with their clubs, and I feared a general war of revenge if I left—for my presence amongst them at least helped to keep the peace.[35] I also was afraid that, if I left, they might not allow me to return to the island—so I declined once more the pleasure of much-needed change and rest. Further, as the *John Williams* brought me the wood for building a Church which I had bought on Aneityum, the Tannese now plainly saw that, though their conduct had been very bad, and I had suffered much on their island, I had no intention of leaving them or of giving up the work of Jehovah.

Too much, perhaps, had I hoped for from the closely succeeding visits of the good Bishop Selwyn, the gallant Captain Vernon, and the Mission ship *John Williams*. The impressions were undoubtedly good, but evanescent;[36] and things soon went on as they had done before among our benighted Tannese, led by Satan at his will, and impelled to the grossest deeds of Heathen darkness. The change by Divine grace, however, we knew to be possible;[37] and for this we labored and prayed incessantly, fainting not, or if fainting, only to rise again and tackle every duty in the name of the Lord who had placed us there.

Fever and ague had now attacked me fourteen times severely, with slighter recurring attacks almost continuously after my first three months on the island, and I now felt the necessity of taking the hint of the Tannese Chief before re-

35. John Paton now became a peacemaker between the warring tribes. "Blessed are the peacemakers, for they shall be called the children of God" (Matt. 5:9).

36. Evanescent means "quickly fading or transient."

37. External threats cannot change the hearts of men. What they need is a supernatural transformation by the work of the Holy Spirit and the preaching of the Gospel.

ferred to—"Sleep on the higher ground." Having also received medical counsel to the same effect, though indeed experience was painfully sufficient testimony, I resolved to remove my house, and began to look about for a suitable site. There rose behind my present site, a hill about two hundred feet high, surrounded on all sides by a valley, and swept by the breezes of the trade-winds, being only separated from the ocean by a narrow neck of land. On this I had set my heart; there was room for a Mission House and a Church, for which indeed Nature seemed to have adapted it. I proceeded to buy up every claim by the Natives to any portion of the hill, paying each publicly and in turn, so that there might be no trouble afterwards.[38] I then purchased from a Trader the deck planks of a shipwrecked vessel, with which to construct a house of two apartments, a bedroom and a small store-room adjoining it, to which I purposed to transfer and add the old house as soon as I was able.

Just at this juncture, the fever smote me again more severely than ever; my weakness after this attack was so great, that I felt as if I never could rally again. With the help of my faithful Aneityumese Teacher, Abraham,[39] and his wife, however, I made what appeared my last effort to creep—I could not climb—up the hill to get a breath of wholesome air. When about two-thirds up the hill, I became so faint that I concluded I was dying. Lying down on the ground, sloped against the root of a tree to keep me from rolling to the bottom, I took farewell of old Abraham, of my Mission work, and of everything around! In this weak state I lay, watched over by my faithful companion, and fell into a quiet sleep. When consciousness returned, I felt a little stronger, and a faint gleam of hope and life came back to my soul.

Abraham and his devoted wife Nafatu lifted me and carried me to the top of the hill. There they laid me on cocoanut leaves on the ground, and erected over me a shade or screen of the same; and there the two faithful souls, inspired surely by something diviner even than mere human pity, gave me the

38. Christians always respect private property and make an honest purchase of land from the natives (as they are willing to sell it).

39. His helper, Abraham, became his most faithful assistant through the worst of his life on Tanna.

cocoanut juice to drink and fed me with native food and kept me living—I know not for how long. Consciousness did, however, fully return. The trade-wind refreshed me day by day. The Tannese seemed to have given me up for dead; and providentially none of them looked near us for many days. Amazingly my strength returned, and I began planning about my new house on the hill. Afraid again to sleep at the old site, I slept under the tree, and sheltered by the cocoanut leaf screen, while preparing my new bedroom.

Here again, but for these faithful souls, the Aneityumese Teacher and his wife, I must have been baffled, and would have died in the effort. The planks of the wreck, and all other articles required, they fetched and carried; and it taxed my utmost strength to get them in some way planted together. But life depended on it. It was at length accomplished; and after that time I suffered comparatively little from anything like continuous attacks of fever and ague. That noble old soul, Abraham, stood by me as an angel of God in sickness and in danger; he went at my side wherever I had to go; he helped me willingly to the last inch of strength in all that I had to do; and it was perfectly manifest that he was doing all this not from mere human love, but for the sake of Jesus. That man had been a Cannibal in his Heathen days, but by the grace of God there he stood verily a new creature in Christ Jesus. Any trust, however sacred or valuable, could be absolutely reposed in him; and in trial or danger I was often refreshed by that old Teacher's prayers, as I used to be by the prayers of my saintly father in my childhood's home. No white man could have been a more valuable helper to me in my perilous circumstances; and no person, white or black, could have shown more fearless and chivalrous devotion.[40]

When I have read or heard the shallow objections of irreligious scribblers and talkers, hinting that there was no reality in conversions, and that Mission effort was but waste, oh, how my heart has yearned to plant them just one week on Tanna, with the "natural" man all around in the person of Cannibal

40. Paton witnessed an amazing transformation in Abraham, who used to be a pagan cannibal like the rest. Now, he was willing to give up his life serving Paton. If there was any question that a native could become a man of faith, courage, and character, this example of Abraham would dispel all doubts!

and Heathen, and only the one "spiritual" man in the person of the converted Abraham, nursing them, feeding them, saving them "for the love of Jesus"—that I might just learn how many hours it took to convince them that Christ in man was a reality after all! All the skepticism of Europe would hide its head in foolish shame; and all its doubts would dissolve under one glance of the new light that Jesus, and Jesus alone, pours from the converted Cannibal's eye.

Perhaps it may surprise some unsophisticated reader to learn, though others who know more will be quite prepared for it, that this removal of our house, as also Mr. Mathieson's for a similar reason, was severely criticized by the people who try to evangelize the world while sitting in easy chairs at home. Precious nonsense appeared, for instance, in the *Nova Scotian Church Magazine*, about my house being planted on the fighting ground of the Natives, and thereby courting and provoking hostilities. As a matter of fact, the hill-top was too narrow to accommodate both the Church and my house, and had to be leveled out for that purpose, and it was besides surrounded by a deep valley on three sides; but the arm-chair critics[41] unwilling to believe in the heathen hatred of the Gospel, had to invent some reason out of their own brains to account for me being so persecuted and plundered. In truth, we were learning by suffering for the benefit of those who should follow us on these Islands—that health could be found only on the higher levels, swept by the breath of the trade winds, and that fever and ague lay in wait near the shore, and especially on the leeward side. Even Mr. Inglis had his house on Aneityum removed also to the higher ground; and no Missionary since has been located in the fever beds by the swamp or shore. Life is God's great gift to be preserved for His uses, not thrown away.

CHAPTER VIII – MORE MISSION LEAVES FROM TANNA
A.D. 1860. Age 36

The Peace party, my band of twenty Chiefs already spoken of, kept all the tribes around the Harbor acting only on the defensive for a season. But the Inland people murdered eight Chiefs from a distance who, after paying a friendly visit to the Harbor people, were returning to their homes.

At the same time, one of the Inland Chiefs, who had pled with his people to give up war and live at peace with surrounding tribes, was overthrown and murdered by his own men, as also his brother and four wives and two children, and was supplanted by another leader more akin to their wishes and tastes. They proceeded, according to their custom of declaring war, to shoot one of the Harbor men and to break down their fences and plantations. So, once again, the blood fiend was unleashed—the young men of Tanna being as eager to get up a battle, as young men of the world at home seem eager to get up a concert or a ball.[1]

The Harbor people advised me to remove a mile further away from these warriors; but the Inland tribes sent me word not to desert my house, lest it might be burned and plundered, for that they themselves had no quarrel against me. Early next morning, I, accompanied by Abraham and another Aneityu-

1. Young men are less judicious and more interested in war, fighting, and even killing.

mese, started off to visit the Bush party, and if possible avert the impending war, but without informing my Harbor people. About four miles from our Station, we met the Chief of our farthest inland friendly tribe with all his fighting men under arms. Forcing me to disclose our errand, he reluctantly allowed us to pass. Praying to Jesus for guidance and protection, we pressed along the path through the thick bush four miles further still. My two attendants, sinking into silence, betrayed growing fear; and I, after trying to cheer them, had at their most earnest appeal to walk on also in silence, my heart and theirs going up to Jesus in prayer. We passed many deserted villages and plantations, but saw no living person. At last, unexpectedly, we stumbled upon the whole host assembled on the Village Common at a great feast; and at sight of us every man rushed for his weapons of war. Keeping my Teachers close beside me, I walked straight into the midst of them, unarmed of course, and cried as loud as I possibly could in their own tongue:

"My love to all you men of Tanna! Fear not; I am your friend; I love you every one,[2] and am come to tell you about Jehovah God and good conduct such as pleases Him!"[3]

An old Chief thereon came and took me by the hand, and, after leading me about among the people, said:

"Sit down beside me here and talk with me; by-and-by the people will not be afraid."

A few ran off to the bush in terror. Others appeared to be beside themselves with delight. They danced round us frantically, striking the ground and beating a canoe with their clubs, while shouting to each other, "Missi is come! Missi is come!" The confusion grew every moment wilder, and there was a fiendish look about the whole scene. Men and boys rushed thronging around from every quarter, all painted in varied and savage devices, and some with their hair stuck full of fantastic feathers. Women and children peered through the bush, and instantaneously disappeared. Even in that anxious moment, it struck me that they had many more children amongst them

2. Paton expressed his love for the people over and over again. This appears somewhat unique in missionary records. He was not afraid to give them the laws of God, as well as the Gospel of Christ.

3. Paton risked his life to stop the war between the Inland tribes and the Harbor tribes, walking eight miles into the bush to prevent the fighting.

than the people around the shores, where women and children are destroyed by the cruelty and vices of "civilized" visitors! After spending about an hour, conversing and answering all questions, they apparently agreed to give up the war, and allowed me to conduct the Worship amongst them. They then made me a present of cocoanuts and sugar-cane and two fowls, which my attendants received from them; and I, in return, presented a red shirt to the principal Chief, and distributed a quantity of fish-hooks and pieces of red calico amongst the rest. The leading men shook hands graciously, and invited us often to come and see them, for after that visit they would harm no person connected with our Mission. Meantime, the Harbor people having learned where we had gone, had concluded that we would all be killed and feasted upon. When we returned, with a present of food, and informed them what we had heard and seen, their astonishment was beyond measure; it had never been so seen after this manner on Tanna! The peace continued for more than four weeks, an uncommonly prolonged truce.[4] All hands were busy at work. Many yam-plantations[5] were completed, and all fences were got into excellent condition for a year.[6]

The prejudices and persecutions of Heathens were a sore enough trial, but sorer and more hopeless was the wicked and contaminating influence of, alas, my fellow-countrymen. One, for instance, a Captain Winchester, living with a native woman at the head of the bay as a Trader, a dissipated wretch, though a well-educated man, was angry forsooth at this state of peace! Apparently there was not the usual demand for barter for the fowls, pigs, etc., in which he traded. He developed at once a wonderful interest in their affairs, presented all the Chiefs around with powder, caps, and balls, and lent among them a number of flash-muskets. He urged them not to be afraid of war, as he would supply any amount of ammunition.[7] I remonstrated, but he flatly told me that peace did not suit his purposes. Incited and encouraged thus, these poor Heathen people were goaded into a most unjust war on neighboring

4. Four weeks was an "uncommonly prolonged truce"! Pagan tribes are constantly vulnerable to total annihilation. This is the pattern of human civilizations — always given to war, sexual degradation, birth implosions (abortion), and disease. Short of the Gospel of Christ, there is no hope for peace, and there is no hope for any civilization.

5. Yams are a staple for the Melanesian people in New Guinea down through the South Pacific.

6. It is amazing how much productive work can be accomplished if the nations would stay out of wars! The yam farms proliferated in the four weeks.

7. Again, the apostate white men became the greatest bane to the missionary in the form of this Captain Winchester (who made money off of the wars of these tribes).

tribes. The Trader immediately demanded a high price for the weapons he had lent; the price of powder, caps, and balls rose exorbitantly with every fresh demand; his yards were crowded with poultry and pigs, which he readily disposed of to passing vessels; and he might have amassed great sums of money but for his vile dissipations. Captain Winchester, now glorying in the war, charged a large hog for a wine-glass full of powder, or three or four balls, or ten gun-caps; he was boastful of his "good luck" in getting rid of all his old muskets and filling his yards with pigs and fowls. Such is the infernal depth to which we can sink, when the misery and the ruin of many are thought to be more than atoned for by the wealth and prosperity of a few who trade in their doom!

Miaki the war Chief had a young brother, Rarip by name, about eighteen years of age. When this war began he came to live with me at the Mission House. After it had raged some time, Miaki forced him to join the fighting men; but he escaped through the bush, and returned to me, saying, "Missi, I hate this fighting; it is not good to kill men; I will live with you!"

Again the war Chief came, and forced my dear young Rarip to join the hosts. Of course, I could only plead; I could not prevent him. This time, he placed him at his own side in the midst of his warriors. On coming in sight of the enemy, and hearing their first yells as they rushed from the bush, a bullet pierced young Rarip's breast, and he fell dead into the arms of Miaki. The body was carried home to his brother's village, with much wailing, and a messenger ran to tell me that Rarip was dead. On hasting thither, I found him quite dead, and the center of a tragic ceremonial. Around him, some sitting, others lying on the ground, were assembled all the women and girls, tearing their hair, wounding themselves with split bamboos and broken bottles, dashing themselves headlong to the earth, painting all black their faces, breasts, and arms, and wailing with loud lamentations! Men were also there, knocking their heads against the trees, gashing their bodies with knives till they ran with streaks of blood, and indulging in every kind of savage symbol of grief and anguish. My heart broke to see them, and to think that they knew not to look to our dear Lord Jesus for consolation.

I returned to the Mission House, and brought a white sheet and some tape, in which the body of dear young Rarip was wrapped and prepared for the grave. The Natives appeared to be gratified at this mark of respect; and all agreed that Rarip should have, under my direction, a Christian burial. The men prepared the grave in a spot selected near to his own house; I read the Word of God, and offered prayer to Jehovah, with a psalm of praise, amidst a scene of weeping and lamentation never to be forgotten; and the thought burned through my very soul—oh, when, when will the Tannese realize what I am now thinking and praying about, the life and immortality brought to light through Jesus?[8]

As the war still raged on, and many more were killed, vengeance threatened the miserable Trader. Miaki attacked him thus, "You led us into this war. You deceived us, and we began it. Rarip is dead, and many others. Your life shall yet go for his."[9]

Captain Winchester, heartless as a dog so long as pigs and fowls came to the yard at whatever cost to others' lives, now trembled like a coward for himself. He implored me to let him and his Mare wife sleep at my house for safety; but I refused to allow my Mission to be in any way identified with his crimes. The Natives from other islands, whom he kept and wrought like slaves, he now armed with muskets for his defense; but, having no faith in their protecting or even warning him, he implored me to send one of my Teachers, to assist his wife in watching till he snatched a few hours of sleep every day, and, if awake, he would sell his life as dearly as he could by aid of musket and revolver. The Teachers were both afraid and disinclined to go; and I could not honestly ask them to do so. His peril and terror became so real that by night he slept in his boat anchored out in the center of the bay, with his arms

8. Funerals became a good opportunity to speak of the resurrection of Christ. The great contrast between a Christian burial and a pagan burial is extremely obvious — hope vs. hopelessness.

9. Jesus said, "Those that take the sword, will perish by the sword" (Matt. 26:52).

10. Paton brought the war to a close by gifts given in secret. "A gift in secret pacifieth anger: and a reward in the bosom strong wrath" (Prov. 21:14).

11. Paton was one to get involved, to take the Gospel to the very center of the warfare. He held worship in the fighting ground every Sunday! And he held worship in both camps! Such courage and boldness is truly amazing, unheard of in the history of Christian missions!

12. Paton thinks he has a handful of converts at this point, about 3 years after arriving on Tanna.

beside him, and a crew ready to start off at the approach of danger and lose everything; while by day he kept watch on shore, armed, and also ready to fly. Thus his miserable existence dragged on, keeping watch alternatively with his wife, till a trading vessel called and carried him off with all that he had rescued—for which deliverance we were unfeignedly thankful! The war, which he had wickedly instigated, lingered on for three months; and then, by a present given secretly to two leading Chiefs, I managed to bring it to a close.[10] But feelings of revenge for the slain burned fiercely in many breasts; and young men had old feuds handed on to them by the recital of their fathers' deeds of blood.

All through this war, I went to the fighting ground every Sabbath, and held worship amongst our Harbor people. Hundreds assembled around me, and listened respectfully, but they refused to give up the war. One day, I determined to go through the bush that lay between and speak and pray with the enemies also. Our Harbor folks opposed me, and one leading man said, "Missi, pray only for us, and your God will be strong to help us and we will not be afraid! You must not pray with the enemy, lest He may help them too."

After this episode, I made it my duty always to visit both Camps, when I went to the fighting ground, and to have worship with both—teaching them that Jehovah my God was angry at all such scenes and would not fight for either, that He commanded them to live at peace.[11]

About this time, our Sabbath audiences at the Mission numbered forty or so. Nowar and three or four more, and only they, seemed to love and serve Jesus.[12] They were, however, changeable and doubtful, though they exerted a good influence on their villages, and were generally friendly to us and to the Worship. Events sometimes for a season greatly increased our usefulness. For instance, one of the Sacred Men when fishing on the coral reef was bitten by a poisonous fish. After great agony, he died, and his relatives were preparing to strangle his two wives that their spirits might accompany and serve him in the other world. Usually such tragedies were completed before I ever heard of them. On this occasion, I had called at the village that very day, and succeeded in persuading them to bury him alone—his wives being saved alive at my appeal. Thus the idea got to be talked of, and the horrible custom was being undermined—the strangling of widows![13]

In connection with such poisonings, I may mention that some of these fishes were deadly poisonous; others were unwholesome, and even poisonous, only at certain seasons; and still others were always nutritious and good. For our own part, we used fish sparingly and cautiously; and the doubtful ones we boiled with a piece of silver in the water. If the silver became discolored, we regarded the fish as unwholesome; if the silver remained pure, we could risk it.

One morning at daybreak I found my house surrounded by armed men, and a Chief intimated that they had assembled to take my life. Seeing that I was entirely in their hands, I knelt down and gave myself away body and soul to the Lord Jesus, for what seemed the last time on earth. Rising, I went out to them, and began calmly talking about their unkind treatment of me and contrasting it with all my conduct towards them. I also plainly showed them what would be the sad consequences, if they carried out their cruel purpose.[14] At last some of the chiefs, who had attended the Worship, rose and said, "Our conduct has been bad; but now we will fight for you, and kill all those who hate you."

Grasping hold of their leader, I held him fast till he promised never to kill any one on my account, for Jesus taught us to love our enemies and always to return good for evil! During this scene, many of the armed slunk away into the bush, and those who remained entered into a bond to be friendly and to protect us. But again their Public Assembly resolved that we should be killed, because, as they said, they hated Jehovah and the Worship; for it made them afraid to do as they had always done. If I would give up visiting the villages, and praying and talking with them about Jehovah, they intimated that they

13. Paton was slowly overcoming the practice of widow-strangling. This was similar to the challenge William Carey faced when he attempted to oppose *sati* (widow burning) in India.

Coral Reefs such as this one abound near Vanuatu.

14. Paton was willing to give up his life for Jesus, but he is also careful to defend himself and argue his case with the enemy.

would like me to stay and trade with them, as they liked the Traders but hated the Missionaries! I told them that the hope of being able to teach them the Worship of Jehovah alone kept me living amongst them; that I was there, not for gain or pleasure, but because I loved them, and pitied their estate, and sought their good continually by leading them to know and serve the only true God.

One of the Chiefs, who had lived in Sydney and spoke English, replied for all the rest:

"Missi, our fathers loved and worshipped whom you call the Devil, the Evil Spirit; and we are determined to do the same, for we love the conduct of our fathers. Missi Turner came here and tried to break down our worship, but our fathers fought him and he left us. They fought also Peta, the Samoan Teacher, and he fled. They fought and killed some of the Samoan Teachers placed on the other side of the Harbor, and their companions left. We killed the last foreigner that lived in Tanna before you came here. We murdered the Aneityumese Teachers, and burned down their houses. After each of these acts, Tanna was good; we all lived like our fathers, and sickness and death left us. Now, our people are determined to kill you, if you do not leave this island; for you are changing our customs and destroying our worship, and we hate the Jehovah Worship."[15]

Streets of Sydney in 1883

15. One of the chiefs had lived in Australia for a while, but he was committed to the heathen practices. His reasoning — whenever they killed the Samoan Teachers (Christians) and the Aneityumese Teachers (Christians), things would go well for them for a while.

But my enemies seldom slackened their hateful designs against my life, however calmed or baffled for the moment. Within a few days of the above events, when Natives in large numbers were assembled at my house, a man furiously rushed on me with his ax; but a Kaserumini Chief snatched a spade with which I had been working, and dexterously defended me from instant death. Life in such circumstances led me to cling very near to the Lord Jesus; I knew not, for one brief hour, when or how attack might be made; and yet, with my trembling hand clasped in the Hand once nailed on Calvary, and now swaying the scepter of the Universe, calmness and peace and resignation abode in my soul.

Next day, a wild Chief followed me about for four hours with his loaded musket, and, though often directed towards me, God restrained his hand. I spoke kindly to him, and attended to my work as if he had not been there, fully persuaded that my God had placed me there, and would protect me till my allotted task was finished. Looking up in unceasing prayer to our dear Lord Jesus, I left all in His hands, and felt immortal till my work was done.[16] Trials and hairbreadth escapes strengthened my faith, and seemed only to nerve me for more to follow; and they did tread swiftly upon each other's heels. Without that abiding consciousness of the presence and power of my dear Lord and Saviour, nothing else in all the world could have preserved me from losing my reason and perishing miserably. His words, "Lo, I am with you alway, even unto the end of the world," became to me so real that it would not have startled me to behold Him, as Stephen did, gazing down upon the scene. I felt His supporting power, as did St. Paul, when he cried, "I can do all things through Christ which strengthened me." It is the sober truth, and it comes back to me sweetly after twenty years, that I had my nearest and dearest glimpses of the face and smile of my blessed Lord in those dread moments when musket, club, or spear was being leveled at my life. Oh the bliss of living and enduring, as seeing "Him who is invisible!"[17]

One evening, I awoke three times to hear a Chief and his men trying to force the door of my house. Though armed with muskets, they had some sense of doing wrong, and were wholesomely afraid of a little retriever dog which had often stood betwixt me and death. God restrained them again; and next morning the report went all round the Harbor that those who tried to shoot me were "smitten weak with fear," and that shooting would not do. A plan was therefore deliberately set on foot to fire the premises, and club us if we attempted to escape.[18] But our Aneityumese Teacher heard of it, and God helped us to frustrate their designs. When they knew their plots were revealed to us, they seemed to lose faith in them-

16. Paton felt immortal until Christ's work was done with him. He was completely confident in the absolute sovereignty of Jesus Christ over all events. Jesus is Lord over all things to the Church (Eph. 1:22).

17. He had a strong sense of the presence of Christ. The promise that Christ would be with us to the end of the age is very encouraging to the Christian worker who is risking all for Him.

18. The attacks are accelerating in force and frequency.

selves, and cast about to circumvent us in some more secret way. Their evil was overruled for good.

Namuei, one of my Aneityumese Teachers, was placed at our nearest village. There he had built a house for himself and his wife, and there he led amongst the Heathen a pure and humble Christian life.[19] Almost every morning he came and reported on the state of affairs to me. Without books or a school, he yet instructed the Natives in Divine things, conducted the Worship, and taught them much by his good example. His influence was increasing, when one morning a Sacred Man threw at him the kawas or killing-stone, a deadly weapon like a scythe stone in shape and thickness, usually round but sometimes angular, and from eighteen to twenty inches long. They throw it from a great distance and with fatal precision. The Teacher, with great agility, warded his head and received the deep cut from it in his left hand, reserving his right hand to guard against the club that was certain to follow swiftly. The Priest sprang upon him with his club and with savage yells. He evaded, yet also received, many blows; and, rushing out of their hands, actually reached the Mission House, bleeding, fainting, and pursued by howling murderers.[20] I had been anxiously expecting him, and hearing the noise I ran out with all possible speed.[21]

On seeing me, he sank down by a tree, and cried, "Missi, Missi, quick! and escape for your life! They are coming to kill you; they say they must kill us all today, and they have begun with me; for they hate Jehovah and the Worship!"

I hastened to the good Teacher where he lay; I bound up, washed, and dressed his wounds; and God, by the mystery of His own working, kept the infuriated Tannese watching at bay. Gradually they began to disappear into the bush, and we conveyed the dear Teacher to the Mission House. In three or four weeks, he so far recovered by careful nursing that he was able to walk about again. Some petitioned for him to return to the village; but I insisted, as a preliminary, that the Harbor Chiefs should unitedly punish him who had abused

19. Namuei came over to Aneityum to help Paton in the work on Tanna.

20. The Sacred Man that attacked Numuei was a chief as well.

21. Reminiscent of the Apostle Paul, the native teacher once murdered people, and now he is willing to die for Jesus' sake. A tremendous witness to the power of Christ in this man's life.

the Teacher; and this to test them, for he had only carried out their own wishes—Nowar excepted, and perhaps one or two others. They made a pretense of atoning by presenting the Teacher with a pig and some yams as a peace-offering; but I said, "No! Such bad conduct must be punished, or we would leave their island by the first opportunity."

Now that Sacred Man, a Chief too, had gone on fighting with other tribes, till his followers had all died or been slain; and, after three weeks' palaver, the other Chiefs seized him, tied him with a rope, and sent me word to come and see him punished, as they did not want us after all to leave the island. I had to go, for fear of more bloody work, and after talk with them, followed by many fair promises, he was loosed.

All appearing friendly for some time, and willing to listen and learn, the Teacher earnestly desired to return to his post. I pled with him to remain at the Mission House till we felt more assured, but he replied, "Missi, when I see them thirsting for my blood, I just see myself when the Missionary first came to my island. I desired to murder him, as they now desire to kill me. Had he stayed away for such danger, I would have remained Heathen; but he came, and continued coming to teach us, till, by the grace of God, I was changed to what I am. Now the same God that changed me to this can change these poor Tannese to love and serve Him. I cannot stay away from them; but I will sleep at the Mission House, and do all I can by day to bring them to Jesus."

It was not in me to keep such a man, under such motives, from what he felt to be his post of duty. He returned to his village work, and for several weeks things appeared most encouraging. The inhabitants showed growing interest in us and our work, and less fear of the pretensions of their Heathen Priest, which, alas! fed his jealousy and anger. One morning during worship, when the good Teacher knelt in prayer, the same savage Priest sprang upon him with his great club and left him for dead, wounded and bleeding and unconscious. The people fled and left him in his blood, afraid of being mixed up

22. In the way of Jesus, this man forgave his murderer as he died.

with the murder. The Teacher, recovering a little, crawled to the Mission House, and reached it about midday in a dying condition. On seeing him, I ran to meet him, but he fell near the Teacher's house, saying, "Missi, I am dying! They will kill you also. Escape for your life."

Trying to console him, I sat down beside him, dressing his wounds and nursing him. He was quite resigned; he was looking up to Jesus, and rejoicing that he would soon be with Him in Glory. His pain and suffering were great but he bore all very quietly, as he said and kept saying, "For the sake of Jesus! For Jesus' sake!" He was constantly praying for his persecutors,[22] "O Lord Jesus, forgive them, for they know not what they are doing. Oh, take not away all Thy servants from Tanna! Take not away Thy Worship from this dark island! O God, bring all the Tannese to love and follow Jesus!"

23. "No bands in death" is a reference to Psalm 73:4. There is no pain to death. "Oh death where is your sting? Oh grave, where is your victory?" That's the cry of the Christian as he is about to die.

To him, Jesus was all and in all; and there were no bands in his death.[23] He passed from us, in the assured hope of entering into the Glory of his Lord. Humble though he may appear in the world's esteem, I knew that a great man had fallen there in the service of Christ, and that he would take rank in the glorious Army of the Martyrs. I made for him a coffin, and dug his grave near the Mission House. With prayers, and many tears, we consigned his remains to the dust in the certainty of a happy resurrection. Even one such convert was surely a triumphant reward for the Missionaries, whom God had honored in bringing him to Jesus. May they have many like Namuri for their crown of joy and rejoicing in the great day!

Immediately after this, a number of Chiefs and followers called on me at the Mission House, professing great friendliness, and said:

"Mr. Turner gave our fathers great quantities of calico, axes, and knives, and they became his friends. If you would give the people some just now they would be pleased. They would stop fighting against the Worship."

I retorted, "How was it then, if they were pleased, that they persecuted Messrs. Turner and Nisbet till they had to leave the island? Your conduct is deceitful and bad. I never will reward you for bad actions and for murder! No present will be given by me."[24]

They withdrew sullenly, and seemed deeply disappointed and offended.

On one occasion, when a Chief had died, the Harbor people were all being assembled to strangle his widow. One of my Aneityumese Teachers, hearing of it, hastened to tell me. I ran to the village, and with much persuasion, saved her life. A few weeks thereafter she gave birth to a young chieftain, who prospered well. If our Harbor people told the truth, the widows of all who fell in war were saved by our pleading. Immediately after the foregoing incident, a Sacred Man was dying, and a crowd of people were assembled awaiting the event in order to strangle his three wives. I spoke to them of the horrid wickedness of such conduct. I further reasoned with them, that God had made us male and female, the sexes so balanced, that for every man that had three or a dozen wives, as many men generally had none, and that this caused great jealousy and quarrelling. I showed them further, that these widows being spared would make happy and useful wives for other kind and loving husbands. After the Worship, I appealed to the Chief and be replied:

"Missi, it was a practice introduced to Tanna from the island of Aneityum. It was not the custom of our fathers here to strangle widows. And, as the Aneityumese have given it up since they became worshippers of Jehovah, it is good that we now should give it up on Tanna too."

Thus these three widows were saved; and we had great hope in Christ that the ghastly practice would soon disappear from Tanna.[25]

An incident of this time created great wonder amongst the Natives; namely, the Sinking of a Well. We had, heretofore, a boiling spring to drink from, the water of which literally required in that climate days to cool down; we had also, a stagnant pool at the lower end of a swamp in which the Natives

24. These peoples were materialistic and deceitful, and they hated the Gospel. Is there anything different about our unbelieving population in the Western world today?

25. John Paton saved many lives. When Christians enter the mission field before abortion clinics today, are they there to save lives or to save souls? Of course, they are interested in both causes, as was John G. Paton.

26. Generally, Paton did the work by paying the natives. If he had not invested in the well, there would have been no significant blessing for the people.

27. In the second book (which is not included in this Study Guide), Paton digs another well on Aniwa (and God uses this as a huge encouragement for the people to faith).

habitually bathed, the only available fresh water bath! Beyond that, no drinking water could be had for six or seven miles. I managed to sink a well, near the Mission House, and got about twelve feet deep a good supply of excellent fresh water, though, strange to say, the surface of the well rose and fell regularly with every tide! This became the universal supply for us and for the Natives all round the Harbor and for miles inland. Hundreds of Natives from all parts of Tanna flocked to examine this greatest wonder they had ever seen—rain rising up out of the earth. I built it round with a kind of stone brought in my boat from the other side of the bay; and for many years it was the only fresh water supply for the Natives all around.[26] Some years later a native Chief sank a well about a mile nearer the entrance to the Harbor at his own village, and built it round with the bricks that I had purchased for house-building; these he grabbed and thus appropriated! Many a vessel, calling at the Harbor, was glad to get her casks refilled at my well, and all were apparently more friendly because of it; but the Sinking of this Well produced no such revolution as on Aniwa—to be hereafter related.[27]

For fully three months, all our available time, with all the native help which I could hire, was spent in erecting a building to serve for Church and School. It was fifty feet long, by twenty-one feet six inches broad. The studs were three feet apart, and all fixed by tenon and mortise into upper and lower wall plates. The beautiful roof of iron-wood and sugar-cane leaf was supported by three massive pillars of wood, sunk deeply into the ground. The roof extended about three feet over the wall plates, both to form a verandah and to carry the raindrops free beyond the walls. It was made of sugar-cane leaf and co-coanut leaves all around. The floor was laid with white coral, broken small, and covered with cocoanut leaf mats, such as those on which the Natives sat. Indeed, it was as comfortable a House of Prayer as any man need wish for in the tropics, though having only open spaces for doors and windows! I bought the heavy wood for it on Aneityum—price, fifty pairs of trousers for Natives; and these again were the gift of my Bible Class in Glasgow, all cut and sewed by their own hands. I gave also one hundred and thirty yards of cloth, along with other things, for other needful wood.[28]

My Tannese people at first opposed the erection of a Church. They did not wish Jehovah to secure a house on their island. On the opening day, only five men, three women, and three children were present, besides our Aneityumese Teachers. But after the morning service, on that day, I visited ten villages, and had worship in each. The people were generally shy and unfriendly. They said that we were the cause of the prevailing sickness and fever. They had no idea of any sickness or death being natural, but believing that all such events were caused by some one nahaking, i.e. bewitching, them. Hence their incessant feuds; and many were murdered in blind revenge.

As we were preparing a foundation for the Church, a huge and singular-looking round stone was dug up, at sight of which the Tannese stood aghast. The eldest Chief said, "Missi, that stone was either brought there by Karapanamun (the Evil Spirit), or hid there by our great Chief who is dead. That is the Stone God to which our forefathers offered human sacrifices; these holes held the blood of the victim till drunk up by the Spirit. The Spirit of that stone eats up men and women and drinks their blood, as our fathers taught us. We are in greatest fear!"[29]

A Sacred Man claimed possession, and was exceedingly desirous to carry it off; but I managed to keep it, and did everything in my power to show them the absurdity of these foolish notions. Idolatry had not indeed yet fallen throughout Tanna; but one cruel idol, at least, had to give way for the erection of God's House on that benighted land.

An ever-memorable event was the printing of my first book in Tannese. Thomas Binnie, Jun., Glasgow, gave me a printing-press and a font of type. Printing was one of the things I had never tried, but having now prepared a booklet in Tannese, I got my printing press into order, and began fin-

28. The first church in Tanna was about 1,000 square feet. Taking all of the islands together, Vanuatu now claims 83% of the natives as Christian, the largest church of which is Presbyterian (32%).

29. Human sacrifices were made to the Karapanamun god in past years — human sacrifice being common among primitive and pagan tribes. The motivation to worship and serve these gods was dread and fear (not a fatherly reverence).

30. Pioneering missionaries had to be very innovative and Jack-of-all-Trades.

gering the type. But book-printing turned out to be for me a much more difficult affair than house-building had been. Yet by dogged perseverance I succeeded at last.[30] My biggest difficulty was how to arrange the pages properly! After many failures, I folded a piece of paper into the number of leaves wanted, cut the corners, folding them back, and numbering as they would be when correctly placed in the book; then folding all back without cutting up the sheet, I found now by these numbers how to arrange the pages in the frame or case for printing, as indicated on each side. And do you think me foolish, when I confess that I shouted in an ecstasy of joy when the first sheet came from the press all correct? It was about one o'clock in the morning. I was the only white man then on the island, and all the Natives had been fast asleep for hours! Yet I literally pitched my hat into the air, and danced like a schoolboy round and round that printing-press;[31] till I began to think, Am I losing my reason? Would it not be like a Missionary to be upon my knees, adoring God for this first portion of His blessed Word ever printed in this new language? Friend, bear with me, and believe me—that was as true worship as ever was David's dancing before the Ark of his God! Nor think that I did not, over that first sheet of God's Word ever printed in the Tannese tongue, go upon my knees too, and then, and every day since, plead with the mighty Lord to carry the light and joy of His own Holy Bible into every dark heart and benighted home on Tanna! But the Tannese had a superstitious dread of books, and especially of God's Book. I afterwards heard that Dr. Turner printed a small primer in Tannese, translated by the help of the Samona Teachers; but this I never saw till near the close of my work on Tanna. Dr. Geddie sent me a copy, but it was more Samoan than Tannese, especially in its spelling, and I could make little or nothing of it.

31. John Paton admits to dancing in joy before the Lord when he was successful at printing his first piece of Scriptural literature.

Shortly after this, I was greatly refreshed by the visit of an American whaler, the Camden Packet, under Captain Allan. he, his chief officer, and many of his company of seamen were decided Christians—a great contrast to most of the traders that had called at Port Resolution.[32] The Captain cordially invited me on board to preach and conduct a religious service. That evening I enjoyed exceedingly—wells in the desert! The Captain introduced me, saying:

"This is my ship's company. My first officer and most of my men are real Christians, trying to love and serve Jesus Christ. We have been three years out on this voyage, and are very happy with each other. You would never hear or see worse on board of this vessel than you see now. And God has given us gratifying success."[33]

He afterwards told me that he had a very valuable cargo of sperm oil on board, the vessel being nearly filled up with it. He was eager to leave supplies, or do something for me, but I needed nothing that he could give. His mate, on examining my boat, found a hole in her, and several planks split and bulged in, as I had gone down on a reef with her when out on Mission work, and narrowly escaped drowning. Next morning, the Captain, of his own accord, set his carpenter to repair the boat, and left it as good as new. Not one farthing of recompense would any of them take from me; their own Christian love rewarded them, in the circumstances. I had been longing for a chance to send it to Sydney for repairs, and felt deeply thankful for such unexpected and generous aid. The Captain would not admit that the delay was any loss to him—his boats spending the day in purchasing cocoanuts and provisions from the Natives for his own ship. Oh, how the Christ-like spirit knits together all true followers of Christ! What other earthly or human tie could have so bound that stranger to me? In the heart of Christ we met as brothers.

Yet dangers darkened round me. One day, while toiling away at my house, the war Chief and his brother, and a large party of armed men, surrounded the plot where I was working. They all had muskets, besides their own native weapons. They watched me for some time in silence, and then every man leveled a musket straight at my head. Escape was impossible. Speech would only have increased my danger. My

32. These whalers were Christian — a rare experience to run into white Christians on these ships. It is touching to see how much they enjoyed Christian fellowship, how much they wanted to bless Paton in his ministry on this far-off island.

33. Christians instantly recognize brothers and sisters in Christ and enjoy fellowship no matter where they are in the world.

34. Paton witnessed the supernatural intervention of Christ on the men threatening to kill him on many occasions.

35. The Westminster Shorter Catechism on the sixth commandment (Thou shalt not murder) tells us, "The sixth commandment requireth all lawful endeavors to preserve our own life, and the life of others." Christians must not commit suicide, and even when taking significant risks (as John G. Paton did on Tanna), they must still do what they can to preserve their lives.

36. Non-Christians are more likely to enslave their men, as we find with this French-American.

eyesight came and went for a few moments. I prayed to my Lord Jesus, either Himself to protect me or to take me home to His Glory. I tried to keep working on at my task, as if no one was near me. In that moment, as never before, the words came to me "Whatsoever ye shall ask in My name, I will do it"; and I knew that I was safe. Retiring a little from their first position, no word having been spoken, they took up the same attitude somewhat farther off, and seemed to be urging one another to fire the first shot. But my dear Lord restrained them once again, and they withdrew, leaving me with a new reason for trusting Him with all that concerned me for Time and Eternity.[34]

Perils seemed, however, to enclose me on every hand, and my life was frequently attempted. I had to move about more cautiously than ever, some days scarcely daring to appear outside my Mission premises. For I have ever most firmly believed, and do believe, that only when we use every lawful and possible means for the preservation of our life, which is God's second greatest gift to man (His Son being the first), can we expect God to protect us, or have we the right to plead His precious promises.[35]

The vessel of one calling himself Prince de Jean Beuve, a French refugee, who had become a naturalized American, visited Port Resolution. He said, he had to escape from his own country for political offences. His large and beautiful ship was fitted up and armed like a Man-of-war. She was manned chiefly by slaves, whom he ruled with an iron hand.[36] What a contrast to Captain Allan's whaler! Yet he also was very sympathetic and kind to me. Having heard rumor of my trials and dangers, he came on shore, as soon as his ship cast anchor, with a body of armed men. He was effusively polite, with all a Frenchman's gush and gesticulation, and offered to do anything possible for me. He would take me to Aneityum or Sydney or wherever I wished. The ship was his own; he was sailing chiefly for pleasure, and he had called at our Islands to see if sufficient trade could be opened up to justify his laying on a line of steamers to call here in their transit. He urged me, I believe sincerely, to give him the pleasure of taking me and my belongings to some place of safety. But I was restrained from leaving, through the fear that I would never be permitted to return, and that Christ's work would suffer. In the still burning hope of being able to lead the Tannese to love and serve Jesus, I declined with much gratitude his genuine kindness.[37] He looked truly sorry to leave me in the circumstances wherein I was placed. After two hours on shore, he returned to his ship towards evening.[38]

Knowing that the Tannese were threatening to burn my former house, which I wished to remove to higher ground and add to the room I now occupied on the hill, I took advantage of the presence of the Prince's vessel, and set my Aneityumese Teachers and some friendly Natives to prepare for the task; but unfortunately, I forgot to send word to the Frenchman regarding my plans and aims. We removed the sugar-cane leaf thatch from the roof of the house, and began burning it on cleared ground, so that I might be able to save the heavy wood which could not be replaced on Tanna. Our French friend, on seeing the flames rising up furiously, at once loaded his heavy guns, and prepared his men for action. Under great excitement, he came ashore with a large number of armed men, leaving the rest on board ready at a given signal to protect them with shot and shell. Leaving one-half of those brought on shore to guard the boats, he came running towards my house, followed by the other half, wet with perspiration, and crying:

"Fer are dey? fer are dey? De scoundrels! I vill do for dem, and protect you. I sail punish dem, de scoundrels!"

He was so excited, he could scarcely compose himself to hear my explanations, which, when understood, he laughed at heartily. He again urged me to leave in his vessel; he could not bear me to lead such a life amongst savages. I explained to him my reasons for not leaving the island, but these he seemed unable to understand. He put his men through drill on shore, and left them under officers, ready for action at a moment's

37. Paton's commitment to love and serve the Tannese is very strong and keeps him steadfast for many years (despite regular threats to his life). Apparently, the word is getting out that Tanna is a dangerous place for these westerners.

38. Unbelievers do not understand why anybody would sacrifice comforts and peace to spread the Gospel to far off lands.

39. The unprincipled traders from Australia and other places were the greatest bane to the missionaries. Paton believes this is the primary source of his troubles with the natives.

40. A whale boat was 27-30 feet long (thin and easily maneuverable). It had a bow on both ends, so it could be rowed in either direction. Captain V wanted to steal Mr. Copeland's newer boat without paying the market price for it (the boat was in Paton's possession).

41. Captain T owned the boats and Captain V worked for him. They were all unprincipled.

warning, saying they would all be the better for a day on shore. He wished to take pot luck with me at our Mission House of one room for all purposes! My humble dinner and tea must have been anything but a treat for him, but he seemed to relish the deliverance for once from all the conventionalisms of the world. Before he left, he sent of his own accord for all the Chiefs within reach, and warned them that if they hurt me or took my life, he would return with his Man-of-war and punish them, by killing themselves and firing their villages; and that a British Man-of-war would also come and set their island on fire. They promised all possible good conduct, being undoubtedly put into great terror. The kind-hearted Frenchman left, with profuse expressions of admiration for my courage and of pity for my lot. No doubt he thought me a foolish dreamer of dreams.

A miserable contrast befell us in the bad impression produced by the conduct of one of Captain T—'s vessels in the Sydney sandal-wood trade.[39] Whale-boats had been sent out with Mr. Copeland and myself from Glasgow, as part of the necessary equipment of every Missionary on these Islands. Mine being rather large and heavy, I had sold it to one of T—'s captains; but the other had also been left to my care. After having used my boat for about twelve months—the best boat in that trade only being expected to last two years—the Captain called on Mr. Copeland, and got a note from him to me regarding the sale of his boat too. He declared, when calling on me, that Mr. Copeland had authorized him to get his boat from me in exchange for mine, which he had now been using for a year. I asked for the letter, and found it to be authority for me to sell his boat for cash only and at the same price as mine.[40] Captain V—[41] then raged at me and stormed, declaring that he would return my old boat, and take the other in defiance of me. Swearing dreadfully, he made for his ship, and returned with a large party of men whom he had picked up amongst the Islands. Collecting also a company of Tannese, and offering them tobacco, he broke down the fence, burst into the boat-house, and began to draw out the boat. Here I reached the spot, and sternly opposed them. He swore and foamed at me, and before the natives knocked and pulled me about, even kicking at me, though I evaded his blows. Standing by, I said in Tannese:

"You are helping that man to steal my boat; he is stealing it as you see."

On hearing this, the Tannese ran away, and his own party alone could not do it. In great wrath, he went off again to his vessel, and brought on shore as much tobacco as could be held in a large handkerchief tied by the four corners; but even for that, our own Natives refused to help him. He offered it then to a crowd of Inland savages, gathered at the head of the bay, who, regardless of my remonstrances, launched the boat, he raging at and all but striking me. Instead of returning, however, the other boat to the house, he merely set it adrift from his vessel, and it was carried on to the reef, where it remained fast, and was knocked about by the waves. After his vessel left, I, with much difficulty, got it off and brought it to the boat-house. Imagine, when such was their tyrannical treatment of a Missionary and a British fellow-subject, how they would act towards these poor native Islanders.

By the earliest opportunity, I wrote all the facts of the case to his employer, Captain T— of Sydney, but got not even a reply, while Captain V— continued in their trade, a scourge to these Islands, and a dishonor to his country and to humanity. Unfriendly Tannese now said:

"When a white man from his own country can so pull and knock the Missionary about and steal his boat and chain without being punished for it, we also may do as we please!"

I hesitate not to record my conviction that that man's conduct had a very bad effect, emboldening them in acts of dishonesty and in attempts upon my life till the Mission Station was ultimately broken up. After I had to escape from Tanna, with bare life in my hand, one of the same Captain's vessels called at Port Resolution and gave the Natives about three pounds weight of useless tobacco, purchasable at Sydney for less than one shilling per pound, to allow them to take away my boat, with oars, sails, mast, and all other belongings. They also purchased all the plunder from my house. Both boats were so large and so strongly built, that by adding a plank or two they turned them into small-decked schooners, admirably suited for the sandal-wood traffic round the shores, while larger vessels lay at safe anchorage to receive what they collected. Once, when Dr. Inglis and I met in Sydney, we called on Captain T— and stated the whole case, asking reasonable payment at least for the boats. He admitted that the boats had been taken and were in his service, and agreed to pay us for the boats if we would repay the large sum invested therein by his Captains. Calling one of his clerks, he instructed him to trace in the office record how much had been paid to the Tannese for the Missionary's boat

The young man innocently returned the reply, "Three pounds of tobacco."

In anger, he said, "I understood that a larger value had been given!"

The clerk assured him, "That is the only record."

Captain T—, after discussing the worth of the boat as being about £80, agreed to give us £60, but in writing out the cheque, threw down the pen and shouted, "I'll see you in __ first!"

Offering £50, to which we agreed, he again reviled, and declared he would not give a penny above £30.[42]

We appealed to him to regard this as a debt of honor, and to cease haggling over the price, as he well knew how we had been wronged in the matter.

Finally we left him declaring, "I am building similar boats just now at £25, apiece; I will send you one of them, and you may either take that or want!"

We left, glad to get away on any terms from such a character; and, though next year he did send one of his promised boats for me to Aneityum, yet the conduct of his degraded

42. These men were making thousands of pounds per year, and yet could not pay John G. Paton 50 pounds to compensate for stealing his boat.

servants engaged in the sandal-wood trade had a great share in the guilt of breaking up and ruining our Mission. Thousands upon thousands were made by it yearly, so long as it lasted; but it was a trade steeped in human blood and indescribable vice, nor could God's blessing rest on them and their ill-gotten gains. Oh, how often did we pray at that time to be delivered from the hands of unreasonable and wicked men! Sandal-wood traders murdered many of the Islanders when robbing them of their wood,[43] and the Islanders murdered many of them and their servants in revenge. White men, engaged in the trade, also shot dead and murdered each other in vicious and drunken quarrels, and not a few put end to their own lives. I have scarcely known one of them who did not come to ruin and poverty; the money that came even to the shipowners was a conspicuous curse. Fools there made a mock at sin, thinking that no one cared for these poor savages, but their sin did find them out, and God made good in their experience His own irrepealable law, "The wages of sin is death."[44]

Ships, highly insured, were said to be sent into our Island trade to be deliberately wrecked. One Sabbath evening, towards dark, the notorious Captain H——, in command of a large ship, allowed her to drift ashore and be wrecked without any apparent effort to save her. Next morning, the whole company were wading about in the water and pretending to have lost everything! The Captain, put in prison when he returned to Sydney for running away with another man's wife and property, imposed on Mr. Copeland and myself, getting all the biscuits, flour, and blankets we could spare for his destitute and shipwrecked company. We discovered afterwards that she was lying on a beautiful bank of sand, only a few yards from the shore, and that everything contained in her could be easily rescued without danger to life or limb! What we parted with was almost necessary for our life and health; of course he gave us an order on Captain T—— for everything, but not one farthing was ever repaid. At first he made a pretence of paying the Natives for food received; but afterwards, an armed band

43. They made their money by murdering many of the natives and stealing their Sandalwood.

44. These men lived by the gun and died by the gun. There was no ultimate profit in any of their work. Many passages apply to them. Psalm 11 says, "But the wicked and the one who loves violence His soul hates. Upon the wicked He will rain coals; fire and brimstone and a burning wind shall be the portion of their cup."

went inland night by night and robbed and plundered whatever came to hand. The Natives, seeing the food of their children ruthlessly stolen, were shot down without mercy when they dared to interfere; and the life of every white man was marked for speedy revenge. Glad were we when a vessel called, and carried away these white heathen Savages.

The same Captain T— also began the shocking Kanaka labor-traffic to the Colonies,[45] after the sandal-wood trade was exhausted, which has since destroyed so many thousands of the Natives in what was nothing less than Colonial slavery, and has largely depopulated the Islands either directly or indirectly. And yet he wrote, and published in Sydney, a pamphlet declaring that he and his sandal-wooders and Kanaka-labor collectors had done more to civilize the Islanders than all our Mission efforts combined. Civilize them, indeed! By spreading disease and vice, misery and death amongst them, even at the best; at the worst, slaving many of them till they perished at their toils, shooting down others under one or other guilty pretence, and positively sweeping thousands into an untimely grave. A common cry on their lips was:[46]

"Let them perish and let the white men occupy these Isles."

It was such conduct as this, that made the Islanders suspect all foreigners and hate the white man and seek revenge in robbery and murder. One Trader, for instance, a sandal-wooder and collector of Kanakas, living at Port Resolution, abominably ill-used a party of Natives. They determined in revenge to plunder his store. The cellar was underneath his house, and he himself slept above the trap-door by which alone it could be entered. Night and day he was guarded by armed men, Natives of adjoining islands, and all approaches to his premises were watched by savage dogs that gave timely warning. He felt himself secure. But the Tannese actually constructed a tunnel underground from the bush, through which they rolled away tobacco, ammunition, etc., and nearly emptied his cellar! My heart bled to see men so capable and clever thus brutally abused and demoralized and swept away.

45. This same Captain T entered the kidnapping and enslavement business. This marked the most evil elements of a materialistic West for centuries.

46. The Kanaka laborers were used on Australian sugar plantations. At least 60,000 of them were used between 1863 and 1906 when the Australian government repatriated them to their various lands.

By the Gospel, and the civilization which it brings, they were capable of learning anything and being trained to a useful and even noble manhood. But all influence that ever I witnessed from these Traders was degrading, and dead against the work of our Missions.[47]

The Chief, Nowar Noukamara, usually known as Nowar, was my best and most-to-be-trusted friend. He was one of the nine or ten who were most favorable to the Mission work, attending the Worship pretty regularly, conducting it also in their own houses and villages, and making generally a somewhat unstable profession of Christianity. One or more of them often accompanied me on Sabbath, when going to conduct the Worship at inland villages, and sometimes they protected me from personal injury. He influenced the Harbor Chiefs and their people for eight or ten miles around to get up a great feast in favor of the Worship of Jehovah. All were personally and specially invited, and it was the largest Assembly of any kind that I ever witnessed on the Islands.

When all was ready, Nowar sent a party of Chiefs to escort me and my Aneityumese Teachers to the feast. Fourteen Chiefs, in turn, made speeches to the assembled multitude; the drift of all being, that war and fighting be given up on Tanna—that no more people be killed by *Nahak*, for witchcraft and sorcery were lies—that Sacred Men no longer profess to make wind and rain, famine and plenty, disease and death—that the dark Heathen talk of Tanna should cease—that all here present should adopt the Worship of Jehovah as taught to them by the Missionary and the Aneityumese—and that all the banished Tribes should be invited to their own lands to live in peace! These strange speeches did not draw forth a single opposing voice. Doubtless these men were in earnest, and had there been one master mind to rule and mould them, their regeneration had dawned. Though for the moment a feeling of friendliness prevailed, the Tannese were unstable as water and easily swayed one way or the other The Tannese are born

47. Racism and Darwinian eugenics was very strong at this time (as John G. Paton brings out in the Second Book of his *Autobiography*). Kanaka is a derogatory term referring to these people as "animal men."

talkers, and can and will speechify on all occasions; but most of it means nothing, bears no fruit.

After these speeches, a scene followed which gradually assumed shape as an idolatrous ceremonial and greatly horrified me.[48] It was in connection with the immense quantity of food that had been prepared for the feast, especially pigs and fowls. A great heap had been piled up for each Tribe represented, and a handsome portion also set apart for the Missionary and his Teachers. The ceremony was this, as nearly as I could follow it. One hundred or so of the leading men marched into the large clear space in the center of the assembled multitudes, and stood there facing each other in equal lines, with a man at either end closing up the passage between. At the middle they stood eight or ten feet apart, gradually nearing till they almost met at either end. Amid tremendous silence for a few moments, all stood hushed; then every man kneeled on his right knee, extended his right hand, and bent forward till his face nearly touched the ground. Thereon the man at the one end began muttering something, his voice rising ever louder as he rose to his feet, when it ended in a fearful yell as he stood erect. Next the two long lines of men, all in a body, went through the same ceremonial, rising gradually to their feet, with mutterings deepening into a howl, and heightening into a yell stood erect. Finally, the man at the other end went through the same hideous forms. All this was thrice deliberately repeated, each time with growing frenzy. And then, all standing on their feet, they united as with one voice in what sounded like music running mad up and down the scale—closing with a long, deep-toned, hollow howl as of souls in pain. With smiles of joy, the men then all shook hands with each other. Nowar and another Chief briefly spoke; and the food was then divided and exchanged, a principal man of each Tribe standing by to receive and watch his portion.

At this stage, Nowar and Nerwangi, as leaders, addressed the Teachers and the Missionary to this effect: "This feast is held to move all the Chiefs and People here to give up fight-

48. John G. Paton was concerned about the synthesis of devil worship (false gods) and Christianity. Thus, he didn't feel that he should eat the food offered to idols and thereby commune with these demons (1 Cor. 10:14-21 speaks directly to this.)

ing, to become friends, and to worship your Jehovah God. We wish you to remain, and to teach us all good conduct. As an evidence of our sincerity, and of our love, we have prepared this pile of food for you."

In reply, I addressed the whole multitude, saying how pleased I was with their speeches and with the resolutions and promises which they all had made. I further urged them to stick fast by these, and that grand fruits would arise to their island, to themselves, and to their children.

Having finished a brief address, I then walked forward to the very middle of the circle, and laid down before them a bundle of stripes of red calico and pieces of white calico, a number of fish-hooks, knives, etc., etc., requesting the two Chiefs to divide my offering of goodwill among the Tribes assembled, and also the pile of food presented to us, as a token of my love and friendship to them all.

Not without some doubt, and under considerable trial, did I take this apparently unfriendly attitude of refusing to take their food. But I feared to seem even to approve of any act of devil-worship, or to confirm them in it, being there to discourage all such scenes, and to lead them to acknowledge only the true God.[49] Yet all the time I felt this qualm—that it might have been better to eat food with men who acknowledged some God and asked his blessing, than with those white Heathens at home, who asked the blessing of no God, nor thanked Him—in this worse than the dog which licks the hand that feeds it! Nowar and Nerwangi explained in great orations what I meant, and how I wished all to be divided amongst the assembled Tribes to show my love. With this, all seemed highly satisfied.

Heathen dances were now entered upon, their paint and feathers and ornaments adding to the wildness of the scene. The men seemed to dance in an inside ring, and the women in an outside ring, at a considerable distance from each other. Music was supplied by singing and clapping of hands. The order was perfect, and the figures highly intricate. But I

49. Mission work that synthesizes with pagan religions turns out to be of no effect in the long run. It takes a great deal of faith to hold out the exclusive claims of Jesus Christ and demand a repudiation of the false gods.

have never been able to associate dancing with things lovely and of good report! After the dancing, all retired to the bush; and a kind of sham fight then followed on the public cleared ground. A host of painted savages rushed in and took possession with songs and shoutings. From the bush, on the opposite side, the chanting of women was heard in the distance, louder and louder as they approached. Snatching from a burning fire flaming sticks, they rushed on the men with these, beating them and throwing burning pieces of wood among them, till with deafening yells amongst themselves and amidst shouts of laughter from the crowd, they drove them from the space, and danced thereon and sang a song of victory. The dancing and fighting, the naked painted figures, and the constant yells and shoutings gave one a weird sensation, and suggested strange ideas of Hell broken loose.[50]

50. The attempts of men to resolve their differences in these heathen feasts or the United Nations are always short-lived and fruitless. There is no possibility of peace outside of Christ.

The final scene approached, when the men assisted their women to fill all the allotted food into baskets to be carried home and eaten there; for the different Tribes do not sit down together and eat together as we would do; their coming together is for the purpose of exchanging and dividing the food presented. And now they broke into friendly confusion, and freely walked about mingling with each other; and a kind of savage rehearsal of Jonathan and David took place. They stripped themselves of their fantastic dresses, their handsomely woven and twisted grass skirts, leaf skirts, grass and leaf aprons; they gave away or exchanged all these, and their ornaments and bows and arrows, besides their less romantic calico and print dresses more recently acquired. The effusion and ceremonial of the gifts and exchanges seem to betoken a loving people; and so they were for the feast—but that laid not aside a single deadly feud, and streams of blood and cries of hate would soon efface all traces of this day.

51. The Mathiesons were on the side of the island. Paton established mission stations and Bible teaching in six places on his side of the island, using native teachers from the island of Aneityum.

I had now six Stations, opened up and ministered to by Aneityumese Teachers, at the leading villages along the coast, and forming links in a chain towards the other mission Establishment on Tanna.[512] And there were villages prepared to receive as many more. These Teachers had all been Cannibals once; yet, with one exception, they proved themselves to the best of my judgment to be a band of faithful and devoted followers of Christ. Their names were Abraham, Kowari, Namuri, Nerwa, Lazarus, and Eoufati. I visited them periodically and frequently, encouraging and guiding them, as well as trying to interest the villagers in their teaching and work. But whenever war broke out they had all to return to the Mission House, and sleep there for safety by night, visiting their Stations, if practicable, by the light of day.[52] My poor dear Teachers, too, had to bear persecutions for Jesus' sake, as the following incident will sorrowfully prove.

A native woman, with some murderous purpose in her heart, pretended great friendship to the excellent wife of one of my fellow-laborers. She was specially effusive in bringing her dishes of food from time to time. Having thus gained confidence, she caught a little black fish of those parts, known to be deadly poisonous, and baked it up in a mess for the unsuspecting Teacher's wife. On returning, she boasted of what she had done, and thereon a friendly neighbor rushed off to warn the other, but arrived just to learn that the fatal meal had been taken. Beyond all reach of human skill, this unknown Martyr for Christ died soon after in great agony, and doubtless received her Master's reward.[53]

In helping to open up new Stations, those dear Native Teachers often bore the greatest hardships and indignities with a noble self-denial and positively wonderful patience. Nothing known to men under Heaven could have produced their new character and disposition, except only the grace of God in Christ Jesus. Though still marred by many of the faults of Heathenism, they were at the roots of their being literally new creatures, trying, according to their best light, to live for and to please their new Master, Jesus Christ. This shone out very conspicuously in these two apostolic souls, Abraham and Kowari, as leaders among all the devoted band.

52. The six teachers would find refuge at the mission house when war broke out between the tribes.

53. The Teacher's wife becomes the second martyr on Tanna.

54. John G. Paton has the reputation of being the great peacemaker on the island. Jesus said, "Blessed are the Peacemakers for they shall be called children of God."

Let me recall another occasion, on which I prevented a war. Early one morning, the savage yells of warring Tribes woke me from sleep. They had broken into a quarrel about a woman, and were fiercely engaged with their clubs. According to my custom, I rushed in amongst them, and, not without much difficulty, was blessed in separating them before deadly wounds had been given or received.[54] On this occasion, the Chiefs of both Tribes, being very friendly to me, drove their people back from each other at my earnest appeals. Sitting down at length within earshot, they had it out in a wild scolding match, a contest of lung and tongue. Meanwhile I rested on a canoe midway betwixt them, in the hope of averting a renewal of hostilities. By and by an old Sacred Man, a Chief, called Sapa, with some touch of savage comedy in his breast, volunteered an episode which restored good humor to the scene. Leaping up, he came dancing and singing towards me, and there, to the amusement of all, reenacted the quarrel, and mimicked rather cleverly my attempt at separating the combatants. Smashing at the canoe with his club, he yelled and knocked down imaginary enemies; then, rushing first at one party and then at the other, he represented me as appealing and gesticulating and pushing them afar from each other, till he became quite exhausted. Thereon he came and planted himself in great glee beside me, and looked around as if to say, "You must laugh, for I have played." At this very juncture, a loud cry of "Sail O!" broke upon our ears, and all parties leapt to their feet, and prepared for a new sensation; for in those climes, everything—war itself—is a smaller interest than a vessel from the Great Unknown Beyond sailing into your Harbor.

Not many days thereafter, a very horrible transaction occurred. Before daybreak, I heard shot after shot quickly discharged in the Harbor. One of my Teachers came running, and cried, "Missi, six or seven men have been shot dead this morning for a great feast. It is to reconcile Tribes that have been at war, and to allow a banished Tribe to return in peace."

I learned that the leading men had in council agreed upon this sacrifice, but the name of each victim was kept a secret till the last moment. The torture of suspense and uncertainty seemed to be borne by all as part of their appointed lot; nor did they prepare as if suspecting any dread assault. Before daylight, the Sacred Men allocated a murderer to the door of each house where a victim slept. A signal shot was fired; all rushed to their doors, and the doomed ones were shot and clubbed to death, as they attempted to escape. Their bodies were then borne to a sacred tree, and hung up there by the hands for a time as an offering to the gods. Being taken down, they were carried ceremoniously and laid out on the shore near my house, placed under a special guard.[55]

Information had reached me that my Teachers and I were also destined victims for this same feast; and sure enough we espied a band of armed men, the killers, dispatched towards our premises. Instantaneously I had the Teachers and their wives and myself securely locked into the Mission House; and, cut off from all human hope, we set ourselves to pray to our dear Lord Jesus, either Himself to protect us or to take us to His glory. All through that morning and forenoon we heard them tramp-tramping round our house, whispering to each other, and hovering near window and door. They knew that there were a double-barreled fowling-piece and a revolver on the premises, though they never had seen me use them, and that may, under God, have held them back in dread. But the thought of using them did not enter our souls even in that awful time. I had gone to save, and not to destroy. It would be easier for me at any time to die, than to kill one of them.[56] Our safety lay in our appeal to that blessed Lord who had placed us there, and to whom all power had been given in Heaven and on Earth. He that was with us was more than all that could be against us. This is strength—this is peace—to feel, in entering on every day, that all its duties and trials have been committed to the Lord Jesus—that, come what may, He will use us for His glory and our own real good!

55. Here was a dreadful human sacrifice of six or seven men, and cannibalism was typically a part of it.

56. Paton kept the guns, but only as a deterrent. He never intended to use them. Every missionary must make the decision whether he is there to give up his life for the Gospel or take other people's lives in the defense of his own. Biblically, we have more of an obligation to defend our family from violence than to defend our own lives.

57. The human sacrifice was intended to reconcile the tribes. This would only last for a very short while, however. The only sacrifice that takes down the walls of separation and establishes peace between God and man (and between man and man) is Christ. He is our peace (Eph. 2:14).

All through that dreadful morning, and far into the afternoon, we thus abode together, feeling conscious that we were united to this dear Lord Jesus; and we had sweet communion with Him, meditating on the wonders of His person and the hopes and glories of His kingdom. Oh, that all my readers may learn something of this in their own experience of the Lord! I can wish them nothing more precious. Towards sundown, constrained by the Invisible One, they withdrew from our Mission House, and left us once more in peace. They bore away the slain to be cooked, and distributed amongst the Tribes, and eaten in their feast of reconciliation; a covenant sealed in blood, and soon, alas, to be buried in blood again![57] For many days thereafter we had to take unusual care, and not unduly expose ourselves to danger; for dark characters were seen prowling about in the bush near at hand, and we knew that our life was the prize. We took what care we could, and God the Lord did the rest; or rather He did all—for His wisdom guided us, and His power baffled them.

Shortly thereafter war was again declared, by the Inland people attacking our Harbor people. It was an old quarrel; and the war was renewed and continued, long after the cause thereof had passed away. Going amongst them every day, I did my utmost to stop hostilities, setting the evils of war before them, and pleading with the leading men to renounce it. Thereon arose a characteristic incident of Island and Heathen life. One day I held a Service in the village where morning after morning their Tribes assembled, and declared that if they would believe in and follow the Jehovah God, He would deliver them from all their enemies and lead them into a happy life. There were present three Sacred Men, Chiefs, of whom the whole population lived in terror—brothers or cousins, heroes of traditional feats, professors of sorcery, and claiming the power of life and death, health and sickness, rain and drought, according to their will. On hearing me, these three stood up and declared they did not believe in Jehovah, nor did they need His help; for they had the power to kill my life by *Nahak* (i.e. sorcery or witchcraft), if only they could get possession of any piece of the fruit or food that I had eaten. This was an essential condition of their black art; hence the peel of a banana or an orange, and every broken scrap of food, is gathered up by the Natives, lest it should fall into the hands of the Sacred Men, and be used for *Nahak*. This superstition was the cause of most of the bloodshed and terror upon Tanna; and being thus challenged, I asked God's help, and determined to strike a blow against it.[58]

A woman was standing near with a bunch of native fruit in her hand, like our plums, called quonquore. I asked her to be pleased to give me some; and she, holding out a bunch, said, "Take freely what you will!"

Calling the attention of all the Assembly to what I was doing, I took three fruits from the bunch, and taking a bite out of each, I gave them one after another to the three Sacred Men, and deliberately said in the hearing of all, "You have seen me eat of this fruit, you have seen me give the remainder to your Sacred Men; they have said they can kill me by *Nahak*, but I challenge them to do it if they can, without arrow or spear, club or musket; for I deny that they have any power against me, or against any one, by their Sorcery."[59]

The challenge was accepted; the Natives looked terror-struck at the position in which I was placed! The ceremony of *Nahak* was usually performed in secret—the Tannese fleeing in dread, as Europeans would from the touch of the plague; but I lingered and eagerly watched their ritual. As the three Chiefs arose, and drew near to one of the Sacred Trees, to begin their ceremonial, the Natives fled in terror, crying, "Missi, Iawé? Alas, Missi!"

But I held on at my post of observation. Amidst wavings and incantations, they rolled up the pieces of the fruit from which I had eaten, in certain leaves of this Sacred Tree, into a shape like a waxen candle; then they kindled a sacred fire near the root, and continued their mutterings, gradually burning a little more and a little more of the candle-shaped things,

58. Most of the wars on Tanna were caused by the superstitious belief that a demonic magical curse could be placed on somebody (if they could get a hold of something they had eaten).

59. Paton performs a test on their powers, not unlike Elijah testing the prophets of Baal on Carmel.

wheeling them round their heads, blowing upon them with their breaths, waving them in the air, and glancing wildly at me as if expecting my sudden destruction. Wondering whether after all they did not believe their own lie, for they seemed to be in dead earnest, I, more eager than ever to break the chains of such vile superstition, urged them again and again, crying, "Be quick! Stir up your gods to help you! I am not killed yet; I am perfectly well!"

At last they stood up and said, "We must delay till we have called all our Sacred Men. We will kill Missi before his next Sabbath comes round. Let all watch, for he will soon die and that without fail."[60]

I replied, "Very good! I challenge all your Priests to unite and kill me by Sorcery or *Nahak*. If on Sabbath next I come again to your village in health, you will all admit that your gods have no power over me, and that I am protected by the true and living Jehovah God!"

Every day throughout the remainder of that week the Conchs were sounded; and over that side of the island all their Sacred Men were at work trying to kill me by their arts. Now and again messengers arrived from every quarter of the island, inquiring anxiously after my health, and wondering if I was not feeling sick, and great excitement prevailed amongst the poor deluded idolaters.

Sabbath dawned upon me peacefully, and I went to that village in more than my usual health and strength. Large numbers assembled, and when I appeared they looked at each other in terror, as if it could not really be I myself still spared and well. Entering into the public ground, I saluted them to this effect, "My love to you all, my friends! I have come again to talk to you about the Jehovah God and His Worship."

The three Sacred Men, on being asked, admitted that they had tried to kill me by *Nahak*, but had failed; and on being questioned, why they had failed; they gave the acute and subtle reply, that I also was myself a Sacred Man, and that my God being the stronger had protected me from their gods.[612]

60. The pagan priests needed more time, like the prophets of Baal who couldn't quite awaken their gods.

61. They had to admit that Jehovah God was stronger than their gods.

Addressing the multitude, I answered thus, "Yea, truly; my Jehovah God is stronger than your gods. He protected me, and helped me; for He is the only living and true God, the only God that can hear or answer any prayer from the children of men. Your gods cannot hear prayer, but my God can and will hear and answer you, if you will give heart and life to Him, and love and serve Him only. This is my God, and He is also your friend if you will hear and follow His voice."

Having said this, I sat down on the trunk of a fallen tree, and addressed them, "Come and sit down all around me, and I will talk to you about the love and mercy of my God, and teach you how to worship and please Him."

Two of the Sacred Men then sat down, and all the people gathered round and seated themselves very quietly. I tried to present to them ideas of sin, and of salvation through Jesus Christ, as revealed to us in the Holy Scriptures.[62]

The third Sacred Man, the highest in rank, a man of great stature and uncommon strength, had meantime gone off for his warrior's spear, and returned brandishing it in the air and poising it at me. I said to the people, "Of course he can kill me with his spear, but he undertook to kill me by *Nahak* or Sorcery, and promised not to use against me any weapons of war; and if you let him kill me now, you will kill your friend, one who lives among you and only tries to do you good, as you all know so well. I know that if you kill me thus, my God will be angry and will punish you."

Thereon I seated myself calmly in the midst of the crowd, while he leaped about in rage, scolding his brothers and all who were present for listening to me. The other Sacred Men, however, took my side, and, as many of the people also were friendly to me and stood closely packed around me, he did not throw his spear. To allay the tumult and obviate further bloodshed, I offered to leave with my Teachers at once, and, in doing so, I ardently pled with them to live at peace. Though we got safely home, that old Sacred Man seemed still to hunger after my blood. For weeks thereafter, go where I would, he

62. This may have been Paton's best opportunity to teach the Gospel on Tanna. He spoke of sin and Christ's salvation to the most influential "Sacred Men."

would suddenly appear on the path behind me, poising in his right hand that same Goliath spear. God only kept it from being thrown, and I, using every lawful precaution, had all the same to attend to my work, as if no enemy were there, leaving all other results in the hands of Jesus. This whole incident did, doubtless, shake the prejudices of many as to Sorcery; but few even of converted Natives ever get entirely clear of the dread of *Nahak*.[63]

63. The fear of false gods and black magic (the demonic world) is strong, especially when it has been engrained for generations.

If not truly converted, the two Priests were fast friends of mine from that day, as also another leading man in the same district. They also received an Aneityumese Teacher to their village, protecting and showing kindness to him; one of the Sacred Men who could speak his language lived almost constantly with him, and some young people were allowed daily to attend our School. These two and a number of others began to wear a kilt, and some a shirt also.[64] Three of them especially, if not Christians, appeared to be not far from the Kingdom of God, and did all that was in their power to protect and to assist me. A few began to pray to Jehovah in their houses offering a kind of rude Family Worship, and breathing out such prayers and desires as I had taught them for the knowledge of the true God and only Saviour.[65] And these, as my companions, accompanied me from place to place when I visited their district.

64. Kilts and shirts would have been traditional Scottish dress. These men were more likely to abandon the cultural nakedness of the pagans.

65. Family Worship was key to any kind of Christian life (in the pagan world or the Western world). Where it is missing in modern families, it is hard to say there is any Christian faith left.

But let us return to the war. Many Chiefs and villages were now involved in it; and a large part of the bush over the country between had been consumed by fire, to prevent surprises. Yet, our Harbor people being assembled one night for consultation, a number of the Inland warriors crept near unobserved and discharged a volley of muskets amongst them. Several were shot dead, and in the darkness and confusion the enemy got clear away. Revenge and self-preservation now united our people as one man, and every man assembled for action on the borders of the hostile Tribes. I again visited them on the fighting ground. As I was seen approaching, the two old Priests, my friends, came to receive and escort me, protected by their clubs and muskets—the one blind of an eye lost in war marching before me, and the other behind me with poised spear and mighty club. Seating me in a central position, they assembled all the warriors, except the watchmen, and these savage men listened attentively to my message, and bowed quietly during prayer. God only knows what may be the fruit in some dark benighted soul. The whole host of them ceased firing, till the two friendly Priests had again conveyed me safely beyond the reach of danger.

Going among them frequently thus, they treated me with exceptional kindness, till one Sabbath I determined to go over and talk with the enemy also, in the hope of getting this sad war put an end to. Our people were sternly opposed to this, not for fear of my safety, but lest I prayed for the enemy and my God might help them in the war. But my two friends, the old Priests, persuaded them to let me go, and to cease their shooting till my return. They had an idea to buy, in this way, my intercession with Jehovah exclusively on their behalf; but I explained to them as on former occasions, that I was there for the good of all alike, that I loved them all and sought to lead them to give up war and bad conduct, for my God would hear and bless only those who feared and loved and obeyed Him. I had a long interview with the enemies also, arguing against the evils of war, and urging them to give it up.[66] They were so far friendly; they allowed me to have worship amongst them, and I returned in safety before another musket was discharged on either side. The war still went on, though more languidly; but after a time the leaders entered into a kind of truce, and peace reigned for a season.

The other Mission Station, on the southwest side of Tanna, had to be visited by me from time to time. Mr. and Mrs. Mathieson, there, were both in a weak state of health, having a tendency to consumption. On this account they visited Aneityum several times. They were earnestly devoted to their work, and were successful as far as health and the time allowed to them permitted. At this juncture, a message reached

66. Paton continually called them to repentance, to give up their wars and bad conduct (sinful lifestyles). Repentance is basic for any Gospel ministry.

me that they were without European food, and a request to send them a little flour if possible. The war made the journey overland impossible. A strong wind and a high sea round the coast rendered it impracticable for my boat to go. The danger to life from the enemy was so great that I could not hire a crew. I pled therefore with Nowar and Manuman, and a few leading men, to take one of their best canoes, and themselves to accompany me. I had a large flat-bottomed pot with a close fitting lid, and that I pressed full of flour; and, tying the lid firmly down, I fastened it right in the center of the canoe, and as far above water-mark as possible. All else that was required we tied around our own persons. Sea and land being as they were, it was a perilous undertaking, which only dire necessity could have justified. They were all swimmers, but as I could not swim, the strongest man was placed behind me, to seize me and swim ashore, if a crash came.

Creeping round near the shore all the way, we had to keep just outside the great breakers on the coral reef, and were all drenched through and through with the foam of an angry surf. We arrived, however, in safety within two miles of our destination, where lived the friends of my canoe's company, but where a very dangerous sea was breaking on the reef. Here they all gave in, and protested that no further could they go; and truly their toil all the way with the paddles had been severe. I appealed to them, that the canoe would for certain be smashed if they tried to get on shore, that the provisions would be lost, and some of us probably drowned. But they turned to the shore, and remained for some time thus, watching the sea. At last their Captain cried, "Missi, hold on! There's a smaller wave coming; we'll ride in now."

67. Through each and every hardship, Paton lifted up a prayer to God for deliverance. We find him resorting to prayer at every obstacle and difficulty along the way.

My heart rose to the Lord in trembling prayer![67] The wave came rolling on; every paddle with all their united strength struck into the sea; and next moment our canoe was flying like a sea-gull on the crest of the wave towards the shore. Another instant, and the wave had broken on the reef with a mighty roar, and rushed passed us hissing in clouds of foam. My company were next seen swimming wildly about in the sea, Manu-man the one-eyed Sacred Man alone holding on by the canoe, nearly full of water, with me still clinging to the seat of it, and the very next wave likely to devour us. In desperation, I sprang for the reef, and ran for a man half-wading, half-swimming to reach us; and God so ordered it, that just as the next wave broke against the silvery rock of coral, the man caught me and partly swam with me through its surf, partly carried me till I was set safely ashore. Praising God, I looked up and saw all the others as safe as myself, except Manuman, my friend, who was still holding on by the canoe in the face of wind and sea, and bringing it with him. Others ran and swam to his help. The paddles were picked up amid the surf. A powerful fellow came towards me with the pot of flour on his head, uninjured by wa-ter! The Chief who held on by the canoe got severely cut about the feet, and had been badly bruised and knocked about; but all the rest escaped without further harm, and everything that we had was saved. Amongst friends at last, they resolved to await a favorable wind and tide to return to their own homes. Singing in my heart unto God, I hired a man to carry the pot of flour, and soon arrived at the Mission Station.[68]

Supplying the wants of our dear friends, Mr. and Mrs. Mathieson, whom we found as well as could be expected, we had to prepare, after a few hours of rest, to return to our own Station by walking overland through the night. I durst not remain longer away, lest my own house should be plundered and broken into. Though weak in health, my fellow-Mission-aries were both full of hope, and zealous in their work, and this somewhat strange visit was a pleasant blink amidst our dark-ness. Before I had gone far on my return journey, the sun went down, and no Native could be hired to accompany me. They all told me that I would for certain be killed by the way. But I knew that it would be quite dark before I reached the hostile districts, and that the Heathen are great cowards in the dark and never leave their villages at night in the darkness, except in companies for fishing and suchlike tasks. I skirted along the

68. Paton made this dangerous trip to deliver flour to the Mathiesons, a reminder of the three mighty men of David (2 Sam. 23) who broke through the Philistines for water from the well of Bethlehem!

sea-shore as fast as I could, walking and running alternately; and, when I got within hearing of voices, I slunk back into the bush till they had safely passed, and then groped my way back near the shore, that being my only guide to find a path.

Having made half the journey, I came to a dangerous path, almost perpendicular, up a great rock round the base of which the sea roared deep. With my heart lifted up to Jesus, I succeeded in climbing it, cautiously grasping roots, and resting by bushes, till I safely reached the top. There, to avoid a village, I had to keep crawling slowly along the brush near the sea, on the top of that great ledge of rock—a feat I could never have accomplished even in daylight without the excitement; but I felt that I was supported and guided in all that life-or-death journey by my dear Lord Jesus.[69] I had to leave the shore, and follow up the bank of a very deep ravine to a place shallow enough for one to cross, and then through the bush away for the shore again. By holding too much to the right, I missed the point where I had intended to reach it. Small fires were now visible through the bush; I heard the voices of the people talking in one of our most Heathen villages.

Quietly drawing back, I now knew where I was, and easily found my way towards the shore; but on reaching the Great Rock, I could not in the darkness find the path down again. I groped about till I was tired. I feared that I might stumble over and be killed; or, if I delayed till daylight, that the savages would kill me. I knew that one part of the rock was steep-sloping, with little growth or none thereon, and I searched about to find it, resolved to commend myself to Jesus and slide down thereby, that I might again reach the shore and escape for my life. Thinking I had found this spot, I hurled down several stones and listened for their splash that I might judge whether it would be safe. But the distance was too far for me to hear or judge. At high tide the sea there was deep; but at low tide I could wade out of it and be safe. The darkness made it impossible for me to see anything. I let go my umbrella, shoving it

69. John Paton relied on Christ's presence and Christ's help in genuine faith along the way. To Paton, the Lord was very near, and he was confident, completely confident of his presence. We find this throughout his experience on Tanna.

down with considerable force, but neither did it send me back any news.

Feeling sure, however, that this was the place I sought, and knowing that to await the daylight would be certain death, I prayed to my Lord Jesus for help and protection, and resolved to let myself go. First, I fastened all my clothes as tightly as I could, so as not to catch on anything; then I lay down at the top on my back, feet foremost, holding my head downwards on my breast to keep it from striking on the rock; then, after one cry to my Saviour, having let myself down as far as possible by a branch, I at last let go, throwing my arms forward and trying to keep my feet well up. A giddy swirl, as if flying through the air, took possession of me; a few moments seemed an age; I rushed quickly down, and felt no obstruction till my feet struck into the sea below. Adoring and praising my dear Lord Jesus, who had ordered it so, I regained my feet; it was low tide, I had received no injury, I recovered my umbrella, and, wading through, I found the shore path easier and lighter than the bush had been. The very darkness was my safety, preventing the Natives from rambling about. I saw no person to speak to, till I reached a village quite near to my own house, fifteen or twenty miles from where I had started; I here left the sea path and promised some young men a gift of fish-hooks to guide me the nearest way through the bush to my Mission Station, which they gladly and heartily did. I ran a narrow risk in approaching them; they thought me an enemy, and I arrested their muskets only by a loud cry:

"I am Missi! Don't shoot; my love to you, my friends!"

Praising God for His preserving care, I reached home, and had a long refreshing sleep. The natives, on hearing next day how I had come all the way in the dark exclaimed:

"Surely any of us would have been killed! Your Jehovah God alone thus protects you and brings you safely home."

With all my heart, I said, "Yes! and He will be your protector and helper too, if only you will obey and trust in Him."

70. It is amazing to think that he walked 15-20 miles through enemy territory, through the rugged bush and over cliffs in the night, and reached home safely in just 8-10 hours of walking.

Certainly that night put my faith to the test. Had it not been the assurance that I was engaged in His service, and that in every path of duty He would carry me through or dispose of me therein for His glory, I could never have undertaken either journey. St. Paul's words are true today and forever—"I can do all things through Christ which strengtheneth me."[70]

※ CHAPTER IX –
DEEPENING SHADOWS
A.D. 1860-1861. Age 36-37

In September, 1860, I had the very great pleasure of welcoming, as fellow-laborers to Tanna, the Rev. S. F. Johnston and his wife, two able and pious young Missionaries from Nova Scotia.[1] Having visited the whole group of the New Hebrides, they preferred to cast their lot on Tanna. During the Rainy Season, and till they had acquired a little of the language, and some preparation had been made of a Station for themselves, I gladly received them as my guests. The company was very sweet to me! I gave them about fourteen Tannese words to be committed to memory every day, and conversed with them, using the words already acquired; so that they made very rapid progress, and almost immediately were of some service in the Mission work. No man could have desired better companions in the ministry of the Gospel.

About this time I had a never-to-be-forgotten illustration of the infernal spirit that possessed some of the Traders towards these poor Natives. One morning, three or four vessels entered our Harbor and cast anchor in Port Resolution. The captains called on me, and one of them, with manifest delight, exclaimed, "We know how to bring down your proud Tannese now! We'll humble them before you!"

1. The Mathiesons from Nova Scotia were on the other side of Tanna. Now the Johnstons (also from Nova Scotia) would join the missionary troop.

I answered, "Surely you don't mean to attack and destroy these poor people?"

He replied, not abashed but rejoicing, "We have sent the measles to humble them! That kills them by the score! Four young men have been landed at different ports, ill with measles, and these will soon thin their ranks."[2]

Shocked above measure, I protested solemnly and denounced their conduct and spirit; but my remonstrances only called forth the shameless declaration, "Our watchword is—Sweep these creatures away and let white men occupy the soil!"[3]

Their malice was further illustrated thus: they induced Kapuku, a young Chief, to go off to one of their vessels, promising him a present. He was the friend and chief supporter of Mr. Mathieson and of his work. Having got him on board, they confined him in the hold amongst natives lying ill with measles. They gave him no food for about four-and-twenty hours; and then, without the promised present, they put him ashore far from his own home. Though weak and excited, he scrambled back to his tribe in great exhaustion and terror. He informed the Missionary that they had put him down amongst sick people, red and hot with fever, and that he feared their sickness was upon him. I am ashamed to say that these Sandal-wood and other Traders were our own degraded countrymen; and that they deliberately gloried in thus destroying the poor Heathen. A more fiendish spirit could scarcely be imagined; but most of them were horrible drunkards, and their traffic of every kind amongst these islands was, generally speaking, steeped in human blood.

The measles, thus introduced, became amongst our islanders the most deadly plague. It spread fearfully, and was accompanied by sore throat and diarrhea. In some villages, man, woman, and child were stricken, and none could give food or water to the rest. The misery, suffering, and terror were unexampled, the living being afraid sometimes even to bury the dead. Thirteen of my own Mission party died of this disease;

2. Western diseases were the primary means by which the native populations on these far off islands were decimated. The Native population in America plunged by 95% due to measles outbreaks, and Hawaii lost about a third of their population. These nations had not formed a long standing immunity or resistance to the disease, and the immediate opening up of trade routes paved the way for these pandemics. What cruelty to purposefully spread the disease on Tanna!

3. "Sweep these creatures away. . . " Darwinian eugenics was an ideology that had captured many of the unbelieving minds of the 19th century. In his second part of the *Autobiography*, Paton finds this same spirit in Australia.

and, so terror-stricken were the few who survived, that when the little Mission schooner John Knox returned to Tanna, they all packed up and left for their own Aneityum, except my own dear old Abraham.[4]

4. The measles also decimated the mission. Only the native missionary, Abraham, remained with Paton.

At first, thinking that all were on the wing, he also had packed his chattels, and was standing beside the others ready to leave with them. I drew near to him, and said, "Abraham, they are all going; are you also going to leave me here alone on Tanna, to fight the battles of the Lord?"

He asked, "Missi, will you remain?"

I replied, "Yes; but Abraham, the danger to life is now so great that I dare not plead with you to remain, for we may both be slain. Still, I cannot leave the Lord's work now."

The noble old Chief looked at the box and his bundles, and, musingly, said, "Missi, our danger is very great now."

I answered, "Yes; I once thought you would not leave me alone to it; but, as the vessel is going to your own land, I cannot ask you to remain and face it with me!"

He again said, "Missi, would you like me to remain alone with you, seeing my wife is dead and in her grave here?"

I replied, "Yes, I would like you to remain; but, considering the circumstances in which we will be left alone, I cannot plead with you to do so."

He answered, "Then, Missi, I remain with you of my own free choice, and with all my heart. We will live and die together in the work of the Lord. I will never leave you while you are spared on Tanna."[5]

5. Such courage and loyalty is hard to find anywhere in the world. Old Abraham is committed to giving his life for the "work of the Lord."

So saying, and with a light that gave the fore-gleam of a Martyr's glory to his dark face, he shouldered his box and bundles back to his own house; and thereafter, Abraham was my dear companion and constant friend, and my fellow-sufferer in all that remains still to be related of our Mission life on Tanna.

Before this plague of measles was brought amongst us, I had sailed round in the *John Knox* to Black Beach on the opposite side of Tanna, and prepared the way for settling Teach-

6. Typically, it was the missionaries that labored the hardest to save the lives of the natives (once they were inflicted with these deadly diseases). This story is told many times in the history of missions.

ers. And they were placed soon after by Mr. Copeland and myself with encouraging hopes of success, and with the prospect of erecting there a Station for Mr. and Mrs. Johnson, the newly arrived Missionaries from Nova Scotia. But this dreadful imported epidemic blasted all our dreams. They devoted themselves from the very first, and assisted me in every way to alleviate the dread sufferings of the Natives. We carried medicine, food, and even water, to the surrounding villages every day, few of themselves being able to render us much assistance. Nearly all who took our medicine and followed instructions as to food, etc., recovered;[6] but vast numbers of them would listen to no counsels, and rushed into experiments which made the attack fatal all around. When the trouble was at its height, for instance, they would plunge into the sea, and seek relief; they found it an almost instant death. Others would dig a hole into the earth, the length of the body and about two feet deep; therein they laid themselves down, the cold earth feeling agreeable to their fevered skins; and when the earth around them grew heated, they got friends to dig a few inches deeper, again and again, seeking a cooler and cooler couch. In this ghastly effort many of them died, literally in their own graves, and were buried where they lay! It need not be surprising, though we did everything in our power to relieve and save them, that the natives associated us with the white men who had so dreadfully afflicted them, and that their blind thirst for revenge did not draw fine distinctions between the Traders and the Missionaries. Both were whites—that was enough.

The 1st January, 1861, was a New Year's Day ever to be remembered. Mr. and Mrs. Johnston, Abraham, and I, had spent nearly the whole time in a kind of solemn yet happy festival. Anew in a holy covenant before God, we unitedly consecrated our lives and our all to the Lord Jesus, giving ourselves away to His blessed service for the conversion of the Heathen on the New Hebrides. After evening Family Worship,[7] Mr. and Mrs. Johnston left my room to go to their own house, only some ten feet distant; but he returned to inform me that there were two

7. John G. Paton continued a morning and evening time of worship every day, even when on the islands.

men at the window, armed with huge clubs, and having black painted faces. Going out to them and asking them, what they wanted, they replied, "Medicine for a sick boy."

With difficulty I persuaded them to come in and get it. At once, it flashed upon me, from their agitation and their disguise of paint, that they had come to murder us. Mr. Johnston had also accompanied us into the house. Keeping my eye constantly fixed on them, I prepared the medicine and offered it. They refused to receive it, and each man grasped his killing-stone. I faced them firmly and said, "You see that Mr. Johnston is now leaving, and you too must leave this room for tonight. Tomorrow, you can bring the boy or come for the medicine."

Seizing their clubs, as if for action, they showed unwillingness to withdraw, but I walked deliberately forward and made as if to push them out, when both turned and began to leave.

Mr. Johnston had gone in front of them and was safely out. But he bent down to lift a little kitten that had escaped at the open door; and at that moment one of the savages, jerking in behind, aimed a blow with his huge club, in avoiding which Mr. Johnston fell with a scream to the ground. Both men sprang towards him, but our two faithful dogs ferociously leapt in their faces and saved his life.[8] Rushing out, but not fully aware of what had occurred, I saw Mr. Johnston trying to raise himself, and heard him cry, "Take care! These men have tried to kill me, and they will kill you!"

Facing them sternly I demanded, "What is it that you want? He does not understand your language. What do you want? Speak with me."

Both men, thereon, raised their great clubs and made to strike me; but quick as lightning these two dogs sprang at their faces and baffled their blows. One dog was badly bruised, and the ground received the other blow that would have launched me into Eternity. The best dog was a little cross-bred retriever with terrier blood in him, splendid for warning us of ap-

8. This is not the first time God used dogs to save the lives of his people. Paton's life was saved a number of times by his dogs.

9. Paton felt it was important to remind the savages of the all-seeing eyes of God, who beholds both the evil and the good. From time to time, we must "warn the unruly" of the judgment of God (1 Thess. 5:14).

10. Paton refers to Psalm 46.

11. Importantly, Paton maintains a healthy fear of God, a reverence for God's final judgment on the Great White Throne. Thus, there is a gravity about his thinking now — but no fear of man.

proaching dangers, and which had already been the means of saving my life several times. Seeing how matters stood, I now hounded both dogs furiously upon them, and the two savages fled. I shouted after them, "Remember, Jehovah God sees you and will punish you for trying to murder His servants!"[9]

In their flight, a large body of men, who had come eight or ten miles to assist in the murder and plunder, came slipping here and there from the bush and joined them, fleeing too. Verily, "the wicked flee, when no man pursueth." David's experience and assurance came home to us, that evening, as very real— "God is our refuge and our strength. . . therefore we will not fear."[10] But, after the danger was all past, I had always a strange feeling of fear, more perhaps from the thought that I had been on the verge of Eternity and so near the great White Throne than from any slavish fear. During the crisis, I felt generally calm, and firm of soul, standing erect and with my whole weight on the promise, "Lo! I am with you alway." Precious promise! How often I adore Jesus for it, and rejoice in it! Blessed be His name.

I, now accustomed to such scenes on Tanna, retired to rest and slept soundly; but my dear fellow-laborer, as I afterwards learned, could not sleep for one moment. His pallor and excitement continued next day, indeed for several days; and after that, though he was naturally lively and cheerful, I never saw him smile again. He told me next morning:

"I can only keep saying to myself, Already on the verge of Eternity! How have I spent my time? What good have I done? What zeal for souls have I shown? Scarcely entered on the work of my life, and so near death! O my friend, I never realized what death means, till last night!" So saying, he covered his face with both hands, and left me to hide himself in his own room.[11]

For that morning, 1st January, 1861, the following entry was found in his Journal: "Today, with a heavy heart and a feeling of dread, I know not why, I set out on my accustomed wanderings amongst the sick. I hastened back to get the

Teacher and carry Mr. Paton to the scene of distress. I carried a bucket of water in one hand and medicine in the other; and so we spent a portion of this day endeavoring to alleviate their sufferings, and our work had a happy effect also on the minds of others." In another entry, on 22nd December, he wrote: "Measles are making fearful havoc amongst the poor Tannese. As we pass through the villages, mournful scenes meet the eye; young and old prostrated on the ground, showing all these painful symptoms which accompany loathsome and malignant diseases. In some villages few are left able to prepare food, or to carry drink to the suffering and dying. How pitiful to see the sufferers destitute of every comfort, attention, and remedy that would ameliorate their suffering or remove their disease! As I think of the tender manner in which we are nursed in sickness, the many remedies employed to give relief, with the comforts and attention bestowed upon us, my heart sickens, and I say, Oh my ingratitude and the ingratitude of Christian people! How little we value our Christian birth, education, and privileges, etc."

Having, as above recorded, consecrated our lives anew to God on the first day of January, I was, up till the 16th of the month, accompanied by Mr. Johnston and sometimes also by Mrs. Johnston on my rounds in the villages amongst the sick, and they greatly helped me. But by an unhappy accident I was laid aside when most sorely needed. When adzing a tree for housebuilding I observed that Mahanan, the war Chief's brother, had been keeping too near me, and that he carried a tomahawk in his hand; and, in trying both to do my work and to keep an eye on him, I struck my ankle severely with the adze. He moved off quickly, saying, "I did not do that," but doubtless rejoicing at what had happened. The bone was badly hurt, and several of the blood-vessels cut. Dressing it as well as I could, and keeping it constantly soaked in cold water, I had to exercise the greatest care. In this condition, amidst great sufferings, I was sometimes carried to the villages

12. Even when unable to walk due to an injury, Paton still was carried to the village so that he could care for the sick and dying. Truly, he was a man willing to give His life for the service of Jesus.

13. Mr. Johnston is a godly man, taking right lessons from the terrible circumstances unfolding on the island. We should be thankful for the medical treatment available to us, providing us with comfort (whereas the people on Tanna suffer without respite from these diseases).

to administer medicine to the sick, and to plead and pray with the dying.[12]

On such occasions, in this mode of transit even, the conversations that I had with dear Mr. Johnston were most solemn and greatly refreshing. He had, however, scarcely ever slept since the 1st of January, and during the night of the 16th he sent for my bottle of laudanum. Being severely attacked with ague and fever, I could not go to him, but sent the bottle, specifying the proper quantity for a dose, but that he quite understood already. He took a dose for himself, and gave one also to his wife, as she too suffered from sleeplessness. This he repeated three nights in succession, and both of them obtained a long, sound and refreshing sleep. He came to my bedside, where I lay in the ague-fever, and said with great animation, amongst other things, "I have had such a blessed sleep, and feel so refreshed! What kindness in God to provide such remedies for suffering man!"[13]

At midday his dear wife came to me crying, "Mr. Johnston has fallen asleep, so deep that I cannot awake him."

My fever had reached the worst stage, but I struggled to my feet, got to his bedside, and found him in a state of coma, with his teeth fixed in tetanus. With great difficulty we succeeded in slightly rousing him; with a knife, spoon, and pieces of wood, we forced his teeth open, so as to administer an emetic with good effects, and also other needful medicines. For twelve hours, we had to keep him awake by repeated cold dashes in the face, by ammonia, and by vigorously moving him about. He then began to speak freely; and next day he rose and walked about a little. For the two following days, he was sometimes better and sometimes worse; but we managed to keep him up till the morning of the 21st, when he again fell into a state of coma, from which we failed to rouse him. At two o'clock in the afternoon he fell asleep—another Martyr for the testimony of Jesus in those dark and trying Isles, leaving his young wife in indescribable sorrow, which she strove to bear with Christian resignation. Having made his coffin and dug his grave, we two alone at sunset laid him to rest beside my own dear wife and child, close by the Mission House.

In Mrs. Johnston's account, in a letter to friends regarding his death, she says:

"Next morning, the 17th, he rose quite well. He slept well the night before from having taken a dose of laudanum.[14] He also gave some to me, as I had been ill all the day, having slept little for two or three nights. . . . Two men helped Mr. Paton to his bedside, as I found him lying very low in fever, yet he waited on Mr. Johnston affectionately. For some time, while he was in Mr. Paton's hands, I could scarcely keep myself up at all. We thought it was from the laudanum I had taken.[15] I had to throw myself down every few minutes. . . . For some weeks after, I was almost constantly bedfast. I ate little; still I felt no pain, but very stupid. . . . At times, we have services with the Natives. For a week past, we have scarcely gone to bed without fears. One night, our house was surrounded with crowds of armed men, ready at any moment to break in upon us for our lives. We have had to sit in the house for days past, with the doors locked, to prevent any of the savages from entering; for every party seems to be united against us now. The great sickness that prevails amongst them is the cause of this rage. They say, we made the disease, and we must be killed for it; that they never died in this way before the religion came amongst them, etc., etc."

Mrs. Johnston recovered gradually, returned by the first opportunity to Aneityum, and for nearly three years taught the girls' School at Dr. Geddie's Station. Thereafter she was married to my dear friend the Rev. Joseph Copeland, and spent with him the remainder of her life on Fotuna, working devotedly in the service of the Mission, seeking the salvation of the Heathen.[16]

The death of Mr. Johnston was a heavy loss. From his landing on Tanna, he appeared to enjoy excellent health, and was always very active, bright, and happy, till after that attack by the savages with their clubs on New Year's Day. From that

14. Laudanum is a tincture of opium (10% concentrate), administered to help them sleep.

15. A single dose of 100-150 mg of laudanum could result in death for an adult not used to this medication. A coma is another possible symptom of an overdose.

16. The widow, Mrs. Johnston, married Joseph Copeland (the single man who was his friend from seminary in Scotland).

night, he never again was the same. He never admitted that he had got a blow, but I fear his nervous system must have been unhinged by the shock and horror of the scene. He was genuinely lamented by all who knew him. Our intercourse on Tanna was very sweet, and I missed him exceedingly. Not lost to me, however; only gone before![17]

17. Paton lost the encouragement and assistance of another missionary when Johnston died. But still, Paton is hopeful in the resurrection.

Another tragedy followed, with, however, much of the light of Heaven amid its blackness, in the story of Kowia, a Tannese Chief of the highest rank. Going to Aneityum in youth, he had there become a true Christian. He married an Aneityumese Christian woman, with whom he lived very happily and had two beautiful children. Some time before the measles reached our island he returned to live with me as a Teacher and to help forward our work on Tanna. He proved himself to be a decided Christian; he was a real Chief amongst them, dignified in his whole conduct, and every way a valuable helper to me. Everything was tried by his own people to induce him to leave me and to renounce the Worship, offering him every honor and bribe in their power. Failing these, they threatened to take away all his lands, and to deprive him of Chieftainship, but he answered "Take all! I shall still stand by Missi and the Worship of Jehovah.

From threats they passed to galling insults, all which he bore patiently for Jesus' sake. But one day a party of his people came and sold some fowls, and an impudent fellow lifted them after they had been bought and offered to sell them again to me. Kowia shouted, "Don't purchase these, Missi; I have just bought them for you, and paid for them!"

Thereon the fellow began to mock at him. Kowia, gazing round on all present, and then on me, rose like a lion awaking out of sleep, and with flashing eyes exclaimed, "Missi, they think that because I am now a Christian I have become a coward! a woman! to bear every abuse and insult they can heap upon me. But I will show them for once that I am no coward, that I am still their Chief, and that Christianity does not take away but gives us courage and nerve."

Springing at one man, he wrenched in a moment the mighty club from his hands, and swinging it in air above his head like a toy, he cried, "Come any of you, come all against your Chief! My Jehovah God makes my heart and arms strong. He will help me in this battle as He helps me in other things, for He inspires me to show you that Christians are no cowards, though they are men of peace. Come on, and you will yet know that I am Kowia your Chief."[18]

All fled as he approached them; and he cried, "Where are the cowards now?" and handed back to the warrior his club. After this they left him at peace.

He lived at the Mission House, with his wife and children, and was a great help and comfort to Abraham and myself. He was allowed to go more freely and fearlessly amongst the people than any of the rest of our Mission staff. The ague and fever on me at Mr. Johnston's death so increased and reduced me to such weakness that I had become insensible, while Abraham and Kowia alone attended to me. On returning to consciousness I heard as in a dream Kowia lamenting over me, and pleading that I might recover, so as to hear and speak with him before he died. Opening my eyes and looking at him, I heard him say, "Missi, all our Aneityumese are sick. Missi Johnson is dead. You are very sick, and I am weak and dying. Alas, when I too am dead, who will climb the trees and get you a cocoanut to drink? And who will bathe your lips and brow?"

Here he broke down into deep and long weeping, and then resumed, "Missi, the Tanna-men hate us all on account of the Worship of Jehovah; and I now fear He is going to take away all His servants from this land, and leave my people to the Evil One and his service!"

I was too weak to speak, so he went on, bursting into a soliloquy of prayer: "O Lord Jesus, Missi Johnston is dead; Thou hast taken him away from this land. Missi Johnston the woman and Missi Paton are very ill; I am sick, and Thy servants the Aneityumese are all sick and dying. O Lord, our Father in

18. The Christian chief, Kowia, was considered a magistrate of sorts, in a rather disorganized world where chiefs were always jockeying for power (and anarchy tended to be the rule of the day). It was appropriate for Kowia to insist on justice and take a strong stance against the thievery that was happening before his eyes. This would have been an appropriate use of Romans 13:1-4, though primitive in form.

Heaven, art Thou going to take away all Thy servants, and Thy Worship from this dark land? What meanest Thou to do, O Lord? The Tannese hate Thee and Thy Worship and Thy servants; but surely, O Lord, Thou canst not forsake Tanna and leave our people to die in the darkness! Oh, make the hearts of this people soft to Thy Word and sweet to Thy Worship; teach them to fear and love Jesus; and oh, restore and spare Missi, dear Missi Paton, that Tanna may be saved!"

Touched to the very fountains of my life by such prayers, from a man once a Cannibal, I began under the breath of God's blessing to revive.

A few days thereafter, Kowia came again to me, and rousing me out of sleep, cried, "Missi, I am very weak; I am dying. I come to bid you farewell, and go away to die. I am nearing death now, and I will soon see Jesus."

I spoke what words of consolation and cheer I could muster, but he answered, "Missi, since you became ill my dear wife and children are dead and buried. Most of our Aneityumese are dead, and I am dying. If I remain on the hill, and die here at the Mission House, there are none left to help Abraham to carry me down to the grave where my wife and children are laid. I wish to lie beside them, that we may rise together in the Great Day when Jesus comes. I am happy, looking unto Jesus! One thing only deeply grieves me now; I fear God is taking us all away from Tanna, and will leave my poor people dark and benighted as before, for they hate Jesus and the Worship of Jehovah. O Missi, pray for them, and pray for me once more before I go!"

He knelt down at my side, and we prayed for each other and for Tanna. I then urged him to remain at the Mission House, but he replied, "O Missi, you do not know how near to death I am! I am just going, and will soon be with Jesus, and see my wife and children now. While a little strength is left, I will lean on Abraham's arm, and go down to the graves of my dear ones and fall asleep there, and Abraham will dig a quiet bed and lay me beside them. Farewell, Missi, I am very near death now; we will meet again in Jesus and with Jesus!"

With many tears he dragged himself away; and my heartstrings seemed all tied round that noble simple soul, and felt like breaking one by one as he left me there on my bed of fever all alone. Abraham sustained him, tottering to the place of graves; there he lay down, and immediately gave up the ghost and slept in Jesus; and there the faithful Abraham buried him beside his wife and children. Thus died a man who had been a cannibal Chief, but by the grace of God and the love of Jesus, changed, transfigured into a character of light and beauty. What think ye of this, ye scoffers at Missions? What think ye of this, ye skeptics as to the reality of conversion? He died, as he had lived since Jesus came to his heart; without a fear as to death, with an ever-brightening assurance as to salvation and glory through the blood of the Lamb of God, that blood which had cleansed him from all his sins, and had delivered him from their power. I lost, in losing him, one of my best friends and most courageous helpers; but I knew that day, and I know now, that there is one soul at least from Tanna to sing the glories of Jesus in Heaven—and, oh, the rapture when I meet him there![19]

Before leaving this terrible plague of measles, I may record my belief that it swept away, with accompanying sore throat and diarrhea, a third of the entire population of Tanna; nay, in certain localities more than a third perished. The living declared themselves unable to bury the dead, and great want and suffering ensued. The Teacher and his wife and child, placed by us at Black Beach, were also taken away; and his companion, the other Teacher there, embraced the first opportunity to leave along with his wife for his own island, else his life would have been taken in revenge. Yet, from all accounts afterwards received, I do not think the measles were more fatal on Tanna than on the other Islands of the group. They appear to have carried off even a larger proportion on Aniwa—the future scene of many sorrows but of greater triumphs.

19. Here is a very emotional parting with this faith-filled Christian brother. Kowia died believing strongly in the resurrection of Jesus Christ and himself. He was one of the first fruits of Tanna, a land hardened in sin, held captive by the Devil for centuries. Here was the worst of the South Sea islanders, but Jesus Christ proved once again that a stronger man could rob the Strong Man's (the Devil's) house.

20. Satan used the ungodly Western traders more than anybody else to destroy the mission on Tanna (as well as kill 1/3 of the population of Tanna with disease). The sheer evil of these Western materialists must never be underestimated or minimized as we consider the history of the last 200 years.

A new incentive was added to the already cruel superstitions of the Natives. The Sandal-wooders, our degraded fellow-countrymen, in order to divert attention from themselves, stirred the Natives with the wild faith that the Missionaries and the Worship had brought all this sickness, and that our lives should be taken in revenge.[20] Some Captains, on calling with their ships, made a pretence of refusing to trade with the Natives as long as I was permitted to live on the island. One Trader offered to come on shore and live amongst the Tannese, and supply them with tobacco and powder, and caps and balls, on condition that the Missionary and Abraham were got out of the way! He knew that these were their greatest wants, and that they eagerly desired these things, but he refused to make any sales to them, till we were murdered or driven away. This was fuel to their savage hate, and drove them mad with revenge, and added countless troubles to our lot.

Hurricane and tempest also fought against us at that time. On the 3rd, and again on the 10th March, 1861, we had severe and destructive storms. They tore up and smashed breadfruit, chestnut, cocoanut, and all kinds of fruit trees. The ground was strewn thick with half-ripe and wasted fruits. Yam plantations and bananas were riven to pieces, and fences and houses lay piled in a common ruin. My Mission House was also greatly injured; and the Church, on which I had spent many weeks of labor, was nearly leveled with the ground. Trees of forty years' growth were broken like straws, or lifted by the roots and blown away. At the other Station, all Mr. Mathieson's premises except one bedroom were swept off in the breath of the hurricane. The sea rose alarmingly and its waves rolled far inland, causing terrible destruction. Had not the merciful Lord left one bedroom at my Station and one at Mr. Mathieson's partly habitable, I know not what in the circumstances we could have done. Men of fifty years declared that never such a tempest had shaken their Islands. Canoes were shivered on the coral rocks, and Villages were left with nothing but ruins to mark where they had been. Though rain poured in torrents, I had to keep near my fallen house for hours and hours to prevent the Natives from carrying away everything I had in this world; and after the second storm, all my earthly belongings had to be secured in the one still-standing room.

Following upon this came another spate of thirst for our blood, which was increased in the following manner. Miaki the war Chief had an infant son, who had just died. They told us that four men were slain at the same time, that their spirits might serve and accompany him in the other world; and that our death also was again resolved upon. For four days they surrounded our diminished premises. We locked ourselves all up in that single bedroom, and armed savages kept prowling about to take our lives. What but the restraining pity of the Lord kept them from breaking in upon us? They killed our fowls. They cut down and destroyed all our remaining bananas. They broke down the fence around the plantation, and tried to burn it, but failed. They speared and killed some of the few goats—my sole supply of milk. We were helpless, and kept breathing out our souls in prayer; and God did preserve us, but, oh, what a trying time![21]

The horror grew, when shortly thereafter we learned that our people near the Harbor had killed four men and presented their bodies to certain Chiefs who feasted on them; and that they in return had given large fat hogs to our people, one for each of ten bodies which our people had formerly presented to them. Within a few months, thirteen or fourteen persons, nearly all refugees or prisoners of war, were reported to us as killed and feasted upon. We generally heard nothing of these murders till all was over, but in any case I would have been helpless against their blood thirst, even had I exposed myself to their savage enmity. They sent two dead bodies to our nearest village, where still we conducted Worship every Sabbath when we durst appear amongst them; but our people refused to receive them, saying, "Now we know that it is wrong to kill and eat our fellow creatures."[22] A Chief from another village,

21. The clouds darkened over the island as Satan let loose his very worst intentions. Murders and cannibalism increased to the highest levels. First John 5 is helpful here. The whole world is under the sway of the wicked one, sitting in the lap of the Devil (vs. 19), "but he who has been born of God keeps himself, and the wicked one does not touch him" (vs. 18).

22. Thankfully, one small village refused to eat the two human bodies. This was a small breakthrough for the Gospel on Tanna.

being present, eagerly received them and carried them off to a great feast for which he was preparing.

At this juncture, our friendly Chief Nowar seemed to become afraid. His life also had been threatened; and our life had been often attempted of late. Society around was all in turmoil, and Nowar urged us all to leave and take refuge in Aneityum till these dangers blew past, and he himself would accompany us. I refused, however, to leave. Indeed, there was no immediate means of escape, except my boat—which would have been almost madness in an open sea voyage of fifty miles, with only Nowar and the Teachers, all inexperienced hands. Nowar, being angry and afraid, took his revenge by laying aside his shirt and kilt, returning to his heathen nakedness and paint, attending the meetings of the savages, and absenting himself from the Sabbath Worship.[23] But after about three weeks he resumed the Christian garments, and, feeling that the danger had for the time passed over, he returned to us as friendly as ever. Poor Nowar! if he only knew what thousands of Christians at home do every day just to save their skins; and then if he only knew how hardly these Christians can speak against Heathen converts!

My first baptism on Tanna was that of a Teacher's child.[24] About fifty persons were present, and Miaki the war Chief was there also. Alas, that child died in the plague of measles, and of course the Worship was blamed. Deaths, hurricanes, all seemed to be turned against us. A thunderstorm came in the wake of the last hurricane. A man and a woman were killed. Not far from my house, the hill was struck, a large mass was dislodged from its shoulder and hurled into the valley below. This was the manifest token to them that the Gods were angry and that we were the cause! God's grace alone kept us from sinking, and the hope of yet seeing them delivered from their Heathenism, and brought to love and serve Jesus Christ. For that everything could be borne; and I knew that this was the post of duty, for it was the Lord undoubtedly that placed me there.

23. Chief Nowar had always been weak and vacillating, and now he returns to the pagan ways. Stony ground hearers show up in every mission work and church work (Matt. 13:1-8).

24. Paton wisely delayed baptisms, except for children born to Christian parents (the Teacher from another island).

One day, about this time, I heard an unusual bleating amongst my few remaining goats, as if they were being killed or tortured. I rushed to the goathouse, and found myself instantly surrounded by a band of armed men. The snare had caught me, their weapons were raised, and I expected next instant to die. But God moved me to talk to them firmly and kindly; I warned them of their sin and its punishment; I showed them that only my love and pity led me to remain there seeking their good, and that if they killed me they killed their best friend. I further assured them that I was not afraid to die, for at death my Saviour would take me to be with Himself in Heaven, and to be far happier than I had ever been on Earth; and that my only desire to live was to make them all as happy, by teaching them to love and serve my Lord Jesus.[25] I then lifted up my hands and eyes to the Heavens, and prayed aloud for Jesus to bless all my dear Tannese, and either to protect me or to take me home to Glory as He saw to be for the best. One after another they slipped away from me, and Jesus restrained them once again.[26] Did ever mother run more quickly to protect her crying child in danger's hour, than the Lord Jesus hastens to answer believing prayer, and send help to His servants in His own good time and way, so far as it shall be for His glory and their good? A woman may forget her child, yet will not I forget thee, saith the Lord. Oh, that all my readers knew and felt this, as in those days and ever since I have felt that His promise is a reality, and that He is with His servants to support and bless them even unto the end of the world!

May, 1861, brought with it a sorrowful and tragic event, which fell as the very shadow of doom across our path; I mean the martyrdom of the Gordons on Erromanga. Rev. G. N. Gordon was a native of Prince Edward Island, Nova Scotia, and was born in 1822. He was educated at the Free Church College, Halifax, and placed as Missionary on Erromanga in June, 1857. Much troubled and opposed by the Sandal-wooders, he had yet acquired the language and was making progress

25. Paton never hesitated to preach, to exhort, to warn, and to call people to repentance (even when they are surrounding him with weapons, poised to kill him). Paton was steadfast, courageous, full of faith — a great example.

26. Paton lifted up his hands and prayed aloud in this time of severe crisis. The power of God in the answer is evident right away as the would-be murderers slink away.

by inroads on Heathenism. A considerable number of young men and women embraced the Christian Faith, lived at the Mission House, and devotedly helped him and his excellent wife in all their work. But the hurricanes and the measles, already referred to, caused great mortality in Erromanga also; and the degraded Traders, who had introduced the plague, in order to save themselves from revenge, stimulated the superstitions of the Heathen, and charged the Missionaries there too with causing sickness and all other calamities. The Sandal-wooders hated him for fearlessly denouncing and exposing their hideous atrocities.

When Mr. Copeland and I placed the Native Teachers at Black Beach, Tanna, we ran across to Erromanga in the *John Knox*, taking a harmonium to Mrs. Gordon, just come by their order from Sydney. When it was opened out at the Mission House, and Mrs. Gordon began playing on it and singing sweet hymns, the native women were in ecstasies.[27] They at once proposed to go off to the bush and cut each a burden of long grass, to thatch the printing-office which Mr. Gordon was building in order to print the Scriptures in their own tongue, if only Mrs. Gordon would play to them at night and teach them to sing God's praises. They joyfully did so, and then spent a happy evening singing those hymns. Next day being Sabbath, we had a delightful season there, about thirty attending Church and listening eagerly. The young men and women living at the Mission House were being trained to become Teachers; they were reading a small book in their own language, telling them the story of Joseph; and the work every way seemed most hopeful. The Mission House had been removed a mile or so up a hill, partly for Mrs. Gordon's health, and partly to escape the annoying and contaminating influence of the Sandal-wooders on the Christian Natives.

On the 20th May, 1861, he was still working at the roofing of the printing-office, and had sent his lads to bring each a load of the long grass to finish the thatching. Meantime a party of Erromangans from a district called Bunk-Hill, under

27. Erromanga was about 30 miles north of Tanna. A harmonium was a pump organ, where the player would pump air with his/her feet applied to pedals. Mrs. Gordon would play the pump organ and sing hymns with the natives.

a Chief named Lovu, had been watching him. They had been to the Mission House inquiring and they had seen him send away his Christian lads. They then hid in the bush and sent two of their men to the Missionary to ask for calico. On a piece of wood he wrote a note to Mrs. Gordon to give them two yards each. They asked him to go with them to the Mission House, as they needed medicine for a sick boy, and Lovu their Chief wanted to see him. He tied up in a napkin a meal of food, which had been brought to him but not eaten, and started to go with them. He requested the native Narubulet to go on before with his companion, but they insisted upon his going in front. In crossing a streamlet, which I visited shortly afterwards, his foot slipped. A blow was aimed at him with a tomahawk, which he caught; the other man struck, but his weapon was also caught. One of the tomahawks was then wrenched out of his grasp. Next moment a blow on the spine laid the dear Missionary low, and a second on the neck almost severed the head from the body. The other Natives then rushed from their ambush, and began dancing round him with frantic shoutings. Mrs. Gordon hearing the noise, came out and stood in front of the Mission House, looking in the direction of her husband's working place, and wondering what had happened. Ouben, one of the party, who had run towards the Station the moment that Mr. Gordon fell, now approached her. A merciful clump of trees had hid from her eyes all that had occurred, and she said to Ouben, "What's the cause of that noise?"

He replied, "Oh, nothing! only the boys amusing themselves!"

Saying, "Where are the boys?" she turned round. Ouben slipped stealthily behind her, sank his tomahawk into her back, and with another blow almost severed her head![28]

Such was the fate of those two devoted servants of the Lord; loving in their lives, and in their deaths not divided—their spirits, wearing the crown of martyrdom, entered Glory together to be welcomed by Williams and Harris,

28. Both Mr. and Mrs. Gordon were martyred on Erromanga for no apparent reason, except that the Traders urged the natives to the deed. Satan worked particularly through the white Traders — materialists who were out to make money on the backs of these natives.

whose blood was shed near the same now hallowed spot for the name and cause of Jesus. They had labored four years on Erromanga, amidst trials and dangers manifold, and had not been without tokens of blessing in the Lord's work. Never more earnest or devoted Missionaries lived and died in the Heathen field. Other accounts, indeed, have been published, and another was reported to me by Mr. Gordon's Christian lads; but the above combines faithfully the principal facts in the story. One young Christian lad from a distance saw Mr. Gordon murdered; and a woman saw Mrs. Gordon fall. The above facts are vouched for by a Mr. Milne, one of the few respectable Sandal-wooders, who was there at the time, and helped the Christian Natives to bury the remains, which he says were painfully mutilated.

Some severe criticisms, of course, were written and published by those angelic creatures who judge all things from their own safe and easy distance. Mr. Gordon's lack of prudence was sorely blamed, forsooth! One would so like to see these people just for one week in such trying circumstances. As my near fellow-laborer and dearest friend, I know what was the whole spirit of the man's life, his watchful care, his ceaseless anxiety to do everything that in his judgment was for God's glory and the prosperity of the Mission, and my estimate of him and of his action to the last fills me with supreme regard to his memory.[29] The Rev. Dr. Inglis of Aneityum, best qualified of all men living to form an opinion, wrote:

"Mr. Gordon was a strong, bold, fearless, energetic, self-denying, and laborious Missionary; eager, earnest, and unwearied in seeking the salvation of the Heathen. . . . Even if Mr. Gordon was to blame for any imprudence, no blame of this kind could be attached to Mrs. Gordon. Hers was a weak, gentle, loving spirit; quiet and uncomplaining, prudent, earnest, and devoted to Christ. She was esteemed and beloved by all who knew her."[30]

My Amen follows, soft and deep, on all that he has written; and I add, Mr. Gordon was doing what any faithful and

29. John Paton was highly displeased with those who criticize missionaries for risking their lives for the Gospel. True men and women of faith have no time for these critics.

30. Readers should be forewarned. Never criticize a martyr or one who has suffered for the Gospel's sake. Never Monday-morning quarterback the one who is on the field, while you are in the grandstands.

devoted Missionary would in all probability for the Master's sake in similar circumstances have done. Those who charge him with imprudence would, doubtless, grievously blame Stephen for bringing that stoning upon himself, which he could so easily have escaped!

Mr. Gordon, in his last letter to me, of date 15th February, 1861, says:

"My Dear Brother,

"I have news of the best and of the worst character to communicate. A young man died in December, in the Lord, as we believe. We are still preserved in health at our work by the God of all grace, whose power alone could have preserved us in all our troubles, which have come upon us by the measles *per* the *Blue Bell*. Ah, this is a season which we will not soon forget. Some settlements are nearly depopulated, and the principal Chiefs are nearly all dead! And oh, the indescribable fiendish hatred that exists against us! There is quite a famine here. The distress is awful, and the cry of mourning perpetual. A few on both sides of the Island who did not flee from the Worship of God are living, which is now greatly impressing some and exciting the enmity of others. I cannot now write of perils. We feel very anxious to hear from you. If you have to flee, Aneityum of course is the nearest and best place to which you can go. Confidence in us is being restored. Mana, a native Teacher, remains with us for safety from the fury of his enemies. I cannot visit as usual. The persecution cannot be much worse on Tanna. I hope the worst is past. Mrs. G. unites in love to you, and to Mr. and Mrs. Johnston. In great haste, I remain, dear Brother, Yours truly,

"G. N. GORDON."

Let every reader, in view of this epistle, like a voice from the World Unseen, judge of the spirit of the man of God who penned it, and of the causes that were even then at work and were bringing about his sorrowful death. Cruel superstition, measles, and the malignant influences of the godless Trad-

31. The blame game was practiced by the natives and the traders, all unbelievers. They always seek a scapegoat when they have felt the devastation of famine, disease, etc. The missionaries became the scapegoats.

32. The Traders brought the same murderers to Tanna in order to kill the last few missionaries on that island, Paton included. By God's grace, the Tannese chiefs sent the Erromangans and Traders packing.

33. Paton would never let lies and public evils continue without correction. A public, prophetic voice is always necessary to correct the wicked who pursue their sin with impunity. Thus, we are thankful every time that a prophet in the Western world preaches publicly against sexual sin, homosexuality, abortion, contraceptives with abortifacient qualities, etc.

ers—these on Erromanga, as elsewhere, were the forces at work that brought hatred and murder in their train.[31]

Immediately thereafter, a Sandal-wood Trader brought in his boat a party of Erromangans by night to Tanna.[32] They assembled our Harbor Chiefs and people, and urged them to kill us and Mr. and Mrs. Mathieson and the Teachers, or allow them to do so, as they had killed Mr. and Mrs. Gordon. Then they proposed to go to Aneityum and kill the Missionaries there, as the Aneityumese Natives had burned their Church, and thus they would sweep away the Worship and the servants of Jehovah from all the New Hebrides. Our Chiefs, however, refused, restrained by the Merciful One, and the Erromangans returned to their own island in a sulky mood.

Notwithstanding this refusal, as if they wished to reserve the murder and plunder for themselves, our Mission House was next day thronged with armed men, some from Inland, others from Mr. Mathieson's Station. They loudly praised the Erromangans! The leader said again and again in my hearing, "The men of Erromanga killed Missi Williams long ago. We killed the Rarotongan and Samoan Teachers. We fought Missi Turner and Missi Nisbet, and drove them from our island. We killed the Aneityumese Teachers on Aniwa, and one of Missi Paton's Teachers too. We killed several white men, and no Man-of-war punished us. Let us talk over this, about killing Missi Paton and the Aneityumese, till we see if any Man-of-war comes to punish the Erromangans. If not, let us unite, let us kill these Missionaries, let us drive the Worship of Jehovah from our land!"

An Inland Chief said or rather shouted in my hearing, "My love to the Erromangans! They are strong and brave men, the Erromangans. They have killed their Missi and his wife, while we only talk about it. They have destroyed the Worship and driven away Jehovah!"

I stood amongst them and protested, "God will yet punish the Erromangans for such wicked deeds. God has heard all your bad talk, and will punish it in His own time and way."[33]

But they shouted me down, amidst great excitement, with the cry, "Our love to the Erromangans! Our love to the Erromangans!"

After I left them, Abraham heard them say, "Miaki is lazy. Let us meet in every village, and talk with each other. Let us all agree to kill Missi and the Aneityumese for the first of our Chiefs that dies."[34]

On Tanna, as on Erromanga, the Natives have no idea of death coming to any one naturally, or sickness or any disease; everything comes by *Nahak*, or sorcery. When one person grows sick or dies, they meet to talk over it and find out who has bewitched or killed him, and this ends in fixing upon some individual upon whom they take revenge, or whom they murder outright. Thus many wars arise on Tanna, for the friends or the tribe of the murdered man generally seek a counter-revenge; and so the blood-fiend is let loose over all the island, and from island to island throughout the whole of the New Hebrides.[35]

The night after the visit of the Erromangan boat, and the sad news of Mr. and Mrs. Gordon's death, the Tannese met on their village dancing-grounds and held high festival in praise of the Erromangans. Our best friend, old Nowar the Chief, who had worn shirt and kilt for some time and had come regularly to the Worship, relapsed once more; he painted his face, threw off his clothing, resumed his bow and arrows and his tomahawk, of which he boasted that it had killed very many men and at least one woman! On my shaming him for professing to worship Jehovah and yet uniting with the Heathen in rejoicing over the murder of His servants on Erromanga, he replied to this effect, "Truly, Missi, they have done well. If the people of Erromanga are severely punished for this by the Man-of-war, we will all hear of it; and our people will then fear to kill you and the other Missionaries, so as to destroy the Worship of Jehovah. Now, they say, the Erromangans killed Missi Williams and the Samoan, Rarotongan, and Aneityumese Teachers, besides other white men, and no Man-of-war

34. The spirit of murder was still in the air. The Tannese chiefs tried to work up the courage to kill Paton. Make no mistake about it, a great deal of evil courage is required to muster up the murder of an innocent man who has given up his life in love for the people on the islands.

35. Murder begets murder, and revenge is constant among these pagan societies.

36. Paton insisted that all things work for God's glory and our own good in the long run (Rom. 8:28).

37. The natives and all unbelievers do not think of "the long run." They look for immediate cause and effect. They get drunk in the evening and never think of the morning after. If they can get away with a sin or a crime for five minutes or five years, they think all is good. They do not realize that "the mills of God grind slowly but very fine." They try not to believe in an all-seeing, all-righteous, all-power-ful, sovereign God over heaven and earth. Their gods are fickle, thought-less, arbitrary, and limit-ed in power and wisdom.

has punished either them or us. If they are not punished for what has been done on Erromanga, nothing else can keep them here from killing you and me and all who worship at the Mission House!"

I answered, "Nowar, let us all be strong to love and serve Jehovah Jesus. If it be for our good and His glory, He will protect us; if not, He will take us to be with Himself.[36] We will not be killed by their bad talk. Besides, what avails it to us, when dead and gone, if even a Man-of-war should come and punish our murderers?"

He shrugged his shoulders, answering, "Missi, by and by you will see. Mind, I tell you the truth. I know our Tannese people. How is it that Jehovah did not protect the Gordons and the Erromangan worshipers? If the Erromangans are not punished, neither will our Tannese be punished, though they murder all Jehovah's people!"[37]

I felt for Nowar's struggling faith, just trembling on the verge of Cannibalism yet, and knowing so little of the true Jehovah.

Groups of Natives assembled suspiciously near us and sat whispering together. They urged old Abraham to return to Aneityum by the very first opportunity, as our lives were certain to be taken, but he replied, "I will not leave Missi."

Abraham and I were thrown much into each other's company, and he stood by me in every danger. We conducted Family Prayers alternately; and that evening he said during the prayer in Tannese, in which language alone we understood each other:

"O Lord, our Heavenly Father, they have murdered Thy servants on Erromanga. They have banished the Aneityumese from dark Tanna. And now they want to kill Missi Paton and me! Our great King, protect us, and make their hearts soft and sweet to Thy Worship. Or, if they are permitted to kill us, do not Thou hate us, but wash us in the blood of Thy dear Son Jesus Christ. He came down to Earth and shed His blood for sinners; through Him forgive us our sins and take us to

Heaven—that good place where Missi Gordon the man and Missi Gordon the woman and all thy dear servants now are singing Thy praise and seeing Thy face. Our Lord, our hearts are pained just now, and we weep over the death of Thy dear servants; but make our hearts good and strong for Thy cause, and take thou away all our fears. Make us two and all Thy servants strong for Thee and for Thy Worship; and if they kill us two, let us die together in Thy good work, like Thy servants Missi Gordon the man and Missi Gordon the woman."[38]

In this manner his great simple soul poured itself out to God; and my heart melted within me as it had never done under any prayer poured from the lips of cultured Christian men![39]

Under the strain of these events, Miaki came to our house, and attacked me in hearing of his men to this effect, "You and the Worship are the cause of all the sickness and death now taking place on Tanna! The Erromanga men killed Missi Gordon the man and also the woman, and they are all well long ago. The Worship is killing us all; and the Inland people will kill us for keeping you and the Worship here; for we love the conduct of Tanna, but we hate the Worship. We must kill you and it, and we shall all be well again."

I tried to reason firmly and kindly with them, showing them that their own conduct was destroying them, and that our presence and the Worship could only be a blessing to them in every way, if only they would accept of it and give up their evil ways. I referred to a poor girl, whom Miaka and his men had stolen and abused—that they knew such conduct to be bad, and that God would certainly punish them for it.[40]

He replied, "Such is the conduct of Tanna. Our fathers loved and followed it, we love and follow it, and if the Worship condemns it, we will kill you and destroy the Worship."[41]

I said, "The Word of the Holy God condemns all bad conduct, and I must obey my God in trying to lead you to give it up, and to love and serve His Son Jesus our Saviour. If I refuse to obey my God, He will punish me."

---

38. Abraham's prayer gives us a great summary of the Christian faith as received and believed by a simple native. Paton must have felt such joy to witness the real spiritual transformation of one heathen man into a servant of the Lord Jesus Christ.

39. Abraham's faith and courage were remarkable under such circumstances.

40. Paton pointed to a very sinful action of which they may have been somewhat ashamed. They had kidnapped a girl and sexually abused her. Paton is hoping they have some little bit of conscience regarding these evils. Paton is simple and direct in his appeals to these wicked men.

41. Miaki's commitment to the "conduct" of Tanna indicates his love for sin and corruption — and his rejection of the call to repentance.

He replied, "Missi, we like many wives to attend us and to do our work. Three of my wives are dead and three are yet alive. The Worship killed them and my children. We hate it. It will kill us all."

I answered, "Miaki, is it good for you to have so many wives, and many of your men to have none? Who waits on them? Who works for them? They cannot get a wife, and so, having to work for themselves, they are led to hate you and all the Chiefs who have more wives than one. You do not love your wives, else you would not slave them and beat them as you do."[42]

42. Paton pointed out the hypocrisy in men who pretend to love their wives and children and yet beat them mercilessly (and often kill them).

But he declared that his heart was good, that his conduct was good, and that he hated the teaching of the Worship. He had a party of men staying with him from the other side of the island, and he sent back a present of four large fat hogs to their Chiefs, with a message as to the killing of the Mathiesons. If that were done, his hands would be strengthened in dealing with us.

Satan seemed to fill that man's heart. He incited his people to steal everything from us, and to annoy us in every conceivable way. They killed one of my precious watch-dogs, and feasted upon it. So sad was the condition of Tanna, that if a man were desperate enough in wickedness, if he killed a number of men and tyrannized over others, he was dignified with the name and rank of a Chief. This was the secret of Miaki's influence, and of his being surrounded by the outlaws and refugees, not only of his own but even other islands. It was all founded upon terror and upheld by cruelty. The Sacred Man, for instance, who murdered my Teacher, and a young man who threw three spears at me, which by God's help I avoided, were both praised and honored for their deeds. But the moment they were laid aside by measles and unable to retaliate, their flatterers turned upon them and declared that they were punished for their bad conduct against Jehovah and His servants and His Worship!

To know what was best to be done, in such trying circumstances, was an abiding perplexity. To have left altogether, when so surrounded by perils and enemies, at first seemed the wisest course, and was the repeated advice of many friends. But again, I had acquired the language, and had gained a considerable influence amongst the Natives, and there were a number warmly attached both to myself and to the Worship. To have left would have been to lose all, which to me was heart-rending; therefore, risking all with Jesus, I held on while the hope of being spared longer had not absolutely and entirely vanished.[43] God only knows how deep and genuine were my pity and affection for the poor Tannese, laboring and longing to bring them from their dark idolatry and heathenism to love and serve and please Jesus Christ as their God and Saviour. True, some of the awfully wise people wrote, as in the case of Mr. Gordon, much nonsense about us and the Tanna Mission. They knew, of course, that I was to blame, and they from safe distances could see that I was not in the path of duty!

Perhaps, to people less omnisciently sure, the following quotation from a letter of the late A. Clark, Esq., J.P., Auckland, New Zealand, will show what Bishop Selwyn thought of my standing fast on Tanna at the post of duty, and he knew what he was writing about. He says:

"Talk of bravery! talk of heroism! The man who leads a forlorn hope is a coward in comparison with him, who, on Tanna, thus alone, without a sustaining look or cheering word from one of his own race, regards it as his duty to hold on in the face of such dangers. We read of the soldier, found after the lapse of ages among the ruins of Herculaneum, who stood firm at his post amid the fiery rain destroying all around him, thus manifesting the rigidity of the discipline among those armies of Ancient Rome which conquered the World. Mr. Paton was subjected to no such iron law. He might with honor, when offered to him, have sought a temporary asylum in Auckland, where he would have been heartily received. But he was moved by higher considerations. He chose to remain,

43. It is extremely difficult for Christians to know what to do when their lives are threatened. We have a duty to protect our own lives and to obey the sixth commandment. But, Jesus also said, "For whoever would save his life will lose it, but whoever loses his life for my sake will save it" (Luke 9:24). Paton held out against multiple threats to his life longer than almost any other missionary in the history of missions. He had made progress with the language and with some converts, and he was reticent to give up the work now. Ultimately, love makes the determination what to do — love for God, love for Christ, love for the people we are serving.

44. The Anglican Bishop, John Selwyn, was a man on the ground in the South Pacific. He rightly viewed Paton as a man of tremendous bravery and heroism.

45. Paton considered himself as one carrying on the legacy of the brave Scottish Covenanters, who were among the most faithful martyrs in the history of the Church.

46. It is beautiful to find true brotherhood between Anglicans and Presbyterians on the battlefield for Christ. When it comes to the real work of faith, denominational distinctions fade.

and God knows whether at this moment he is in the land of the living!' When the Bishop told us that he declined leaving Tanna by *H.M.S. Pelorus*, he added, 'And I like him all the better for so doing!"[44]

For my part I feel quite confident that, in like circumstances, that noble Bishop of God would have done the same. I, born in the bosom of the Scottish Covenant, descended from those who suffered persecution for Christ's honor, would have been unworthy of them and of my Lord had I deserted my post for danger only.[45] Yet not to me, but to the Lord who sustained me, be all the praise and the glory! On his next visit to these Islands, the good Bishop brought a box of Mission goods to me in his ship, besides £90 for our work from Mr. Clark and friends in Auckland. His interest in us and our work was deep and genuine, and was unmarred on either side by any consciousness of ecclesiastical distinctions. We were one in Christ, and, when next we meet again in the glory of our Lord, Bishop and Presbyter will be eternally one in that blessed fellowship.[46]

The following incident illustrates the depth of native superstition. One morning two Inland Chiefs came running to the Mission House, breathless, and covered with perspiration. One of them held up a handful of half-rotten tracts, crying:

"Missi, is this a part of God's Word, the sacred Book of Jehovah? Or is it the work, the words, the book of man?"

I examined them and replied, "These are the work, the words, and the book of man, not of Jehovah."

He questioned me again: "Missi, are you certain that it is not the Word of Jehovah?"

I replied, "It is only man's work and man's book."

He continued then, "Missi, some years ago, Kaipai, a sacred Chief, and certain Tannese, went on a visit to Aneityum, and Missi Geddie gave him these books. On his return, when he showed them to the Tannese, the people were all so afraid of them, for they thought they were the sacred Books of Jehovah, that they met for consultation and agreed solemnly to bury them. Yesterday, some person in digging had disinterred them, and at once our Inland people said that our dead Chief had buried a part of Jehovah's Word, which made Him angry, and that He had therefore caused the Chief's death and the plague of measles, etc.[47] Therefore they were now assembled to kill the dead Chief's son and daughter in revenge! But, before that should be done, I persuaded them to send these books, to inquire of you if this be part of Jehovah's Book, and if the burying of it caused all these diseases and deaths."

I assured him that these books never caused either sickness or death to any human being; and that none of us can cause sickness or death by sorcery; that burying these Tracts did not make Jehovah angry, nor cause evil to any creature. "You yourselves know," I said, "the very ships that brought the measles and caused the deaths; and you killed some of the young men who were landed sick with the disease."[48]

The Inland Chief declared, "Missi, I am quite satisfied; no person shall be put to death over these books now."

They went off, but immediately returned, saying, "Missi, have you any books like these to show to us? And will you show us the sacred Book of Jehovah beside them?"

I showed them a Bible, and then a handful of Tracts with pictures like those they had brought; and I offered them the Bible and specimens of these Tracts, that they might show both to the people assembled. The Tracts they received, but the Bible they refused to touch. They satisfied the Inland people and prevented bloodshed; but oh, what a depth of superstition to be raised out of! and how easily life might be sacrificed at every turn!

On another occasion I had the joy of saving the lives of Sandal-wood Traders, to whom neither I nor the Mission owed anything, except for Christ's sake. The *Blue Bell* cast anchor in the Harbor on a beautiful morning, and the Captain and Mate immediately came on shore. They had letters for me; but, on landing, they were instantly surrounded by the Chiefs and people, who formed a ring about them on the beach and

47. Human thinking always wants to know the purposes of the gods (or God) in bringing this disease or that disease. We must be careful not to fall into these superstitious practices or to press into the purposes of God (which He does not choose to share with us).

48. The natives wanted to associate John Paton with the Traders.

49. Paton put his life on the line for the Traders (who themselves had dealt very wickedly).

called for me to come. The two white men stood in the midst, with many weapons pointed at them, and death if they dared to move. They shouted to me:[49]

"This is one of the Vessels which brought the measles. You and they made the sickness, and destroyed our people. Now, if you do not leave with this vessel, we will kill you all."

Of course, their intention was to frighten me on board just as I was, and leave my premises for plunder! I protested:

"I will not leave you; I cannot leave you in this way; and if you murder these men or me, Jehovah will punish you. I am here for your good; and you know how kind I have been to you all, in giving you medicine, knives, axes, blankets, and clothing. You also know well that I have never done ill to one human being, but have constantly sought your good. I will not and cannot leave you thus."

In great wrath they cried, "Then will we kill you and this Captain and Mate."

I kept reasoning with them against such conduct, standing firmly before them and saying, "If you do kill me, Jehovah will punish you; the other men in that vessel will punish you before they sail; and a Man-of-war will come and burn your villages and canoes and fruit trees."

I urged the two men to try and get into their boat as quickly as possible, in silence, while I kept arguing with the Natives. The letters which they had for me, the savages forbade me to take into my hands, lest thereby some other foreign disease should come to their island. Miaki exclaimed in great wrath that my medicine had killed them all; but I replied:

"My medicine with God's blessing saved many lives. You know well that all who followed my rules recovered from the measles, except only one man, and are living still. Now, you seek to kill me for saving your lives and the lives of your people!"[50]

50. Paton responded with the facts. His medicine had saved almost everybody he treated (except one man).

I appealed to Yorian, another Chief, if the medicine had not saved his life when he appeared to be dying, which he admitted to be the truth. The men had now slipped into their boat and were preparing to leave. Miaki shouted:

"Let them go! Don't kill them today." Then he called to the Captain, "Come on shore and trade with us tomorrow."

Next day they foolishly came on shore and began to trade. Natives surrounded the boat with clubs and tomahawks. But Miaki's heart failed him when about to strike; and he called out:

"Missi said that, if we kill them, a Man-of-war will come and take revenge on us."[51]

In the altercation that followed, the men thrust the boat into deep water and forced it out of the grasp of the savages; but they caught the Captain's large Newfoundland dog and kept it prisoner. As a compensation for this disappointment, Miaki urged that my life and Abraham's be at once taken, but again Nowar's firm opposition and God's goodness rescued us from the jaws of the lion. The *Blue Bell* left next morning, and the dog remained behind, as no one from the vessel would venture ashore.

Revenge for the murder of the four men killed to accompany Miaki's child, threatened to originate another war; but the Chiefs for eight miles around met, and, after much speechifying, agreed that as they were all weak for war, owing to the measles and the want of food through the hurricanes, they should delay it till they all grew stronger. Nowar was, however, greatly excited, and informed me that Miaki had urged the people of an inland district to shoot Nowar and Abraham and me, and he pled with us again to take him and flee to Aneityum—impossible except by canoe, and perhaps impossible even so. That night and the following night they tried to break into my house. On one occasion my valuable dog was let out, and cleared them away. Next night I shouted at them from inside, when they thought me asleep, and they decamped again. Indeed, our continuous danger caused me now oftentimes to sleep with my clothes on, that I might start at a moment's warning. My faithful dog would give a sharp bark and awake me.[52] At other times, she would leap up and pull at the clothes till I awoke, and then she turned her head

51. Paton's life was on a thin thread. Chief Nowar saves his life this time.

52. Paton had to sleep with his clothes on now, relying on his dog to protect him.

quietly and indicated by a wondrous instinct where the danger lay. God made them fear this precious creature, and often used her in saving our lives. Soon after this, six Inland Chiefs came to see me. We had a long talk on the evils of war, and the blessings of the Worship of Jehovah. I gave each a knife and a fork and a tin plate, and they promised to oppose the war which Miaki was forcing on. A man came also with a severe gash in his hand, which a fish had given him; I dressed it, and he went away very grateful and spread everywhere the news of healing, a kind of Gospel which he and they could most readily appreciate.[53]

Another incident made them well-disposed for a season; namely, the use of a fishing-net. Seeing that the Natives had so little food—there being, in fact, a famine after the hurricane—I engaged an inland Tribe to make a net forty feet long and very broad. Strange to say, the Inland people who live far from the sea make the best fishing materials, which again they sell to the Harbor people for the axes, knives, blankets, and other articles obtained from calling vessels. They also make the killing-stones, and trade with them amongst the shore people all round the island. This kawas or killing-stone is made of blue whinstone, eighteen to twenty-four inches long, an inch and a half across, perfectly straight, and hewn as round and neat as any English tradesman could have done it, exactly like a large scythe-stone, such as they use on the harvest fields in Scotland. The kawas seems to be peculiar to Tanna, at least I have not seen it on any other island. The Natives, with pieces of very hard heavy wood of the same size and shape, are taught to throw it from infancy at a given mark; in warfare, it is thrown first; where it strikes it stuns or kills, and then they spring forward with their large double-handed heavy club. Every man and boy carries his killing-stone and other weapons, even when moving about peaceably in his own village, war being, in fact, the only regular occupation for men![54]

Well, these same Inland people, the sort of artisans of the island, being mostly the women and the girls, manufactured

53. Paton was always helpful — providing the free use of the fishing net, providing food and medicine to the peoples. He is the consummate peacemaker. He is the one bringing the Gospel of Christ. And he is the one who the Devil wants killed off the island.

54. Among pagans, war seems to be the regular occupation of the men. Meanwhile, the women do all the productive work. This is never healthy for economies, as is obvious with these primitive tribes.

for me this huge fishing-net. The cord was twisted from the fiber made out of the bark of their own trees, and prepared with immense toil and care; and not without touches of skill and taste, when woven and knotted and intertwined. This net I secured, and lent about three days each to every village all round the Harbor and near it. One night I saw them carrying home a large hog, which they had got from an Inland Chief for a portion of the fish which they had taken. I thought it right to cause them to return the net to the Mission House every Saturday evening, that they might not be tempted to use it on Sabbath. It was a great help to them, and the Harbor yielded them much wholesome food in lieu of what the hurricane had destroyed.

When, about this time, the *John Knox* came to anchor in the bay, a Native was caught in the act of stealing from her. Angry at being discovered, he and his friends came to shoot me, pretending that it was because the *John Knox* knew they were in want of food and had not brought them a load of Taro from Aneityum. Taro is a plant of the genus *Arum*, the *Esculentum*, or *Colocasia Esculenta*, well known all through Polynesia.[55] The Natives spread it in a very simple way. Cutting off the leaves, with a very little of the old bulb still attached, they fix these in the ground, and have the new Taro about a year after that. It is of several kinds and of a great variety of colors—white, yellow, blue, etc. It grows best in ground irrigated by streams of pure water, or in shallow, swampy ground, over which the water runs. The dry-ground Taro is small and inferior compared to the water-grown roots. Nutritious and pleasant, not unlike the texture of cheese when laid in slices on the table, in size and appearance like a Swedish turnip, it can be either boiled or baked. Hurricanes may destroy all other native food, but the Taro lies uninjured below the water; hence on islands, where it will grow, it forms one of the most permanent and valuable of all their crops.

Our people also demanded that the *John Knox* should bring them kava and tobacco. Kava[56] is the plant, *Piper Methys-*

55. Taro was a staple among the Hawaiians as well.

56. The method for creating this Kava drink is rather grotesque. It is chewed and spit into a vat first, that the men may drink and become intoxicated with it.

ticum, from which they make a highly intoxicating drink. The girls and boys first chew it, and spit the juice into a basin; there it is mixed with water, and then strained through a fibrous cloth-like texture, which they get from the top of the cocoanut trees, where it surrounds the young nuts, and drops off with them when they are ripe. This they freely drink; it does not make them violent, but stupefies them and induces sleep like opium. A portion is always poured out to their Gods; and the dregs in every mouth after drinking are always spit out with the exclamation, "That's for you, Kumesam!" It is sometimes offered and partaken of with very great ceremony; but its general use is as a soporific by the men, regularly after the evening meal. Women and children are not allowed to drink it. Many men have been attacked and murdered at night, when lying enfeebled and enfolded by kava. That, indeed, is their common mode of taking revenge and of declaring war. These angry men, who came to me about the *John Knox*, tried to smash in my window and kill my faithful dog; but I reasoned firmly and kindly with them, and they at last withdrew.

At that time, though my life was daily attempted,[57] a dear lad, named Katasian, was coming six miles regularly to the Worship and to receive frequent instruction. One day, when engaged in teaching him, I caught a man stealing the blind from my window. On trying to prevent him, he aimed his great club at me, but I seized the heavy end of it with both my hands as it swung past my head, and held on with all my might. What a prayer went up from me to God at that dread moment! The man, astonished and abashed at my kind words and appeal, slunk away and left me in peace.[58]

I had planted a few Yams, of the genus *Dioscoria*; a most valuable article of food, nearly as precious as potatoes were to the poor in Ireland, and used very much in the same way. Years after, when I went to Melbourne, I took one from Aniwa, by no means the largest, weighing seventy-two pounds, and another, forty-two.[59] The things, however, that I planted on Tanna the Natives stole and carried away, making them-

57. Daily attempts were made on Paton's life at this point.

58. A kind word, a soft word, seemed to dissipate wrath. Paton's practice to defend his life was never to hurt his attackers. He would disarm them first and then give them a kind word. This sort of Christian treatment is very rare in the world.

59. Some Yam "tubers" can grow to 150 pounds (5 feet in length)!

selves extremely troublesome. But God never took away from me the consciousness that it was still right for me to be kind and forgiving, and to hope that I might lead them to love and imitate Jesus.[60]

For a season thereafter, the friendly feeling grew on every side. The Natives prepared, for payment, an excellent foundation for a new Church, by leveling down the hill near to my Mission House. Any number of men offered to work for calico, knives, axes, etc. All the fences were renewed, and the Mission premises began to look nice once more, at least, in my eyes. My work became encouraging, and I had many opportunities of talking with them about the Worship and Jehovah. This state of matters displeased Miaki and his men; and one day, having been engaged thus, I rushed back only in time to extinguish a fire which they had kindled under the verandah and close to the door of my house. Our watch had to be un-relaxing. A cousin of Miaki's, for instance, sold me a fish as good for food which he knew to be poisonous, but Nowar saw in time and warned me of its deadly character. Miaki then threatened to shoot any of the Inland people who came to work or to receive instruction, yet larger numbers came than before, but they came fully armed![61] Nouka, the high Chief of the Harbor, Miaki's uncle, came and sat beside us often, and said:

"Miaki breaks my heart! He deceives Missi. He hates the Worship of Jehovah."

For some time, Nouka and his wife and daughter—a handsome girl, his only child—and Miaki's principal wife and her two sons, and nine Chiefs attended Worship regularly at the Mission House, on Sabbaths and on the afternoon of every Wednesday. In all, about sixty persons somewhat regularly waited on our ministrations at this time; and amidst all perils I was encouraged, and my heart was full of hope. Yet one evening, when feeling more consoled and hopeful than ever before, a musket was discharged at my very door, and I was

60. Paton would forgive the people who stole his food.

61. Often, God's work grows in the middle of great tribulation and persecutions. This is the best time for harvest! May Christian workers come to understand this *modus operandi* of the kingdom.

constrained to realize that we were in the midst of death. Father, our times are in Thy hand.

As my work became more encouraging, I urgently applied to the Missionaries on Aneityum for more Teachers, but none could be found willing to return to Tanna. The plague of measles had almost demoralized them. Even on Aneityum, where they had medicine and would follow the Missionaries' advice, no fewer than eleven hundred had been cut off; and the mortality was very much greater on such islands as Tanna, Aniwa, etc., where they were still Heathen, and either had not or would not follow medical counsels. Of my Teachers and their wives ten were swept away in the epidemic, and the few that were left were so disheartened that they escaped to their own land at the first opportunity, as before recorded, excepting only dear old faithful Abraham. But I need not wonder; smaller perils deter God's people at home from many a call of duty.

In my Mission School, I offered as a prize a red shirt for the first Chief who knew the whole Alphabet without a mistake. It was won by an Inakaki Chief, who was once a terror to the whole community. Afterwards, when trying to teach the A B C to others, he proceeded in something like this graphic style:

"A is a man's legs with the body cut off; B is like two eyes; C is a three-quarters moon; D is like one eye; E is a man with one club under his feet and another over his head; F is a man with a large club and a smaller one," etc., etc.; L was like a man's foot; Q was the talk of the dove, etc. Then he would say, "Remember these things; you will soon get hold of the letters and be able to read. I have taught my little child, who can scarcely walk, the names of them all. They are not hard to hold, but soft and easy. You will soon learn to read the book, if you try it with all your heart!"[62]

But Miaki was still our evil genius, and every incident seemed to be used by him for one settled purpose of hate. A Kaserumini Chief, for instance, and seven men took away a young girl in a canoe to Aniwa, to be sold to friends there for

62. Paton continued to teach the natives how to read, despite the constant threats to his life.

tobacco leaf, which the Aniwans cultivated extensively. They also prepared to take revenge there for a child's death, killed in their belief by the sorcery of an Aniwan. When within sight of the shore, the canoes were upset and all were said to have been devoured by sharks, excepting only one canoe out of six. This one returned to Tanna and reported that there were two white Traders living on Aniwa, that they had plenty of ammunition and tobacco, but that they would not come to Tanna as long as a Missionary lived there. Under this fresh incitement, a party of Miaki's men came to my house, praising the Erromangans for the murder of their Missionaries and threatening me.

Even the friendly Nowar said, "Miaki will make a great wind and sink any Man-of-war that comes here. We will take the Man-of-war and kill all that are on board. If you and Abraham do not leave us we will kill you both, for we must have the Traders and the powder."

Just as they were assuming a threatening attitude, other Natives came running with the cry, "Missi, the *John Knox* is coming into the Harbor, and two great ships of fire, Men-of-war behind her, coming very fast!"

I retorted upon Nowar and the hostile company, "Now is your time! Make all possible haste! Let Miaki raise his great wind now; get all your men ready; I will tell them that you mean to fight, and you will find them always ready!"

Miaki's men fled away in unconcealed terror; but Nowar came to me and said, "Missi, I know that my talk is all lies, but if I speak the truth, they will kill me!"

I answered, "Trust in Jehovah, the same God who sent these vessels now, to protect us from being murdered."

But Nowar always wavered.

And now from all parts of the island those who were most friendly flocked to us. They were clamorous to have Miaki and some others of our enemies punished by the Man-of-war in presence of the Natives; and then they would be strong to speak in our defence and to lead the Tannese to worship Jehovah.[63]

63. John Paton never passed over an opportunity to press them on their threats and big talk. By God's providence, two British Man-of-war ships come into the harbor as the chiefs brag of their powers to arouse the gods to destroy these ships.

64. Paton saw himself as standing in the way of the utter destruction of the mission work and the buildings as well as the killings of the few converts on the island. He didn't think he could leave now.

65. Even the British Commodore was certain that the worship of Jehovah would do them good. Thankfully, the British government was willing to protect John G. Paton's life as best as possible.

Commodore Seymour, Captain Hume, and Dr. Geddie came on shore. After inquiring into everything, the Commodore urged me to leave at once, and very kindly offered to remove me to Aneityum, or Auckland, or any place of safety that I preferred. Again, however, I hesitated to leave my dear benighted Tannese, knowing that both Stations would be instantly broken up, that all the influence gained would be thrown away, that the Church would lose all that had been expended, and above all, that those friendly to us would be left to persecution and destruction.[64] For a long time I had seldom taken off my clothes at night, needing to be constantly on the alert to start at a moment's notice; yet, while hope burned within my soul I could not withdraw, so I resolved to risk all with my dear Lord Jesus, and remained at my post. At my request, however, they met and talked with all the leaders who could be assembled at the Mission House. The Natives declared frankly that they liked me but did not like the Worship. The Commodore reminded them that they had invited me to land among them, and had pledged their word more than once to protect me; he argued with them that as they had no fault to find with me, but only with the Worship, which could do them only good, they must bind themselves to protect my life.[65] Miaki and others promised and gave him their hands to do so. Lathella, an Aneityumese Chief, who was with Dr. Geddie, interpreted for him and them, Dr. Geddie explaining fully to Lathella in Aneityumese what the Commodore said in English, and Lathella explaining all to the Tannese in their own tongue.

At last old Nouka spoke out for all and said, "Captain Paddan and all the Traders tell us that the Worship causes all our sickness and death. They will not trade with us, nor sell us tobacco, pipes, powder, balls, caps, and muskets, till we kill our Missi like the Erromangans, but after that they will send a Trader to live among us and give us plenty of all these things. We love Missi. But when the Traders tell us that the Worship makes us sick, and when they bribe us with tobacco and powder to kill him or drive him away, some believe them and our hearts do bad conduct to Missi. Let Missi remain here, and we will try to do good conduct to Missi; but you must tell Queen 'Toria of her people's bad treatment of us, and that she must prevent her Traders from killing us with their measles, and from telling us lies to make us do bad conduct to Missi! If they come to us and talk as before, our hearts are very dark and may again lead us to bad conduct to Missi."

After this little parley, the Commodore invited us all on board, along with the Chiefs. They saw about three hundred brave marines ranked up on deck, and heard a great cannon discharged. For all such efforts to impress them and open their eyes, I felt profoundly grateful; but too clearly I knew and saw that only the grace of God could lastingly change them![66]

They were soon back to their old arguments, and were heard saying to one another, "If no punishment is inflicted on the Erromangans for murdering the Missi there, we fear the bad conduct of the Tannese will continue."

No punishment was inflicted at Erromanga, and the Tannese were soon as bold and wicked as ever. For instance, while the Man-of-war lay in the Harbor, Nowar kept himself closely concealed; but no sooner had she sailed than the cowardly fellow came out, laughing at the others, and protesting that he was under no promise and was free to act as he pleased! Yet in the hour of danger he generally proved to be our friend; such was his vacillating character. Nor was Miaki very seriously impressed. Mr. Mathieson shortly thereafter sent his boat round to me, being again short of European food. On his crew leaving her to deliver their message to me, some of Miaki's men at once jumped into the boat and started off round the island in search of kava. I went to Miaki, to ask that the boat might be brought back soon, but on seeing me he ran for his club and aimed to strike me. I managed to seize it, and to hold on, pleading with God and talking with Miaki, till by the interference of some friendly Natives his wrath was assuaged a little. Returning home, I sent food overland to keep them going till

66. Paton saw clearly that the powers of the British government could not change the hearts of these natives. They might deter a murder for a week or two. But only the power of the Holy Spirit of God could change the hearts of these people.

67. Paton was quite brave in his attempts to restrain the thievery and to disarm the war chief of his club, again.

the boat returned, which she did in about eight days. Thus light and shadow pursued each other, the light brightening for a moment, but upon the whole the shadows deepening.[67]

❧ CHAPTER X – FAREWELL SCENES
A.D. 1861-1862. Age 37-38

A time of great excitement amongst the Natives now prevailed. War, war, nothing but war was spoken of! Preparations for war were being made in all the villages far and near. Fear sat on every face, and armed bands kept watching each other, as if uncertain where the war was to begin or by whom. All work was suspended, and that war spirit was let loose which rouses the worst passions of human nature. Again we found ourselves the center of conflict, one party set for killing us or driving us away; the other wishing to retain us, while all old bitter grievances were also dragged into their speeches.[1]

Miaki and Nouka said, "If you will keep Missi and his Worship, take him with you to your own land, for we will not have him to live at the Harbor."

Ian, the great Inland Chief, rose in wrath and said, "On whose lands does the Missi live, yours or ours? Who fight against the Worship and all good, who are the thieves and murderers, who tell the lies, you or we? We wish peace, but you will have war. We like Missi and the Worship, but you hate them and say, 'Take him to your own land!' It is our land on which he now lives; it is his own land which he bought from you, but which our fathers sold Missi Turner long ago. The land was not yours to sell; it was really ours. Your fathers stole it from us long ago by war; but we would not have asked

1. Paton became a bargaining chip in the war negotiations. The inland tribes took the side with "Missi," and the harbor tribes led by Miaki opposed him.

it back, had you not asked us to take Missi away. Now we will defend him on it, and he will teach us and our people in our own land!" So meeting after meeting broke into fiery speech, and separated with many threats.

To the next great meeting I was invited, but did not go, contenting myself with a message pleading that they should live at peace and on no account go to war with each other. But Ian himself came for me. I said, "Ian, I have told you my whole heart. Go not to that meeting. I will rather leave the island or die, than see you going to war about me!"

He answered, "Missi, come with me, come now!"

I replied, "Ian, you are surely not taking me away to kill me? If you are, my God will punish it."

His only reply was, "Follow me, follow me quickly."

I felt constrained to go. He strode on before me till we reached the great village of his ancestors. His followers, armed largely with muskets as well as native weapons, filled one half the Village Square or dancing-ground. Miaki, Nouka, and their whole party sat in manifest terror upon the other half. Marching into the center, he stood with me by his side, and proudly looking round, exclaimed, "Missi, these are my men and your friends! We are met to defend you and the Worship." Then pointing across to the other side, he cried aloud, "These are your enemies and ours! The enemies of the Worship, the disturbers of the peace on Tanna! Missi, say the word, and the muskets of my men will sweep all opposition away, and the Worship will spread and we will all be strong for it on Tanna. We will not shoot without your leave; but if you refuse they will kill you and persecute us and our children, and banish Jehovah's Worship from our land."[2]

I said, "I love all of you alike. I am here to teach you how to turn away from all wickedness, to worship and serve Jehovah, and to live in peace. How can I approve of any person being killed for me or for the Worship? My God would be angry at me and punish me, if I did!"[3]

2. Ian's words sound like the Devil's temptation to Jesus. The Kingdom of Jesus does not come by war. It comes by preaching the Word to both sides, to both tribes. This is Paton's priority.

3. As always, Paton used this as an opportunity to preach to both sides concerning Jesus Christ who died to save us.

He replied, "Then, Missi, you will be murdered and the Worship destroyed."

I then stood forth in the middle before them all and cried, "You may shoot or murder me, but I am your best friend. I am not afraid to die. You will only send me the sooner to my Jehovah God, whom I love and serve, and to my dear Saviour Jesus Christ, who died for me and for you, and who sent me here to tell you all His love. If you will only love and serve Him and give up your bad conduct, you will be happy. But if you kill me, His messenger, rest assured that He will in His own time and way punish you. This is my word to you all; my love to you all!"

So saying, I turned to leave; and Ian strode suddenly away and stood at the head of his men, crying, "Missi, they will kill you! they will kill us, and you will be to blame!"

Miaki and Nouka, full of deceit, now cried out, "Missi's word is good! Let us all obey it. Let us all worship."[4]

An old man, Sirawia, one of Ian's under-chiefs, then said, "Miaki and Nouka say that the land on which Missi lives was theirs; though they sold it to him and he has paid them for it, they all know that it was ours, and is yet ours by right; but if they let Missi live on it in peace, we will all live at peace, and worship Jehovah. And if not, we will surely claim it again."

Miaki and his party hereon went off to their plantations, and brought a large present of food to Ian and his men as a peace-offering. This they accepted; and the next day Ian and his men brought Miaki a return present and said, "You know that Missi lives on our land? Take our present, be friends, and let him live quietly and teach us all. Yesterday you said his word was good; obey it now, else we will punish you and defend the Missi."

Miaki accepted the token, and gave good promises for the future. Ian then came to the hill-top near our house, by which passed the public path, and cried aloud in the hearing of all, "Abraham, tell Missi that you and he now live on our land. This path is the march betwixt Miaki and us. We have this day bought back the land of our fathers by a great price to prevent

4. Ian was more supportive of Paton than Miaki and the Harbor tribes.

war. Take of our breadfruits and also of our cocoanuts what you require, for you are our friends and living on our land, and we will protect you and the Worship!"

For some time things moved on quietly after this. An inland war, however, had continued for months. As many as ten men, they said, were sometimes killed in one day and feasted on by the warriors. Thousands had been thereby forced down from the mountains, and sought protection under Ian and his people. All the people claiming connection with his Tribe were called Naraimini; the people in the Volcano district were called the Kaserumini; and the Harbor Tribes were the Watarenmini; and so on all over the island. In such divisions, there might be from two to twenty Chiefs and Villages under one leader, and these stood by each other for purposes defensive and offensive. Now Nouka and Miaki had been frustrated in all their plans to get the Inland and the Harbor people involved in the war, as their own followers were opposed to it. In violation of his promises, however, Nouka invited all the men who wished to go to the war to meet him one morning, and only one appeared! Nouka, in great wrath, marched off to the war himself, but, as no one followed, he grew faint-hearted, and returned to his own village. On another morning, Miaki summoned all his fighting men; but only his own brother and six lads could be induced to accompany him, and with these he started off. But the enemy, hearing of his coming, had killed two of his principal allies the night before, and Miaki, learning this, turned and fled to his own house, and was secretly laughed at by his tribe.

Next day, Nouka came to me professing great friendship and pleading with me to accompany him and Miaki to talk with the Kaserumini, and persuade them to give up the war. He was annoyed and disappointed when I refused to go. Nowar and others informed me, two days thereafter, that three persons had died in that district, that others were sick, and that the Heathen there had resolved to kill me in revenge as the cause of all.[5] As Nouka's wife was one of the victims, this

5. Paton had friends on the island, who were always willing to warn him of the latest threats on his life.

scheme was concocted to entrap me. I was warned on no account to leave my house at night for a considerable time, but to keep it locked up and to let no one in after dark. The same two men from that district who had tried to kill Mr. Johnston and me, were again appointed and were watching for Abraham and me, lurking about in the evenings for that purpose. Again I saw how the Lord had preserved me from Miaki and Nouka! Truly all are safe who are in God's keeping; and nothing can befall them, except for their real good and the glory of their Lord.

Chafed at the upsetting of all their plans and full of revenge, Nouka and Miaki and their allies declared publicly that they were now going to kill Ian by sorcery, by *Nahak*, more feared by the poor Tannese than the field of battle. Nothing but the grace of God and the enlightenment of His Spirit through the Scriptures has ever raised these Natives above that paralyzing superstition. But, thank God, there are now, while I write this (1887), about twelve thousand in the New Hebrides who have been thus enlightened and lifted out of their terrors, for the Gospel is still, as of old, the power of God unto salvation![6] Strange to say, Ian became sick shortly after the Sacred Men had made the declaration about their *Nahak*-sorcery. I attended him, and for a time he recovered, and appeared very grateful. But he soon fell sick again. I sent him and the Chief next under him a blanket each; I also gave shirts and calico to a number of his leading men. They wore them and seemed grateful and pleased. Ian, however, gradually sank and got worse. He had every symptom of being poisoned, a thing easily accomplished, as they know and use many deadly poisons. His sufferings were very great, which prevented me from ascribing his collapse to mere superstitious terror. I did all that could be done; but all thought him dying, and of course by sorcery. His people were angry at me for not consenting before to their shooting of Miaki; and Miaki's people were now rejoicing that Ian was being killed by *Nahak*.[7]

6. Paton marvelled at the power of the Gospel to deal with very deep-seated fears of *Nahak* (sorcery). Here we have insight into what has happened by the year 1887 (26 years later). Twelve thousand natives converted to a saving knowledge of the Lord Jesus Christ. The population for this nation was about 100,000 in 1976. A significant percentage had become Christians in the first 30-40 years of missionary work on these islands.

7. Deceit is always strong in these false religions. Evidently, somebody poisoned the chief (while of course his enemies would claim power over the demonic world through sorcery).

One night, his brother and a party came for me to go and see Ian, but I declined to go till the morning for fear of the fever and ague. On reaching his village, I saw many people about, and feared that I had been led into a snare; but I at once entered into his house to talk and pray with him, as he appeared to be dying. After prayer, I discovered that I was left alone with him, and that all the people had retired from the village; and I knew that, according to their custom, this meant mischief. Ian said, "Come near me, and sit by my bedside to talk with me, Missi."

I did so, and while speaking to him he lay as if lost in a swoon of silent meditation. Suddenly he drew from the sugar-cane leaf thatch close to his bed a large butcher-like knife, and instantly feeling the edge of it with his other hand, he pointed it to within a few inches of my heart and held it quivering there, all atremble with excitement. I durst neither move nor speak, except that my heart kept praying to the Lord to spare me, or if my time was come to take me home to Glory with Himself. There passed a few moments of awful suspense. My sight went and came. Not a word had been spoken, except to Jesus; and then Ian wheeled the knife around, thrust it into the sugar-cane leaf, and cried to me, "Go, go quickly!"[8]

8. Another rather elaborate attempt was made on Paton's life, foiled by the power of the living Christ working on the dying man (in whose hand lay the knife).

Next moment I was on the road. Not a living soul was to be seen about the village. I understood then that it had been agreed that Ian was to kill me, and that they had all withdrawn so as not to witness it, that when the Man-of-war came to inquire about me, Ian would be dead, and no punishment could overtake the murderer. I walked quietly till quite free of the village, lest some hid in their houses might observe me. Thereafter, fearing that they, finding I had escaped, might overtake and murder me, I ran for my life a weary four miles till I reached the Mission House, faint yet praising God for such a deliverance. Poor Ian died soon after, and his people strangled one of his wives and hanged another, and took out the three bodies together in a canoe and sank them in the sea.[9]

9. These are dangerous and evil tribes as they kill Ian's wives for his burial.

Miaki was jubilant over having killed his enemy by *Na-hak*; but the Inland people now assembled in thousands to help Sirawia and his brother to avenge that death on Miaki, Nouka, and Karewick. These, on the other hand, boasted that they would kill all their enemies by *Nahak*-sorcery, and would call up a hurricane to destroy their houses, fruit trees, and plantations. Miaki and a number of his men also came to the Mission House; but, observing his sullen countenance, I asked kindly after his wife who was about to be confined, and gave a blanket, a piece of calico, and a bit of soap as a present for the baby. He seemed greatly pleased, whispered something to his men, and peaceably withdrew. Immediately after Miaki's threat about bringing a storm, one of their great hurricanes actually smote that side of the island and laid everything waste. His enemies were greatly enraged, and many of the injured people united with them in demanding revenge on Miaki. Hitherto I had done everything in my power to prevent war, but now it seemed inevitable, and both parties sent word that if Abraham and I kept to the Mission House no one would harm us. We had little faith in any of their promises, but there was no alternative for us.[10]

On the following Saturday, 18th January, 1862, the war began. Musket after musket[11] was discharged quite near us, and the bush all around rang with the yell of their war-cry, which if once heard will never be forgotten. It came nearer and nearer, for Miaki fled, and his people took shelter behind and around our house. We were placed in the heart of danger, and the balls flew thick all around us. In the afternoon Ian's brother and his party retired, and Miaki quickly sent messengers and presents to the Inikahimini and Kaserumini districts, to assemble all their people and help him "to fight Missi and the Tannese who were friends of the Worship." He said, "Let us cook his body and Abraham's, and distribute them to every village on this side of the island!"[12]

Yet all the while Miaki assured me that he had sent a friendly message. The war went on, and poor Nowar the Chief

10. In His providence, God brought a storm in conjunction with Miaki's threats. The war became inevitable because God ordained it. This island was not yet prepared to receive the Gospel. More judgment and slaughter appeared to be in order.

11. The natives used guns provided them by the Traders. Sadly, Western technology was used to great harm on these islands (before the Gospel took root).

12. Deceit, murder, and mayhem are now completely unleashed upon the missionary and his helper, Abraham.

protected us, till he had a spear broken into his right knee. The enemy would have carried him off to feast on his body; but his young men, shouting wildly his name and battle-cry, rushed in with great impetuosity and carried their wounded Chief home in triumph. The Inland people now discharged muskets at my house and beat against the walls with their clubs. They smashed in the door and window of our storeroom, broke open boxes and casks, tore my books to pieces and scattered them about, and carried off everything for which they cared, including my boat, mast, oars, and sails. They broke into Abraham's house and plundered it; after which they made a rush at the bedroom, into which we were locked, firing muskets, yelling, and trying to break it in. A Chief, professing to be sorry for us, called me to the window, but on seeing me he sent a tomahawk through it crying, "Come on, let us kill him now!"

I replied, "My Jehovah God will punish you; a Man-of-war will come and punish you, if you kill Abraham, his wife, or me."

He retorted, "It's all lies about a Man-of-war! They did not punish the Erromangans. They are afraid of us. Come on, let us kill them!"

He raised his tomahawk and aimed to strike my forehead, many muskets were uplifted as if to shoot, so I raised a revolver in my right hand and pointed it at them. The Rev. Joseph Copeland had left it with me on a former visit. I did not wish it, but he insisted upon leaving it, saying that the very knowledge that I had such a weapon might save my life. Truly, on this occasion it did so. Though it was harmless they fell back quickly. My immediate assailant dropped to the ground, crying, "Missi has got a short musket! He will shoot you all!"[13]

After lying flat on the ground for a little, they all got up and ran to the nearest bush, where they continued yelling about and showing their muskets. Towards nightfall they left, loaded with the plunder of the store and of Abraham's house. So God once more graciously protected us from falling into their cruel hands.

13. It is amazing how lacking in courage wicked men always turn out to be. "The wicked flee when no one pursues, but the righteous are bold as a lion" (Prov. 28:1). Paton is determined not to use violence to defend himself on the island. The pistol was brandished merely as a deterrent.

In the evening, after they left, I went to Miaki[14] and Nouka. They professed great sorrow at what had taken place and pretended to have given them a present of food not to do us further injury. But Nowar informed us that, on the contrary, they had hired them to return and kill us next morning and plunder everything on the Mission premises. Miaki, with a sneer, said, "Missi, where was Jehovah today? There was no Jehovah today to protect you. It's all lies about Jehovah. They will come and kill you, and Abraham, and his wife, and cut your bodies into pieces to be cooked and eaten in every village upon Tanna."

I said, "Surely, when you had planned all this, and brought them to kill us and steal all our property, Jehovah did protect us, or we would not have been here!"

He replied, "There was no Jehovah today! We have no fear of any Man-of-war. They dare not punish us. They durst not punish the Erromangans for murdering the Gordons. They will talk to us and say we must not do so again, and give us a present. That is all. We fear nothing. The talk of all Tanna is that we will kill you and seize all your property tomorrow."

I warned him that the punishment of a Man-of-war can only reach the body and the land, but that Jehovah's punishment reached both body and soul in Time and in Eternity.[15]

He replied, "Who fears Jehovah? He was not here to protect you today!"

"Yes," I said, "my Jehovah God is here now. He hears all we say, sees all we do, and will punish the wicked and protect His own people."

After this, a number of the people sat down around me, and I prayed with them. But I left with a very heavy heart, feeling that Miaki was evidently bent on our destruction.

I sent Abraham to consult Nowar, who had defended us till disabled by a spear in the right knee. He sent a canoe by Abraham, advising me to take some of my goods in it to his house by night, and he would try to protect them and us. The risk was so great we could only take a very little. Enemies

14. It was very courageous for Paton to march into Miaki's presence and challenge him this last time. This was the man that was contracting Paton's murder.

15. Paton reminded Miaki that the Man-of-war is far less to be feared than God Almighty, Judge of the Earth, and Maker of the Universe. He referred to the words of Jesus in Matthew 10:28 here: "And do not fear those who kill the body but cannot kill the soul. Rather fear him who can destroy both soul and body in hell."

16. Paton called himself a Calvinist, which means he was absolutely certain of God's sovereignty over every thing that happens to us. The Calvinist believes that God ordained the arch-crime of history in accordance with Acts 2:23: "This Jesus, delivered up according to the definite plan and foreknowledge of God, you crucified and killed by the hands of lawless men." Nonetheless, the Calvinist is not a fatalist. He still realizes that he has responsibility to make wise decisions. Paton determined that the door to Tanna had closed tightly and that there was no more opportunity for survival or for doing any more work there. Thus, he took the signal and ran for his life (along with his native helpers).

17. Paton lost almost everything, except for the Bible and his translations of the Bible (the most precious possessions of all). Here we see the true priorities of a man's life. He abandoned all of his earthly possessions and only later regained access to a few of his books.

were on every hand to cut off our flight, and Miaki, the worst of all, whose village had to be passed in going to Nowar's. In the darkness of the Mission House, we durst not light a candle for fear of some one seeing and shooting us. Not one of Nowar's men durst come to help us. But in the end it made no difference, for Nowar and his men kept what was taken there, as their portion of the plunder. Abraham, his wife, and I waited anxiously for the morning light. Miaki, the false and cruel, came to assure us that the Heathen would not return that day. Yet, as daylight came in, Miaki himself stood and blew a great conch not far from our house. I ran out to see why this trumpet-shell had been blown, and found it was the signal for a great company of howling armed savages to rush down the hill on the other side of the bay and make straight for the Mission House. We had not a moment to lose. To have remained would have been certain death to us all, and also to Matthew, a Teacher just arrived from Mr. Mathieson's Station. Though I am by conviction a strong Calvinist,[16] I am no Fatalist. I held on while one gleam of hope remained. Escape for life was now the only path of duty. I called the Teachers, locked the door, and made quickly for Nowar's village. There was not a moment left to carry anything with us. In the issue, Abraham and his wife and I lost all our earthly goods, and all our clothing except what we had on. My Bible, the few translations which I had made into Tannese, and a light pair of blankets I carried with me.[17]

To me the loss was bitter, but as God had so ordered it, I tried to bow with resignation. All my deceased wife's costly outfit, her piano, silver, cutlery, books, etc., with which her dear parents had provided her, besides all that I had in the world; also a box worth £56, lately arrived, full of men's clothing and medicine, the gift of my dear friends, Samuel Wilson, Esq., and Mrs. Wilson, of Geelong. The Sandal-wood Traders bought all the stolen property for tobacco, powder, balls, caps, and shot. One Trader gathered together a number of my books in a sadly torn and wasted condition and took them to

Aneityum, demanding £10 from Dr. Geddie for his trouble. He had to pay him £7 10s., which I repaid to him on my second return to the Islands. This, by way of digression, only to show how white and black Heathenism meet together.

Let us return to the morning of our flight. We could not take the usual path along the beach, for there our enemies would have quickly overtaken us. We entered the bush in the hope of getting away unobserved. But a cousin of Miaki, evidently secreted to watch us, sprang from behind a bread-fruit tree, and swinging his tomahawk, aimed it at my brow with a fiendish look. Avoiding it, I turned upon him and said in a firm bold voice:

"If you dare to strike me, my Jehovah God will punish you. He is here to defend me now!"

The man, trembling, looked all round as if to see the God who was my defender, and the tomahawk gradually lowered at his side. With my eye fixed upon him, I gradually moved backwards in the track of the Teachers, and God mercifully restrained him from following me.[18]

On reaching Nowar's village unobserved, we found the people terror-stricken, crying, rushing about in despair at such a host of armed savages approaching. I urged them to ply their axes, cut down trees, and blockade the path. For a little they wrought vigorously at this; but when, so far as eye could reach, they saw the shore covered with armed men rushing on towards their village, they were overwhelmed with fear, they threw away their axes and weapons of war, they cast themselves headlong on the ground, and they knocked themselves against the trees as if to court death before it came. They cried:

"Missi, it's of no use! We will all be killed and eaten today! See what a host are coming against us."

Mothers snatched up little children and ran to hide in the bush. Others waded as far as they could into the sea with them, holding their heads above the water. The whole village collapsed in a condition of indescribable terror. Nowar, lame with his wounded knee, got a canoe turned upside-down and

18. There seems to be some fear of God, a dread of God in this man's mind (Miaki's cousin). This is somewhat foreign to the modern humanist who attends Western schools and universities.

sat upon it where he could see the whole approaching multitude. He said:

"Missi, sit down beside me, and pray to our Jehovah God, for if He does not send deliverance now, we are all dead men. They will kill us all on your account, and that quickly. Pray, and I will watch!"[19]

19. The village was utterly defenseless against the men. Only prayer could save them now, and that is exactly what happened. We find that God often saves at the very last moment of desperation.

They had gone to the Mission House and broken in the door, and finding that we had escaped, they rushed on to Nowar's village. For, as they began to plunder the bed-room, Nouka said:

"Leave everything. Missi will come back for his valuable things at night, and then we will get them and him also!"

So he nailed up the door, and they all marched for Nowar's. We prayed as one can only pray when in the jaws of death and on the brink of Eternity. We felt that God was near, and omnipotent to do what seemed best in His sight. When the savages were about three hundred yards off, at the foot of a hill leading up to the village, Nowar touched my knee, saying:

"Missi, Jehovah is hearing! They are all standing still."

Had they come on they would have met with no opposition, for the people were scattered in terror. On gazing shorewards, and round the Harbor, as far as we could see, was a dense host of warriors, but all were standing still, and apparently absolute silence prevailed. We saw a messenger or herald running along the approaching multitude, delivering some tidings as he passed, and then disappearing in the bush. To our amazement, the host began to turn, and slowly marched back in great silence, and entered the remote bush at the head of the Harbor. Nowar and his people were in ecstasies, crying out:

"Jehovah has heard Missi's prayer! Jehovah has protected us and turned them away back."[20]

20. This answer to prayer was certainly a faith-building moment for this village on Tanna.

We were on that day His trusting and defenseless children; would you not, had you been one of our circle, have joined with us in praising the Lord God for deliverance from the jaws of death? I know not why they turned back; but I have no doubt it was the doing of God to save our lives.

We learned that they all assembled in a cleared part of the bush and there held a great wrangling palaver.[21] Nouka and Miaki advised them first to fight Manuman and his people. They said:

"His brother, the Sacred Man Kanini, killed Ian by *Nahak*. He is a friend of Missi and of the Worship. He also sent the hurricane to destroy us. They have plenty of yams and pigs. Let us fight and plunder them, and when they are out of the way, we will be strong to destroy Missi and the Worship."[22]

On this the whole mass went and attacked Manuman's first village, where they murdered two of his men, two women, and two children. The inhabitants fled, and all the sick, the feeble, and the children who fell into their hands were reported to us to be murdered, cooked, and eaten. Led on by Miaki, they plundered and burned seven villages.

About mid-day, Nouka and Miaki sent their cousin Jonas, who had always been friendly to me, to say that I might return to my house in safety, as they were now carrying the war inland. Jonas had spent some years on Samoa, and been much with Traders in Sydney, and spoke English well; but we felt they were deceiving us. That night, Abraham ventured to creep near the Mission House, to test whether we might return, and save some valuable things, and get a change of clothing. The house appeared to stand as when they nailed up the door. But a large party of Miaki's allies at once enclosed Abraham, and, after asking many questions about me, they let him go since I was not there. Had I gone there, they would certainly that night have killed me. Again, at midnight, Abraham and his wife and Matthew went to the Mission House, and found Nouka, Miaki, and Karewick near by, concealed in the bush among the reeds. Once more they enclosed them, thinking I was there too, but Nouka, finding that I was not, cried out:

"Don't kill them just now! Wait till Missi comes."

21. Palavar is "a prolonged and idle discussion."

22. For some reason, they viewed Missi (the missionary Paton) as the most formidable enemy on the island. This is surprising in that Paton never used arms against them. They must have felt the presence of the true and living God upon him.

Hearing this, Matthew slipped into the bush and escaped. Abraham's wife waded into the sea, and they allowed her to get away. Abraham was allowed to go to the Mission House, but he too crept into the bush, and after an anxious waiting they all came back to me in safety. We now gave up all hope of recovering anything from the house.

Towards morning, when Miaki and his men saw that I was not coming back to deliver myself into their hands, they broke up my house and stole all they could carry away. They tore my books, and scattered them about. They took away the type of my printing-press, to be made into bullets for their muskets. For similar uses they melted down the zinc lining of my boxes, and everything else that could be melted. What they could not take away, they destroyed. I lay on the ground all night, concealed in an outhouse of Nowar's, but it was a sleepless and anxious night, not only to me and my Aneityumese, but also to Nowar and his people.

Next day, the attack was renewed by the three Chiefs on the district of my dear friend Manuman. His people fled; the villages were burned; all who came in their way were killed, and all food and property carried away. At night they returned to keep watch over Nowar and me. When darkness was setting in, Miaki sent for me to go and speak with him, but Nowar and the Aneityumese were all so opposed to it that I did not go. Messages were sent to Nowar, threatening to kill him and his people for protecting me, and great excitement prevailed.[23]

Another incident added horror to the memories of this day. A savage from Erromanga, living with Nowar, had gone to the war that day. He got near a village unobserved, climbed into a tree, and remained there watching. After midday, Kamkali, a true friend of mine, the Chief of his village, came home wearied from the war, got his blanket, stealthily crept into a quiet place in the bush, rolled himself up, and lay down to sleep; for, according to their custom, the leading warriors in times of conflict seldom sleep in their own houses, and seldom twice in the same place even in the bush, for fear of personal

23. Now, Miaki and his troops were killing Paton's allies on the island.

danger. The Erromangan, having watched till he was sound asleep, crept to where he lay, raised his club and smashed in his skull. He told, when he came home, how the blood ran from nose, mouth, and ears, with a gurgling sound in his throat, and after a few convulsive struggles all was over! And the people around Nowar praised him for his deed. Cocoanuts were brought for him to drink, and food was presented before him in large quantities, as to one who had done something noble. For safety, he was put into the same house where I had to sit, and even Nowar honored him. I watched for the workings of a natural man's conscience under the guilt of murder. When left alone, he shook every now and then with agitation, and started round with a terrified gaze. He looked the picture of a man who felt that he had done to his neighbor what he would not have liked another to do to him. I wonder if that consciousness ever dies out, in the lowest and worst, that last voice of God in the soul?[24]

That very night, Nowar declared that I must leave his village before morning, else he and his people would be killed for protecting me. He advised me, as the sea was good, to try for Mr. Mathieson's Station; but he objected to my taking away any of my property—he would soon follow with it himself! But how to sail? Miaki had stolen my boat, mast, sails, and oars, as also an excellent canoe made for me and paid for by me on Aneityum; and he had threatened to shoot any person that assisted me to launch either the one or the other. The danger, however, was so great that Nowar said:

"You cannot remain longer in my house! My son will guide you to the large chestnut tree in my plantation in the bush. Climb up into it, and remain there till the moon rises."

Being entirely at the mercy of such doubtful and vacillating friends, I, though perplexed, felt it best to obey. I climbed into the tree, and was left there alone in the bush. The hours I spent there live all before me as if it were but of yesterday. I heard the frequent discharging of muskets, and the yells of the savages. Yet I sat there among the branches, as safe in the arms

24. Paton was in the same room with a murderer directly after he committed the deed. He perceives the man's conscience is still very much alive.

of Jesus! Never, in all my sorrows, did my Lord draw nearer to me, and speak more soothingly in my soul, than when the moonlight flickered among these chestnut leaves, and the night air played on my throbbing brow, as I told all my heart to Jesus. Alone, yet not alone! If it be to glorify my God, I will not grudge to spend many nights alone in such a tree, to feel again my Saviour's spiritual presence, to enjoy His consoling fellowship. If thus thrown back upon your own soul, alone, all, all alone, in the midnight, in the bush, in the very embrace of death itself, have you a Friend that will not fail you then?[25]

Gladly would I have lingered there for one night of comparative peace! But Nowar sent his son to call me down from the tree, and to guide me to the shore where he himself was, as it was now time to take to sea in the canoe. Pleading for my Lord's continuing presence, I had to obey. My life and the lives of my Aneityumese now hung upon a very slender thread; the risk was almost equally great from our friends so-called, or from our enemies. Had I been a stranger to Jesus and to prayer, my reason would verily have given way, but my comfort and joy sprang out of these words, "I will never leave thee, nor forsake thee; lo, I am with you alway!" Pleading these promises, I followed my guide. We reached the beach, just inside the Harbor, at a beautiful white sandy bay on Nowar's ground, from which our canoe was to start. A good number of the Natives had assembled there to see us off. Arkurat, having got a large roll of calico for the loan of his canoe, hid it away, and then refused the canoe, saying that if he had to escape with his family he would require it. He demanded an ax, a sail for his canoe, and a pair of blankets. As Koris had the ax and another had the quilt, I gave the quilt to him for a sail, and the ax and blankets for the canoe, in fact, these few relics of our earthly all at Nowar's were coveted by the savages and endangered our lives, and it was as well to get rid of them altogether. He cruelly proposed a small canoe for two; but I had hired the canoe for five, and insisted upon getting it, as he had been well paid for it. As he only laughed and mocked us, I prepared to start

25. The peace of God that passes all understanding keeps us in Christ Jesus (Phil. 4:7). This, Paton experienced first hand in the middle of the mayhem and war.

and travel overland to Mr. Mathieson's Station. He then said, "My wrath is over! You may take it and go."

We launched it, but now he refused to let us go till daylight. He had always been one of my best friends, but now appeared bent on a quarrel, so I had to exercise much patience with him and them. Having launched it, he said I had hired the canoe but not the paddles. I protested, "Surely you know we hired the paddles too. What could we do without paddles?"

But Arkurat lay down and pretended to have fallen asleep, snoring on the sand, and could not be awaked. I appealed to Nowar, who only said, "That is his conduct, Missi, our conduct!"

I replied, "As he has got the blankets which I saved to keep me from ague and fever, and I have nothing left now but the clothes I have on, surely you will give me paddles."

Nowar gave me one. Returning to the village, friends gave me one each till I got other three. Now Arkurat started up, and refused to let us go. A Chief and one of his men, who lived on the other side of the island near to where we were going, and who was hired by me to go with us and help in paddling the canoe, drew back also and refused to go.[26] Again I offered to leave the canoe, and walk overland if possible, when Faimungo, the Chief who had refused to go with us, came forward and said, "Missi, they are all deceiving you! The sea is so rough, you cannot go by it; and if you should get round the weather point, Miaki has men appointed to shoot you as you pass the Black Rocks, while by land all the paths are guarded by armed men. I tell you the truth, having heard all their talk. Miaki and Karewick say they hate the Worship, and will kill you. They killed your goats, and stole all your property yesterday. Farewell!"

The Teachers, the boy, and I now resolved to enter the canoe and attempt it, as the only gleam of hope left to us. After Faimungo came, the man to whom the canoe belonged had withdrawn from us, it having transpired that Miaki would not attack us that night, as other game had attracted his savage

26. The demonic resistance to Paton's flight was obvious in the deceitful wrangling with Arkurat.

eyes. My party of five embarked in our frail canoe; Abraham first, I next, Matthew after me, the boy at the steering paddle, and Abraham's wife sitting in the bottom, where she might hold on while it continued to float. For a mile or more we got away nicely under the lee of the island, but when we turned to go south for Mr. Mathieson's Station, we met the full force of wind and sea, every wave breaking over and almost swamping our canoe. The Native lad at the helm paddle stood up crying, "Missi, this is the conduct of the sea! It swallows up all who seek its help."

I answered, "We do not seek help from it, but from Jehovah Jesus."

Our danger became very great, as the sea broke over and lashed around us. My faithful Aneityumese, overcome with terror, threw down their paddles, and Abraham said, "Missi, we are all drowned now! We are food for the sharks. We might as well be eaten by the Tannese as by fishes; but God will give us life with Jesus in heaven!"

I seized the paddle nearest me; I ordered Abraham to seize another within his reach; I enjoined Matthew to bail the canoe for life, and the lad to keep firm in his seat, and I cried, "Stand to your post, and let us return! Abraham, where is now your faith in Jesus? Remember, He is Ruler on sea as on land. Abraham, pray and ply your paddle! Keep up stroke for stroke with me, as our lives depend on it. Our God can protect us. Matthew, bail with all your might. Don't look round on the sea and fear. Let us pray to God and ply our paddles, and He will save us yet!"

Dear old Abraham said, "Thank you for that, Missi. I will be strong. I pray to God and ply my paddle. God will save us!"

With much labor, and amid deadly perils, we got the canoe turned; and after four hours of a terrible struggle, we succeeded, towards daylight as the tide turned, in again reaching smooth water. With God's blessing we at last reached the shore, exactly where we had left it five hours ago![27]

27. Paton engaged the terrible situation with great faith, action, and leadership. It took four hours to return to their original position (Nowar's village). Now the little group of Christians had no support at all from any village.

Now drenched and weary, with the skin of our hands sticking to the paddles, we left the canoe on the reef and waded ashore. Many Natives were there, and looked sullen and disappointed at our return. Katasian, the lad who had been with us, instantly fled for his own land; and the Natives reported that he was murdered soon after. Utterly exhausted, I lay down on the sand and immediately fell into a deep sleep. By and by I felt someone pulling from under my head the native bag in which I carried my Bible and the Tannese translations—the all that had been saved by me from the wreck! Grasping the bag, I sprang to my feet, and the man ran away. My Teachers had also a hedging knife, a useless revolver, and a fowling-piece, the sight of which, though they had been under the salt water for hours, God used to restrain the savages. Calling my Aneityumese near, we now, in united prayer and kneeling on the sands, committed each other unto the Lord God, being prepared for the last and worst.

As I sat meditating on the issues, Faimungo, the friendly Inland Chief, again appeared to warn us of our danger, now very greatly increased by our being driven back from the sea. All Nowar's men had fled, and were hid in the bush and in rocks along the shore; while Miaki was holding a meeting not half a mile away, and preparing to fall upon us. Faimungo said, "Farewell, Missi, I am going home. I don't wish to see the work and the murders of this morning."

He was Nowar's son-in-law. He had always been truthful and kindly with me. His home was about half-way across the island, on the road that we wanted to go, and under sudden impulse I said, "Faimungo, will you let us follow you? Will you show us the path? When the Mission Ship arrives, I will give you three good axes, blankets, knives, fish-hooks, and many things you prize."

The late hurricanes had so destroyed and altered the paths, that only Natives who knew them well could follow them. He trembled much and said, "Missi, you will be killed. Miaki and Karewick will shoot you. I dare not let you follow. I have

28. Nowar's son-in-law is reluctant to help.

only about twenty men, and your following might endanger us all."[28]

I urged him to leave at once, and we would follow of our own accord. I would not ask him to protect us; but if he betrayed us and helped the enemy to kill us, I assured him that our God would punish him. If he spared us, he would be rewarded well; and if we were killed against his wishes, God would not be angry at him. He said, "Seven men are with me now, and thirteen are to follow. I will not now send for them. They are with Miaki and Nouka. I will go; but if you follow, you will be killed on the way. You may follow me as far as you can."

Off he started to Nowar's, and got a large load of my stolen property, blankets, sheets, etc., which had fallen to his lot. He called his seven men, who had also shared in the plunder, and, to avoid Miaki's men, they ran away under a large cocoanut grove skirting the shore, calling, "Be quick! Follow and keep as near to us as you can."

Though Nowar had got a box of my rice and appropriated many things from the plunder of the Mission House besides the goods entrusted to his care, and got two of my goats killed and cooked for himself and his people, yet now he would not give a particle of food to my starving Aneityumese or myself, but hurried us off, saying, "I will eat all your rice and keep all that has been left with me, in payment for my lame knee and for my people fighting for you!"[29]

29. Nowar proved to be the thorny ground hearer at this point (Matt. 13:1-8). He fails to stand firm during a time of great tribulation and persecution.

My three Aneityumese and I started after Faimungo and his men. We could place no confidence in any of them; but, feeling that we were in the Lord's hands, it appeared to be our only hope of escaping instant death. We got away unobserved by the enemies. We met several small parties of friends in the Harbor, apparently glad to see us trying to get away. But about four miles on our way, we met a large party of Miaki's men, all armed, and watching as outposts. Some were for shooting us, but others hesitated. Every musket was, however, raised and leveled at me. Faimungo poised his great spear and said,

"No, you shall not kill Missi today. He is with me." Having made this flourish, he strode off after his own men, and my Aneityumese followed, leaving me face to face with a ring of leveled muskets.

Sirawia, who was in command of this party, and who once, like Nowar, had been my friend, said to me, Judas like, "My love to you, Missi." But he also shouted after Faimungo, "Your conduct is bad in taking the Missi away; leave him to us to be killed!" I then turned upon him, saying, "Sirawia, I love you all. You must know that I sought only your good. I gave you medicine and food when you and your people were sick and dying under measles; I gave you the very clothing you wear. Am I not your friend? Have we not often drunk tea and eaten together in my house? Can you stand there and see your friend shot? If you do, my God will punish you severely."[30]

He then whispered something to his company which I did not hear; and, though their muskets were still raised, I saw in their eyes that he had restrained them. I therefore began gradually to move backwards, still keeping my eyes fixed on them, till the bush hid them from my view, whereon I turned and ran after my party, and God kept the enemy from following. I would like to think that Sirawia only uttered the cruel words which I heard as a blind to save his own life; for at this time he was joined to Miaki's party, his own people having risen against him, and had to dissemble his friendly feelings towards me. Poor Sirawia! Well I knew that Miaki would only use him as a tool for selfish interests, and sacrifice him at last. All this showed how dangers grew around our path. We trusted in Jehovah Jesus, and pressed on in flight.

A second hostile party encountered us, and with great difficulty we also got away from them. Soon thereafter a friendly company crossed our path. We learned from them that the enemies had slaughtered other two of Manuman's men, and burned several villages with fire. Another party of the enemy encountered us, and were eager for our lives. But this time Faimungo withstood them firmly, his men encircled us, and

30. Sirawia was Ian's under chief, once claiming to be a protector of Paton (against Miaki). Now, he's a turncoat, referred to by Paton as another Judas Iscariot (who betrayed Jesus).

he said, "I am not afraid now, Missi; I am feeling stronger near my own land!"

Hurrying still onwards, we came to that village on their high ground called Aneai, i.e. Heaven. The sun was oppressively hot, the path almost unshaded, and our whole party very exhausted, especially Faimungo, carrying his load of stolen goods. So here he sat down on the village dancing-ground for a smoke, saying, "Missi, I am near my own land now. We can rest with safety."

In a few minutes, however, he started up, he and his men, in wild excitement. Over a mountain, behind the village and above it, there came the shoutings, and anon the tramp, tramp of a multitude making rapidly towards us. Faimungo got up and planted his back against a tree. I stood beside him, and the Aneityumese woman and the two men stood near me, while his men seemed prepared to flee. At full speed a large body of the tallest and most powerful men that I had seen on Tanna came rushing on and filled the dancing-ground. They were all armed, and flushed with their success in war. A messenger had informed them of our escape, probably from Miaki, and they had crossed the country to intercept us.

Faimungo was much afraid, and said, "Missi, go on in that path, you and your Aneityumese; and I will follow when I have had a smoke and a talk with these men."

I replied, "No, I will stand by your side till you go; and if I am killed, it will be by your side, I will not leave you."

He implored us to go on, but that I knew would be certain death. They began urging one another to kill us, but I looked round them as calmly as possible, saying, "My Jehovah God will punish you here and hereafter, if you kill me or any of His servants."

A killing stone, thrown by one of the savages, grazed poor old Abraham's cheek, and the dear soul gave such a look at me, and then upwards, as if to say, "Missi, I was nearly away to Jesus." A club was also raised to follow the blow of the killing stone, but God baffled the aim. They encircled us in a deadly ring, and one kept urging another to strike the first blow or fire the first shot. My heart rose up to the Lord Jesus; I saw Him watching all the scene. My peace came back to me like a wave from God. I realized that I was immortal till my Master's work with me was done. The assurance came to me, as if a voice out of Heaven had spoken, that not a musket would be fired to wound us, not a club prevail to strike us, not a spear leave the hand in which it was held vibrating to be thrown, not an arrow leave the bow, or a killing-stone the fingers, without the permission of Jesus Christ, whose is all power in Heaven and on Earth. He rules all Nature, animate and inanimate, and restrains even the savage of the South Seas. In that awful hour I saw His own words, as if carved in letters of fire upon the clouds of Heaven: "Seek, and ye shall find. Whatsoever ye shall ask in My name, that will I do, that the Father may be glorified in the Son." I could understand how Stephen and John saw the glorified Saviour as they gazed up through suffering and persecution to the Heavenly Throne.[31]

Yet I never could say that on such occasions I was entirely without fear. Nay, I have felt my reason reeling, my sight coming and going, and my knees smiting together when thus brought close to a violent death, but mostly under the solemn thought of being ushered into Eternity and appearing before God. Still, I was never left without hearing that promise in all its consoling and supporting power coming up through the darkness and the anguish, "Lo, I am with you alway."[32] And with Paul I could say, even in this dread moment and crisis of being, "I am persuaded that neither death nor life. . . nor any other creature, shall be able to separate us from the love of God which is in Christ Jesus our Lord."

Faimungo and others now urged us to go on in the path. I said, "Faimungo, why are we to leave you? My God heard your promise not to betray me. He knows now what is in your heart and in mine. I will not leave you; and if I am to die, I will die by your side."

He replied, "Now, I go on before; Missi, keep close to me."

31. Here is the most dangerous encounter with the savages in the story. John G. Paton speaks of seeing Jesus Christ, as Stephen did on his martyrdom (Acts 7:55-56). The Lord Jesus will make His presence known and bring great peace to His servants when they are placed in the most difficult conditions. Not many Christians can testify to seeing Christ. Paton is absolutely convinced of Ephesians 1:22: "He [Christ] is head over all things to the church."

32. The absolute sovereignty of Christ over every single force in the universe is an essential belief for the Christian.

33. There is no explanation for the restraint on these men, except the power of God keeping the lions' mouths shut.

34. These are exceedingly strong, faith-building testimonies. The reader should be great encouraged by this. Spend a little more time contemplating this experience of faith for Paton.

35. Again, Paton is more filled with the holy fear of God (and the final judgment), than he is of these men wielding a few weapons.

His men had gone, and I persuaded my Aneityumese to follow them. At last, with a bound, Faimungo started after them. I followed, keeping as near him as I could, pleading with Jesus to protect me or to take me home to Glory. The host of armed men also ran along on each side with their weapons ready; but leaving everything to Jesus, I ran on as if they were my escort, or as if I saw them not. If any reader wonders how they were restrained, much more would I, unless I believed that the same Hand that restrained the lions from touching Daniel held back these Savages from hurting me![33] We came to a stream crossing our path. With a bound all my party cleared it, ran up the bank opposite, and disappeared in the bush. "Faint yet pursuing," I also tried the leap, but I struck the bank and slid back on my hands and knees towards the stream. At this moment I heard a crash above my head amongst the branches of an overhanging tree, and I knew that a Kawas had been thrown, and that that branch had saved me. Praising my God, I scrambled up on the other side, and followed the track of my party into the bush.[34] The savages gazed after me for a little in silence, but no one crossed the stream; and I saw them separate into two, one portion returning to the village and another pressing inland. With what gratitude did I recognize the Invisible One who brought their counsels to confusion.[35]

I found my party resting in the bush, and amazed to see me escaped alive from men who were thirsting for my blood. Faimungo and his men received me with demonstrations of joy, perhaps feeling a little ashamed of their own cowardice. He now ascended the mountain and kept away from the common path to avoid other Native bands. At every village enemies to the Worship were ready to shoot us. But I kept close to our guide, knowing that the fear of shooting him would prevent their shooting at me, as he was the most influential Chief in all that section of the island.

One party said, "Miaki and Karewick said that Missi made the sickness and the hurricanes, and we ought to kill him."

Faimungo replied, "They lie about Missi! It is our own bad conduct that makes us sick."

They answered, "We don't know who makes the sickness, but our fathers have taught us to kill all Foreign men."

Faimungo, clutching club and spear, exclaimed, standing betwixt them and us, "You won't kill Missi today!"

In the flight we passed springs and streamlets, but though parched with sickening thirst, not one of us durst stoop down to drink, as we should have been almost certainly killed in the act.[36] Faimungo now sent his own men home by a near path, and guided us himself till we were close upon the shore. There, sitting down he said:

"Missi, I have now fulfilled my promise. I am so tired, I am so afraid, I dare not go farther. My love to you all. Now go on quickly! Three of my men will go with you to the next rocks. Go quickly! Farewell."[37]

These men went on a little, and then said, "Missi, we dare not go! Faimungo is at war with the people of the next land. You must keep straight along this path." So they turned and ran back to their own village.

To us this district was especially perilous. Many years ago the Aneityumese had joined in a war against the Tannese of this tribe, and the thirst for revenge yet existed in their hearts, handed down from sire to son. Most providentially the men were absent on a war expedition, and we saw only three lads and a great number of women and children, who ran off to the bush in terror. In the evening the enraged savages of another district assaulted the people of the shore villages for allowing us to pass, and, though sparing their lives, broke in pieces their weapons of war—a very grievous penalty. In the next district, as we hasted along the shore, two young men came running after us, poising their quivering spears. I took the useless revolver out of my little native basket, and raising it cried, "Beware! Lay down your spears at once on the sand, and carry my basket to the next landing at the Black Rocks."

36. They would not lower their heads to drink, for any person would have taken advantage and killed them.

37. The thin thread of Faimungo does not break during the escape, only by the grace of God. Faimungo was not enthusiastic about helping Paton from the beginning.

They threw their spears on the sand, lifted the bag, and ran on before us to the rocks which formed the march betwixt them and their enemies. Laying it down, they said appealingly, "Missi, let us return to our home!" And how they did run, fearing the pursuit of their foes.

In the next land we saw none. After that we saw crowds all along, some friendly, others unfriendly, but they let us pass on, and with the blessing of Almighty God we drew dear to Mr. Mathieson's Station in safety. Here a man gave me a cocoanut for each of our party, which we greatly required, having tasted nothing all that day, and very little for several days before. We were so weak that only the struggle for life enabled us to keep our feet; yet my poor Aneityumese never complained and never halted, not even the woman. The danger and excitement kept us up in the race for life; and by the blessing of God we were now approaching the Mission House, praising God for His wonderful deliverances.[38]

Hearing of our coming, Mr. Mathieson came running to meet me. They had heard of our leaving my own Station, and they thought I was dead! They were themselves both very weak; their only child had just been laid in the grave, and they were in great grief and in greater peril.[39] We praised the Lord for permitting us to meet; we prayed for support, guidance, and protection; and resolved now, in all events, to stand by each other till the last.

Before I left the Harbor I wrote and left with Nowar letters to be given to the Captains of any vessels which called, for the first, and the next, and the next, telling them of our great danger, that Mr. Mathieson was almost without food, and that I would reward them handsomely if they would call at the Station and remove any of us who might be spared thence to Aneityum. Two or three vessels called, and, as I afterwards learned, got my letters; but, while buying my stolen property from the Natives for tobacco, powder, and balls, they took no further notice of my appeals, and sailed past Mr. Mathieson's,

38. The entire journey would have been 25-30 miles in length, almost entirely through dangerous territory, over rough terrain, and on foot. They had almost no food for the journey, but by God's grace survived it.

39. The Mathiesons were also suffering greatly, having lost a child.

straight on to Aneityum. "The tender mercies of the wicked are cruel!"[40]

Let me now cull the leading events from my Journal, that intervened betwixt this date and the break-up of the Mission on Tanna—at least for a season—though, blessed be God! I have lived to see the light rekindled by my dear friends Mr. and Mrs. Watt, and shining more brightly and hopefully than ever. The candle was quenched, but the candlestick was not removed![41]

On Wednesday, 22nd January, 1862, we heard that other three of Manuman's people had been killed and a district burned with fire. Though this poor man was one of Nowar's chief friends, yet I heard him say before my flight, "When so many children are being killed, why do they not send one for food to me and my family? They are as tender and good as the young fowls!" A remark like this lets you see deep into the heart of a Cannibal, and he a sort of half-converted one, if I may use such an expression; certainly not one of the worst type by any means.

On the 23rd January, 1862, Mr. Mathieson sent for Taura, Kati, and Kapuku, his three principal Chiefs, to induce them to promise protection till a vessel called to take us away. They appeared friendly, and promised to do their best. Alas! the promises of the Tannese Chiefs had too often proved to be vain.

On Friday, 24th January, report reached our Station that Miaki and his party, hearing that a friendly Chief had concealed two of Manuman's young men, compelled him to produce them and club them to death before their eyes. Also, that they surrounded Manuman's party on a mountain, and hemmed them in there, dying of starvation, and trying to survive on the carcasses of the dead and on bark and roots. Also, that Miaki had united all the Chiefs, friends and foes alike, in a bond of blood, to kill every one pertaining to the whole Mission on Tanna. Jesus reigns!

40. The Traders were more interested in making money than saving lives.

41. About six years later (1868), William and Agnes Watt (Presbyterians) re-established the mission work on Tanna. William finally baptized two men and four women in 1880 (after 12 full years of labor).

42. The missionaries continued to hold worship services in various villages despite the danger.

On Sunday, the 26th January, thirty persons came to worship at the Mission House. Thereafter, at great risk, we had Worship at three of the nearest and most friendly villages. Amidst all our perils and trials we preached the Gospel to about one hundred and sixteen persons. It was verily a sowing time of tears; but, despite all that followed, who shall say that it was vain! Twenty years have passed, and now when I am writing this, there is a Church of God singing the praises of Jesus in that very district of Tanna.[42] On leaving the second village, a young lad affectionately took my hand to lead me to the next village; but a sulky, down-browed savage, carrying a ponderous club, also insisted upon accompanying us. I led the way, guided by the lad. Mr. Mathieson got the man to go before him, while he himself followed, constantly watching. Coming to a place where another path branched off from ours, I asked which path we took, and, on turning to the left as instructed by the lad, the savage, getting close behind me, swung his huge club over his shoulder to strike me on the head. Mr. Mathieson, springing forward, caught the club from behind with a great cry to me; and I, wheeling instantly, had hold of the club also, and betwixt us we wrested it out of his hands. The poor creature, craven at heart however bloodthirsty, implored us not to kill him. I raised the club threateningly, and caused him to march in front of us till we reached the next village fence. In terror lest these villagers should kill him, he gladly received back his club, as well as the boy his bow and arrows, and they were lost in the bush in a moment.

At the village from which this man and boy had come, one savage brought his musket while we were conducting Worship, and sat sullen and scowling at us all the time. Mocking questions were also shouted at us, such as, "Who made the rains, winds, and hurricanes? Who caused all the disease? Who killed Missi Mathieson's child?" They sneered and scoffed at our answers, and in this Taura the Chief joined the rest.

On the 27th, at daylight, a vessel was seen in the offing, as if to tantalize us. The Captain had been at the Harbor, and had received my letter from Nowar. I hoisted a flag to induce him to send or come on shore, but he sailed off for Aneityum, bearing the plunder of my poor Mission House, purchased for ammunition and tobacco for the Natives. He left the news at Aneityum that I had been driven from my Station some time ago, and was believed to have been murdered.

On the 29th of January, the young Chief Kapuku came and handed to Mr. Mathieson his own and his father's war-gods and household idols. They consisted chiefly of a basket of small and peculiar stones, much worn and shining with use. He said, "While many are trying to kill you and drive the Worship of Jehovah from this island, I give up my gods, and will send away all Heathen idols from my land."[43]

43. A young chief gave up his idols to serve the true and living God.

On the 31st, we learned that a party of Miaki's men were going about Mr. Mathieson's district inciting the people to kill us. Faimungo also came to inform us that Maiki was exerting all his artifice to get us and the Worship destroyed. Manuman even sent, from inland, Raki, his adopted son, to tell me of the fearful sufferings that he and his people were now passing through, and that some were killed almost every day. Raki's wife was a Chief's daughter, who, when the war began, returned to her father's care. The savages of Miaki went to her own father's house and compelled him to give her up as an enemy. She was clubbed and feasted on.

On Sabbath, 2nd February, thirty-two people attended the Morning Service. I addressed them on the Deluge,[44] its causes and lessons. I showed them a doll, explaining that such carved and painted images could not hear our prayers or help us in our need, that the living Jehovah God only could hear and help. They were much interested, and after Worship carefully examined the doll. Mr. Mathieson and I, committing ourselves to Jesus, went inland and conducted Worship at seven villages, listened to by about one hundred people in all. Nearly all appeared friendly. The people of one village had been in-

44. The Deluge refers to Noah's flood.

45. God saved their lives again. He had rescued them hundreds of times in remarkable ways.

46. Miaki, at this point, became the major force on the entire island. He was bound and determined to kill the missionaries (a true Judas).

47. While the natives were not to be counted on, Paton's dog (Clutha) was faithful to the end. The dog knows to be silent but warns his master of danger.

cited to kill us on our return; but God guided us to return by another way, and so we escaped.[45]

During the day, on 3rd February, a company of Miaki's men came to the Mission House,[46] and forced Mrs. Mathieson to show them through the premises. Providentially, I had bolted myself that morning into a closet room, and was engrossed with writing. They went through every room in the house and did not see me, concluding I had gone inland. They discharged a musket into our Teacher's house, but afterwards left quietly, greatly disappointed at not finding me. My heart still rose in praise to God for another such deliverance, neither by man nor of man's planning!

Worn out with long watching and many fatigues, I lay down that night early, and fell into a deep sleep. About ten o'clock the savages again surrounded the Mission House. My faithful dog Clutha, clinging still to me amid the wreck of all else on earth, sprang quietly upon me, pulled at my clothes, and awoke me, showing danger in her eye glancing at me through the shadows.[47] I silently awoke Mr. and Mrs. Mathieson, who had also fallen asleep. We committed ourselves in hushed prayer to God and watched them, knowing that they could not see us. Immediately a glare of light fell into the room! Men passed with flaming torches; and first they set fire to the Church all round, and then to a reed fence connecting the Church and the dwelling-house. In a few minutes the house, too, would be in flames, and armed savages waiting to kill us on attempting an escape!

Taking my harmless revolver in the left hand and a little American tomahawk in the right, I pleaded with Mr. Mathieson to let me out and instantly to again lock the door on himself and wife. He very reluctantly did so, holding me back and saying, "Stop here and let us die together! You will never return!"

I said, "Be quick! Leave that to God. In a few minutes our house will be in flames, and then nothing can save us."

He did let me out, and locked the door again quickly from the inside; and, while his wife and he prayed and watched for me from within, I ran to the burning reed fence, cut it from top to bottom, and tore it up and threw it back into the flames, so that the fire could not by it be carried to our dwelling-house. I saw on the ground shadows, as if something were falling around me, and started back. Seven or eight savages had surrounded me, and raised their great clubs in air. I heard a shout—"Kill him! Kill him!" One savage tried to seize hold of me, but, leaping from his clutch, I drew the revolver from my pocket and leveled it as for use, my heart going up in prayer to my God. I said, "Dare to strike me, and my Jehovah God will punish you. He protects us, and will punish you for burning His Church, for hatred to His Worship and people, and for all your bad conduct. We love you all; and for doing you good only, you want to kill us. But our God is here now to protect us and to punish you."[48]

They yelled in rage, and urged each other to strike the first blow, but the Invisible One restrained them. I stood invulnerable beneath His invisible shield, and succeeded in rolling back the tide of flame from our dwelling-house.

At this dread moment occurred an incident, which my readers may explain as they like, but which I trace directly to the interposition of my God. A rushing and roaring sound came from the South, like the noise of a mighty engine or of muttering thunder. Every head was instinctively turned in that direction, and they knew, from previous hard experience, that it was one of their awful tornadoes of wind and rain. Now, mark, the wind bore the flames away from our dwelling-house; had it come in the opposite direction, no power on earth could have saved us from being all consumed! It made the work of destroying the Church only that of a few minutes; but it brought with it a heavy and murky cloud, which poured out a perfect torrent of tropical rain. Now, mark again, the flames of the burning Church were thereby cut off from extending to and seizing upon the reeds and the bush; and,

48. Paton, always the most courageous and willing to give up his life for others, exits the house to interact with the enemy.

49. In His good providence, God sends a tremendous rainstorm to halt the plans of the natives to burn down the house in which the missionaries were hiding.

besides, it had become almost impossible now to set fire to our dwelling-house. The stars in their courses were fighting against Sisera![49]

The mighty roaring of the wind, the black cloud pouring down unceasing torrents, and the whole surroundings, awed those savages into silence. Some began to withdraw from the scene, all lowered their weapons of war, and several, terror-struck, exclaimed, "That is Jehovah's rain! Truly their Jehovah God is fighting for them and helping them. Let us away!"

A panic seized upon them; they threw away their remaining torches; in a few moments they had all disappeared in the bush; and I was left alone, praising God for His marvelous works. "O taste and see that God is good! Blessed is the man that trusteth in Him!"[50]

50. Paton verified Psalm 34:8 by experience and by this life of faith.

Returning to the door of the Mission House, I cried, "Open and let me in. I am now all alone."

Mr. Mathieson let me in, and exclaimed, "If ever, in time of need, God sent help and protection to His servants in answer to prayer, He has done so tonight! Blessed be His holy Name!"

In fear and in joy we united our praises. Truly our Jesus has all power, not less in the elements of Nature than in the savage hearts of the Tannese. Precious Jesus! Often since have I wept over His love and mercy in that deliverance, and prayed that every moment of my remaining life may be consecrated to the service of my precious Friend and Saviour![51]

51. The right response to these marvelous deliverances is to recommit our lives to His service (with a new-found dedication).

All through the remainder of that night I lay wide awake keeping watch, my noble little dog lying near me with ears alert. Early in the morning friends came weeping around us. Our enemies were loudly rejoicing. It had been finally resolved to kill us at once, to plunder our house and then to burn it. The noise of the shouting was distinctly heard as they neared the Mission premises, and our weeping, friendly Natives looked terror-struck, and seemed anxious to flee for the bush. But just when the excitement rose to the highest pitch, we heard, or dreamed that we heard, a cry higher still, "Sail O!"[52]

We were by this time beginning to distrust almost our very senses; but again and again that cry came rolling up from the shore, and was repeated from crowd to crowd all along the beach, "Sail O! Sail O!"

The shouts of those approaching us gradually ceased, and the whole multitude seemed to have melted away from our view. I feared some cruel deception, and at first peered out very cautiously to spy the land. But yonder in very truth a vessel came sailing into view. It was the *Blue Bell*, Captain Hastings. I set fire to the reeds on the side of the hill to attract his attention. I put a black shawl as a flag on one end of the Mission House and a white sheet on the other.

This was one of the vessels that had been to Port Resolution, and had sailed past to Aneityum some time ago. I afterwards saw the mate and some of the men wearing my shirts, which they had bought from the Tannese on their former visit. At the earnest request of Messrs. Geddie and Copeland, Mr. Underwood, the owner, had sent Captain Hastings to Tanna to rescue us if yet alive.[53] For this purpose he had brought twenty armed men from Aneityum, who came on shore in two boats in charge of the mate, the notorious Ross Lewin. He returned to the ship with a boat-load of Mr. Mathieson's things, leaving ten of the Natives to help us to pack more and carry them down to the beach, especially what the Missionary thought most valuable.

The two boats were now loaded and ready to start. It was about two o'clock in the afternoon, when a strange and painful trial befell us. Poor dear Mr. Mathieson, apparently unhinged, locked himself all alone into what had been his study, telling Mrs. Mathieson and me to go, for he had resolved to remain and die on Tanna. We tried to show him the inconsistency of praying to God to protect us or grant us means of escape, and then refuse to accept a rescue sent to us in our last extremity. We argued that it was surely better to live and work for Jesus

52. A ship sailed into harbor, just in the nick of time. Again, God's deliverances are often right when Pharaoh's armies are descending on the people of God.

53. Paton insists that to stay means their immediate murders. At this last moment, it makes the most sense to leave the island.

than to die as a self-made martyr, who, in God's sight, was guilty of self-murder. His wife wept aloud and pleaded with him, but all in vain! He refused to leave or to unlock his door. I then said, "It is now getting dark. Your wife must go with the vessel, but I will not leave you alone. I shall send a note explaining why I am forced to remain; and as it is certain that we shall be murdered whenever the vessel leaves, I tell you God will charge you with the guilt of our murder."

At this he relented, unlocked the door, and accompanied us to the boats, in which we all immediately left.

Meantime, having lost several hours, the vessel had drifted leeward; darkness suddenly settled upon us, and when we were out at sea we lost sight of her and she of us. After tumbling about for some hours in a heavy sea, and unable to find her, those in charge of the boats came near for consultation, and, if possible, to save the lives of all. We advised that they should steer for Port Resolution by the flame of the volcano—a never failing lighthouse, seen fifty miles away—and there await the vessel. The boats were to keep within hearing of each other by constant calling; but this was soon lost to the ear, though on arriving in the bay we found they had got to anchor before us. There we sat in the boats and waited for the coming day.[54] As the light appeared, we anchored as far out as possible, beyond the reach of musket shots; and there without water or food we sat under a tropical sun till midday came, and still there was no sign of the vessel. The mate at last put all the passengers and the poorest seamen into one boat and left her to swing at anchor, while, with a strong crew in the other, he started off in search of the vessel.[55]

In the afternoon, Nowar and Miaki came off in a canoe to visit us. Nowar had on a shirt, but Miaki was naked and frowning. He urged me to go and see the Mission House, but as we had seen a body of men near it I refused to go. Miaki declared that everything remained as I had left it, but we knew that he lied. Old Abraham and a party had slipped on shore in a canoe, and had found the windows smashed and everything

54. The two boats were supposed to rendezvous with the ship, but could not find the ship in the darkness. They returned to Port Resolution (the other side of the island where Paton used to live).

55. The mate took the one boat out to find the ship in the morning. The others crowded into the remaining little boat.

gone except my books, which were scattered about and torn in pieces. They learned that Miaki had sold everything that he could sell to the Traders. The mate and men of the *Blue Bell* had on my very clothes. They boasted that they had bought them for a few figs of tobacco and for powder, caps, and balls. But they would not return a single shirt to me, though I was without a change. We had all been without food since the morning before, so Nowar brought us off a cocoanut each, and two very small roasted yams for the ladies.[56] Those, however, only seemed to make our thirst the more severe, and we spent a trying day in that boat under a burning sun.

Miaki said, "As our fathers did not destroy Missi Turner's house, we will not destroy yours." But after a time, failing to persuade me to accompany him and fall into a trap, he muttered— "We have taken everything your house contained, and would take you too if we could; for we hate the Worship, it causes all our diseases and deaths; it goes against our customs, and it condemns the things we delight in."

Nowar informed me that only a few nights before this, Miaki and his followers went inland to a village where last year they had killed ten men. Having secretly placed a savage at the door of every house, at a given signal they yelled, and when the terrified inmates tried to escape, they killed almost every man, woman, and child. Some fled into the bush, others rushed to the shore. A number of men got into a canoe to escape, but hearing women and children crying after them they returned, and taking those they could with them, they killed the rest, lest they should fall alive into Miaki's hands. These are surely "they who through fear of death are all their lifetime subject to bondage." The Chief and nearly his whole village were cut off in one night![57] The dark places of the Earth are "full of the habitations of horrid cruelty." To have actually lived amongst the Heathen and seen their life gives a man a new appreciation of the power and blessings of the Gospel, even where its influence is only very imperfectly allowed to guide

56. Nowar was still acting kindly to the missionaries.

57. An entire village was massacred, man, woman, and child. This becomes a final sign of the degradation of these islands.

and restrain the passions of men. Oh, what it will be when all men in all nations love and serve the glorious Redeemer!

This Miaki and his followers were a scourge and terror to the whole island of Tanna. They intensely hated Nowar, because he would not join in their cruelties. Yet he and Manuman and Sirawia and Faimungo continued to survive long after war and death had swept all the others away. The first three lived to be very old men, and to the last they made a profession of being Christians, though their knowledge was very limited and their inconsistencies very grave and very numerous. Happy is it for us that we are not the judges, for souls either of the white or the dark skin, as to how many and grievous things may be forgiven, and whether there be or be not that spark of love, that grain of faith which the Lord the Pitiful will graciously accept and increase![58]

58. Nowar, Manuman, and Sirawia lived out their old age as Christians. What a remarkable testimony to Christ's victory and the Devil's loss! Their sins of cannibalism and murder are forgiven, and Paton glories in this.

About five o'clock in the evening the vessel hove in sight. Before dark we were all on board, and were sailing for Aneityum. Though both Mr. and Mrs. Mathieson had become very weak, they stood the voyage wonderfully. Next day we were safely landed. We had offered Captain Hastings £20 to take us to Aneityum, but he declined any fare. However, we divided it amongst the mate and crew, for they had every one shown great kindness to us on the voyage.

59. Many missionaries gave their lives on the mission field in the 19th century. The average lifespan of missionaries in Africa during the 19th century was seven years. They were told to build a graveyard before they built a church. The diseases, the hardships, and so forth were part and parcel of discipling these nations for Christ.

After arriving on Aneityum, Mrs. Mathieson gradually sank under consumption, and fell asleep in Jesus on 11th March, 1862, and was interred there in the full assurance of a glorious resurrection. Mr. Mathieson, becoming more and more depressed after her death, went over to Mr. Creagh's Station, on Mare, and there died on 14th June, 1862, still trusting in Jesus, and assured that he would soon be with Him in Glory.[59] Never more earnest or more faithful souls entered the Mission field; but they both suffered from weakness and ill-health during all their time on Tanna, and had frequently to seek change by removal for a short period from the island. Their memory is very fragrant to me as follow-laborers in the Gospel of Jesus.

After their death I was the only one left alive in all the New Hebrides Mission north of Aneityum, to tell the story of those pioneer years, during which were sown the seeds of what is now fast becoming a glorious harvest. Twenty-five years ago, all these dear brethren and sisters who were associated with me in the work of the Mission were called home to Glory, to cast their crowns at the feet of Jesus and enjoy the bliss of the redeemed; while I am privileged still to toil and pray for the salvation of the poor Islanders, and plead the cause of the Mission both in the Colonies and at home, in which work the Lord has graciously given me undreamt-of success. My constant desire and prayer are that I may be spared to see at least one Missionary on every island of the group, or trained Native Teachers under the superintendence of a Missionary, to unfold the riches of redeeming love and to lead the poor Islanders to Jesus for salvation.

What could be taken in three boats was saved out of the wreck of Mr. Mathieson's property; but my earthly all perished, except the Bible and the translations into Tannese. Along with the goods pertaining to the Mission, the property which I had to leave behind would be under-estimated at £600, besides the value of the Mission House, etc. Often since have I thought that the Lord stripped me thus bare of all these interests that I might with undistracted mind devote my entire energy to the special work soon to be carved out for me, and of which at this moment neither I nor any one had ever dreamed. At any rate, the loss of my little Earthly All, though doubtless costing me several pangs,[60] was not an abiding sorrow like that which sprang from the thought that the Lord's work was now broken up at both Stations, and that the Gospel was for the time driven from Tanna.

In the darkest moment I never doubted that ultimately the victory there, as elsewhere, would be on the side of Jesus, believing that the whole Earth would yet be filled with the glory of the Lord.[61] But I sometimes sorely feared that I might never live to see or hear of that happy day! By the goodness of

60. Paton saw four years of work (in buildings and capital) go up in smoke. But what remained were the seeds planted in the hearts of men and women still left on Tanna. These brought forth fruit in years to come.

61. Paton retained an optimistic view of history. This is characteristic of 19th-century missionaries who knew that "[Christ] must reign until he has put all his enemies under his feet" (1 Cor. 15:25). The kingdom must grow like the mustard seed into a tree that covers the world. It was only the 20th century that brought a more pessimistic eschatology and a less aggressive kingdom-seeking force among Western evangelicals.

the Ever-merciful One I have lived to see and hear of a Gospel Church on Tanna, and to read about my dear fellow-Missionaries, Mr. and Mrs. Watt, celebrating the Holy Supper to a Native Congregation of Tannese, amid the very scenes and people where the seeds of faith and hope were planted not only in tears, but tears of blood—"in deaths oft."

My own intention was to remain on Aneityum, go on with my work of translating the Gospels, and watch the earliest opportunity, as God opened up my way, to return to Tanna. I had, however, got very weak and thin; my health was undoubtedly much shaken by the continued trials and dangers through which we had passed; and therefore, as Dr. and Mrs. Inglis were at home carrying the New Testament through the press in the language of Aneityum, and as Tanna was closed for a season—Dr. Geddie, the Rev. Joseph Copeland, and Mr. Mathieson all urged me to go to Australia by a vessel then in the Harbor and leaving in a few days. My commission was to awaken an interest among the Presbyterian Churches of our Colonies in this New Hebrides Mission which lay at their doors, up till this time sustained by Scotland and Nova Scotia alone. And further, and very specially, to raise money there, if possible, to purchase a new Mission Ship for the work of God in the New Hebrides—a clamant necessity, which would save all future Missionaries some of the more terrible of the privations and risks of which a few examples have in these pages already been recorded.[62]

After much prayerful deliberation with my brethren and with my own heart before God, I somewhat reluctantly felt constrained to undertake the task. If my story was to be the means of providing more Missionaries for the Islands, and of providing a commodious Ship for the service of the Mission alone, to keep open their communications with the outer world and with Christian influences, not to speak of carrying their provisions at fixed periods, or rescuing them when in troubles and perils from the jaws of death, I was not unwilling to tell it again and again, if the Lord would open up my path.

62. Paton would spend a few years raising funds in Australia, especially to purchase their own ship (that would carry missionaries in safety to the various islands throughout the South Pacific). He became a tremendous fundraiser for missions, as can be imagined from the commitment he shares in this testimony.

God knows my heart, and any one who really knows me will easily admit, that no selfish or egotistical motive has influenced me in reciting through all the Australasian Colonies, New Zealand, Scotland, and latterly in many parts of England and Ireland, the incidents of my career and experience, first of all on Tanna, and thereafter for nearly twenty years—as the Second Part of my biography will relate—on the neighboring island of Aniwa; an island entirely given to me by the Lord, the whole population of which became Christian; and they and their race will be my crown of joy and rejoicing in the day of the Lord Jesus.[63]

With regrets, and yet with unquenchable hope for these Islands, I embarked for Australia, having received the solemn promise of my brethren, that in entering upon this great effort I was to be left absolutely free of all control, and empowered to carry out the work as God might seem to guide me, and open up my way. I had only spoken to one man in Sydney; all the doors to influence had therefore to be unlocked, and I had no helper, no leader, but the Spirit of my Lord. The Second Part of this Autobiography, should God spare me to write it, will record His marvelous goodness in using my humble voice and pen and the story of my life for interesting thousands and tens of thousands in the work of Missions, and especially for binding together the children of the Sabbath Schools of Australasia in a Holy League of help to the New Hebrides, which has already borne precious fruit to His glory, and will continue to do so for ages to come.

Oftentimes, while passing through the perils and defeats of my first years in the Mission field on Tanna, I wondered, and perhaps the reader hereof has wondered, why God permitted such things. But on looking back now, I already clearly perceive, and the reader of my future pages will, I think, perceive, that the Lord was thereby preparing me for doing, and providing me materials wherewith to accomplish, the best work of all my life—the kindling of the heart of Australian Presbyterianism with a living affection for these Islanders of

63. In the second volume of his *Autobiography,* John Paton tells more of the tremendous success he achieved by the grace of God on the island of Aniwa. Practically the whole island was converted to Christ.

their own Southern Seas—the binding of all their children into a happy league of shareholders, first in one Mission Ship, and finally in a larger and more commodious Steam-Auxiliary, and, last of all, in being the instrument under God of sending out Missionary after Missionary to the New Hebrides, to claim another island and still another for Jesus. That work, and all that may spring from it in time and Eternity, never could have been accomplished by me, but for first the sufferings and then the story of my Tanna enterprise![64]

64. John Paton can see how God used the severe trials on Tanna to open up a much greater outreach to the whole island chain. God used these trials to break down Satan's kingdom and to bring the Church of Christ to these dark isles.

Some unsophisticated souls who read these pages will be astonished to learn, but others who know more of the heartless selfishness of human creatures, will be quite prepared to hear, that my leaving Tanna was not a little criticized, and a great deal of nonsense was written, even in Church Magazines, about the breaking up of the Mission. All such criticism came, of course, from men who were themselves destitute of sympathy, and who, probably, never endured one pang for Jesus in all their comfortable lives. Conscious that I had, to the last inch of life, tried to do my duty, I left all results in the hands of my only Lord, and all criticisms to His unerring judgment.[65] Hard things also were occasionally spoken to my face. One dear friend, for instance, said:

65. Paton was criticized for risking his life in the New Hebrides, and then he was criticized for not risking his life to the point of losing it. Those with the "gift of criticism" should take their gift somewhere other than this area of missionary work.

"You should not have left. You should have stood at the post of duty till you fell. It would have been to your honor, and better for the cause of the Mission, had you been killed at the post of duty like the Gordons and others."

I replied—"I regard it as a greater honor to live and to work for Jesus, than to be a self-made martyr. God knows that I did not refuse to die; for I stood at the post of duty, amid difficulty and danger, till all hope had fled, till everything I had was lost, and till God, in answer to prayer, sent a means of escape. I left with a clear conscience, knowing that in doing so I was following God's leading, and serving the Mission too. To have remained longer would have been to incur the guilt of self-murder in the sight of God."

Never for one moment have I had occasion to regret the step then taken. The Lord has so used me, during the five-and-twenty years that have passed over me since my farewell to Tanna, as to stamp the event with His own most gracious approval. Oh, to see a Missionary, and Christian Teachers, planted on every island of the New Hebrides! For this I labor, and wait, and pray. To help on the fulfilment thereof is the sacred work of my life, under God. When I see it accomplished, or in a fair way of being so, through the organization that will provide the money and call forth the men, I can lay down my head as peacefully and gratefully as ever warrior did, with the shout of victory in his ears—"Lord, now lettest Thou Thy servant depart in peace!"

List of Images

The Confessions of Augustine

BOOK I
1. Romanesque baptismal font from Grotlingbo Church, Sweden | Wikimedia Commons | Public Domain
2. Bust of Virgil from the Tomb of Virgil in Naples, Italy | Wikimedia Commons | Public Domain
3. Depiction of Homer, British Museum | Wikimedia Commons | Public Domain

BOOK II
1. Landscape of Souk Ahkras, modern day Tagaste | Wikimedia Commons | Public Domain

BOOK III
1. Ruins of Carthage | Wikimedia Commons | Public Domain
2. Roman Theater in Amman, Jordan | Wikimedia Commons | Public Domain
3. Marcus Cicero (106–43 BC), a Roman politician, lawyer, and orator | Wikimedia Commons | Public Domain

BOOK IV
1. Hippocrates of Kos (460 – c. 370 BC) | Wikimedia Commons | Public Domain
2. Aristotle (384–322 BC), a Greek philosopher and pupil of Plato | Wikimedia Commons | Public Domain

BOOK V
1. Manichean priests depicted in a Chinese mural | Wikimedia Commons | Public Domain
2. Early New Testament manuscript (c. 400–440) | Wikimedia Commons | Public Domain
3. One of the first churches in Milan, Basilica of San Lorenzo | Wikimedia Commons | Public Domain

BOOK VI
1. Augustine and his mother Monica | Wikimedia Commons | Public Domain
2. Ambrose (c. 340 – 4 April 397), bishop of Milan | Wikimedia Commons | Public Domain
3. Ruins of ancient Rome | Pixabay | Public Domain

BOOK VII
1. "The Expulsion of Adam and Eve from Paradise" by Benjamin West
    | Wikimedia Commons | Public Domain
2. Apostle Paul, preaching to the Athenians | Wikimedia Commons | Public Domain
3. Paul the Apostle by Rembrandt (1657) | Wikimedia Commons | Public Domain

BOOK VIII
1. Plotinus (AD 204–270), a Greek-speaking Platonic philosopher
    | Wikimedia Commons | Public Domain
2. St. Anthony (AD 251–356) | Wikimedia Commons | Public Domain
3. The Conversion of St. Augustine by Fra Angelico | Wikimedia Commons | Public Domain

Patrick's Confessions & Breastplate

CHAPTER I: KIDNAPPED
1. Ballintoy, Northern Ireland | iStock.com

CHAPTER II: ESCAPE FROM IRELAND
1. Sheep in Downpatrick, Northern Ireland | Wikimedia Commons | Public Domain

CHAPTER III: PATRICK'S CALL TO IRELAND
1. Ruins of Monasterboice, founded in the 5th century in Ireland
    | Wikimedia Commons | Public Domain

CHAPTER IV: PATRICK'S MINISTRY
1. Mt. Croagh Patrick in Ireland | Wikimedia Commons | Public Domain

CHAPTER V: PATRICK'S CONFESSION
1. Patrick's gravesite in Down Cathedral | Wikipedia | Public Domain

The History of the Reformation of Religion Within the Realm of Scotland

Grace Abounding to the Chief of Sinners

CHAPTER III: INTERNAL WRESTLINGS

CHAPTER IV: TEMPTATIONS TO DOUBT

CHAPTER VII: DELIVERANCE

A BRIEF ACCOUNT OF THE AUTHOR'S IMPRISONMENT

The Autobiography of John B. Paton

CHAPTER I: THE HOME LIFE

CHAPTER II: SCHOOL AND EARLY COLLEGE DAYS

CHAPTER III: IN GLASGOW CITY MISSION

CHAPTER IV: FOREIGN MISSION CLAIMS

CHAPTER V: THE NEW HEBRIDES

APOLOGETICS IN ACTION

DISCOVER HOW THE BIBLE PROVES ITSELF, AND THE INSIGHT YOU NEED TO STRENGTHEN YOUR FAITH AND DEFEND GOD'S WORD

978-1-68344-046-8

978-0-89051-661-4

978-0-89051-633-1

978-0-89051-649-2

978-0-89051-600-3

5 BOOK SET 978-0-89051-848-9

Daily Lesson Plans

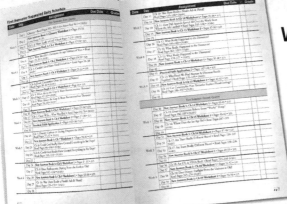

WE'VE DONE THE WORK FOR YOU!

PERFORATED & 3-HOLE PUNCHED
FLEXIBLE 180-DAY SCHEDULE
DAILY LIST OF ACTIVITIES
RECORD KEEPING

HOMESCHOOL
Master Books® Homeschool Curriculum

Faith-Building Books & Resources
Parent-Friendly Lesson Plans
Biblically-Based Worldview
Affordably Priced

Master Books® is the leading publisher of books and resources
based upon a Biblical worldview that points to God as our Creator.

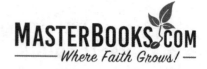

MASTERBOOKS.COM
— *Where Faith Grows!* —